SQL SERVER 7

In Record Time

SQL SERVER® 7

In Record Time™

Mike Gunderloy
Mary Chipman

San Francisco • Paris • Düsseldorf • Soest

Associate Publisher: Amy Romanoff
Contracts and Licensing Manager: Kristine O'Callaghan
Acquisitions & Developmental Editor: Melanie Spiller
Editor: Jane Ross
Project Editor: Davina Baum
Technical Editor: Karen Jaskolka
Book Designers: Franz Baumhackl, Patrick Dintino, Catalin Dulfu
Graphic Illustrator: Tony Jonick
Electronic Publishing Specialist: Kris Warrenburg Design
Production Coordinators: Jeremy Crawford, Shannon Murphy
Indexer: Rebecca Plunkett
Cover Designer: Design Site
Cover Photographer: Adri Berger/Tony Stone Images

Library of Congress Card Number: 98-88334
ISBN: 0-7821-2155-1

Manufactured in the United States of America

10 9 8 7 6 5 4 3 2 1

To Melanie, who believed in us.

Acknowledgments

This book, just like any other, is not solely the product of the authors. We'd like to thank some of the people who helped us get from that first sketchy outline to a published work. Naturally, none of them are responsible for any remaining mistakes within these covers—we claim exclusive ownership of those. But we'd like to thank:

Melanie Spiller, Davina Baum, and Jane Ross for attempting to turn our prose into something resembling English, and Karen Jaskolka for checking the veracity of same. Jeremy Crawford, Shannon Murphy, and Kris Warrenburg for keeping the production side of things in tip-top shape.

Tom Kreyche, Tom Casey, Gert Drapers, and Al Comeau from the SQL Server group and Debra Dove from the Jet group at Microsoft for providing additional insight and technical information and for answering our occasionally boneheaded questions.

Di Schaffhauser, Shelley Doyle, and Steve White for driveways and home-made beer.

Andy Baron for his unconditional support, encouragement, and critiques, and Bar Biszick for being there during the writing process.

Contents at a Glance

Table of Contents

Introduction

Thanks for picking up *SQL Server 7 In Record Time*. You may have noticed that this is a relatively short book as computer books go. SQL Server 7 ships with nearly 10MB of hypertext documentation in SQL Server Books Online. We don't think it's necessary to lead you through all the ins and outs of that documentation; nor, frankly, is it even possible to do so in a reasonably sized book. What we can do here is give you a tour of SQL Server 7 that assumes you already know the basics of using the software. There's a lot to tour in this new version. Some of the highlights of SQL Server 7 include the following:

- Dynamic self-management of things like memory and locking
- Dynamic locking granularity
- Very large database support
- Better performance
- Windows 95 server support
- Better integration with Windows NT security
- More flexible replication
- Full-text indexing and search support
- Full Unicode support
- Centralized management for multiple sites
- Data warehousing and OLAP support
- Many new wizards
- Microsoft Management Console integration
- Improved Data Transformation Services
- Row-level locking
- Parallel query support
- Distributed query support
- OLE DB support
- Scripting support in jobs

In the pages that follow, we'll visit these and other new features, as well as the core features of SQL Server that haven't changed. Our goal is not to tell you everything about the product, but to tell you the things that you really need to know to get up and running.

- If you're an experienced SQL Server developer or administrator, this book will clue you in to new and improved features that will help you write more efficient applications and develop more reliable and robust databases.
- If you're used to desktop databases such as Microsoft Access or Microsoft Foxpro, we'll teach you enough about SQL Server to get going, and show you how a client-server database differs from a desktop database.
- If you're moving from another client-server database such as Oracle, this book can help you quickly find out how SQL Server does things. You should also keep an eye out for SQL Server features that give it more flexibility than your current server.

Before you start this book, you should be familiar with basic Windows operation. We won't give every single procedure in excruciating detail or just repeat material that's in Books Online. Our goal is to provide an advanced-level introduction to SQL Server 7, aimed at an audience that can handle technical material.

What's in This Book

This book is divided into two major sections. The first eight skills will get you started on the basics of using SQL Server as a database. These skills will teach you to set up your database, put data in it, and retrieve that data as required. (If you also need to know how to install the software, take a look at Appendix A.) The last nine skills cover more advanced topics. If you're already familiar with SQL Server basics, you might want to skip ahead and check these skills out first to see what's new in Web interaction, server administration, replication, and SQL Server security, among other topics.

Throughout the book, we've tried to flag important information so you can find it quickly. In particular, look for three specific types of paragraph:

NOTE Notes contain important information that will help you better understand SQL Server 7 and its operation.

TIP Tips are designed to help you do your work more quickly and efficiently.

WARNING Warnings will help you avoid some of the dangerous pitfalls that surround any complex product.

We really enjoyed writing this book in part because SQL Server 7 is such a terrific product. It's fun being able to write about exploring so many new, exciting features. This book isn't long enough to do them all justice, but we fervently hope that it will serve as the starting point for your own explorations.

SKILL 1

Evaluating SQL Server

- Understanding SQL Server architecture
- Pinpointing what's new
- Outlining supporting programs

In this book we'll be digging into Microsoft SQL Server 7 (formerly code-named "Sphinx"). Over the next 17 skills, we'll get into both basic and advanced features of Microsoft's high-end enterprise database server. Before we start looking at specifics, though, let's get a high-level view of the whole system. SQL Server is a huge and complex program, and it helps to have some idea of the big picture before delving into the details. In this chapter, we'll cover the overall architecture of SQL Server, highlight the new features that make this version a significant upgrade over SQL Server 6.5, and take a quick look at some of the other programs in the SQL Server box.

System Architecture

SQL Server is a SQL-based, client-server database. *SQL-based* means that it uses the ANSI (American National Standards Institute) version of Structured Query Language, or SQL. *Client-server* means that SQL Server is designed to store data in a central location (the server) and deliver it on demand to numerous other locations (the clients). As you'd expect, SQL Server is actually a collection of many different components. These include SQL Server itself, the SQL Server Agent, SQL Mail, and the Distributed Transaction Coordinator. In addition, the default SQL Server installation creates several databases known as the system databases.

NOTE Although SQL Server supports ANSI-92 SQL, it also allows various enhancements to and deviations from the standard, just as other database servers do. You can use the `SET ANSI DEFAULTS` statement to force closer compliance with the standard if you're concerned about interoperation with other databases.

SQL Server

SQL Server itself is implemented as the MSSQLServer service on Windows NT, and as the `SQLSERVR.EXE` program on Windows 95. This service is the core database engine and is the only SQL Server component that actually modifies data. It acts as a sort of "traffic cop" for clients, deciding which data requests to service first and allocating resources between multiple competing users.

SQL Server is the component that knows what to do with SQL statements. That is, it's able to take a statement such as

```
SELECT CustomerName FROM Customers WHERE CustomerID = 117
```

and return the appropriate data to the client that made the request. This is the key feature of a client-server database: all of the selection of data happens on the server, and clients are given only the exact data they request.

SQL Server also protects your valuable data by carefully screening the actions that clients are allowed to take. This includes actions such as:

- Enforcing business rules defined in stored procedures and triggers
- Preventing two users from updating the same data at the same time
- Enforcing logical consistency between data stored in different places

NOTE Although SQL Server is launched differently on Windows 95, this is only because Windows 95 does not support services. Generally, the server runs the same way on all supported operating systems.

SQL Server Agent

SQL Server Agent (formerly SQL Executive) provides scheduling services to SQL Server. SQL Server Agent can execute *jobs*, which consist of multiple steps to be performed at a specific time. A step might be a single Transact-SQL statement, an operating system command, or even a script written with an active scripting language such as VBScript.

SQL Server Agent also supports the concept of sending *alerts* to *operators*. For example, if a serious error occurs when trying to retrieve data from a particular database, SQL Server Agent can automatically send e-mail to an operator, or even use that operator's pager to notify them that something is wrong.

We'll cover alerts and jobs in some detail in Skill 15, *Administering a Server*.

SQL Mail

Another important component of SQL Server is the SQL Mail engine. This component uses extended stored procedures to communicate with MAPI-compliant electronic mail systems.

NOTE Extended stored procedures are pieces of SQL Server programming that are stored in a separate DLL (dynamic link library). You'll learn more about extended stored procedures in Skill 7, *Altering Data*.

SQL Mail is able to read, to delete, and to send electronic mail messages from an account dedicated to the particular server. But this doesn't capture the full flavor of SQL Server's integration with electronic mail. For example, you can configure your SQL Server to accept Transact-SQL statements from clients in e-mail and to send back result sets as e-mail messages. You'll see how to set this up in Skill 15, *Administering a Server*.

Distributed Transaction Coordinator

With the explosive growth of networking and the Internet, it's getting more and more common for large databases to be distributed—that is, to have components installed on more than one server. For example, a large bank might keep records relating to saving accounts on one server and records relating to checking accounts on another server. Splitting a database in this way allows better performance (because more processors and more network bandwidth are available to service requests) but opens the question of how to handle transactions that cross database boundaries (for a refresher on transactions, see the sidebar below). For example, a hypothetical bank using two different servers to manage savings and checking information must ensure that money transferred away from one server actually shows up at the other server.

Handling these distributed transactions is the job of *Microsoft Distributed Transaction Coordinator* (usually known as MS DTC). MS DTC handles distributed transactions through a system known as two-phase commit. In the first phase, it asks all the servers involved to prepare to execute their part of the transaction. If every server is able to do this, then in the second phase it tells them all to go ahead and do their part. If any one of the servers is unable to commit the transaction, then it tells all the servers to forget about it, and the transaction is rolled back.

TIP Microsoft Transaction Server (a feature of the Windows NT 4 Options Pack) can use MS DTC and other interfaces to help transactions span not just databases but many other operations. While MTS is beyond the scope of this book, it's worth looking into if you're designing complex server operations.

What's a Transaction?

One of the key concepts in database development is that of a *transaction*. Transactions are units of work characterized by the ACID properties. *ACID* is an acronym to help you remember these properties: Atomicity, Consistency, Isolation, and Durability.

Atomicity means that the transaction is treated as a single item. No matter how many updates you make to multiple database tables spread across multiple database servers, if these updates are contained within a transaction, either they all succeed or they all fail. You'll never see a situation where some updates within a transaction commit even though others are aborted.

Consistency is usually expressed by saying the transactions "preserve the state invariants" of the system. A simpler way to think of this is that transactions don't break the rules of the software they're working with. If you change the name of a database table, for example, then the indexes for the old name are seamlessly transferred to the new name, rather than hanging loose in the system somewhere. Software in general, not just transactional software, is generally designed to be consistent.

Isolation means that incomplete transactions have no effect on one another. Suppose one transaction is trying to put money into an account while a different transaction is trying to take money out. The second transaction will only see the money from the first transaction if the entire first transaction is committed—not if it's in progress. Isolation is sometimes called serializability, since isolated transactions can always be treated as happening one after the other rather than simultaneously.

Durability means that the effects of committed transactions survive system failures. Once the attempt to commit a transaction succeeds, you're guaranteed that any changes it made to database tables are already written to those tables, even if both the transaction manager and the database server crash immediately after the transaction is committed.

System Databases

SQL Server is a good example of a self-contained system: It manages tables of data according to rules that are themselves held in tables of data. When you install the SQL Server software, it automatically creates four databases known as the *system databases*. In general, you'll want to avoid making any changes to the system databases, since by modifying them you could cause your server to stop functioning. However, it's a good idea to know what's in these four databases, which are named master, model, tempdb, and msdb.

The master Database

As the name would suggest, the *master* database records information that is used in SQL Server's most basic operations. This is the database that contains user accounts and system-configuration information. It also holds information that tells SQL Server where to find other, user-created databases. If something should happen to your master database, you'd be in big trouble. You should back up the master database on a regular basis (see Skill 5, *Moving Data* for more information on SQL Server's backup and restore capabilities).

The model Database

The *model* database is the only system database that you might want to modify in the regular course of events. Whenever you create a new database (see Skill 2, *Managing Databases*), SQL Server starts by making a copy of the model database. If there is some object that you'd like to have present in all databases on your server (for example, a custom datatype that's important to your business), adding it to the model database is a worthwhile thing to do since it will cause that datatype to automatically be created along with any new databases.

WARNING Don't try to remove the model database! Because SQL Server uses it as the template for a new tempdb database every time your server is started, SQL Server will not run without this database.

The tempdb Database

The *tempdb* database is SQL Server's scratchpad. This is where it stores all of its temporary working tables and temporary stored procedures. The tempdb database is automatically re-created every time you start SQL Server, and there's never any reason for you to mess with it.

The msdb Database

Finally, the *msdb* database is used by SQL Server Agent to store the information it needs to process jobs and alerts. You should never modify msdb directly. Always use the user interface to create, modify, or delete SQL Server Agent objects.

What's New in SQL Server 7

SQL Server is a mature application at this point, but it isn't a static one. If you're familiar with previous versions, such as SQL Server 6 or SQL Server 6.5, you're naturally wondering what's new in this version. We cover new features throughout the book, but this section will give you a quick overview. Many of the new features focus on two areas: ease of use (including better administrative tools and, for the first time, a Windows 95 version of SQL Server) and high-end features (including row-level locking, OLAP support, and single-console management of multiple servers).

It seems like new versions are always larger, and SQL Server 7 is no exception. Table 1.1 gives you a quick look at some of the key numbers for this version.

TABLE 1.1: Comparison of SQL Server 6.5 and 7

Feature	SQL Server 6.5	SQL Server 7
Bytes per character or binary column	255	8000
Bytes per text, ntext, or image column	2GB-2	2GB-2
Bytes per GROUP BY, ORDER BY	900	8060
Columns in GROUP BY, ORDER BY	16	Limited only by number of bytes
Bytes per index or key	900	900
Columns per index or key	16	16
Bytes per row	1962	8060
Bytes in source text of a stored procedure	65025	Batch size (128K if network supports 1K packets)
Clustered indexes or constraints per table	1	1

TABLE 1.1 CONTINUED: Comparison of SQL Server 6.5 and 7

Feature	SQL Server 6.5	SQL Server 7
Columns or expressions in a GROUP BY WITH CUBE or WITH ROLLUP statement	10	10
Columns per base table	250	1024
Columns per SELECT statement	4096	4096
Columns per INSERT statement	250	1024
Database size	1 TB	1,048,516TB
Files per database	32	32,767
File size (data)	32GB	32TB
File size (log)	32GB	4TB
FOREIGN KEY constraints per table	31	253
Foreign key table references per table	16	63
Identifier length (in characters)	30	128
Index key size (bytes)	900	900
Nested subqueries	16	64
Nested trigger levels	16	32
Nonclustered indexes or constraints per table	249	249
Parameters per stored procedure	255	1024
Tables per SELECT statement	16	32
Triggers per table	3	Limited by number of objects in a database (2 billion or so)
UNIQUE constraints per table	249	249 nonclustered and 1 clustered
Unicode support	No	Yes

You can see immediately that one big change is in the amazing amount of data that SQL Server 7 can manage: over one million terabytes! That's enough to store over 100 megabytes of data for every man, woman, child, and dog on the face of the planet, with room to spare. It's unlikely that you'll hit this limit before you run out of money to buy mass storage devices.

TIP One good application for this sort of extremely large database is for storing images. For example, Microsoft TerraServer (`http://terraserver.microsoft.com`) is hosted on SQL Server 7.

What's New in Queries

At the simplest level, the purpose of a database is to store data and retrieve it on demand. This means that a database's query engine must be fast and robust, and the SQL Server designers were careful to address this issue. Query improvements include OLE DB support, heterogeneous distributed query support, parallel query execution, improved index utilization, and a better user interface for query analysis.

OLE DB is Microsoft's relatively new standard for communication between heterogeneous database components via COM interfaces. The SQL Server query processor has been completely revamped to use OLE DB to communicate with data stores. This is important because it automatically provides support for heterogeneous and distributed queries. In general, if you have an OLE DB driver for a data source, you can include tables and fields from that data source in a SQL Server 7 query. You'll learn more about OLE DB in Skill 12, *OLE DB Fundamentals*.

TIP If you'd like to know more about OLE DB and related technologies, check out Microsoft's Universal Data Access Web site at `http://www.microsoft.com/Data`.

If you have multiple processors, SQL Server 7 will automatically generate parallel execution plans to speed up queries that benefit from parallelism. For example, a query that involves sorting a very large result set will execute faster if two or more processors help out with the sorting process.

SQL Server will now use multiple indexes on a single table to resolve a query, and it automatically maintains index statistics. It will use the intersection or union of multiple indexes to resolve queries (old database hands will recognize this as Foxpro's "Rushmore" optimization). The speed of update for multiple nonclustered indexes on a single table that also has a clustered index has been significantly improved by implementing new methods of index storage.

The new graphical Query Analyzer (shown in Figure 1.1) is an incremental improvement to the previous ISQL/W interface. It's not a completely new tool, but it has better help than the previous version, color coding, execution to a grid, and it can analyze your query in a new graphical format.

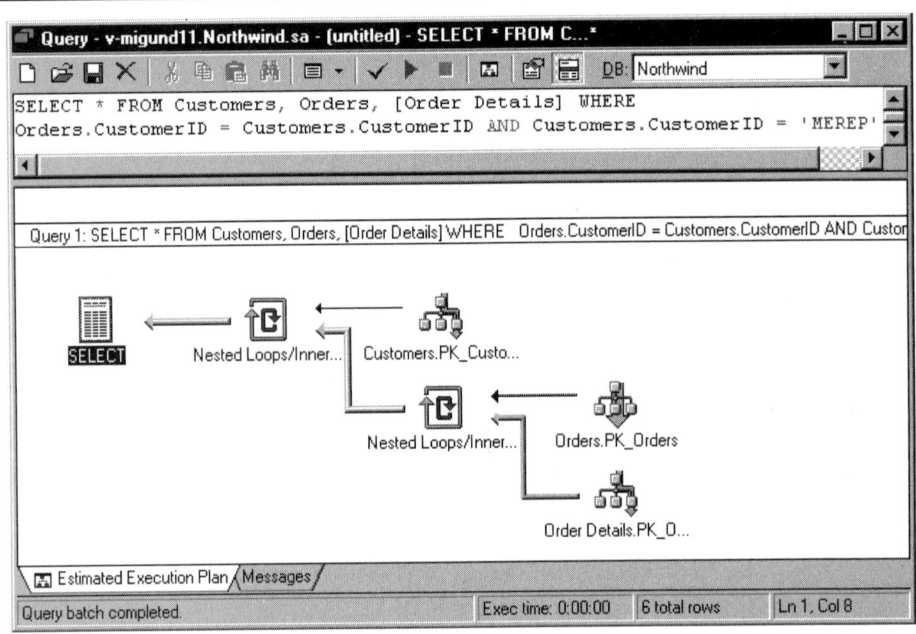

FIGURE 1.1: Query Analyzer

What's New in Data Storage

SQL Server 7 also features a number of improvements to data storage. Key new features include multiple-trigger support, fatter tables, Unicode support, and row-level locking.

Past versions of SQL Server supported only one insert, one update, and one delete trigger on each table. (A *trigger* is a bit of SQL code that is automatically run when data is altered. We'll cover triggers in Skill 6, *Retrieving Data*.) Now you can have essentially unlimited triggers per table. This change makes triggers much more useful for enforcing business rules. If a table is affected by multiple business rules, you can maintain each one with a separate trigger, rather than a single hard-to-debug trigger full of conditional logic.

While it may have seemed expansive in SQL Server 4.21, the limits of 250 columns per table and 1962 bytes per row have forced suboptimal schemas in the case of many databases. Raising these limits in SQL Server 7 to 1024 columns and 8060 bytes means that many more logical entities can be represented as a single physical table. The expansion of char and binary columns from 255 to 8000 bytes maximum also helps.

If you've worked with SQL Server in the past, you know about the hassles of having to choose a "code page" for each server, limiting the characters that can be stored on that server and the even worse hassles of changing your mind about a code page later on. Now, SQL Server identifiers can use any Unicode character, and there are new data types (nchar, nvarchar, and ntext) that allow you to store Unicode characters in your database.

SQL Server 7 also introduces dynamic row-level locking. Developers have been asking for the ability to lock a single row, rather than a whole data page, for several years now, and with this release Microsoft finally delivers. The optimizer will automatically choose row locking instead of page locking when it makes sense for a particular operation. Table scans, for example, still benefit from page locking, because they quickly read all the data on a page. Row inserts, on the other hand, are a prime example of an operation that benefits from row locking. The result should be increased concurrency for many databases.

WARNING Although you can fine-tune locking behavior using locking hints for SELECT, DELETE, INSERT, and UPDATE statements, you should always let SQL Server choose a locking strategy first and only change this strategy if absolutely necessary.

What's New in Replication

One of the key features of SQL Server is *replication*: the ability to keep two or more copies of a database synchronized so that changes in one copy are reflected in other copies. This is an area of intense competition between database manufacturers, and Microsoft has made major improvements in this release. SQL Server now supports merge replication, Internet replication, new wizards, and better heterogeneous replication support.

Merge replication allows replicated data to be changed at multiple sites and then later reconciled. This opens up many new uses for replication that SQL Server 6.5's model of a single read-write master database did not allow.

SQL Server 7 allows anonymous pull subscriptions. This allows servers on the Internet to subscribe to data published by another server without having to register with the publishing server. This model allows hundreds or thousands of servers to participate in a single replication scheme.

New wizards are provided to step the user through some of the more difficult parts of replication. For example, there's a conflict resolution wizard, modeled after the one provided with Microsoft Access, to help you reconcile data discrepancies that can arise with merge replication.

SQL Server 6.5 could replicate out to other databases—SQL Server 7 adds the ability to accept data from other databases. This will make, for example, complete two-way replication with Microsoft Access 2000 databases a reality.

You'll find more information on replication in Skill 14, *Using Replication*.

What's New in Administration

A major theme of SQL Server 7 is ease of administration. This shows up in dynamic self-management, the elimination of devices, multi-site management via Microsoft Management Console, more job options, Web administration, and the Windows 95/98 version of SQL Server 7.

Dynamic self-management means that SQL Server 7 monitors its own operations and adjusts parameters as necessary. This removes a whole area of work that the SQL Server DBA was once responsible for. For example, you don't have to worry about setting a maximum number of locks with this release; if the server needs more locks, it will allocate them itself. The same applies to memory. If the server needs more RAM and it's available from the operating system, SQL Server will request that RAM without the DBA having to intervene. And since the self-management is dynamic, it will also give back that RAM once it's no longer needed for SQL Server operations.

NOTE Speaking of memory, if you run SQL Server 7 on Windows NT 5 on a DEC Alpha system, the server can use up to 32GB of physical memory.

Anyone who's worked with previous releases knows what a nuisance device management could be—it meant having to allocate files to devices, to extend and link those devices, and to generally manage a whole intermediate layer of storage between your databases and your hard drive. With SQL Server 7, those days are gone. Databases are now created directly on top of files, and extensions to the `CREATE DATABASE` syntax allow you to specify the size and location of those files.

Even better, databases will grow automatically when they need more space (you can specify the increment of growth and a maximum size). A nice extra touch is that the operating-system file is automatically deleted if the database is dropped.

Microsoft Management Console (MMC) is a new interface for managing server operations of all types—not just SQL Server, but many other products from Microsoft as well. This console, similar to Windows Explorer, gives you a point-and-click interface for performing nearly all server operations and is wonderfully customizable. You can manage multiple servers from a single console with ease. Figure 1.2 shows MMC in action.

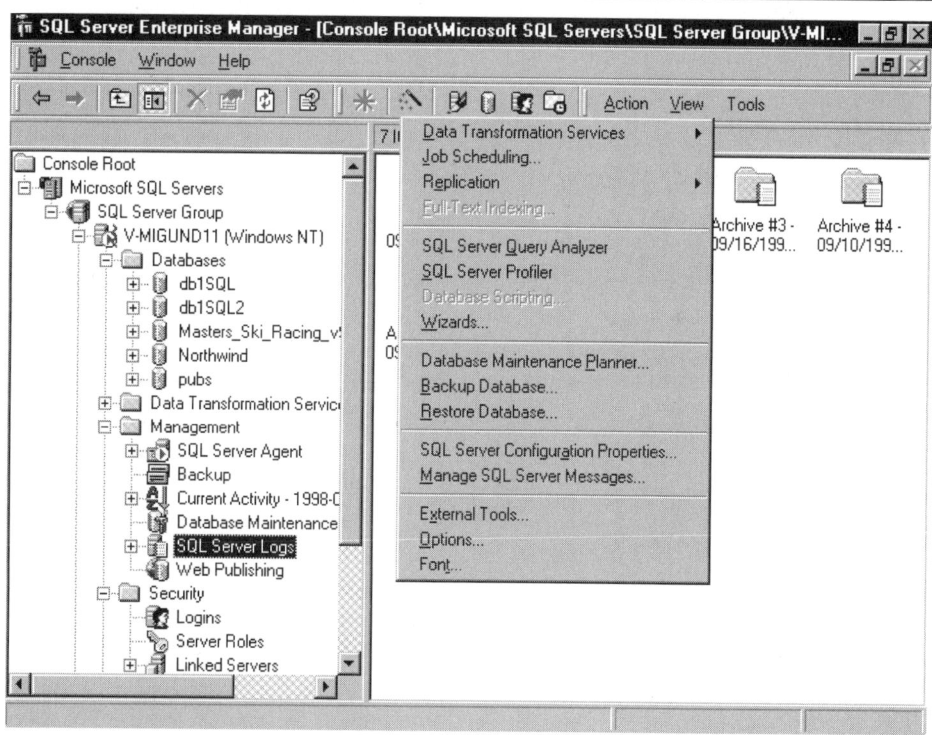

FIGURE 1.2: Microsoft Management Console

SQL Server jobs have been significantly enhanced. Jobs can be spread across multiple servers, and job steps can have conditional logic, allowing branching within a single job. VBScript, Java scripting, and Windows NT command files can all be used to create job steps.

SQL Server 7 can also be managed remotely from almost any location via a Web browser. (Imagine managing your server from a Windows CE handheld!) Internet management pages are supplied when you install the server.

The Windows 95/98 version of SQL Server is built from the same source as the Windows NT version. There's nothing new for the administrator to learn with this version; it can be managed with precisely the same tools as its big brother. With the improved integration between Access 2000 and SQL Server 7, Microsoft will have an impressively scalable database at last.

What's New in Data Warehousing

Data warehousing is another key competitive area in enterprise databases, and everything is new here, since there was no data warehousing support to speak of in previous versions of SQL Server. But SQL Server 7 is designed to support data warehousing in a big way. Key features here include Data Transformation Services, Microsoft OLAP Server and Microsoft Data Cube Service, and the Microsoft Repository.

Data Transformation Services (DTS) is designed to move schemas and data between multiple heterogeneous databases. Once the transformation is defined, it can be run interactively or on a regularly scheduled basis without user intervention. This makes it easy to construct OLAP databases that pick up their data from sources scattered around an enterprise. DTS can read data from OLE DB, ODBC, or plain-text providers.

The *Microsoft OLAP Server* (code-named "Plato") is designed to quickly aggregate data from a variety of data sources. It provides essential support for huge CUBE statements, and is designed with a flexible storage architecture to support many versions of OLAP. The companion *Microsoft Data Cube Service* provides client-side caching and easy access to SQL Server CUBE data from COM clients such as Visual Basic or Microsoft Office.

The *Microsoft Repository* is intended to provide an industry-wide standard for storing and accessing database metadata. This standard is currently undergoing an open review process designed to help multiple vendors participate in OLAP and DTS operations seamlessly.

Miscellaneous Improvements

In addition to the major areas enumerated above, there's a grab bag of miscellaneous improvements to SQL Server 7. These include backup improvements, bcp improvements, security improvements, Internet improvements, and the Microsoft Visual Database Tools.

SQL Server 7 supports incremental backups for faster backup and recover. Backup also now supports the Microsoft Tape Format, which means that your SQL Server backups can co-exist on the same tape media as your Windows NT backups.

The bulk copy program, *bcp*, has been rewritten to use OLE DB to communicate with SQL Server, which makes it faster than before. Loading data via bcp now checks constraints and fires triggers as well. Among other things, this means that bcp-loaded data can automatically participate in replication.

On the security front, SQL Server security is integrated more seamlessly with Windows NT security. You can assign database permissions to Windows NT users or groups directly. There's also a SQL Server group analog called a role, which provides increased flexibility for server administration since users can now be assigned to multiple roles.

For the Internet, the SQL Server Web Assistant can now import data from an HTML table (in addition to exporting to one). It can also post and read directly from HTTP or FTP locations. SQL Server is also integrated directly with Microsoft Proxy Server to permit safe and secure access by authorized users to SQL Server data over the Internet. Skills 9 and 10 highlight the Internet features in this release of SQL Server.

The *Microsoft Visual Database Tools* (found in products such as Visual Studio and Visual Basic) provide easy tools for performing many complex database tasks. Query design and schema design in particular are simplified, and there's no need to learn Transact-SQL for operations such as adding a field or creating a trigger. These tools are also integrated with SQL Server Enterprise Manager. Figure 1.3 shows these tools at work designing a new SQL Server view. Note that you can see a graphical design, the SQL for the view, and the results of the query at the same time!

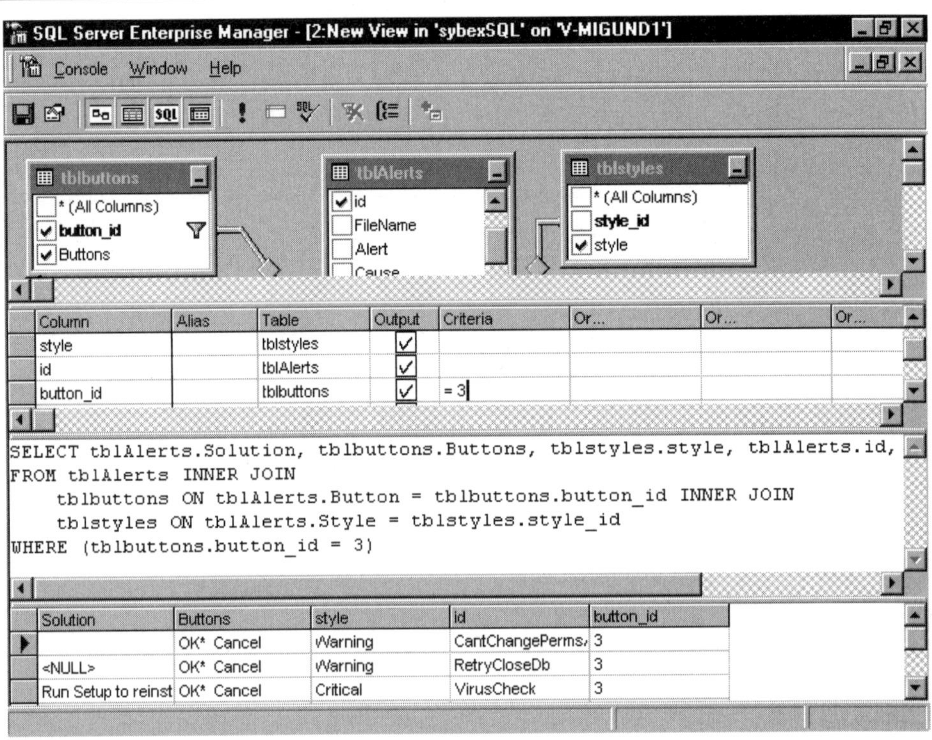

FIGURE 1.3: Visual Database Tools in action

Supporting Programs

In addition to the core database files, SQL Server ships with several supporting utilities and applications. This section lists these other pieces of the puzzle. The most important of these utilities are covered in more depth later in the book.

Client Network Utility

SQL Server can communicate with clients over a variety of mechanisms. The default is Named Pipes, which is suitable for most networks, but other choices include AppleTalk, TCP/IP, and Vines. The Client Network Utility (shown in Figure 1.4) provides a way to maintain your server's communications configuration and to troubleshoot problems caused by version conflicts.

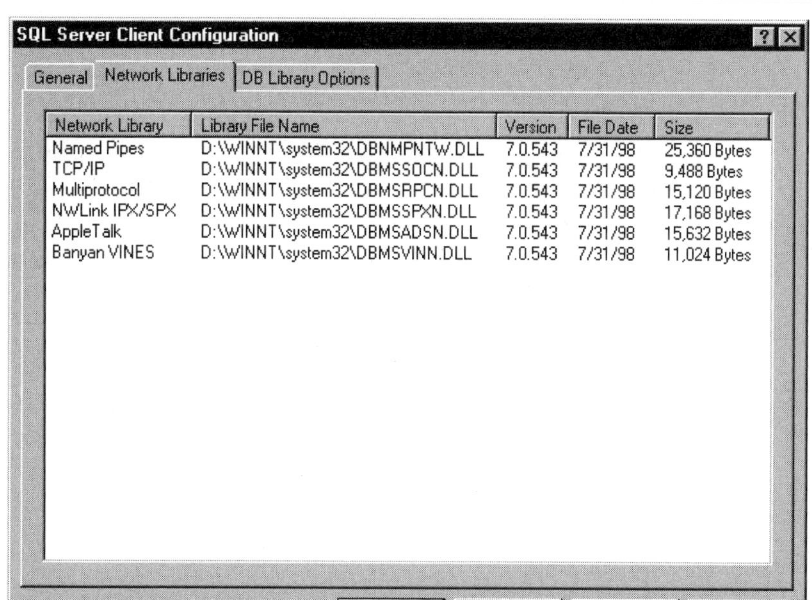

FIGURE 1.4: Client Network Utility

MS DTC Administrative Console

The *MS DTC Administrative Console* is a tool for working with the Distributed Transaction Coordinator. Its tabbed interface lets you start and stop the service, see what transactions are in progress, and check statistics on overall transaction performance. Skill 15, *Administering a Server,* will show you MS DTC in action.

SQL Server Profiler

The *SQL Server Profiler* tool lets you see just what your servers are up to. If you've got a problem with performance and you're not sure what's going on, this is probably the first place to look. Profiler is a "sniffer" tool that intercepts conversations between the server and its clients and shows you what those conversations contain. You can also see how long each action took the server to complete, and quickly zero in on time-consuming queries. Profiler also features extensive filtering capabilities and can also capture a conversation for later "replay" to the server so you can analyze problem interactions in non-peak hours.

Query Analyzer

Query Analyzer was mentioned earlier, in the "What's New in Queries" section. In addition to providing a quick way to execute SQL Statements against a server, Query Analyzer is home to two key tuning functions. First, the SQL Execution Plan view will show you exactly how the server proposes to execute your query. If you think it's making the wrong decision, you can employ query hints in your SQL statements to fine-tune the server's operation. Second, you can launch the Index Analyzer from Query Analyzer. *Index Analyzer* looks at your proposed query and the actual data in the tables and suggests additional indexing that could make the query more efficient. It can even create the indexes for you if you'd like.

Microsoft English Query

Microsoft English Query 2 is another layer on top of SQL Server. The administrator uses the English Query tools to provide information on the logical domain represented by the database. English Query then processes questions submitted in plain English and transforms them into appropriate SQL Server queries. This capability can be accessed from Visual Basic or Visual C++, or even over Web pages deployed with Microsoft Internet Information Server. We'll look at English Query in Skill 8, *Using SQL Server Tools*.

Performance Monitor

Performance Monitor is built into Windows NT to track system performance of all sorts. Although SQL Server doesn't include this tool, it does install a number of extra "counters" (statistics that Performance Monitor can track). In conjunction with SQL Mail, this feature allows additional flexibility in server management. For example, you can track whether SQL Server is allocating an excessive number of locks (often a sign that some process is out of control) and automatically send mail to an operator warning of the condition.

Are You up to Speed?

Now you can...

- ☑ get your head around SQL Server architecture
- ☑ understand the new features in SQL Server 7
- ☑ understand the programs that come with SQL Server

SKILL 2

Managing Databases

- Managing databases
- Estimating disk usage
- Device mirroring
- Databases on removable media

Now that you've seen the big picture of SQL Server's capabilities, it's time to begin learning the actual mechanics of working with SQL Server data. Before you can do anything with your data, however, you need to have a place to put it. In this skill, we'll discuss databases (the logical grouping of related data). In Skill 3, *Working with Tables*, we'll introduce SQL Server tables, which actually hold your data. Then we'll use the rest of the book to see just what you can do with that data.

Databases

A SQL Server database is a container that holds many different types of SQL Server objects:

- Tables
- Views
- Stored procedures
- Defaults
- Rules
- Triggers
- Indexes
- Data types
- Constraints
- Database diagrams

You'll learn about all of these objects in later skills. In this skill we'll cover basic database concepts and demonstrate how to create and maintain databases.

Understanding SQL Server Databases

Before we cover the mechanics of creating and using SQL Server databases, let's take a quick look at a couple of key ideas. One way in which SQL Server protects your data is through the use of transaction logs, special databases that keep track of client activity. SQL Server uses the underlying physical storage concepts of pages, extents, and files to keep databases on your hard drive. We'll discuss these in the following sections.

Transaction Logs

When you create a database, SQL Server automatically creates a *transaction log* for that database. A transaction log is a special file that records all activity in the database. Whenever a user adds, deletes, or modifies data in the database, a record is written to the transaction log. By default, the transaction log has the same name as the database and it uses the extension `.ldf`, but you can name the log file anything you want when you create the database. (Creating databases is discussed later in this skill.)

The transaction log provides additional data security for SQL Server data. In case of failure, it's possible to apply the transactions in the log to another copy of the database. Suppose, for example, that you back up your customer database on Monday at 10 A.M. If the device holding the customer database fails on Friday at 5 P.M., you can apply the transactions for the week from the transaction log to the backup copy of the database and so recover the week's work.

TIP To deliver protection from hardware failures, the transaction log should be stored on a different physical device from that which holds the database itself. For maximum protection, you should mirror both of these devices. In addition, you must back up the main database regularly so that you can keep the size of the transaction log trimmed.

SQL Server uses a write-ahead strategy to maintain the transaction log. As data is modified, SQL Server goes through these steps:

1. The change is noted in the transaction log.
2. The changed data pages are read into the in-memory storage cache.
3. The changes are made in the cached pages.
4. The checkpoint process writes the changes to disk.

The checkpoint process is an internal SQL Server process that writes all changes from the cache back to the physical drive the data is stored on. SQL Server automatically executes the checkpoint process at frequent intervals. You can also manually execute the `CHECKPOINT` statement in Transact-SQL to force an immediate checkpoint process.

WARNING

Never use a write-caching disk controller for a drive that stores SQL Server databases. SQL Server depends on complex internal logic to ensure that data can be recovered whatever the state of the transaction log at the time of a failure. It depends in part on knowing when the checkpoint process has forced writes to the physical drive. A write-caching disk controller interferes with this process by storing disk writes internally and actually writing them when the system is less busy.

Pages, Extents, and Files

There are three terms referring to SQL Server storage that you should be familiar with:

- Pages
- Extents
- Files

A *page* is the smallest unit of SQL Server storage. One page is 8K, or 8,192 bytes. Any page within a database will only contain data from a single object (for example, rows from one table), although most objects will occupy multiple pages. Each page has 96 bytes set aside to track information, such as the owning object and the amount of free space left on the page. Because a row of data cannot cross multiple pages, rows in a SQL Server table are limited to about 8K of data each.

An *extent* is eight contiguous pages, or 64K of data. In previous versions of SQL Server, a new object was allocated an entire extent. With SQL Server 7, this logic has changed somewhat. Now new objects are given a single page in an existing extent that may contain pages belonging to other objects. When a table or index grows to the point where it occupies eight pages in mixed extents, it's moved to its own uniform extent. SQL Server then allocates additional extents as needed, until you reach the limit of available space on the device.

SQL Server stores data directly in operating system *files*. By default, three file extensions are used:

- Files with an `.mdf` extension are the primary data files.
- Files with an `.ndf` extension are secondary data files, holding additional data for a database defined in a primary data file.
- Files with an `.ldf` extension are log files.

Previous versions of SQL Server stored data in devices and stored devices in files. This added an additional level of management to physical storage operations. This concept has been eliminated in SQL Server 7. We won't discuss devices in this book.

SQL Server files will grow automatically as data is added to them. You can specify the growth increment and an optional maximum size when you create the database.

Managing Databases

Managing databases may be the job of either the database administrator or the developer. As you design applications that use SQL Server, you'll need to create and maintain databases. You may also need to delete obsolete databases. You should also know how to maintain the transaction log.

Creating Databases

The easiest way to create a new database is to use the Create Database Wizard. This is one of the many new wizards in SQL Server 7 that are designed to make common administrative tasks simpler. Like most of the new tools for working with SQL Server, the Create Database Wizard is available from the SQL Enterprise Manager interface. SQL Enterprise Manager is the Microsoft Management Console application for SQL Server that you saw in Skill 1. You can start SQL Enterprise Manager from the Windows Start menu by choosing Enterprise Manager from the Microsoft SQL Server 7 menu.

To launch the wizard, choose Tools ➢Wizards from the MMC menus, or click the Run a Wizard button on the MMC toolbar. This will display a list of all the SQL Server wizards, shown in Figure 2.1. You can expand the tree and double-click Create Database Wizard to bring up the wizard itself, shown in Figure 2.2.

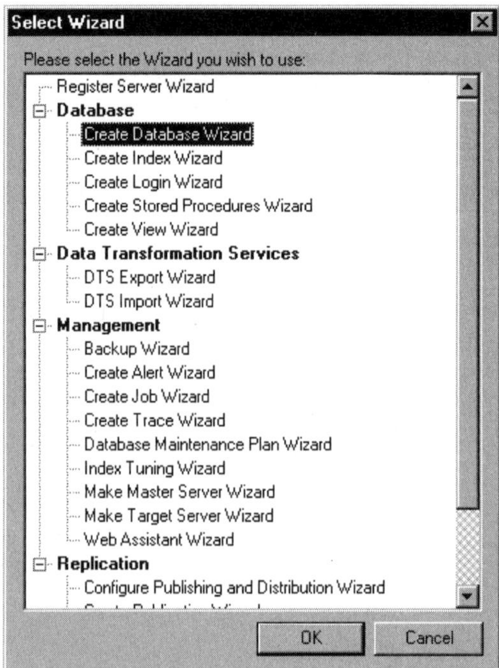

FIGURE 2.1: Choosing a wizard

FIGURE 2.2: The Create Database Wizard

Tools for Managing SQL Server

SQL Server provides a very flexible management environment. In general, there are several ways to perform any database-management task using SQL Server tools:

- By running wizards from within SQL Server Enterprise Manager
- By executing SQL statements with the Query Analyzer tool
- By using menus, icons, and dialog boxes within SQL Enterprise Manager
- By running the wizards from an application using the SQL-NS object

Some developers are adamant about using SQL statements from a tool such as Query Analyzer to perform management tasks, since they prefer to work without lifting their hands from the keyboard. Others are just as strongly in favor of using the more recent graphical tools. In this book, we'll describe the use of the graphical tools and also show you the equivalent SQL, so that you can perform management tasks no matter which style you prefer.

The wizard gives you some control over the creation of a new database, but it deliberately hides more advanced options. To create a database using these options from SQL Enterprise Manager, right-click Databases in the Server Manager window and choose New Database. SQL Server displays the dialog box shown in Figures 2.3–2.5. The figures show the various tabs as they might appear when creating an actual database.

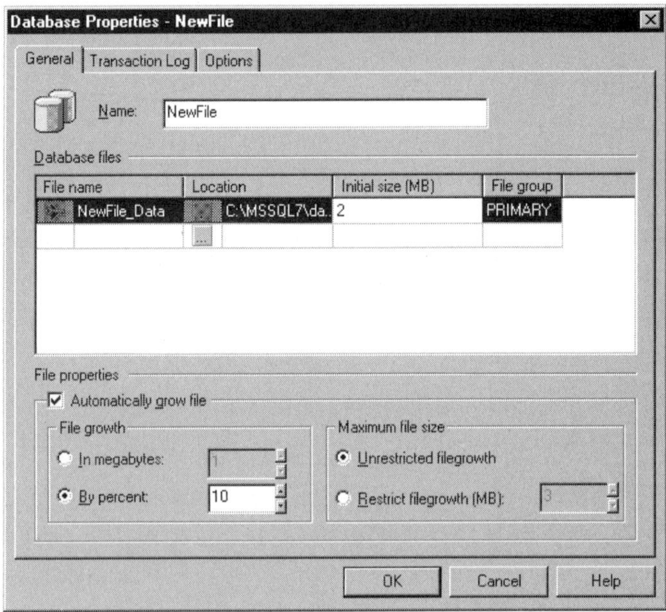

FIGURE 2.3: Creating a new database—the General tab

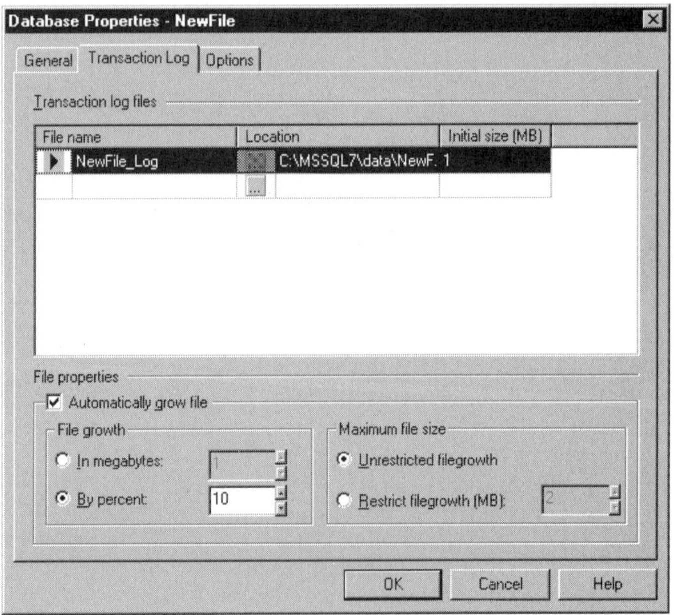

FIGURE 2.4: Specifying the transaction log for a new database

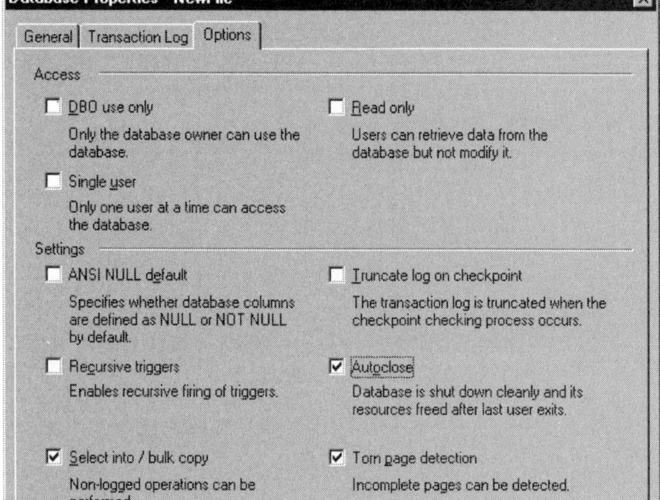

FIGURE 2.5: Setting options for a new database

To use this dialog box, fill in the name of your database and click OK. If you take this simple route, SQL Server will automatically assign database and log file names and set the files to automatically grow by 10 percent each time that they fill. You can also use the General tab to define your file or set of files for the database, and the Transaction Log tab to do the same for logs. The settings you can make on the Options tab are covered in detail later in this skill.

In addition to using the dialog boxes in SQL Server Enterprise Manager, you can also create a database by using the `CREATE DATABASE` Transact-SQL statement:

```
CREATE DATABASE database_name
 [ON [PRIMARY]
  [<filespec> ...n]
 ]
 [ LOG ON {<filespec>}]

<filespec> ::=
 ([NAME=logical_file_name,]
   FILENAME= 'operating_system_file_name'
   [, SIZE = size]
   [, MAXSIZE = {max_size | UNLIMITED}]
   [, FILEGROWN = increment])
```

NOTE

In Transact-SQL statements in this book, italics indicate parameters you should supply, and square brackets indicate optional parameters. Curly braces with vertical bars indicate choices from a fixed list. An ellipsis (...) indicates that an option can be repeated multiple times. Angle brackets indicate part of the syntax that is later expanded.

TIP

The Transact-SQL statements in this book do not include every single option that the language supports. Instead, we've chosen to present only those options that are most useful when you're learning the language. For full Transact-SQL syntax, refer to the SQL Server Books Online *Transact-SQL Reference*. If you use Transact-SQL to modify SQL Server objects, the changes won't show up immediately in SQL Enterprise Manager. To see recent changes, just right-click the folder holding the objects you're working with and select Refresh.

SQL Server Identifiers

The logical name of a database must be a valid SQL Server identifier. Identifiers follow these rules:

- They must be at least one character and no more than 128 characters.
- They must start with a letter or the symbols @, _, or #. "Letter" means any character that's defined as a letter by the Unicode standard, which includes *a* through *z*, *A* through *Z*, and most foreign characters.
- An identifier starting with @ can only be a local variable.
- An identifier starting with # can only be a local temporary object.
- An identifier starting with ## can only be a global temporary object.
- Characters after the first character can be letters, digits, or the symbols #, $, or _.
- Spaces and other special characters can only be used if the identifier is always quoted with double quotation marks.

These identifier rules apply to all object names within SQL Server, including names of databases, tables, columns, and stored procedures.

The *database_name* parameter must follow the rules for SQL Server identifier naming (see sidebar). At the minimum, you must specify the operating system filename to use for the primary file for the database, and you can specify information on other files. Size parameters default to megabytes (not extents, pages, or allocation units); however, you can use KB and MB as suffixes to specify kilobytes or megabytes. If you specify more than one filename, SQL Server will distribute the database's tables across those files.

TIP

One reason to distribute a database across multiple files is to improve performance in multiuser situations. If the different files are serviced by different drive controllers, data updates can be completed more quickly.

NOTE

The new database will contain a copy of all of the objects in the model database that SQL Server creates on the master device. If there is some object that you'd like to have present in all new databases (for example, a custom data type that is used throughout your business), add the object to the model database.

Deleting Databases

To delete a database using SQL Server Enterprise Manager, right-click the database and choose Delete from the Context menu. Once you confirm the deletion, SQL Server will remove the database.

NOTE

Deleting a database removes all references to it from the master database, deletes the databases and all objects within it, and removes the database's files from the operating system. You can't delete a database that is being used, i.e., open for reading or writing by any user.

From Transact-SQL, you can use the `DROP DATABASE` statement to delete databases:

```
DROP DATABASE database_name [, database_name …]
```

You can specify multiple databases to drop with the `DROP DATABASE` statement.

WARNING Unlike the equivalent SQL Enterprise Manager action, `DROP DATABASE` won't prompt for confirmation. If you're writing SQL statements directly, SQL Server assumes you know what you're doing. The only way to recover a dropped database is by restoring a backup!

Modifying Databases

As you work with SQL Server, you may discover that your original database creation choices need to be revised, perhaps to enhance performance. SQL Server allows you to add files to a database or transaction log if you ever need to do so. There are also a number of special-purpose options you can set on individual databases.

Expanding Databases To expand a database using SQL Enterprise Manager, right-click the database in the Server Manager window and choose Properties. Figure 2.6 shows the General tab on the Database Properties dialog box for the Northwind database.

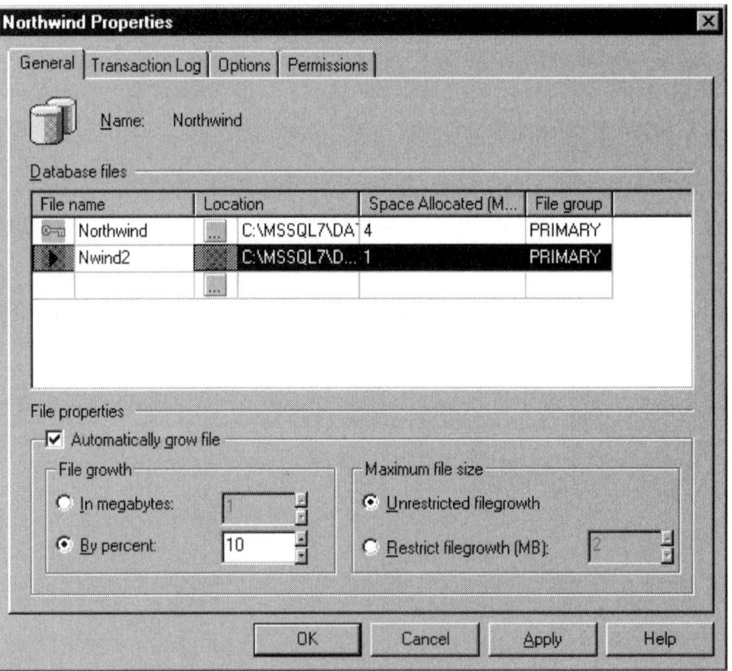

FIGURE 2.6: Expanding a database

NOTE

We'll only discuss three of the four tabs on this dialog box in this skill. The Permissions tab is covered in Skill 16, *Managing SQL Server Security*.

To add a new file, add a filename to the list (as we're doing here for the NWind2 file) and specify its growth properties. You can perform the same operation for transaction logs on the Transaction Log tab of this dialog box.

You can also use the Transact-SQL ALTER DATABASE statement to expand a database:

```
ALTER DATABASE database_name
 {ADD FILE <filespec>
  | ADD LOG FILE <filespec>
  | REMOVE FILE logical_file_name
  | MODIFY FILE <filespec>
 }

<filespec> ::=
 ([NAME=logical_file_name,]
   FILENAME= 'operating_system_file_name'
   [, SIZE = size]
   [, MAXSIZE = {max_size | UNLIMITED}]
   [, FILEGROWN = increment])
```

To use ALTER DATABASE, you specify your database name and choose what you'd like to do with its files. If you're adding a file, you specify the properties for that file using the same syntax that the CREATE DATABASE statement uses.

TIP

You can't shrink a database to a size smaller than was originally allocated for the database, nor can you make it too small to hold all the objects it currently contains.

Database Options

You can use the Options tab on the Database Properties dialog box to set a variety of other database options, as shown in Figure 2.7.

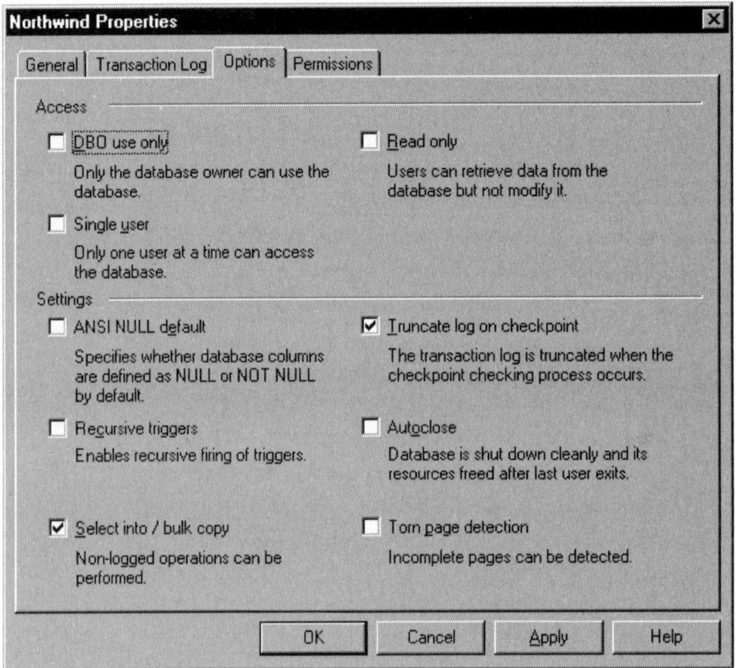

FIGURE 2.7: Database options

Table 2.1 lists these options, their effects, and the equivalent Transact-SQL option. You can execute these options in Transact-SQL by calling the `sp_dboption` stored procedure:

```
sp_dboption [database_name, option_name, {true | false}]
```

SQL Server understands any unique portion of the option name. If there's a space in the option name, you must enclose the entire option name in single quotes, as shown here.

```
sp_dboption Northwind 'dbo use only', true
```

TABLE 2.1: Database Options

Option	Effect	sp_dboption
DBO use only	Allows only the owner of the database (generally, the user who created the database) to use the database.	dbo use only

TABLE 2.1 CONTINUED: Database Options

Option	Effect	sp_dboption
Single user	Allows only one user into the database. New users may not use the database until this option is set to false.	single user
Read only	Allow users to retrieve data but not change data	read only
ANSI NULL default	If checked, columns allow Null unless explicitly defined with NOT NULL	ANSI null default
Recursive triggers	Allows a trigger on a table to cause another trigger on the same table to be executed	recursive triggers
Select into/bulk copy	Allows unlogged bulk data loading	select into/ bulkcopy
Truncate log on checkpoint	Destroys the contents of the transaction log each time the Checkpoint process commits them to disk (usually once per minute)	trunc. Log on chkpt.
Autoclose	Shuts down the database cleanly when the last user stops using it	autoclose
Torn page detection	Causes SQL Server to check for incomplete data pages	torn page detection
	Prevents writing a record to a database after loading transactions. Useful if you're periodically updating a backup that you want to remain an exact copy of the original database	no chkpt on recovery
	Tells SQL Server to periodically check the database for automatic shrinking	Autoshrink
	Sets the ANSI null behavior that one NULL compared to another NULL yields UNKNOWN rather than TRUE	ANSI nulls
	Causes errors to be issued for conditions such as divide by zero	ANSI warnings
	The result of any concatenation including NULL is NULL.	concat null yields null
	Automatically closes cursors when a transaction is committed	cursor close on commit
	Causes all cursors against this database to default to LOCAL	default to local cursor
	Allows a database to be published for merge replication	merge publish

TABLE 2.1 CONTINUED: Database Options

Option	Effect	sp_dboption
	Places the database offline	offline
	Allows a database to be published for replication	published
	Allows double quotation marks to be used to delimit identifiers	quoted identifier
	Allows a database to be subscribed for replication	subscribed

NOTE As you can see, many options can only be set using `sp_dboption`. These are generally more advanced options for specific purposes.

WARNING Setting the Truncate Log On Checkpoint option to True is useful during development, because it will keep your transaction log from filling up with information from testing. Make sure, though, that you set this option to False when you place a database in production! Otherwise, the transaction log won't contain the information needed to recover from potential disasters.

Managing the Transaction Log

One of the most important jobs of the database administrator is to manage the transaction logs for production databases. Even though the amount of data in the database might be relatively constant, if the data is being changed, the transaction log will continue to grow. That's because every operation that changes data adds rows to the transaction log, which are never removed (and a good thing, too, since they're necessary to recover from database failure).

If you're responsible for the health of a database, you should follow these steps to safely maintain the transaction log of the database:

1. Place the transaction log on a separate physical device from the database itself to avoid having a hardware failure wipe out both the database and the log.
2. Monitor the transaction log file in the operating system periodically to make sure you're in no danger of running out of space for the log to grow.

3. Keep regular backups of the log, and truncate the backed-up data by using the `DUMP TRANSACTION` statement. (See Skill 6, *Retrieving Data*, for information on using `DUMP TRANSACTION`). These backups should be on a device that is physically distinct from both the database device and the log device.

You'll also need to keep track of backups of both the database and the transaction log. It's important not to overwrite log backups between database backups. An example will help make this clear. Suppose you back up the database at 5 P.M. each Monday and back up the log at 5 P.M. Tuesday through Sunday. If the drive containing the database fails on Saturday, you'll need Monday's database backup, plus the log backups from Tuesday through Saturday, to restore the database. Each log backup holds the changes since the last log backup. Once the full database is backed up again on Monday, you can safely overwrite the previous week's log backups.

Estimating Disk Usage

As you're creating devices and databases, you need to be concerned with the physical implications of your actions. In addition to designing a viable mirroring strategy and maintaining transaction log dumps, you'll need to consider the amount of disk space that the planned database will occupy. In this section, we'll look at some rules of thumb for estimating these space requirements.

Database Size

Estimating the size of a database is something between a science and an art. If you have perfect knowledge of both the data and the use it will be put to, you can come up with an accurate estimate. Often, though, this is not the case. You might not know the actual number of rows of data that will be generated each day, for example. Or you might discover after creating the database that a particular query is too slow and that you need to add an index to a table, resulting in additional storage space for that table

Data Type Size Estimating the size of a database starts with estimating the size of each table in the database. This in turn depends on the data types of the columns that make up that table (for discussion of tables and data types, turn to Skill 3, *Working with Tables*). Table 2.2 shows the size (in bytes) of the various standard

SQL Server data types. If your database contains user-defined data types, you can determine their size by summing the sizes of their constituent parts.

TABLE 2.2: Data Type Sizes

Data Type	Size in Bytes
char	Defined size
varchar	Size of data actually stored in the field
nchar	Two times the defined size
nvarchar	Two times the size of the data actually stored in the field
binary	Defined size
varbinary	Size of the data actually stored in the field
int	4
smallint	2
tinyint	1
float	8
float(*b*) (precision 1-7)	4
float(*b*) (precision 8-15)	8
double precision	8
real	4
money	8
smallmoney	4
datetime	8
smalldatetime	4
bit	1
text	16, plus 8KB for each row that actually holds data
image	16, plus 8KB for each row that actually holds data
timestamp	8
decimal or numeric, precision 0-2	2
decimal or numeric, precision 3-4	3
decimal or numeric, precision 5-7	4
decimal or numeric,, precision 8-9	5

Skill 2

TABLE 2.2 CONTINUED: Data Type Sizes

Data Type	Size in Bytes
`decimal` or `numeric, precision 10-12`	6
`decimal` or `numeric, precision 13-14`	7
`decimal` or `numeric, precision 15-16`	8
`decimal` or `numeric, precision 17-19`	9
`decimal` or `numeric, precision 20-21`	10
`decimal` or `numeric, precision 22-24`	11
`decimal` or `numeric, precision 25-26`	12
`decimal` or `numeric,, precision 27-28`	13
`decimal` or `numeric, precision 29-31`	14
`decimal` or `numeric, precision 32-33`	15
`decimal` or `numeric, precision 34-36`	16
`decimal` or `numeric, precision 37-38`	17
`uniqueidentifier`	128

Row Size Armed with the size of the individual columns in a table, you can calculate the size of a row. Depending on whether there is variable data (varchar or varbinary data types), you need to use a slightly different formula to calculate the row size, to allow for the overhead SQL Server incurs in storing variable length data. If your table has no variable columns, then the row size is simply the sum of the column sizes plus two. If the table has variable columns, use these formulas:

Subtotal = sum of column sizes

Row size = Subtotal + (Subtotal/256) + Number of variable columns + 4

TIP

When summing the column sizes for variable columns, you can err on the safe side by always using the maximum size of the column, or take a riskier estimate and guess the average size of the data that will be stored in these columns.

Data Pages Once you have the row size for your table, you can combine this with your best estimate of the number of rows that will be stored in the table to determine the number of data pages that the table will require:

8,060 / row size = Number of data rows per page

Number of rows / Number of rows per page = Number of pages required

TIP Round down the results of both of these divisions. The magic number 8,060 comes from the page size less a fixed overhead.

Index Size You'll also have to calculate the size of the indexes on your table. There are different formulas for this depending on whether the indexes are clustered or non-clustered, and on whether they contain variable columns. A *clustered* index is one which sorts the rows of data on the drive, while a *non-clustered* index merely keeps track of rows. You'll learn more about indexing in Skill 3, *Working with Tables.*

For a clustered index without variable columns:

Index row size = 5 + sum of column sizes

For a clustered index with variable columns:

Subtotal = 5 + sum of column sizes

Index row size = Subtotal + (Subtotal / 256) + 4 + number of variable columns

For a nonclustered index without variable columns:

Index row size = 7 + sum of column sizes

For a nonclustered index with variable columns:

Subtotal = 10 + sum of column sizes

Index row size = Subtotal + (Subtotal / 256) + 1

Index Pages Given the index row size and the number of data pages in the table, you can calculate the number of data pages required for the index. Again, this calculation depends on whether the index is clustered or nonclustered.

For clustered indexes:

(8,060 / Index row size) – 2 = Index rows per page

Number of data pages / Index rows per page = Level 0 index pages

If there is more than one index page at level 0, you need to calculate the index pages at level 1:

> Number of index pages at last level / Index rows per page = Number of index pages at next level

Continue this division until you reach a level with only a single index page. The number of required index pages is given by the sum of the number of index pages at all levels.

For nonclustered indexes:

> (2,016 / Index row size) – 2 = Leaf rows per page
>
> Number of rows in table / Leaf rows per page = Leaf pages
>
> Index row size + 4 = Size of nonleaf index row
>
> 2,016 / Size of nonleaf index row = Number of pages at level 1

If there is more than one index page at level 1, you need to calculate the index pages at level 2:

> Number of index pages at last level / Index rows per page = Number of index pages at next level

Continue this division until you reach a level with only a single index page. The number of required index pages is given by the sum of the number of index pages at all levels, including the leaf pages.

Table and Database Size Once you know the number of data pages a table requires, and the number of pages each index for the table requires, you can calculate the number of data pages for the entire table by summing the requirements for the data and each index.

Finally, given the sizes of all the tables in the database, you can sum these to get an idea of the disk space required by the entire database. You'll need to round this number up to the next allocation unit, of course. And if you're very close to a full number of allocation units, add one more to allow for stored procedures, rules, and other miscellaneous objects.

Log Size

You can derive an initial estimate for log size by using 25 percent of the database size. But you should treat this only as an estimate. Regular monitoring of your log file will give you a feel for how quickly your log actually grows under real use. You can combine this figure with your backup frequency to determine how large a log device you need to allow for. For example, if your log grows by an average of 4MB each day of use, and you back up the log once every five days, you'd need a 20MB log device. Prudence dictates adding a safety margin of 10–25 percent to this number, just in case. If your log ever fills up during use, database activities will come to a complete halt, and your users will be very unhappy.

Again, the "25 percent of the database size" rule is just a rule of thumb. Here are some of the factors that can require you to allocate additional log space:

- Frequent use of bulk inserts, updates, or deletes
- Transactions that go a long period of time without being committed
- Database use that is so heavy that the backup process never gets time to execute

Device Mirroring

One of the characteristics that distinguishes SQL Server from desktop databases (such as Microsoft Access or Microsoft FoxPro) is that SQL Server is designed to have more robust protection for your data. It does this by supporting automatic backups, object-level logon security, and transaction logging. *Device mirroring* provides another level of security by storing critical data in multiple locations. When you mirror a device, you create an exact copy of an existing device. Future changes to the data will be saved to both copies at practically the same time. Data loss is minimized in case of a system failure. You can mirror devices in two ways:

- With Windows NT software mirroring
- With Windows NT hardware mirroring

Using Windows NT Software Mirroring

The Windows NT operating system offers a software alternative to SQL Server device mirroring: *RAID* in software. RAID stands for *Redundant Array of Inexpensive Disks* and refers to a method of distributing data among multiple disk drives. In addition to distributing the data, RAID writes additional information that can be used to help recover from hardware failures.

Device mirroring is only available if you're running SQL Server on Windows NT Server rather than on Windows NT Workstation or Windows 95. To establish a mirror of a Windows NT disk, run the Disk Administrator utility and choose Fault Tolerance ➢ Establish Mirror.

Using Windows NT Hardware Mirroring

Windows NT also supports specialized hardware that supplies mirroring functionality. Compaq, DEC, Hitachi, Micropolis, and other manufacturers supply disk subsystems that automatically store every disk write on more than one hard drive. These systems can be very expensive, but they provide protection from hardware failure with no software overhead at all.

Distributing Databases on Removable Media

You can create SQL Server databases on removable media, such as disks, CD-ROMs, or WORM drives. A single database can span up to 16 disks or CDs. These databases can then be distributed and installed on other SQL Servers. Because of the differences between different installations of SQL Server (for example, the only user that's guaranteed to be on every server is the SA user), you'll need to use some special procedures when creating and developing a database for distribution in this fashion.

Creating a Removable-Media Database

SQL Server supplies a stored procedure for creating databases that will later be placed on removable media, `sp_create_removable`:

```
sp_create_removable dbname,
 syslogical, 'sysphysical', syssize,
 loglogical, 'logphysical', logsize,
 datalogical1, 'dataphysical1', datasize1
 [..., datalogical16, 'dataphysical16', datasize16]
```

A database that will be distributed on removable media must use at least three devices: one for the system tables, one for the transaction log, and one for the actual data tables. The `sp_create_removable` stored procedure creates all of these devices and places the database on these devices. For each device, you need to supply the logical name, physical name, and size in megabytes. You can supply additional data device information if you anticipate that you will need to distribute the database on multiple disks.

Limitations for Removable-Media Databases

Once you've created your removable-media database, you can proceed to develop it just as you would any other database, adding tables, defaults, stored procedures, and other database objects. There are a few limitations you need to be aware of when developing specifically for removable-media databases:

- Don't add any other databases or logs to the storage devices created by `sp_create_removable`. Keep these devices for the exclusive use of the removable database.
- Keep the SA user as the DBO of the database. Don't transfer database ownership to another user.
- Don't add users to the database. (You can safely add groups to the database.)
- Don't change user permissions on database objects. (You can safely change group permissions.)
- Don't reference objects outside of the database from views, stored procedures, triggers, or other objects within the database.

When you are done developing and are ready to transfer the database to removable media, you should check to be sure that you haven't accidentally broken one of these rules. You can do this with the `sp_certify_removable` stored procedure, which also prepares the database for the transfer to removable media:

```
sp_certify_removable database_name, [AUTO]
```

If you include the AUTO parameter, the stored procedure will transfer ownership of all objects back to SA (if any are owned by other users). This stored procedure also truncates the transaction log, moves the log to the system device, drops the log device, and marks the database as being offline. These changes ensure that the database is in a consistent state and ready to be moved to removable media.

Once the database has been certified, you can copy its physical files (the `*.dat` files that hold the database devices) on to disks or CDs and distribute those media to other SQL Server administrators. You'll also need to include the information returned by `sp_certify_removable`: the physical and logical names and sizes of the system and data devices. These will be used by the administrator who installs a copy of the database.

Installing a Removable-Media Database

If you've received a database on removable media, you can follow these steps to install it on your own SQL Server:

1. Run sp_dbinstall to install the system device:

   ```
   sp_dbinstall database_name, system_logical_dev_name,
   ➥'system_physical_dev_name', size, 'SYSTEM', location.
   ```

   The logical and physical device names and size should match those for the system device as reported by sp_certify_removable. The location parameter indicates the full path and filename to use for the system device on your computer.

2. Run sp_dbinstall to install the each data device:

   ```
   sp_dbinstall database_name, data_logical_dev_name,
   ➥'data_physical_dev_name', size, 'DATA', location.
   ```

   The logical and physical device names and size should match those for the data device as reported by sp_certify_removable. The location parameter indicates the full path and filename to use for the system device on your computer. If there are multiple data devices, you need to run the stored procedure once for each device.

3. Run sp_dboption to put the database online:

   ```
   sp_dboption database_name, offline, FALSE.
   ```

4. Back up your master database, since this procedure makes changes to device and database information in the system tables.

Now that you know how to create devices and databases, you're ready to work with actual data. In the next skill, you'll learn how to create and manipulate SQL Server tables, which will store this data.

Are You up to Speed?

Now you can...

- ☑ create and drop SQL Server databases
- ☑ set database options
- ☑ maintain transaction logs
- ☑ estimate the storage requirements for a database
- ☑ distribute databases on removable media

SKILL 3

Working with Tables

- System data types
- User-defined data types
- Creating tables
- Modifying tables

Tables consist of a collection of columns that contain all of the data in the database and define the attributes of the data being stored. Each row in a table contains information about a single, unique record. When you design a database, you define tables by deciding what type of data each column will contain, and you set the length of each column and whether or not it can accept a null value. Additionally, you need to decide when and where to add constraints, defaults, indexes, and rules, and to decide which columns are to be primary or foreign keys.

Working with tables entails understanding a wide variety of SQL Server objects. This skill introduces the system data types and how to create your own data types, as well as how to create, drop, and alter tables. Other objects, such as constraints, rules, and triggers, are discussed in later skills.

TIP It is unlikely that you will ever come close to this limit, but a SQL Server database can hold up to 2 billion tables.

Data Types

When you create tables in SQL Server, you must define the columns in them. Defining columns requires that you specify a data type for the column as well as define other properties, such as name, length, precision, scale, and whether to allow nulls or not. The number of rows and total size of the table are limited only by the available storage.

WARNING The maximum number of bytes SQL Server can store per row is 8,092. You will get a warning message if you create a table with `varchar`, `nvarchar`, or `varbinary` columns whose total defined width exceeds 8,060 bytes. If you actually try to stuff data that amounts to more than 8,060 bytes into that row, you'll get another error message and the operation will fail.

Data types in SQL Server determine the types of values that are allowed in a column. If you define a column as numeric, then you will not be allowed to enter character data in that column. This enforcement of data types is one of the reasons why you should use a database, such as SQL Server, to store data, rather than a spreadsheet, where you can enter anything you like into a cell, as there are no restrictions. You can prevent bad data from entering the system in the first place by restricting the type of data that goes into a column as it's being entered. In later skills, we'll see how to use rules, defaults, and triggers to further enforce data integrity.

SQL Server supplies a variety of system data types for standard needs, such as storing dates, numbers, or text. You can also define your own custom data types if the built-in ones don't meet your specifications. In addition, SQL Server 7 now supports Unicode, which allows you to store any character from any character set that is defined by the Unicode Standard. This amounts to just about every character set in every known language, living or dead.

SQL Server Unicode Support

SQL Server supports Unicode data with the following three data types:

- `ntext`
- `nchar`
- `nvarchar`

These are similar to their ANSI counterparts except for the wider range of characters supported and the increased storage space required—twice as much as non-Unicode types. This is because each Unicode character requires two bytes to store, while ANSI characters only require one byte.

System Data Types

When you define a data type for each column in your table you can either use the system data types "out of the box" or define your own named data types, which are made up of the system data types. These are the system data types that you will be learning about in this skill:

- Binary (`binary`, `varbinary`)
- Text and image (`ntext`, `text`, `image`)
- Character (`char`, `varchar`, `nchar`, `nvarchar`)

- Date and time (`datetime`, `smalldatetime`)
- Exact numeric (`decimal`, `numeric`)
- Approximate numeric (`float/double precision`, `real`)
- Integer (`int`, `smallint`, `tinyint`)
- Monetary (`money`, `smallmoney`)
- Bit (`bit`)
- Timestamp (`timestamp`)
- Unique identifier

Binary

The binary data type includes two variations in syntax.

Syntax: binary[(*n*)] The `binary` data type holds a maximum of 8,000 bytes of fixed-length binary data where *n* is a value between 1 and 8,000. The storage size is *n* + 4 additional bytes. `Binary` is a fixed-length data type, so if you define a field as `binary(5)` it will always take 5 bytes of disk space (plus the additional 4) to store, whether you enter that much data in the field or not. Use `binary` when data entries will all be close to the same size.

Syntax: varbinary[(*n*)] `Varbinary` is similar to `binary`, except that it can hold up to 8,000 bytes of variable-length binary data. Only the actual length of the data entered is stored, with the maximum allowable length being specified by *n* (longer entries will be truncated). Use `varbinary` when the length of the binary data is unknown or may vary in length. If the binary data being stored exceeds the 8K byte limit, use the `image` data type.

TIP

If your binary data is almost always the same size with only occasional differences, consider using a `binary` column instead of a `varbinary` column. `Binary` columns are generally faster because the fixed-length storage allows SQL Server to retrieve data more efficiently.

Text and Image

Both text and image data consist of character or binary data stored as linked 2KB data pages. These are managed so that they appear to be stored in a table row, but what is actually stored in the table is a pointer to the first linked data page. When the column is initialized prior to using text or image data, a 2KB data page is allocated.

WARNING This linked storage introduces some limits on the use of these data types. You can't use text or image columns in ORDER BY, COMPUTE, or GROUP BY clauses, in an index, or as a local variable.

Syntax: text The text data type contains literal non-Unicode string data up to 2,147,483,647 characters. Text values are entered by delimiting them with single quotation marks (') and can be used with wildcard characters and the LIKE keyword. If you convert text data to char or varchar, it will be truncated to fit. The default length is 16.

Syntax: ntext ntext columns can hold data up to 1,073,741,823 Unicode characters long, which are stored as twice the number of bytes as characters entered.

Syntax: image The image data type can hold up to 2,147,483,647 bytes of binary data. If you enter image data using the INSERT statement, you have to precede the value by 0x. The image data type can't be used for variables or parameters in stored procedures or in a WHERE clause.

Character

The character data type stores values as strings which are entered by delimiting the data with single quotation marks ('). These values can be any combination of characters, symbols, or numbers. The character data type can also store either a null or an empty string (''). Use char for fixed-length characters and varchar when columns vary in the number of characters stored. Both char and varchar cannot exceed 8KB.

Syntax: char[(*n*)] char is a fixed-width data type which can contain from 1 to 8,000 ANSI characters, which means that *n* is the actual storage size regardless of the actual length of the data. Any unused storage is padded with trailing blanks.

Use char when data entered in a column will be the same length, since access times are slightly faster than for varchar. The default length is 10.

Syntax: varchar[(*n*)] varchar is similar to char in that it can contain from 1 to 8,000 ANSI characters, but *n* in this case refers to the maximum length of the string since varchar is variable width, which means only the data actually contained in the column is stored. Use varchar when you need to store null values or the data varies in length. The default length is 50.

TIP

There are tradeoffs between the char and varchar data types. Data stored in a char can be retrieved faster, since the fixed-length format helps SQL Server locate the data. On the other hand, if there's a lot of variation in the length of data, char can waste a lot of space compared to varchar. In general, store data which has a constant length (such as social security numbers) in char fields, and data that varies widely (such as city names) in varchar fields.

Syntax: nchar[(*n*)] nchar is a fixed-length data type which can contain from 1 to 4,000 Unicode characters.

Syntax: nvarchar[(*n*)] nvarchar is a variable-length data type which can contain from 1 to 4,000 Unicode characters.

NOTE

Unicode characters use 2 bytes per character, whereas ANSI characters only use 1 byte.

WARNING

Any data that is too long to fit in the specified character format is truncated at the *n*th character.

Date and Time

SQL Server supports two different date and time data types, datetime and smalldatetime. Date and time data are alphanumeric and are entered by enclosing the values with single quotation marks ('). When you enter data, the date and time parts are processed separately, so it doesn't matter whether you enter the time or date portion of the value first. However, it is important that you enter time components in their proper order: hours, minutes, seconds, milliseconds; AM, am, PM, or pm.

You also need to enter either a colon (:) or an am/pm signifier for time values to be properly recognized. You can enter spaces between different components or not. Either of the following examples will be stored correctly as January 1, 1997, 2:00 P.M.:

```
2:00 PM 1/1/97
1/1/97 2:00 PM
```


SQL Server and the Year 2000

If you are concerned about Year 2000 issues—and who isn't?—you don't need to worry with SQL Server since it is already compliant. It can hold values through 9999, so you can enter dates for many centuries to come and they will be accurate.

Syntax: datetime The `datetime` data type consists of two 4-byte segments: 4 bytes for the number of days before or after the base date of 1/1/1900, and another 4 bytes for the number of milliseconds after midnight. The data type is only valid for dates between 1753 and 9999. If you omit either the date part or both parts, `datetime` defaults to 1/1/1900. If you omit just the time part, then that segment defaults to 12:00:00:000 A.M. For example, if you type

```
1/1/97
```

it will be stored internally as January 1, 1997, 12:00:00:000 A.M. Conversely, if you type only

```
3:00 PM
```

it will be stored as January 1, 1900, 3:00:00:000 P.M.

Syntax: smalldatetime `smalldatetime` is a less precise version of `datetime`, using only 4 bytes of storage, one small integer for the number of days after 1/1/1900, and one small integer for the number of minutes past midnight. It is only valid for dates between 1/1/1900 and 6/6/2079 and with time accuracy only to the minute.

Exact Numeric

The two exact numeric data types in SQL Server, `decimal` and `numeric`, are identical in order to comply with ANSI compatibility, so we will consider them as one. They both consist of scaled numeric data with accuracy preserved to the least-significant digit. Each can contain an integer part to the left of the decimal point and a fractional part to the right of the decimal point.

Syntax: decimal[(*p*[, *s*])] and numeric[(*p*[, *s*])] The scale (*s*) is the maximum number of digits that can be stored to the right of the decimal point, and it must be less than or equal to the precision. When specifying the precision, use a value of 1 through a maximum of 28 (although you can get around this limitation if you have to by using the `/p` parameter with `SQLSERVER.EXE`). If you don't specify a scale or precision, the default precision is 18, and the default scale is 0. The storage for exact numeric data depends on the precision (*p*) required, precision being the maximum total number of digits that can be stored on both sides of the decimal point. Table 3.1 illustrates the storage needed for varying ranges of precision. The storage requirements are the same for both decimal and numeric data and depend on the total number of digits for the data and the number of decimal digits to the right of the decimal point. For example, more bytes are required to store 11111.11111 than 1.1.

TABLE 3.1: Storage Requirements for Decimal and Numeric Data

Precision	Storage in Bytes
1 – 9	5
10 – 19	9
20 – 28	13
29 – 38	17

Approximate Numeric

Approximate numeric data types are necessary when you need to store large floating-point numbers that can't be stored in an exact numeric data type. These are stored as accurately as possible, although some floating-point numbers, such as those ending in .3, are impossible to store accurately in a binary numbering system and require rounding. SQL Server rounds up, but results may vary.

Don't use floating-point columns where you need a precise match, such as in a `WHERE` clause. Since floating-point values are not stored precisely, you may not get a match where you expect one. See Skill 7, *Altering Data*, for more information on how to build queries.

Syntax: float[(*n*)] and double precision A `double precision`, or `float`, data type uses eight bytes of storage and can hold either a positive or negative number with a binary precision up to 15 digits. Its range of possible positive values is approximately 2.23×10^{-308} through 1.79×10^{-308} and its range of negative values is approximately -2.23×10^{-308} through -1.79×10^{-308}. Floats can also include an exponent.

`double precision` is an exact synonym for `float`, added for compliance with the ANSI SQL standards.

Syntax: real Think of a `real` as a smaller `float`, using only 4 bytes of storage and with a binary precision up to seven digits. Its range of positive values is from 1.18×0^{-38} through 3.40×10^{38}, and its range of negative values is -1.18×10^{-38} through -3.40×10^{38}.

Integer

An integer consists of numeric data with precision to a whole number. SQL Server has three flavors, with different storage and ranges: `int`, `smallint`, and `tinyint`.

Syntax: int `int` takes 4 bytes of storage and has a range of whole numbers from -2×10^{31} through 2×10^{31}.

Syntax: smallint `smallint` takes 2 bytes of storage and has a range of whole numbers from –32,768 through 32,767.

Syntax: tinyint `tinyint` takes 1 byte of storage and has a range of whole numbers from 0 through 255.

Monetary

Monetary data types are used for decimal currency values and are scaled to four digits of precision. Values computed using monetary data types are rounded up to the nearest cent, with accuracy to a ten-thousandth of a monetary unit.

Syntax: money `money` takes 8 bytes of storage and can store values ranging from –992,337,293,685,477.5808 through +922,337,203,685,447.5807 and is represented as a double-precision integer.

Syntax: smallmoney `smallmoney` takes 4 bytes of storage and can store values from –214,748.3648 through +214, 748.3647, with values being rounded up to two places.

TIP

The `money` and `smallmoney` data types are useful for many purposes besides currency. They preserve the values entered exactly, without rounding beyond the four digits of precision. So if you've got exact figures in engineering or other fields that don't require more than four decimal places, you might want to use the `money` data type.

Bit

The `bit` data type uses 1 byte of storage and can hold a value of either 1 or 0. Use the `bit` data type for True/False and Yes/No types of data where you don't need to store a null value.

Syntax: bit SQL Server will collect multiple `bit` fields into bytes for efficient storage. Up to eight `bit` fields will be stored in a single byte.

Timestamp

A `timestamp` is an auto-incrementing data type that is updated every time the row containing a `timestamp` column is inserted or updated. The `timestamp` has nothing to do with the `datetime` data type or the actual time on your computer clock, but is a monotonically increasing counter whose values are always guaranteed to be unique within a database. SQL Server uses the `timestamp` column to indicate the sequence of activity on that row and to speed up certain operations. A table can only have one `timestamp` column. It requires 8 bytes of storage and is unique within the database.

Unique Identifier

The `uniqueidentifier` consists of a 16-byte hexadecimal number, or GUID (globally unique identification number). This is useful when a row must be unique and there is no other candidate column in the table.

Synonyms

Data type synonyms are included in SQL Server for compatibility with ANSI SQL-92 standards. Table 3.2 illustrates the mapping between user-defined data types and system data types.

TABLE 3.2: User-Defined and System Data Types

User-Defined	System
`binary varying`	`varbinary`
`char varying`	`varchar`
`character`	`char`
`character`	`char(1)`
`character(n)`	`char(n)`
`character varying(n)`	`varchar(n)`
`dec`	`decimal`
`double precision`	`float`
`float[(n)] for n = 1-7`	`real`
`float[(n)] for n = 8-15`	`float`
`integer`	`Int`
`numeric`	`decimal`
`national character(n)`	`nchar(n)`
`national char(n)`	`nchar(n)`
`varying(n)`	`nvarchar(n)`
`national char varying(n)`	`nvarchar(n)`
`national text`	`ntext`

User-Defined Data Types

User-defined data types are composed of system data types. Each system data type has specific parameters. You can specify these parameters when designing a user-defined data type for a column, thus both fine-tuning and documenting the type of data the column can store.

When to Use a User-Defined Data Type

SQL Server allows you to create your own data types when you want a more specific data type than the built-in data types. For example, you can create a user-defined data type named `localphone`, which would consist of `varchar` data for the seven digits of a local phone number. The names are case-insensitive. If you include your data type in the model database, it will be automatically included in all subsequently created databases.

TIP You can also use user-defined data types to indicate an association between business rules and data. For example, if discounts are represented by exact numeric data with four digits of precision throughout your database, you might define a discount data type to represent this concept.

Creating User-Defined Data Types

You can create user-defined data types two ways: through the Enterprise Manager and by using the stored procedure `sp_addtype`.

To create a user-defined data type with SQL Enterprise Manager, follow these steps:

1. Expand the server group and then the database that will use the data type.
2. Right-click the database.
3. Click New, and then click User-Defined Data Type on the shortcut menu.
4. Fill in the options for the new data type as shown in Figure 3.1, which creates a `localphone` data type to hold a seven-digit phone number.

You can create your own data types using the system stored procedure `sp_addtype` and you can drop them using `sp_droptype`:

```
sp_addtype {type}, [, system_data_type] [, 'null_type']
```

{type} is the unique name of the new data type, which must obey all the rules for identifiers. *system_data_type* is the built-in SQL Server data type being used. The optional argument, *null_type*, specifies whether the default can be null or not null. To define the same data type we used in the example shown in Figure 3.1, a user-defined `localphone` of seven characters and able to contain null values, type:

```
sp_addtype localphone, 'varchar(7)', 'NULL'
```

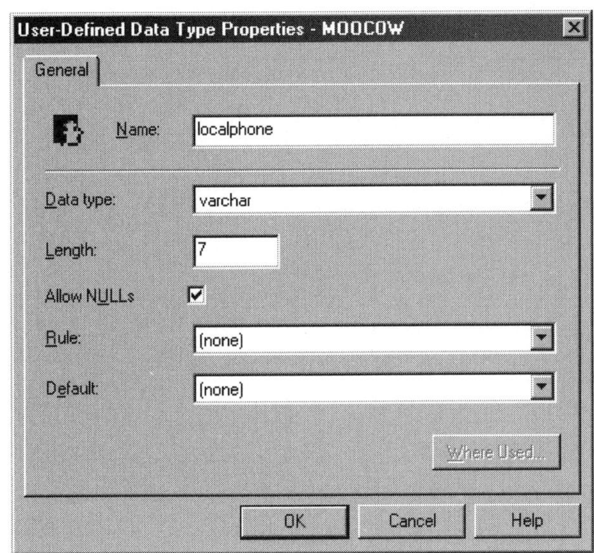

FIGURE 3.1: Creating a User-Defined data type using the Enterprise Manager

To drop a user-defined data type with SQL Enterprise Manager, expand the database window and then the User-Defined Data Types folder. Select the user-defined data type and click the Delete button.

If you want to remove a user-defined data type, you drop it by executing the `sp_droptype` system stored procedure. The syntax is `sp_droptype` *`typename`*.

To drop the `localphone` data type previously defined, type:

```
sp_droptype 'localphone'
```

Figure 3.2 shows running the stored procedure in the Query Analyzer.

NOTE

Note that you won't be able to drop `localphone` if you've used it in a table definition, rule, or default.

Skill 3

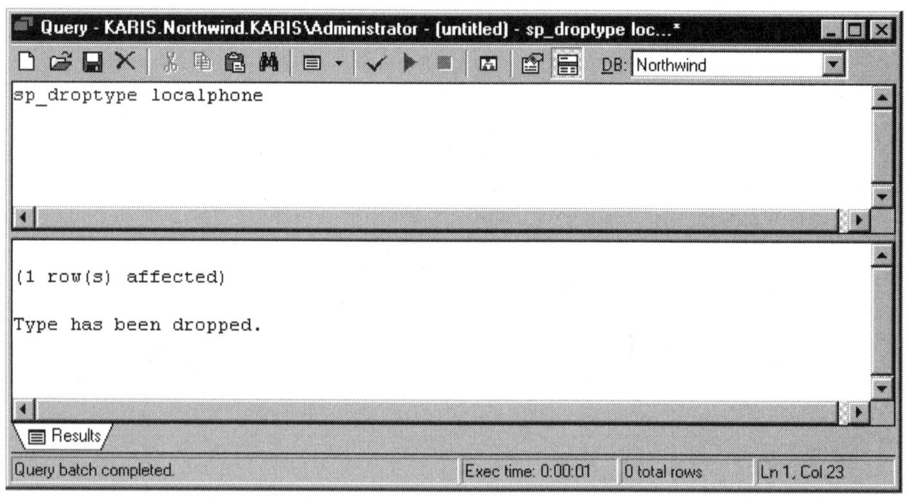

FIGURE 3.2: Deleting a user-defined data type with a stored procedure

Creating, Dropping, and Altering Tables

A database contains many tables, which store information. This section discusses how to create, delete, and modify tables in your application. All SQL Server tables possess certain common features of a relational DBMS, such as:

- Each table must have a unique name. It's a good idea to name the table something which identifies the subject or the type of information contained in the table.
- Tables are composed of rows (sometimes called records) and columns (sometimes called fields).
- Each row in a table must be unique and describe one set of related information about the subject of the table. The uniqueness of each row is ensured by the primary key, which consists of a column or columns with unique values.
- Each column or field describes a single characteristic of a set. Column names must be unique within a table.
- The order of the rows or columns should not be significant. In other words, storage should carry no information nor convey any meaning.

There are three main statements dealing with manipulating tables in SQL Server: `CREATE TABLE`, `DROP TABLE`, and `ALTER TABLE`. You can use either the Enterprise Manager or Transact-SQL to create and drop tables.

TIP SQL Server table and column names must follow the rules for identifiers listed in the sidebar, "SQL Server Identifiers," in Skill 2.

Creating Tables

In SQL Server you can create regular database tables as well as temporary tables, which can be either local (visible only to the current session) or global (visible to all sessions). Table names have to be unique within a database and follow the normal conventions for naming objects. Since creating a table involves creating the columns within the table at the same time, this skill will briefly discuss columns.

Guidelines for Creating Columns

Tables consist of columns that you define when you create the table. In order to optimize the benefits of using a relational DBMS, there are certain rules that you have to follow when creating your columns. The first and most important rule is: *Columns should be non-decomposable, that is, contain information that cannot be divided into smaller columns.*

If you can break down information further, then you need to make another column. The most common example of this is a column containing a person's name. A `PersonName` column that contained the first name, middle initial, and last name is not non-decomposable since it can be broken down into three columns: `FirstName`, `MiddleInitial`, and `LastName`.

Non-decomposable columns are easier to maintain since you can set separate rules. For example, you can set separate rules requiring an entry in the `LastName` field and a separate rule allowing null values in the `MiddleInitial` field. They are also a whole lot easier to query. If you store all three values in a single `PersonName` field, and you want a list of all people whose first name is Fred and who have no middle initial, you will have to write a program to examine every `PersonName` and then use string parsing functions to pick apart the name elements. On the other hand, designing a select query with a `WHERE` clause on the `FirstName` and `Middle-Initial` fields is a piece of cake.

NOTE For a complete discussion of data normalization and table and column design principles, see Skill 4, *Organizing and Normalizing Data*.

Setting Column Restrictions

You can restrict the data entered in columns by setting restrictions, or constraints, on the types of values allowed. Restrictions are placed on columns as part of creating tables. There are five types of constraints that you can set on columns, as shown in Table 3.3. These are explained in the following section on creating tables.

TABLE 3.3: Column Restrictions

Constraint	Meaning
PRIMARY KEY	Identifies the column(s) which uniquely identify a row in a table
FOREIGN KEY	Identifies the column(s) participating in a relationship between tables
NOT NULL	Requires that an entry be made in a column before the record can be saved
CHECK	Limits values that can be entered in a column
UNIQUE	Requires that each entry in a column be unique

Creating Tables

When you create a table in SQL Server, you have to define all of the columns, along with their constraints, all at once.

In Transact-SQL, use the CREATE TABLE statement, which has the following syntax:

```
CREATE TABLE table_name
(    {     <column_definition>
         | column_name AS computed_column_expression
         | <table_constraint>
    } [, ...n]
)
[ON {filegroup | DEFAULT} ]
[TEXTIMAGE_ON {filegroup | DEFAULT} ]
<column_definition> ::= { column_name data_type }
[ NULL | NOT NULL ]
[ IDENTITY [(seed, increment )
```

```
            [NOT FOR REPLICATION] ] ]
[ ROWGUIDCOL ]
[ <column_constraint> ::=
    [CONSTRAINT constraint_name]
    {     { PRIMARY KEY | UNIQUE }
            [CLUSTERED | NONCLUSTERED]
            [WITH [FILLFACTOR = fillfactor]
            ]
            [ON {filegroup | DEFAULT} ]
        | [FOREIGN KEY]
            REFERENCES ref_table
            [ ( ref_column ) ]
            [NOT FOR REPLICATION]
        | DEFAULT constant_expression
        | CHECK [NOT FOR REPLICATION]
            (logical_expression)
    }
] [ ...n]

<table_constraint> ::= [CONSTRAINT constraint_name]
{     [ { PRIMARY KEY | UNIQUE }
        [ CLUSTERED | NONCLUSTERED]
        { ( column[,...n] ) }
        [ WITH [FILLFACTOR = fillfactor]
        ]
        [ON {filegroup | DEFAULT} ]
    ]
    | FOREIGN KEY
            [(column[,...n])]
            REFERENCES ref_table [(ref_column[,...n])]
            [NOT FOR REPLICATION]
    | CHECK [NOT FOR REPLICATION]
        (search_conditions)
}
```

The `table_name` is the name of the table, which must be unique in the database and conform to the rules for identifiers.

The `computed_column_expression` defines the value of a computed column, which is not physically stored in the table, but computed from the values in other columns in the same table.

TIP You can't use computed columns as a key column in an INDEX, PRIMARY KEY, UNIQUE, FOREIGN KEY, or DEFAULT constraint definition. It also can't be the target of an INSERT or UPDATE statement. However, you can use them in select lists, WHERE and ORDER BY clauses, or in expressions.

`ON filegroup` specifies the file group on which the table is stored.

`TEXTIMAGE_ON filegroup` indicates that text and image columns are stored on the specified filegroup.

The `<column_definition>` section has the following syntax:

```
<column_definition> ::= { column_name data_type }
[ NULL | NOT NULL ]
[ IDENTITY [(seed[, increment] )
                        [NOT FOR REPLICATION] ] ]
[ ROWGUIDCOL ]
[ <column_constraint> ::=
     [CONSTRAINT constraint_name]
     {       { PRIMARY KEY | UNIQUE }
                     [CLUSTERED | NONCLUSTERED]
                     [WITH [FILLFACTOR = fillfactor]
                     [[,] {SORTED_DATA
                             | SORTED_DATA_REORG}]]
                     [ON filegroup]
             | [FOREIGN KEY]
                     REFERENCES ref_table
                     [ ( ref_column ) ]
                     [NOT FOR REPLICATION]
             | DEFAULT constant_expression
             | CHECK [NOT FOR REPLICATION]
                     (logical_expression)
     }
] [ ...n]
```

The *column_name* is the name of a column, which must be unique in the table and conform to the rules for identifiers.

The *data_type* specifies the column data type, which can be either system or user-defined.

The *constraint_name* is the name of a constraint, which must be unique in that database.

`ROWGUIDCOL` indicates that the column is a row global unique identifier. You can only have one per table.

The `<table_constraint>` section has the following syntax:

```
<table_constraint> ::= [CONSTRAINT constraint_name]
{     [ { PRIMARY KEY | UNIQUE }
              [ CLUSTERED | NONCLUSTERED]
              { ( column[,...n] ) }
              [ WITH [FILLFACTOR = fillfactor]
                     [[,] {SORTED_DATA
                             | SORTED_DATA_REORG} ]
              ]
```

```
            [ON filegroup]
        ]
        | FOREIGN KEY
                    [(column[,...n])]
                    REFERENCES ref_table [(ref_column[,...n])]
                    [NOT FOR REPLICATION]
        | CHECK [NOT FOR REPLICATION]
              (search_conditions)
}
```


You can create PRIMARY KEY, UNIQUE, FOREIGN KEY, DEFAULT, and CHECK constraints in a table. A table can have only one PRIMARY KEY and DEFAULT constraint, but up to 249 UNIQUE constraints. FOREIGN KEY constraints can reference up to 63 tables in the same database and can also reference other columns in the same table. They can only reference PRIMARY KEY or UNIQUE constraints in the referenced table. DEFAULT constraints can contain constants, functions, ANSI-standard niladic functions, or Null. They can't refer to other columns, tables, views, or stored procedures or be created on timestamp or identity columns. You can have as many CHECK constraints as you want, with the condition containing multiple logical expressions.

NOTE A niladic function is a built-in function that does not retrieve information from SQL Server. It is usually used when inserting data to provide a default value if one is not supplied.

To create a new table in the pubs database using the Enterprise Manager, right-click the database you want the table to be in and select New, then select the Table option. Fill in the options, as shown in Figure 3.3. This will create a table named Person, with LastName, FirstName, and MiddleInitial fields in the pubs database. Only the LastName column will not allow null values.

2:New Table in 'Northwind' on 'KARIS'

Column Name	Datatype	Length	Precision	Scale	Allow Nulls	Default Value	Identity	Identity Seed	Identity Increment	Is RowGuid
LastName	varchar	50	0	0	☐		☐			☐
FirstName	varchar	50	0	0	☑		☐			☐
MiddleInitial	varchar	3	0	0	☑		☐			☐

FIGURE 3.3: Creating the Person table using the Enterprise Manager

To create the Person table discussed above using the `CREATE TABLE` syntax, with `LastName`, `FirstName` and `MiddleInitial` where only the `LastName` field is required, you would use the following syntax:

```
CREATE TABLE Person
(
    LastName        varchar(50)       NOT NULL,
    FirstName       varchar(50)       NULL,
    MiddleInitial   varchar(3)       NULL
)
```

TIP The default for new columns in SQL Server is Not Null, so don't omit this argument if you want to allow null values in a column.

The Identity Property

If you set a column's property to `IDENTITY`, it will generate a value that uniquely identifies each row in a table. You can use the `IDENTITY` property as a surrogate primary key in a table. You must use a data type of `tinyint`, `smallint`, `int`, `decimal`, or `numeric`. To add the `IDENTITY` property using the Enterprise Manager, select the table from the Tables folder, right-click, and select the Design Table option. Fill in the options for a new column named `PersonID`, making it a `smallint`, and check the Identity box as shown in Figure 3.4. The seed value will default to 1 with an increment value of 1. This will cause the numbering to start automatically at 1 when the first record is entered into the table and increase by one with each new record entered. To make the `PersonID` field a primary key, click the gold key icon on the toolbar. A key icon will then appear in the row selector next to `PersonID`.

2:Design Table 'Person'

Column Name	Datatype	Length	Precision	Scale	Allow Nulls	Default Value	Identity	Identity Seed	Identity Increment	Is RowGuid
LastName	varcha	50	0	0	☐		☐			☐
FirstName	varcha	50	0	0	☑		☐			☐
MiddleInitial	varcha	3	0	0	☑		☐			☐
PersonID	smallint	2	5	0	☐		☑	1	1	☐

FIGURE 3.4: Adding an IDENTITY property to the Person table using the Enterprise Manager

The correct syntax for this process is `identity [(seed, increment)]`. For example, if we wanted to add a column to the Person table which would generate a unique value to be used as a primary key, we could set the `IDENTITY` property to begin numbering at 1 and to increase by 1 each time a record is added:

```
IDENTITY(1,1)
```

The completed code to create the Person table with a primary key would look like:

```
CREATE TABLE Person
(
  PersonID      smallint     IDENTITY(1,1) PRIMARY KEY CLUSTERED,
  LastName      varchar(25) NOT NULL,
  FirstName     varchar(25) NULL,
  MiddleInitial varchar(25) NULL
)
```

TIP The `IDENTITY` property will automatically number each row in a table and is guaranteed to be unique within that table. However, other tables in the same database may also have the same `IDENTITY` property. If you need a globally unique identifier that is unique across the entire database, use the `uniqueidentifier` data type and set its `Identity Seed` property to the newid() function and set its `IsRowGUID` property to true.

Temporary Tables

You can create either global temporary tables, which are visible to all sessions, or local temporary tables, which are visible in only the current session. All temporary tables are stored in the sysobjects table in the tempdb database. Local temporary tables are automatically dropped at the end of a session and global temporary tables are automatically dropped when the session that created the table ends.

Since temporary tables are not persistent objects, you don't use the Enterprise Manager to create them. Create a local temporary table by assigning a single pound sign as a prefix to the name of the table (`#localtablename`) or a double pound sign for a global temporary table (`##globaltablename`). You have a limit of 128 characters for a local temporary table, including the # signs. You can create any kind of a constraint definition except foreign key constraints.

Dropping Tables

The way you delete a table is to drop it. Once you drop a table, all of the data in the table is deleted. Any indexes and permissions will be deleted along with the table. Rules and defaults bound to the table are not deleted, but they are no longer bound. Constraints and triggers are automatically dropped, but if you have a view based on a dropped table, you must drop the view in a separate step since it will not automatically be deleted when the table is dropped.

You can drop a table through the Enterprise Manager by selecting the table and pressing the Delete key, which will bring up the Drop Objects dialog box, as shown in Figure 3.5. To view any objects that depend on the table, or that the table depends on, click the Show Dependencies button.

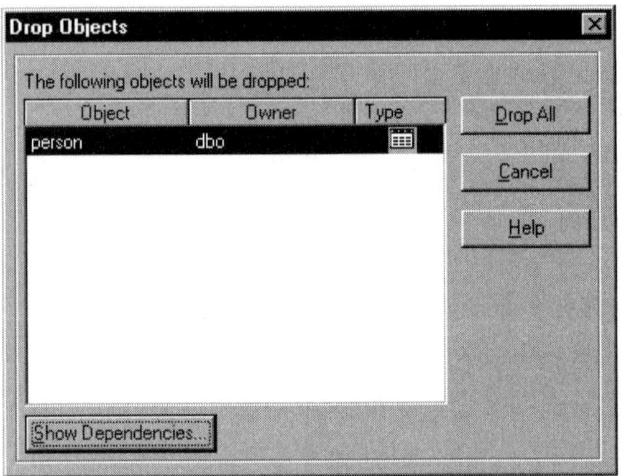

FIGURE 3.5: Dropping a table with Enterprise Manager

DROP TABLE

You can also use the `DROP TABLE` statement, which has the following syntax:

```
DROP TABLE table_name
```

The following will drop the Person table created above:

```
DROP TABLE Person
```

Limits on Dropping Tables

You can drop any table that you create; however, there are some tables that you won't be able to drop:

- Any of the system tables in the master database or any other database
- Any table that is being referenced by a foreign key constraint
- Any table that you do not own, unless you are the database owner or system administrator

Modifying Tables

You can modify your tables using the Enterprise Manager or the `ALTER TABLE` statement. You can alter the following details:

- Add or remove columns.
- Add new table- or column-level constraints.
- Enable or disable foreign key constraints.
- Enable or disable triggers.
- Defer constraints during replication.

To add columns to an existing table, right-click it and select the Design Table option, which will allow you to modify the table. Figure 3.6 shows a new column added for the Social Security number to the Person table. Click the Save button to save the new column.

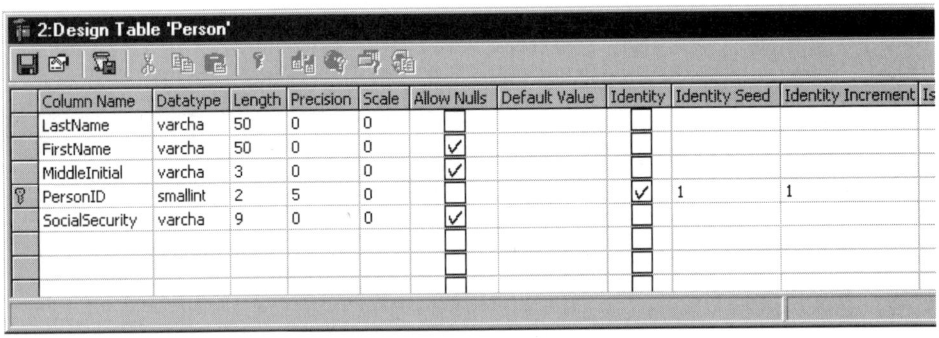

2:Design Table 'Person'

	Column Name	Datatype	Length	Precision	Scale	Allow Nulls	Default Value	Identity	Identity Seed	Identity Increment	Is
	LastName	varcha	50	0	0	☐		☐			
	FirstName	varcha	50	0	0	☑		☐			
	MiddleInitial	varcha	3	0	0	☑		☐			
🔑	PersonID	smallint	2	5	0	☐		☑	1	1	
	SocialSecurity	varcha	9	0	0	☑		☐			

FIGURE 3.6: Adding columns to a table with the Enterprise Manager

ALTER TABLE

The ALTER TABLE statement has the following syntax:

```
ALTER TABLE table
{
    [WITH CHECK | WITH NOCHECK]
    {       [ALTER COLUMN column_name
                    {
                            [ new_data_type [ (precision[, scale] ) ]
                                            [ NULL | NOT NULL ] ]
                            | [ {ADD | DROP} ROWGUIDCOL ]
                    }
            ]
            | ADD
                    {       [ <column_definition> ]
                            |  column_name AS computed_column_expression
                            | [ <table_constraint> ]
                    }[,...n]
            | DROP
                    {       [CONSTRAINT] constraint
                            | COLUMN column
                    }[,...n]
            | {CHECK | NOCHECK} CONSTRAINT
                    {ALL | constraint[,...n]}
            | {ENABLE | DISABLE} TRIGGER
                    {ALL | trigger[,...n]}
    }
}
```

The *table* argument specifies which table to alter. The `WITH NOCHECK` option will allow you to add constraints without checking the existing data for possible pre-existing violations. `ADD` lets you add a constraint. The `[<column_definition>]` part of the syntax is shown here:

```
<column_definition> ::= { column_name data_type }
[ NULL | NOT NULL ]
[ IDENTITY [(seed[, increment] )
                    [NOT FOR REPLICATION] ] ]
[ ROWGUIDCOL ]
[ <column_constraint> ::=
     [CONSTRAINT constraint_name]
     {       { PRIMARY KEY | UNIQUE }
                    [CLUSTERED | NONCLUSTERED]
                    [WITH [FILLFACTOR = fillfactor]
                    [[,] {SORTED_DATA
                            | SORTED_DATA_REORG}]]
                    [ON filegroup]
             | [FOREIGN KEY]
                    REFERENCES ref_table
                    [ ( ref_column ) ]
                    [NOT FOR REPLICATION]
             | DEFAULT constant_expression
             | CHECK [NOT FOR REPLICATION]
                    (logical_expression)
     }
] [ ...n]
```

column_name and *data_type* are the name and data type of the column in a table. The `<column_constraint>` part of the syntax contains the different properties that you can set, as well as any constraints and their properties.

To add new columns to the Person table, use the following syntax:

```
ALTER TABLE Person ADD
    address1 varchar(50) NULL,
    address2 varchar(50) NULL,
    areacode varchar(3) NULL,
    phone localphone NULL,
    deptID char(5) NULL
```

TIP

Remember that `localphone` is a custom data type we defined using the sp_addtype stored procedure at the beginning of this skill.

Skill 3

PLACING TABLES ON FILEGROUPS

You can create a table to be located on a specific filegroup instead of the default filegroup. This allows you to spread out the table across different physical disks, each with its own disk controller. Any queries on the table will also be spread out across the disks, improving performance.

You can also specify any `text`, `ntext`, or `image` columns to be created on a separate filegroup from the base table. When editing a table using the Enterprise Manager, right-click the column and then click Properties. Select the filegroup to which you want the column to belong from the Text File Group. To place the entire table on another filegroup, you can select the filegroup from the Table File Group.

Adding Constraints

You can add constraints with `ALTER TABLE` for:

- One primary key per table.
- Any number of foreign keys. This will require a matching record for that column in another table.
- One `DEFAULT` constraint per column. This will provide a default value if data is not initially entered in it.
- One `CHECK` constraint per column. `CHECK` is used to enforce domain integrity by limiting the possible values that can be entered in a column.
- One `UNIQUE` constraint per column. This will ensure that no duplicate values may be entered in that column.

To modify the additional columns added above, we can create constraints to add a `FOREIGN KEY` constraint to the `DeptID` field, which will check to make sure there is a related record in the Dept table, and a `CHECK` constraint to the area code to ensure that only numeric data is entered.

The easiest way to use the Enterprise Manager to add a FOREIGN KEY constraint is to create a Database Diagram.

1. Right-click the Diagrams folder, select New Database Diagram, and follow the wizard, selecting the tables you want to modify.
2. In this case, we want to create a relationship between the Person table and the Department table, with the DeptID column being the foreign key in the Person table. Starting from the Department table, select and drag the DeptID column and drop it on the Person table.
3. Fill in the dialog box as shown in Figure 3.7.

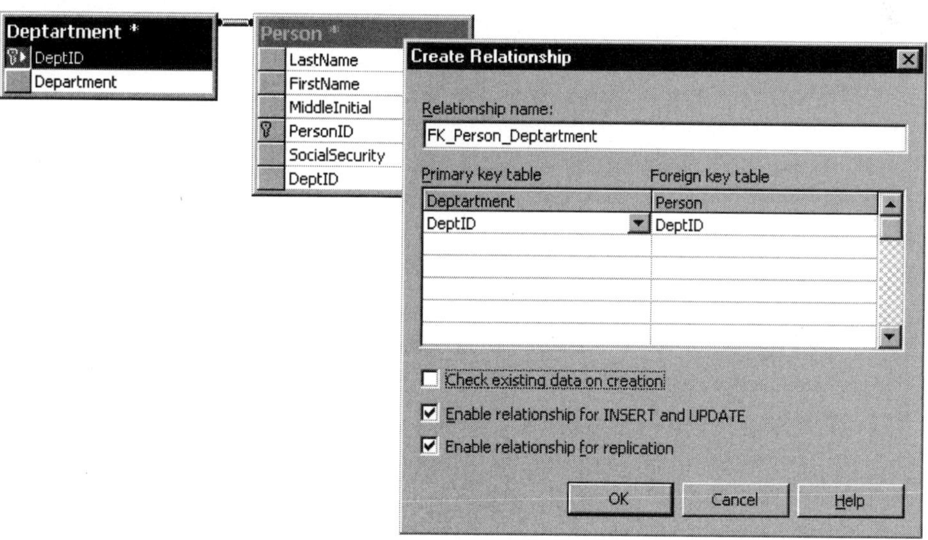

FIGURE 3.7: Adding a FOREIGN KEY constraint using the Database Diagrams view

You can also add the FOREIGN KEY constraint, as well as an areacode constraint, using the ALTER TABLE statement:

```
ALTER TABLE Person
ADD

CONSTRAINT FK_person_dept FOREIGN KEY (DeptID) REFERENCES
   department(DeptID),

CONSTRAINT ck_areacode CHECK (areacode LIKE '[0-9][0-9][0-9]')
```

NOTE Why would you add a constraint to a table? Most of the time, you'll do this to help enforce integrity rules on your data. These rules are discussed in Skill 4.

Renaming Tables

To rename a table through the Enterprise manager, follow these steps:

1. Right-click the table and select Rename.
2. Retype the name as shown in Figure 3.8 below. You will be prompted to confirm since any stored procedures, views, or triggers that depend on the table will become invalid. You can also view the list of dependent objects by clicking the View Dependencies button.

Name	Owner	Type	Create Date
Categories	dbo	User	1998-08-10 16:21:03.297
CustomerCustomerDemo	dbo	User	1998-08-10 16:22:06.967
CustomerDemographics	dbo	User	1998-08-10 16:22:07.077
Customers	dbo	User	1998-08-10 16:21:03.687
Dept	dbo	User	1998-09-16 17:32:34.067
dtproperties	dbo	System	1998-08-10 16:21:04.280

FIGURE 3.8: Renaming a table using the Enterprise Manager

sp_rename

The `sp_rename` system stored procedure lets you rename any user-defined object, such as tables, columns, indexes, or user-defined data types. You can't change the names of most systems objects and you can only change the names of objects that you own.

The syntax is:

```
sp_rename {'object_name'} [, 'new_name'] [, 'object_type']
```

In this statement, *`object_name`* is the name the object currently has, and *`new_name`* is the name you wish it to have. The *`object_type`* parameter allows you to specify exactly which object you're renaming in cases where, for example, a column in one table has the same name as an index in another table. To rename our Person table to be the Employee table, type the following:

```
sp_rename Person, Employee
```

TIP

Instead of renaming stored procedures and views, you should drop them and re-create them with the new name. If you rename them instead, you have to make sure to flush the procedure cache to ensure that dependent views and stored procedures are recompiled.

NOTE

Information about views and stored procedures is automatically updated in the sysobjects system table when you rename them. When a `PRIMARY KEY` or `UNIQUE` constraint is renamed, any associated indexes are updated. If you rename an index, which is tied to a primary key, then the primary key will also be renamed.

Using Indexes

Although you can store data in a table as soon as you create the table, you will probably want to do some additional work to make your data easier to work with. One thing you can do to speed up data access is to add appropriate indexes to your tables.

What Is an Index?

An index in SQL Server provides a logical order to data in your tables and can speed access to this data. If you didn't create any indexes, SQL Server would have to read the data in each row and column to find the rows you are trying to retrieve. Indexes work a lot like indexes in a book, which specify a page where specific information is located. When you create an index on a column in a table, SQL Server can locate information more quickly, without having to scan the entire table to look for it.

NOTE

There are two types of indexes, *clustered* and *non-clustered.* A clustered index sorts rows based on the key values. This means that there can only be one clustered index per table since rows can only be sorted in one order at a time. A non-clustered index does not sort based on the key since the index data structure is separate from the data rows. A table without a clustered index is a heap, and its rows are not stored in any particular order. Having to locate a row in a heap is going to be a lot slower than locating a row with a clustered index.

When Should You Index a Table?

Indexes speed queries that join tables, that search for specific information in a WHERE clause, or that use ORDER BY and GROUP BY operations. Indexes also speed up updates and deletes since SQL Server has to find the row before it can update or delete it. You can also use an index to specify uniqueness on a column. However, not every column should be indexed, since adding too many indexes can also lessen performance since indexes take up additional disk space. When data is added or deleted, indexes must also be modified.

In general, you should only index columns based on high selectivity. In other words, just a few rows would be returned that meet the criteria. You would not want to create an index on a column with only two values, since too many rows would likely be selected.

You should index columns which meet the following criteria:

- You search the columns frequently or use them with a WHERE clause.
- You use the columns in sorting data.
- The columns are primary keys, foreign keys, or any other columns used in joins.

Don't index columns in the following cases:

- You won't need to sort or search.
- Too many rows are going to be returned.
- The data in the column exceeds 20 bytes.
- The column contains only a few unique values.

TIP In some situations, you may need to benchmark performance times for certain operations in order to determine whether you are achieving the maximum benefit from indexing. There are no hard-and-fast rules since every database is different, and performance times may vary depending on the amount of data actually being stored.

You can create indexes using the Enterprise Manager or through Transact-SQL. In Transact-SQL, use the CREATE INDEX statement to create and name an index.

Use `CREATE TABLE` with any of the following constraints to create an index at the same time as the table itself:

- `PRIMARY KEY` to create a primary key
- `UNIQUE` to create a unique index
- `CLUSTERED` to create a clustered index
- `NON CLUSTERED` to create a non-clustered index

Setting the Fill Factor

Indexes have a *fill factor*, which determines how densely the index is packed when it is created. If the table is going to have many updates and inserts, then create an index with a low fill factor to leave room for the future keys to be inserted. However, if the table is read-only or will otherwise not change much, then a high fill factor will reduce the physical size of the index, lowering the number of disk reads needed. The fill factor only applies when you create the index—indexes stabilize at a certain density over time as keys are inserted and deleted.

Calculating Fill Factors

Whenever an index page becomes full, the page splits in order to accommodate more data when index values change. If you specify a factor of 100 percent as the fill factor, then each index node page will fill completely, except for space for two entries. This is only useful for read-only data that will never change.

Use smaller values, such as 10, for tables that contain only a fraction of the data they will eventually contain. A smaller fill factor will cause each index to take up more space.

A clustered index with a fill factor will affect the amount of storage space since SQL Server must redistribute the data when it creates the clustered index.

Creating an Index

There are two ways to create an index using the Enterprise Manager. The easiest way is to use the Create Index Wizard.

1. From the Enterprise Manager, select Tools ➢ Wizards.
2. Expand the Database option and double-click Create Index Wizard, as shown in Figure 3.9.

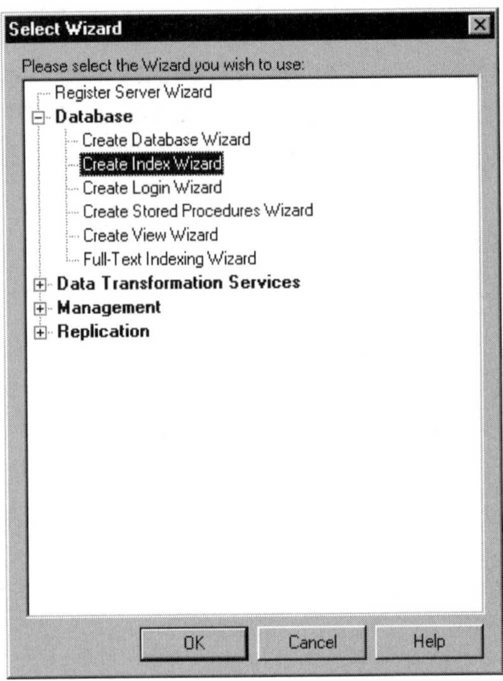

FIGURE 3.9: Select the Create Index Wizard in the Enterprise Manager

The wizard will walk you through the steps of creating an index, from selecting the database and table, showing you existing indexes, selecting the column to index, through specifying the index characteristics such as clustered, unique, fill factor, and name.

To create an index using the Enterprise Manager without the Create Index Wizard:

1. Right-click the table and select the Design Table option.

2. Select Properties by either right-clicking to bring up the shortcut menu or clicking the Properties toolbar button.
3. Select the Indexes/Keys tab and click New.
4. Fill in the options and click the Finish button. This will create a non-unique index on the `LastName` column. The properties of the new index are shown in Figure 3.10.

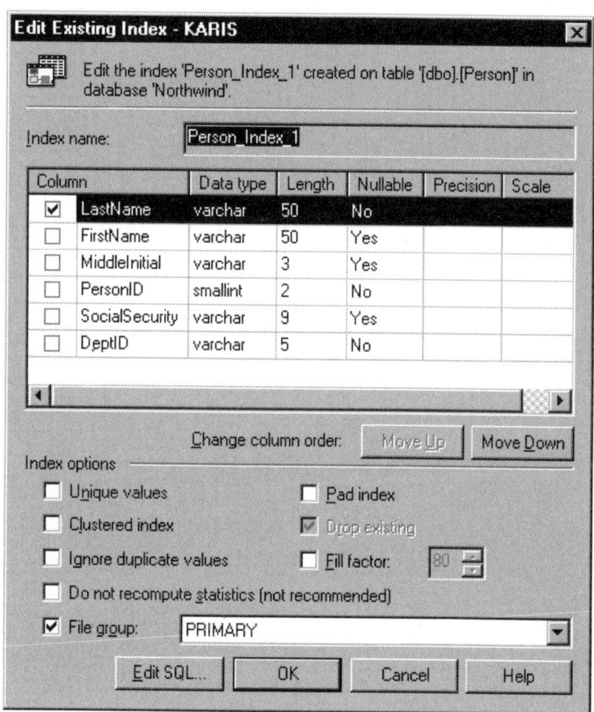

FIGURE 3.10: Creating an index using the Enterprise Manager

The Transact-SQL syntax for creating an index is:

```
CREATE [UNIQUE] [CLUSTERED | NONCLUSTERED]
     INDEX index_name ON table (column [, ...n])
[WITH
            [PAD_INDEX]
            [[,] FILLFACTOR = fillfactor]
            [[,] IGNORE_DUP_KEY]
```

```
                [[,] SORTED_DATA_REORG]
                [[,] {IGNORE_DUP_ROW | ALLOW_DUP_ROW}]
                [[,] DROP_EXISING]
                [[,] STATISTICS_NORECOMPUTE
]
[ON filegroup]
```

Use the following Transact-SQL syntax to create a unique, non-clustered index on the `LastName` column with a fill factor of 10 percent:

```
CREATE UNIQUE NONCLUSTERED INDEX IX_LastName
   ON Person (LastName)
   WITH FILLFACTOR = 10
```

Clustered and Non-Clustered Indexes

The difference between clustered and non-clustered indexes is that clustered indexes reflect the physical ordering of the data while non-clustered indexes represent a logical ordering of the same data. Therefore you can only have one clustered index on a table since data can only be stored in one physical order at a time, but you can have many logical orderings, or non-clustered indexes, of the same data.

Every table should have a clustered index to speed retrieval of data. Here's what you need to consider when you create your clustered index:

- Choose a column that has a high percentage of unique values or is used in joins. A primary key column is often a good choice, but other columns may be better—you may need to test based on the distribution of data in your particular database.
- Create the clustered index before you create any non-clustered indexes so non-clustered indexes don't have to be rebuilt after a clustered index is created.
- Use the `FILLFACTOR` option (discussed above) to ensure adequate free space on existing leaf pages.
- Use the `SORTED_DATA` option to reduce the space required to create the clustered index.

A non-clustered index specifies a logical ordering only, so you can create more than one on a table. Consider the following guidelines when creating non-clustered indexes:

- Add indexes only when they are useful, since every index created requires additional maintenance overhead.

- Index columns that are used in highly selective queries or are used for joins, ORDER BY clauses, in GROUP BY clauses, or WHERE clauses which return few duplicates.
- If the structure of a non-clustered index resembles the clustered index, don't bother—there won't be much performance gain. Use the clustered index instead.
- Don't use non-clustered indexes for range selections that are different from the physical data order unless the range reflects a small percentage of the values in the table.

TIP If you create an index and don't specify whether it is clustered or non-clustered, it will default to non-clustered.

You can create a clustered index using the Enterprise Manager by selecting the Create as Clustered checkbox in the Indexes dialog box.

To create a clustered index in Transact-SQL, type:

```
CREATE UNIQUE CLUSTERED INDEX IX_PersonID
   ON Person (PersonID)
```

TIP When creating indexes, use a naming convention that gives you some idea of the kind of information being stored and the relationship between tables. For example, a primary key index on the Authors table named AUTHORS_IDENT is a lot clearer than the same index named FRED.

Composite Indexes

A composite index consists of two or more columns, indexed together, with a maximum of 16 columns to a combined size of 900 bytes allowed. Composite indexes require less overhead than single-column indexes during data manipulation and can be used in place of multiple single-column indexes. You can also create a clustered, composite index. Consider the following issues when creating a composite index:

- Smaller indexes are more efficient than large (three-or-more column) indexes.
- Create a composite index when you search two or more columns as a unit.
- First list the column which has the most unique values, since the query optimizer will look there first to see if it's worthwhile using the index or not.

- Create a composite index for any columns which are accessed frequently, such as lookup tables.
- Don't index columns that get too large (more than 8 bytes) since it takes too long to retrieve the data.

NOTE If you index a table on `Column1`, `Column2`, and `Column3` and the `WHERE` clause only refers to `Column2` and `Column3`, then SQL Server can't use the index. In this case a separate index on each column would be faster since SQL Server could choose the most efficient one.

To create a composite index using the Enterprise Manager:

1. Right-click the table and select the Design Table option.
2. Select Properties by either right-clicking to bring up the shortcut menu or clicking the Properties toolbar button.
3. Select the Indexes/Keys tab and click New.
4. Fill in the options for the new index, which creates a composite index named `IX_Person_1` on the `LastName` and `FirstName` columns. The properties are shown in Figure 3.11.

The following will create a unique, non-clustered composite index using the `CREATE INDEX` statement:

```
CREATE INDEX IX_FullName
  ON Person (LastName, FirstName)
```

TIP The order in which columns are specified in a `WHERE` clause which uses a composite index does not matter as long as you specify the leftmost column in the index in the `WHERE` clause.

Using the Index Tuning Wizard

You can examine existing indexes using the SQL Server Profiler.

1. Choose Tools ➢ Wizards and expand the Management item.
2. Double-click Index Tuning Wizard to start it up and then run the wizard, completing the options.

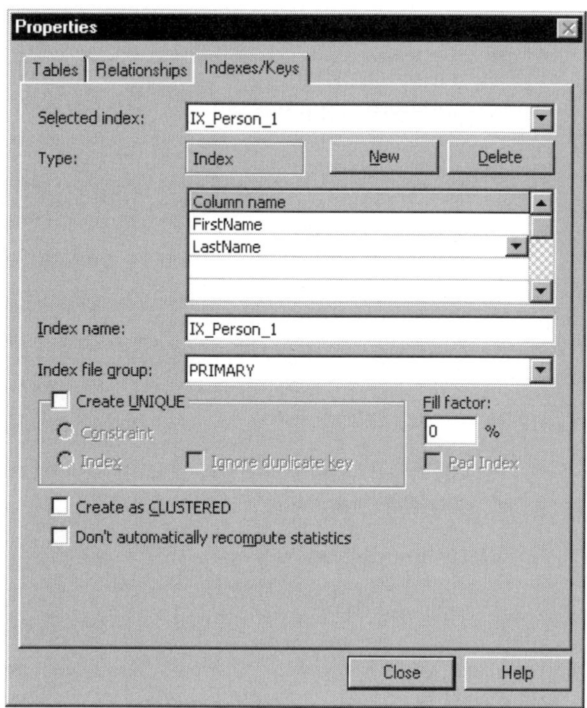

FIGURE 3.11: A composite index

Make sure to back up the database before you start, in case the wizard drops some indexes you may want back.

3. You will be prompted to select the server and database and whether or not to keep existing indexes, as well as whether or not you wish to perform a thorough analysis (which will be slower). Then you select whether or not you already have a saved workload file, which is a saved SQL Server Profiler trace, or whether you will create one on your own. (You have to create the trace file before you run the Index Tuning Wizard.)

4. Once you specify the trace file, you can set advanced options by clicking the Advanced Options button. These include maximum queries to tune, maximum space, and maximum number of columns per index.

5. The wizard defaults to selecting all the tables in the database, but you can select tables you want it to ignore. The wizard will then display its recommendations, as shown in Figure 3.12.
6. You can then elect to apply the changes and/or save to a script file.

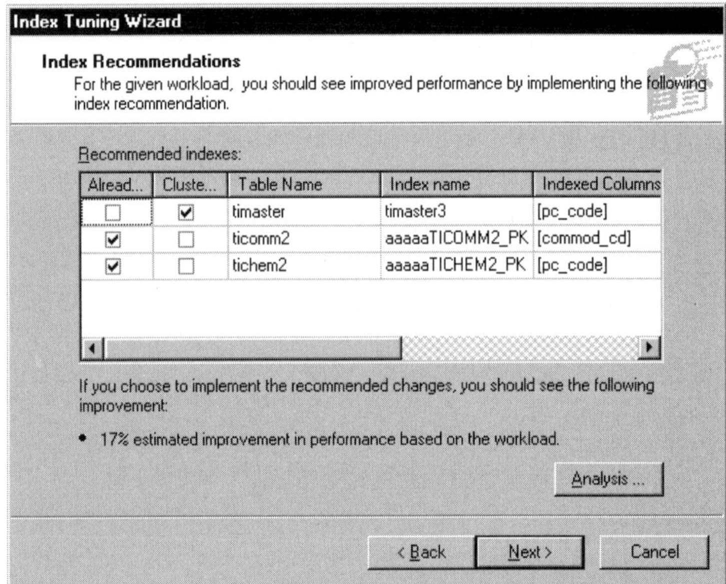

FIGURE 3.12: The Index Tuning Wizard's recommendations

Using sp_helpindex

You can also use the system stored procedure `sp_helpindex` to examine existing indexes. In a query window, execute the following:

```
sp_helpindex Person
```

You can then examine the output, as shown in Figure 3.13.

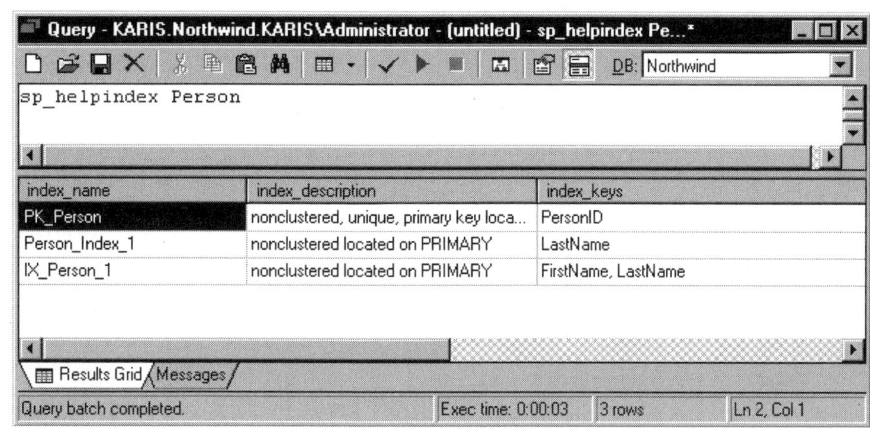

FIGURE 3.13: Examining the output of `sp_helpindex` in the Query Analyzer

Using UPDATE STATISTICS

The main tool used for maintaining indexes is the `UPDATE STATISTICS` stored procedure, which runs automatically when you create an index on a table that already contains data. You can run `UPDATE STATISTICS` yourself whenever the distribution of data changes due to modifications. The syntax is:

```
UPDATE STATISTICS {table} [index | (index_or_column [, ...n])]
     [WITH
            [
                   [FULLSCAN]
                   | [[,] SAMPLE number {PERCENT | ROWS}]
            ]
            [[,] NORECOMPUTE]
            [[,] [INDEX | COLUMNS | ALL]
     ]
```

To update statistics for all indexes on a table, type the following:

```
UPDATE STATISTICS table_name
```

To update statistics for a specific index in a table, type:

```
UPDATE STATISTICS table_name index_name
```

NOTE You should seldom need to update statistics by hand in SQL Server 7. That's because SQL Server now auto-updates statistics on a regular basis by sampling data in the tables. If you've recently imported a great deal of data to a table, you might want to update its statistics rather then relying on the random sampling.

The Database Consistency Checker (DBCC) provides the following tools that allow you to examine the state of indexes in a particular database:

- DBCC DBREINDEX
- DBCC SHOWCONTIG
- DBCC CHECKTABLE
- DBCC CHECKDB
- NOINDEX

TIP If you are converting your database from an earlier version of SQL Server, make sure to check out the different output for certain DBCC statements since some earlier ones are no longer supported.

You can also execute a query with the option `SET SHOWPLAN_ALL` or `SET SHOWPLAN_TEXT`, which will report information on the final access method that the query optimizer selected for that particular query. You can use it to verify that the indexes you created are actually being used. A query executed with the `SET STATISTICS IO` option will report the number of pages already in data cache as well as the number of pages that must be retrieved from the disk.

You can also specify an optimizer hint in a query, which will allow fine-tuning of an index selection. This acts as a "tip" for the optimizer in suggesting that a particular index be used. The following query will suggest using the index named `aunmind` for querying the Authors table in the pubs database:

```
SELECT au_lname, au_fname, phone FROM authors
(INDEX = aunmind)
WHERE au_lname = ' Blotchet-Halls'
```

NOTE For more information on querying, see Skill 7.

Dropping an Index

To drop an index from the Enterprise Manager, follow these steps:

1. Right-click the table and select the Design Table option.
2. Select Properties by either right-clicking or clicking the Properties toolbar button.
3. Select the Indexes/Keys tab and then select the index you want to delete from the drop-down list box. Click the Delete button, as shown in Figure 3.14 below.

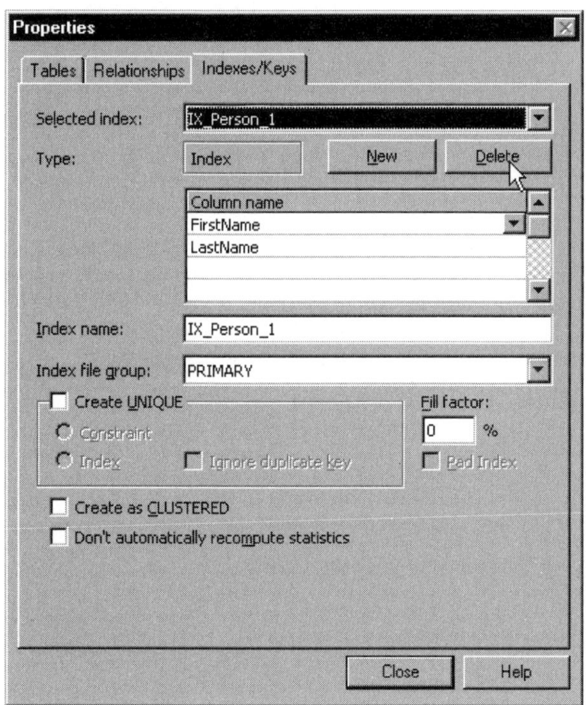

FIGURE 3.14: Dropping an index

The syntax for dropping an index in Transact-SQL is:

```
DROP INDEX {'table.index'} [, ...n]
```

The optional argument *n* is a placeholder indicating that you can drop multiple indexes.

To drop the FullName index in the Person table in the pubs database, use the following syntax:

```
DROP INDEX FullName.Person
```

Are You up to Speed?

Now you can . . .

- ☑ work with existing SQL Server data types
- ☑ create your own custom data types
- ☑ create your own tables and columns
- ☑ modify existing tables and columns
- ☑ set and modify primary and foreign keys
- ☑ set and modify constraints
- ☑ drop existing tables
- ☑ work with indexes

SKILL 4

Organizing and Normalizing Data

- Data integrity
- Data normalization
- Tools for data integrity
- Primary and foreign keys
- Declarative Referential Integrity

Now you know how to set up SQL Server to store your data—but you may still be a bit uncertain about *what* data to store. Understanding the creation process for tables is necessary to using SQL Server, but it's not sufficient. The purpose of a database is to provide a computer representation of some real-world problem. You can think of this as a data model. But the real world is much messier and more chaotic than any computer database. When you finish with this skill, you'll know how to take your real-world situation, analyze it, and create an efficient and useful set of tables to represent that situation.

Data Normalization

Normalization is a fancy word for a simple topic. Think of your database like your sock drawer (or, at least, like your mother wanted your sock drawer to be). There should be a place for everything, and everything should be in its place. If you keep unmatched socks in multiple random places, you'd never find a matching pair to wear to work in the morning. And if you mixed your socks with your swimfins in the same place, you might look pretty funny if you weren't paying attention when you got dressed.

Normalization is the process of taking a tangled mass of data and untangling it, to make tables with logical places for each piece of the tangle. The notion of data *integrity* works hand in hand with normalization: integrity rules help you identify units of data in order to protect the data; normalization rules help you decide where to store these units. We'll learn about both integrity and normalization in this skill.

NOTE The whole concept of relational database theory was developed by Dr. Codd at IBM back in the 1960s and is based on set theory and predicate logic. You don't have to immerse yourself in the scientific and technical underpinnings of Dr. Codd's work in order to understand and implement a sound database design, but you do need to understand the basic concepts, which apply to all relational databases—not just SQL Server 7.

Integrity Concepts

Integrity rules are designed to keep your data consistent, correct, and compliant with your business rules. You've undoubtedly heard the computer maxim

"Garbage in, garbage out." The main reason we use databases rather than spreadsheets or word processors to store our data is that databases are designed to use integrity rules to help prevent garbage from getting into the database in the first place. We'll look at four data integrity concepts in this skill:

- Entity integrity
- Domain integrity
- Referential integrity
- User-defined integrity

Entity Integrity

The basic idea of *entity integrity* is that you must be able to identify each entity that you store in a database. An entity is any real-world thing (either an object, a subject, or an event) that you choose to represent in the database. For example, suppose you were developing a patient-tracking system for an HMO. Entities in this system might include:

- Patients
- Prescriptions
- Physicians
- Drugs
- Appointments

Each entity needs to have a *primary key*, which consists of a unique characteristic or set of characteristics that distinguish it from other entities of the same type.

NOTE If you can locate a single column that serves to identify records in a table, you've found a *simple primary key*. If it takes a combination of columns to do this, the table is said to have a *composite primary key*.

As you're developing a database *schema* (a set of tables with interrelationships) to represent your real-world problem, you'll create a table to store each entity and a field (or group of fields) to store the primary key for each entity. Table 4.1 shows one possible set of tables, fields, and primary key fields for our hypothetical HMO.

TABLE 4.1: A Set of Tables and Keys

Table	Fields (* indicates primary key)
Patients	Patient Name*, Address, Age
Prescriptions	Patient*, Drug*, Date*, Amount, Pharmacy, Cautions
Physicians	Physician Name*, Specialty
Drugs	Drug Name*, Manufacturer
Appointments	Patient*, Physician*, Date*, Reason

Identifying key fields is the first step in enforcing entity integrity. Think about the Prescriptions table, for example. If we know that our physicians never prescribe the same drug twice for the same patient in the same day, then the combination of patient name, drug name, and prescription date is enough to uniquely identify the prescription. Put another way, if we know those three pieces of information, we can look up the amount and pharmacy in our Prescriptions table and know we've found the correct information since those three columns are the unique identifiers for every prescription.

Once you've identified the key fields for your tables, you can use a variety of SQL Server features to enforce entity integrity. You could create a unique index on the field, as discussed in Skill 3, to prevent users from entering duplicate key values. You can also use `PRIMARY KEY` or `UNIQUE KEY` constraints, or the `IDENTITY` property, to enforce entity integrity. These features are discussed later in this skill.

Domain Integrity

Just as entity integrity keeps watch over the values entered in a table, *domain integrity* enforces restrictions on the values you can enter in a particular column. For any given piece of data—say, the physician name or the prescription date in our HMO database—there is some *domain* of values that is valid for entry in that field. Another way to think of domain is as the business rules that govern each column. At the simplest level, the data type assigned to the column enforces domain integrity. For example, you won't be able to enter text in a domain that is defined as a date. The more you can do to limit the data that can be entered into the field for this domain, the higher your chance of keeping bad data from entering your database.

SQL Server (like most other database products) can store a special value called Null. A Null is a placeholder for unknown data: it's not equal to anything else, not even another Null. As you're considering the domain integrity rules for your database, you should consider the special case of whether a field should allow Nulls or whether to require users to enter a value when they create a new record. SQL Server uses the `NOT NULL` clause in a `CREATE TABLE` statement to specify that a particular field should not accept Null values. If you do specify `NOT NULL` on a field, you won't be able to save the record until the value is supplied.

Table 4.2 specifies the domain of each field in our hypothetical HMO database. If you are just starting a new database design, you may wish to construct a table like this to help guide you in your choice of domain integrity rules.

TABLE 4.2: Field Domains

Table	Field	Domain	Nulls OK?
Patients	Patient Name	Names of people	No
	Address	Addresses in our city	No
	Age	Between 1 and 115	No
Prescriptions	Patient	Must be in our Patients table	No
	Drug	Must be in our Drugs table	No
	Date	Between 1/1/80 and 12/31/2099	No
	Amount	Integer, 1 to 500	No
	Pharmacy	Names of pharmacies	Yes
	Cautions	0–1000 text characters	Yes
Physicians	Physician Name	Names of people	No
	Specialty	Names of specialties	Yes
Drugs	Drug Name	Names of drugs	No
	Manufacturer	Names of companies	Yes
Appointments	Patient	Must be in our Patients table	No
	Physician	Must be in our Physicians table	No
	Date	Between 1/1/80 and 12/31/2099	No
	Reason	0–1000 text characters	Yes

SQL Server provides a variety of tools for enforcing domain integrity. These include:

- Data types
- User-defined data types
- `DEFAULT` constraints
- `CHECK` constraints
- Rules
- `FOREIGN KEY` constraints

Referential Integrity

If you look back at Table 4.2, you'll see that there are some fields whose acceptable values are defined in terms of fields in other tables. For example, it wouldn't make sense for the Appointments table to contain the name of a doctor who isn't in the Physicians table. Enforcing relationships such as this and ensuring that we do not have orphan records—appointments without doctors—is the job of *referential integrity*. If we preserve referential integrity between the Appointments and Physicians tables in this example, we must constrain, or limit, a number of possible database actions:

- We can't add an appointment for a non-existent physician.
- We can't change the physician name for an existing appointment, unless the new name is already in our table of physicians.
- We can't delete a physician who has appointments.
- We can't change the physician name of a physician who has appointments.

These rules are not as arbitrary as they might seem at first glance. The basic idea is that no matter what actions you perform in the database, you always have to be able to match each appointment to a corresponding physician. Referential integrity states that there are immutable relationships between tables in our database that need to be enforced.

TIP In the real world, of course, physicians do sometimes change their names. We could allow for this in our database by using a different unique characteristic, say employee number, as the primary key of the Physicians table and the linking field, or *foreign key*, of the Appointments table. Such a key, which provides uniqueness but no real-world information, is called a *surrogate key*.

The relations between tables in a database can be represented as shown in Figure 4.1. Here the lines between the tables show the relationships that referential integrity will preserve, and the key symbols show the primary key fields. This diagram was created using SQL Server's own Database Diagram tool.

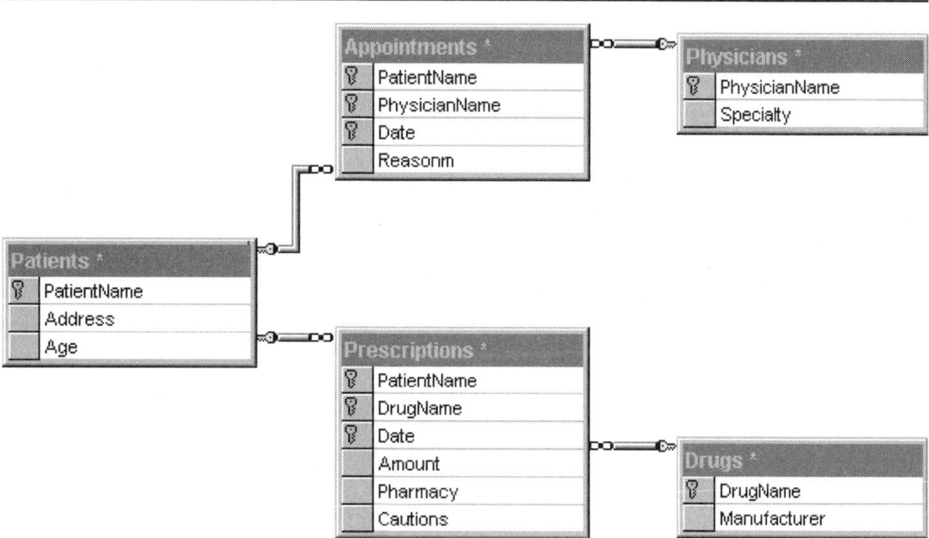

FIGURE 4.1: Schema for the HMO database

Referential integrity may be modified by introducing the concepts of cascading updates and cascading deletes. Cascading increases the range of allowable database actions while still preserving the relationships between different tables. If you implement cascading updates, you can change the primary key of a table on the parent side of a relationship, and the foreign keys on the child side will be automatically updated to match. If you implement cascading deletes, you can delete a record from a parent table, and any matching child rows will be automatically deleted as well.

SQL Server provides several tools for maintaining referential integrity:

- `FOREIGN KEY` constraints
- `CHECK` constraints
- Triggers and stored procedures

Generally speaking, implementing cascading updates causes little harm, but you need to carefully consider whether implementing cascading deletes makes sense in a given relationship. For example, if you have implemented cascading deletes between the doctor table and the patient table, accidental deletion of a doctor will trigger deleting all of the related patient rows as well. In this case cascading deletes is a bad idea—without it, users would be prevented from deleting a doctor if there were related records in the patient table. When deciding whether or not you need to implement cascading deletes in a given situation, ask yourself whether or not you want all the historical data on the child side to be permanently deleted. If the answer is no, then don't implement cascading deletes.

NOTE Although `FOREIGN KEY` constraints have largely replaced triggers and stored procedures for implementing referential integrity, the latter are still necessary if you need cascading updates or cascading deletes.

User-Defined Integrity

Entity integrity, domain integrity, and referential integrity are all formal database concepts. *User-defined integrity* encompasses all other "business rules" that don't fit neatly into one of these concepts. For example, we might know that the Cautions field of the Prescriptions table should include "Do not operate heavy machinery" any time it also includes "Do not drive while using this prescription." Such a rule can't be expressed through integrity rules and can only be implemented using triggers, rules, or stored procedures on the server, or through logic implemented in whatever client program we use to retrieve data from the database.

Normalizing Data

As you design databases with entity, domain, and referential integrity, you'll begin to recognize patterns in the way that you organize the data. For example, the search for primary keys will encourage you to separate dissimilar data into different tables. These rules have been codified as the *normal forms*, a progression of structural ideas that have been shown to lead to well-behaved databases. Advanced books on the subject (such as C. J. Date's classic, *An Introduction to Database Systems*) identify half a dozen or more normal forms, but the higher forms are mainly of academic interest. For most straightforward business databases you'll only need to be concerned with the first three normal forms.

Each normal form includes the previous ones, so that a database in Third Normal Form is automatically in First Normal Form and Second Normal Form as well. As you're gaining experience in database design, you may want to explicitly apply the rules of each normal form in turn to your original inchoate sea of data, moving through the process of *normalizing* the data. As you grow more experienced, you'll find that you tend to automatically put your data in Third Normal Form, and may just need to review the final database schema to make sure you haven't introduced any inconsistencies on the way.

TIP As you're learning the normal forms, it's important to concentrate on the concepts, rather than knowing precisely which normal form enforces which rules.

First Normal Form

Before you even start normalizing your data, it is assumed that every table has a primary key. Having a primary key for each table in your database schema is not a part of the normalization process; it is the prerequisite.

The rules for First Normal Form are simple: each field in a table must contain only a single type of data, and each piece of data must only be stored in one place. This requirement is sometimes phrased as a requirement for *atomic data*. There are two ways in which First Normal Form is commonly violated in incomplete database designs. First, related data may be lumped into a single field. An example of this would be a single Address field containing street address, city, state, postal code, and country. In this case, getting to First Normal Form would mean breaking this field up into at least five separate fields (Address, City, State, PostalCode, and Country).

Another common violation of First Normal Form is the repeating field. For example, suppose you were creating a database to track invoice information. You might define an Invoice table with fields such as Quantity1, Part1, Amount1, Quantity2, Part2, Amount2, Quantity3, Part3, and Amount3. A structure such as this runs into problems because it is not flexible enough, wastes space, and is an inefficient structure for quickly retrieving data once it's entered. For example, if you only need a single line on a particular invoice, you're wasting space with all the empty columns. If you need four lines, you'd need to create extra columns since there's nowhere to put the fourth one. You can solve this problem temporarily by entering multiple rows in the table, but the real solution is to break out a separate InvoiceLine table and use referential integrity to relate it back to the main Invoice table.

As with the other normalization rules, putting a database into First Normal Form is a matter of judgment. You must consider not just the formal arrangement of your data, but the business scenarios you'll use it for. Think about people's names, for example. If you just use the name as a customer identifier, and you almost never get repeat business or need to find a particular customer, you can probably get by with a single Name field. But the moment you need to sort people alphabetically by last name, or search for a particular person by last name, you'll find it necessary to have FirstName and LastName fields. The business requirements in this case dictate that a single Name field is not atomic, while in other circumstances, such as storing a company name, it can be.

Second Normal Form

To achieve Second Normal Form, you must make sure that your tables contain data about one and only one entity. Operationally, you can check this by making sure that you can identify a primary key for every table, and that all non-key fields are dependent on the primary key and not on other fields in the table.

Some violations of Second Normal Form are easy to spot. For example, in an invoicing database, you might decide to put both customers and suppliers in a single BusinessParty table, since they share the same fields (Name, Address, City, State, and so on). But this structure would violate Second Normal Form, which requires separate Customer and Supplier tables. More importantly, if you did not separate these tables, you'd find certain fundamental operations very hard to implement. For example, you might want to present your users with an easy way to select the supplier for an invoice. How could you do this if customers and suppliers were all muddled up in a single table?

When a table has a composite primary key, violations of Second Normal Form can be harder to spot. For example, in our hypothetical Appointments table (which has a key of Physician, Patient, and Date), you might be tempted to include the Specialty field, since the specialty is dependent on the physician. But this too would be a violation of Second Normal Form, since the specialty is not dependent on the entire primary key of the table. Storing the specialty in the Appointments table would waste space, since you'd have to repeat it with every appointment, instead of storing it once in the Physician table where it belongs.

Third Normal Form

The rule for Third Normal Form is that all non-key fields must be mutually independent. That is, you should be able to change the value of any field without needing to recalculate or "fix up" any other field. The most obvious violations of Third Normal Form are calculated fields. If you design an Invoice table that includes Quantity, Price, and TotalPrice fields (with TotalPrice being simply Quantity multiplied by Price), you've violated Third Normal Form. You can derive the total price any time you need it by knowing the Quantity and Price values for the record. Storing it requires you to make multiple changes to keep the record self-consistent any time you must change one of these fields.

Third Normal Form also helps you see that some tables need to be split into multiple pieces. If we stored patient data in our Appointments table in the HMO database, for example, we'd quickly find that changing a patient's address is a nightmare, requiring us to search through the entire table and change the address for every appointment belonging to that patient. We're much better off to split out the Patient table separately, so that changing a patient's address affects only a single row of data.

THE RULES OF NORMALIZATION

The following rules pertain to normalization:

- Each table must have a primary key.
- All fields must contain atomic data.
- There must be no repeating fields.
- Each table must contain information about a single entity.
- Each field in a table must depend on all fields in the primary key.
- All non-key fields must be mutually independent.

Tools for Enforcing Data Integrity

Understanding the principles of data normalization is one thing, but how do you enforce these rules using SQL Server? As we've mentioned above, SQL Server provides a wide variety of tools for enforcing data integrity. In this section, we'll discuss identity columns, constraints, rules, and declarative referential integrity (DRI). You can also use triggers and stored procedures for some complex operations, such as maintaining user-defined integrity or implementing referential integrity with cascades. These more advanced tools are discussed in Skill 7, *Altering Data.*

Identity Columns

A simple tool for enforcing entity integrity is the *identity column*. An identity column is a column in a table that SQL Server automatically supplies values for. By default, the first value is 1 and each succeeding value is one more than the previous value, but both the starting value (the "seed") and the increment can be specified by the database designer.

To create a table including an identity column using SQL Server Enterprise Manager, right-click Tables and choose New Table. Choose a name for your new table, and then fill in field names and sizes for your table in the New Tables window shown in Figure 4.2.

TIP This table design tool is completely new to SQL Server with this release, but it will be familiar to users of Visual Studio. It's part of a new set of shared tools called the Microsoft Visual Design Tools. These tools, which include the table and view designers and the database diagrammer, are becoming the standard for all Microsoft products that manipulate data.

When you're ready to choose the identity column for your table (in this case, EmployeeID), click the checkbox in the Identity column of the table designer in the row for the field you've chosen. If you like, you can specify a seed value and increment to use for this column, or you can accept the system-supplied defaults.

TIP In general, you can use the same SQL Server Enterprise Manager dialog boxes to alter constraints that you use to add them in the first place. Just right-click the table and choose Design Table.

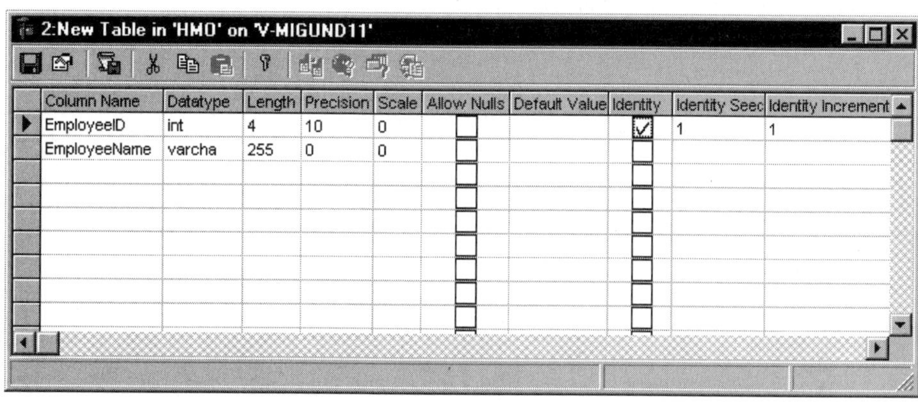

FIGURE 4.2: Creating a table with an identity column

You'll notice that you receive an error message if you try to click the Identity checkbox on some rows. That's because SQL Server Enterprise Manager automatically recognizes the limits on which columns can be identity columns. These limits are:

- Data type can only be `tinyint`, `smallint`, `int`, `decimal[p,0]` or `numeric[p,0]`.
- The column must not allow null values.
- There can only be one identity column per table.
- There cannot be a default bound to the column.

In Transact-SQL, you specify the identity column during the `CREATE TABLE` statement. To create the table shown in Figure 4.2, you could use this Transact-SQL statement:

```
CREATE TABLE Employee (
     EmployeeId int IDENTITY (1, 1) NOT NULL ,
     EmployeeName varchar (255) NOT NULL
)
```

TIP For the complete syntax of the `CREATE TABLE` statement, see Skill 3. To add an identity column to an existing table with Transact-SQL, use the `ALTER TABLE` statement, also covered in Skill 3.

For the most part, you can treat an identity column just like any other column when using your database. However, you cannot insert data into the identity column unless you first use the special `SET IDENTITY_INSERT` statement. SQL Server provides a global variable, `@@IDENTITY`, which contains the last identity value generated by any `INSERT` statement executed in the database.

TIP In `SELECT`, `UPDATE`, `INSERT`, and `DELETE` statements, you can use the special keyword `IDENTITYCOL` to refer to the identity column in the table, rather than specifying it by name.

Constraints

SQL Server uses *constraints* to enforce limitations on the data that can be entered into a particular column in a table. You can use `UNIQUE`, `DEFAULT`, and `CHECK` constraints to enforce entity, domain, and user-defined integrity. In addition, SQL Server uses `PRIMARY KEY` and `FOREIGN KEY` constraints to implement referential integrity. These two types of constraints are discussed in their own section later in this skill.

TIP If a constraint is violated, the command that caused the violation is terminated and has no effect. However, if this command is part of a batch transaction, the transaction will continue. If statements in a transaction may violate constraints, you should check the value of the `@@ERROR` global variable and execute a `ROLLBACK TRANSACTION` statement if the `@@ERROR` variable is not equal to zero.

Unique Constraints

A `UNIQUE` constraint specifies that all values in a given column must be unique, that is, the column must have a different value in every row in the table. A table can have multiple `UNIQUE` constraints, in which case they must all be satisfied for every row. `UNIQUE` constraints obviously bring entity integrity to a table, since they guarantee that every row is different.

To add a `UNIQUE` constraint to a table using SQL Server Enterprise Manager, you can use the Indexes/Keys tab of the Properties dialog box of the table designer, as shown in Figure 4.3. (To open this dialog box, first open your table in the designer and then click the Table and Index Properties toolbar button, second from the left in the designer.) Click the New button to add the constraint and select the column name in the Column Name grid. Click the Create Unique checkbox. SQL Server will generate a name for the new constraint.

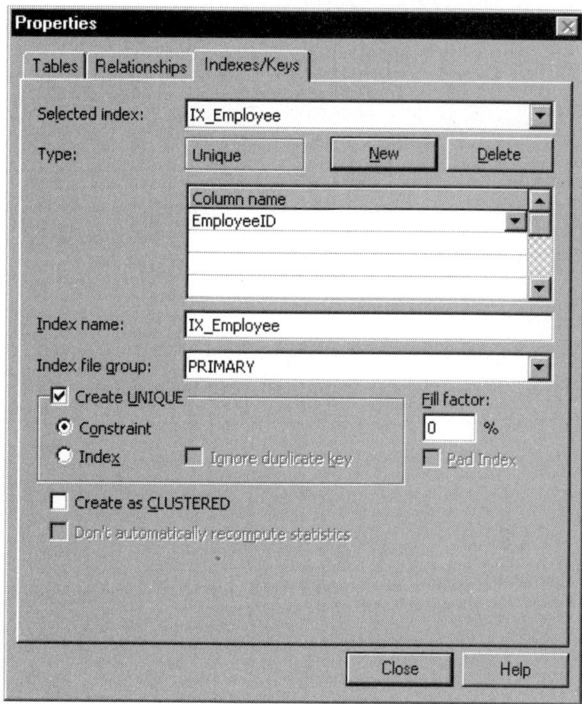

FIGURE 4.3: Adding a UNIQUE constraint to an existing table

In Transact-SQL, you can create a UNIQUE constraint with the CREATE TABLE statement:

```
CREATE TABLE Employee (
     EmployeeId int IDENTITY (1, 1) NOT NULL ,
     EmployeeName varchar (255) NOT NULL ,
     CONSTRAINT Unique1 UNIQUE NONCLUSTERED
     (
             EmployeeId
     )
)
```

In this example, `Unique1` is the name of the constraint to be created. Whenever SQL Server creates a `UNIQUE` constraint, it automatically creates an index on the field as well. By default, this is a non-clustered index, but you can specify either the `CLUSTERED` or `NONCLUSTERED` keyword explicitly if you'd like to control this. Clustered and non-clustered indexes are discussed in Skill 3.

WARNING If you've used Microsoft Access, you might expect a SQL Server Identity column to automatically enforce entity integrity, but this is not the case. You can insert duplicated values into an Identity column. To enforce entity integrity, you should also apply a `UNIQUE` constraint to the column.

Default Constraints

A `DEFAULT` constraint gives you a way to supply a default value for a column in any table. That is, the constraint provides the value that will be stored with new rows in the data when the value for the column is not otherwise specified. `DEFAULT` constraints can help enforce domain integrity by providing reasonable values for new records. They also help with some user-defined integrity problems: for example, all new customers might start with an account balance of zero.

`DEFAULT` constraints can be specified in the Default Value column of the table designer, as shown in Figure 4.4. You can specify a constraint for any column except timestamp columns or identity columns. Note that you must supply the constraint in this dialog box using legal Transact-SQL syntax; that is, character values must be enclosed in single quotes.

Name	Datatype	Length	Precision	Scale	Allow Nulls	Default Value	Identity	Identity Seed	Iden
eeID	int	4	10	0			✓	1	1
eeName	varchar	255	0	0					
eeTitle	varbinary	50	0	0	✓	('Salesperson')			

FIGURE 4.4: A table with a `DEFAULT` Constraint

In Transact-SQL, you use a CONSTRAINT clause to create a DEFAULT constraint, as in this example:

```
CREATE TABLE Employee (
     EmployeeId int IDENTITY (1, 1) NOT NULL ,
     EmployeeName varchar (255) NOT NULL ,
      EmployeeTitle varchar (50) NULL
      CONSTRAINT EmployeeTitleDefault DEFAULT ('Salesperson')
)
```

TIP You can't implement a DEFAULT constraint on a column that is defined with a user-defined data type that itself has a default bound to it.

The value supplied for a DEFAULT constraint (in this example, 'Salesperson') can be a constant, a function, NULL, or a niladic-function. *Niladic-functions* are functions supplied by SQL Server that do not take arguments. Table 4.3 lists the niladic-functions that are supplied by SQL Server.

TABLE 4.3: Niladic-Functions

Function	Returns
CURRENT_TIMESTAMP	The date and time from the clock of the machine running SQL Server
CURRENT_USER	User's database username
SESSION_USER	User's database username
SYSTEM_USER	User's Windows NT login name
USER	User's database username

Check Constraints

A CHECK constraint allows you to control the data entered into a particular column by evaluating an expression. The expression must return a Boolean value. If the return value is False, the constraint has been violated and the command that caused the violation will be terminated. CHECK constraints are useful for setting limits on acceptable data to enforce domain integrity, as well as for enforcing more complex user-defined integrity rules.

The Tables tab of the Property dialog box in the SQL Server Enterprise Manager table designer allows you to add CHECK constraints. Figure 4.5 shows the process of adding a CHECK constraint to an existing table. This particular constraint enforces a pattern on invoice numbers, so that they must start with two letters, followed by four numbers.

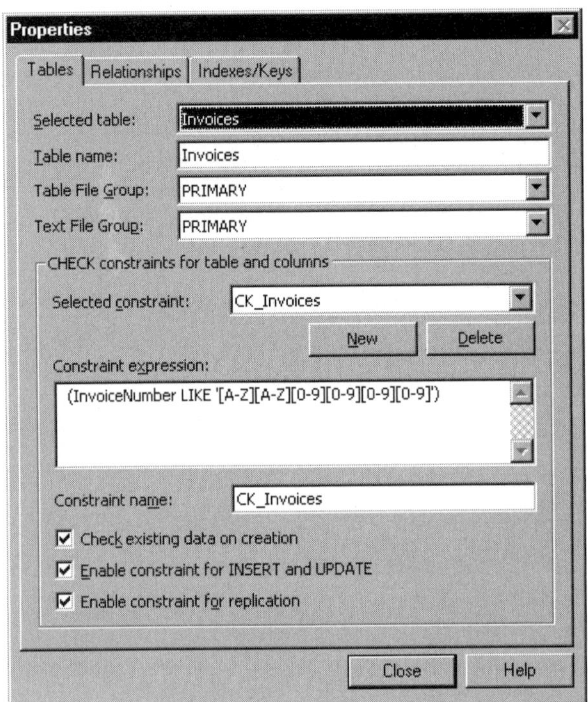

FIGURE 4.5: Adding a CHECK constraint

TIP

When you add a new CHECK constraint, SQL Server offers the option of checking the existing data in your table. If you're using the constraint to enforce integrity rules, you should check this option.

You could use this Transact-SQL to create the constraint as shown in the figure:

```
CREATE TABLE Invoices (
     InvoiceNumber char (6) NULL ,
     InvoiceAmount money NULL ,
     CONSTRAINT InvoiceNumberCheck
      CHECK ((InvoiceNumber LIKE '[A-Z][A-Z][0-9][0-9][0-9][0-9]'))
)
```

In this example, InvoiceNumberCheck is the name of the constraint.

TIP

In a SQL Server `LIKE` clause, you can specify a range of characters with the syntax `[a-z]`. This particular expression would match any character from lowercase *a* through lowercase *z*.

Table 4.4 shows some possible `CHECK` constraint expressions.

TABLE 4.4: Sample `CHECK` Constraints

Constraint	Result
`NetDays <= 30`	Allows values equal to or less than 30 in the NetDays column
`Sex IN ('M', 'F')`	Allows *M* or *F* in the Sex column
`((Age > 0) AND (Age < 100))`	Allows values between zero and 100 in the Age column

Rules

Rules provide another means of enforcing domain and user-defined integrity rules within your database. The easiest way to think of a rule is as a reusable constraint. A rule is a separate SQL Server object that can be bound to one or more columns in one or more tables.

To add a rule using SQL Server Enterprise Manager, right-click Rules in the main Server Manager window and choose New Rule. This will open the dialog box shown in Figure 4.6. To define the rule, enter an expression that returns a Boolean value and a name for the rule. Just as with `CHECK` constraints, if this expression evaluates to False, the operation that triggered the evaluation will be canceled. This expression can use one local variable to refer to the value being entered into the column. You can use any name to refer to this constant, but it must start with an @ sign.

You use the buttons at the bottom of this dialog box to bind this rule to as many columns as you like. Binding a rule to a column is the operation that tells SQL Server to use that rule when values are entered or changed in that column.

To create a rule with Transact-SQL, use the `CREATE RULE` statement:

```
CREATE RULE [owner.]rule_name AS expression
```

To bind a rule to a column using Transact-SQL, use the `sp_bindrule` system stored procedure:

```
sp_bindrule rule_name, column_name
```

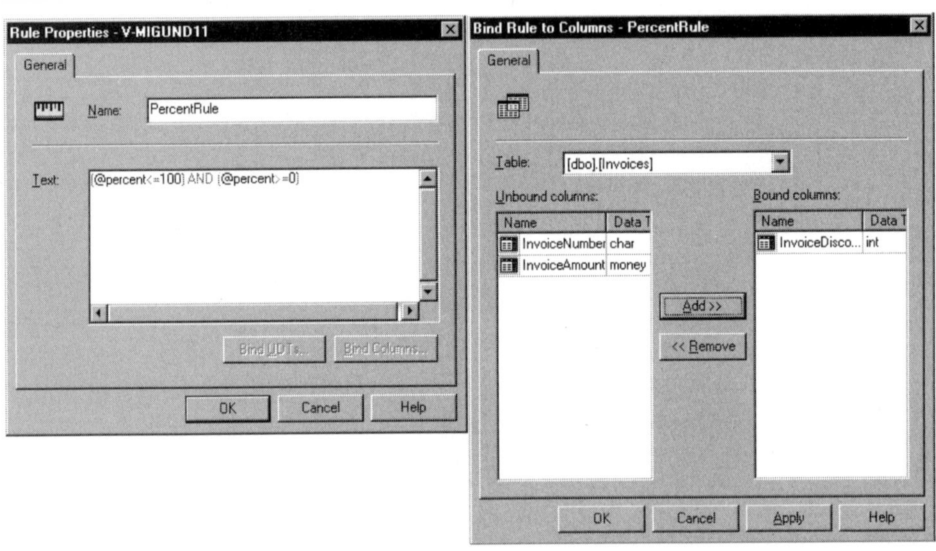

FIGURE 4.6: Managing a rule with SQL Server Enterprise Manager

In addition to binding a rule to a column, you can bind a rule directly to a user-defined data type. This will put this rule into effect for all columns of that data type.

TIP A single column can only have one rule bound to it. If you need multiple constraints on one column, use CHECK constraints instead of rules.

Denormalizing Data

Just as normalization is the process of arranging data in a very organized fashion, *denormalization* is the process of deliberately introducing redundancy to your data. Theoretically, of course, one should never denormalize data. However, in the real world things are not quite that simple. Sometimes it may be necessary to denormalize data in the interest of performance. An over-normalized database can be slow on a network due to the number of joins that have to be performed to retrieve data from multiple tables.

TIP When you are forced to denormalize data for performance, make sure you document your decision, so that some other developer doesn't think you simply made a mistake.

If your normalized data model produces tables with multi-part primary keys, particularly if those keys have four or more columns in them and are used in joins with other tables, you should consider denormalizing the data by introducing arbitrary surrogate keys. Identity columns, combined with `UNIQUE` constraints, provide a convenient means for creating these surrogate keys. You can then add arbitrary foreign keys to tables that join back to the main table and enforce the join on the surrogate keys instead. This will often provide a substantial performance benefit.

If producing calculated values, such as maximum historic prices, involves complex queries with many joins, you should consider denormalizing the data by adding calculated columns to your tables to hold these values. You can use triggers to ensure that these calculated columns are updated whenever one of the columns that they depend on is updated (for more on triggers, see Skill 8, *Using SQL Server Tools*).

If your database contains extremely large tables, you should consider denormalizing the data by creating multiple redundant tables instead. You may do this either by column or by row. For example, if the Employees table contains many columns, and some of these (such as hire date) are very infrequently used, it may help to move the less frequently used columns to their own table. By reducing the volume of data in the main table, you can make it faster to access this data. If the Employees table is worldwide and most queries are only interested in employees from one region, you can speed up the queries by creating separate tables for each region.

If data is no longer "live" and is being used for archiving or is otherwise read-only, denormalizing by storing calculated values in fields can make certain queries run faster.

TIP If you split a table into multiple tables by row, you can still query all the data by using the Transact-SQL `UNION` operator.

If queries on a single table frequently use only one column from a second table, consider including a copy of that single field in the first table. For example, you might choose to include a PhysicianName field in an Appointment table, even though the table already includes the PhysicianNumber, because you always list appointments by physician name. In this case, of course, you'll need to write code to ensure that the PhysicianName field is updated every time the PhysicianNumber is changed.

Remember, you should never denormalize your data without a specific business reason for the denormalization! Careless denormalization can ruin the integrity of your data, and lead to slower performance as well.

Using Declarative Referential Integrity (DRI)

Declarative Referential Integrity (usually just called DRI) is a process that allows you to notify SQL Server of the referential integrity between tables and to have the server automatically enforce these relationships. Prior to the implementation of DRI, keeping referential integrity enforced required writing trigger code for every table to perform appropriate actions under developer control. Now that SQL Server can do this automatically, performance has improved and the developer has more time to work on other parts of the application.

As with other integrity support, DRI is implemented using constraints on tables. There are two types of constraints used: `PRIMARY KEY` and `FOREIGN KEY`. We'll look at each of these in turn.

Primary Keys

In most relational databases, the primary key of a table performs two duties. First, since it is guaranteed to be unique on every record, it enforces entity integrity. Second, it serves as an anchor for referential integrity relationships from other tables. Before we look at the mechanism for creating primary keys in SQL Server, let's take a moment to discuss selecting primary keys.

Choosing Primary Keys

Given a table without a primary key, the developer usually has a choice as to what to choose for this primary key. Remember, a key may consist of one or more columns. The technical requirement is that the union of the data in all the primary key columns be unique for every row in the table (including rows that will be added in the future). Every column or combination of columns that fits this requirement is called a *candidate key*. So, in an Employees table, the Employee number might be one candidate key, but so might the combination of employee name and Social Security number.

NOTE Once you've chosen a primary key from among all possible candidate keys, the remaining candidate keys are called *alternate keys*.

So how do you decide which candidate key to actually use for your primary key? Two useful criteria are *minimality* and *stability*.

A minimal key is a key with the fewest columns. Thus, if you have a choice of a simple key or a composite key to be your primary key, take the simple key. This rule flows from the fact that, generally speaking, manipulating a single column is faster than manipulating multiple columns. Like other rules of thumb, there are exceptions to this. For example, a combination of two integer columns would be faster to work with than a single large `varchar` column.

Stability is a characteristic of the data in your table. Because the primary key will be used in relationships, it's important that the data in the primary key column change as little as possible—ideally, it should never change. This avoids the necessity to implement cascading updates and once again makes your database a bit faster. Thus, candidate keys such as employee number are usually preferable to candidate keys such as employee name.

Finally, remember the advice from the section on denormalization. If your table's natural primary key includes many fields, you're usually better off creating a surrogate key and making that the primary key of the table.

Creating Primary Keys

To add a primary key using SQL Server Enterprise Manager, select the row containing the field in the table designer and click the Set Primary Key toolbar button (the one with the little key on it). This will put the primary key on the row, as shown in Figure 4.7.

Using Transact-SQL, the primary key is selected with a `PRIMARY KEY` clause in the `CREATE TABLE` statement:

```
CREATE TABLE Customers (
     CustId varchar (6) NOT NULL ,
     CustName varchar (50) NOT NULL ,
     CONSTRAINT CustomersPK PRIMARY KEY CLUSTERED
     (
             CustId
     )
)
```

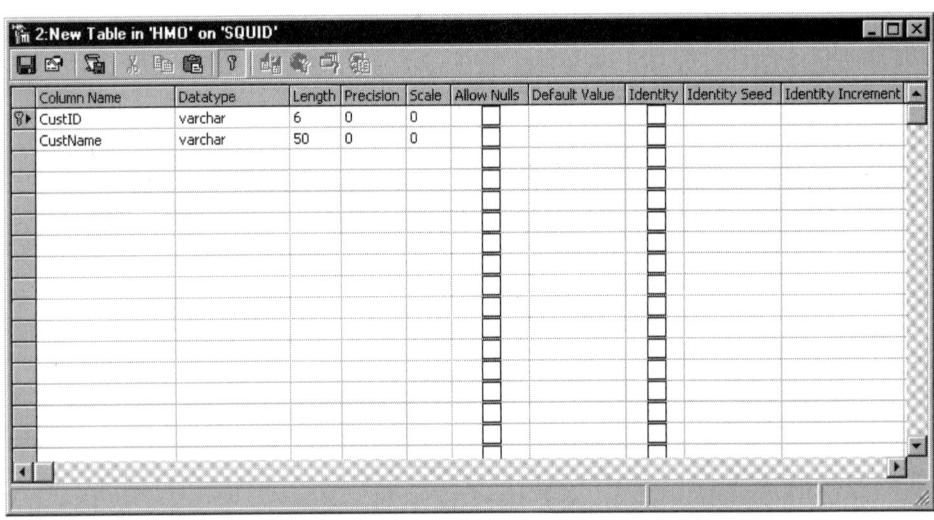

FIGURE 4.7: Adding a primary key

Here `CustomersPK` is the name of the new constraint. When you create a new `PRIMARY KEY` constraint you must specify the field list for the key. In this example, there's just one field in the field list.

All columns that are part of a primary key must be defined as `NOT NULL`. Some other products, such as Microsoft Access, do not enforce this same limitation. If you're importing a table from one of these other systems, you may have to enforce referential integrity with triggers instead of constraints.

A table can only have one `PRIMARY KEY` constraint. SQL Server automatically creates an index on the primary key.

Removing Primary Keys

Sometimes you may have to remove primary keys from tables. For example, the data might have changed sufficiently or the table grown large enough to force you to implement a surrogate key in place of the natural primary key. Before you can create the new key, you must remove, or *drop*, the old primary key. To drop a primary key using SQL Server Enterprise Manager, just select the row with the key and click the Set Primary Key button a second time.

To drop a primary key using Transact-SQL, you must use the ALTER TABLE statement:

```
ALTER TABLE [database.[owner.]]table_name
     DROP CONSTRAINT
     primary_key_name
```

NOTE Dropping a primary key is one of many actions you can perform with the ALTER TABLE statement. For the complete syntax of ALTER TABLE, see Skill 3.

Foreign Keys

Foreign keys, in conjunction with primary keys, provide the other half of SQL Server's implementation of referential integrity. A foreign key is a copy of the primary key in the parent table that is inserted in the child table in order to create a relationship between the two. Just like primary keys, foreign keys are implemented with CONSTRAINT clauses. Unlike primary keys, a single table can have multiple foreign keys.

Creating Foreign Keys

To add a foreign key using SQL Server Enterprise Manager, you use the Database Diagrammer, another of the Visual Data Tools.

1. In the main tree, right-click Diagrams and select New Database Diagram. This will launch the Create Diagram Wizard, which will prompt you for tables to include on the diagram.
2. Choose the table that you want to add the foreign key to and the table that contains the primary key that this foreign key will reference.
3. Drag and drop the primary key to the foreign key. The dialog box shown in Figure 4.8 will appear to allow you to confirm the columns that you wish to relate. You must select compatible columns from the current table to match each column in the primary key.

TIP The data types and sizes of columns in a foreign key must match exactly to the corresponding columns in the primary key.

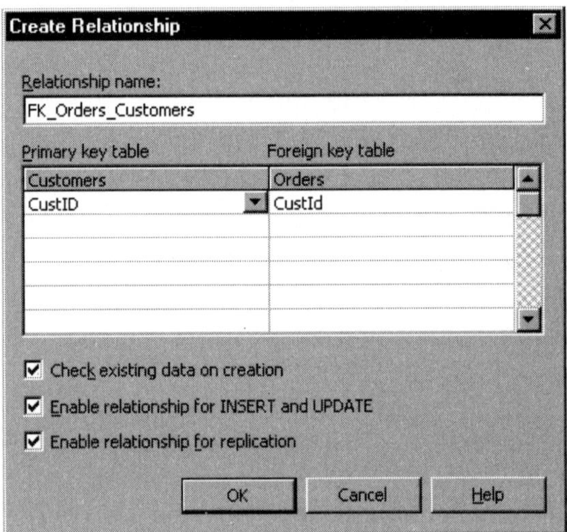

FIGURE 4.8: Adding a foreign key

In Transact-SQL, you add a foreign key with a `FOREIGN KEY` constraint. Here's the Transact-SQL for the table in Figure 4.8:

```
CREATE TABLE Orders (
     OrderId varchar (6) NOT NULL ,
     CustId varchar (6) NOT NULL ,
     OrderAmount money NOT NULL ,
     CONSTRAINT OrderCustFK FOREIGN KEY
     (
            CustId
     ) REFERENCES Customers (
            CustId
     )
)
```

As with any other constraint, you must provide a name for the new foreign key—here it's `OrderCustFK`. Creating a foreign key requires providing two lists of columns. The first list is the list of columns in the current table that make up the foreign key. The second list is the list of columns in the primary table that match the new foreign key.

The name of the PRIMARY KEY constraint is not used when creating a FOREIGN KEY constraint. Be sure you list the names of the columns in the key.

In contrast to primary keys, the value in a column included in a foreign key in SQL Server can be NULL. Foreign keys can only reference tables in the same database. If you need to enforce cross-database referential integrity, you need to use triggers.

Foreign keys are not automatically indexed by SQL Server. To speed up referential integrity operations, you should use CREATE INDEX to create your own index on the foreign key columns.

Removing Foreign Keys

To drop a foreign key using Transact-SQL, you must use the ALTER TABLE statement:

```
ALTER TABLE [database.[owner.]]table_name
     DROP CONSTRAINT
     foreign_key_name
```

Integrity and Replication

In Skill 14, *Using Replication*, you'll learn about SQL Server replication, which allows you to maintain synchronized copies of your data on multiple servers. SQL Server does this by recording changes on one server and replaying them on another. This can create some unique problems. For example, if you have a table with an Identity column defined, SQL Server will not let you insert arbitrary values into that column. But if a record is created with an identity value on Server One, you want it to retain that same value in the copy of the table on Server Two. Fortunately, SQL Server supports syntax within Transact-SQL to cover just this problem.

In the CREATE TABLE statement, SQL Server supports the optional NOT FOR REPLICATION clause in several places:

- Identity columns
- FOREIGN KEY constraints
- CHECK constraints

This clause allows you to create constraints that are enforced on users but not on the replication process. Such a constraint on an Identity column takes care of the distributed insert problem we've already mentioned. A constraint on a foreign key that's not checked on replication allows you to replicate only part of a database without referential integrity problems. And a CHECK constraint can prevent users from inserting rows but still allow those rows to be inserted by the replication process.

A CREATE TABLE statement using these clauses might look like this:

```
CREATE TABLE Orders (
     OrderId INT IDENTITY(1,1) NOT FOR REPLICATION ,
     CustId varchar (6) NOT NULL ,
     OrderAmount money NOT NULL ,
     CHECK NOT FOR REPLICATION (OrderAmount < 100)
     CONSTRAINT OrderCustFK FOREIGN KEY
     (
            CustId
     ) REFERENCES Customers (
            CustId
     ) NOT FOR REPLICATION
)
```

Are You up to Speed?

Now you can...

- ☑ **use entity, domain, referential, and user-defined integrity**
- ☑ **design a database in Third Normal Form**
- ☑ **add Identity columns to a table**
- ☑ **implement Unique, Default, and Check constraints**
- ☑ **implement rules**
- ☑ **use Declarative Referential Integrity to enforce table relationships**
- ☑ **use integrity with replication**

SKILL 5

Moving Data

- Importing and exporting data
- Working with Data Transformation Services
- Using the bcp utility
- Backing up and restoring your data

When using SQL server, you may need to work with data by importing, exporting, or transferring it, either from SQL Server sources or from other sources. You may also need to upgrade from an earlier version.

Importing, Exporting, and Transforming Data

Data can be exchanged between applications by importing and exporting to a common format. For example, SQL Server supports importing data from text files, databases, and spreadsheets. Transforming data makes it suitable for storage in the destination database, whether that is SQL Server or some other format. Some values may be calculated from one or more source fields, or single fields may be broken up for storage in separate columns. Transformations make it easy to implement complex data validation and to facilitate scrubbing and enhancement during import and export.

This section will cover the two tools you can use to transfer data: Data Transformation Services (which you can run from the Enterprise Manager) and the Bulk Copy Program, or bcp. This version of SQL Server uses improved index maintenance strategies that make loading data into tables with indexes more efficient than earlier versions. Bulk copy operations in general are also much faster.

NOTE Another method of moving data is through replication, which has many new improvements and capabilities in SQL Server 7. Replication is designed to maintain the same data at multiple sites, rather than just to move it from one site to another. You can now modify data at multiple sites using update replication, which allows the bi-directional flow of data. Heterogeneous replication through COM interfaces that open store-and-forward replication services is also supported. For a complete discussion of replication, see Skill 14, *Using Replication*.

Using the Data Transformation Services Import and Export Wizards

Data Transformation Services (or DTS) now incorporates the functionality that used to be found in the Transfer Manager, which became obsolete in SQL Server 6.5. Data Transformation Services makes it easy to import, export, and transform heterogeneous data—not just to SQL Server, but also between any two OLE DB compatible data sources. The data source can be relational or non-relational, text or database files, from the desktop, from the same server, or from different servers. For example, you could use DTS to move data from an Access database to an Oracle database.

In addition, DTS provides:

- Access to native OLE DB providers (SQL Server, Access, Excel, and Word)
- Access to ODBC data sources (Access, Oracle, DB2 using the OLE DB Provider for ODBC)
- Access to fixed-length and delimited ASCII text files
- Support for high-speed nonlogged inserts (SQL Server versions 6 and later)
- Support for transforming and publishing HTML data
- Ability to create pivot tables in Excel
- Support for creating customized data sources and destinations.

Triggers, stored procedures, rules, defaults, constraints, and user-defined data types are not supported by Data Transformation Services (DTS) when converting data between heterogeneous data sources.

Some of the data sources supported are:

- SQL Server databases
- ODBC data sources
- Microsoft Access databases
- Microsoft FoxPro databases
- dBase or Paradox databases
- Microsoft Excel spreadsheets
- ASCII fixed-length field text files

Although it's beyond the scope of this book, you can also use DTS to:

- Build data warehouses and data marts by importing and transforming data from multiple heterogeneous data sources either interactively or through scheduling.

- Create custom transformation objects for integration into third-party products.
- Use third-party OLE DB providers to access applications to be used as sources and destinations of data.

You can use Data Transformation Services to transform data between different SQL Servers and any OLE DB, ODBC, or text file format. Transforming data entails a sequence of operations applied to each row in a source rowset prior to sending it to the destination. Transformation operations are all managed by central metadata with support for business rules and data lineage, and these include:

- Data validation for missing values, scrubbing, and exception handling
- Data integration for eliminating duplicates and heterogeneous queries
- Data transformation for value mapping and merging/splitting columns
- Data aggregation

NOTE

You can use the predefined authoring tools using the DTS wizards or write code in VB Script, JavaScript, or any COM programming language. See Skill 13 for more information on programming SQL Server. For more information on OLE DB, see Skill 12, *OLE DB Fundamentals*.

DTS works with a DTS package, which is a self-contained definition of all the tasks to be performed as part of a transformation. These packages can be executed from the Enterprise Manager by a script, they can be saved to a server or a file and scheduled for later execution, or executed from the command line. Each package contains multiple steps that can be executed either serially or in parallel. Steps can also be executed conditionally. Transactions are also supported across the steps.

Using the DTS Wizard

The DTS Wizard allows you to create DTS packages to import, export, validate, and transform heterogeneous data through OLE DB and ODBC. You can use the DTS Wizard to copy schema and data between relational databases. However, indexes, stored procedures, or referential integrity constraints will not be copied. DTS will check to see if a destination table already exists and will give you the option to drop and re-create it.

DTS will attempt to define the best possible data type matches between the source and destination, which you can override by specifying different destination data types, sizes, precision, and scale properties. DTS will use the source object's name as a default. You must add double quotes or brackets around table and column names that contain spaces.

TIP DTS functionality may be further limited by the capabilities of specific DBMS or OLE DB drivers. In addition, you may be limited in the way BLOBs (binary large objects) are handled. A destination ODBC database requires that a table only contain one BLOB column and a unique index.

You can run the DTS Wizard from the Enterprise Manager or from a command-line prompt. The DTS Wizard will then create a package, which you can choose to execute immediately or save for scheduling later. Whether you run the wizard from the Enterprise Manager or a command line, you will be asked to supply the following information:

- The source, or destination, of the data
- Whether to copy an entire table or the results of a query
- The destination table for the copied data
- How to perform any necessary transformations of the data
- Whether to execute the package immediately or at a later time
- Whether to save the package so that it can be reused

TIP When you launch the DTS Wizard from the command prompt, using the dtswiz utility, you can specify options that cause certain wizard dialog boxes to be bypassed. When you launch the DTS Wizard from the Enterprise Manager, the wizard prompts you for all required information.

Let's look at a concrete example of using DTS. In this case, we'll transfer existing data from Microsoft Access to SQL Server. In order to transfer data using DTS to import an Access database, you first need to create a destination database on your SQL Server to contain the tables. DTS will create the tables for you if they do not already exist, but not an entire database. Choose Tools ➢ Wizards from the main console and expand the Data Transformation Services option. Double-click DTS Import Wizard, which will load with an introductory screen. Click Next. The dialog box prompting you for the source of the import data is shown in Figure 5.1. This database is not secured, so specify the username Admin with no password.

TIP If you are working with a secured Access database and need to specify the workgroup file, click the Advanced button and specify the fully-qualified path and filename under the JetOLEDB: System database option.

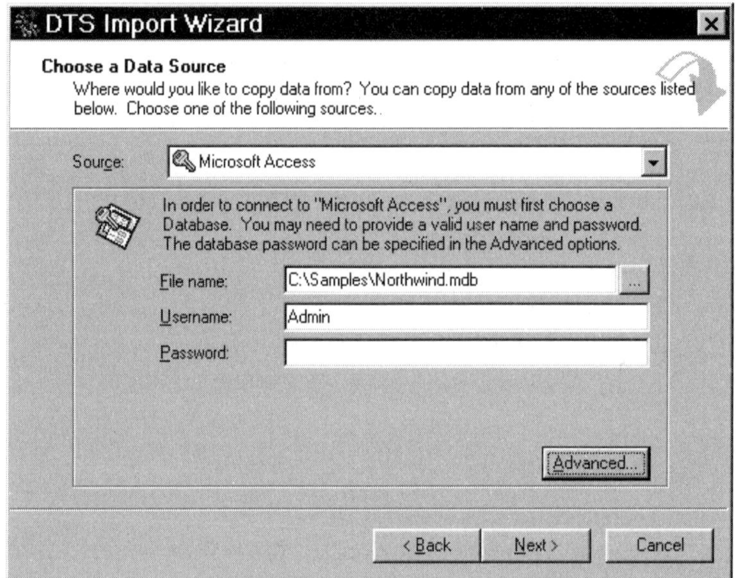

FIGURE 5.1: Choosing a data source with the DTS Import Wizard

The next dialog box prompts you for the destination database. For this example we have created a database named NwindSample on the SQL Server, as shown in Figure 5.2. Security on the server has been set up to use integrated NT security.

You will then be asked whether you are copying tables or copying data from a query, as shown in Figure 5.3. In this example we are copying all the tables from the Northwind database. If you elect to copy the tables into an empty database, the tables will be created for you. The next dialog box allows you to select the tables to be copied, as shown in Figure 5.4.

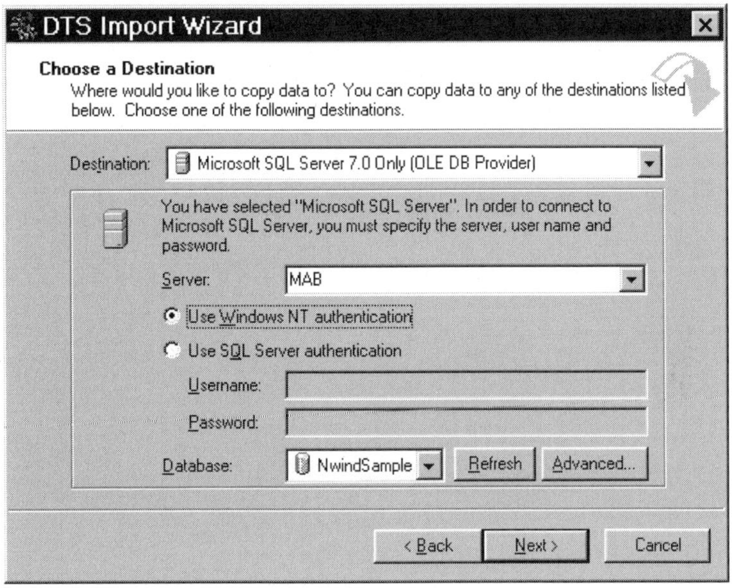

DTS Import Wizard

Choose a Destination

Where would you like to copy data to? You can copy data to any of the destinations listed below. Choose one of the following destinations.

Destination: Microsoft SQL Server 7.0 Only (OLE DB Provider)

You have selected "Microsoft SQL Server". In order to connect to Microsoft SQL Server, you must specify the server, user name and password.

Server: MAB

Use Windows NT authentication

Use SQL Server authentication

Username:

Password:

Database: NwindSample Refresh Advanced...

< Back Next > Cancel

FIGURE 5.2: Choosing a destination database with the DTS Import Wizard

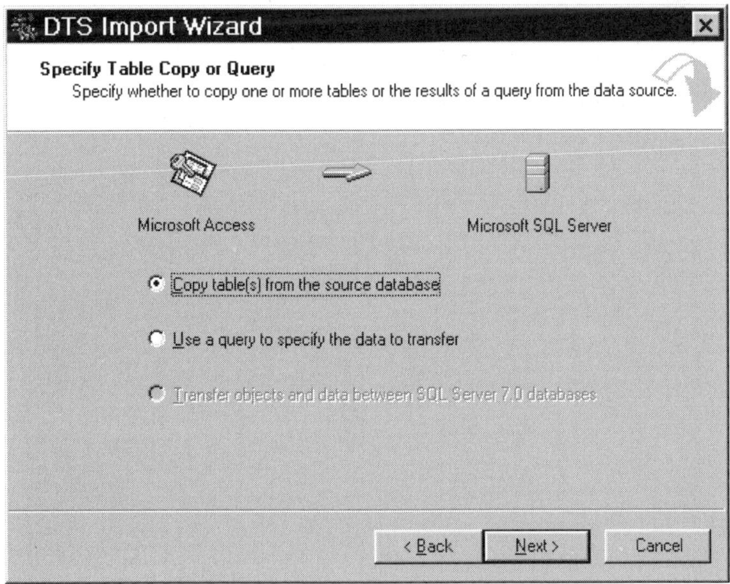

FIGURE 5.3: Selecting copying tables or using a query

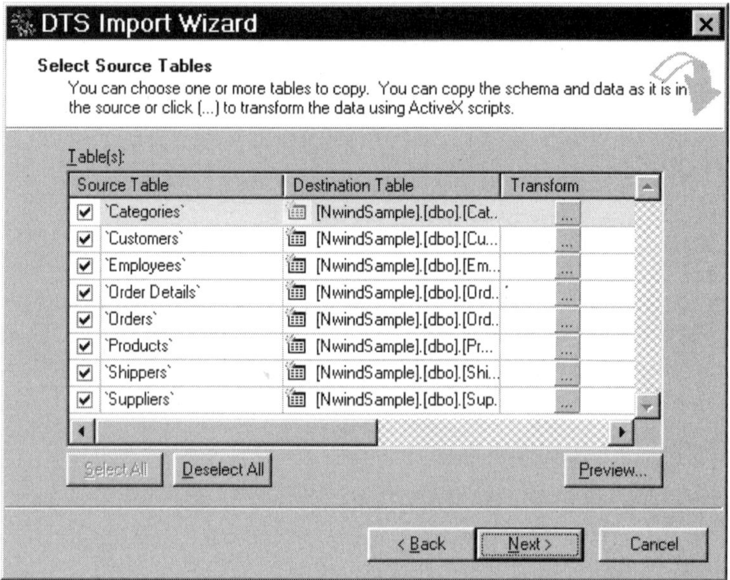

FIGURE 5.4: Selecting the tables to be copied

Select the Employees table and click the corresponding button in the Trans--form column. You can then view or change the properties for individual fields on the Column Mappings tab, as shown in Figure 5.5. Note that you have the option of deciding whether to create a new table, delete any existing data, or append new rows.

The Transformations tab allows you to write a script in either VBScript or JScript to perform any necessary transformations, as shown in Figure 5.6.

In this example there isn't much to do since we are just going to create a new table and use the existing data and data types, so we'd be better off using the option to copy the source columns directly to the destination columns. Clicking the Advanced button here gives us the options shown in Figure 5.7. Note that you can also set custom transformations.

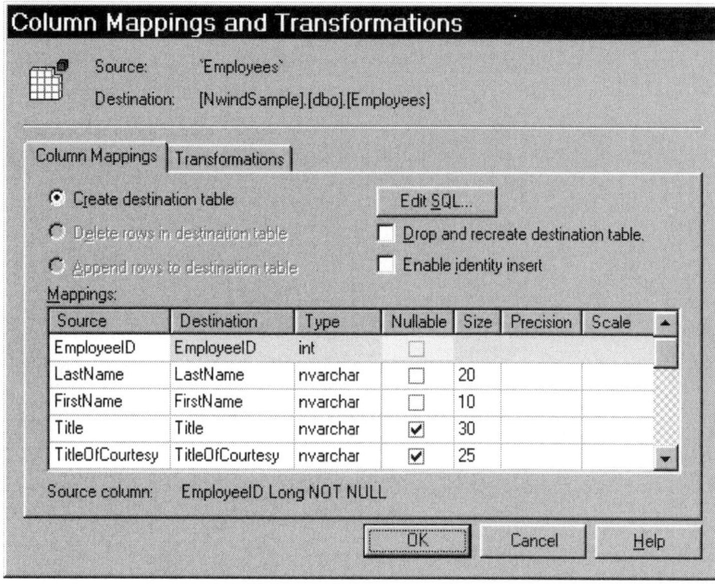

FIGURE 5.5: Setting transformation options—Column Mappings

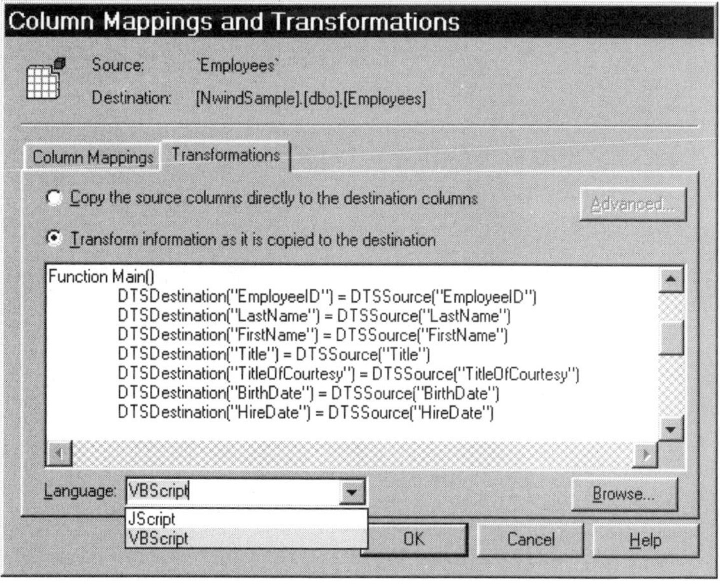

FIGURE 5.6: Setting transformation options—Transformations

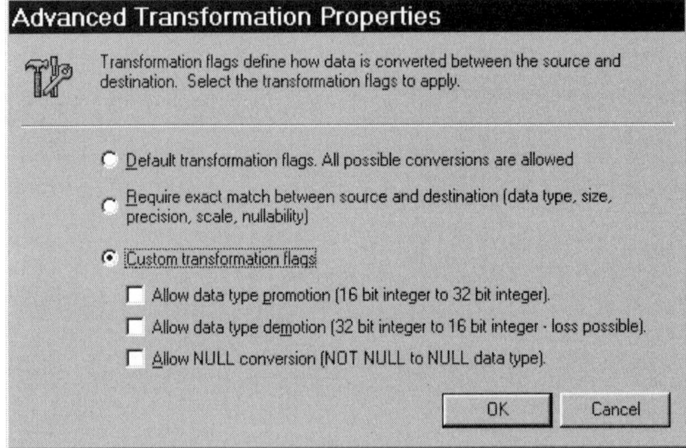

FIGURE 5.7: Setting Advanced options

You can then select whether to run immediately, to create a replication publication, to save the package, or to schedule it for later execution. All the examples are shown checked in Figure 5.8 for the purpose of illustrating that they are there—it's doubtful you'd ever actually use them all at once.

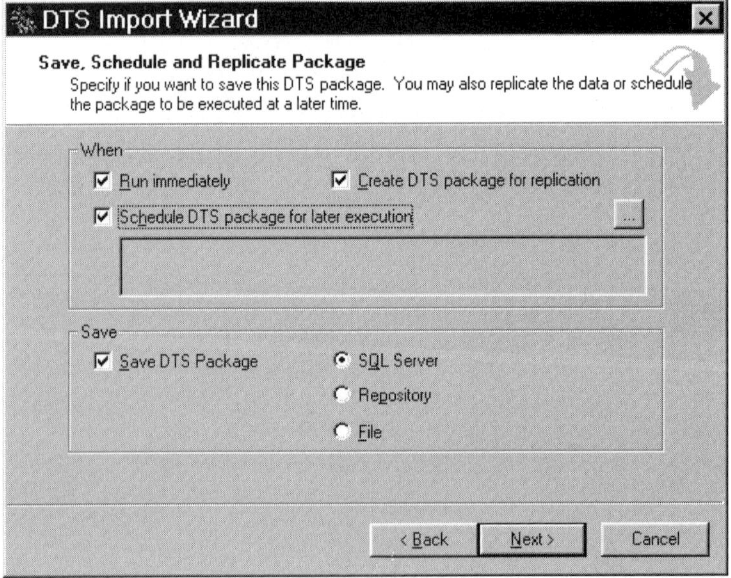

FIGURE 5.8: Save options for the DTS package

Clicking the builder button (labeled "...") next to the Schedule DTS Package for Later Execution option will let you schedule it, as shown in Figure 5.9.

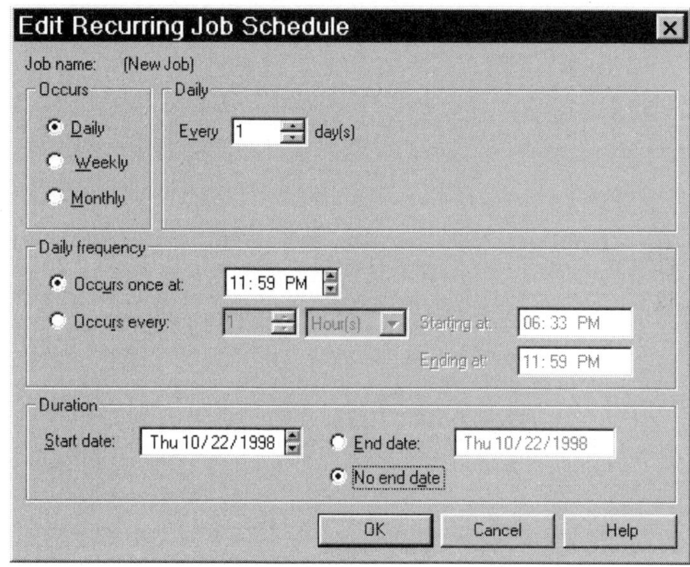

FIGURE 5.9: Scheduling the DTS package to run later

The final screen gives you a summary of the databases and tables involved. Click Finish to complete the wizard and the tables will be imported. If you are using DTS to convert an Access database to SQL Server, you will now need to modify the tables the DTS Wizard created to create primary keys, relationships, indexes, and any constraints you may need. Since we elected to run the DTS package immediately, a progress dialog box will keep us informed of the progress being made, as shown in Figure 5.10.

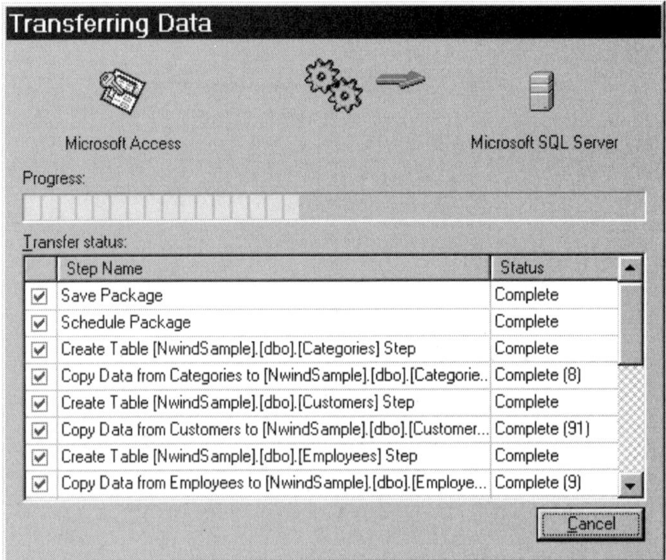

FIGURE 5.10: The DTS Wizard progress meter

Calling the DTS Wizard from the Command Line

You can also call the DTS wizard from the command line using the following syntax:

```
dtswiz [/f filename] [/i | /x] [/r provider_name]
[/s server_name] [/u login_id] [/p password] [/n]
[/d database_name] [/y]
```

The arguments are shown in Table 5.1:

TABLE 5.1: Arguments to dtswiz

Argument	Description
/f	Specifies the name of the DTS package the wizard will create
/i	Imports to SQL Server
/x	Exports from SQL Server
/r	Name of the provider, i.e., MSDASQL for the OLE DB provider for ODBC

TABLE 5.1 CONTINUED: Arguments to dtswiz

Argument	Description
/s	Name of the SQL Server
/u	Login ID to connect to SQL Server
/n	Specifies a trusted connection
/p	Password
/d	SQL Server database used for import or export
/y	Hides the master, model, msdb, and tempdb systems databases so they won't show up in the import or export list boxes

If you don't specify the arguments listed above, then the DTS Wizard will interactively request any required values that you didn't supply. To invoke the DTS Export Wizard, use the following syntax. This will export the data from the NwindSample.

```
dtswiz /i /n /rMSDASQL /sKARIS /dNwindSample
```


The DTS Package Designer

The DTS Wizard is limited to creating single import or export tasks. For more complex DTS packages, you can use the DTS Package Designer, which is available by selecting New Package from the shortcut menu for the Data Transformation Services nodes in SQL Server Enterprise Manager.

We don't have space to cover the DTS Package Designer in detail in this book. For more information, check the SQL Server Books Online chapter titled *Data Transformation Services*. Some of the things you can do with the DTS Package Designer include:

- Specify multiple transformations as part of a single package.
- Specify workflow within a package, including sequence of actions and conditional branching.
- Add pure Active Script tasks that do not execute within a particular transformation.
- Edit the properties of any DTS object.

Figure 5.11 shows the DTS Package Designer in action.

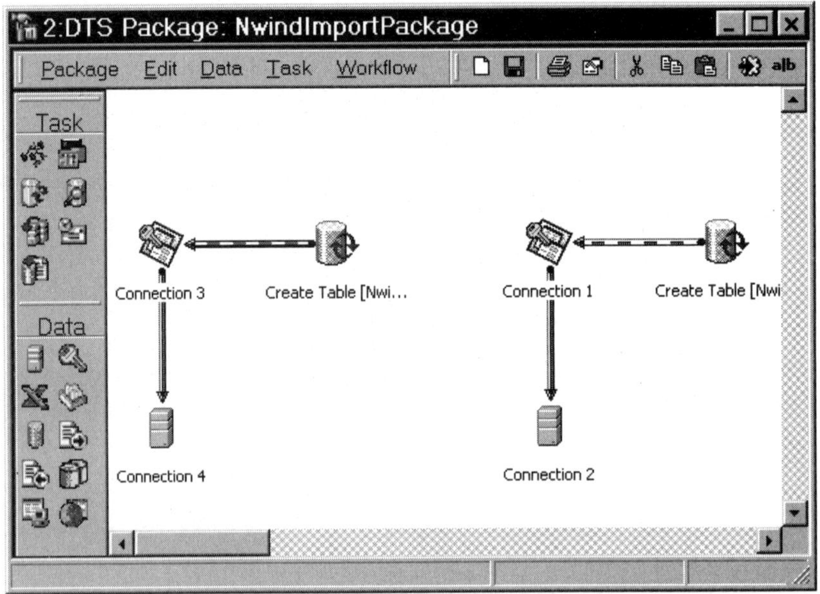

FIGURE 5.11: The DTS Package Designer

Using the Bulk Copy Program (bcp)

The *Bulk Copy Program*, or bcp, is a command-prompt utility that enables you to copy SQL Server data to or from a data file in a user-specified format. It's most commonly used when you have large volumes of data to transfer, since it allows table loads to be performed as non-logged operations. Bcp copies data to an intermediate data file on disk and then either imports or exports it.

NOTE The bcp utility is written using the ODBC bulk copy API, which you can use when programming ODBC, OLE DB and DB-Library based applications.

Bcp works in conjunction with the query processor to optimize the actual queries, index maintenance, constraint checking, and parallel data load operations, so it's a good choice when you have large amounts of data to be passed back and forth. In addition, you an also customize file format definitions, select specific columns, choose delimited ASCII or binary formatted data, and perform inter-platform transfers, such as between a mainframe and SQL Server.

Since bcp moves data into an operating system file that can be easily imported into another application, you can also use it as an intermediary step when you need to transfer data to any other application that can read text files, such as word processors and spreadsheets.

Before using bcp, the table to be loaded must already exist, although the number of fields in the data file doesn't have to match exactly the number of columns in the table. The data file must be formatted as text-only or in a format generated by bcp itself, such as native format. The columns in the table must match the data type of the field in the data file being copied.

To perform a non-logged bulk copy, you need to meet the following conditions or else the bulk copy will be logged:

- The database option Select Into/Bulk Copy is set to True.
- The target table has no triggers.
- The target table is not being replicated.

TIP If you are copying a large number of rows into a table with indexes, you can improve performance by dropping all the indexes, performing the bulk copy, and then re-creating the indexes.

After running a non-logged bulk copy, you need to back up the database before you can back up the log. That is because data inserted without being logged won't show up if the database has to be reloaded and the transaction log applied.

NOTE You need to set the `select into/bulk copy` option for the database to True before a user can do non-logged copies with bcp. `select into/bulk copy` is set to False by default in newly created databases. To change the default value, set `select into/bulk copy` to True in the model database. You'll find this option on the Options tab of the Properties dialog box for the database. For more details on setting database options, see Skill 2.

Bcp has a wide variety of optional switches. Here's the syntax. Table 5.3 explains the meaning of the syntax and switches.

```
bcp [[database_name.]owner.]table_name {in | out | format} data_file
[-m max_errors] [-f format_file] [-e err_file]
[-F first_row] [-L last_row] [-b batch_size]
[-n] [-c] [-w] [-N] [-6] [-C code_page]
[-t field_term] [-r row_term]
[-i input_file] [-o output_file] [-a packet_size]
-U login_id [-P password] [-S server_name]
[-T] [-v] [-k] [-E] [-h "hint [, …n]"]
```

TABLE 5.2: bcp Syntax Parameters

Syntax/Parameter	Description
database_name	The database name.
owner	The owner's name.
table_name	The table or view to copy.
`in | out | format`	The direction of the copy: `in` copies from a file into the database table; `out` copies from the database table or view to a file. The `format` option creates a format file based on the `n`, `-c`, `-w`, or `-6` options. If you use the `format` option, then you need to specify the `-f` option as well.
data_file	The fully-qualified path of an operating-system file when copying to or from a hard-disk file or a single disk.
`-m` *max_errors*	The maximum number of errors allowed in a bcp operation. The default is 10.
`-f` *format_file*	Creates a format file. If you don't create a format file or use the `-n`, `-c`, `-w`, or `-6` options, then bcp requests format information.
`-e` *err_file*	Creates an error file to store rows that did not transfer. If you don't specify this option, then no error file is created.
`-F` *first_row*	Specifies the first row to copy (the default is the first row).
`-L` *last_row*	Specifies the number of the last row to copy (the default is the last row).
`-b` *batch_size*	Sets size of batch file. This allows you specify the number of rows per batch. Do not use in conjunction with the `-h "ROWS_PER_BATCH = bb"` option.
`-n`	Sets native format. Use this option when copying from one SQL Server to another SQL Server; it saves time by preventing unnecessary conversion of data types into and out of character format.
`-c`	Sets character formats by using the char format as the default storage type for all columns, no prefixes, \t (tab) as the default field separator, and \n (new line) as the default row terminator.
`-w`	Uses Unicode characters as the default. This option does not prompt for each field; it uses nchar as the default storage type, no prefixes, \t (tab) as the default field separator, and \n (new line) as the default row terminator.
`-N`	Uses the native data types of the data for noncharacter data and Unicode characters for character data.
`-6`	Use in conjunction with character (`-c`) or native (`-n`) format to perform the copy operation using SQL Server version 6 or 6.5 data types as the default. This option does not prompt for each field; it uses the default values. Use this option when using bcp files generated from SQL Server version 6 or 6.5.

TABLE 5.2 CONTINUED: bcp Syntax Parameters

Syntax/Parameter	Description
-C *code_page*	Specifies the code page of the data in the data file.
-t *field_term*	Field terminator.
-r *row_term*	Row terminator.
-i *input_file*	Creates an input file to redirect input to bcp.
-o *output_file*	Creates an output file.
-a *packet_size*	Specifies the number of bytes, per network packet, sent to and from the server.
-U *login_id*	Login ID.
-P *password*	User-specified password.
-S *server_name*	Specifies which SQL Server to connect to.
-T	Connects with a trusted connection.
-v	The current bcp version number.
-k	Retain nulls in columns with no data rather than inserting any default values.
-E	Specifies that identity columns are present in the file being imported
-h "hint [, …n]"	Use hints during bulk copy. Only valid for SQL Server version 6.5 or later.

If you don't specify the -n, -c, or -w parameters, then bcp will prompt for information on:

- File storage type
- Prefix length
- Field length
- Field terminator

Some data formats may not be compatible with data structures expected by other programs, so bcp allows more detailed information to be specified interactively. The default values bcp supplies are based on the SQL Server data type of the source or destination column. Accepting these defaults produces the same result as native format (-n).

If you use interactive bcp to specify the `-n`, `-c`, or `-w` parameters, then you'll be prompted to save this information in a format file, which is used to store the format information for each field in the data file. The format file can be reused in the future to copy data without needing to re-specify the format. The default name for the format file is `bcp.fmt`, but you can name it something else if you prefer.

TIP You can use the bulk copy API in ODBC, OLE DB, and DB-Library from your applications to bulk copy data to SQL Server.

Other Ways of Copying Data

You can also copy data from one SQL Server database to another by using the following methods:

- Create an `INSERT` or an `INSERT...SELECT` statement to add data to an existing table.
- Use a cursor.
- Use the `WRITETEXT` statement to write to text or image columns.
- Write a trigger for an `INSERT` action.
- Use the `BULK INSERT` statement.

The following Transact-SQL statement will insert a row in the employees table in the Northwind sample database:

```
INSERT employees (LastName, FirstName)
  VALUES ('Wilde', 'Oscar')
```

You can also add data from one table to another. The following statement will copy data from the employees table to a new TempEmployee table in the Northwind database. Note that the column order in TempEmployee must be the same as the column order in the `SELECT` statement.

```
INSERT TempEmployee
  SELECT EmployeeID, LastName, FirstName
  FROM Employees
  WHERE LastName = 'Wilde'
```

The WRITETEXT statement is used to add or update an existing text, ntext, or image column. The default is not to log the statement, so the Transaction Log does not fill up with large amounts of data. The syntax is:

```
WRITETEXT {table.column text_ptr}
    [WITH LOG] {data}
```

You can also use a BULK INSERT statement. BULK INSERT bulk copies data into SQL Server much the same way the bcp utility does, except you don't have to use the command prompt. However, you can't use it to bulk copy SQL Server data back to a text file. The syntax is:

```
BULK INSERT [['database_name'.]['owner'].]{'table_name' FROM data_file}
[WITH
(
[ BATCHSIZE [ = batch_size]]
[[,] CHECK_CONSTRAINTS]
[[,] CODEPAGE [ = ACP | OEM | RAW | code_page]]
[[,] DATAFILETYPE [ =
{'char' | 'native'| 'widechar' | 'widenative'}]]
[[,] FIELDTERMINATOR [ = 'field_terminator']]
[[,] FIRSTROW [ = first_row]]
[[,] FORMATFILE [ = 'format_file_path']]
[[,] KEEPIDENTITY]
[[,] KEEPNULLS]
[[,] LASTROW [ = last_row]]
[[,] MAXERRORS [ = max_errors]]
[[,] ORDER ({column [ASC | DESC]} [, ...n])]
[[,] ROWTERMINATOR [ = 'row_terminator']]
[[,] TABLOCK]
)
]
```

If you were going to use it to bulk insert data into the Northwind Customers table from a comma-delimited text file, your code would look like this:

```
BULK INSERT Northwind.dbo.Customers
    FROM 'D:\orders\NewCust.txt'
    WITH
        (
            FIELDTERMINATOR = ',',
            ROWTERMINATOR = '\n'
        )
```

Applications can use various automatic means to launch one of these methods of inserting data. For example, an application could contain a trigger that specified a row to add to a History table whenever a row was modified in a Customer table. Or an application might use a cursor to hold all the rows currently in a table and add rows by manipulating the rowset contained in the cursor. We'll discuss triggers in Skill 6, *Retrieving Data*, and cursors in Skill 13, *Programming SQL Server*.

Backup and Restore

Backing up and restoring both systems databases and user databases is an important part of administering a SQL Server. Data can be lost in myriad ways: through user actions, through all kinds of disasters from power spikes to fires and floods, viruses, incompetent or malicious users, corruption or other damage to the physical disk device, and theft. Recovering from these situations requires a good backup strategy that is relevant to your business needs. You can back up and restore your database using either the Enterprise Manager or by the BACKUP and RESTORE commands.

NOTE SQL Server uses the Microsoft Tape Format, which allows backups to share the same tape media with other programs' backups. For example, you could store both a Windows NT system backup and a SQL Server database backup on the same tape. This simplifies tape management and hardware configuration for servers.

In the normal course of events, SQL Server uses transactions to update data. When a transaction initiates, the database is in a consistent state. The application makes updates to data and, as the updates are processed, they are either committed or rolled back. Transactions are recorded in the log so that, if something happens in the middle of a transaction before it is either committed or rolled back, there is enough information in the log to either roll back (undo) or roll forward (redo) a transaction. If the server stops for any reason, the next time it starts it will automatically recover all outstanding transactions. It does this by writing all uncommitted transactions still in the log to disk and rolling back any transactions that had not been completed at the time the server went down. When you restore a backup, all outstanding uncommitted transactions at the time the backup was made are also restored.

NOTE Earlier versions of SQL Server used the terms *dump* (for backup) and *load* (for restore). The DUMP and LOAD statements have only been included in this version of SQL Server for backward compatibility.

The type of backup you perform and how often you back up depends on the volume of transactions and the amount of work that might be lost in the event of a crash, as well as on how difficult it would be to re-create the results of that work. If you have a database with a high volume of transactions, you might want to back up daily with the transaction logs backed up hourly. If your database is used primarily for decision support and the data does not change frequently, you may only need to back up weekly and have the transaction log backed up daily.

Backup Strategy

You need to have a backup plan in place before you roll out your application since it is a key part of any robust system. If the data is critical, you may need to recover to the point of failure, which means backing up the log between database backups. When you back up logs, recovery is more complicated. If the data is not critical, then loading the last database backup might be sufficient and restores easier. You may need to get back online in the shortest possible time and need more frequent backups or a standby server. You can also elect to do both database and incremental backups, which saves time since you only have to restore the latest backup and the latest incremental backup. Another option is backing up to multiple devices. This speeds up the backup and restore process by taking advantage of parallel IO.

Once you have determined a plan suitable for your database, test and time it thoroughly. A backup is no good if you can't recover from it quickly and efficiently. You need to simulate failures and test your restoration procedures for any weaknesses. You also need to determine whether the frequency of backup is adequate for your needs and how long it takes to restore, and adjust your strategy accordingly.

When you back up a database, everything is copied, including portions of the log. You can also make a separate log backup that only copies the log. The backup copy is a snapshot of the database or log at the time the backup was made. It contains copies of all the data pages and log images from a starting point to the end of the log at the time the backup finishes.

You can also back up individual files or filegroups or make incremental backups that contain only pages that have been changed since the last full database backup.

Restoring loads the backup of the database (or file, filegroup, or log). All data pages in the log are copied into the database, all transactions from the log pages are rolled forward and written to the data pages, and any uncompleted transactions from the log pages are then rolled back.

WARNING If you are making log backups, make sure to back up the database if you perform any of the following operations: running a non-logged bulk copy operation with the `select into/bulk copy` option set to True ; a `SELECT INTO` statement with the `select info/bulk copy` option set to True; running a non-logged text/ntext/image modification; or running `BACKUP LOG` with the `TRUNCATE ONLY` or `NO_LOG` options set. These will cause a break in the chain of log backups. If you need to restore, you could only do so up to the point where the break occurred.

If you elect to back up both the database and the log, you can restore to the point of failure as long as you haven't lost the disks containing the log files or the server. The way this works is that in between database backups you periodically back up the log. If you need to restore, you restore the most recent database backup and then restore the logs in the same order in which they were written. If you lose a log backup, you can only restore to the log just before the lost one.

NOTE SQL Server 7 also supports standby servers and failover servers. A standby server holds a second copy of a database that is automatically and periodically refreshed with transactions from the primary server. A standby server can be quickly activated if the primary server fails. A failover server is a second server that shares the same physical hard drive with the primary server, via Microsoft Clustering Services, and that will be instantly activated if the primary server fails. Standby servers and failover servers are advanced topics that aren't covered in this book.

Backing Up Using the Enterprise Manager

To back up an entire database or the transaction log or to perform an incremental backup, choose Tools ➢ Backup Database from the main console. This will open the dialog box shown in Figure 5.12, which allows you to fill in the options for the backup on the General tab.

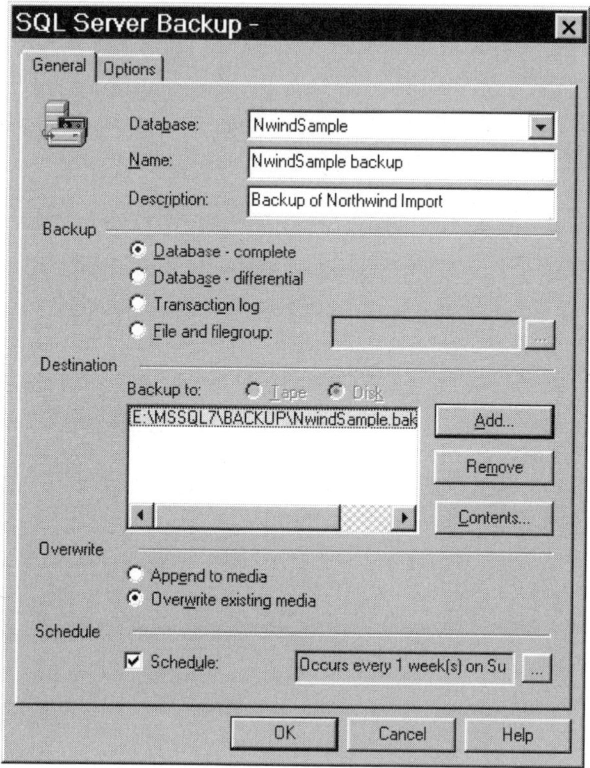

FIGURE 5.12: Setting general options for backing up the Northwind database

After you fill in the options under the General tab, click the Options tab to verify the backup on completion, to set the backup expiration date, and to set additional options, as shown in Figure 5.13.

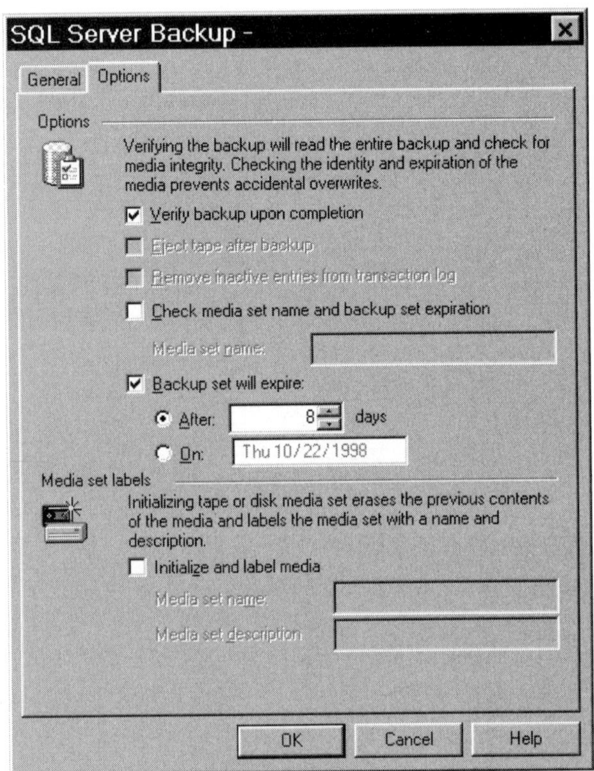

FIGURE 5.13: Setting Backup options on the Options tab

Once you click OK, the backup will proceed.

Transaction Log Backups

If you want to restore a database to the exact point of failure, it is necessary to back up both the database and the transaction log. Unless you have a lot of very heavy transactions in your database, the transaction log backup will generally use fewer resources than a full database backup. This means you can run them more frequently than database backups, reducing the window of time in which a failure could occur since the last backup and also reducing the amount of potential data loss.

If any kind of data loss would prove catastrophic, then the following sequence of backing up and restoring the database and log would minimize your losses:

1. Back up the database daily (or at a regular interval).
2. Back up the transaction log hourly (or more frequently for very active systems).

In case of a failure, follow these steps:

1. Back up the current transaction log, if possible. It may not be possible if the disk itself has failed.
2. Restore the most recent full database backup.
3. Apply all the transaction log backups in the order in which they were created subsequent to the database backup.
4. If you were able to complete step 1, apply the final transaction log, which will restore the database to the point of failure.

To create a transaction log backup, follow these steps:

1. Expand the server group and database you want to create the transaction log for. Right-click the database to bring up the Task shortcut menu and select All Tasks. Then select the Backup Database option.
2. Fill in the options on the General tab for Name and Description.
3. Under Backup, select Transaction Log.
4. Under Destination, click Add to add an existing backup device or to create a new one, as shown in Figure 5.14.
5. Fill in the rest of the options and click OK to finish.

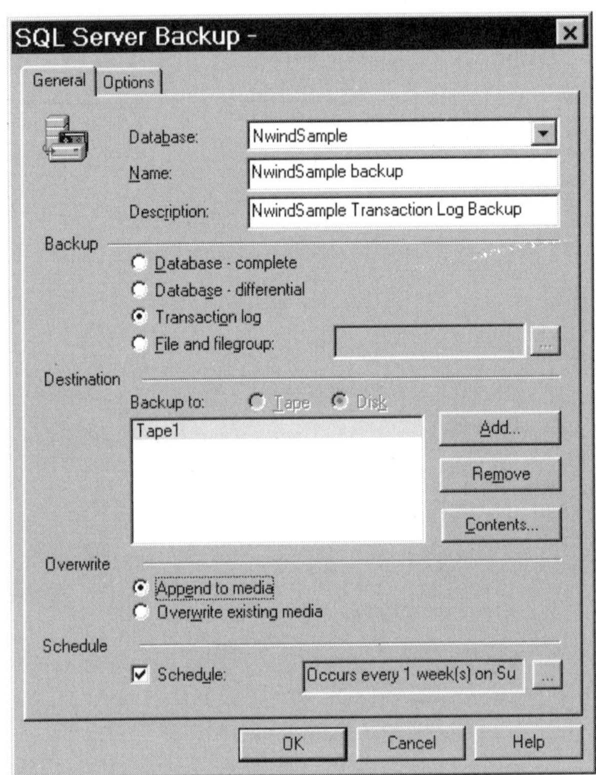

FIGURE 5.14: Setting options for a transaction log backup

Differential Database Backups

Differential database backups record only changes made to the database since the last backup, thereby reducing the amount of time it takes for the backup to run. Differential backups should also be used after non-logged transactions, since otherwise data might be lost in the event of a failure. By using a combination of database, differential database, and transaction log backups, recovery time and the amount of potential data loss due to failure can be minimized.

Creating a differential database backup is the same as creating a full database backup, except that the Database - Differential option should be checked, as shown in Figure 5.15.

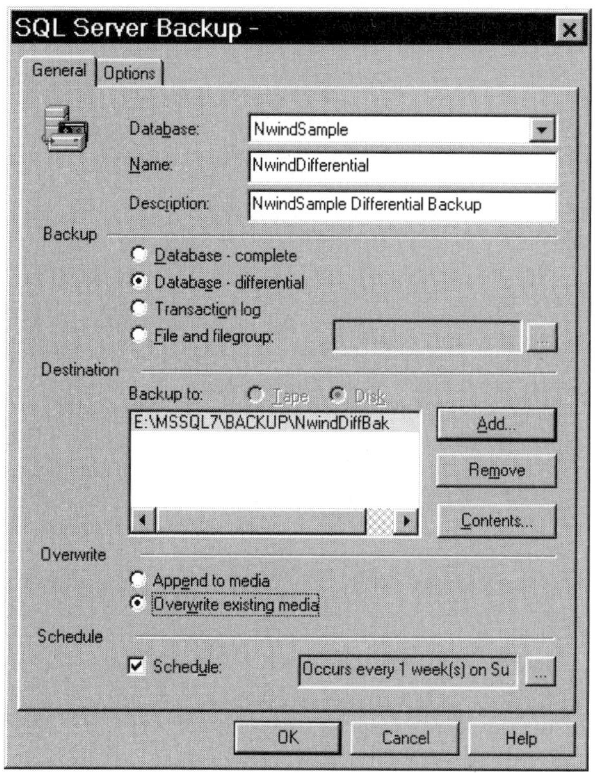

FIGURE 5.15: Creating a differential database backup

Differential backups have some limitations that full backups do not have. Some operations are not allowed during a differential database backup, such as:

- Creating or deleting database files
- Creating indexes
- Nonlogged operations
- Shrinking a database

If any of the above operations are in progress when a differential database backup is attempted, then the backup will fail. If the differential backup is already in progress, then the operation will fail and the backup continue.

Backing Up the System Databases

It isn't enough to back up just your user databases; you also need to think about backing up the following systems databases in the event of a system or database failure, or if the disk fails:

- The master database
- The msdb database
- The distribution database (if the server is configured as a replication Distributor)
- The model database (if you've modified it)

If the master database is damaged due to media failure, then SQL Server may not be able to start, so you should back it up in the same way you do a user database. It should be backed up after any procedure that changes information in the system tables in master. For example, if you create a new database before backing up master, when master is restored the new user database won't exist because there won't be any entries in the systems tables in the restored master for the new database.

If you can't restore master, you may have to rebuild it using the Rebuild Master utility, which also rebuilds the msdb and model databases. If any databases are restored or attached after master is rebuilt, it is necessary to specify the same sort order, code page, and Unicode collation when rebuilding master as used by those databases. If the same sort order, code page, and Unicode collation are not used, then it will not be possible to restore or attach those databases.

The model database is used as a template for creating other databases. If model is damaged and can't be restored, any user-specific template information will need to be re-created manually. The msdb database stores data such as scheduling information and backup and restore history for SQL Server, the Enterprise Manager, and SQL Server Agent. If msdb can't be restored, then scheduling information will need to be re-created manually. The distribution database is used for replication, so if it is lost, all replication information used by the SQL Server replication utilities will need to be re-created. Back up these databases in the same way you would a user database—and more frequently if they are changed.

Verifying Backups

Once you've created your backup, you need to verify it to ensure that all necessary files have been written and that they are readable in the event that a restore becomes necessary. Verifying a backup checks that it is physically intact but does not ensure that the structure of the data contained within it is correct. If there is some kind of database integrity problem present that could compromise the backup set, you need to verify the structure of the data before creating the backup by running a database consistency check using the Database Maintenance Plan or using the DBCC CHECKDB procedure.

To verify the backup using Transact-SQL, run RESTORE VERIFYONLY. Using the Enterprise manager, select the option Verify Backup Upon Completion from the Options tab of the Backup Database dialog box, as shown earlier in this skill.

Backing Up Using Transact-SQL

To back up the pubs database using Transact-SQL, you first need to create a backup device by using the sp_addumpdevice stored procedure. Then use the BACKUP DATABASE statement:

```
USE master
EXEC sp_addumpdevice 'disk', 'pubsbak', 'c:\mssql7\backup\pubsbak.dat'

BACKUP DATABASE pubs TO pubsbak
```

To back up the log, you also need to create the device first. The syntax is similar to backing up the database:

```
USE master
EXEC sp_addumpdevice 'disk', 'pubslogbak', 'c:\mssql7\backup\pubslog-
bak.dat'

BACKUP LOG pubs TO pubslogbak
```

Backing Up Using the Database Maintenance Plan Wizard

Perhaps the simplest way of all to back up a database and its transaction log is to use the Database Maintenance Plan Wizard. Of course, it does a few more things than just back up the database—it will also perform data verification and optimization tests for you as well. Setting up a plan is easy; you can load the wizard either from the main console by choosing Tools ➢ Database Maintenance Planner or by right-clicking the Database Maintenance Plans folder and choosing New Maintenance Plan. Once you open the wizard, you'll get to specify which databases to include in the plan. You can have one plan for all databases, or you can create separate plans for individual databases. In this example, we will create a plan for a single database. Figure 5.16 shows how you choose a database to be used in this plan.

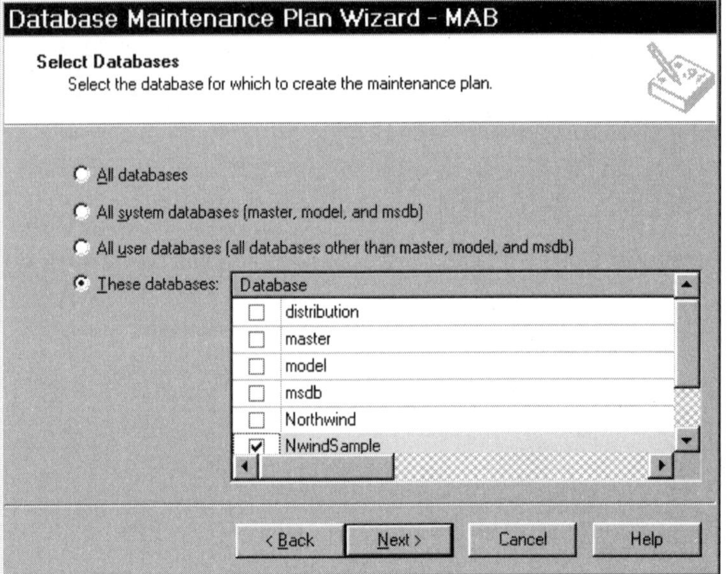

FIGURE 5.16: Selecting the databases to participate in the plan

The next screen, shown in Figure 5.17, asks you if you want to update data optimization information. Note that you can schedule this separately from your backups if you do not need to run it as frequently.

You can also schedule data integrity tests, as shown in Figure 5.18.

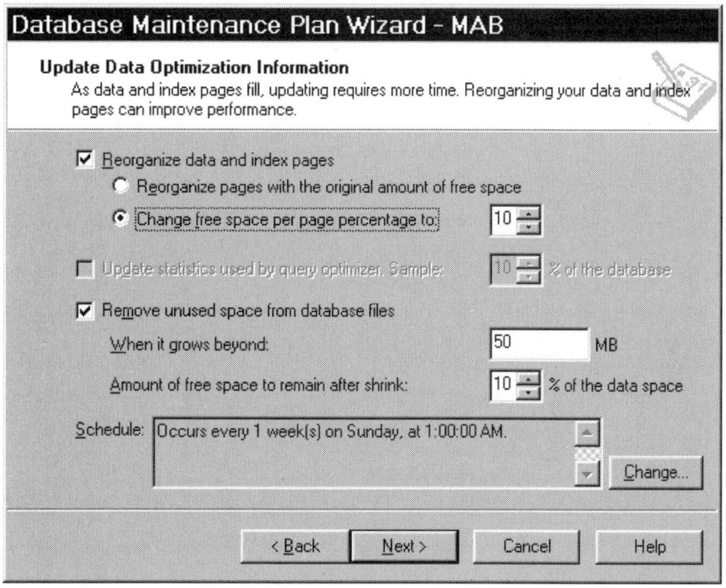

FIGURE 5.17: Scheduling data optimization information

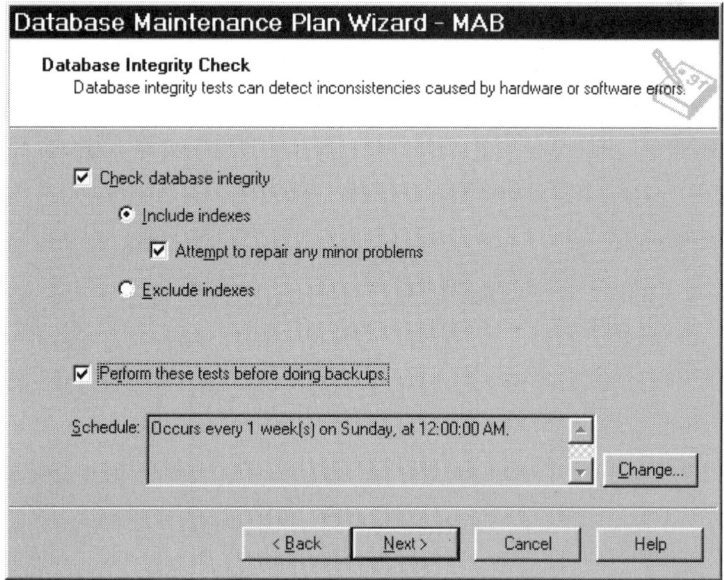

FIGURE 5.18: Scheduling data integrity tests

Figure 5.19 displays the screen for specifying the database maintenance plan backup.

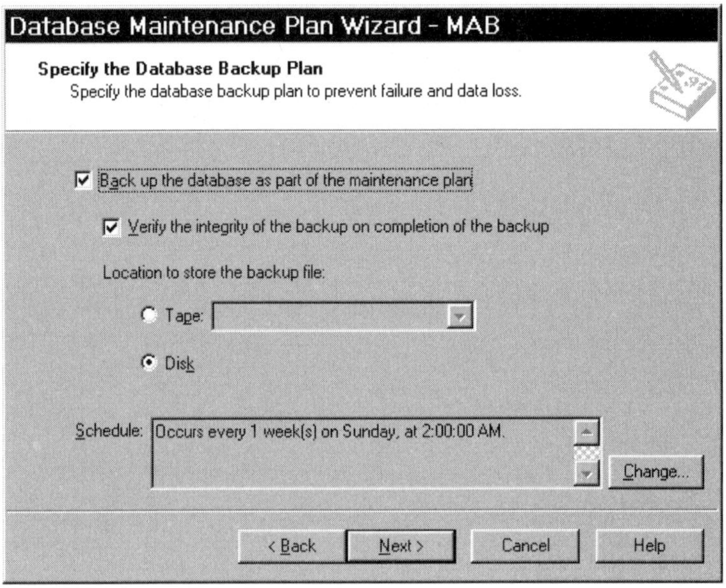

FIGURE 5.19: Specifying the backup

You can then specify the drive or tape location, as shown in Figure 5.20. You can also elect to remove old backup files. Each time the backup is run, a new file will be created.

Figure 5.21 shows the options for backing up the transaction log. Note that in this instance the log is going to be backed up every two hours.

You also need to specify the drive or tape location for the transaction log, as shown in Figure 5.22.

Figure 5.23 displays the options for any reports you may want to generate.

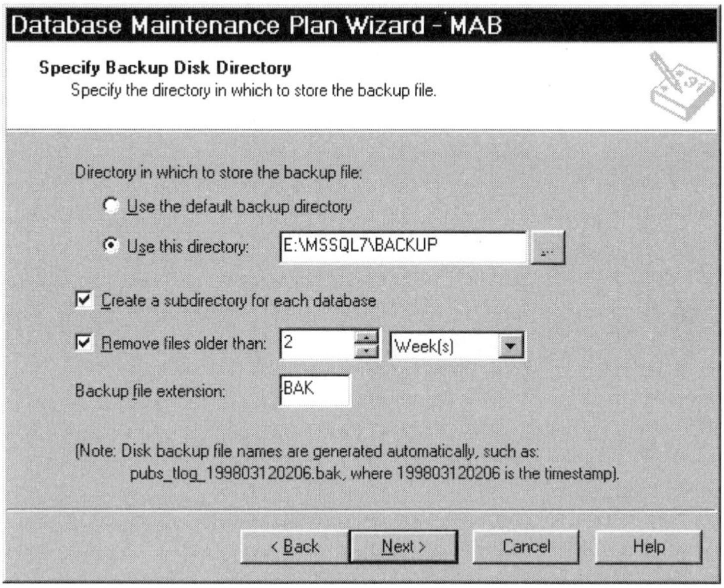

Database Maintenance Plan Wizard - MAB
Specify Backup Disk Directory
Specify the directory in which to store the backup file.
Directory in which to store the backup file:
Use the default backup directory
Use this directory:
E:\MSSQL7\BACKUP
Create a subdirectory for each database
Remove files older than:
2
Week(s)
Backup file extension:
BAK
(Note: Disk backup file names are generated automatically, such as:
pubs_tlog_199803120206.bak, where 199803120206 is the timestamp).
< Back
Next >
Cancel
Help

FIGURE 5.20: Specifying the location of the backup files

Database Maintenance Plan Wizard - MAB
Specify the Transaction Log Backup Plan
Specify the transaction log backup plan to prevent failures and operator errors.
Back up the transaction log as part of the maintenance plan
Verify the integrity of the backup on completion of the backup
Location to store the backup file:
Tape:
Disk
Schedule:
Occurs every 1 week(s) on Monday, Tuesday, Wednesday, Thursday, Friday, Saturday, at 12:00:00 AM.
Change...
< Back
Next >
Cancel
Help

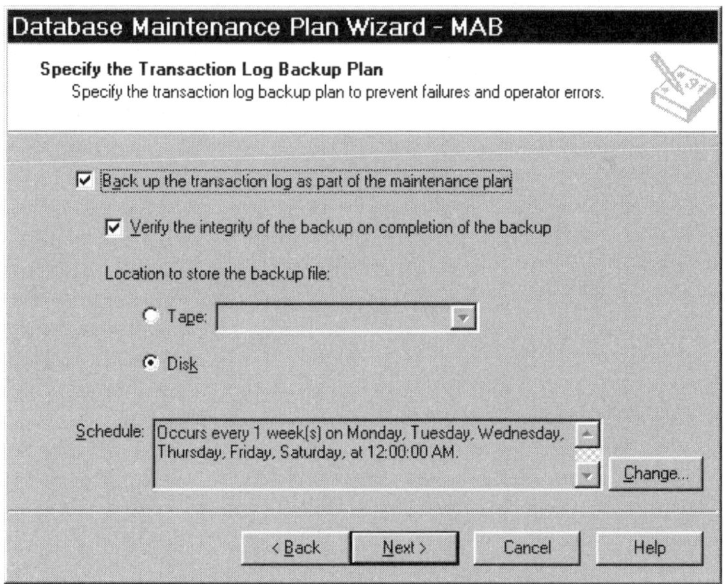

FIGURE 5.21: Specifying backing up the transaction log

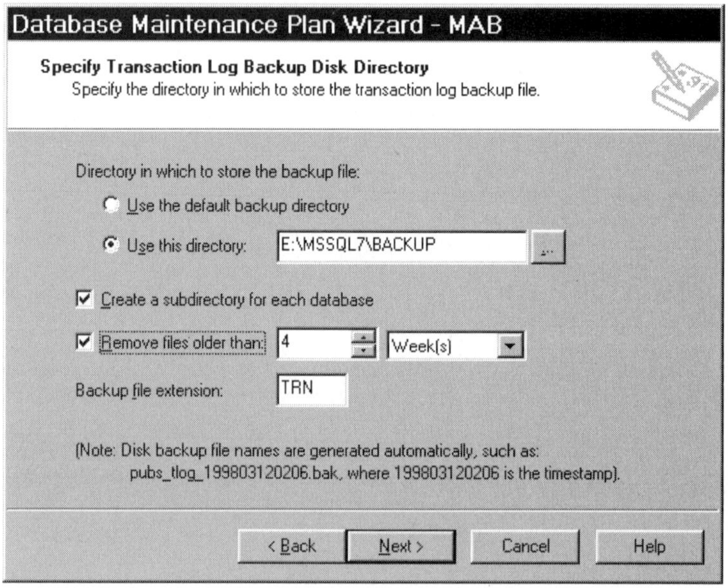

Database Maintenance Plan Wizard - MAB

Specify Transaction Log Backup Disk Directory
Specify the directory in which to store the transaction log backup file.

Directory in which to store the backup file:
Use the default backup directory
Use this directory: E:\MSSQL7\BACKUP ...
Create a subdirectory for each database
Remove files older than: 4 Week(s)
Backup file extension: TRN

(Note: Disk backup file names are generated automatically, such as:
pubs_tlog_199803120206.bak, where 199803120206 is the timestamp).

< Back Next > Cancel Help

FIGURE 5.22: Specifying backing up the transaction log location

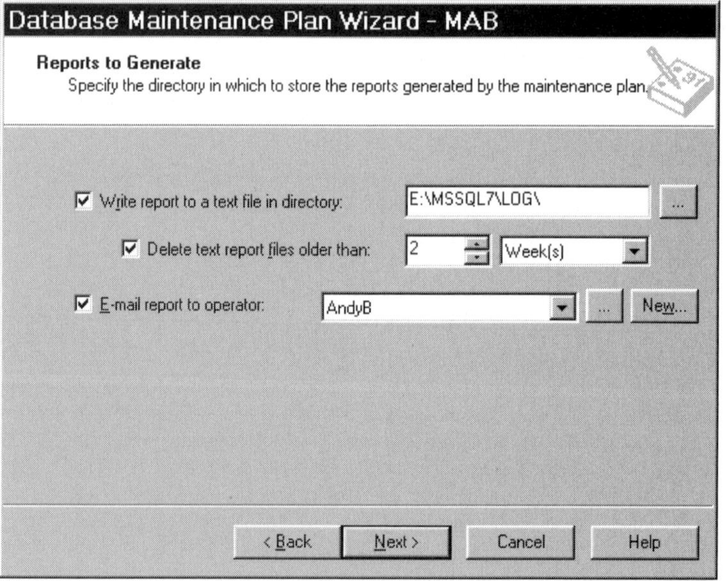

FIGURE 5.23: Specifying report options

You can also elect whether to record the actions performed on the server or on a remote server, as shown in Figure 5.24.

Figure 5.25 shows the final screen of the Maintenance Plan Wizard, where you name the plan and click the Finish button to implement it. Once you've created and saved the plan, you can just double-click it in the Database Maintenance Plans window to edit or revise it. The wizard won't run again, but you'll be able to edit all the options you set when you ran the wizard.

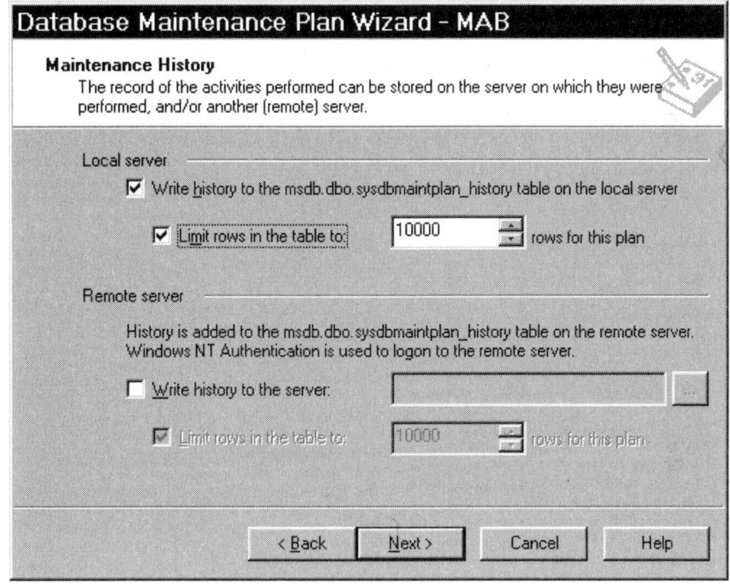

FIGURE 5.24: Maintenance history options

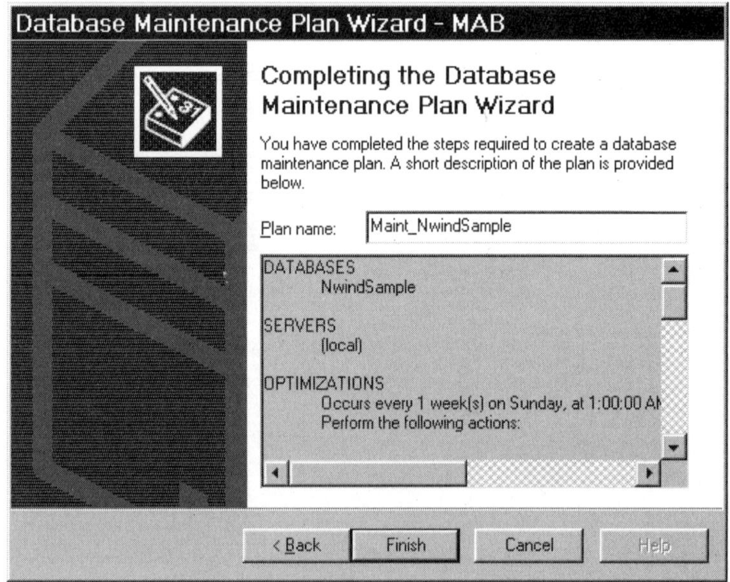

FIGURE 5.25: Naming the plan and finishing up

Restoring Using the Enterprise Manager

You can restore a database by right-clicking the Databases folder, selecting the Tools menu, and then clicking the Restore Database option. This will load the options screen where you can select the backup you want to restore. In this case, the backup of the Northwind database is displayed, as shown in Figure 5.26.

Click the Options tab to display further options, such as whether you want to restore over an existing database and the recovery completion state desired, as shown in Figure 5.27.

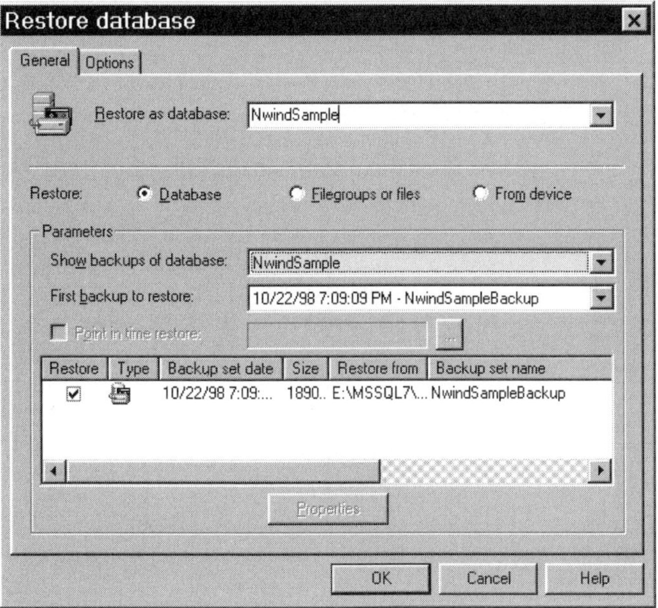

FIGURE 5.26: Restoring the Northwind database from a backup

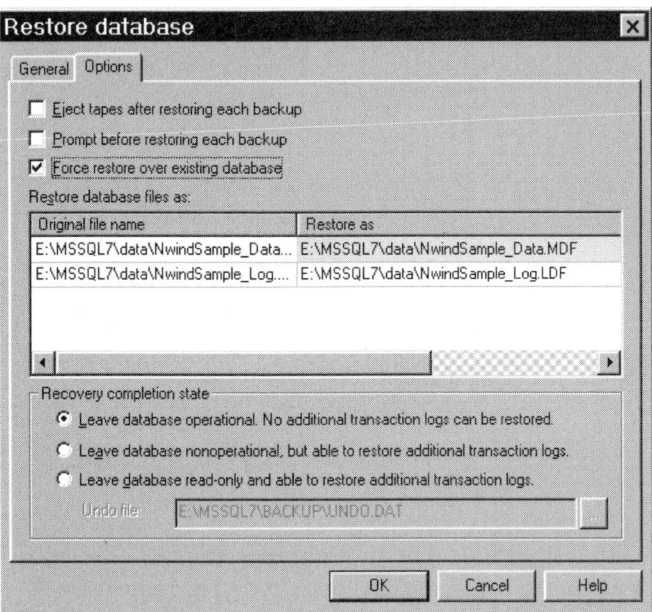

FIGURE 5.27: Additional options for restoring a database

Restoring Using Transact-SQL

To restore a database from a full backup, use the following syntax:

```
RESTORE DATABASE pubs
  FROM pubs_backup
```

To restore both the database and an incremental backup, use the following syntax:

```
RESTORE DATABASE pubs
  FROM pubs_backup

RESTORE LOG pubs_log
  FROM pubs_lg1
```

Are You up to Speed?

Now you can...

- ☑ **import or export using Data Transformation Services, bcp, or Transact-SQL**
- ☑ **back up and restore both your database and transaction log**

SKILL 6

Retrieving Data

- Creating queries and subqueries
- Using joins
- Using functions in queries
- Using cursors
- Creating summary queries
- Using parallel queries, full-text querying, and distributed queries
- Creating views

In this skill you will learn to use the SQL Server Query Analyzer to create queries using Transact-SQL, become familiar with Transact-SQL basics, work with different data types, and understand joins. You will also create more advanced queries and views and learn about how SQL Server handles data concurrency and record locking.

Creating Queries

Once you've entered data into your SQL Server database, you need to have a way to retrieve it, to change it, to add or insert new data, or to delete existing data. You request information from SQL Server by using a query, which is composed of SQL statements.

SQL (or Structured Query Language) employs a uniform syntax across multiple platforms in order to retrieve data. Transact-SQL in SQL Server 7 complies with the Entry Level of the American National Standards Institute (ANSI) SQL-92 standard but also supports many additional features and extensions not explicitly defined in the SQL-92 standard. SQL-92 is also often referred to as ANSI SQL.

There are several tools you can use to access and change data in SQL Server:

- Form-based or graphical tools, such as those found in Access or Visual Basic, which allow you to work with the data and do not require any knowledge of SQL.
- Interactive SQL Server tools, such as the osql utility and the SQL Server Query Analyzer, which you can use to directly enter Transact-SQL statements and view results.
- Programming APIs that are employed from an application, such as ADO, OLE DB, and ODBC, and allow programmers to build applications that can retrieve and manipulate data. The programmer needs to know Transact-SQL, but users of the application do not. Programming APIs are covered in Skills 12 and 13.

No matter which of these tools you employ, you are sending Transact-SQL statements to the SQL Server to be processed.

THE osql COMMAND-PROMPT UTILITY

You can use osql from the command prompt to interactively enter Transact-SQL statements and have them display in the command prompt. You can also submit an osql job and have the output directed to a text file instead of having it display in the command prompt, where it isn't terribly useful.

The osql utility uses the ODBC API and is a replacement for the older isql utility which used the DB-Library API. Isql does not support some SQL Server 7 features, such as those dealing with Unicode data types. If you have an older application that relies on isql, you can replace it with osql and not lose any of the functionality of isql.

Transact-SQL Basics

You can use Transact-SQL to communicate directly with SQL Server. Transact-SQL allows you to work with data, create and manipulate database objects, and work with stored procedures, which are compiled static SQL statements. Four basic Transact-SQL statements make up the core of the SQL language:

- The `SELECT` statement is used to retrieve existing data.
- The `UPDATE` statement is used to edit existing data.
- The `INSERT` statement is used to add new data.
- The `DELETE` statement is used to delete data.

NOTE Stored procedures allow an application's processing logic to be shifted from the application to the server. Since they are precompiled, they don't have to be parsed each time the procedure is executed. Stored procedures are written with Transact-SQL statements and control-of-flow syntax. See Skill 13, *Programming SQL Server*, for information on batch processing and control language.

In this skill we are going to learn how the SELECT statement creates a query—retrieving data from the server and then presenting the result set to the user. The result set is a tabular arrangement of the data that is returned by the SELECT statement and contains columns and rows. Figure 6.1 shows the result set of a query of the LastName and FirstName fields in the Employees table in the sample Northwind database when executed into the Results Grid of the SQL Server Query Analyzer.

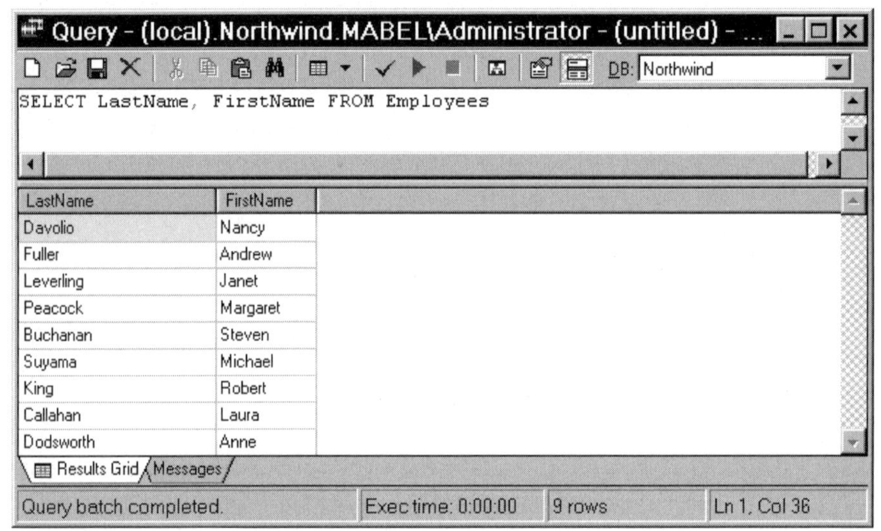

FIGURE 6.1: The result set of a query

Using the SQL Server Query Analyzer

The SQL Server Query Analyzer allows you to create ad hoc queries and scripts and run them interactively. You can also use text files containing Transact-SQL statements, execute them, and view the results in the Results pane or the Results Grid. The Query Analyzer has a color-coded editor to assist you with checking your syntax. It also has context-sensitive Help as well as Transact-SQL Help. In addition to executing the query and displaying the results, you can also do the following:

- View a graphical representation of a query's execution plan.
- Perform index analysis.

- View statistical information about an executed query.
- Display the execution plan.
- Run query analysis.

GETTING HELP IN THE QUERY ANALYZER

Use the following shortcuts to quickly get help in the Query Analyzer:

- Press F1 or click Help and select one of the menu options to get help on the Query Analyzer itself.
- Select all or part of a Transact-SQL statement and press Shift+F1 to get Transact-SQL syntax help.
- Select a database object within the Transact-SQL statement and press Alt+F1 to get help on that object's properties.

The Transact-SQL online Help includes help not only for Transact-SQL syntax, but also for system stored procedures, functions, global variables, data types, and a list of new features in this version of Transact-SQL. This is a good place to look for information, since Transact-SQL is far too complex to completely document in detail in this book.

You can set options for the result set by clicking the Query Options button on the toolbar or choosing Query ➢ Current Connection Options from the menu bar. Figure 6.2 shows the General tab in the Current Connection Options dialog box where the row count limit has been set to 50. Figure 6.3 shows the Advanced tab, which allows you to format the result set.

NOTE For a more complete discussion of the different options available in the Query Analyzer, see Skill 8, *Using SQL Server Tools*.

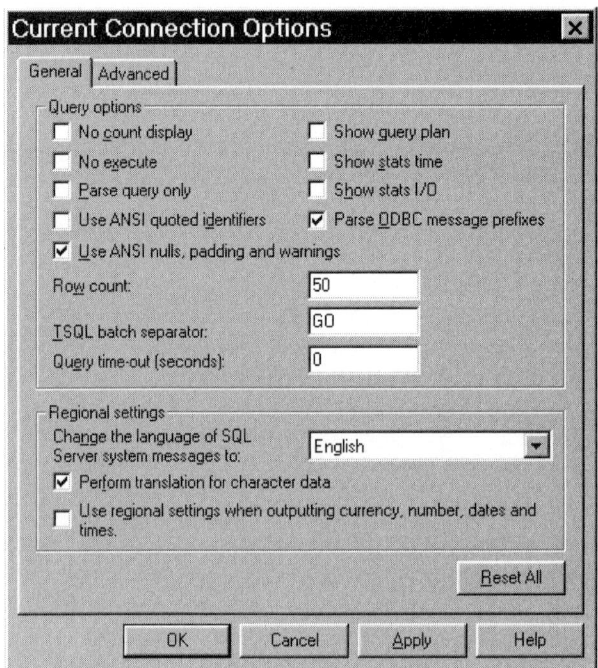

FIGURE 6.2: SQL Server Query Analyzer advanced options for query execution

To use the Query Analyzer, simply type a SQL statement into the top pane and select one of the following options from the toolbar buttons or from the Query menu:

- Execute Query
- Execute Query into Grid
- Display SQL Execution Plan
- Perform Index Analysis

In this skill we're going to execute the query. Figure 6.1 showed executing the query into a grid, and Figure 6.4 shows executing the same query using the Execute Query option.

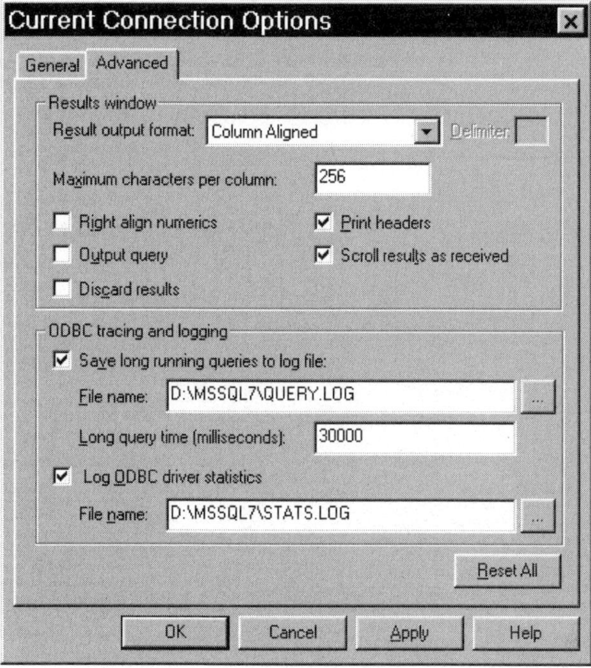

FIGURE 6.3: SQL Server Query Analyzer Advanced options for formatting the result set

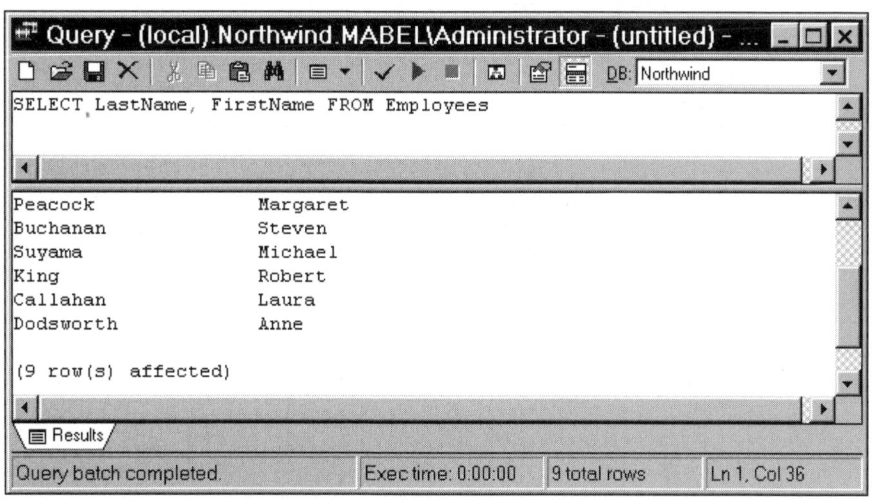

FIGURE 6.4: The result set displayed by the Execute Query option

Using the SELECT Statement to Retrieve Data

The SELECT statement retrieves rows and columns from a table and presents you with a result set. It can also be used to join tables together or to retrieve a subset of columns from one or more tables. The full syntax is as follows:

```
SELECT
[ALL | DISTINCT] [TOP n [PERCENT] [WITH TIES]]
{ <result_data> :: =
  { *
    | [column_heading = ] column_name
    | column_name [[AS] column_heading]
    | column_name AS expression
    | expression [AS] column_heading]
    | GROUPING (column_name)
    | IDENTITYCOL
    | ROWGUIDCOL
    | local_or_global_variable
    | new_column_name = IDENTITY(data_type, seed, increment)
  } [, ...n]
  | <variable_assignment> :: = {@local_variable = expression } [, ...n]
}
[INTO new_table_name]
[FROM
{ <table_or_view>
  | (select_statement) [AS] alias
  | <table_or_view> CROSS JOIN <table_or_view>
  | <table_or_view>
    [{ INNER | {LEFT | RIGHT | FULL} [OUTER] }
    [<join_hint>]] JOIN
    <table_or_view> ON search_conditions
}[, ...n]
]
[WHERE search_conditions]
[GROUP BY [ALL] {aggregate_free_expression} [, ...n]
  [WITH {CUBE | ROLLUP}]
]
[HAVING search_conditions]
[ORDER BY
{ {  {table. | view.}column_name
    | select_list_number
    | expression
  } [ASC | DESC]
}  [, ...n]
]
[COMPUTE row_aggregate({expression | column_name}[, ...n])
```

```
    [BY {expression | column_name}[, …n]]
]
[FOR BROWSE]
[OPTION (<query_hint> [, ... n])]

<table_or_view> ::=
   { table [[AS] alias] [<table_hint>]
   | view [[AS] alias] }
   | OpenRowset('provider_name', {'datasource';'user_id';'password' |
        'provider_string'}, {[catalog.][schema.]object_name | 'query'})
   | OpenQuery(linked_server, 'query')}

<table_hint> ::=
   ([INDEX = {index_name | index_id}[, …n]] [FASTFIRSTROW]
      [HOLDLOCK] [NOLOCK] [PAGLOCK] [READCOMMITTED]
      [READPAST] [READUNCOMMITTED] [REPEATABLEREAD]
      [ROWLOCK] [SERIALIZABLE] [TABLOCK] [TABLOCKX]
      [UPDLOCK])
<join_hint> ::=
   {LOOP | HASH | MERGE}
<query_hint> :: =
   {  {HASH | ORDER} GROUP
      | {MERGE | HASH | CONCAT} UNION
      | FAST n
      | FORCE ORDER
      | ROBUST PLAN
   }
```

As you can see, the full syntax of the SELECT statement is rather complex. We won't cover some of the more esoteric options; refer to Books Online for more information. Let's examine the following SELECT statement, which retrieves the names of employees with an employee ID greater than six and then sorts the result set by the last name:

```
SELECT LastName, FirstName
FROM Employees
WHERE EmployeeID > 6
ORDER BY LastName
```

Let's break down more simply what's going on here.

- The column names are always listed immediately after the SELECT keyword—these columns form the Select list, which tells us that the query has two columns.

- The name of the table from which the data is to be retrieved, Employees, is listed immediately after the `FROM` keyword.
- The `SELECT` and the `FROM` keywords are required—the other parts of the query are optional.
- The `WHERE` clause specifies that only employee names having an employee ID greater than six will be listed.
- The `ORDER BY` clause specifies that the result set be sorted in ascending order on the `LastName` column.

Here's the result set from this query:

```
LastName             FirstName
-------------------  ----------
Callahan             Laura
Dodsworth            Anne
King                 Robert

(3 row(s) affected)
```

All queries that you create will have their elements in this basic order, although you may add other elements as well, such as `GROUP BY` and `HAVING` clauses, which we will cover later in this skill.

When you refer to database objects, you must make sure that the reference is not ambiguous. For example, it is possible to create multiple objects with the same name in a database as long as they have different owners. In this case you'd need to qualify the table name with the owner's name, as shown here, where you want to work with the `LastName` field in Norman's Employees table:

```
SELECT LastName from Norman.Employees
```

If the database you are working with is not the current database, you need to refer to it explicitly by qualifying the object name with the database name and the database owner:

```
SELECT LastName from Northwind.dbo.Employees
```

If you are joining multiple tables, there may be column names that are the same in both tables. In the following query, which selects the `EmployeeID` from both the Employees table and the Orders table, you need to qualify the column name with the table name:

```
SELECT DISTINCT Orders.EmployeeID, Employees.EmployeeID
FROM Orders
```

```
JOIN Employees
ON (Orders.EmployeeID = Employees.EmployeeID)
```

You can also use aliases to refer to columns and tables using the AS keyword as shown in the next example. Here the EmployeeID column is aliased as OrdID, the Orders table is aliased as Ord in the FROM clause, and the Employees table is aliased as Emp in the join. The query lists the ID numbers of employees who have related records in the Orders table.

```
SELECT DISTINCT Ord.EmployeeID as OrdID
FROM Northwind.dbo.Orders as Ord
JOIN Northwind.dbo.Employees as Emp
ON (Ord.EmployeeID = Emp.EmployeeID)
```

Working with the Select List

The Select list defines the columns returned in the result set of a SELECT statement. These are returned in the same order that they are listed. You can also use expressions in the Select list to define the following attributes of the result set columns:

- Data type, precision, and scale
- The column name displayed in the result set by using the AS keyword
- The values displayed in the result set resulting from an expression applied to each row

To return only certain columns in the result set, list them out by name. The following SELECT statement will display only the FirstName and LastName columns from the Employees table:

```
SELECT FirstName, LastName FROM Employees
```

If you want to return all of the columns in a given table, use the asterisk (*). The following SELECT statement will return all of the rows in the Employees table:

```
SELECT * FROM Employees
```

You can compute values in the Select list by creating expressions. The result set contains columns that do not exist in the underlying tables. The following query will count all of the orders taken by the employee whose ID is three:

```
SELECT Count(*) AS NumOrders
FROM Orders
WHERE EmployeeID = 3
```

You can also use certain keywords to modify the records returned:

- The `DISTINCT` keyword eliminates duplicate rows. `SELECT DISTINCT EmployeeID FROM Orders` returns nine rows while `SELECT EmployeeID FROM Orders` returns 830 rows.
- The `TOP n` keyword specifies that only the first *n* rows of a result set are returned after an `ORDER BY` specification is applied. The following query selects the top three employees who have placed the most orders:

```
SELECT TOP 3 EmployeeID, Count(*) as NumOrders
FROM Orders
GROUP BY EmployeeID
ORDER BY NumOrders DESC
```

The result set will be:

```
EmployeeID  NumOrders
----------  ---------
4           156
3           127
1           123
```

You can also use the `PERCENT` qualifier with `TOP n`:

```
SELECT TOP 30 PERCENT EmployeeID, Count(*) as NumOrders
FROM Orders
GROUP BY EmployeeID
ORDER BY NumOrders DESC
```

Working with the FROM Clause

The `FROM` clause is a comma-delimited list of the table names and views which contain the columns specified in the Select list and `WHERE` clause. You can specify one or more tables or views, as shown in the following example, which selects all of the records from the Employees table:

```
SELECT * FROM Employees
```

You can also use it to specify the joins between two tables or views:

```
SELECT DISTINCT Orders.EmployeeID, Employees.LastName
FROM Orders
JOIN Employees
ON (Orders.EmployeeID = Employees.EmployeeID)
```

TIP

You don't need a FROM clause if you are not returning data from a table or view with your SELECT statement. A statement can be used to select data from a local variable or Transact-SQL function. The following example will return the version of SQL Server you are currently running: SELECT @@version.

Specifying Rows in a WHERE or HAVING Clause

The optional WHERE and HAVING clauses in a query act as filters to limit the number of rows returned based on conditions you specify. Only those rows that match your conditions are displayed in the result set. The following simple example uses a WHERE clause to return all of the employees who live in Seattle:

```
SELECT LastName
FROM Employees
WHERE City = 'Seattle'
```

The HAVING clause works the same way as the WHERE clause, except that it is used in conjunction with a GROUP BY clause to further filter the data. It is applied after the WHERE clause. The following query selects all the employees with an employee ID greater than three and counts the number of orders they have taken. It then uses the HAVING clause to further filter the result set to show only those records where the number of orders is greater than 50:

```
SELECT EmployeeID, Count(*) AS NumOrders
FROM Orders
WHERE EmployeeID > 3
GROUP BY EmployeeID
HAVING Count(*) > 50
```

You can use different kinds of search conditions and comparison operators when constructing WHERE and HAVING clauses. Table 6.1 lists the different comparison operators you can use in a query.

TABLE 6.1: Comparison Operators

Operator	Meaning
=	Equal to
>	Greater than
<	Less than
>=	Greater than or equal to

TABLE 6.1 CONTINUED: Comparison Operators

Operator	Meaning
<=	Less than or equal to
< > (ANSI-compatible)	Not equal to
!>	Not greater than
!<	Not less than
!=	Not equal to

The following example would list all of the employees with an employee ID greater than three:

```
SELECT EmployeeID
FROM Orders
WHERE EmployeeID > 3
```

You can also specify ranges and lists. Table 6.2 lists the syntax you can use to return ranges and lists.

TABLE 6.2: Ranges and Lists

Search Condition	Example in WHERE Clause
BETWEEN, NOT BETWEEN	WHERE EmployeeID BETWEEN 1 AND 3 WHERE EmployeeID NOT BETWEEN 1 AND 3
IN, NOT IN	WHERE City IN ('Seattle', 'Redmond') WHERE City NOT IN ('Seattle', 'Redmond')
LIKE, NOT LIKE	WHERE LastName LIKE 'd%' WHERE LastName NOT LIKE 'd%'
IS NULL, IS NOT NULL	WHERE Region IS NULL WHERE Region IS NOT NULL
AND	WHERE LastName LIKE 'd%' AND FirstName LIKE 'n%'
OR	WHERE LastName LIKE 'd%' OR FirstName LIKE 'n%'

TIP Try to avoid using negative conditions in your search criteria, such as NOT IN. Negative conditions slow down performance since the query parser can't optimize them.

NOTE

Any arithmetic or bitwise operators are evaluated before logical operators in a statement. When more than one logical operator is used, NOT is evaluated first, then AND, and finally OR. If you want to force a certain order, then use parentheses () to enclose the part of the statement you want evaluated first.

You can choose from the list of wildcard operators shown in Table 6.3 when using the LIKE keyword.

TABLE 6.3: Wildcard Operators

Wildcard	Description
_	A single character
%	A string of any length
[]	Any single character within the range enclosed in brackets
[^]	Any single character not within the range enclosed in brackets

TIP

The other wildcard character, the asterisk (*), is used for selecting all of the columns from a table or joined tables and is not for use in a WHERE clause.

The following example lists all employee names with the string *ing* anywhere in them:

```
WHERE LastName LIKE '%ing%'
```

The following example lists all employee names with five letters, the last four of which are *aura*:

```
WHERE FirstName LIKE '_aura'
```

The following example lists all employees named Catherine or Katherine:

```
WHERE FirstName LIKE '[CK]atherine'
```

The following example lists all names that start with letters between *M* and *Z* and whose other characters are *ilson*:

```
WHERE LastName LIKE '[M-Z]ilson'
```

The following example lists all names that start with the letter *M* and whose second character is not *e*:

```
WHERE FirstName LIKE 'M[^e]%'
```

TIP Don't use wildcard characters to begin an expression unless you absolutely must—it will degrade query performance since an index cannot be used. Wildcards used in the middle or at the end of an expression are OK since an index can be used in those cases.

To search for wildcard characters that might appear inside of strings, use the ESCAPE keyword. The following example will return all description rows that contain the string *20%*:

```
WHERE Description LIKE '%20/%%' ESCAPE '/'
```

You can also enclose the wildcard character in brackets. The following example will return all rows that have a dash in them:

```
WHERE Description LIKE '[-]'
```

Sorting the Results with ORDER BY

If you want to specify the order of the columns, use the ORDER BY clause. You can sort in either ascending (ASC) or descending (DESC) order. If you don't specify ASC or DESC, then ascending is assumed.

If you sort on more than one column, then the sorts are nested. The following SELECT statement sorts first on the CategoryID column in ascending order, and then on the UnitPrice column in descending order:

```
SELECT CategoryID, ProductName, UnitPrice
FROM Products
ORDER BY CategoryID, UnitPrice DESC
```

The first few rows of the results returned look like this:

```
CategoryID  ProductName                      UnitPrice
----------  ------------------------------  ----------
1           Côte de Blaye                    263.5000
1           Ipoh Coffee                      46.0000
1           Chang                            19.0000
1           Chai                             18.0000
1           Steeleye Stout                   18.0000
1           Chartreuse verte                 18.0000
1           Lakkalikööri                     18.0000
```

TIP You can't sort columns defined as text or image.

Using the HAVING Clause

You can use the HAVING clause to restrict rows returned by group, instead of individually, as a WHERE clause does. The WHERE clause is evaluated first, then a GROUP BY is applied. Only then do you put in a HAVING, which works like a WHERE, but only on the rows returned by the GROUP BY. The following example first selects all the pub_id's from the Titles table, and sums the advance and price where the price is greater than or equal to $5. Only then does it select those records where the sum of the advance is greater than $15,000:

```
USE pubs
SELECT pub_id, SUM(advance), AVG(price)
FROM titles
WHERE price >= $5
GROUP BY pub_id
HAVING SUM(advance) > $15000
ORDER BY pub_id
```


Using Joins

Joins in a query let you retrieve data from tables based on the relationship between them and the join operator employed. A join typically specifies foreign key relationships between the tables along with a logical operator to be used in comparing values from the join columns. Join types include the following:

- *Inner join*, or *equi-join*, which is based on an operator (=, >, <, <>), matches rows between two tables based on their common values
- *Outer join*, in which all rows from one of the tables will be included, even if there are no matching values in the related table
- *Cross join*, or *full outer join*, in which all rows from both tables will be included, even if there are no matching values in either related table

TIP Although you can specify a join in either the FROM or the WHERE clause, the FROM clause is recommended since it is SQL-92 compliant and less likely to create an ambiguous situation.

The syntax for a join is as follows:

```
FROM first_table join_type second_table [ON (join_condition)]
```

The following simple example selects the company name from the Customers table and the order ID from the Orders table. The join is on the `CustomerID` field, which is a foreign key in the Orders table, and the column by which the two tables are related to each other. Only customers with matching orders are shown since we're using the equality operator (=) in the join.

```
SELECT CompanyName, OrderID
FROM Customers JOIN Orders
ON (Customers.CustomerID = Orders.CustomerID)
```

TIP Queries using joins can often be rewritten as subqueries, which are discussed later in this skill.

Inner Joins

Joins can also be expressed in a SQL statement by using the `INNER` and `OUTER` keywords to specify the join type. For example, if you wanted to find all the customers and suppliers located in the same city, you would use an inner join:

```
SELECT Customers.CompanyName AS Cust, Suppliers.CompanyName AS Supp
FROM Customers INNER JOIN Suppliers
ON Customers.City = Suppliers.City
```

Figure 6.5 shows a sample inner join, in which one record in the first table is related to many records in the second table and a single record in the second table is related to only one record in the first table.

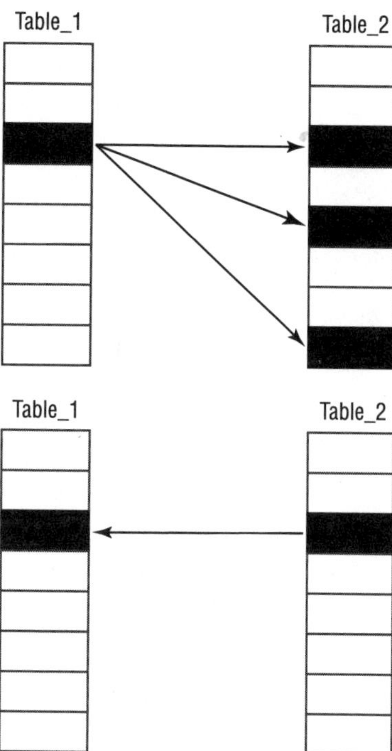

FIGURE 6.5: A sample inner join: one record in the first table is related to many records in the second table, and one record in the second table is related to only one record in the first table.

Outer Joins

In this case only equal matches would be returned. If you wanted to see all of the customers listed, and only those suppliers in a matching customer city, you would use an outer join:

```
SELECT Customers.CompanyName AS Cust, Suppliers.CompanyName AS Supp
FROM Customers LEFT OUTER JOIN Suppliers
ON Customers.City = Suppliers.City
```

This is what the first few rows of the result set look like. Note the null values for customers who do not have a supplier located in their city.

```
Cust                                     Supp
---------------------------------------- ----------------------------
Alfreds Futterkiste                      Heli Süßwaren GmbH & Co. KG
Ana Trujillo Emparedados y helados       NULL
Antonio Moreno Taquería                  NULL
Around the Horn                          Exotic Liquids
Berglunds snabbköp                       NULL
```

Outer joins can be either `LEFT OUTER JOIN`, which returns all the records on the leftmost table in the join, or `RIGHT OUTER JOIN`, which returns all the records on the rightmost table in the join. The nulls in the result set reflect the other side of the join where there are no matching values. All records from one side of the join and only records with matching values from the other side are returned in an outer join. Figure 6.6 illustrates an outer join.

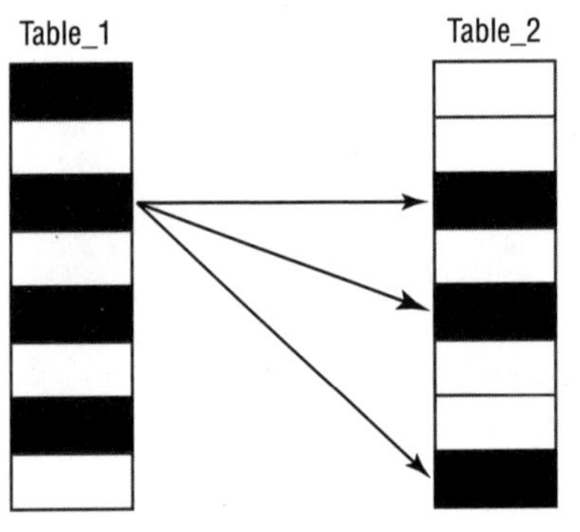

FIGURE 6.6: An outer join

Joining with a WHERE Clause

In addition to the `INNER` and `OUTER JOIN` keywords, you can also use a `WHERE` clause to create joins. The following query returns the same result set as the `INNER JOIN` query listed above since the `WHERE` clause restricts the rows returned to those with matching values in both tables.

```
SELECT Customers.CompanyName AS Cust, Suppliers.CompanyName AS Supp
FROM Customers, Suppliers
WHERE Customers.City = Suppliers.City
```

TIP

If there are null values in either one of the columns of the tables being joined, you must use an outer join unless the WHERE clause excludes null values.

Self Joins

A *self join* is a type of inner join. You can use self joins to find records in a table that are related to other records in the same table, as shown in Figure 6.7. For example, if you wanted to find all the customers located in the same city, you would use the following syntax. Note that there is an additional join using the less-than operator (<) on the CustomerID field, which restricts duplicates as well as customer cities matching to themselves:

```
SELECT Customers.City, Customers.CompanyName AS Cust,
  Customers1.CompanyName AS Cust1
FROM Customers
INNER JOIN Customers Customers1
ON Customers.City = Customers1.City
AND Customers.CustomerID < Customers1.CustomerID
ORDER BY Customers.City
```

The first few rows of the result set would look like this:

```
City           Cust                           Cust1
-------------- ------------------------------ ----------------------
Buenos Aires   Cactus Comidas para llevar     Océano Atlántico Ltda.
Buenos Aires   Cactus Comidas para llevar     Rancho grande
Buenos Aires   Océano Atlántico Ltda.         Rancho grande
Lisboa         Furia Bacalhau e Frutos do Mar Princesa Isabel Vinhos
```

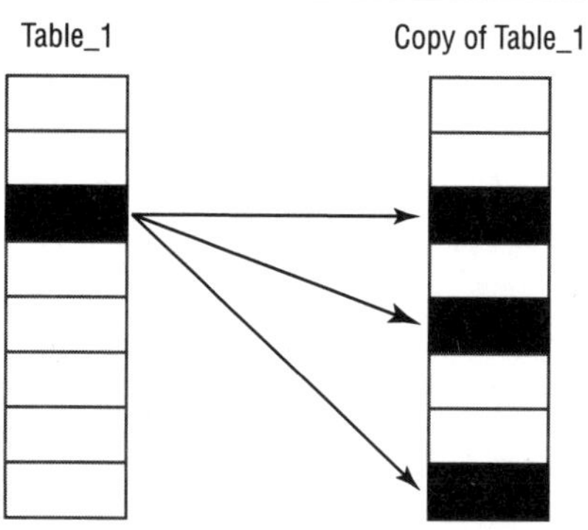

FIGURE 6.7: Self joins

Skill 6

Cross Joins

A *cross join*, or full outer join, produces a Cartesian product since there are no matching columns in either table, as shown in Figure 6.8. The number of rows produced by a Cartesian product is the number of rows in the first table multiplied by the number of rows in the second table. The following query selects the `LastName` from the Employees table and the `CompanyName` from the Customers table. If there are ten records in the Employees table and 91 records in the Customers table, the result set will contain 910 rows.

```
SELECT LastName, CompanyName
FROM Employees CROSS JOIN Customers
```

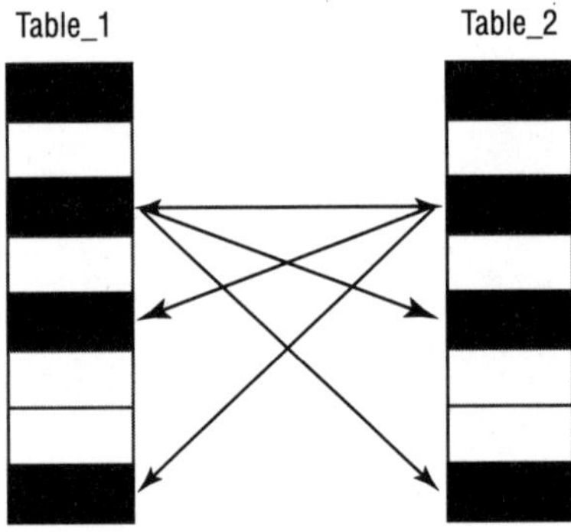

FIGURE 6.8: Cross joins

However, if you include a `WHERE` clause, the cross join behaves as an inner join and no longer produces a Cartesian product. The following query restricts the result set to returning 27 rows instead of 910:

```
SELECT Employees.City, Employees.LastName, Customers.CompanyName
FROM Employees CROSS JOIN Customers
WHERE Employees.City = Customers.City
ORDER BY Employees.City
```

Using Subqueries

Subqueries are most often used to save steps in operations that would normally require two separate queries in order to locate information. Subqueries are `SELECT` statements nested inside other `SELECT`, `INSERT`, `UPDATE`, or `DELETE` statements, other subqueries, or in any allowable expression (the expression that includes the subquery must return True or False). Subqueries are most often found nested inside the WHERE or HAVING clause of an outer SELECT, INSERT, UPDATE, or DELETE statement, or inside another subquery. Many SQL statements that include subqueries can also be formulated as joins. The syntax is:

```
expression comparison_operator [ANY | ALL | SOME] (subquery)
expression [NOT] IN (subquery)
 [NOT] EXISTS (subquery)
```

Suppose you want to find all of the products that cost the same as Longlife Tofu. The following query uses a WHERE clause comparing the unit price against the WHERE clause in the subquery which locates the price of Longlife Tofu:

```
SELECT ProductName, UnitPrice
FROM Products
WHERE UnitPrice =
  (SELECT UnitPrice
  FROM Products
  WHERE ProductName = 'Longlife Tofu')
```

The result set looks like this:

```
ProductName                       UnitPrice
------------------------------    ----------
Aniseed Syrup                     10.0000
Sir Rodney's Scones               10.0000
Longlife Tofu                     10.0000
```


The SELECT statement of a subquery (or inner query) is always enclosed in parentheses and cannot include an ORDER BY, COMPUTE, or FOR BROWSE clause. You can nest subqueries inside the WHERE or HAVING clauses of the outer query and there is no limit on the level of nesting. Columns from a subquery cannot be included in the output of the outer query unless the table they are drawn from also appears in the outer query. You can use the following statement formats in the subquery:

```
WHERE expression [NOT] IN (subquery)

WHERE expression comparison_operator [ANY | ALL] (subquery)

WHERE [NOT] EXISTS (subquery)
```

You can use a WHERE EXISTS clause to find out whether any records exist that match certain criteria. For example, you might want to select only the order IDs that have an order for a beverage, whose CategoryID equals 1. The outer query looks in the Order Details table and has a WHERE clause which then selects records from the Products table where the ProductID matches the Order Details ProductID and the CategoryID is 1:

```
SELECT OrderID
```

```
FROM [Order Details]
WHERE EXISTS
     (SELECT *
      FROM Products
      WHERE ProductID = [Order Details].ProductID
        AND CategoryID = 1
     )
```

A correlated (or repeating) subquery depends on the outer query for its values, as shown in the following query which looks for the amount specified in the WHERE...IN clause to find all orders with 10 units in stock. The subquery is then executed repeatedly, once for each row selected by the outer query.

```
SELECT DISTINCT OrderID
FROM [Order Details]
WHERE 10 IN
    (SELECT UnitsInStock
     FROM Products
     WHERE Products.ProductID = [Order Details].ProductID)
```

Correlated subqueries cannot be resolved independently of the main query since the main query supplies a value which is evaluated in the subquery.

Using Functions in Queries

You can use functions, which are Transact-SQL extensions, to return values from queries. We will briefly discuss the different kinds of functions that you can use.

Aggregate Functions

Aggregate functions generate summary values. They can be applied to all rows in a table, to rows specified by a WHERE clause, or to groups of rows in a table. Aggregate functions generate a single value from each set of rows and consist of the functions shown in Table 6.4.

TABLE 6.4: Aggregate Functions

Aggregate Functions				
AVG	COUNT	COUNT(*)	MAX	MIN
STDEV	STDEVP	SUM	VAR	VARP

You can use aggregate functions in conjunction with the `GROUP BY` clause. For example, the following query finds the total products sold:

```
SELECT ProductID, "sum" = SUM(UnitPrice)
FROM [Order Details]
GROUP BY ProductID
ORDER BY ProductID
```

Date Functions

Date functions are used for manipulating `datetime` and `smalldatetime` values, performing arithmetic operations, and extracting their components:

- `DATEADD`
- `DATENAME`
- `DATEDIFF`
- `DATEPART`
- `GETDATE`

The general syntax for the `date` functions, except for `GETDATE`, which returns the current system date and time, is:

```
DATE_FUNCTION (parameters)
```

For example, if you wanted to calculate the date one month past the date when an order was shipped, you could add one month to the `ShippedDate` field in the Orders table for all orders which have already gone out:

```
SELECT OrderID, PmtDue = DATEADD(month, 1, ShippedDate)
FROM Orders
WHERE ShippedDate IS NOT NULL
ORDER BY OrderID
```

The first few rows of the result set looks like this:

```
OrderID     PmtDue
----------  -----------------------
10248       1994-09-16 00:00:00.000
10249       1994-09-10 00:00:00.000
10250       1994-09-12 00:00:00.000
10251       1994-09-15 00:00:00.000
```

Mathematical Functions

As their name implies, mathematical functions perform numeric operations. The data types with which you can use mathematical functions are: `decimal`, `numeric`, `integer`, `float`, `real`, `money`, `smallmoney`, `smallint`, and `tinyint`. The functions you can use in Transact-SQL are shown in Table 6.5.

TABLE 6.5: Mathematical Functions

Mathematical Functions		
ABS	DEGREES	RAND
ACOS	EXP	ROUND
ASIN	FLOOR	SIGN
ATAN	LOG	SIN
ATN2	LOG10	SQRT
CEILING	PI	SQUARE
COS	POWER	TAN
COT	RADIANS	

Their common syntax is:

```
FUNCTION_NAME(parameters)
```

The following query sums the freight charges for each customer and then rounds the result to a whole dollar amount:

```
SELECT CustomerID, TotFreight = ROUND(SUM(Freight), 0)
FROM Orders
GROUP BY CustomerID
ORDER BY CustomerID
```

The first few rows of the result look like this:

```
CustomerID TotFreight
---------- ----------
ALFKI      226.0
ANATR      97.0
ANTON      269.0
AROUT      472.0
```

String Functions

You can use the string functions shown in Table 6.6 on binary data, character strings, or expressions.

TABLE 6.6: String Functions

String Functions		
ASCII	LTRIM	RTRIM
CHAR	PATINDEX	SOUNDEX
CHARINDEX	QUOTENAME	SPACE
DIFFERENCE	REPLACE	STR
LEFT	REPLICATE	STUFF
LEN	REVERSE	SUBSTRING
LOWER	RIGHT	UPPER

Most string functions are used with `char`, `nchar`, `varchar`, and `nvarchar` data types and a few of them on `binary` and `varbinary` data. For example, if you wanted to select a string inside of another string, you would use the `SUBSTRING` function. The following example takes the first three letters of the publisher name and converts them to upper case:

```
SELECT CompanyName, UPPER(SUBSTRING(CompanyName, 1,3))
FROM Customers
```

The first few rows of the result set look like this:

```
CompanyName
---------------------------------------- ---
Alfreds Futterkiste                      ALF
Ana Trujillo Emparedados y helados       ANA
Antonio Moreno Taquería                  ANT
Around the Horn                          ARO
```

System Functions

The system functions shown in Table 6.7 return information about values, objects, and settings in SQL Server.

TABLE 6.7: System Functions

System Functions	
CAST	IS_MEMBER
COALESCE	IS_SRVROLEMEMBER
COL_LENGTH	ISDATE
COL_NAME	ISNULL
COLUMNPROPERTY	ISNUMERIC
CONVERT	NEWID
CURRENT_TIMESTAMP	NULLIF
CURRENT_USER	OBJECT_ID
CURSOR_STATUS	OBJECT_NAME
DATABASEPROPERTY	OBJECTPROPERTY
DATALENGTH	PARSENAME
DB_ID	PERMISSIONS
DB_NAME	SESSION_USER
FILE_ID	STATS_DATE
FILE_NAME	SUSER_ID
FILEGROUP_ID	SUSER_NAME
FILEGROUP_NAME	SUSER_SID
GETANSINULL	SUSER_SNAME
GETCHECKSUM	SYSTEM_USER
HOST_ID	TYPEPROPERTY
HOST_NAME	USER
IDENT_INCR	USER_ID
IDENT_SEED	USER_NAME
INDEX_COL	

System functions are mainly useful for querying the system tables. The general syntax is:

```
SELECT FUNCTION_NAME(parameters)
```

For example, the following query will give you the name and ID of the server you are currently connected to:

```
SELECT HOST_NAME(), HOST_ID()
```

Text and Image Functions

The text and image functions shown in Table 6.8 perform operations on text and image data.

TABLE 6.8: Text and Image Functions

Text and Image Functions		
DATALENGTH	WRITETEXT	SUBSTRING
READTEXT	PATINDEX	TEXTPTR
UPDATETEXT	SET TEXTSIZE	TEXTVALID

TEXTPTR obtains a pointer to the first text page and the TEXTVALID function checks to see whether the pointer is valid.

The following function declares a local variable and then puts the text pointer into it. This is supplied to the READTEXT statement and then returns the first 45 bytes of data:

```
DECLARE @var varbinary(16)
SELECT @var = textptr(pr_info) FROM pub_info
WHERE pub_id = '0736'
READTEXT pub_info.pr_info @var 0 45
```

The results look like this:

```
pr_info
---------------------------------------------
This is sample text data for New Moon Books,
```

Conversion Functions

There are two type-conversion functions, CONVERT and CAST. They are both used for converting expressions from one data type into another; CAST is the ANSI-compliant synonym for CONVERT. The syntax for CONVERT is:

```
CONVERT (datatype[(length)], expression [, style])
```

The syntax for CAST is:

```
CAST(expression AS data_type)
```

For example, if you wanted to concatenate ytd_sales in the titles table with the literal string 'YTD Sales: ', you would use the following syntax with CONVERT:

```
SELECT title_id, 'YTD Sales: ' + CONVERT(char(12), ytd_sales)
FROM titles
```

Use this syntax for CAST:

```
SELECT title_id, 'YTD Sales: ' + CAST(ytd_sales AS char(12))
FROM titles
```

This is what the first few rows of the result set would look like, regardless of which one you use. Note the blank where the ytd_sales value was null.

```
title_id
-------  ----------------
BU1032   YTD Sales: 4095
BU1111   YTD Sales: 3876
BU2075   YTD Sales: 18722
BU7832   YTD Sales: 4095
MC2222   YTD Sales: 2032
MC3021   YTD Sales: 22246
MC3026   YTD Sales:
PC1035   YTD Sales: 8780
PC8888   YTD Sales: 4095
```

Using the UNION Statement to Combine Results

The UNION operator allows you to combine two separate queries into a single result set. The syntax is:

```
select_statement UNION [ALL] select_statement
[UNION [ALL] select_statement][,...n]
```

The UNION operator removes any duplicates returned by the two queries. If you want to see the duplicates, use UNION ALL instead. The ALL operator will not remove the duplicates.

The following example shows combining two SELECT statements, one selecting the LastName column from the Employees table, and the other selecting the ContactName column from the Customers table. The ORDER BY clause comes last, after the second SELECT statement:

```
SELECT LastName FROM Employees
UNION
SELECT ContactName FROM Customers
ORDER BY LastName
```

The first few rows of the result set look like this:

```
LastName
--------------------
Alejandra Camino
Alexander Feuer
Ana Trujillo
Anabela Domingues
André Fonseca
Ann Devon
Annette Roulet
Antonio Moreno
Aria Cruz
Art Braunschweiger
```

Note that if you specify an ORDER BY clause, it has to be on column names in the first SELECT statement, not the second one. Since there is no join in a UNION query, the only rule is that each SELECT statement must contain the same number of columns of a compatible data type. For example, the following UNION query combines the title_id column from the Roysched table with the lname column from the Employees table:


```
SELECT LastName FROM Employees
UNION
SELECT CategoryName FROM Categories
ORDER BY LastName
```

The first few rows of the result set look like this:

```
LastName
----------
Beverages
Buchanan
Callahan
Condiments
```

Using Cursors

When you use a SELECT statement, the rows returned are known as the result set. Cursors are an extension to result sets that allow an application to work with one row (or a small block of rows) instead of having to deal with the entire result set as a unit. Some of the things cursors can do are:

- Position at specific rows.
- Retrieve rows from the current position in the result set.

- Modify data at the current position in the result set.
- Show changes to result set data made by other users.

You can request a cursor through Transact-SQL or through the following database APIs:

- OLE DB
- ODBC
- ADO
- DB-Library

SQL Server defaults to returning a complete result set, known as a default result set, if neither a Transact-SQL nor API cursor has been requested. The process for Transact-SQL cursors and API cursors is the same, even though the syntax is different. The following steps detail how to use a cursor:

1. Associate the cursor with a result set and define its characteristics.
2. Execute the Transact-SQL statement to populate the cursor.
3. Fetch the rows you intend to use.
4. Perform any update operations at the current position.
5. Close the cursor.

NOTE See Skill 13, *Programming SQL Server*, for more information on how to use cursors with OLE DB, ODBC, and ADO.

The four types of cursors you can specify are:

- Static
- Dynamic
- Forward-only
- Keyset-driven

They vary in their ability to detect changes to the underlying tables in the cursor and in the amount of memory and resources they consume. Static cursors consume few resources while scrolling but detect few changes. Dynamic cursors detect all the changes but consume the most resources while scrolling. Keyset-driven cursors are somewhere in between, detecting most changes but consuming fewer resources than dynamic cursors. In SQL Server, forward-only is an option that can be applied to static, keyset-driven, and dynamic cursors, while it is considered to be a distinct type of cursor by the database APIs.

To use a cursor in Transact-SQL, use the DECLARE CURSOR statement to associate a cursor with the result set of a SQL SELECT statement. Then use the FETCH statement to get the rows.

TIP

You can have multiple active cursors on a single connection.

There are two forms of syntax for DECLARE CURSOR. The first form is the SQL-92 standard:

```
DECLARE cursor_name [INSENSITIVE] [SCROLL] CURSOR
FOR select_statement
[FOR {READ ONLY | UPDATE [OF column_list]}]
```

The second form employs a set of Transact-SQL extensions:

```
DECLARE cursor_name CURSOR
[LOCAL | GLOBAL]
[FORWARD_ONLY | SCROLL]
[STATIC | KEYSET | DYNAMIC]
[READ_ONLY | SCROLL_LOCKS | OPTIMISTIC]
FOR select_statement
[FOR {READ ONLY | UPDATE [OF column_list]}]
```

Table 6.9 describes the arguments for DECLARE CURSOR for both the SQL-92 and the Transact-SQL extensions.

TABLE 6.9: Arguments for DECLARE CURSOR

Argument	Description
cursor_name	Name of cursor being identified. Must conform to rules for identifiers
INSENSITIVE	Makes a temporary copy of the data to be used by the cursor in tempbd and does not allow modifications. Changes made to base tables by other users won't be reflected in data fetched by this cursor.
SCROLL	Specifies that all fetch options (first, last, prior, next, relative, absolute) are available.
select_statement	The SELECT statement that defines the result set of the cursor.

TABLE 6.9 CONTINUED: Arguments for DECLARE CURSOR

Argument	Description
READ_ONLY	Prevents updates
UPDATE [OF *column_list*]	Defines which columns can be updated
LOCAL	Defines the scope of a cursor as being local to a particular batch, stored procedure, or trigger. The cursor name is only valid within the scope defined.
GLOBAL	The scope of the cursor is global to the connection and only implicitly de-allocated at disconnect.
FORWARD ONLY	The cursor can only scroll from the first row to the last, and not backwards.
STATIC	Read-only cursor. Changes made to base tables are not reflected in the data returned by fetches to this cursor.
KEYSET	The membership and order of rows are fixed when the cursor is opened. The keys that uniquely identify the rows are copied into tempdb. Changes made to non-key values in the base tables are visible. If a row is deleted and then fetched, @@fetch_status will show –2. If a row is inserted, it will not be visible.
DYNAMIC	All data changes made to rows in the result set will be visible.
SCROLL_LOCKS	Positioned updates or deletes are guaranteed to succeed since SQL Server locks the rows as they are read into the cursor.
OPTIMISTIC	Positioned updates or deletes made through the cursor will not succeed since no rows are locked as they are read into the cursor. If a row was modified, the positioned update or delete will fail.

Once you declare a cursor in Transact-SQL, it can't be used by any of the database APIs or DB-Library functions. You can only fetch rows using the Transact-SQL FETCH statement, whose syntax is as follows:

```
FETCH
[ [NEXT | PRIOR | FIRST | LAST
| ABSOLUTE {n | @nvar} | RELATIVE {n | @nvar}]
FROM ] { { [GLOBAL] cursor_name } | cursor_variable_name}
[INTO @variable_name[,...n] ]
```

NEXT returns the row immediately following the current row, PRIOR returns the previous row, FIRST returns the first row in the cursor, and LAST returns the last row in the cursor. ABSOLUTE returns the row that is *n* rows from the cursor, and RELATIVE returns the row that is *n* rows behind the current row. The following example opens a cursor on the Customers table and selects the company names whose city name starts with a P. It then loops through the records as long as there are records in the cursor (`@@FETCH_STATUS = 0`). The cursor is then closed and the `DEALLOCATE` statement removes the cursor reference and de-allocates the data structure.

```
DECLARE CustCursor CURSOR FOR
SELECT CompanyName FROM Customers
WHERE City LIKE 'P%'
ORDER BY CompanyName

OPEN CustCursor
FETCH NEXT FROM CustCursor

WHILE @@FETCH_STATUS = 0
    BEGIN
     FETCH NEXT FROM CustCursor
    END

CLOSE CustCursor
DEALLOCATE CustCursor
```

Once you declare a cursor, you can use the system stored procedures shown in Table 6.10 to determine its characteristics.

TABLE 6.10: Stored Procedures to Determine a Cursor's Characteristics

System Stored Procedure	Description
`sp_cursor_list`	Lists the cursors currently opened by the current connection
`sp_describe_cursor`	Describes attributes, such as forward-only or scrolling
`sp_describe_cursor_columns`	Describes column attributes
`sp_describe_cursor_tables`	Describes the base tables accessed by the cursor

Some of the things you need to consider when choosing a cursor are:

- The size of the result set
- The percentage of the data likely to be needed
- Performance when opening the cursor
- Options needed, such as positioned updates or scrolling
- The need to see changes made by other users

If the result set is small and you don't need to update it, then the default settings work well. Dynamic cursors work well for large result sets where the user won't need to retrieve many of the rows. The following are some guidelines to follow when choosing a cursor type:

1. Use the default settings for small result sets or singleton selects.
2. Use the default settings when fetching an entire result set to the client application. It's faster.
3. Don't use the default settings if you need a positioned update or multiple active statements.
4. Use the default result set when generating multiple result sets.
5. Dynamic cursors open faster than static or keyset-driven cursors since a dynamic cursor doesn't need internal temporary work tables.
6. Static and keyset-driven cursors increase tempdb usage.
7. Keyset-driven and static cursors are faster than dynamic cursors in joins.
8. Absolute fetches require keyset-driven or static cursors.
9. Use block cursors with a reasonably large number of rows to minimize round trips to the server during FETCH functions.

Summarizing Data

There are many ways to generate summary data, both in Transact-SQL and by using Microsoft Decision Support Services. We're going to examine how to use Transact-SQL to summarize data. Decision Support Services is covered briefly in Skill 11, *Creating Client-Server Applications*.

Using GROUP BY

GROUP BY is almost always used when you are creating queries using aggregate functions, in which case a value is produced for each group. It is used in SELECT statements to group by either the column name or the results when using numeric data types. You can't group columns of bit, text, or image data types. You can group by an expression as long as it doesn't contain any aggregate functions.

NOTE The technical term for values returned for each group is *vector aggregate*. A *scalar aggregate* is a single value produced by an aggregate function that does not have a GROUP BY clause.

The syntax for the GROUP BY clause is:

```
GROUP BY [ALL] aggregate_free_expression [, ...n]
```

For example, the following query finds the average product price for each category:

```
SELECT CategoryID, AVG(UnitPrice)
FROM Products
GROUP BY CategoryID
```

If the grouping column contains nulls, then the null values are put into a group. The following query counts the cities in each region.

```
SELECT Region, Count(City)
FROM Customers
GROUP BY Region
```

The first few rows of the result set look like this:

```
Region
-------------- ---
NULL           60
AK             1
BC             2
CA             1
Co. Cork       1
DF             1
```


You can also nest groups, as in the following example, which finds both the average unit price and the units on hand, grouped by supplier ID and category ID:

```
SELECT SupplierID, CategoryID, 'AvgPrice' = AVG(UnitPrice), 'SumUnits'
= sum(UnitsInStock)
FROM Products
GROUP BY SupplierID, CategoryID
ORDER BY SupplierID
```

The first few rows of the result set look like this:

```
SupplierID  CategoryID  AvgPrice              SumUnits
----------  ----------  --------------------  ------------
1           1           18.5000               56
1           2           10.0000               13
2           2           20.3500               133
3           2           32.5000               126
```

You can use the ALL keyword in the GROUP BY clause when the SELECT statement includes a WHERE clause. This causes all rows to be shown even if they don't meet the condition in the WHERE clause. If you don't use ALL, then you won't see rows that don't meet the search conditions. The following query shows the average unit price where the number of units in stock is greater than 100, grouped by category ID.

```
SELECT CategoryID, AVG(UnitPRice)
FROM Products
WHERE UnitsInStock > 100
GROUP BY ALL CategoryID
```

The first few rows of the result set display the groups and null for the rows which don't match the criteria.

```
CategoryID
----------  ----------
1           10.8750
2           26.7500
3           NULL
4           2.5000
```

The result set of the same query without the ALL keyword does not display the groups that don't match the criteria:

```
CategoryID
----------  ----------
1           10.8750
2           26.7500
4           2.5000
```

You can also add an ORDER BY clause to sort the results as long as the ORDER BY clause comes after the GROUP BY clause. The same query used above could be rewritten to sort the results on the average unit price:

```
SELECT CategoryID, AVG(UnitPRice)
FROM Products
WHERE UnitsInStock > 100
GROUP BY CategoryID
ORDER BY AVG(UnitPrice)
```

The result set would be:

```
CategoryID
----------  ----------
4           2.5000
1           10.8750
8           17.4666
5           21.0000
```

Use COMPUTE BY and COMPUTE when you want to generate subtotals and totals in the result set. For example, the following query will compute the average price for each category whose price is greater than $25. Using the COMPUTE BY clause creates group subtotals showing the average price per group, whereas the total price of all the books is created from the COMPUTE on the last line.

```
SELECT CategoryID, UnitPrice
FROM Products
WHERE UnitPrice > 25
ORDER BY CategoryID
COMPUTE AVG(UnitPrice) BY CategoryID
COMPUTE SUM(UnitPrice)
```

The first group of the result set looks like this:

```
CategoryID  UnitPrice
----------  ----------
1           263.5000
1           46.0000

(2 row(s) affected)

avg
---------------------
154.7500

(1 row(s) affected)
```


Using CUBE and ROLLUP

The CUBE and ROLLUP options allow you to perform dimensional analysis on your data, which is useful for reporting. SQL Server ships with Microsoft Decision Support Services, which provides you with a better way to compute many of the totals that CUBE and ROLLUP can deliver. However, Decision Support Services requires installing additional software and can take an enormous amount of hard drive space. For occasional use, the CUBE and ROLLUP operators in Transact SQL may be a better choice.

TIP If you need to analyze your data on multiple dimensions on a frequent basis, you should install and learn Microsoft Decision Support Services instead of using CUBE and ROLLUP.

The CUBE operator generates additional rows in a result set when used with any aggregate function, such as SUM, MAX, MIN, AVG, and COUNT. Columns included in the GROUP BY clause are cross-referenced to produce a superset of groups. The aggregate function specified in the Select list is applied to these groups to produce summary values for the additional super-aggregate rows. The number of extra groups in the result set is determined by the number of columns included in the GROUP BY clause.

The maximum size of a GROUP BY column list is 900 bytes, and there is a maximum limit of 10 columns or expressions when using WITH CUBE or WITH ROLLUP. The use of GROUP BY ALL is not permitted; you must specify the columns or expressions in the GROUP BY clause. In addition, all CUBE and ROLLUP operators are disabled when trace flag 204 is on.

NOTE

The CUBE operator got its name because every possible combination of the columns or expressions in the GROUP BY clause is used to produce super-aggregates, which mathematically form an *n*-dimensional cube. If you have *n* columns or expressions, there are 2*n*–1 possible super-aggregate combinations.

The following example shows the quantity of books ordered by stor_id:

```
SELECT stor_id, "qty" = SUM(qty)
FROM sales, titles
WHERE sales.title_id = titles.title_id
GROUP BY stor_id
WITH CUBE
```

The result set looks like this:

```
stor_id qty
------  ----
6380    8
7066    125
7067    90
7131    130
7896    60
8042    80
NULL    493
```

Note that the null row under stor_id is the sum of the total quantity ordered for all stores. In other words, for each store, this query performs a GROUP BY query. The results of all of these queries are combined into a single result set.

Use the ROLLUP operator when you want to produce only summary results with your aggregate functions. ROLLUP gives you the capability to create cumulative aggregates, such as running sums or running averages. The main difference between it and the CUBE operator is that it is sensitive to the column's position in the GROUP BY clause. Aggregate groupings are made up of columns to the right of the current column value.

The following query shows the use of ROLLUP to show the number of books each store ordered, grouped by publisher:

```
SELECT stor_id, pub_name, "qty" = SUM(qty)
FROM publishers, sales, titles
WHERE publishers.pub_id = titles.pub_id
AND sales.title_id = titles.title_id
GROUP BY stor_id, pub_name
WITH ROLLUP
```

The result set shows the total quantity for each store with the grand total on the bottom row:

```
stor_id pub_name                                 qty
------  ---------------------------------------- ------
6380    Algodata Infosystems                     5
6380    New Moon Books                           3
6380    NULL                                     8
7066    Algodata Infosystems                     50
7066    New Moon Books                           75
7066    NULL                                     125
7067    Binnet & Hardley                         80
7067    New Moon Books                           10
7067    NULL                                     90
7131    Binnet & Hardley                         45
7131    New Moon Books                           85
7131    NULL                                     130
7896    Algodata Infosystems                     15
7896    Binnet & Hardley                         10
7896    New Moon Books                           35
7896    NULL                                     60
8042    Algodata Infosystems                     65
8042    Binnet & Hardley                         15
8042    NULL                                     80
NULL    NULL                                     493
```

Parallel Queries

If your computer has more than one processor, you can take advantage of parallel queries. Parallel queries allow SQL Server to perform a query in parallel by using several operating system threads. This process allows for large amounts of data to be queried much more quickly than the same query executing on a single processor.

SQL Server identifies queries that might benefit from parallel execution during query optimization and inserts *exchange operators* into the execution plan. Exchange operators provide process management, data redistribution, and flow control, which results in a *parallel query execution plan*. Unlike non-parallel query execution plans, parallel query execution plans can use more than one thread, the actual number of which is called the *degree of parallelism*.

When the query executes, SQL Server determines whether the current system workload and configuration information permit parallel query execution. If so, SQL Server allocates the number of threads and spreads the execution across those threads, using the same number of threads until the query completes. A query can execute one time on a single thread and another time on multiple threads since each time the query runs, SQL Server reexamines the optimal number of thread decisions.

Graphical Showplan displays the parallelism operators, which can have one of three argument values:

`Distribute Stream` for operators causing distribution of a single data stream into multiple streams, each processed by a separate thread

`Gather Streams` for operators gathering multiple data streams into a single stream.

`Redistribute Stream` for operators redistributing multiple data streams into a new set of data streams

`SET SHOWPLAN_TEXT` or `SET SHOWPLAN_ALL` will also show a parallelism operator once a parallel query execution plan has been generated.

You don't need to set any special configuration options to achieve optimal parallel query execution. You can use the SQL Server Profiler to monitor parallel query execution with the `Degree of Parallelism` event subclass.

NOTE If you're running SQL Server on a computer with only one CPU, SQL Server will not waste time trying to compute a parallel executing plan that it can't use.

Full-Text Querying

Chances are a sizable amount of the data stored in your SQL Server database is text, stored in `char`, `nchar`, `varchar`, `nvarchar`, `text`, and `ntext` columns. In SQL Server 6.*x* you can use pattern matching in criteria to retrieve text, but there's no way for SQL Server to look up words and phrases that might be in close proximity to one another, which would involve combining a full-text query with a regular, structured relational query. SQL Server 7 allows you to issue full-text queries against plain-character-based data in SQL Server tables. You can perform a linguistic search of words, phrases, or multiple forms of a word or phrase. This operates on words and phrases—unlike pattern matching, which utilizes character patterns. An added bonus is that the full-text search feature can weigh query terms and report on how well a particular match scored against the search term.

Full-text indexes are only supported for the server version of SQL Server 7. If you are running SQL Server on Windows 95/98 or Windows NT Workstation, you will be unable to configure full-text querying.

There are several tasks involved in implementing a full-text search:

1. Register the tables and columns that will be involved with full-text searches.
2. Index the data in the registered columns and then populate the indexes with essential words.
3. Query the registered columns for populated full-text indexes.
4. Make sure that subsequent changes to the data stay synchronized with the index.

Full-text indexes differ from regular SQL Server indexes in the following ways:

- They are stored in the file system but are administered through the database, whereas a regular index is stored directly in the database.
- Only one full-text index is allowed per table.
- Full-text indexes must be repopulated by request or scheduled. Regular indexes are updated automatically when data is modified.
- A full-text catalog is created to group together one or more full-text indexes.
- You use stored procedures to create, manage, and drop full-text indexes whereas regular indexes are created and dropped using SQL statements.

As you can see from the above list, there's a lot more administration involved in implementing a full-text search. Some of the tasks you need to perform include:

- Setting server properties such as the connection timeout when retrieving data to be indexed
- Enabling a database to use full-text searches
- Creating and populating a full-text catalog

- Registering a table to support full-text queries, at which time metadata is created for that table's full-text index
- Adding or dropping columns that support full-text queries from inactive registered tables

TIP Don't be scared away by the amount of work in setting up full-text indexing. If your application requires free text search, this work pays off in immensely faster query execution than is possible using the standard LIKE operator.

You can use the Full-Text Indexing Wizard, the SQL Server context menus for tables, and the Full-Text Catalog object in the Enterprise Manager to perform these administrative tasks interactively. You can also use the full-text stored procedures and scalar functions.

The Full-Text Indexing Wizard, shown in Figure 6.9, will take you through all of the steps necessary to create a full-text index. Select Tools ➢ Wizards ➢ Database ➢ Full-Text Indexing Wizard from the Management Console to load the wizard. The wizard will take you through the task of setting up your full-text index, basically following the same steps in the same order as you would using Transact-SQL, which follows next.

FIGURE 6.9: The Full-Text Indexing Wizard

You can also perform the same steps using Transact-SQL to run the necessary stored procedures.

1. To see if a database is already enabled or not, use the following syntax:

```
SELECT DatabaseProperty ('Northwind', 'IsFulltextEnabled' )
```

2. This will return 1 if the database is enabled for full-text searching, and 0 if it is not. To enable it, use the `sp_fulltext_database` stored procedure:

```
sp_fulltext_database 'enable'
```

3. Run the `sp_fulltext_catalog` stored procedure, which creates the metadata about a full-text catalog in the database's system tables and builds an empty full-text catalog in the file:

```
sp_fulltext_catalog 'NwindCatalog', 'create'
```

4. Create the metadata for the full-text index by registering the table for full-text processing by running the `sp_fulltext_table` stored procedure:

```
sp_fulltext_table 'Products', 'create', 'NwindCatalog',
   'PK_Products'
```

5. Specify the names of the columns that will support full-text queries by invoking the stored procedure once for each column:

```
sp_fulltext_column 'Products', 'ProductName', 'add'
```

6. The tables then need to be registered in the catalog using the `sp_fulltext_table` stored procedure with the activate argument so that their data will be included in the next population:

```
sp_fulltext_table 'Products', 'activate'
```

7. To populate the full-text catalog, use the `sp_fulltext_catalog` stored procedure. Since the population is an asynchronous operation, it is likely that the full-text indexes will not have been completely populated by the return to the caller of the procedure.

```
sp_fulltext_catalog 'NwindCatalog', 'start_full'
```

8. You can verify the progress of the population procedure by interrogating the `FullTextCatalogProperty`, which will return 0 if the service is idle (completed) and will return 1 if it's still busy populating the index.

```
SELECT FulltextCatalogProperty ('NWindCatalog', 'PopulateStatus')
```

Once you're done populating the full-text index, you can start testing it by running some queries against it. The Transact-SQL predicates you need are `CONTAINS` and `FREETEXT`, which can be used in any search condition (such as a `WHERE` clause) in a `SELECT` statement. The two rowset-valued functions, `CONTAINSTABLE` and `FREETEXTTABLE`, can be used in the `FROM` clause of a `SELECT` statement. The following query lists all the products that have the word *Organic* in their name:

```
SELECT ProductName
FROM Products
WHERE CONTAINS(ProductName, ' "Organic" ')
```

You can also use wildcards, as in the following query, which selects all the products that start with *ice*:

```
SELECT ProductName
FROM Products
WHERE CONTAINS(ProductName, ' "ice*" ')
```

The following query searches for any form of *ice*, such as *ice*, *iced*, or *icing*. You can search for different tenses of a verb or both the singular and plural forms of a noun.

```
SELECT ProductName
FROM Products
WHERE CONTAINS (Description, 'FORMSOF (INFLECTIONAL, "ice")')
```

You can also search for words or phrases that are close to one another, as shown in this query, which looks for the words *hot* and *sauce* in the name of the product:

```
SELECT ProductName
FROM Products
WHERE CONTAINS (Products, 'hot NEAR() sauce')
```

TIP You can replace `NEAR()` with a tilde (~), which produces the same results and requires less typing.

You can search using `FREETEXT`, which is less precise than `CONTAINS`, as in the following example, which searches for products with *hot*, *sauce*, *piquante*, *salsa*, *chile*, or *relish* in the name.

```
SELECT ProductName
FROM Products
WHERE FREETEXT (Products, 'hot sauce piquante salsa chile relish')
```

There are also several Transact-SQL properties and functions you can use to return information about your full-text queries:

- The `IsFullTextEnabled` property indicates whether a database has been enabled for full-text querying and is called by the `DatabaseProperty` function.
- The `TableHasActiveFulltextIndex` property indicates whether a table has been enabled for full-text querying and is called by the `ObjectProperty` function.
- The `IsFullTextIndexed` property indicates whether a column has been enabled for full-text querying and is called by the `ColumnProperty` function.
- The `TableFullTextKeyColumn` property provides the column ID of the full-text unique key column and is called by the `ObjectProperty` function.

There is a lot to full-text querying that is beyond the scope of this book. For more information, refer to Books Online.

Distributed Queries

Distributed queries allow you to access data stored on the same or different computers, distributed data stored in multiple computers running SQL Server, or heterogeneous data stored in various relational and non-relational data sources. Distributed queries to heterogeneous data sources require that there be either an OLE DB provider or an ODBC driver. If you are using an OLE DB provider, you can access the data in a rowset, which SQL Server treats just like a SQL Server table. This means you can write a Transact-SQL statement against it that is identical to a statement against a normal SQL Server table. Distributed queries in SQL Server are very similar to the linked (or *attached*) table functionality that has been present in Microsoft Access for years. It is now built into SQL Server with OLE DB as the interface to the external data. When you install SQL Server, you also install the OLE DB providers for ODBS, SQL Server, Jet, and Oracle databases.

In order to use external data from an OLE DB data source, you need to provide the following information:

- The name of the OLE DB provider
- Whatever information the OLE DB provider requires to locate the data source
- Any necessary login IDs for the data source

- Either the name of an object (a remote table) or a query (pass-through query) that will cause the OLE DB provider to expose a rowset

If you are using distributed queries frequently, you will probably want to use the linked server name for accessing the OLE DB data source, which you define using the `sp_addlinkedserver` system stored procedure. You then map local SQL Server logins to logins on the linked server using `sp_addlinkedsrvlogin`, as shown here:

```
sp_addlinkedserver @server = N'LinkServer',
    @srvproduct = N' ',
    @provider = N'SQLOLEDB',
    @datasrc = N'ServerNetName',
    @catalog = N'Northwind'
GO
SELECT *
FROM LinkServer.Northwind.dbo.Shippers
GO
```

If you rarely use distributed queries, you can use an ad hoc connector name without defining a linked server name with the `OPENROWSET` function, which specifies the name of the information needed to connect to the OLE DB data source and the name of the object or query that generates a rowset:

You need to generate a rowset from an OLE DB provider by referencing an object in the data source, such as a table or query, that provides a rowset. You can also use the ICommand interface, which allows you to use pass-through queries. A pass-through query can be used with either the `OPENROWSET` or `OPENQUERY` functions. A pass-through query is a Transact-SQL statement written in the dialect that the OLE DB data source understands and is not interpreted by SQL Server, as shown in this ad hoc distributed query which selects Paris-based customers from the Access Northwind database:

```
SELECT * FROM OpenRowset('Microsoft.Jet.OLEDB.4.0',
  'c:\samples\northwind.mdb';'admin'; '',
    'SELECT CustomerID, CompanyName
       FROM Customers
       WHERE City = ''Paris'' ')
```

NOTE You can't create new tables or modify existing ones using distributed queries. You can only use a static or insensitive cursor to reference a view on a linked server.

You can update and delete data on a remote table only if it has a unique index. The OLE DB provider must also support bookmarks and the IRowsetLocate and IRowsetChange interfaces on the rowset. You can insert data if the OLE DB provider supports IRowsetChange with the `InsertRow` method.

Using Views

Views in SQL Server give you a way to home in on your data and simplify it for the end-user's consumption. Instead of presenting entire tables, views can be fine-tuned to display just the necessary columns. You can use views for manipulation of data as well as presentation by defining frequently used joins, projections, and selections so that users don't have to specify them when performing data operations. Views can be used to customize data by allowing different users to see the data in different ways. Views are also useful for exporting data for use in other applications, such as Word or Excel, or as a direct data source, such as linking views directly in Microsoft Access. In short, think of a view as either a virtual table or a saved query, which can represent data in any way you choose.

Here are the rules for creating views:

- You can create views only in the current database.
- View names must be unique for each user and follow naming rules for identifiers.
- Views can be based on other views and on procedures that reference views.
- Views can't have indexes, rules, defaults, or triggers.
- You can't create views on temporary tables or create temporary views.
- You don't have to specify column names since SQL Server gives columns the same name and data type as the referenced columns, unless you want to include two with the same name. However, if you derive columns from an expression or function, then you must provide unique column names.
- You need to have the necessary permissions (`CREATE VIEW`) granted by the database owner as well as permissions to the underlying tables or views you intend to use as the data source for your view.

Creating Views Using the Enterprise Manager

You can create a new view by expanding the Databases folder and then expanding the database folder in which you want to create the new view. Right-click the Views folder and select New View from the shortcut menu. This will bring up an empty view. You can then add tables by dragging them from the Enterprise Manager and dropping them on the new view in the Diagram pane or by clicking the plus (+) sign on the toolbar. Select the fields you want for the view from the Grid pane and check the options you want. The SQL statements will automatically be filled in, in the SQL pane. Alternatively, type in the SQL statements in the SQL pane and the Grid pane will be filled in. You can then execute the query to view the results in the Show Results pane. Figure 6.10 shows a simple view for selecting orders after a certain date.

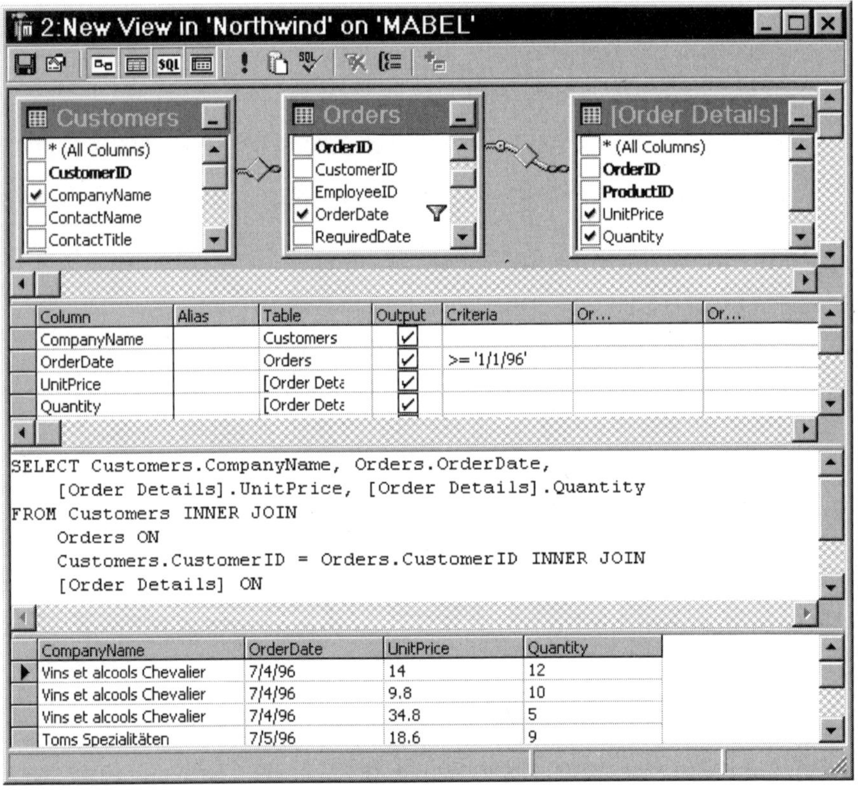

FIGURE 6.10: Creating a new view

You can also set various options for the view by right-clicking and choosing Properties from the shortcut menu or clicking the Properties toolbar button, as shown in Figure 6.11.

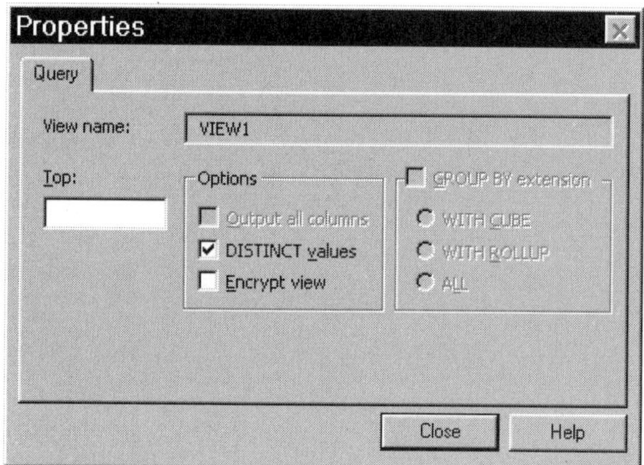

FIGURE 6.11: Setting view properties

When you have defined the view, you can then save it by clicking the Save button.

To create a view using the Create View Wizard, choose Tools ➢ Wizards ➢ Database from the Enterprise Manager and double-click the Create View Wizard. The wizard will walk you through the steps of creating the view. First you'll be asked to select the database. Next you can select the tables to be used in the view, as shown in Figure 6.12.

The next screen asks you to select the columns you want to display, as shown in Figure 6.13.

Create View Wizard - MABEL\Northwind

Select Tables
Select one or more tables to be referenced by the view.

Table Name	Include in View
Categories	☐
CustomerCustomerDemo	☐
CustomerDemographics	☐
Customers	☑
Employees	☐
EmployeeTerritories	☐
Order Details	☑
Orders	☑
Products	☐
Region	☐
Shippers	☐

< Back | Next > | Cancel

FIGURE 6.12: Selecting tables in the Create View Wizard

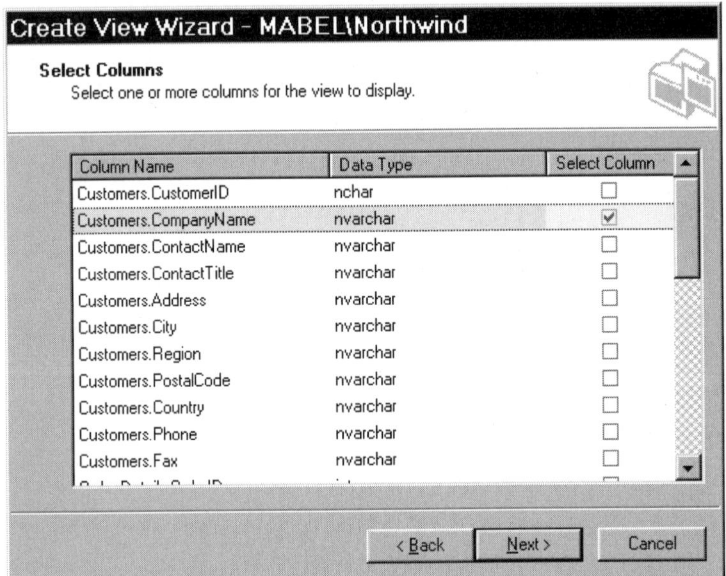

FIGURE 6.13: Selecting columns in the Create View Wizard

If you want to define a restriction, you can type in a `WHERE` clause, as shown in Figure 6.14.

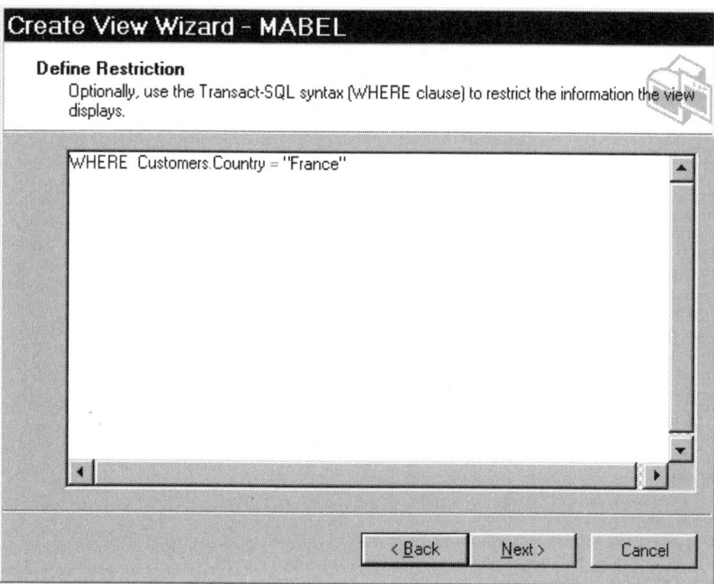

FIGURE 6.14: Creating a WHERE clause in the Create View Wizard

Then you are prompted to name the view. The final dialog box shows you the Transact-SQL that will be used to create the view, as shown in Figure 6.15. You can edit it if you like. Click Finish to save the view.

You can view the Transact-SQL that defines the view by double-clicking it in the Views folder. To edit the view, right-click the view and choose Design View. You will be able to edit the view in Design View mode (see Figure 6.10).

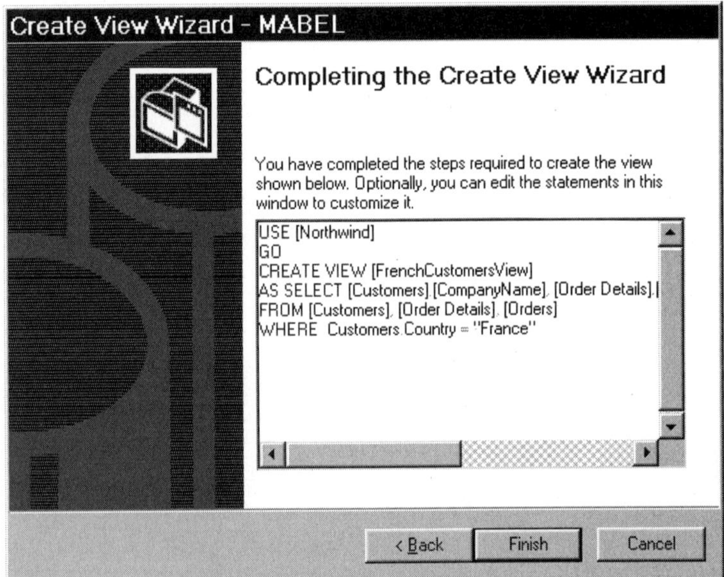

FIGURE 6.15: Transact-SQL in the Create View Wizard

Creating Views in Transact-SQL

Transact-SQL has three statements that work with views:

- `CREATE VIEW`
- `ALTER VIEW`
- `DROP VIEW`

To create a view in Transact-SQL, use the following syntax:

```
CREATE VIEW view_name [(column [, ...n])]
[WITH ENCRYPTION]
AS
     select_statement
[WITH CHECK OPTION]
```

The `WITH ENCRYPTION` clause is used protect sensitive views so that their definition cannot be obtained. The `WITH CHECK OPTION` clause ensures that the rows in the view's result set are present, even if the data is updated through the view and no longer meets the view's WHERE clause criteria.

The following sample creates a simple view consisting of the author name and year-to-date sales:

```
CREATE VIEW AuthorSales_view
AS
SELECT au_fname, au_lname, ytd_sales
FROM authors, titles, titleauthor
WHERE titleauthor.au_id = authors.au_id
AND titles.title_id = titleauthor.title_id
```

The statement does not return any rows, so after creating the view, you need to select the records in it:

```
SELECT * FROM AuthorSales_view
ORDER BY au_lname
```

The first few rows of the result set look like this:

```
au_fname            au_lname                                 ytd_sales
------------------- ---------------------------------------- ---------
Abraham             Bennet                                   4095
Reginald            Blotchet-Halls                           15096
Cheryl              Carson                                   8780
Michel              DeFrance                                 22246
```

ALTER VIEW lets you modify a view without affecting any dependent stored procedures and without changing permissions. The syntax is:

```
ALTER VIEW view_name
[(column [,...n])]
[WITH ENCRYPTION]
AS
select_statement
[WITH CHECK OPTION]
```

For example, to modify the view created above, we could use ALTER VIEW to eliminate the author's first name by re-defining the SELECT statement the view is based on:

```
ALTER VIEW AuthorSales_view
AS
SELECT au_lname, ytd_sales
FROM authors, titles, titleauthor
WHERE titleauthor.au_id = authors.au_id
AND titles.title_id = titleauthor.title_id
```

Selecting all the records in the AuthorSales_view will now look like the following:

```
au_lname                                  ytd_sales
----------------------------------------  ---------
Bennet                                    4095
Blotchet-Halls                            15096
Carson                                    8780
DeFrance                                  22246
```

If you want to remove a view, use the DROP VIEW statement, as follows:

```
DROP VIEW AuthorSales_view
```

Using Views for Security

Views give you a mechanism for presenting only a subset of the rows or columns available in an entire table to a user. For example, if you have a salary column that you don't want certain users to see, you can restrict their access to the data in the table to a view in which you do not include the salary column.

You can create views for users to query and modify data without granting permissions to the underlying tables by using the WITH CHECK OPTION statement. WITH CHECK OPTION forces all data modification statements executed against the view to adhere to the criteria set within the SELECT statement defining the view. By defining different views and selectively granting permissions on them, you can fine-tune your user's access to specific subsets of data, by row or by column. A view might select only certain columns or a view might restrict rows returned with a WHERE clause, or a combination of both. Or perhaps you want certain users to only have access to summary or statistical data, and not the core data. All these things are possible using views.

NOTE For more information on using GRANT and REVOKE to restrict database access, see Skill 16, *Managing SQL Server Security*.

Are You up to Speed?

Now you can...

- ☑ create simple queries using Transact-SQL
- ☑ search for data using search operators and wildcard characters
- ☑ use different kinds of joins in a query
- ☑ create advanced queries to summarize information
- ☑ create cursors
- ☑ use functions in queries
- ☑ use parallel queries
- ☑ create a full-text index
- ☑ use a distributed query to obtain information from another database
- ☑ create views

SKILL 7

Altering Data

- Inserting, deleting, and updating data
- Catalog, system, and extended stored procedures
- Creating your own stored procedures
- Using triggers

So far you've learned how to set up a database efficiently, how to create tables, and how to retrieve data from tables. You've also seen in Skill 5 how you can import large amounts of data to a new table. But databases are very rarely static. In the real world, you often need to add additional data to a table, update existing data in a table, or delete obsolete data from a table. Fortunately, SQL Server provides a variety of tools for altering data. Queries allow you to alter the data in one row or in many rows. Stored procedures allow you to store a complex series of actions directly on your server for later activation. Triggers can make automatic changes based on user actions. In this skill, you'll learn how to use these SQL Server objects to make your database dynamic.

Using Queries

If you're new to SQL, you might think of Transact-SQL at this point as just a language for creating objects and retrieving data. But there are Transact-SQL keywords to allow you to alter data as well. In this section you'll learn how to use the `INSERT`, `DELETE`, and `UPDATE` keywords to change the data in your database tables. Because these keywords are instructions to the server, and SQL Server can decide on the best means to carry out the instructions, queries using these keywords can be a very efficient tool.

TIP If you're designing a complex query, you can use the SQL Query Analyzer to help you understand how SQL Server will carry out the query. See Skill 8, *Using SQL Server Tools*, for information on SQL Query Analyzer.

Inserting Rows in a Table

Before you can do anything with data in a table, you have to get data into that table in the first place. In Skill 5, we saw how you could use `RESTORE` or the bcp tool to move large amounts of data into a table. But what if you only want to insert a small amount of data? That's where `INSERT` queries come in. Think of an `INSERT` query as a tool for moving data from a Transact-SQL statement into a table.

TIP For more information on the various ways you can send a query to SQL Server for execution, see Skill 2 and Skill 11.

The INSERT Statement

To insert a new row into a table, use an INSERT query. Here's the syntax outline for INSERT:

```
INSERT [INTO]
 {[database.][owner.]tablename | viewname} [(column_list)]
 {
 DEFAULT VALUES
 | VALUES ({DEFAULT | constant_expression} [,…n])
 | select_statement
 | execute_statement}
```

Here the INSERT keyword (and the optional INTO, which adds no functionality) specifies the type of the query. The tablename or viewname specifies where the inserted rows should go, and the optional column_list narrows down the columns you wish to add data to. The remainder of the syntax gives you choices as to how to derive the data you want to insert.

Simple Data Insertion

To insert a single row in the stores table in the pubs database, you could use a query like this:

```
INSERT stores
VALUES ('1234', 'Pyramid Books', '2317 5th Street',
 'Chicago', 'IL', '60601')
```


The VALUES clause contains a single value for each column in the table. Since all the columns in this table are type char or varchar, you must use quotation marks (either single or double) around each value. If any of the columns were numeric, you wouldn't use any delimiters around the values for those columns.

Inserting Default Values

You don't always have to supply values for every column in a table, since SQL Server can store a default value for each column in a table. Figure 7.1 shows the design of the jobs table in the pubs database. In this table, the job_id column is an identity column, and the job_desc column has a default value.

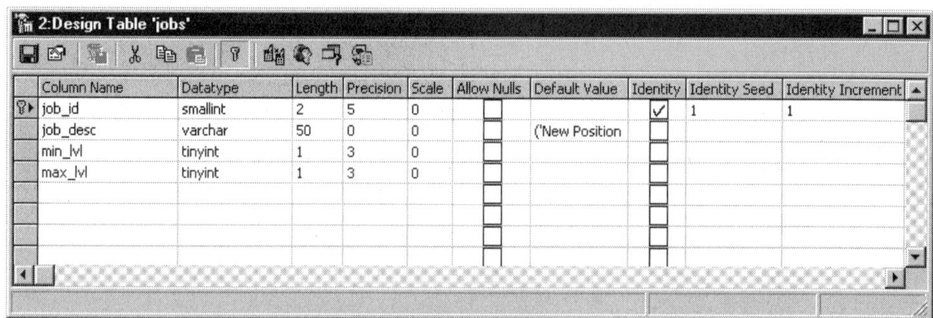

FIGURE 7.1: Design of the jobs table

Since SQL Server can determine the default values for job_id and job_desc, you need not supply values for those columns. For example, you could insert a new row in this table with this query:

```
INSERT INTO jobs (min_lvl, max_lvl)
 VALUES (75, 100)
```

Note the use of the `column_list` argument in this query to specify which columns the supplied data maps to. SQL Server expects one value for each column in the table, in the same order that they appear in the table definition, and it's up to you to tell it otherwise.

TIP A column list does not have to be in the same order as the columns in the table. The SQL statement `INSERT INTO jobs (max_lvl, min_lvl) VALUES (150, 25)` is also perfectly legal.

If you prefer, you can use the `DEFAULT` keyword to specify explicitly that a particular column should use its default value:

```
INSERT INTO jobs (job_desc, min_lvl, max_lvl)
 VALUES (DEFAULT, 75, 100)
```

If a table has default values for all columns, you can use a simple syntax to insert all of these values into a new row. For example, this is syntactically valid Transact-SQL:

```
INSERT jobs
DEFAULT VALUES
```

If you actually try to run this query in the sample pubs database, it will fail, because there is no default for the max_lvl column, and it is defined not to accept null as a legal value.

Omitting Columns from the Column List

You don't have to specify a value for every column in a table in an INSERT statement, but SQL Server has to be able to determine a value from the table definition for any column that you omit. The rules SQL Server follows to determine the value for an omitted column are fairly straightforward. In order, they are:

1. If the column has the IDENTITY property set, use the next incremental identity value.
2. If the column has a default value, use the default value.
3. If the column is of the timestamp data type, use the current timestamp value.
4. If the column was defined as nullable, use NULL.

If none of these conditions is true, and you don't supply a value for the column, then the insert will fail.

Inserting Identity Values

Ordinarily SQL Server prohibits you from inserting values into a column with the IDENTITY property set. For example, this query will fail in the pubs database:

```
INSERT INTO jobs
 VALUES (77, "Sales Manager", 100, 150)
```

However, SQL Server recognizes that there are times when you will wish to insert a specific value in an identity column. The SET IDENTITY_INSERT *tablename* ON statement temporarily turns off the prohibition in inserting identity values for a particular table. You can patch the previous query to work by modifying it to include a SET IDENTITY_INSERT statement:

```
SET IDENTITY_INSERT jobs ON
GO
INSERT INTO jobs (job_id, job_desc, min_lvl, max_lvl)
 VALUES (77, "Sales Manager", 100, 150)
GO
```

 **TIP**

You can only insert a value in an identity column if you specify an explicit column list in the INSERT statement—this applies even if you're inserting values into every column in the table.

When you insert an explicit value into an identity column, SQL Server does not check to see that it is unique. This is the reason that you should always create a UNIQUE or PRIMARY KEY constraint on any identity column. IDENTITY_INSERT can only be on for one table in a database at a time. If you must insert identity values in multiple tables, you need to set this for each table in turn.

Inserting Unique Identifier Values

There are two ways to insert data into a column with the uniqueidentifier data type. We'll demonstrate these syntaxes using a new table, which was created with this statement:

```
CREATE TABLE Contacts
(
 con_id uniqueidentifier NOT NULL,
 con_fname varchar(30) NOT NULL,
 con_lname varchar(50) NOT NULL
)
```

The first syntax uses a string representation of the unique identifier value, using the standard GUID syntax:

```
INSERT INTO Contacts
 VALUES ('12345678-ABCD-DCBA-0123-1234567890AB',
 'Simon', 'Jasperson')
```

 **TIP**

Some development environments use curly braces around GUID values. SQL Server isn't one of these.

The second syntax uses the built-in NEWID keyword to generate an arbitrary unique identifier for the inserted row:

```
INSERT INTO Contacts
 VALUES (NEWID(),
'Francis', 'Drake')
```

In most cases, you'll probably want SQL Server to come up with the unique value, so the second syntax is generally more useful.

WARNING

When you insert an explicit value into a `uniqueidentifier` column, SQL Server does not check to see that it is unique. This is the reason that you should always create a `UNIQUE` or `PRIMARY KEY` constraint on any `uniqueidentifier` column.

Truncation and Padding

If you're inserting values into `char`, `varchar`, or `varbinary` columns, these rules apply:

- Columns with the `char` data type are padded with spaces until they're the full defined width of the column.
- Columns with the `varchar` data type are stored as is, with no truncation or padding.
- Columns with the `varbinary` data type are stored as is, with no truncation or padding.
- Inserting a value consisting entirely of spaces into a `varchar` column results in inserting a single space.
- Inserting an explicit empty string (two single quotes with no characters between them) into a `text` or `varchar` column inserts an empty string into that column. However, you can use the `sp_dbcmptlevel` stored procedure to return to the SQL Server 6 and 6.5 behavior in this situation, which is to insert a single space in the column.

The behavior specified above is compatible with ANSI padding standards. You can also use the statement `SET ANSI_PADDING OFF` when you create the table for compatibility with previous versions of SQL Server. In that case, these rules apply:

- Columns with the `char` data type have trailing spaces removed.
- Columns with the `varchar` data type have trailing spaces removed. That is, if you insert "Somedata   ", what actually gets inserted is "Somedata".
- Columns with the `varbinary` data type have trailing zeros removed.

Inserting Data through a View

SQL Server allows inserting data into a view as well as directly into a table. The syntax of the insert is exactly the same in both cases. The important thing to remember is that the order of columns in the INSERT statement must be the order of columns in the view, not that in the underlying table.

For example, you could create a view in the pubs database by executing this statement:

```
CREATE VIEW joblevels AS
SELECT min_lvl, max_lvl FROM jobs
```

To insert new data through this view you could execute:

```
INSERT INTO joblevels
VALUES (101, 105)
```

Note that this INSERT would fail if the view did not contain all the columns that required data. That is, if we left min_lvl out of the view, we would not be able to use it to insert data, since there's no way for SQL Server to determine a default value for that column.

Inserting from a Select or Execute

The data inserted into a table with the INSERT statement need not be supplied directly in a VALUES clause. You can use other Transact-SQL statements that return the appropriate data. For example, you could create the following table in the pubs database:

```
CREATE TABLE storenames
(
 stor_id char(4) NOT NULL,
 stor_name varchar(40)
)
```

To copy all of the store names and IDs from the existing stores table you could then use this query:

```
INSERT storenames
SELECT stor_id, stor_name FROM stores
```

NOTE This example is just to show you the syntax of an INSERT with a SELECT. In a real application, this would be a useless violation of the normalization rules you learned in Skill 4.

You can also use the EXECUTE keyword with the name of a stored procedure in an INSERT statement to insert the rows returned by the stored procedure. (Stored procedures are discussed later in this skill.)

Errors during Insertion

If the data you're inserting into a table violates a rule or constraint on the table, is incompatible with the data type of a column in the table, or specifies a value for an identity column without executing the SET IDENTITY_INSERT ON statement, SQL Server returns an error, and no row is inserted into the table.

If any of the data in a multi-row insert (from a SELECT or EXECUTE statement) cannot be inserted in the table, SQL Server returns an error message and the entire INSERT fails. SQL Server will never insert only some of the rows from a SELECT or EXECUTE statement.

Deleting Data from a Table

Of course, just as you can insert data into a table, you can delete data from a table. SQL Server supplies a pair of Transact-SQL statements to handle deletions: DELETE and TRUNCATE TABLE. The DELETE statement is more flexible, but TRUNCATE TABLE can be faster and has less impact on the database log. You'll learn about both methods of deleting data in this section.

TIP

If you want to remove an entire table from your database, don't bother with either of these techniques. Just use the DROP TABLE statement we covered in Skill 3.

The DELETE Statement

The DELETE statement has several options:

```
DELETE [FROM] {[database.][owner.]tablename | viewname}
 [FROM
  { table_or_view
   | table_or_view CROSS JOIN table_or_view
   | table_or_view JOIN table_or_view
    ON search_conditions
  } [,…n]
 ]
[WHERE search_conditions]
```

DELETE is the keyword that tells SQL Server you're deleting rows. The FROM keyword is optional. The second FROM keyword, and the clause it introduces, allow you to use another table or a combination of tables to specify which rows should be deleted from the first table or view. The search_conditions clauses are useful for limiting the number of rows deleted.

Deleting All Rows from a Table

To delete all the data from a table, you can use a simple DELETE query:

```
DELETE contacts
```

If you like, you can include the FROM keyword, but it isn't necessary. This statement deletes each row from the contacts table, logging each deletion separately.

Deleting Selected Rows from a Table

You can also specify a WHERE clause in a DELETE statement. This allows you to delete only the selected rows. The syntax for the WHERE clause is exactly the same as it would be in a SELECT statement. For example, to delete all the stores in Illinois from our database, we could use this statement:

```
DELETE FROM stores
WHERE state = 'IL'
```

Deleting Rows Specified by a Second Table

You may also find it useful to use one table to specify the rows to delete from a second table. For example, you might have a table of stores that have been closed and want to delete those rows from the existing stores table. To do this, you would use this Transact-SQL statement:

```
DELETE stores
FROM stores, closedstores
WHERE stores.stor_id = closedstores.stor_id
```

Here the part of the SQL statement starting with the FROM clause is similar to what you would find in a SELECT statement. The FROM and WHERE clauses act to select a set of rows from the stores table. Those rows are then deleted from the table.

The TRUNCATE TABLE Statement

The `TRUNCATE TABLE` statement has the same effect as a `DELETE` statement with no `WHERE` clause. Therefore it deletes all the rows in the specified table. For example, to delete all the rows in the contacts table, you could use the statement:

```
TRUNCATE TABLE contacts
```

Unlike the `DELETE` statement, `TRUNCATE TABLE` simply de-allocates the data storage pages without logging the delete operations. That makes it much faster in cases where you want to flush all the data out of a table. For example, you might want to do this to reuse a temporary table.

TIP

Because `TRUNCATE TABLE` is not a logged operation, it cannot be rolled back by rolling back an enclosing transaction.

NOTE

When you use `TRUNCATE TABLE` to delete all the rows from a table with an identity column, the identity counter is reset to the seed for that column. In contrast, if you delete all the rows with `DELETE`, the identity counter remains unchanged.

Errors during Deletions

If any error occurs during a delete operation, whether it's done with `DELETE` or with `TRUNCATE TABLE`, the entire operation fails. SQL Server will not delete only some of the rows specified. If it can't delete all the specified rows, it leaves them all intact.

`DELETE` can remove rows from a table that is referenced by a foreign key from another table, so long as the removed rows are not actually referenced by any rows in the foreign table. `TRUNCATE TABLE` cannot be used on a table that is referenced by a foreign key from another table.

Updating Rows in a Table

You could update data in your tables the brute force way: by using `DELETE` to remove the old data and `INSERT` to place the changed data back into the table. But Transact-SQL offers a better alternative for this pair of operations: the

UPDATE statement. With an UPDATE query, you can make changes directly to the data stored in your tables.

The UPDATE Statement

The syntax for an UPDATE statement is quite similar to that for INSERT or DELETE:

```
UPDATE {[database.][owner.]tablename | viewname }
 SET
 { column = {expression | DEFAULT }
  | @variable = expression} [,…n]
 [FROM
  { table_or_view
   | table_or_view CROSS JOIN table_or_view
   | table_or_view JOIN table_or_view
    ON search_conditions
  }[,…n]
 ]
 WHERE search_conditions]
```

Here the UPDATE clause specifies the table or view to be updated, and the SET clause supplies the new data to be inserted. The FROM clause allows you to use a join with another table to limit the rows to be updated. The WHERE clause allows you to specify a restriction, so that only certain rows are updated.

Updating a Single Column

To change the state field of every row in the stores table to FL, you could use this UPDATE statement:

```
UPDATE stores
 SET state = 'FL'
```

As with other queries, of course, the delimiters used around any data in the SET clause must match the type of data being passed.

Of course, you usually don't want to change the data in every row of an existing table. That's why the UPDATE statement supports the WHERE and join clauses to limit the rows changed. For example, to just move store number 6,380 to Florida, you could use this single-row UPDATE:

```
UPDATE stores
 SET state = 'FL'
 WHERE stor_id = '6380'
```

Updating Multiple Columns

You can also use an UPDATE statement to change the values of more than one column at a time. You might have to change the entire address for a store, for example, which can be accomplished simply by setting multiple columns in the SET clause:

```
UPDATE stores
 SET
  stor_address = "2317 Fifth Ave.",
  city = 'Miami',
  state = 'FL',
  zip = '33305'
 WHERE stor_id = '6380'
```

Returning the Default Value to a Column

An UPDATE statement can also be used to return a column to its original default value. To change the description of a particular row in the jobs table to its default value you could use this statement:

```
UPDATE jobs
 SET job_desc = DEFAULT
 WHERE job_id = 77
```


Update-in-Place

SQL Server chooses between two different strategies when carrying out an update. The first, called a deferred update, is actually a delete followed by an insert—just what you would do if you were performing the action without an UPDATE statement. This is an internal translation and you'll never see the delete and insert, but both statements are executed and logged.

The second strategy SQL Server uses is called update-in-place. In this mode, SQL Server actually changes directly the row that's stored in the database. An update-in-place is faster than a deferred update, because SQL Server only has to carry out and log a single action.

You don't have any direct control over which of these alternatives SQL Server chooses for any given update. If any of the updated columns are part of a clustered index, SQL Server uses a deferred update. Otherwise, it uses an update-in-place.

Limits on Updates

These rules apply when you're using UPDATE to change the values in a table:

- Identity columns cannot be updated. If you need to change a value in an identity column, delete the row, use SET IDENTITY_INSERT ON, and then insert a new row with the desired value.
- Data inserted into char columns is right-padded with spaces. Data inserted into varchar columns has trailing spaces removed.
- If an update violates any constraint or rule, has a data type incompatible with the column definition, or changes a value that's used by a foreign key in another table, SQL Server returns an error and the entire update fails.

Using Stored Procedures

All of the Transact-SQL statements we've worked with so far are transient: they are sent to the database and evaluated every time you evaluate them from SQL Query Analyzer, for example. Stored procedures provide permanent bits of SQL Server programming that are stored on the server itself and remain available across sessions.

There are four types of stored procedures. Catalog stored procedures, system stored procedures, and extended stored procedures are shipped with SQL Server (though you can add additional extended stored procedures). User stored procedures are created in a particular database using the CREATE PROCEDURE statement. We'll look at each of these types of stored procedures in turn.

Catalog Stored Procedures

Like any other database product, SQL Server stores information about the data it contains in a set of tables, called the *system catalog*. Parts of the system catalog describe each column in every table in your database. The catalog stored procedures allow you to retrieve information from this system catalog, just as you can use regular SELECT statements to retrieve information from your database's tables.

NOTE The rest of this section presents a few of the most useful catalog stored procedures. For the complete list, refer to SQL Server Books Online.

The sp_databases Stored Procedure

You can execute `sp_databases` to retrieve a list of all the databases on the server. The `DATABASE_NAME` column of the result set gives you a complete list of the databases available to you to execute statements on the current server. To direct future queries to another database, you can execute the `USE` statement. Table 7.1 shows the columns returned by `sp_databases`.

TABLE 7.1: Results Returned by sp_databases

Column	Datatype	Contents
DATABASE_NAME	char(32)	Name of the database
DATABASE_SIZE	int	Size of the database, in kilobytes
REMARKS	int	Always NULL

The sp_columns Stored Procedure

The `sp_columns` stored procedure returns information on the columns in a specified table. The full syntax of this stored procedure is:

```
sp_columns object[, owner][, qualifier][, column][, ODBCver]
```

The `object` argument, of course, is the name of the table or view that you want to analyze with this stored procedure. `Owner` is the owner of the object (if the specified user doesn't own an object by that name, SQL Server returns information on an object with that name owned by the dbo user). `Qualifier` can be used to specify the name of the database containing the table. `Column` can be used to specify a single column, or a group of columns (using wildcards). If no column is specified, information is returned for all columns in the table. `ODBCver` specifies the version of the ODBC standard to use when interpreting information—only two or three can be specified, and if no value or an illegal value is specified, three is assumed.

Skill 7

TIP Some of the data returned by `sp_columns` may seem irrelevant for SQL Server development. That's because this stored procedure is a wrapper around the ODBC function for retrieving column information, and some of this information is of interest mainly to ODBC developers. You can use a SQL Server ODS Gateway to execute stored procedures against other data sources, which may return different values in some columns.

Table 7.2 shows the information returned by sp_columns.

TABLE 7.2: Results Returned by sp_columns

Column	Data type	Contents
TABLE_QUALIFIER	varchar(32)	Database containing the table.
TABLE_OWNER	varchar(32)	Owner of the table.
TABLE_NAME	varchar(32)	Name of the table.
COLUMN_NAME	varchar(32)	Name of the column (this will, of course, be different for each row of the result set).
DATA_TYPE	Smallint	Integer representing the ODBC data type of the column.
TYPE_NAME	varchar(13)	The SQL Server data type.
PRECISION	Int	Number of significant digits for the column.
LENGTH	Int	Size of the data in bytes.
SCALE	Smallint	Number of digits to the right of the decimal point for numeric data types.
RADIX	Smallint	Base for numeric data types.
NULLABLE	Smallint	1 if the column allows nulls; 0 if the column was defined as NOT NULL.
REMARKS	varchar(254)	Always NULL.
COLUMN_DEF	varchar(254)	Default value for the column.
SQL_DATA_TYPE	Smallint	The SQL type, as defined by ODBC.
SQL_DATETIME_SUB	Smallint	Subtype for datetime and interval data types.
CHAR_OCTET_LENGTH	Smallint	Maximum length in bytes for integer or character columns. NULL for all other columns.
ORDINAL_POSITION	Int	Ordinal position of the column in the table. The first column is position 1.
IS_NULLABLE	varchar(254)	YES or NO, depending on whether the column can accept nulls.
SS_DATA_TYPE	Smallint	Data type as defined for Open Data Services (ODS).

The results from sp_columns may seem like a lot of irrelevant information for most applications. Why should you care about this information? If you're writing a utility that has to work on arbitrary tables, of course, it's essential to have some method such as this to retrieve information about the tables. But even day-to-day business applications may have need for this information. For instance, you might be building a client-side query interface to allow users to submit queries to the database without writing Transact-SQL. In that case, you'll probably want to present the users with a list of columns they can use to restrict the data returned, and `sp_columns` is the obvious tool to return that list.

The sp_pkeys Stored Procedure

You can also use catalog stored procedures to retrieve information on the relationships between tables. For example, the `sp_pkeys` stored procedure will return information on the primary key columns in any table. The syntax is:

```
sp_pkeys name, owner, qualifier
```

Once again, `name` is the name of the table, `owner` is the owner of the table, and `qualifier` is the database name. Table 7.3 shows the information returned by `sp_pkeys`.

TABLE 7.3: Results Returned by sp_pkeys

Column	Data type	Contents
TABLE_QUALIFIER	varchar(32)	The database name.
TABLE_OWNER	varchar(32)	Owner of the table.
TABLE_NAME	varchar(32)	Name of the table.
COLUMN_NAME	varchar(32)	Name of a column in the primary key for the table.
KEY_SEQ	Smallint	Position of the key in a multipart primary key. This will be 1 for a single-column primary key.
PK_NAME	varchar(32)	SQL Server identifier for the primary key.

The sp_server_info Stored Procedure

Some stored procedures return information on SQL Server itself. Chief among these is `sp_server_info`, which returns a variety of miscellaneous information. The result set has columns for `ATTRIBUTE_ID`, `ATTRIBUTE_NAME` and `ATTRIBUTE_VALUE`. Table 7.4 shows the rows returned in this result set.

TABLE 7.4: Results Returned by sp_server_info

ATTRIBUTE_ID	ATTRIBUTE_NAME	ATTRIBUTE_VALUE
1	DBMS_NAME	"Microsoft SQL Server"
2	DBMS_VER	Full version string for the server
10	OWNER_TERM	"owner"
11	TABLE_TERM	"tablev"
12	MAX_OWNER_NAME_LENGTH	Maximum number of characters in an owner name
13	TABLE_LENGTH	Maximum number of characters in a table name
14	MAX_QUAL_LENGTH	Maximum number of characters in a database name
15	COLUMN_LENGTH	Maximum number of characters in a table name
16	IDENTIFIER_CASE	MIXED if SQL Server is running in case-insensitive mode, SENSITIVE if it's running in case-sensitive mode
17	TX_ISOLATION	ANSI Transaction isolation level
18	COLLATION_SEQ	Information on the character set and sort order used by the server
19	SAVEPOINT_SUPPORT	"Y" for SQL Server, which supports named save points
20	MULTI_RESULT_SETS	"Y" for SQL Server, which supports stored procedures returning multiple result sets
22	ACCESSIBLE_TABLES	"Y" for SQL Server, where sp_tables only returns tables that the current user can see
100	USERID_LENGTH	Maximum number of characters in a user name
101	QUALIFIER_TERM	"Database"
102	NAMED_TRANSACTIONS	"Y" for SQL Server, which supports named transactions
103	SPROC_AS_LANGUAGE	"Y" for SQL Server, which supports stored procedures

TABLE 7.4 CONTINUED: Results Returned by sp_server_info

ATTRIBUTE_ID	ATTRIBUTE_NAME	ATTRIBUTE_VALUE
104	ACCESSIBLE_SPROC	"Y" for SQL Server, where sp_stored_procedures only returns procedures the current user can execute
105	MAX_INDEX_COLS	Maximum columns an index can contain
106	RENAME_TABLE	"Y" for SQL Server, which allows renaming tables
107	RENAME_COLUMN	"Y" for SQL Server, which allows renaming columns
108	DROP_COLUMN	"N" for SQL Server, which does not allow dropping columns
109	INCREASE_COLUMN_LENGTH	"N" for SQL Server, which does not allow making columns wider
110	DDL_IN_TRANSACTION	"Y" for SQL Server, which allows DDL statements within transactions
111	DESCENDING_INDEX	"N" for SQL Server, which does not support descending indexes
112	SP_RENAME	"N" for SQL Server, which does not allow renaming stored procedures
113	REMOTE_SPROC	"Y" for SQL Server, which allows remote execution of stored procedures
500	SYS_SPROC_VERSION	Current version of the catalog of stored procedures on this server

The sp_statistics Stored Procedure

The `sp_statistics` stored procedure can be used to retrieve information on the indexes defined on a particular table and the columns within those indexes. The full syntax to call this stored procedure is:

```
sp_statistics tablename[,owner][,qualifier][,index][,is_unique]
```

Here `tablename`, `owner`, and `qualifier` serve to identify the table to work with, just as they do in the other catalog stored procedures we've already seen. `Index` allows you to specify a particular index to retrieve information for, and `is_unique` can be set to `"Y"` if you only want information on unique indexes.

Table 7.5 shows the information returned by this stored procedure.

TABLE 7.5: Results Returned by `sp_statistics`

Column	Data type	Contents
TABLE_QUALIFIER	varchar(32)	Name of the table.
TABLE_OWNER	varchar(32)	Owner of the table.
TABLE_NAME	varchar(32)	Name of the table.
NON_UNIQUE	Smallint	0 if this is a unique index, 1 if this is a non-unique index.
INDEX_QUALIFIER	varchar(32)	Owner of the index. In SQL Server, this will always be the same as the owner of the table.
INDEX_NAME	varchar(32)	Name of the index.
TYPE	Smallint	0 if this is a plain index, 1 if this is a clustered index, 2 if this is a hashed index (not used by SQL Server), 3 for other types of index.
SEQ_IN_INDEX	Smallint	Position of this column within the index.
COLUMN_NAME	varchar(32)	Name of this column.
COLLATION	char(1)	"A" for ascending (the only values SQL Server will return), or "D" for descending.
CARDINALITY	Int	Number of unique values in the index.
PAGES	Int	Number of pages used to store the index.
FILTER_CONDITION	varchar(128)	Not used by SQL Server.

The sp_tables Stored Procedure

As you've probably guessed by now, `sp_tables` returns information on the tables in the current database. It also returns information about the system tables (the ones that store the catalog) and the views in the database. You can, of course, specify that less information be retrieved by supplying additional parameters:

```
sp_tables [name][,owner][,qualifier][,type]
```

`Name` allows you to specify the name of a particular table. `Owner` lets you limit the results to tables owned by a particular user. `Qualifier` lets you specify a database. The type parameter can be set to 'TABLE', 'SYSTEM TABLE', or 'VIEW' to return information on particular types of objects.

Table 7.6 shows the information returned by this stored procedure.

TABLE 7.6: Results Returned by sp_tables

Column	Data type	Contents
TABLE_QUALIFIER	varchar(32)	Name of the database
TABLE_OWNER	varchar(32)	Owner of the table
TABLE_NAME	varchar(32)	Name of the table
TABLE_TYPE	varchar(32)	'TABLE', 'SYSTEM TABLE', or 'VIEW'
REMARKS	varchar(254)	Not used by SQL Server

System Stored Procedures

The *system stored procedures* are a second group of stored procedures supplied by SQL Server. You can think of these as management tools for SQL Server. In most cases, there are visual alternatives to these stored procedures. For example, the action of sp_addserver can be duplicated by adding a new server with SQL Server Enterprise Manager. However, it's important that you know that system stored procedures exist, because you'll find them in use in many existing SQL Server installations. They also provide a way to automate actions that would otherwise need to be done by hand.

SQL Server supplies dozens of system stored procedures. We're not going to list or analyze them all (you can find a full list in SQL Server Books Online). Rather, we'll just pick a few of the most useful to give you an idea of what these procedures can do for you.

The sp_addserver Stored Procedure

The sp_addserver stored procedure allows you to tell this server that another server exists. There are three reasons you might want to do this:

- Before you can run stored procedures on a remote server, you must add that server.
- To set up a fallback server, you must add that server.

- To change the name of the local server, you can add it using a new name (however, unless you have a very good reason, you should leave the name of the server the same as that of the computer it's installed on).

The stored procedure has options to distinguish which of these cases you want to execute:

```
sp_addserver servername, [,{LOCAL | FALLBACK}]
```

To rename the local server, you must include the `LOCAL` parameter; to add a fallback server, you must include the `FALLBACK` parameter.

The sp_configure Stored Procedure

The `sp_configure` stored procedure is a dual-purpose stored procedure. It can either display the current configuration of the server, or alter that configuration. Figure 7.2 shows the results of running sp_configure with no parameters in Query Analyzer. In this case, it displays the current server configuration.

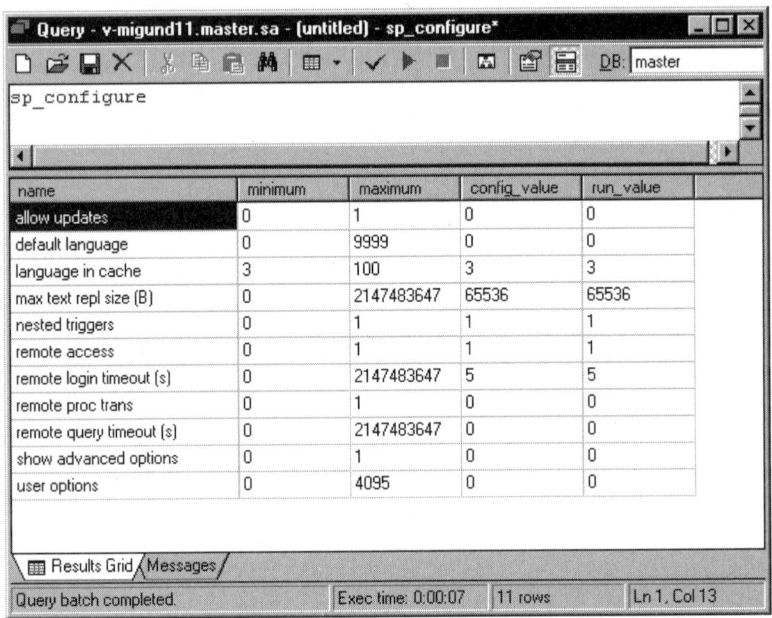

name	minimum	maximum	config_value	run_value
allow updates	0	1	0	0
default language	0	9999	0	0
language in cache	3	100	3	3
max text repl size (B)	0	2147483647	65536	65536
nested triggers	0	1	1	1
remote access	0	1	1	1
remote login timeout (s)	0	2147483647	5	5
remote proc trans	0	1	0	0
remote query timeout (s)	0	2147483647	0	0
show advanced options	0	1	0	0
user options	0	4095	0	0

FIGURE 7.2: Output from `sp_configure`

To use sp_configure to change an option, you add parameters to tell it the option name (one of the names listed in the first column in Figure 7.2) and the new value you'd like to use for that option. You can use any unique string to identify the name. Changes do not take effect immediately. Rather, you need to run the RECONFIGURE command to tell the server to change the next time it's started, or RECONFIGURE WITH OVERRIDE to tell it to change immediately.

For example, this script will show you the advanced options for sp_configure itself:

```
sp_configure 'advanced', 1
GO
RECONFIGURE
GO
sp_configure
```

NOTE The Advanced Options are immediately shown even if you don't use RECONFIGURE WITH OVERRIDE.

WARNING You shouldn't change any of the advanced options without a very good reason. For example, Microsoft tech support might instruct you to change one of these options when troubleshooting a problem.

To immediately change the number of available user connections, you'd need to use RECONFIGURE WITH OVERRIDE, as shown in this script:

```
sp_configure 'user connections', 25
GO
RECONFIGURE WITH OVERRIDE
GO
sp_configure
```

The sp_help Stored Procedure

The sp_help stored procedure provides a variety of information on database objects. You can either run it with no arguments, or supply the name of an object.

With no arguments, sp_help returns a list of all views, tables, stored procedures, extended stored procedures, constraints, defaults, and users in the database. Any of these can be used as an argument to sp_help. For example, executing sp_help stores will return information on the stores table.

If you execute sp_help on a table or view, it returns information on the table, columns, identity columns, indexes, constraints, and any tables referencing the specified table via a foreign key. If you execute sp_help on a view, it returns information on the stored procedure.

The sp_helpdb Stored Procedure

Executing sp_helpdb without a database name returns information on all of the databases on the current server. This information includes the database name, size, owner, creation date, and status information. You can also add the name of a particular database, for example:

```
sp_helpdb pubs
```

The sp_helptext Stored Procedure

The sp_helptext stored procedure gives you a way to return the text that defines a SQL Server object. The types of object you can investigate this way are:

- Rule
- Default
- Stored procedure
- Trigger
- View

For example, executing

```
sp_helptext reptq1
```

in the pubs database returns the output shown in Figure 7.3.

TIP You can prevent sp_helptext from showing the text of a view, trigger, or stored procedure by using the WITH ENCRYPTION option in the CREATE VIEW, CREATE TRIGGER, or CREATE PROCEDURE statement.

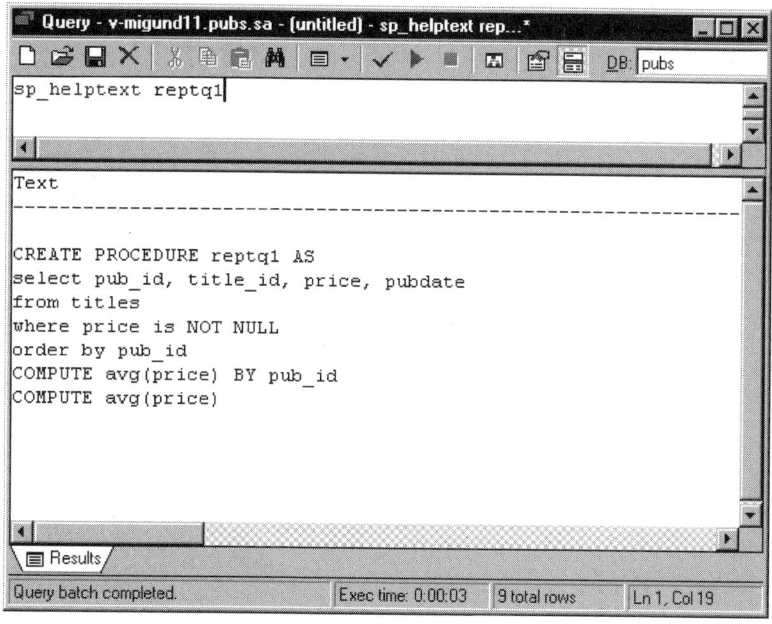

FIGURE 7.3: Text of a stored procedure

The sp_lock Stored Procedure

The `sp_lock` stored procedure returns a report on all the locks currently in place on a server. Figure 7.4 shows sample output from `sp_lock` on a lightly loaded server (a production server in active use would show many more locks than this).

This stored procedure comes in very handy when you're having locking problems, as it's a critical part of tracking down who is holding locks on a table. To determine which user has a lock on any object, follow these steps:

1. Run a query to retrieve the ID from the sysobjects table corresponding to the object name. For example, to determine the ID for the stores table, you'd execute `SELECT id FROM sysobjects WHERE name = 'stores'`.
2. Run the `sp_lock` stored procedure to list all locks. Examine the `ObjId` column of the output to find locks on the table you're interested in.

3. Run the sp_who stored procedure (see below) to find the user corresponding to the spid for the lock of interest.

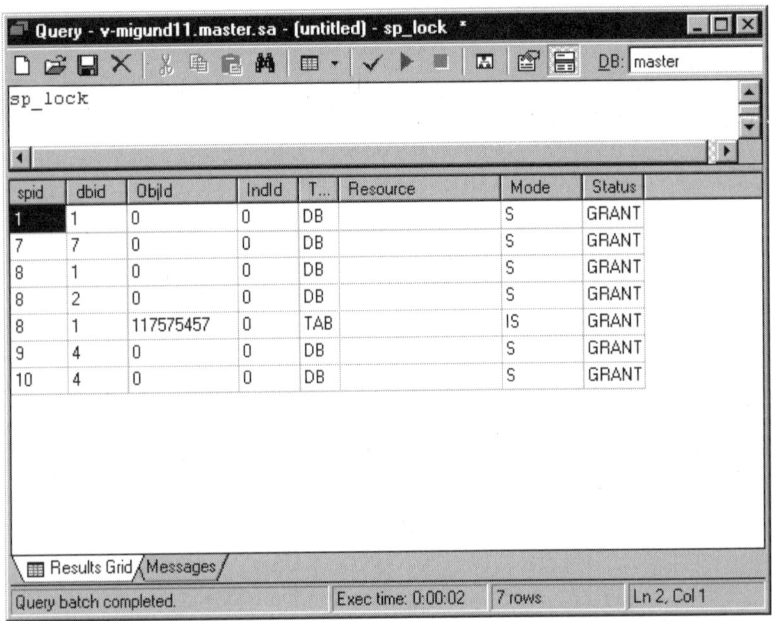

spid	dbid	ObjId	IndId	T...	Resource	Mode	Status
1	1	0	0	DB		S	GRANT
7	7	0	0	DB		S	GRANT
8	1	0	0	DB		S	GRANT
8	2	0	0	DB		S	GRANT
8	1	117575457	0	TAB		IS	GRANT
9	4	0	0	DB		S	GRANT
10	4	0	0	DB		S	GRANT

FIGURE 7.4: Output from sp_lock

The sp_who Stored Procedure

The sp_who stored procedure is designed to return information on active users on the server and to link them to process ID's (spids). When you run sp_who, the following information is returned for each connection to the server:

- The spid for the process
- The process status
- The user's login name
- The host server name
- The spid for any process that is blocking this process

- The database name the user is using
- The SQL Server command currently executing for the process

Extended Stored Procedures

Extended stored procedures are implemented as separate libraries outside of SQL Server, although a number of these are loaded when you install SQL Server. Generally, they're used for interfacing with other applications or the operating system itself, rather than for doing work within SQL Server. We'll look at a few of the most useful built-in extended stored procedures here.

Some of the issues involved in creating your own extended stored procedures are discussed in Skill 13, *Programming SQL Server*.

The xp_cmdshell Stored Procedure

The xp_cmdshell extended stored procedure provides a way to execute Windows operating system commands directly from SQL Server. Any output from the command is returned as a single-column result set (you can use the optional NO_OUTPUT parameter to suppress this result set). For example, to retrieve a list of files from the operating system you could execute


```
master..xp_cmdshell "dir *.*"
```

The master.. part of this statement tells SQL Server which database contains this particular extended stored procedure.

You can use xp_cmdshell to do anything you could do from the Windows command prompt, including launching programs or command (batch) files. You can even use it to shut down SQL Server itself:

```
master..xp_cmdshell "net stop sqlserver", NO_OUTPUT
```

By default only the sa user and members of the Windows NT Local Administrators group can use the xp_cmdshell procedure. You should be very careful about granting permission to other users, since they could use the procedure to execute any command, even potentially damaging ones.

The xp_sendmail Stored Procedure

The xp_sendmail stored procedure provides an interface to your mail server. The full syntax of this stored procedure is a bit daunting:

```
xp_sendmail 'recipient' [;...recipient]
 [,'message']
 [,query]
 [,attachments]
 [,'copy_recipient [;...copy_recipient]]
 [,blind_copy_recipientname [;...blind_copy_recipientname]]
 [,subject]
 [,type]
 [,attach_results]
 [,no_output]
 [,no_header]
 [,width]
 [,separator]
 [,echo_error]
 [,user]
 [,database]
```

Table 7.7 gives further details on these parameters. Fortunately, as you can see, they're nearly all optional. To simply send a message to a user, you need only supply the recipient and the user:

```
xp_sendmail 'Admin', 'This is a Test Message'
```

TABLE 7.7: Parameters for xp_sendmail

Parameter	Use
recipient	One or more recipients for the mail, separated by semicolons
message	Message text
query	A SELECT query, the results of which are sent as the mail message
attachment	An operating system file to attach to the mail message
copy_recipient	One or more recipients of copies of the mail, separated by semicolons
blind_copy_recipient	One or more recipients of blind copies of the mail, separated by semicolons
subject	The subject line for the message. If not specified, the subject is set to "SQL Server Message"
type	Custom message type. Generally you should leave this set to Null, which will cause the message to appear in the recipient's inbox.

TABLE 7.7 CONTINUED: Parameters for xp_sendmail

Parameter	Use
attach_result	If set to True, the results of any query are sent as an attachment. If set to False, query results are included in the message.
no_output	Set to True to suppress output of `xp_sendmail` back to the client that calls it.
no_header	False to include column headers with any query, True to suppress the column headers.
width	Wrap width of the mail message and any embedded query results.
separator	Character to use between columns of any embedded query results.
echo_error	If set to True, any errors are appended to the mail message.
user	Security context the query should run under.
database	Database to execute the query in.

You can specify any or all of these parameters just by separating them with commas, but you can also use the @variable syntax to fill in just a few parameters. For example, to run a query and send the results as an attachment you might execute the following:

```
xp_sendmail @recipients='Admin',
 @query = 'select * from stores'
 @attach_results = 'TRUE'
```

Before you can use `xp_sendmail` to send a message, you must use `xp_startmail` to log on to your mail server. The syntax of `xp_startmail` is:

```
xp_startmail 'user', 'password'
```

User-Defined Stored Procedures

In addition to using the built-in stored procedures (catalog, system, and extended) you can also create your own stored procedures. Stored procedures can offer significant advantages to client-side applications such as Microsoft Access or Microsoft Visual Basic. If one of these clients submits a query, SQL Server must compile the query into an execution plan when it receives the query. If the same query is stored as a stored procedure on the server, the execution plan is precompiled. Either way, the results to the client are the same.

Creating Stored Procedures

The basic tool for creating your own stored procedures is the CREATE PROCEDURE statement:

```
CREATE PROC[EDURE] name [;number]
 [({@parameter_name} data type [= default] [OUTPUT])]
 [...n]
 [WITH { RECOMPILE | ENCRYPTION | RECOMPILE, ENCRYPTION }]
 [FOR REPLICATION]
 AS sql_statement [...n]
```

The name argument supplies the name you want to assign to the stored procedure. You may optionally assign a number to group procedures together. The only effect that grouping has is to make using DROP PROCEDURE simpler when you want to remove multiple procedures. For example, if you create stock;1 and stock;2 as separate procedures with CREATE PROCEDURE, they can both be removed with DROP PROCEDURE stock.

Parameter names, data types, and defaults let you supply information that will be plugged into the stored procedure at runtime (similar to the way that a function definition works in most programming languages). The sql_statement argument supplies the statement or statements that should be executed when the stored procedure is invoked.

A Simple Stored Procedure

For example, if you found that your client applications often need to know which titles are stocked by which stores, you could instruct them to run this query to retrieve the information:

```
SELECT stor_name, title
 FROM stores, sales, titles
 WHERE stores.stor_id = sales.stor_id AND
  sales.title_id = titles.title_id
 ORDER BY title, stor_name
```

But every time client applications submit this query, SQL Server needs to calculate the execution plan. Instead, you can get more efficiency by creating a stored procedure to run the same query:

```
CREATE PROC stortitles
AS
 SELECT stor_name, title
  FROM stores, sales, titles
```

```
  WHERE stores.stor_id = sales.stor_id AND
   sales.title_id = titles.title_id
  ORDER BY title, stor_name
```

Once you've created this stored procedure, client applications can retrieve the same data by running any of these statements:

```
EXECUTE stortitles
EXEC stortitles
stortitles
```

TIP The third syntax, without any part of the EXECUTE keyword, only works as the initial statement in a batch.

A Stored Procedure with Parameters

You can also use parameters with stored procedures. Suppose you needed to retrieve only the stores that sold a particular title. In that case, you could create this stored procedure:

```
CREATE PROC stortitles2
 @findtitle varchar(80)
AS
 SELECT stor_name, title
  FROM stores, sales, titles
  WHERE stores.stor_id = sales.stor_id AND
   sales.title_id = titles.title_id AND
   titles.title = @findtitle
  ORDER BY title, stor_name
```

Here `@findtitle` is an input parameter, a piece of data to be supplied to the stored procedure by the user. You can specify input parameters by name or by position, so any of these syntaxes will work to retrieve sales on a particular title:

```
EXECUTE stortitles2 'Is Anger the Enemy?'
EXECUTE stortitles2 @findtitle = 'Is Anger the Enemy?'
EXEC stortitles2 'Is Anger the Enemy?'
EXEC stortitles2 @findtitle = 'Is Anger the Enemy?'
stortitles2 'Is Anger the Enemy?'
stortitles2 @findtitle = 'Is Anger the Enemy?'
```

You can also define stored procedures with output parameters, which allow the stored procedure to return calculated values to the caller.

Recompile, Encryption, and Replication Arguments

It's possible that a particular stored procedure won't benefit from a permanently stored execution plan. For example, you might have a stored procedure that retrieves information based on wildcards, and depending on which wildcard value the user supplies, SQL Server should use multiple execution plans. In that case, you should use the `WITH RECOMPILE` clause to tell SQL Server to re-evaluate the execution plan whenever the stored procedure is called.

TIP When in doubt, store the execution plan. SQL Server is very smart about finding optimal plans.

The `ENCRYPTION` clause stores the actual text of the stored procedure in scrambled form. This means that it's not accessible to the sp_help system stored procedure, nor can it be retrieved by a query on the sysobjects table.

The `FOR REPLICATION` clause is used to mark a particular stored procedure as being a filter procedure that will be executed only by the replication engine.

NOTE See Skill 14, *Using Replication*, for more information on replication.

Stored Procedure Limits

You can create a stored procedure that refers to nonexistent database objects, although you'll receive a warning. For example, the following statement will execute without error, even if `badtable` does not exist:

```
CREATE PROCEDURE badproc
AS
SELECT * FROM badtable
```

This is an aid to developers, since it means that they need not create all tables and other objects before writing stored procedures. The object must exist when the procedure is executed, of course. This feature is called *delayed name resolution.*

`SET` statements executed within a stored procedure only affect the operation of that procedure.

Object names in some statements must be qualified with an owner name in stored procedures. These statements are affected:

- ALTER TABLE
- CREATE TABLE
- DROP TABLE
- TRUNCATE TABLE
- CREATE INDEX
- DROP INDEX
- UPDATE STATISTICS
- DBCC

You can create temporary stored procedures by prefacing the name of the procedure with # or ##, in the same manner that you can use to create temporary tables.

SQL Server 7 includes deferred name resolution for stored procedures. What this means is that you can create a stored procedure that refers to a table or column that does not yet exist. Of course, if you execute the stored procedure before creating the table or column, an error results.

Startup Stored Procedures

You can create stored procedures that execute automatically when SQL Server is started. To create one of these startup stored procedures, follow these steps:

1. Log on as the sa user.
2. Create a stored procedure in the master database.
3. Use `sp_procoption` to mark the stored procedure as a startup stored procedure. For example, to mark the stored procedure `stproc` as a startup stored procedure, you would execute `sp_procoption 'stproc', 'startup', 'True'`.

If you accidentally create a startup stored procedure that interferes with normal system startup, you can override it by using the `-f` flag at startup. To use a startup flag, you launch SQL Server from the command line instead of as a service:

```
sqlservr -f
```

Using Triggers

So far, we've looked at ways to alter data that are initiated by the user of the application. You can also have changes to the data cause Transact-SQL code to execute, and some of this code could even make other data changes. SQL Server supplies *triggers* that can be executed when you insert, delete, or update rows in a table. In this section you'll learn how to create and use triggers.

Creating Triggers

To create a trigger, you use the `CREATE TRIGGER` statement:

```
CREATE TRIGGER triggername
 ON tablename
 [WITH ENCRYPTION]
 {
  {FOR { [INSERT][,UPDATE][,DELETE]}
   [WITH APPEND]
   [NOT FOR REPLICATION]
   AS
    sql_statement [...n]
   }
   |
   {FOR {[INSERT][,UPDATE]}
    [WITH APPEND]
   [NOT FOR REPLICATINO]
   AS
   IF UPDATE(columnname)
   [{AND | OR| UPDATE(columnname) [,...n]]
    sql_statement [...n]
   }
 }
```

The `triggername` argument, of course, is the name you want to assign to the trigger, and the `tablename` argument specifies which table this trigger will be attached to. The `WITH ENCRYPTION` option prevents `sp_help` from showing the text for this trigger. The `FOR` clause specifies which actions should fire this trigger. Normally you'll write separate triggers for inserts, updates, and deletes, but there's nothing to prevent you from having one trigger fired by multiple events.

The `WITH APPEND` clause is used to add an additional trigger of an existing type to a table. This was required with SQL Server 6.5, but is unnecessary in SQL Server 7, which automatically allows multiple triggers of the same type per table. The `NOT FOR REPLICATION` clause prevents this trigger from being fired by the actions of replication stored procedures. This can help when you are using replication to copy data from multiple tables and don't want earlier inserts confusing things for later ones.

The AS clause introduces the Transact-SQL statements that this trigger should execute. You can use multiple statements by wrapping them in BEGIN and END. If you need an update trigger that is specific to updates on a single column, you can use the IF UPDATE(*columnname*) syntax to check whether any particular column was updated by the insert.

The Inserted and Deleted Tables

Two special tables are maintained during trigger operations. These tables are named *inserted* and *deleted*, and you can examine the data in them from within the trigger if you need more information on the data changes that are taking place.

- During a delete, rows are removed from the main table and transferred to the delete table. Then the delete trigger fires.
- During an insert, rows are added to both the main table and the inserted table. Then the insert trigger fires.
- During an update, the old data is added to the deleted table, and the new data is added to the main table and the inserted table. Then the update trigger fires.

Maintaining Summary Values

One common use for triggers is to maintain values in denormalized summary tables. For example, you could use a trigger on the sales table to automatically update a total sales column in the titles table:

```
CREATE TRIGGER ins_update_sum
ON sales
FOR INSERT AS
 UPDATE titles
 SET ytd_sales = ytd_sales +
  (SELECT SUM(qty)
   FROM inserted
   WHERE titles.title_id = inserted.title_id)
 WHERE titles.title_id IN
  (SELECT title_id FROM inserted)
```

The SUM() function is necessary to handle situations where multiple rows are inserted at once, because the trigger only fires once for each insert operation.

Conditional Insert Triggers

You can also use triggers to only allow some inserts in a table. To do this, you write an insert trigger that examines the rows in the insert table and then deletes the rows that you do not approve of. For example, you could create this trigger on the sales table to refuse sales with less than 100 units:

```
CREATE TRIGGER largesalesonly
 ON sales
 FOR INSERT AS
  IF
  (SELECT COUNT(*) FROM titles, inserted
   WHERE titles.title_id = inserted.title_id AND
         inserted.qty >= 100) <> @@rowcount
    BEGIN
     DELETE sales FROM sales, inserted
     WHERE sales.title_id = inserted.title_id AND
           inserted.qty < 100
           PRINT "Not all sales accepted"
    END
```

NOTE Note the use of the BEGIN and END statements to have the trigger carry out a series of operations.

Transactions and Triggers

Triggers can be useful for keeping undesired changes out of a database. A trigger can contain the ROLLBACK TRANSACTION statement. If this statement is executed because one statement in a batch caused the trigger to fire, then all of the statements in the batch are rolled back. In other words, from the trigger's point of view the active transaction is the batch of statements that are executing.

For example, the following trigger would prevent any batch of statements that involved deleting a row from the stores table:

```
CREATE TRIGGER nodelstores
 ON stores
 FOR DELETE
 ROLLBACK TRANSACTION
```

It's unlikely that you would want to cancel every attempt to delete a row from a table, of course. A more sophisticated trigger might check the results of a SELECT statement and prevent the deletion of stores with open invoices.

Nested Triggers

The action of one trigger can cause another trigger to execute. For example, a delete trigger might save an archive copy of the deleted record to a second table. If this second table has an insert trigger, that trigger will be fired as a result of the first trigger's actions. This is referred to as *nested triggers*.

NOTE Triggers can be nested up to 32 levels deep without causing an error. If the nesting goes deeper than this, further trigger actions are aborted.

Removing Triggers

You can remove a trigger from the database by executing the DROP TRIGGER statement:

```
DROP TRIGGER triggername
```

If you use DROP TABLE to remove a table from the database, then all of the triggers for that table are automatically removed as well.

Are You up to Speed?

Now you can...

- ☑ use INSERT statements to add rows to a table
- ☑ use DELETE statements to remove rows from a table
- ☑ use UPDATE statements to alter existing rows in a table
- ☑ retrieve schema information with catalog stored procedures
- ☑ execute system stored procedures
- ☑ send mail and execute commands with extended stored procedures
- ☑ create your own stored procedures
- ☑ use triggers to react to data changes

SKILL 8

Using SQL Server Tools

- SQL Server Enterprise Manager
- Other Windows-based tools
- Command-line utilities
- Microsoft English Query

When you install SQL Server, you get more than a powerful database engine. You also get a whole suite of integrated tools that can help you control and extend your SQL Server's capabilities. Some of these are traditional command-line tools, enabling you to perform specific tasks quickly from a command prompt or a batch file. Others are full-blown Windows applications. In this skill, we'll review these tools and give you an idea of what you can do with them.

Windows Tools

The primary Windows-based tool is, of course, SQL Server Enterprise Manager. We've seen bits and pieces of this application in previous skills, but here we'll take a look at its overall capabilities. We'll also discuss five other applications:

- Query Analyzer
- Client Network Utility
- MS DTC Administrative Console
- SQL Server Profiler
- SQL Server Performance Monitor

SQL Server Enterprise Manager

SQL Server Enterprise Manager is an example of a Microsoft Management Console (MMC) application. MMC is the new management interface that will be widely used within Windows NT 5. MMC is designed to let you perform common management tasks from a single window. Indeed, as we'll see later in this section, you can even customize your MMC installation to mix SQL Server tasks with disk management tasks or many other management tasks.

Within the main MMC window, application objects are arranged in a hierarchy. The SQL Server hierarchy is especially complex, since it's a view of a complex application. Once you've located the proper node in the hierarchy, you can use the custom menus for that node to perform actions on the selected object. You can also use the MMC's own menus to customize the way your console looks and works.

The SQL Server Hierarchy

You can use the MMC to organize your SQL Servers into groups. A SQL Server Group is an administrative unit, designed to help you keep track of servers that are used for similar purposes.

TIP SQL Server is designed for remote administration. If you have more than one server in your organization, adding all of the servers to a single group will allow you to manage them all from a single instance of SQL Server Enterprise Manager.

To create a new SQL Server group, right-click Microsoft SQL Servers and choose New SQL Server Group. This will bring up the dialog box shown in Figure 8.1. Enter a name for your new group, click OK, and it will be added to the SQL Server hierarchy. If you have existing groups in your hierarchy (as this figure shows), you can also choose to make the new group a subgroup rather than a top-level group.

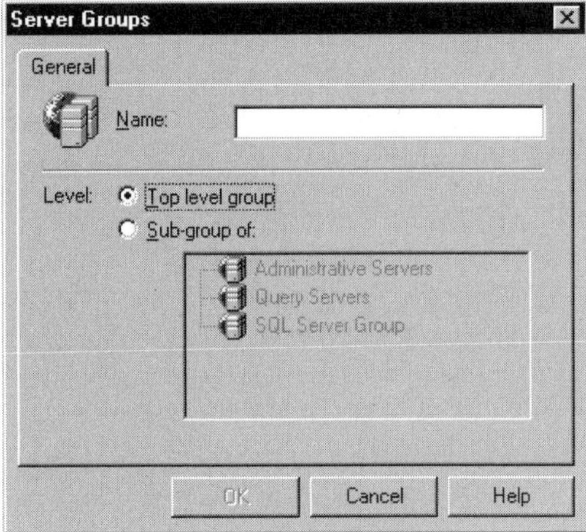

FIGURE 8.1: Creating a new SQL Server group

Once you've created your groups, you can add your servers to them. Right-click the group that you want to add a server to, and choose New SQL Server Registration. This will open the Register SQL Server Wizard, shown in Figure 8.2, which will step you through the necessary choices to add any available server to your MMC hierarchy.

Skill 8

FIGURE 8.2: Registering a SQL Server

Figure 8.3 shows the contents of the Databases node. This node contains one object for each database on the selected server (this particular server has only the two default sample databases that SQL Server installs). You can expand each node to view the list of object types within a database, and by selecting one of these types you can perform operations on these objects. For example, by right-clicking a particular database in the right window in the MMC, you can import or export data, back up or restore the database, and so on.

Each SQL Server within the MMC has its own hierarchy of objects. These objects are divided into five groups:

- Databases
- Data Transformation Services
- Management
- Security
- Support Services

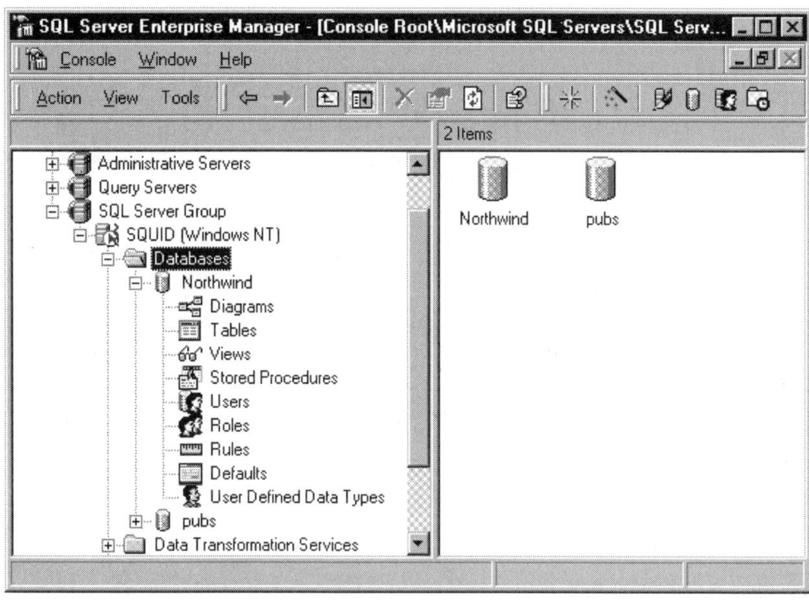

FIGURE 8.3: SQL Server Enterprise Manager Databases node

NOTE Operations on individual database objects are covered in other skills.

Figure 8.4 shows the contents of the Data Transformation Services node and the Management node. Data Transformation Services, the automated interface between SQL Server and other databases, is discussed in Skill 5, *Moving Data*.

The children of the Management node provide access to many of the routine tasks that SQL Server administrators may need to perform:

- The SQL Server Agent node allows you to manage jobs, operators, and alerts. These tasks are discussed in Skill 15, *Administering a Server*.
- The Backup node manages backup and restore operations, which are discussed in Skill 5, *Moving Data*.
- The Current Activity node is designed to allow administrators to perform quick, ad hoc server monitoring. Objects within this window can show you what processes are running on the server and which server objects are locked by which users. This can aid in quickly tracking down blocked and blocking transactions or in seeing which users are on the system.

- The Database Maintenance Plans node is your interface to the Database Maintenance Plan Wizard, also discussed in Skill 5, *Moving Data.*
- The SQL Server Logs node lets you drill down into the current log or recent logs to analyze SQL Server activity.
- The Web Publishing node launches the Web Assistant wizard, which helps you publish data on the Internet. This wizard is covered in Skill 9, *Publishing SQL Server Data on the Web.*

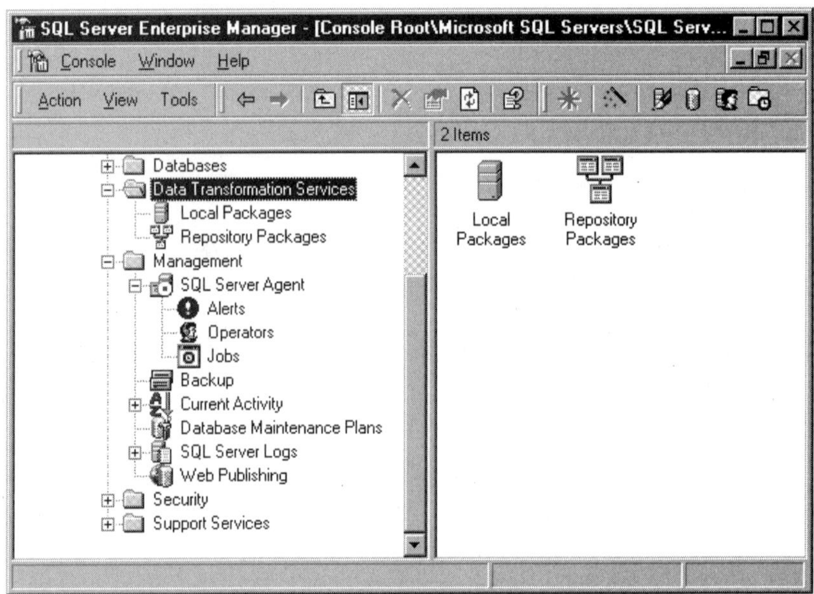

FIGURE 8.4: Data Transformation Services and Management nodes in SQL Server Enterprise Manager

The Security node of each database provides you with the tools you need to manage user- and group-level security on that database. These tools are covered in Skill 16, *Managing SQL Server Security.* Security and Support Services nodes in SQL Server Enterprise Manager are shown in Figure 8.5.

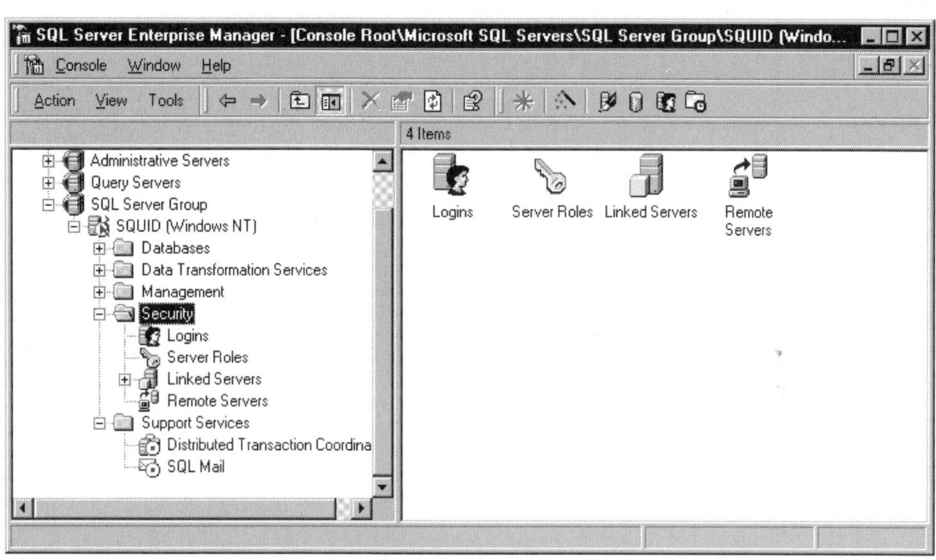

FIGURE 8.5: Security and Support Services nodes in SQL Server Enterprise Manager

Managing Multiple Applications with MMC

NOTE Information in this section is based on public information on beta versions of Windows NT 5. It is possible that some of this information will have changed when Windows NT 5 is released.

SQL Server Enterprise Manager is the first major application to use the MMC to host its main user interface, but it won't be the last. Microsoft has been widely previewing Windows NT 5, which uses MMC for all computer management applications. There are several attractive features to this approach. First, once you learn how one management application works, you have a good idea how all the others work. Second, you can take advantage of MMC's customizability to put together your own custom management interface. Each application that can be used with MMC delivers one or more installable interfaces called *snap-ins*.

For example, suppose you are responsible for managing a Windows NT installation that includes Microsoft SQL Server and Microsoft Transaction Server. You'd also like to keep track of the computer's overall activity. Rather than run three different management applications, you can customize your own user interface by following these steps.

1. From the Start Menu, choose Run and then enter the command line **mmc /a**. This will open a new blank instance of the MMC.
2. Choose Console ➢ Add/Remove Snap-In, from the MMC menus.
3. Click the Add button in the Add/Remove Snap-In dialog box. This will open the Add Standalone Snap-In dialog box, which includes all of the snap-ins installed on your computer.
4. Choose Computer Manager, Microsoft SQL Enterprise Manager, and Microsoft Transaction Server from the list of snap-ins.
5. Click Close and then OK to dismiss the dialog boxes.

Figure 8.6 shows the completed custom console.

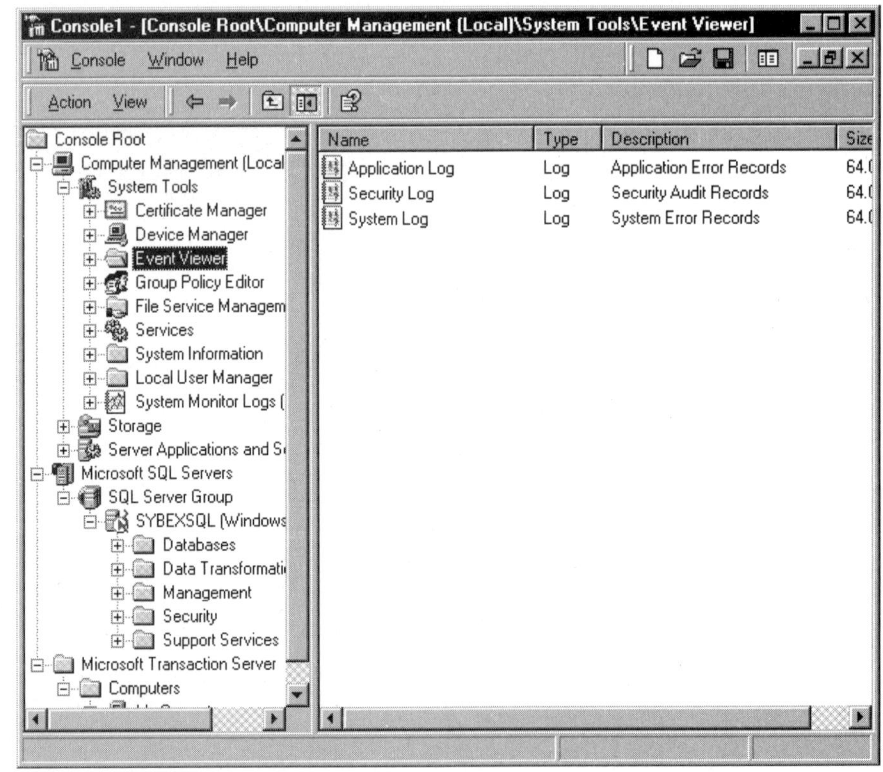

FIGURE 8.6: Managing multiple applications simultaneously

Database Diagrams

SQL Server Enterprise Manager is also the host for some data management tools. One of these is the Database Diagram, which is a window that not only shows the structure of your database, but actually allows you to modify that structure interactively. The Database Diagram thus functions as a sort of entity-relationship design tool within the confines of SQL Server Enterprise Manager.

TIP Database Diagrams are a part of the Microsoft Visual Data Tools. These tools are also hosted by both Microsoft Visual Studio and Microsoft Office 2000. Experience gained in any one of these hosts will help you work within the others.

To create a new database diagram, expand the database you're working with and then right-click the Diagrams node and choose New Database Diagram. This will open the Create Database Diagram Wizard. This wizard will prompt you to choose the tables that you'd like to work with. Optionally, it will automatically add related tables to the diagram for you. The wizard will also do its best to arrange the diagram in a sensible manner. Figure 8.7 shows part of a database diagram created from the sample Northwind database.

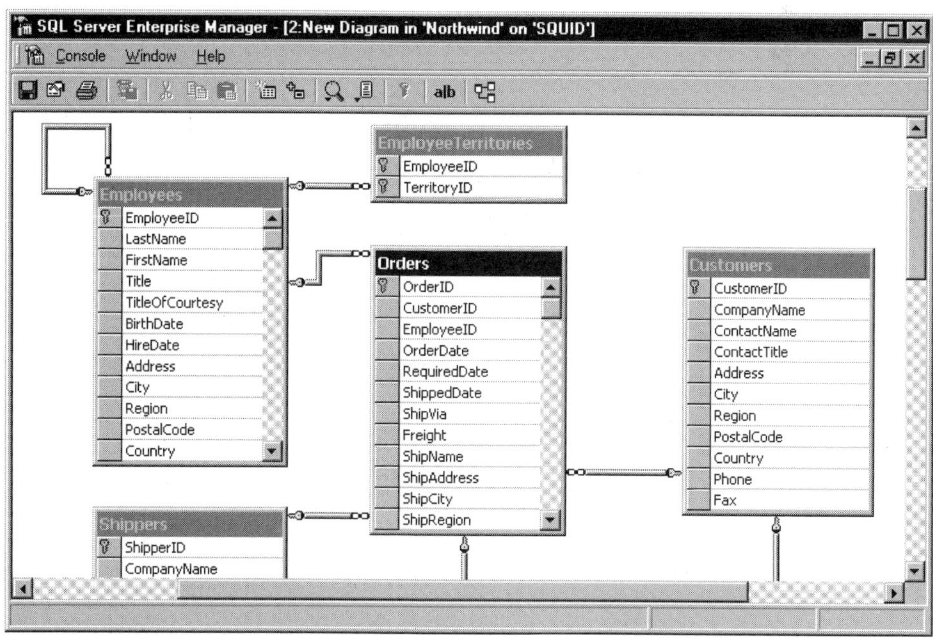

FIGURE 8.7: A database diagram

By default, tables are displayed with only the names of fields showing, and with little key symbols marking the fields in the primary key. By right-clicking a table in the diagram, you can choose any of five different views. These views can be chosen independently for each table, so you can choose to focus on only the tables that are important to you at the moment:

Column Properties shows you the entire set of design properties for every field in the table and lets you modify them, as well.

Column Names is the default view.

Keys shrinks the view by only showing fields that are primary keys or foreign keys.

Name Only hides all the fields in the table. This view is useful if you're trying to get an overview of the database's structure.

Custom displays field names and a few important properties. By default, Custom displays column name, data type, and nullability, but you can modify this by selecting other properties to display.

The database diagram also displays relationships that are enforced between tables with Declarative Referential Integrity (DRI). Primary keys are indicated by a yellow key symbol, while foreign keys are indicated by the infinity symbol. The line from Employees to itself in Figure 8.7 indicates a self-join. For more information on DRI, see Skill 4, *Organizing and Normalizing Data*.

You can perform a wide variety of table and relationship design chores from directly within a database diagram. Indeed, if you like, almost all design work can be done here rather than with SQL statements.

To create a new relationship within a database diagram, use the mouse to drag the primary key from one table and drop it on the foreign key field in the other table. This will open the Create Relationship dialog box shown in Figure 8.8. You can also delete a relationship from the database by right-clicking the relationship line and choosing Delete Relationship From Database.

There are also many table design tasks that can be performed by right-clicking a table in a database diagram. These include:

- Insert a new column into the table.
- Delete a column from the table.

- Delete a table from the diagram (this does not remove it from the database).
- Delete a table from the database.
- Modify other table properties, including constraints and indexes.

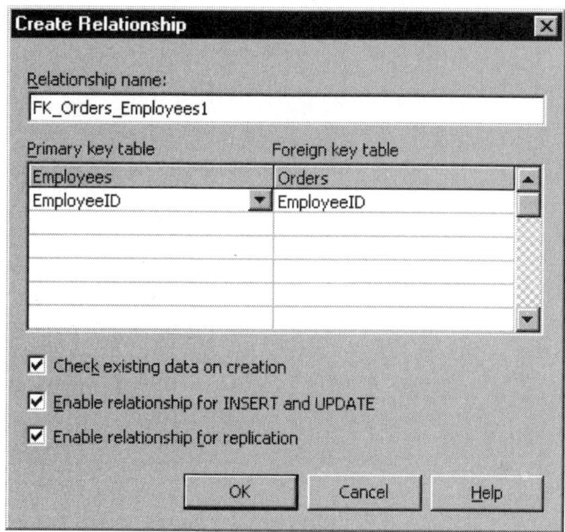

FIGURE 8.8: Adding a new relationship to a database

Finally, you can make field-level changes to a table by choosing to display it in Column Properties or Custom view. You can change almost any property here, including such things as column name, nullability, and data type.

When you choose to save a database diagram, SQL Server Enterprise Manager offers you a chance to decide whether to save your changes by displaying the dialog box shown in Figure 8.9. If you choose Yes, all of your changes are written back to the database. If you choose No, all of your changes are discarded. If you're not sure about the changes, you can also have the database diagram save a *change script*, a set of SQL statements that will apply the proposed changes.

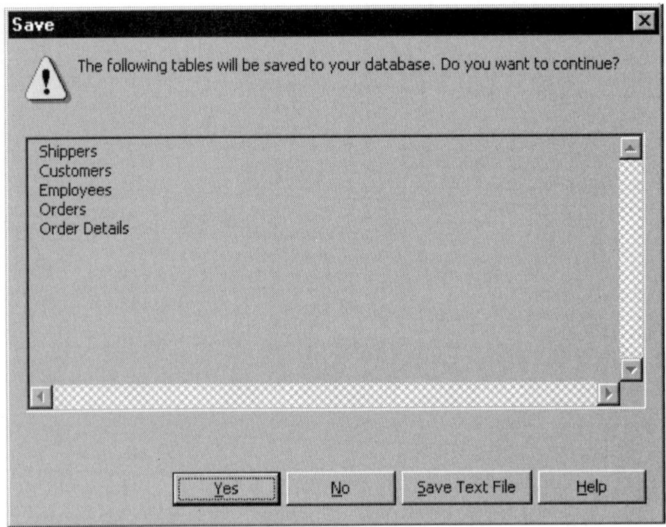

FIGURE 8.9: Save confirmation dialog box

Query Tools

Another of the Visual Data Tools that's hosted in SQL Server Enterprise Manager is the View Designer. To use the designer, right-click the Views node of any database and choose New View. This opens a blank view window, as shown in Figure 8.10. The four panes, from top to bottom, are used to show the following:

- The source tables for the view
- The columns displayed in the view
- The SQL statement for the view
- The data retrieved by the view

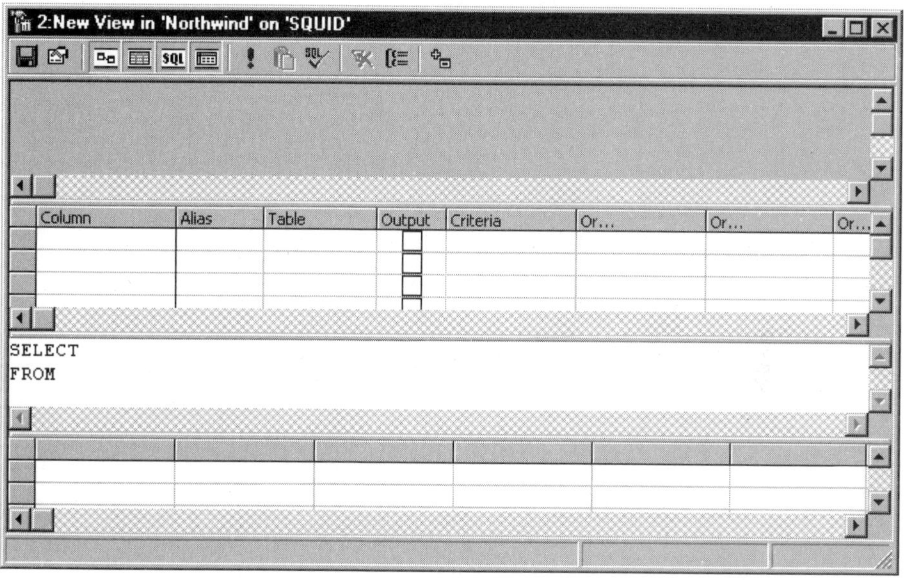

FIGURE 8.10: Blank View Designer

To design a new view, click the Add Table button in the View Designer toolbar and choose the tables (or other views) that are the base tables for your view. The View Designer will automatically draw join lines between the tables if you've used DRI within your database. Next, drag columns from the tables in the top pane and drop them on the field list in the second pane. As an alternative, you can just check the fields you want in the top pane and they'll automatically appear in the second pane.

You can use the Criteria columns in the second pane to implement a `WHERE` clause for your view. Or you can edit the `WHERE` clause directly into the third pane of the View Designer. When you're done designing the view, click the Run button in the toolbar to see the data retrieved to the fourth pane. Figure 8.11 shows an example of a completed view.

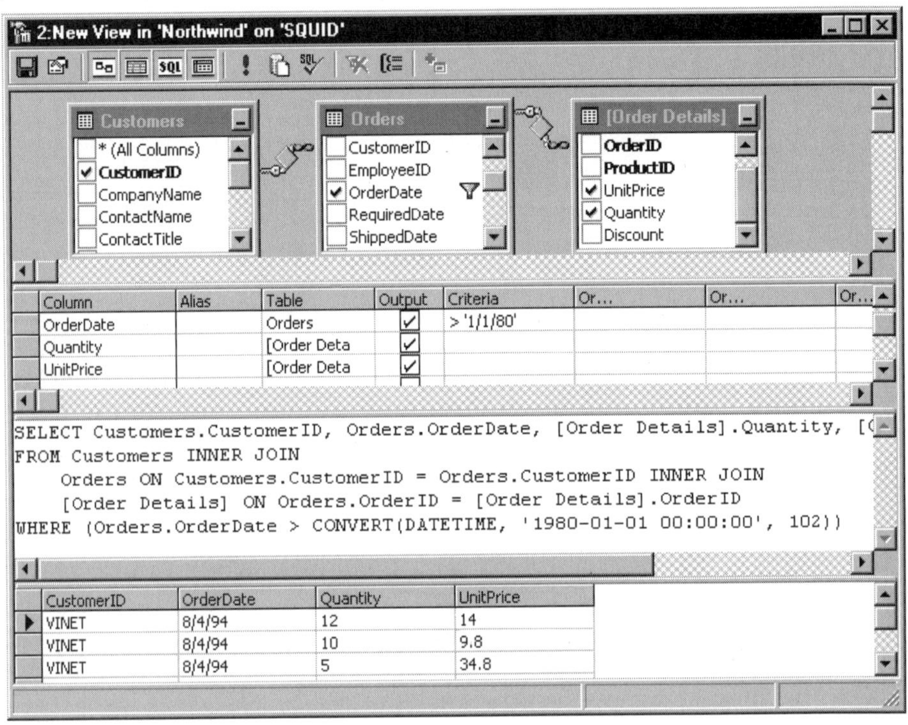

FIGURE 8.11: A finished view

Although the View Designer is similar to the Query Designer that Microsoft Access has had for years, it is not exactly the same. Still, if you've used Access in the past for client-side querying, you'll feel right at home with this tool.

Query Analyzer

We briefly discussed Query Analyzer in Skill 6, *Retrieving Data*. You can launch Query Analyzer by selecting it from the Microsoft SQL Server 7 group in the Start menu. Now it's time to look at a few of the features that Query Analyzer brings to the product other than just executing SQL statements.

Connection Options

Figure 8.12 shows the General tab of the Connection Options dialog box. You can open this dialog box by clicking the Current Connection Options toolbar button in any query window, or by choosing Query ➢ Current Connection Options from the menu. Some of these options you're not likely to need to change; for example, returning system messages in Croatian is likely to be of little use to most readers of this book. However, you should be aware of these options:

No Count Display turns off the line that displays the number of records retrieved when you execute a query.

Parse Query Only will check the query for syntax errors without actually executing it on the server.

Show Query Plan will generate a text version of the query execution plan instead of a results set. You won't need this for ad hoc query analysis, but it's easier to save to a file than the new Graphical Showplan.

Show Stats Time and Show Stats I/O generate detailed information about the load that a particular query generates on your server.

Row Count allows you to specify a maximum number of rows that should be returned. This can be helpful when you're testing new queries against a production server.

Query Timeout allows you to limit the amount of time that Query Analyzer will wait for data to be returned from the server.

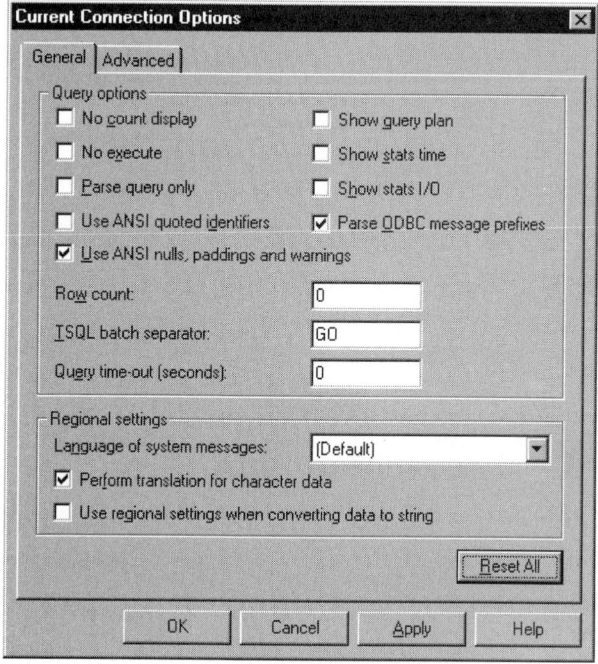

FIGURE 8.12: Query Analyzer Connection Options

Results Formats

At its simplest, Query Analyzer is easy to use. Just type a SQL statement into the window and press the Execute button (or F5 or Ctrl-E) to view its results. However, there are a few extra tricks here that you should know about. First, you can choose whether to display the results in text form or in grid form by selecting from the Current Mode toolbar button drop-down list. Text mode is the default. Figure 8.13 shows a query with its results in grid mode. If you execute a query to grid mode, you can hold down the Shift key and drag the mouse over it to copy any rectangular region of the results to the Windows clipboard.

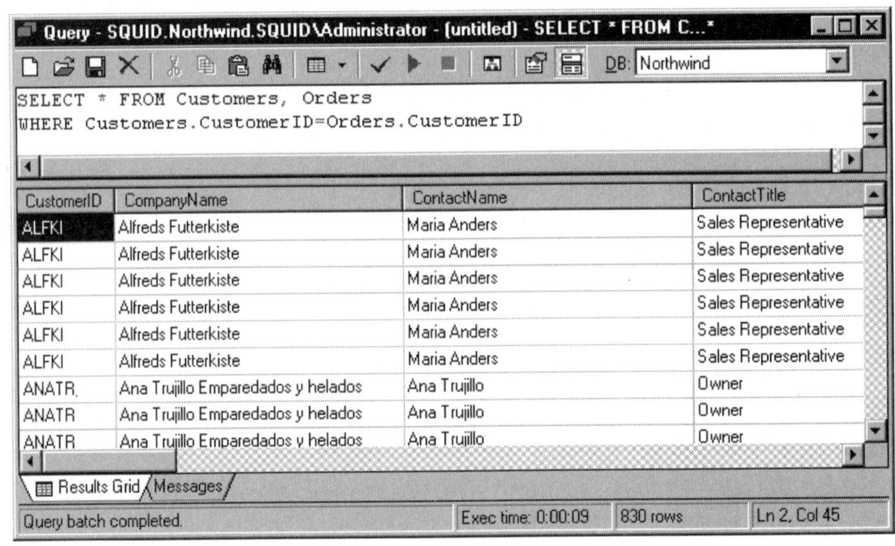

FIGURE 8.13: Query results in grid mode

Query Analyzer can also execute entire batches at one time, with SQL Statements separated by the `GO` keyword. If you have a batch loaded and would like to execute only part of it, use the mouse to highlight just that part and then press F5.

Execution Plans

Query Analyzer also includes the ability to graphically analyze the *execution plan* for a query. Whenever you submit a query to SQL Server for execution, it develops an internal list of the steps that it will carry out to retrieve the requested data. This list is known as the query's execution plan. You can use Query Analyzer to generate a graphical representation of this plan. A sample execution plan for a rather simple query is shown in Figure 8.14.

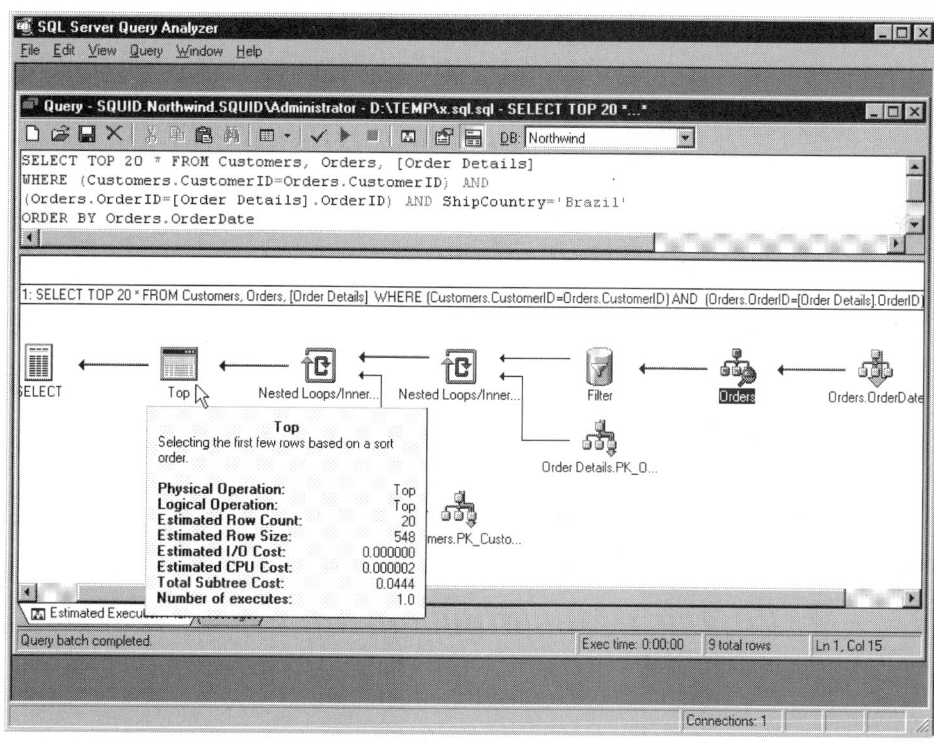

FIGURE 8.14: Execution plan in Query Analyzer

NOTE Learning how to analyze execution plans in detail is beyond the scope of this book. However, you should at least understand some of the basic principles involved. For more information on execution plans see one of Sybex's Developer's Handbooks.

Each step in the execution plan has both a logical and a physical component. The logical step describes what SQL Server will do, and the physical step includes details about how the logical step will be performed.

The execution plan reads generally right to left. As you can see in the sample, it may involve multiple threads of operation. If SQL Server is running on a computer with more than one CPU, it will actually parcel these threads out to the various CPUs automatically.

Each logical step is shown on the diagram with its own icon. For example, the query shown in Figure 8.14 starts out by performing scans or seeks on the indexes of the three tables involved. Intervening operations include filtering rows and using a nested loop to perform an inner join.

If you hover the cursor over any one of the logical steps, you can see the physical work involved in that step. In Figure 8.14, you can see how long the server estimates that it will take to retrieve the desired top 20 rows from the entire result set of 548 rows.

If you're responsible for identifying bottlenecks on your server, you'll find that analyzing execution plans is a very powerful tool.

Client Network Utility

Even though its name says Client, you can launch this utility by choosing Start ➢ Programs ➢ Microsoft SQL Server 7 ➢ Client Network Utility on the server as well as on any client where you've installed the SQL Server Client utilities. If you run it on the server, you're changing the means by which utilities such as SQL Enterprise Manager communicate with the rest of the server. If you run it on a client, you're changing the way in which that client communicates with servers.

The Client Network Utility is used to select a network library. You can think of the network library as the language that the server speaks to the clients. Both the server and the client must be speaking the same language for them to communicate. For the most part, you should be able to avoid using this utility. By default, SQL Server sets up the server and any clients to use Named Pipes as the network protocol, which has been SQL Server's standard library for many years

However, because they're useful in specific circumstances, you should know what libraries you can choose with this utility.

Here are the Libraries available with this utility:

- Named Pipes is the SQL Server default library. However, Named Pipes is not fully supported for SQL Servers running on Windows 95 (the servers will not broadcast their existence to the network). If your server is installed on Windows 95, you'll probably want to add another library besides Named Pipes.
- TCP/IP Sockets provides support for just about any operating system that can run TCP/IP. Of course, you should test carefully if you're using a non-Microsoft operating system to run your clients.
- The MultiProtocol net library is designed to make configuring clients as easy as possible. MultiProtocol clients will try multiple low-level network protocols, including IPX/SPX, TCP/IP, and Named Pipes, until it finds one that talks to the server. If you're having trouble with Named Pipes, try the MultiProtocol net library.
- NWLink IPX/SPX provides an implementation of the native protocol used by Netware networks. It's a good choice if your organization uses Netware servers to run its network.
- AppleTalk is designed for Apple-based networks.
- Vines is designed for Banyan networks.

To install any of these protocols, choose the Add button on the Client Network Utility. This will bring up the dialog box shown in Figure 8.15. Choose the network library you want to add, assign a name for the server, and click OK.

TIP

The Network Libraries tab of the Client Network Utility lists all of the installed libraries together with their version numbers. This can be extremely useful when you're troubleshooting communications problems. One of the first things to check is that the server and client are both running the same version of the same network library.

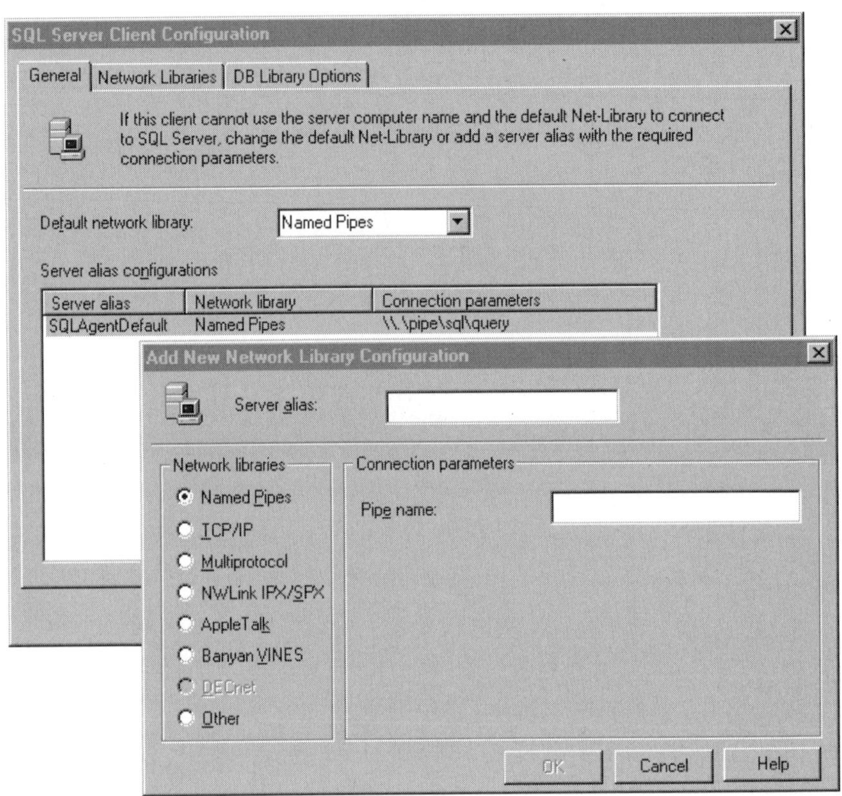

FIGURE 8.15: Installing network libraries

MS DTC Administrative Console

MS DTC is the Microsoft Distributed Transaction Coordinator. This is a software service that manages transactions spread across multiple servers. (For a review of transactions, see Skill 1, *Evaluating SQL Server*.) We'll cover MS DTC briefly in Skill 13, *Programming SQL Server*. You'll find that the MS DTC Administrative Console, shown in Figure 8.16, is your chief tool for monitoring the work of the MS DTC.

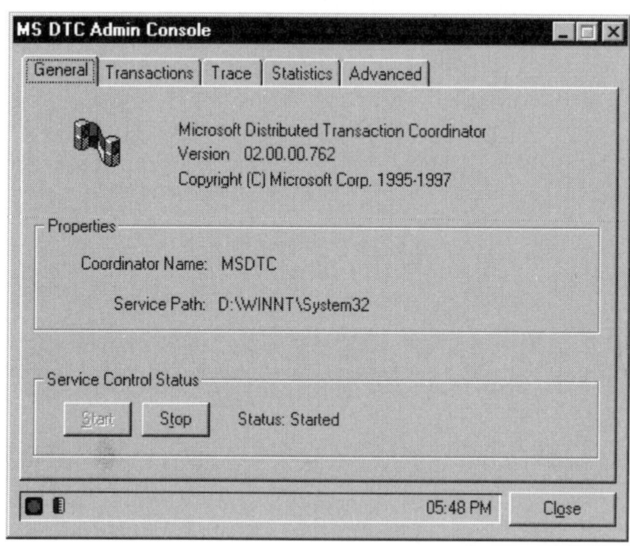

FIGURE 8.16: MS DTC Administrative Console

SQL Server Profiler

SQL Server Profiler is a tool for snooping on your server. When things are running well, you need not be concerned with the details of how SQL Server is talking to its clients. But when there's a problem, you may need to see the actual traffic between client and server, rather than just queries and their results. You can think of SQL Server Profiler as an interception utility. It interposes itself between client and server, passing on all of their traffic but keeping a copy that you can analyze.

To start using SQL Server Profiler, choose Start ➢ Programs ➢ Microsoft SQL Server 7 ➢ Profiler. This will open a blank Profiler session. Next, you need to define a new trace by choosing File ➢ New ➢ Trace. A trace is a way to filter the events that the Profiler captures. If you don't do any filtering, you'll see every single communication your server sends or receives, which on a busy server would be completely overwhelming.

Let's look at the trace options in some detail, since they're the most critical part of making sure you get the information that you need to solve a problem. There are four tabs on the Trace Properties dialog box. Figure 8.17 shows the General tab for a new trace we're in the process of defining. Every trace has to have a name that you can use to refer to it. Since SQL Server 7 is designed to be a distributed system, you can pick any server you can administer to trace; here we're choosing the default local server. Note that you can also save the entire trace to either a file or a database table for later analysis. You might want to save a trace to a table to use a querying tool to see which tables are most frequently accessed, for example.

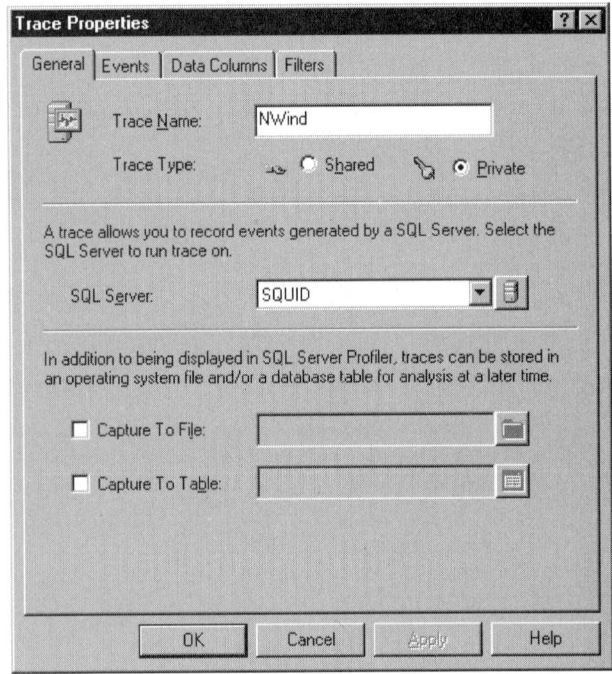

FIGURE 8.17: General trace options

Trace files can get very large in a very short time. If you're unsure how much traffic you're tracing, you should profile it to screen and make sure the amount is reasonable before you choose to save it. You can always open a trace and make changes to it by clicking the Properties icon in the trace window.

The Events tab (shown in Figure 8.18) is used to define precisely what to listen for. In this case, we've left the default events chosen. These will show you clients connecting and disconnecting and provide a broad overview of their activities. However, by choosing additional events from the Available Events list, you can tailor a trace to listen for very specific problems. For example, if you're having a problem with deadlocks on your server, you can expand the Locks node and choose Lock: Deadlock as one of the events to trace.

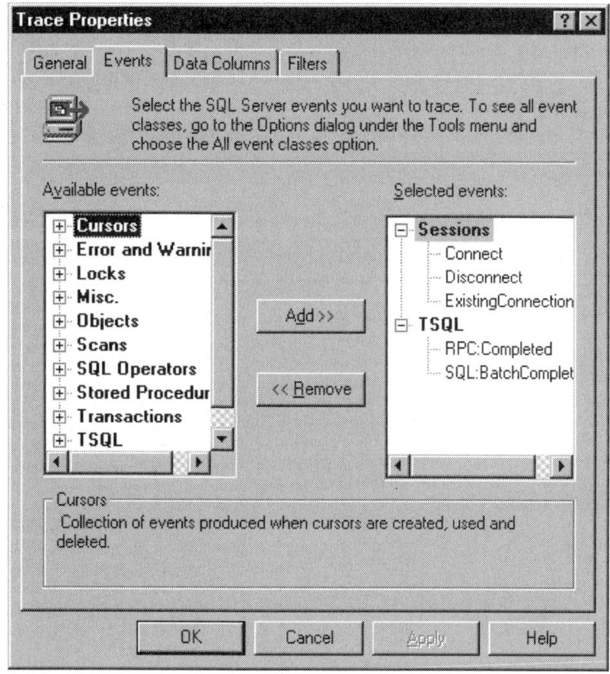

FIGURE 8.18: Events trace options

You should, of course, be cautious when choosing events to trace. If you select all the available events, you'll be buried in a large pile of mostly meaningless details very quickly.

Figure 8.19 shows the Data Columns tab of the Trace Properties dialog box. Once again, you should probably start by leaving the options at their default values. Occasionally, you may need to add extra information to be recorded for every captured event. For example, if you're having locking problems, the Data Columns tab can be useful to capture the Object ID for comparison with log entries and other information you can see in SQL Server Enterprise Manager.

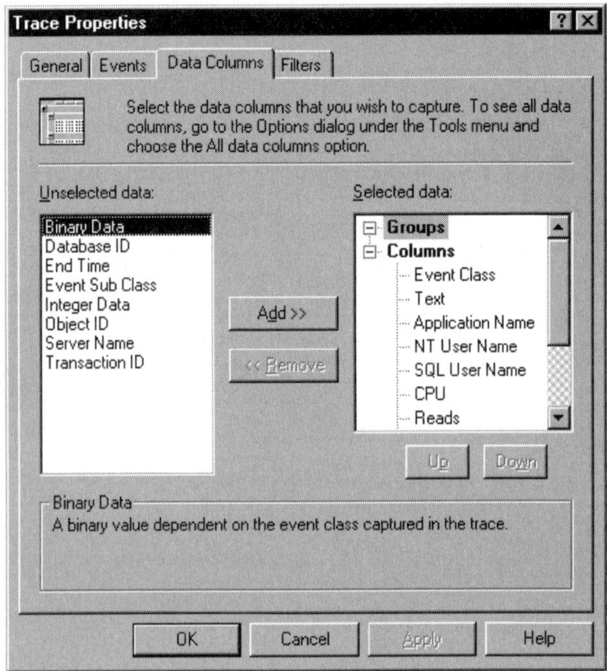

FIGURE 8.19: Data Columns trace options

The Filters tab (shown in Figure 8.20) is the most important one for cutting down the amount of information in a trace. You can choose to include or exclude events based on these criteria:

- Application name supplied by the client
- SQL Server Connection ID
- Amount of CPU time taken to process the event
- SQL Server Database ID
- Amount of clock time taken to process the event
- NT username supplied by the client
- SQL Server Object ID
- Number of logical reads required to process the event

- Server name
- SQL Server Process ID
- SQL Server username supplied by the client
- Text contained in the event
- Number of physical writes required to process the event

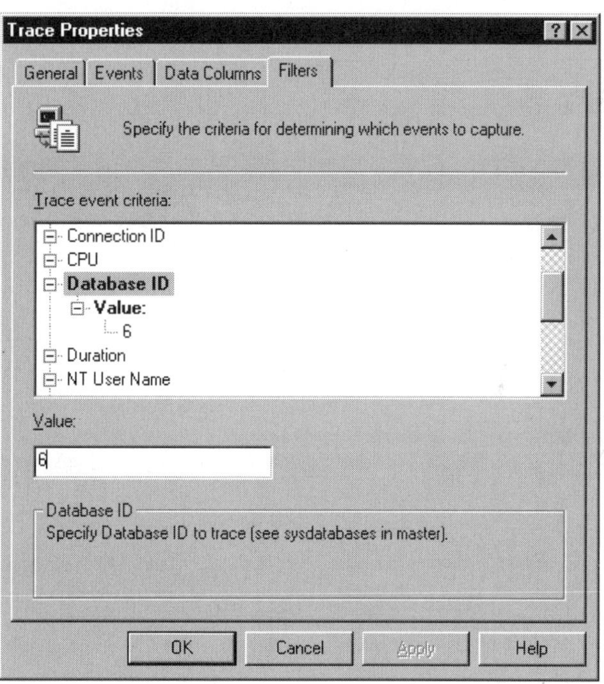

FIGURE 8.20: Filters trace options

So, given any clues as to the nature of a problem, you can use this tab to isolate just the events that you think might be involved. Perhaps a particular client is having trouble connecting or a particular long-running query is using too much CPU time. Here we've chosen to limit the trace to events affecting the Northwind database, identified by its database ID.

TIP

To determine the database IDs of databases on your server, execute the query `SELECT * FROM sysdatabases` on the master database in the server and check the dbid column.

Once you've defined the options for your trace, click OK and SQL Profiler will open a new window showing the results of that trace. Figure 8.21 shows some trace results from our Northwind trace. As you can see, SQL Profiler captures information about the events that we specified and shows a summary in the trace window. As new events are added, old ones scroll off the top. To see details of any particular event, just click that event. Here, the highlighted event shows a Microsoft Access client executing a stored procedure on the server to update a record.

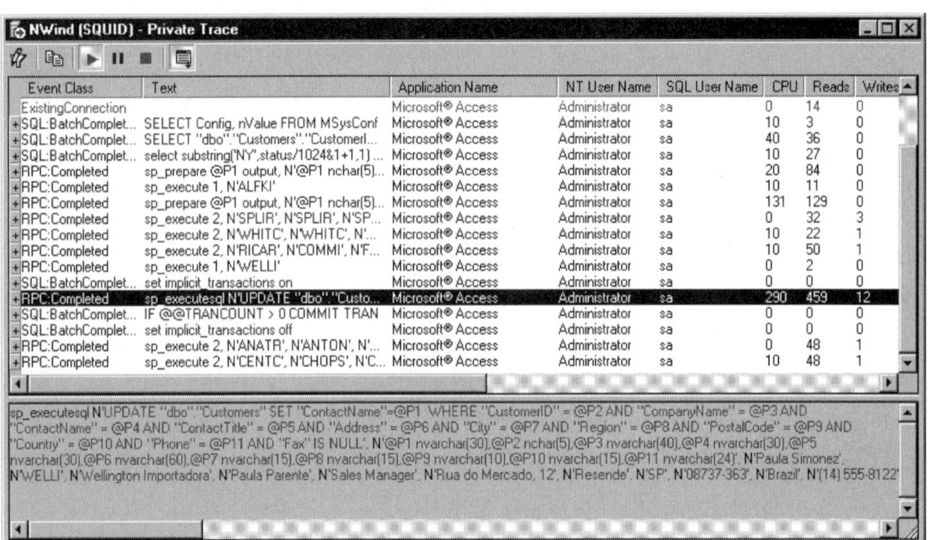

FIGURE 8.21: Trace results

Although SQL Profiler's basic task is to capture information, it also has a number of other functions. Using the SQL Profiler menus, you can perform these tasks:

- Save traces so that they can be reloaded later. This saves the trace definition, not the data.

- Start, stop, or pause traces already loaded.
- Open multiple traces at one time. Be careful, though, as tracing too many events could have a significant performance impact on the server.
- Save a trace to a database table or a file, even if that wasn't turned on in the trace options.
- Open a saved trace file or database table.
- Replay a trace. This powerful tool lets you capture events from a production server and replay them on a development server so you can analyze their effects at your leisure.
- Create and immediately run Transact-SQL Scripts.

For more information on these and other details of SQL Profiler, see the SQL Profiler online help.

SQL Server Performance Monitor

SQL Server Performance Monitor is really just Windows NT's own built-in Performance Monitor with some extensions added by SQL Server. Windows NT Performance Monitor is a tool that can keep track of objects and counters within the Windows NT operating system. When you start the SQL Server version of Performance Monitor by choosing Start ➢ Programs ➢ Microsoft SQL Server 7 ➢ Performance Monitor, you will see a window like the one shown in Figure 8.22.

Performance Monitor can display graphs like the one shown in the figure to help you get a sense of server activity. It can also be configured to trigger alerts. For example, if SQL Server starts consuming too much memory, you could run a program to e-mail an operator to come and look at the problem. Performance Monitor will also save its results in report form for later analysis.

Performance Monitor was designed as an extensible application, so that any other application on the system can add its own counters to be monitored. SQL Server adds a large number of objects and counters. These are summarized in Table 8.1.

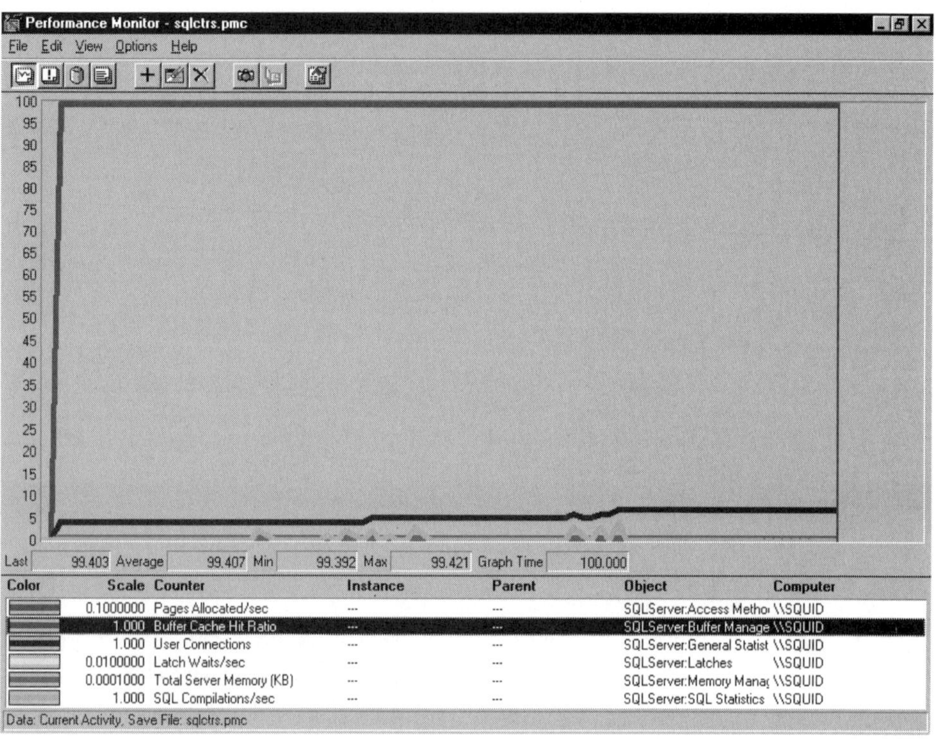

FIGURE 8.22: Performance Monitor in action

TABLE 8.1: SQL Server Objects

Object	Explanation
Access Methods	Tracks SQL Server disk activity
Backup Device	Tracks backup performance
Buffer Manager	Tracks whether requested data is in memory
Cache Manager	Tracks efficiency of object caching
Databases	Tracks gross database operations
General Statistics	Tracks logins and logouts
Latches	Tracks latch responsiveness
Locks	Tracks locks and deadlocks

TABLE 8.1 CONTINUED: SQL Server Objects

Object	Explanation
Memory Manager	Tracks SQL Server memory usage
Replication Agents	Tracks number of replication agents running
Replication Dist.	Tracks efficiency of replication distribution tasks
Replication Logreader	Tracks efficiency of replication logreader tasks
Replication Merge	Tracks efficiency of replication merge tasks
Replication Snapshot	Tracks efficiency of replication snapshot tasks
SQL Statistics	Tracks overall use of the SQL parser
User Settable	Tracks counters defined by the database administrator

For a detailed explanation of any of the counters provided by these objects, open Performance Monitor and select Edit ➢ Add to Chart. Select the counter that you'd like information on, click the Explain button, and you'll see a summary of this counter within the Add to Chart dialog box, as shown in Figure 8.23.

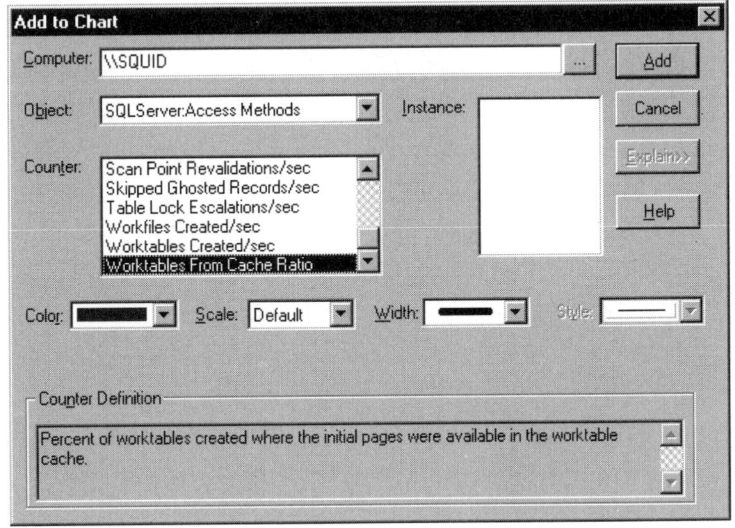

FIGURE 8.23: Retrieving information on a counter

Command-Line Tools

In addition to the Windows-based tools we've already seen, SQL Server 7 still ships with some command-line tools. Most of these are holdovers from previous versions, but they can still be useful in specific circumstances. These tools include:

- The osql and isql utilities.
- The makepipe and readpipe utilities.
- The Bulk Copy Program (bcp).

We've already discussed bcp in Skill 5, *Moving Data*. The other command-line utilities are briefly reviewed in this section. In addition, we'll look at starting SQL Server from a command prompt.

The osql and isql Utilities

Osql and isql are a pair of utilities designed to allow you to submit SQL Server queries directly from a Windows command prompt. Isql has shipped with previous versions of SQL Server, while osql is new in this version. Isql uses the old DB-Library API to communicate with the server. Osql uses the newer ODBC API. What this means is that osql can retrieve some information that isql cannot, since DB-Library was not upgraded for SQL Server 7. In particular, isql cannot retrieve data from `ntext` columns, and it truncates `char`, `varchar`, `nchar`, and `nvarchar` columns after 255 bytes. Since the two utilities function in almost exactly the same way, we'll only cover osql in any detail here.

TIP Unless you have some legacy process that absolutely relies on isql, you should use osql instead.

Figure 8.24 shows a short osql session in action. The `osql -Usa` command starts the session and attempts to login to the server as the user named sa. The numbered prompts are supplied by osql. As you can see, you can use any Transact-SQL syntax you like within an osql session. There's no special formatting on the results, which makes them ideal for capture to a file that can be processed by other utilities.

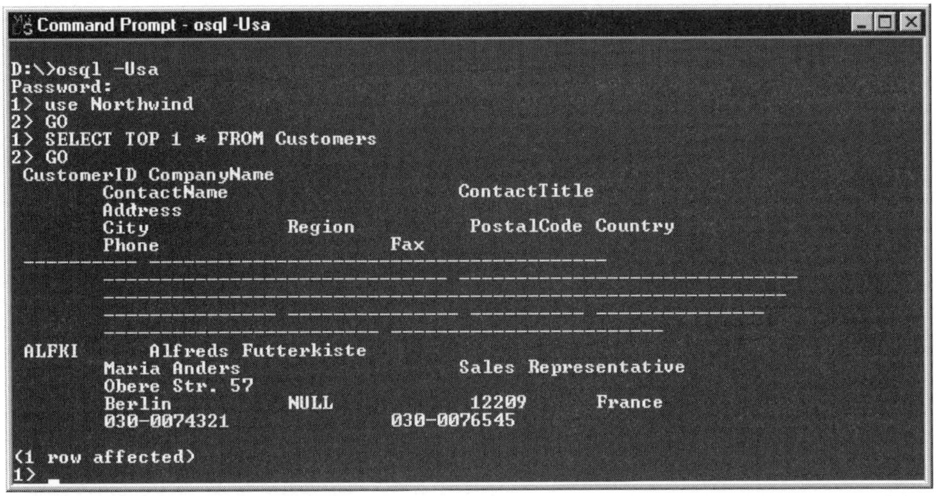

```
Command Prompt - osql -Usa

D:\>osql -Usa
Password:
1> use Northwind
2> GO
1> SELECT TOP 1 * FROM Customers
2> GO
 CustomerID CompanyName
        ContactName                     ContactTitle
        Address
        City            Region           PostalCode Country
        Phone                    Fax
 ---------- ----------------------------------------
        ------------------------------ ------------------------------
        ------------------------------------------------------------
        --------------- --------------- ---------- ---------------
        ------------------------ ------------------------
 ALFKI      Alfreds Futterkiste
        Maria Anders                    Sales Representative
        Obere Str. 57
        Berlin          NULL             12209      France
        030-0074321              030-0076545

(1 row affected)
1>
```

FIGURE 8.24: Simple osql session

Osql also takes a large number of command-line arguments. This helps make it useful in batch files. The full syntax for launching osql is as follows:

```
osql -U login_id [-e] [-E] [-p] [-n] [-d db_name] [-q "query"]
[-Q "query"]
[-c cmd_end] [-h headers] [-w column_width] [-s col_separator]
[-t time_out] [-m error_level] [-L] [-?] [-r {0 | 1}]
[-H wksta_name] [-P password] [-R]
[-S server_name] [-i input_file] [-o output_file] [-u] [-a packet_size]
[-b] [-O] [-l time_out]
```


Table 8.2 explains the various arguments available in this statement. These arguments are case-sensitive, so be careful!

TABLE 8.2: Arguments for osql

Argument	Meaning
-U	User login ID
-e	Echo all input to the screen
-E	Uses a trusted NT connection
-p	Print performance statistics
-n	Removes prompt from input lines

TABLE 8.2 CONTINUED: Arguments for osql

Argument	Meaning
-d	Uses the specified database as the default
-q	Executes the supplied query
-Q	Executes the supplied query and immediately exits osql
-c	Specifies a command terminator (GO is the default)
-h	Number of rows to print between column headers
-w	Specifies screen width in characters
-s	Column separator (blank space by default)
-t	Timeout in seconds
-m	Error level
-L	Lists available servers
-?	Displays a syntax summary
-r	Redirects messages to stderr
-H	Specifies workstation name to use
-P	Password
-R	Uses client settings for date, time, and currency output
-S	Server name
-i	Input file
-o	Output file
-u	Stores the output file in unicode
-a	Packet size
-b	Exits and returns DOS ERRORLEVEL on any error
-O	Matches isql behavior as closely as possible
-l	Login timeout

In addition to executing Transact-SQL statements, osql understands six special commands:

- `GO` executes all statements since the previous `GO`.
- `RESET` clears statements without executing them.

- `ED` invokes the DOS editor (yes, there still is one, even in Windows NT).
- `!!`*`command`* executes the specified operating system command.
- `QUIT` or `EXIT` ends the osql session.
- Ctrl+C ends a query and returns to the osql prompt.

The Makepipe and Readpipe Utilities

Makepipe and readpipe are a pair of very simple utilities with only one purpose: to help you diagnose Named Pipes connection problems. Since Named Pipes is the default net library for SQL Server, it's useful to at least know that these utilities exist. Typically, you would run makepipe on the server and readpipe on the client to establish that they're talking to one another correctly.

The makepipe syntax is:

```
makepipe [/h] [/w] [/p pipe_name]
```

The `/h` switch displays a help message. The `/w` switch specifies a delay between reads and writes; by default this is zero seconds. The `/p` switch specifies a pipe name. If you omit `/p`, the pipe name will be `abc`.

Readpipe has a few more switches. The full readpipe syntax is:

```
readpipe /Sserver_name /Dstring [/n] [/q] [/w] [/t] [/p pipe_name] [/h]
```

The readpipe switches are as follows:

- `/S` specifies the server name to query.
- `/D` specifies the data to write and read.
- `/n` specifies the number of iterations to test.
- `/q` queries the pipe for incoming data.
- `/w` specifies a number of seconds to pause between iterations.
- `/t` asks for a Transact SQL pipe.
- `/h` displays a help message.

Figure 8.25 shows both halves of a makepipe/readpipe session.

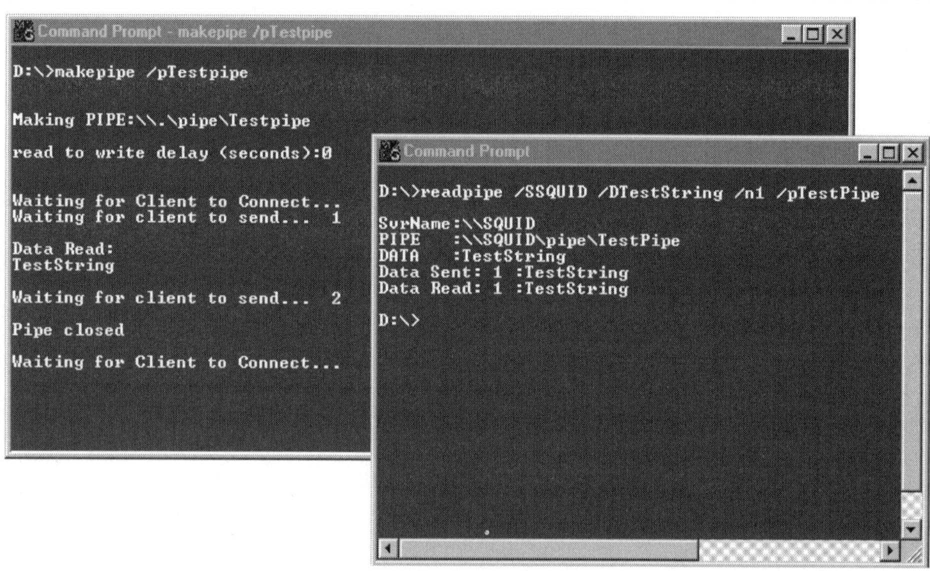

FIGURE 8.25: Using makepipe and readpipe

Starting SQL Server from the Command Line

Most SQL Server installations today are probably started as a Windows NT service when the computers that host them are rebooted. However, that's not the only way to launch SQL Server. There's also a command-line interface for running SQL Server. There are several reasons why you might want to use this interface. First, you might need to start the server with particular options for troubleshooting. Second, you might want the server to autostart on Windows 95, which does not have a services manager to do it for you. In this case, you can still autostart the server by putting a command-line in a batch file and adding the batch file to your Startup Group.

The command-line syntax for launching SQL Server is:

```
sqlservr [-c] [-dmaster_path] [-f] [-eerror_log_path]
 [-lmaster_log_path] [-m] [-n] [-pprecision_level]
 [-sregistry_key] [-Ttrace#] [-v] [-x]
```

Table 8.3 explains the various switches available on the command line.

TABLE 8.3: SQL Server Command-Line Switches

Switch	Meaning
`-c`	Starts SQL Server as a program rather than a service, even on Windows NT
`-d`	Fully qualified path to the master database
`-f`	Starts the Server in a minimal mode. This is useful if you've messed up its configuration and need to use `sp_configure` to fix things but are having trouble starting the server.
`-e`	Fully qualified path to the error log file
`-l`	Fully qualified path to the master transaction log file
`-m`	Starts SQL Server in single-user mode. Useful if you need to repair problems with the system database
`-n`	Don't log SQL Server events to the Windows NT Application Log. You should always specify `-e` if you specify `-n`.
`-s`	Specifies a registry key containing launch parameters
`-T`	Sets a trace flag. This is a debugging option that you may be asked to set by technical support.
`-v`	Displays the version number
`-x`	Disables maintaining CPU statistics

Microsoft English Query

Not everyone wants to learn the intricacies of Structured Query Language to retrieve information from a database. That's what impelled Microsoft to ship Microsoft English Query with SQL Server 7. Microsoft English Query is an application that allows your users to submit queries to a database in plain English. Of course, it's not magic. First, you have to use the Domain Editor to teach English Query about the structure of your database. Then you need to write an application to talk to English Query. But once you've done those two things, the end-user experience is a whole new way of retrieving data.

Although English Query ships with SQL Server, it's not a part of the core product and may not be widely deployed. This section is meant to give you an overview of its functionality rather than to provide a detailed tutorial, which could take a book of its own.

The Domain Editor

Figure 8.26 shows the English Query Domain Editor. The Files and Database tabs are relatively unimportant; they just give you a quick look at what English Query knows about and where it's stored. The real action is on the Semantics tab shown here. This is where you define the mapping between the formal structure of the database and the informal structure of the English language.

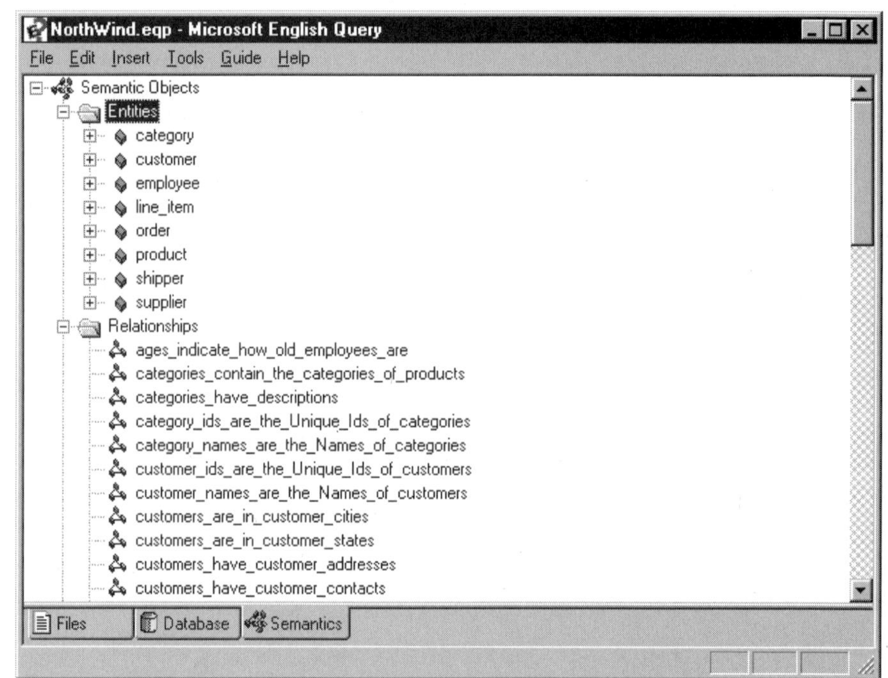

FIGURE 8.26: English Query Domain Editor

As you can see in the figure, the main things you have to define are entities and relationships. Entities are the things that your database contains, while relationships specify how those entities are related to one another.

Figure 8.27 shows a typical entity definition within the English Query domain editor. You can view any existing definition by double-clicking its node in the tree. In this case, we're looking at the definition for the `ShippedDate` field in the Orders table. The most important thing to note is that you can define synonyms for a field, so that people don't have to know the exact field name to ask questions of the database.

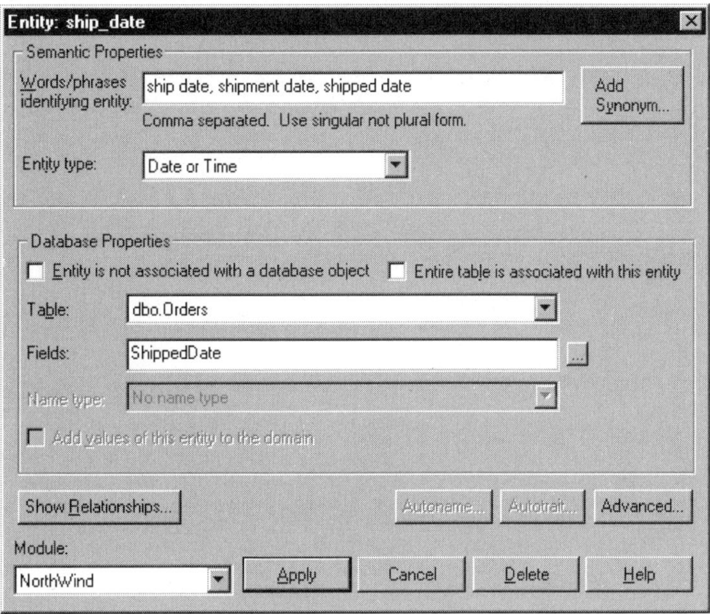

FIGURE 8.27: Entity definition in English Query

Also note that the `ship_date` entity is explicitly identified as a date. This helps English Query to do the right thing with words such as "yesterday" or "before" in user questions.

Although it would be tedious to define every entity and relationship using this dialog box, English Query offers some tools to help you build a new application from an existing database. First, select File ➢ New and choose to build a new project from an existing database. Supply an ODBC connection to that database, and English Query will go through it, retrieving the raw schema information. When this is finished, choose Guide ➢ Guided Application to launch the Guided Application Wizard.

The wizard starts by asking you for the names of three or four key entities in your database. You don't need to use actual table names or field names for this. For example, if you're building an English Query application based on the Northwind sample database, you might choose "customer, order, product, employee" as your key entities. Use singular words, not plurals, and separate entries with commas.

Next, the wizard asks you to pick an entity from the list you supplied and to choose a table that holds information on that entity. The wizard will also ask you for the plural form of the word, what type of questions are appropriate for this entity (see Figure 8.28), what fields to display when the entity is the answer to a question, and so forth. Once you've defined all of your entities this way, you can proceed through further steps in the wizard to define relationships.

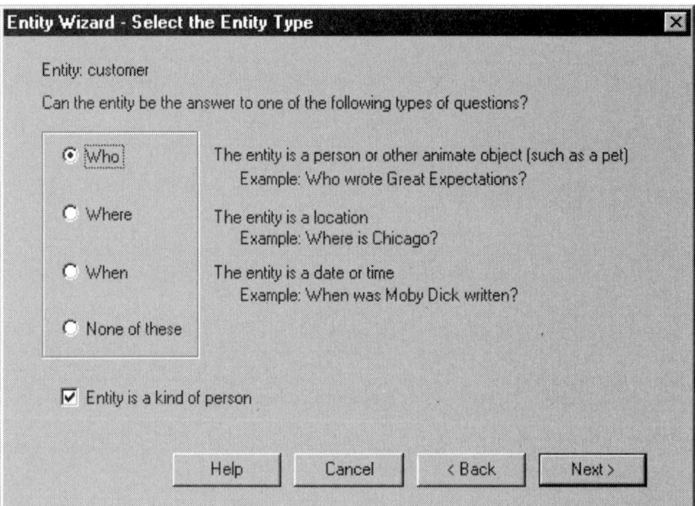

FIGURE 8.28: Defining an entity with the wizard

Retrieving Results from an Application

Once the structure of an English Query application is defined using the Domain Editor, you still have to provide users with a means to retrieve information from the application. English Query enables this by providing a COM server layer that can be used from any COM client application, including standalone applications or Active Server Pages on a Web server. Figure 8.29 shows a bit of a sample application (built using Visual Basic) that ships with English Query. In this case, it's retrieving some information from the pubs database. Although the question may look relatively complex, it's certainly easier for the average user to grasp than the SQL that English Query generates for it:

```
select #t001.title as "Title", #t001.pubdate as "Publication Date",
#t001.au_fname as "First Name", #t001.au_lname as "Last Name" from
#t001 where #t001.pubdate=(select min(t1.pubdate) from #t001 t1)
```

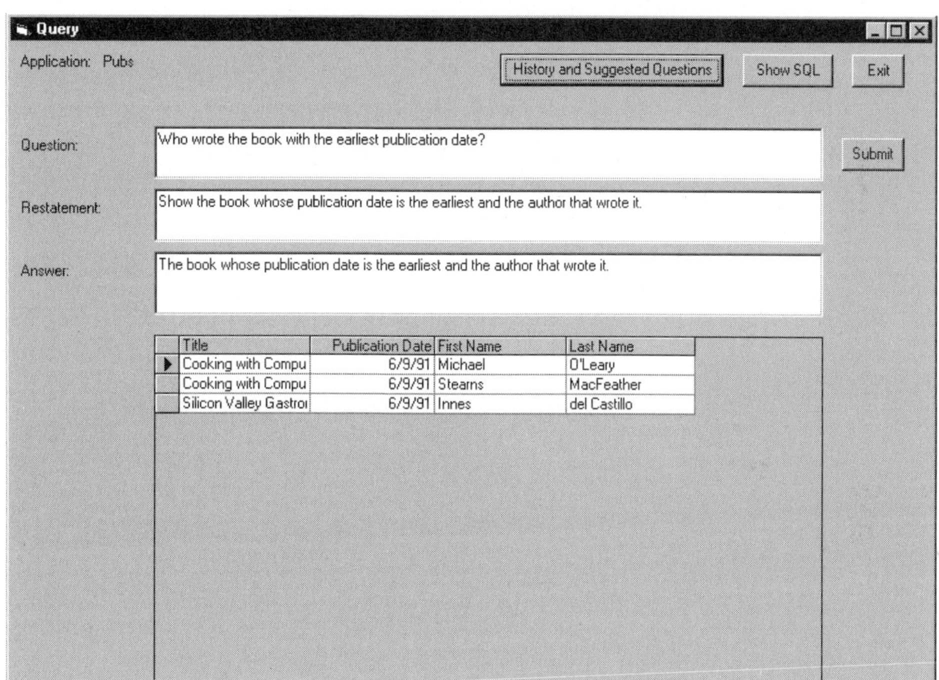

FIGURE 8.29: Retrieving data from English Query

For the details of the English Query object model, refer to the English Query documentation. You'll probably want to start with the `Session` object, which encapsulates most user communications with the parsing engine, and its `ParseRequest` method.

Are You up to Speed?

Now you can...

- ☑ use SQL Enterprise Manager to manage your SQL Server
- ☑ use MMC to manage multiple applications simultaneously
- ☑ create and manipulate database diagrams
- ☑ use the Visual Data Tools View Designer
- ☑ use Query Analyzer to view execution plans
- ☑ choose client and server network libraries
- ☑ monitor SQL Server activity with SQL Profiler and Performance Monitor
- ☑ execute queries with osql
- ☑ test pipes with makepipe and readpipe
- ☑ use Microsoft English Query to ask questions of your data

SKILL 9

Publishing SQL Server Data to the Web

- SQL Server Web Assistant
- Web stored procedures

It's easy to create HTML files using the new and improved SQL Server Web Assistant. It not only exports SQL Server data out to an HTML file, but it can also go the other way and import tabular data from an HTML file into SQL Server. In addition, it can post to and read from HTTP and FTP locations. In this skill you will learn how to:

- Use the SQL Server Web Assistant to publish data to the Web.
- Use the SQL Server Web stored procedures to publish data to the Web.

NOTE To learn how to publish data to the Internet using replication, see Skill 14, *Using Replication*.

The SQL Server Web Assistant

The SQL Server Web Assistant assists you in the task of generating HTML (Hypertext Markup Language) files from your SQL Server data. It is installed by default when you install SQL Server. It uses queries, stored procedures, and extended stored procedures to generate HTML pages. You can generate these pages one time only or as a regularly scheduled Web Assistant Job. Jobs can be scheduled to run dynamically when data changes or at regularly scheduled intervals.

Using the Web Assistant to Publish Data

To run the Web Assistant Wizard, choose Tools ➢ Wizards ➢ Management ➢ Web Assistant Wizard from the main console, or right-click the Web Assistant Jobs after expanding the Server folder and select New Web Assistant Job. This will load the wizard, as shown in Figure 9.1.

You then need to select the database that contains the data you want published. After that you must specify the name of the Web Assistant Job that the wizard will create for you, as shown in Figure 9.2. You also need to select whether the data will come from a table, from the result set of a stored procedure, or from a Transact-SQL statement. In this example, we'll select data from a table.

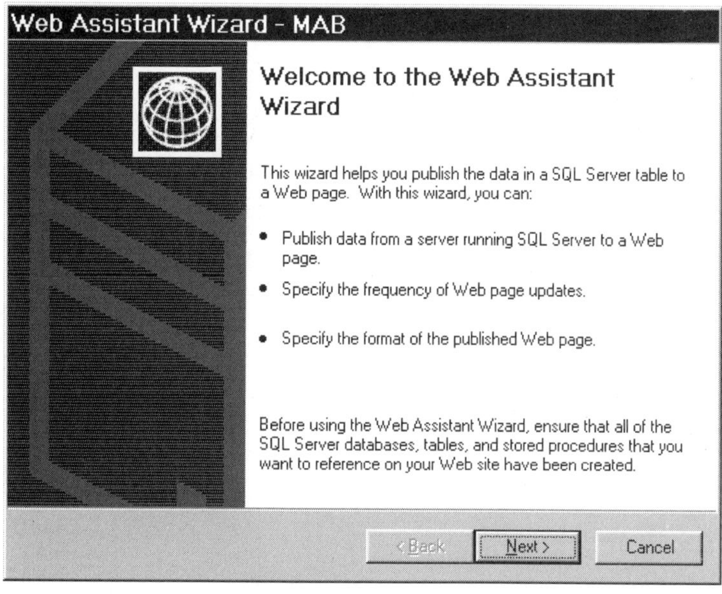

FIGURE 9.1: The opening dialog box for the Web Assistant Wizard

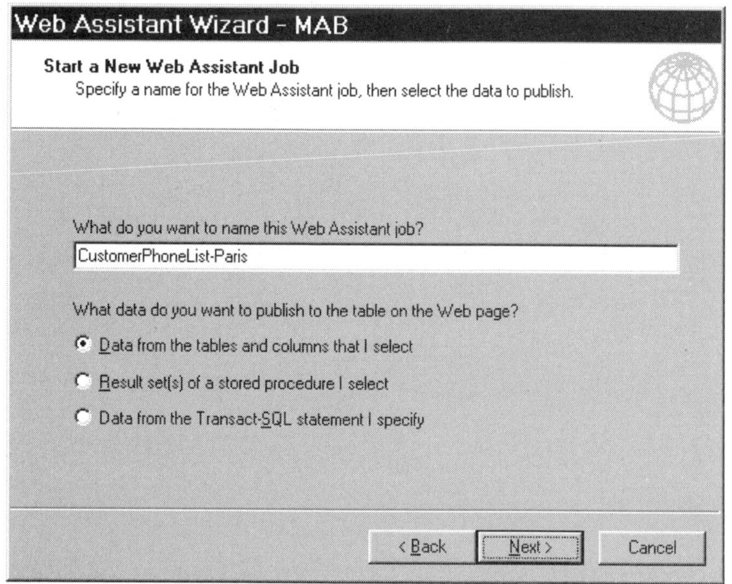

FIGURE 9.2: Selecting the Web Assistant task to be performed

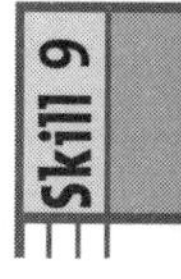

Figure 9.3 shows the dialog box used to select the table and columns to be displayed.

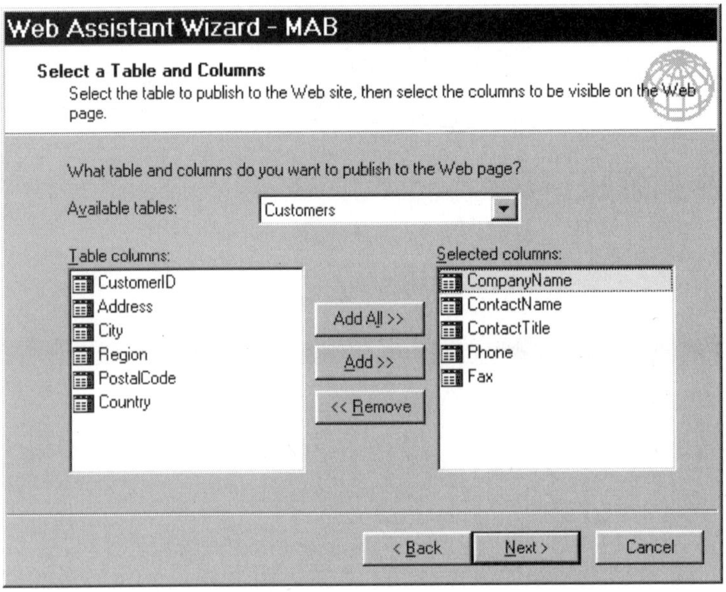

FIGURE 9.3: Selecting the table and columns to be displayed

You can then limit the rows displayed by specifying criteria or typing in a Transact-SQL `WHERE` clause, as shown in Figure 9.4. In this example, only customers living in Paris will be returned.

The next wizard screen allows you to schedule when the Web page is updated, as shown in Figure 9.5.

Your options for specifying when the Web page is generated include:

- Only once, when the wizard is completed
- On demand
- Only once, at a specified time
- When the data changes
- At regularly scheduled intervals

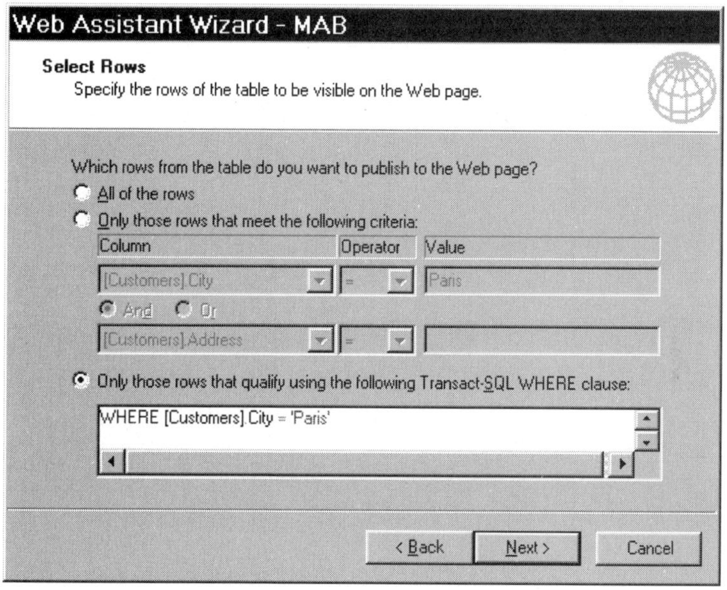

FIGURE 9.4: Specifying criteria to limit rows

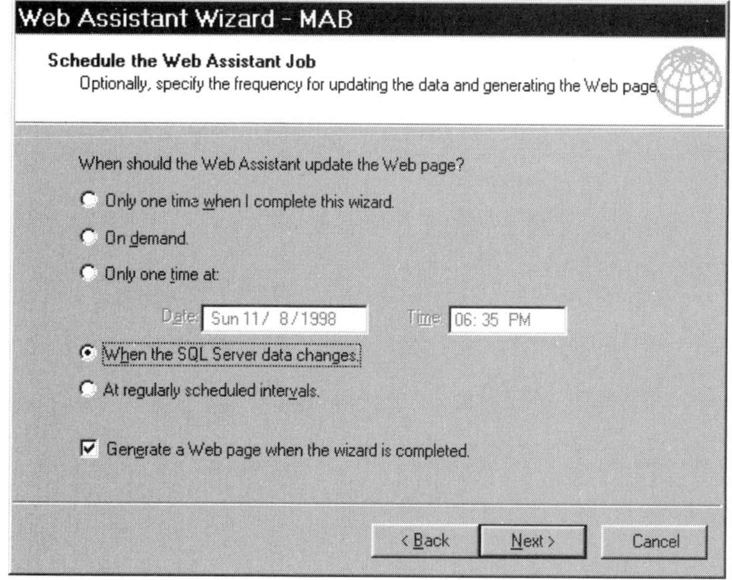

FIGURE 9.5: Scheduling when the Web page will be generated

If you've selected the option When The SQL Server Data Changes, you will then be prompted for the name of the table and the columns you want monitored, as shown in Figure 9.6.

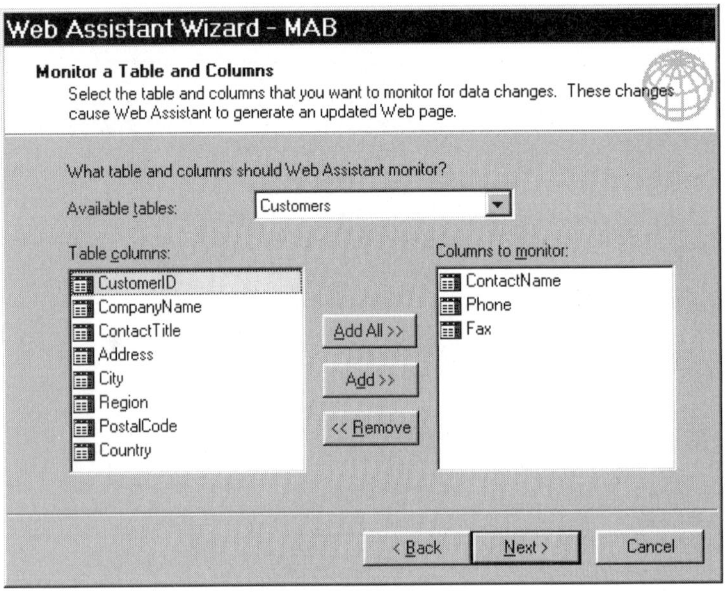

FIGURE 9.6: Selecting the table and columns to monitor

You then need to specify a path and filename where the Web page will be located, as shown in Figure 9.7. Make sure that it is a location that is accessible to the SQL Server.

You then have the option of using your own templates for the formatting of your HTML page or you can let the Web Assistant do it. You can also select the code page for the output, as shown in Figure 9.8.

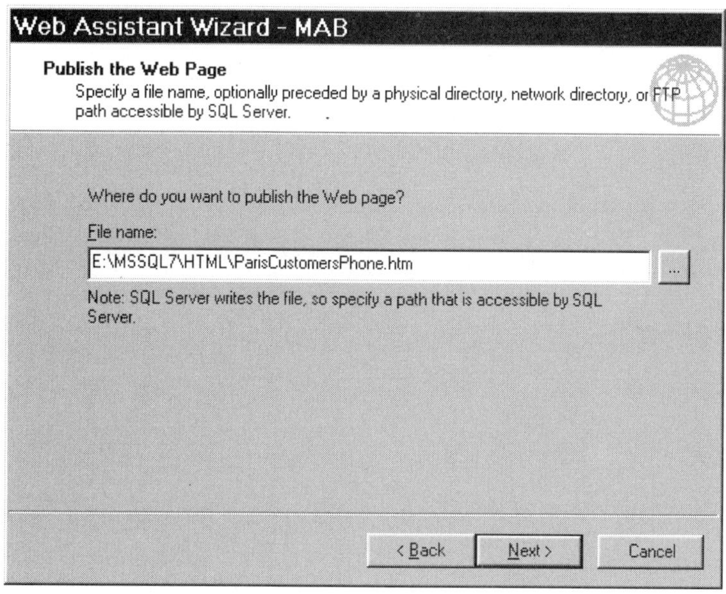

FIGURE 9.7: Specifying the Web filename and location

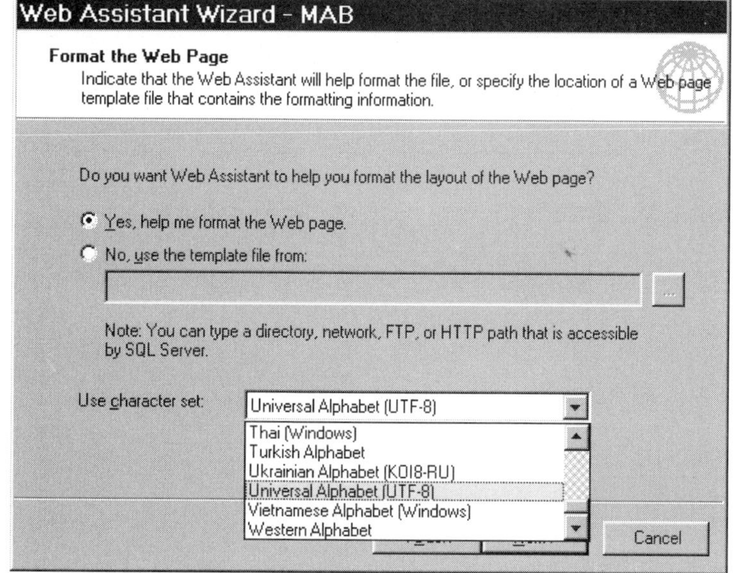

FIGURE 9.8: Formatting options for the HTML page

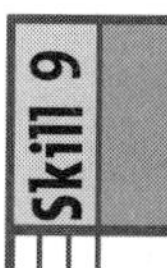

Figure 9.9 shows the remaining options for naming both the HTML page and the HTML table. You also have the option of choosing the font size for the title, which is the HTML page name. Your choices are Large, Larger, Largest, Medium, Smaller, Smallest. These are standard sizes that will be interpreted by the end-user's Web browser to make sense on their own platform. We've selected the timestamp option for the Web page as well.

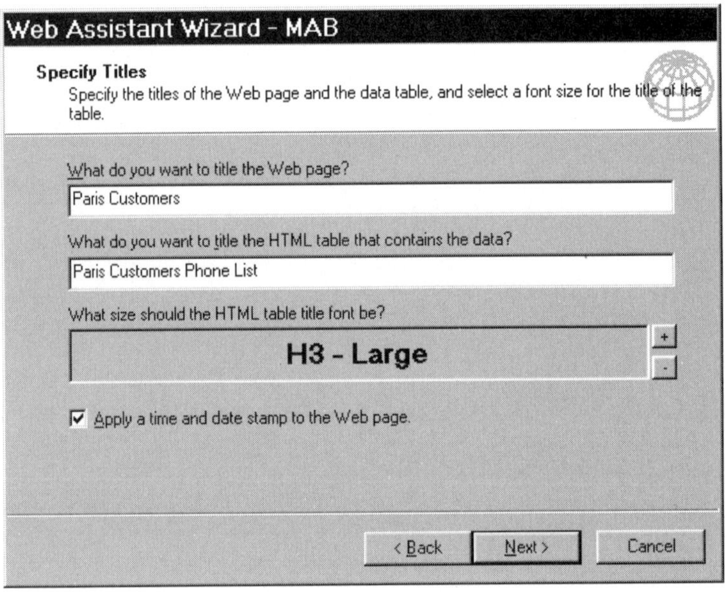

FIGURE 9.9: Naming the HTML page and table and selecting a font size

Figure 9.10 displays the options for formatting the body of the table. You can choose whether or not to display column names and font characteristics and whether or not you want a border around the table. We've chosen not to display the column names with a proportional font.

You can also add hyperlinks to your page, as shown in Figure 9.11. You can add a single hyperlink or add multiple links by selecting them from a table.

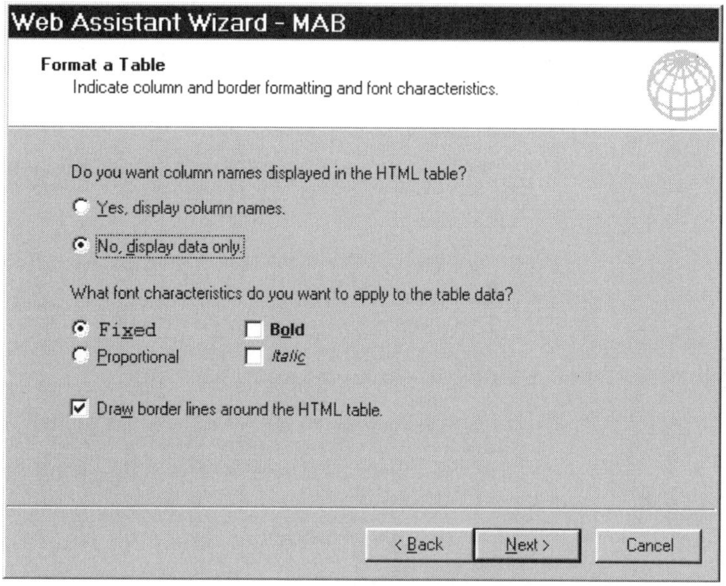

FIGURE 9.10: Display and font options for the table body

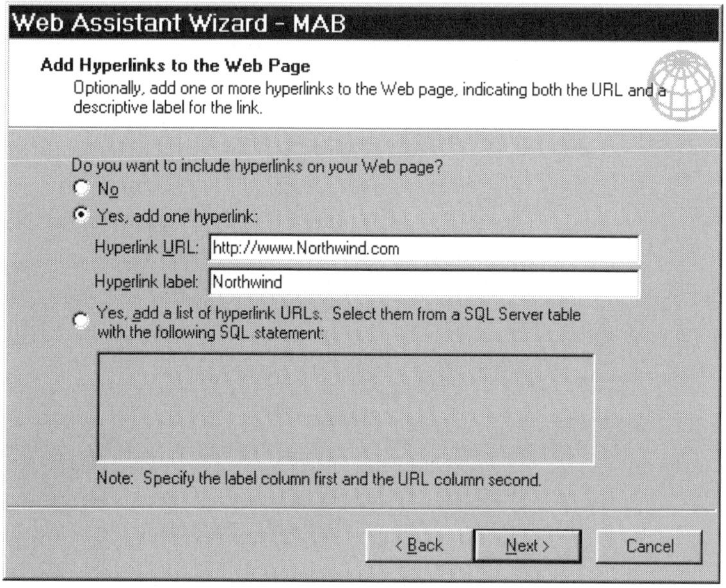

FIGURE 9.11: Adding hyperlinks

If the data you are publishing is quite lengthy, you will probably want to limit the number of rows that are displayed. Figure 9.12 shows the options available for controlling how much data is displayed at a time. We've chosen to return all the data but to only display 20 rows on a page.

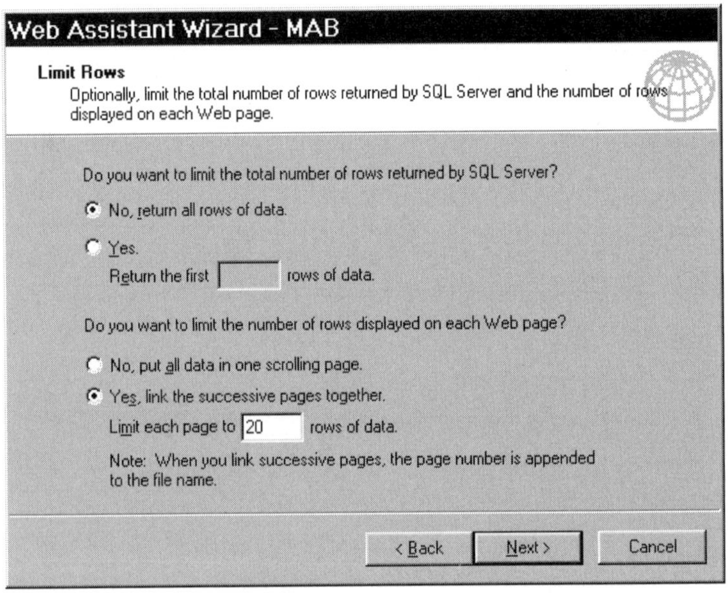

FIGURE 9.12: Limiting the data displayed on a Web page

The final page of the Web Assistant, shown in Figure 9.13, displays the description of the task being created and also lets you write the SQL used in generating the task to a file. Click the Write Transact-SQL To File button to create a text file. The SQL generated looks like this:

```
EXECUTE sp_makewebtask @outputfile =
➥N'C:\MSSQL7\HTML\ParisCustomers.htm', @query=N'SELECT [CompanyName],
➥[ContactName], [ContactTitle], [Phone], [Fax] FROM [Customers] WHERE
➥[Customers].City = ''Paris''', @fixedfont=0, @colheaders=0,
➥@HTMLheader=3, @webpagetitle=N'Paris Customers', @resultstitle=N'Phone
➥List', @URL=N'http://Northwind.com', @reftext=N'Northwind',
➥@dbname=N'Northwind', @whentype=10, @nrowsperpage=20,
➥@datachg=N'TABLE=Customers
➥COLUMN=ContactName,Phone,Fax',@procname=N'CustomerPhoneList',
➥@codepage=65001,@charset=N'utf-8'
```

Click the Finish button to conclude running the Web Assistant.

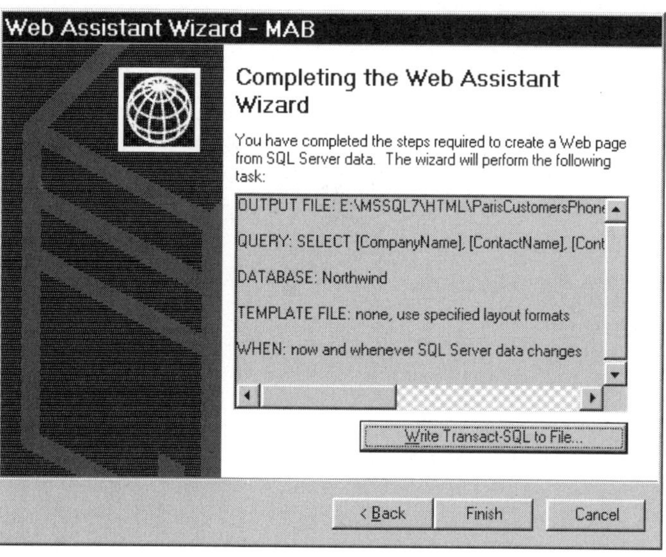

FIGURE 9.13: Writing SQL to file and finishing

The Web Assistant will then create the HTML files in the location you specified and will create the Web page if you've chosen to do so. It will also add an object to the Web Assistant Jobs folder. To edit the job later, right-click and choose Properties. Figure 9.14 shows a completed Web page.

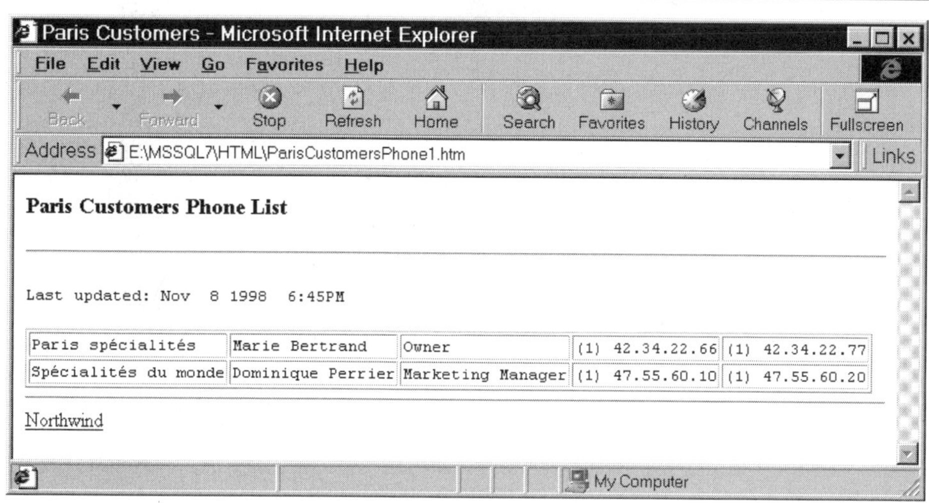

FIGURE 9.14: The completed Web page

SQL Server Web Stored Procedures

The SQL Server Web Assistant provides a graphical interface for the stored procedure sp_makewebtask. There are three SQL Server Web stored procedures: sp_makewebtask, sp_runwebtask, and sp_dropwebtask. These stored procedures are performing the tasks you specify in using the Web Assistant in Transact-SQL. We'll dig in a little deeper and explore the syntax for each.

The sp_makewebtask Stored Procedure

The system stored procedure sp_makewebtask produces an HTML document, as well as creating a task, such as updating the HTML document at specified intervals. The syntax is:

```
sp_makewebtask {[@outputfile =] 'outputfile'} [, [@query =] 'query']
  [, [@fixedfont =] fixedfont] [, [@bold =] bold] [, [@italic =]
➥italic]
  [, [@colheaders =] colheaders] [, [@lastupdated =] lastupdated]
  [, [@HTMLHeader =] HTMLHeader] [, [@username =] username]
  [, [@dbname =] dbname] [, [@templatefile =] 'templatefile']
  [, [@webpagetitle =] 'webpagetitle'] [, [@resultstitle =]
➥'resultstitle']
  [
    [, [@URL =] 'URL', [@reftext =] 'reftext']
    | [, [@table_urls =] table_urls, [@url_query =] 'url_query']
  ]
  [, [@whentype =] whentype] [, [@targetdate =] targetdate]
  [, [@targettime =] targettime] [, [@dayflags =] dayflags]
  [, [@numunits =] numunits] [, [@unittype =] unittype]
  [, [@procname =] procname ] [, [@maketask =] maketask]
  [, [@rowcnt =] rowcnt] [, [@tabborder =] tabborder]
  [, [@singlerow =] singlerow] [, [@blobfmt =] blobfmt]
  [, [@nrowsperpage =] n] [, [@datachg =] table_column_list]
  [, [@charset =] characterset]]
  [, [@codepage =] codpage
```

That's quite a few arguments for one stored procedure. Table 9.1 is an overview of the arguments and their definitions. A more detailed description of each argument can be found in Books Online.

TABLE 9.1: Arguments for sp_makewebtask

Argument	Definition
`@outputfile`	Specifies the location of the generated HTML file. Can be a UNC name and has a maximum of 255 characters
`@query`	Specifies the query to be run
`@fixedfont`	The default value of 1 will display results in a fixed font. A value of 0 will display in a proportional font.
`@bold`	Displays results in bold
`@italic`	Displays results in italic
`@colheaders`	The default value of 1 displays results with column headers. A value of 2 displays results without headers.
`@lastupdated`	The default value of 1 displays a last updated timestamp; 0 does not display a timestamp.
`@HTMLHeader`	Specifies the HTML formatting code for displaying the text contained in the `@resultstitle` variable. Values are 1 to 6 for HTML formatting codes H1 to H6.
`@username`	Default is the current user. Specifies the username for executing the query
`@dbname`	Default is the current database. Specifies the database name to run the query in
`@templatefile`	The path of the template file used to generate the HTML document
`@webpagetitle`	The title of the HTML document
`@resultstitle`	The title displayed above the query results in the HTML document
`@URL`	Places a hyperlink to another HTML document after the query results. If this parameter is specified, `@reftext` must also be specified, and `@table_urls` and `@url_query` cannot be specified.
`@reftext`	Description of the specified hyperlink
`@table_urls`	A value of 1 specifies whether hyperlinks will be included on the HTML document and whether the hyperlinks will come from a SELECT statement executed on Microsoft SQL Server. The default value of 0 indicates that there is no query that will generate hyperlinks for the HTML. If `@table_urls = 1`, then `@url_query` must be included to specify the query to be executed for retrieving hyperlink information, and `@URL` and `@reftext` cannot be specified. Information is specified either in `@URL` and `@reftext`, or in `@url_query` and `@table_urls`.
`@url_query`	The `SELECT` statement to create the URL and its hyperlink text, which come from a SQL Server table. Allows you to generate multiple URLs with associated hyperlinks. Use `@url_query` with `@table_urls`.

TABLE 9.1 CONTINUED: Arguments for sp_makewebtask

Argument	Definition
`@whentype`	When to run the task that creates the HTML document. A value of 1 creates the page now; 2 creates the page later; 3 creates the page every *n* days; 4 creates the page every *n* minutes, hours, days, or weeks; 5 creates the page upon request; 6 creates the page now and later; 7 creates the page now and every *n* days of the week; 8 creates the page now and periodically thereafter; 9 creates the page now and upon request; 10 creates the page now and when data changes.
`@targetdate`	Specifies the date the page should be built. Format is *YYYYMMDD*.
`@targettime`	Specifies the time the HTML document should be created. The default is 12:00 A.M. (midnight).
`@dayflags`	Specifies what days to update the HTML document by adding the values together. Day of week values are: 1 Sunday (the default); 2 Monday; 3 Tuesday; 8 Wednesday; 16 Thursday; 32 Friday; 64 Saturday.
`@numunits`	How often to update the HTML document. Values range from 1 (the default) to 255.
`@unittype`	How often the HTML document should be updated for `@numunits = 4` (periodic) or `@whentype = 8` (now and later). Use 1 (hours), 2 (days), 3 (weeks), or 4 (minutes). If not specified, will default to 1 (hourly).
`@procname`	The procedure or task name for the HTML document.
`@maketask`	The default value of 1 specifies that a task should be created to execute an internal stored procedure that generates an HTML document. A value of 0 creates the stored procedure.
`@rowcnt`	Specifies the maximum number of rows to display in the generated HTML document.
`@tabborder`	The default value of 1 specifies that a border should be drawn around the results table; 0 specifies no border.
`@singlerow`	The default value of 0 specifies that the results all appear on the same page and in the same table. A value of 1 causes a new HTML page to be generated for every qualifying row in the result set.
`@blobfmt`	Specifies whether all columns of text or image data types should be embedded in the same results page (the default is `NULL`) or whether these fields should be saved in another page and linked to the main HTML document by a URL.
`@nrowsperpage`	Specifies that the result set should be displayed in multiple pages of *n* rows each and that the successive pages are linked with next and previous URLs. Default value is 0, meaning all results are to be displayed in a single page. This value cannot be used if `@singlerow` is specified.
`@datachg`	Specifies the table and optional column names that will trigger the new page creation when the data changes.

The sp_runwebtask Stored Procedure

The stored procedure sp_runwebtask executes a previously defined Web task and generates an HTML document. The syntax is:

```
sp_runwebtask [[@procname =] 'procname'] [,[@outputfile = ]
➥'outputfile']
```

The task is identified by the procedure name, the procname argument, or the output file name, the outputfile argument, or both. The output file is the actual HTML file, so you can view it using almost any viewer or word processing software. The following example runs the job we defined earlier using the wizard.

```
sp_runwebtask @procname = 'Customer Phone List',
  @outputfile = 'C:\MSSQL7\HTML\CustPhone.htm'
```

Since you are not required to supply both the procname and outputfile arguments, you can also run the same job using either:

```
sp_runwebtask @procname = 'Customer Phone List'
```

or

```
sp_runwebtask @outputfile = 'C:\MSSQL7\HTML\CustPhone.htm'
```

If you'd like to run this task on a regular basis but don't want to use the Web Assistant Wizard, you can create a SQL Server job to do so. Jobs are discussed in Skill 15, *Administering a Server*. You could also use insert, delete, and update triggers to automatically run this stored procedure whenever the data in a table is changed. You can learn more about triggers in Skill 7, *Altering Data*.

The sp_dropwebtask Stored Procedure

The sp_dropwebtask stored procedure lets you remove previously scheduled Web tasks. The syntax is:

```
sp_dropwebtask [[@procname =]'procname'|NULL][, 'outputfile'
```

The procname argument is the name of the procedure which defines the query for the task and the outputfile argument is the name of the HTML document to be deleted. The procedure accepts either argument or both. The following example will delete the Web task we defined in the previous example:

```
sp_dropwebtask @procname = 'Customer Phone List'
```

Calling Web Stored Procedures from a Client

You can call the Web stored procedures from any client which has VBA. There is nothing different about running Web stored procedures compared to any other stored procedure. The following function, `DoWebTasks()`, executes a stored procedure, which is passed in as the `strSQL` argument. The function is written in Access and uses Jet syntax to specify the ODBCDirect workspace and database objects. The `strConnect` argument specifies the `.Connect` property to connect to the local server:

```
Function DoWebTasks(strConnect As String, strSQL _
  As String) As Boolean
    ' Uses ODBCDirect workspace to execute stored
    ' procedure, which is passed in as the strSQL
    ' argument. strConnect is the connect string for
    ' the current server
    Dim ws As Workspace
    Dim db As Database
    Dim qdf As QueryDef
    Dim con As Connection
    Dim errX As Error
    Dim strErrors As String

    On Error GoTo HandleErr

    Set ws = CreateWorkspace("ODBCws", CurrentUser(), _
      "", dbUseODBC)
    Set con = ws.OpenConnection("ODBCconnection", _
      dbDriverNoPrompt, True, strConnect)
    Set db = CurrentDb
    Set qdf = db.CreateQueryDef("")
    With qdf
        .Connect = strConnect
        .ReturnsRecords = False
        .SQL = strSQL
        .Execute dbSQLPassThrough
    End With

    DoWebTasks = True

ExitHere:
    On Error Resume Next
    con.Close
    ws.Close
    Exit Function
```

```
HandleErr:
    DoWebTasks = False
    For Each errX In Errors
        strErrors = strErrors & Err & ": " & _
          Err.Description & vbCrLf
    Next errX
    MsgBox strErrors, , "Errors in DoWebTasks"
    Resume ExitHere
    Resume
End Function
```

For example, to execute the `sp_makewebtask` stored procedure, make sure to specify the correct Transact-SQL syntax for the `strSQL` argument, as shown in the following VBA code snippet. The SQL syntax needed for a pass-through query is not parsed by Jet, so use SQL Server syntax for the `sp_makewebtask` stored procedure.

```
strSQL = "sp_makewebtask @outputfile = 'C:\WEBTEST\MULTIPLE.HTM', " _
  & "@query = 'SELECT title, price FROM titles SELECT au_lname, " _
  & "au_fname FROM authors SELECT pub_id, pub_name FROM publishers " _
  & "SELECT au_lname, au_fname FROM authors', @templatefile = " _
  & "'C:\WEBTEST\MULTIPLE.TPL', @dbname = 'PUBS', @rowcnt = 5, " _
  & "@whentype = 9"
```

To run an existing Web task using the `sp_runwebtask` stored procedure, you would define your `strSQL` variable as follows:

```
strSQL = "sp_runwebtask @procname ='C:\WEBTEST\MULTIPLE.HTM'"
```

You can specify the name of the HTML file as the `procname` argument, which will refresh it with new data.

To drop a Web task with the stored procedure `sp_dropwebtask`, define the `strSQL` variable as follows:

```
strSQL = "sp_dropwebtask @procname ='C:\WEBTEST\MULTIPLE.HTM'"
```

To save an HTML table back to the SQL Server database with the `sp_savehtmltable` stored procedure, define the strSQL variable as follows:

```
strSQL = "sp_savehtmltable 'C:\WEBTEST\MULTIPLE.HTM', multiple, pubs"
```

NOTE For more information on using stored procedures with client applications, see Skill 13, *Programming SQL Server.*

Are You up to Speed?

Now you can...

☑ use the Web Assistant to publish data to the Web, to transfer data from HTML to tables, and to schedule related tasks

☑ use the SQL Server Web stored procedures to publish data

SKILL 10

Retrieving SQL Server Data from the Web

- Internet Information Server
- Internet Data Connector
- Active Server Pages

SQL Server is designed to be an integrated part of the Microsoft BackOffice suite. As such, it's designed to work well with the other parts of that suite, including the Internet Information Server (IIS). This allows a lot of flexibility in making SQL Server data available to clients across the World Wide Web. In this skill, we'll survey some of the ways that you can make this data available.

Internet Information Server

Internet Information Server (IIS) is Microsoft's server product for the World Wide Web. At first, IIS was a commercial product of its own, but it's now available free to anyone who cares to download it from the Microsoft BackOffice Web site at `http://backoffice.microsoft.com`. You can also get IIS as a part of the Windows NT 4 Option Pack. As of this writing, the current version of IIS is version 4.

Setting Up IIS

The easiest way to install IIS is through the Windows NT 4 Option Pack. The Option Pack includes many other server components:

- Certificate Server
- Front Page Server Extensions
- Internet Connection Services for RAS
- Microsoft Data Access Components 1.5
- Microsoft Index Server
- Microsoft Management Console
- Microsoft Message Queue
- Microsoft Script Debugger
- Microsoft Site Server Express
- Microsoft Transaction Server
- Windows Scripting Host

If your server space is limited, you may want to do a custom install and to deselect some of the other option pack components.

Integration of IIS and SQL Server

There are several ways to retrieve data from SQL Server through IIS. In this skill, we'll consider two of them: using the Internet Data Connector and using Active Server Pages. The Internet Data Connector provides an easy way to do simple data integration tasks with no programming. If you have a basic understanding of Hypertext Markup Language (HTML), you can use the Internet Data Connector to populate those pages with live data from your SQL Server. Active Server Pages provide a more advanced and programmable method of data integration. With Active Server Pages, you can actually cause a program to run on your server whenever a page is downloaded. This program can include Active Data Objects (ADO) code to retrieve data from the server. Active Server Pages take more work than the Internet Data Connector but also provide a great deal more functionality.

Internet Data Connector

The Internet Data Connector (IDC) is the easiest way to get data from SQL Server to a Web page. It works best for data that you want relatively static formatting for, such as a list of customers or prices. Once you construct the appropriate files to drive the IDC, anyone who browses to them will receive the most current data.

Let's look at the basic operation of the IDC, followed by a more in-depth discussion of some of the options you can use to customize its actions.

Understanding the IDC

Internet Information Server is designed to act as an intermediary between the data that you have stored in SQL Server and clients out on the Internet. IIS accepts HTTP (Hypertext Transfer Protocol) requests from Web clients and decides what to do with them. If it gets a properly formatted request for SQL Server data, it will send the request out through the Internet Database Connector. IDC is an ISAPI (Internet Server API) library that uses Open Database Connectivity (ODBC) to retrieve data from SQL Server or other data sources. IIS then turns the data into a formatted HTML page and returns it to the client. Figure 10.1 shows this process schematically.

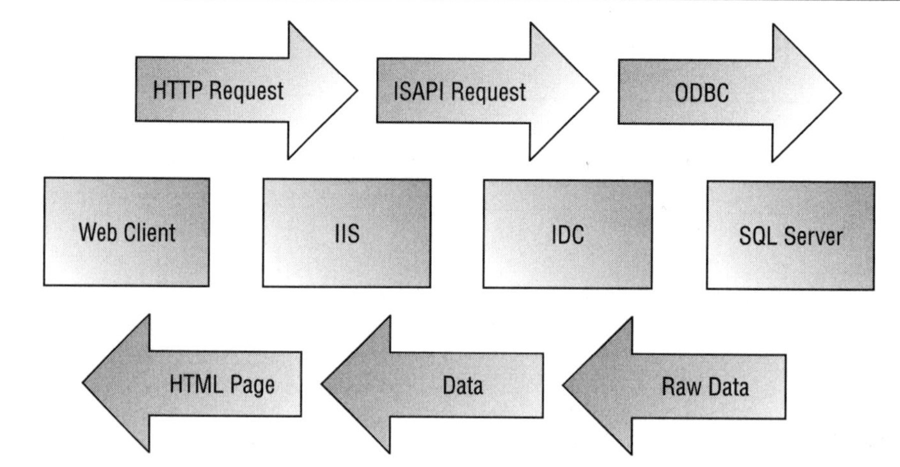

FIGURE 10.1: Retrieving data via the IDC

Files Used by the IDC

The operation of the IDC is controlled by a pair of files for each database. These are:

- An Internet Data Connector (`.idc`) file
- An HTML extension (`.htx`) file

The `.idc` file contains the information that IDC uses to get to a specific data source (we'll use a SQL Server data source, but you can also use IDC to retrieve data from other ODBC data sources). This includes the ODBC connection information and the name and location of the `.htx` file to use.

The `.htx` file is a template for an HTML document. It can contain static text as well as placeholders that will be replaced by data retrieved from the specified data source. IDC takes the data and merges it with the `.htx` file to make the HTML page that is ultimately returned to the Web client.

TIP If you install the samples that ship with IIS, you'll find sample `.idc` and `.htx` files in the Exploration Air sample.

IDC Performance

Because there's very little plumbing involved with the IDC, it provides a high-performance way to retrieve server-side data. Assuming your server has enough memory, it's likely that all of the pieces will remain in memory. The only potential exception to this is the IDC itself. IIS can be set to load ISAPI applications each time they're used or to keep them resident. For maximum performance, you should set IIS to keep the application resident. You can do this by following these steps:

1. Launch Internet Service Manager.
2. Select your application in the IIS tree, and choose Properties from its context menu.
3. Click Configure.
4. Make sure the checkbox for Cache ISAPI Applications is checked, as shown in Figure 10.2.

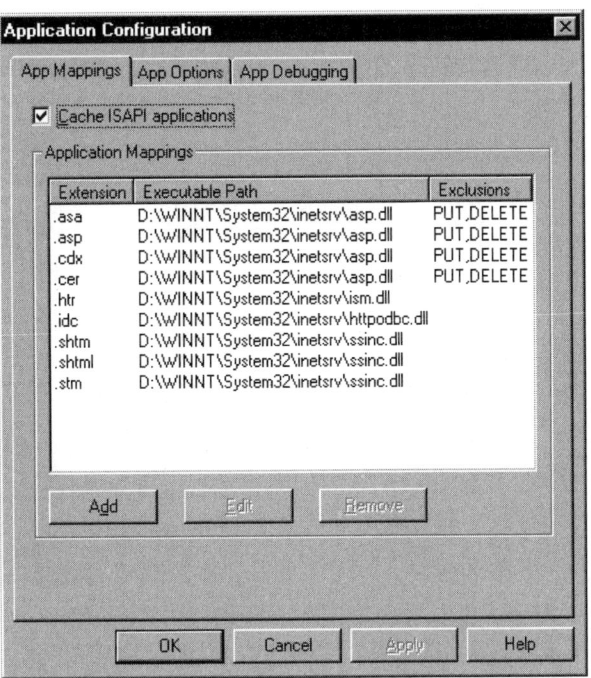

FIGURE 10.2: Configuring ISAPI for maximum performance

Using IDC to Retrieve Data

Let's see how to use the IDC to retrieve data in response to a request from a Web client. This section assumes you've installed the sample Northwind file that comes with SQL Server 7.

Creating the ODBC Connection

The first step is to create an ODBC connection that IDC can use to find the data it's going to return. The easiest way to do this is to use the ODBC Data Sources applet in the Windows Control Panel. Choose to add a System DSN, and then choose the SQL Server driver.

TIP Make sure you create a System DSN rather than a File DSN, so that Windows services, such as IIS, can use the DSN.

Fill in the information requested by the ODBC driver. This includes the name, description, and server name for the connection, as shown in Figure 10.3. It also includes the name of the database to use and the authentication method. The safest authentication method is Windows NT authentication, since IIS will automatically set up its own account to use on your server.

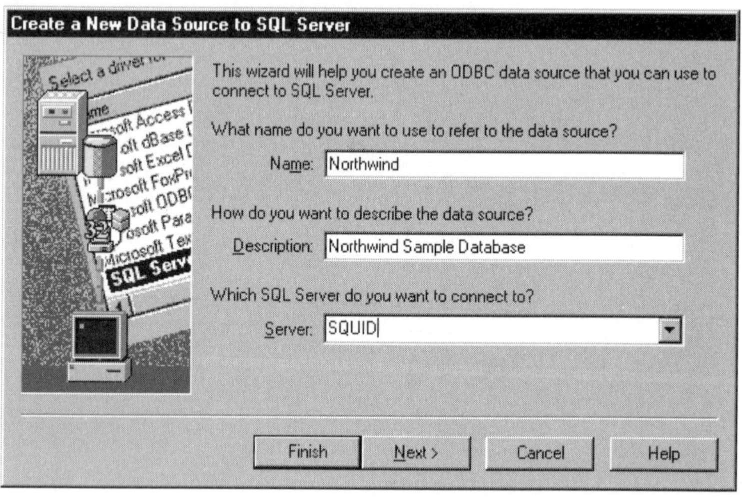

FIGURE 10.3: Creating an ODBC data source

TIP Be sure to use SQL Server's security features to give the IIS account read permissions on whatever database you want to retrieve data from.

Creating the IDC File

You can create an IDC file with any text editor, from Notepad on up. It's just a text file of information for the server to use. The `.idc` file contains options that tell the IDC application how to connect to the server and what data to retrieve. For our purposes, this can be fairly simple:

```
Datasource: Northwind
Username: IUSR_SQUID
Template: Northwind.htx
SQLStatement: SELECT * FROM Customers
```

Each line in the `.idc` file provides a property name and a value for that property. There are four essential properties:

- `Datasource` is the name of the ODBC DSN that this connection should use.
- `Username` is the name of the account that you want to sign on to SQL Server with.
- `Template` is the name of the `.htx` file that will be used to format the results of this query. You can supply a path, but it's simpler to just keep this file in the same folder as the `.idc` file.
- `SQLStatement` is the query you want to send to the server.

So, in this case, we're telling the IDC library to log on to the server as `IUSR_SQUID` and retrieve all the customers from the Northwind DSN. These will be passed back to IIS for formatting with the specified `.htx` file.

NOTE In this case, the `SQLStatement` property is retrieving more data than we actually need. We've kept it simple, but in real life you'd want to use a `SELECT` with only the columns that your page will display.

Creating the .htx File

The `.htx` file does not have to be much more complex than the `.idc` file. For our sample, we'll use this `.htx` file:

```
<HTML>
<HEAD><TITLE>Customers</TITLE></HEAD>
<BODY>
<H1>Our Customers</H1>
<P><TABLE border="1">
<TR><TD><B>Company</B></TD>
<TD><B>Contact</B></TD></TR>
<%begindetail%>
<TR><TD><%CompanyName%></TD>
<TD><%ContactName%><br></TD></TR>
<%enddetail%>
</TABLE>
</BODY>
</HTML>
```

Most of this sample is just routine HTML formatting to place a title and header on the page and to format the results of the query as a table. The tags with percent signs around them are commands to the IDC:

- `<%begindetail%>` and `<%enddetail%>` tell the IDC where the detail section of this page is. The IDC will fill in this section once for each row in the query.
- `<%CompanyName%>` and `<%ContactName%>` are field names from the query. IDC will replace these tags with the data in the field each time it retrieves a row of data.

WARNING If you have database fields named `BeginDetail` or `EndDetail`, there's no way to display their contents using IDC, so stay away from those names for databases you intend to use on the Web.

The completed page from this example is shown in Figure 10.4.

TIP We don't have room in this book to discuss the HTML formatting used in this file. If you'd like to know more about HTML, a good reference is *Effective Web Design: Master the Essentials* by Ann Navarro and Tabinda Khan (Sybex, 1998).

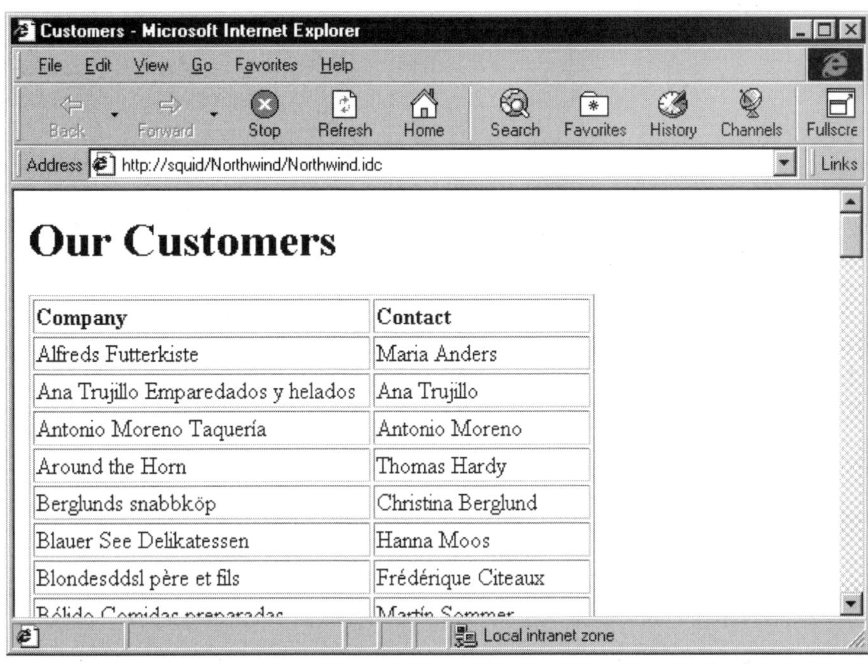

FIGURE 10.4: Data retrieved using the IDC

Additional IDC Options

Only the `Datasource`, `Template`, and `SQLStatement` fields are required in the `.idc` file. However, there are a number of other properties you can use to fine-tune IDC performance. Table 10.1 lists the more important of these and explains what they can do for you.

Skill 10

TABLE 10.1: Advanced IDC Properties

Property	Meaning
`Expires`	Time in seconds that a cached page should be used. If two clients request the same page within this many seconds, IDC will not return to the database to request new data. By default there is no caching, which means that every client request causes a separate database access.

TABLE 10.1 CONTINUED: Advanced IDC Properties

Property	Meaning
`MaxFieldSize`	Maximum size of data (in bytes) that IDC will retrieve for a single field. The default is 8,192.
`MaxRecords`	Maximum number of records that IDC will retrieve in response to a single query. If you don't set this, it defaults to four billion, so this is a good option to set!
`Password`	Password that corresponds to the username, if any. You won't need to set this if you're using Windows NT integrated security on your server.
`SQL_LOGIN_TIMEOUT`	Maximum number of seconds to wait for the server to respond. This is useful if you don't want Web queries to just hang on a heavily used server.

More Advanced IDC Use

You need not limit yourself to simple unparameterized queries with the IDC. It's easy to pass a parameter from a Web browser all the way back to the server. For example, you can modify the `.idc` file this way:

```
Datasource: Northwind
Username: IUSR_SQUID
Template: Northwind.htx
SQLStatement: SELECT CompanyName, ContactName FROM Customers
+WHERE CompanyName LIKE '%Initial%%'
```

You can use a single `.idc` file like this to retrieve the set of customers whose company names start with the letter specified in the variable `%Initial%%`. You do this by using CGI syntax for passing variables. For example, browsing to the HTML page `Northwind.idc?Initial=A` will return the results shown in Figure 10.5.

NOTE Note the + sign used to concatenate multiple lines into a single SQL statement. Also note that `%Initial%%` ends with two percent signs. The first closes the `IDC` variable; the second is the SQL Server wildcard character.

FIGURE 10.5: Retrieving specific customers

You can also use IDC to execute a stored procedure instead of a query. Since IDC passes whatever SQL statement you type straight to the server, you simply need to use the `Execute` keyword. For example, the Northwind sample database contains a stored procedure, `CustOrdersOrders`, which is defined as follows:

```
CREATE PROCEDURE CustOrdersOrders @CustomerID nchar(5)
AS
SELECT OrderID,
     OrderDate,
     RequiredDate,
     ShippedDate
FROM Orders
WHERE CustomerID = @CustomerID
ORDER BY OrderID
```

This stored procedure accepts a single parameter, `@CustomerID`, and returns all the orders for that customer. You can create an `.idc` file to call it like this:

```
Datasource: Northwind
Username: IUSR_SQUID
Template: Northwind.htx
SQLStatement: Execute CustOrdersOrders %CustomerID%
```

The matching `.htx` file might look like this:

```
<HTML>
<HEAD><TITLE>Order Review Page</TITLE></HEAD>
<BODY>
<H1>Orders for <%CustomerID%></H1>
<P><TABLE border="1">
<TR><TD><B>Order ID</B></TD>
<TD><B>Order Date</B></TD>
<TD><B>Required Date</B></TD>
<TD><B>Shipped Date</B></TD></TR>
<%begindetail%>
<TR><TD><%OrderID%></TD>
<TD><%OrderDatee%></TD>
<TD><%RequiredDate%></TD>
<TD><%ShippedDate%><br></TD></TR>
<%enddetail%>
</TABLE>
</BODY>
</HTML>
```

TIP Of course, since you can use any SQL statement in an `.idc` file, you can also use IDC to change data on your server by including UPDATE, DELETE or INSERT statements on particular pages. But you should be careful before you make such pages accessible from the Internet!

Active Server Pages and ADO

The other major alternative for retrieving SQL Server data over the Web via IIS is Active Server Pages (ASP). Active Server Pages contain code that's interpreted on the server. Active Server Pages can use Active Data Objects (ADO) to connect to SQL Server. We'll discuss ADO more fully in Skill 12, *OLE DB Fundamentals*.

With Active Server Pages, the sequence of events looks like this:

1. The client browses to an Active Server Page.
2. The server reads and interprets any scripting (code) on the page.
3. This code can retrieve data from SQL Server.
4. The server uses the retrieved data plus any HTML in the Active Server Page to construct a static HTML page, which is then delivered to the client.

As you can see, in an ASP scenario, all of the code runs on the server rather than on the Web client. This leads to improved performance (since code never needs to be sent over the wire) as well as better security (since source code isn't available for clients to read).

An Active Server Pages Example

SQL Server 7 ships with a sample ASP application that you can activate once you've installed IIS. This sample lets you use Web pages to review and manage the inventory in the Northwind sample database. After you've installed SQL Server and IIS, you can activate this sample by following these steps:

1. Launch the Internet Service Manager. If you did a default NT Option Pack install, you'll find this at Start ➢ Programs ➢ Windows NT 4 Option Pack ➢ Microsoft Internet Information Server ➢ Internet Service Manager.
2. Right-click your server's name and choose New ➢ Web Site. This will open the New Web Site Wizard.
3. When the wizard asks for a home directory, fill in `C:\MSSQL7\DevTools\samples\ADO\Web`.
4. Open the `global.asa` file in that folder with a text editor and fill your server's name in where indicated.

When you finish installing the sample, you should be able to right-click the site name in Internet Service Manager, choose Browse, and have the default page for the sample (shown in Figure 10.6) open in your browser. We'll use this sample to explore some of the issues involved in ASP programming.

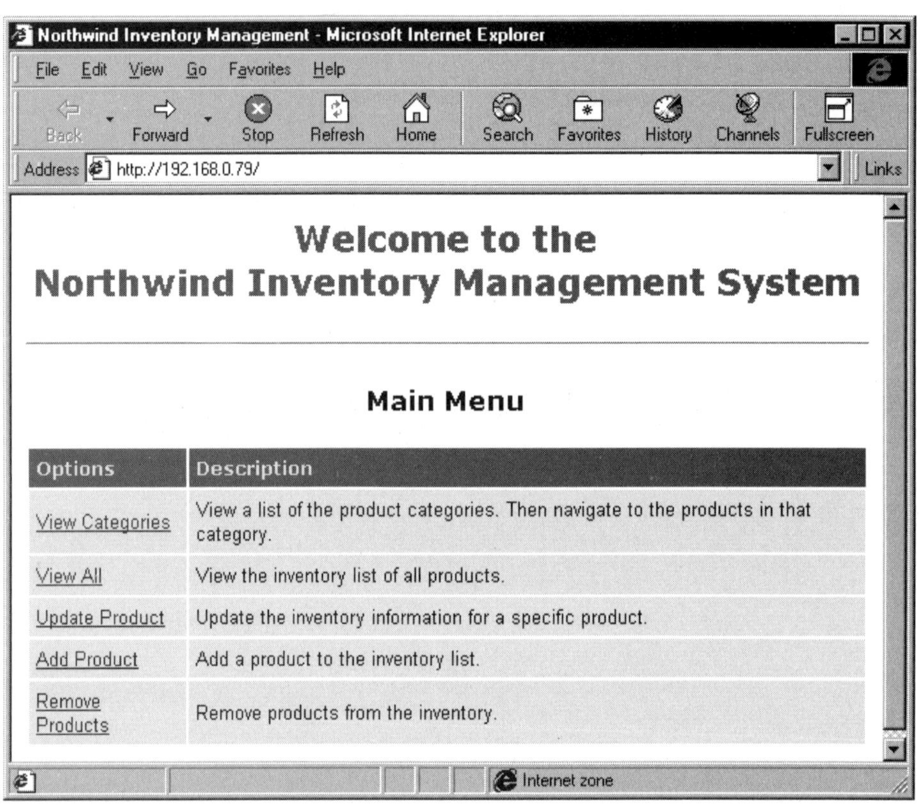

FIGURE 10.6: Northwind Inventory Management System

The global.asa File

Active Server Pages are typically combined into an application, and the Northwind Inventory Management System is no exception. One important part of an ASP application is a file called `global.asa`, which is stored in the same folder as the `.asp` files that make up the user interface of the application. This file contains important application-wide settings and code. Here's the `global.asa` file from the sample application:

```
<SCRIPT LANGUAGE="VBScript" RUNAT="Server">

Sub Session_OnStart
```

```
    'Create an ADO Connection
    Set cn = Server.CreateObject("ADODB.Connection")

    ' Specify the OLE DB provider.
    cn.Provider = "sqloledb"

    ' Specify connection string on Open method.
    ' To run the sample, edit this line to reflect your server's name.
    ProvStr = "Server=SQUID;Database=Northwind;UID=sa;PWD=;"
    cn.Open ProvStr

    Set Session("cnn") = cn

END Sub

Sub Session_OnEnd

    'Close the data connection
    cn.Close

END Sub

</SCRIPT>
```

The `<SCRIPT>` and `</SCRIPT>` tags tell the server that this section is code, not material to be displayed on screen. As you can see, Active Server Pages use an event-driven programming model. The `global.asa` file contains events related to the site as a whole: in this case, some code to be run whenever a user connects to the site and another piece of code to be run whenever a user disconnects from the site.

In this case, when the user connects, a VBScript variable named `cn` is created to represent an ADO connection to a server. The `Server.CreateObject` method in ASP can create any automation object on the server where the ASP code is being executed. This connection is then opened on the appropriate SQL Server. The line `Set Session("cnn")=cn` makes this connection available to all of the pages within this application.

Introduction to ADO Objects

Although we won't cover ADO in depth in this skill, we do need to introduce a few ADO objects that are useful in communicating between ASP pages and SQL Server. ADO provides an application API to communicate to OLE DB, Microsoft's latest set of database interfaces. ADO employs a very simple object model, so that you can do a lot with very little programming, as shown with the following objects used in this sample:

- The Connection object represents a communication between client and server. In our case, we'll use a Connection object to talk to the server from our ASP application.
- The Command object represents a single SQL statement sent to the server.
- The Recordset object represents a group of records retrieved from the server.
- The Field object represents the data in a single column.

With just these four objects, we can browse, insert, update, and delete records. We'll learn more about ADO and OLE DB in Skill 12, *OLE DB Fundamentals*.

Using Active Server Pages for Data Retrieval

There are two parts to retrieving data with Active Server Pages. First, you need to get the data back from the SQL Server. Second, you need to format an HTML page to contain the data. Let's look at both of these tasks using the Product Categories page shown in Figure 10.7.

To retrieve the data from SQL Server, you need to create a recordset. Since variables in VBScript are all variants, there's no need to declare anything. You can just name your variables and go about your business:

```
'Reference the Session connection variable
cn = Session("cnn")
'Create a recordset
Set CategoryInfo = Server.CreateObject("ADODB.Recordset")
'Create a query string
querystr = "SELECT CategoryName, Description, CategoryID FROM
Categories Order By CategoryID, CategoryName"
'Open the Recordset with the query string on the connection cn.
CategoryInfo.Open querystr, cn
```

This code starts by retrieving the `connection` variable that was created in the `global.asa` file. Given this variable, it's easy to open a recordset by supplying a SQL string. Since the ADO object model is very simple, this is enough to retrieve data. After calling the `Open` method on the `CategoryInfo` variable, you'll be holding a recordset containing all of the matching data from the server. The only remaining question is how to put this data on to the HTML page.

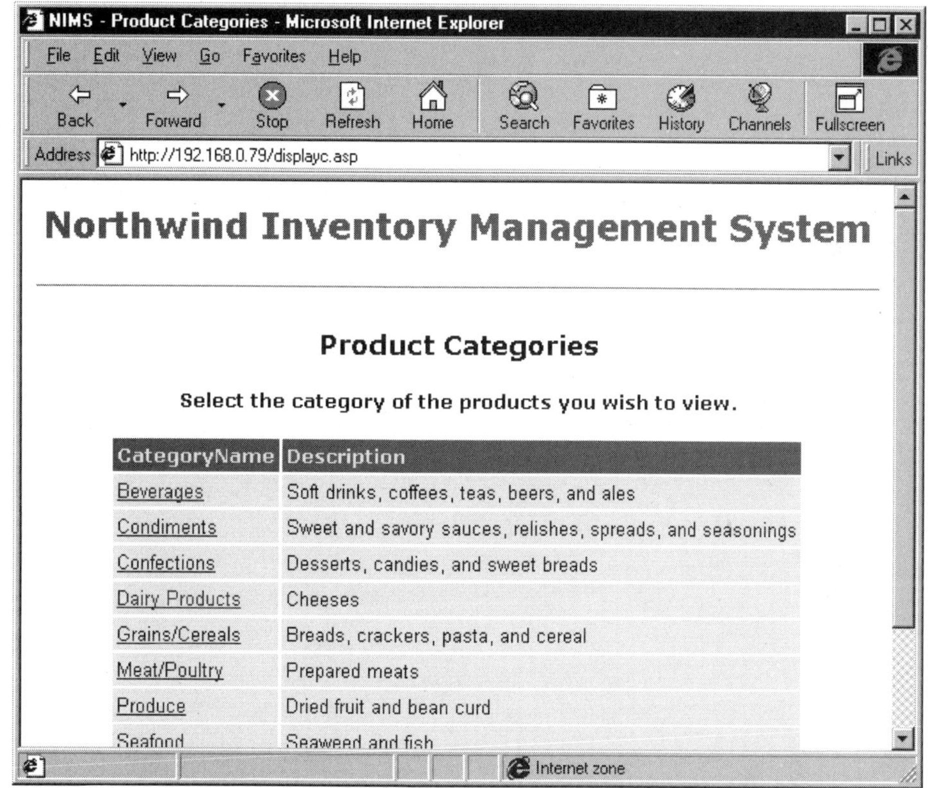

FIGURE 10.7: Product Categories page

The answer to this is that your VBScript code can take advantage of the `Response` object in ASP to create an HTML page, line by line. The `Response` object supports a `Write` method that adds its argument to the HTML being built up. Here's the essential part of the loop that `displayc.asp` uses to create the table we saw in Figure 10.7:

```
<!- Output the table of categories and their descriptions ->
<TABLE CELLPADDING=3 BORDER=0 COLSPAN=8>
```

```
<TR>
        <% 'Output the table headers
        For i = 0 To 1
                Response.Write "<TD CLASS=header>" &
CategoryInfo.Fields(i).Name & "</TD>"
        NEXT %>
</TR>
<% 'Loop through the recordset and output the table values
Do While Not CategoryInfo.EOF
        Response.Write "<TR>"
        For i = 0 to 1
                Response.Write "<TD>"
                IF i = 0 THEN
                        <A
HREF="displayp.asp?CategoryID=<%=CategoryInfo.Fields(2)%>&op=<%=op%>">
                        <%Response.Write
CategoryInfo.Fields(i).Value & "</A>"
                ELSE
                        Response.Write CategoryInfo.Fields(i).Value
                END IF
                Response.Write "</TD>"
        NEXT
        Response.Write "</TR>"
        CategoryInfo.MoveNext
LOOP %>

</TABLE>
```

The core code here is a loop that uses the ADO recordset's `MoveNext` method to visit each record in turn. The Fields collection is used to retrieve first the category name and then the category description. The `Response.Write` method builds these bits of data into the returned HTML page, along with all the other code needed to make an HTML table and create the category names as hyperlinks.

Using Active Server Pages to Alter Data

You can also use ASP pages to allow people to update records in your database via the Web. One way to do this is to use the ADO Command object to execute SQL statements on the server. This is the method used by the Remove Products page shown in Figure 10.8.

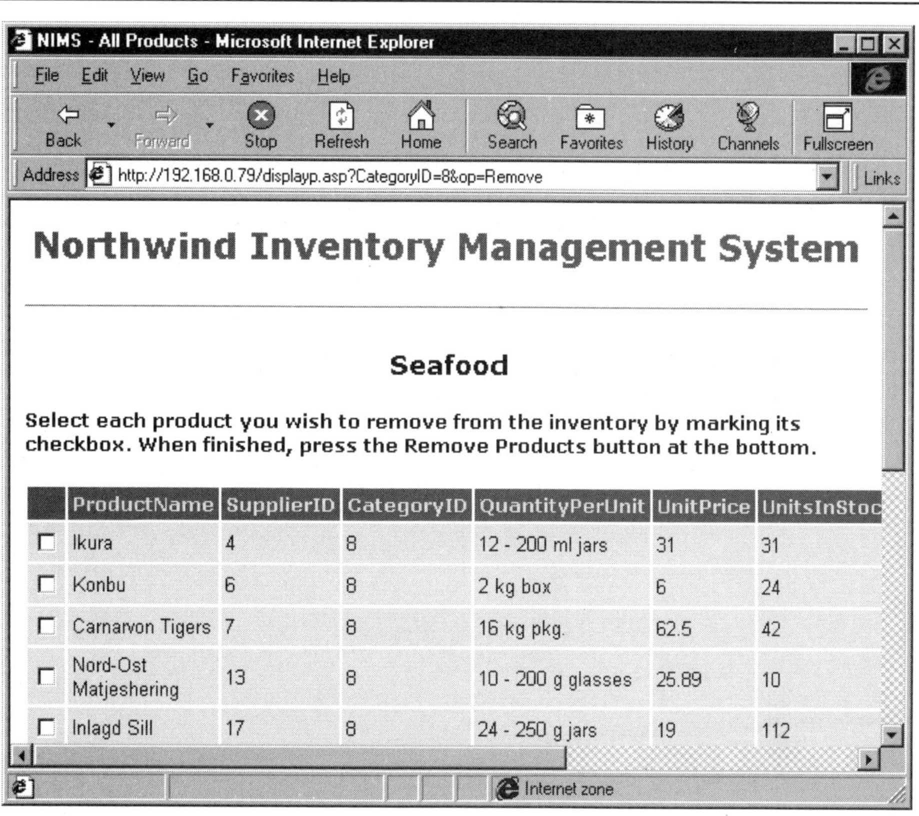

FIGURE 10.8: Removing data via a Web page

When you choose a product and click the button on this page, here's the code that runs:

```
' Create the first part of the T-SQL statement to be executed
sqlcmd = "DELETE Products WHERE "

' Generate WHERE clause of the SQL command by adding all
' selected ProductIDs to it.
FOR i = 1 TO Request.Form("ProductID").Count
     sqlcmd = sqlcmd & " ProductID = " & Request.Form("ProductID")(i)
     IF i <> Request.Form("ProductID").Count THEN
            sqlcmd = sqlcmd & " OR"
```

```
        END IF
    NEXT

    'Reference the Session connection variable
    cn = Session("cnn")

    ' Create the remove command and set its properties
    Set cmd = Server.CreateObject("ADODB.Command")
    cmd.CommandText = sqlcmd
    cmd.ActiveConnection = cn

    ' Execute the command on the Active Connection
    cmd.Execute nRecordsAffected
```

Again, this is very straightforward. The code uses string functions to build up a SQL statement based on the choices that the user has made on the HTML form. Then it retrieves the existing ADO session, creates a new Command object, and uses that object to pass the SQL statement back to the server for execution.

Obviously, you can use a similar technique to insert or to update records. In fact, if you can do it in Transact-SQL, you can use this ADO method to do it in ASP.

Are You up to Speed?

Now you can...

- ☑ **install Internet Information Server to work with SQL Server**
- ☑ **retrieve data using the Internet Data Connector**
- ☑ **retrieve data using ASP and ADO**
- ☑ **alter data using ASP and ADO**

SKILL 11

Creating Client-Server Applications

- Multiple tier client-server architecture
- DAO, ODBCDirect, and RDO
- Client-side design and optimization techniques
- Using SQL-DMO and SQL-NS

As powerful as SQL Server is, there's not much you can do with it by itself. There are many pieces you need in order to put together a functional application, of which SQL Server is but one. A successful client-server application is one that achieves a balance across the various components. In this skill you will learn about designing a client-server application, different data access techniques, and optimization techniques. You will also learn how to use SQL Distributed Management Objects (SQL-DMO) and SQL Namespace (SQL-NS) to administer a server from your client-side application.

NOTE SQL Server 7 includes an updated ODBC SQL Server 3.*x* driver, which is compliant with the ODBC 3 standard, and a beta release of the ODBC 3.5 Driver Manager. The ODBC SQL Server driver fully supports SQL Server 7 and 6.*x* servers. Microsoft recommends that you use ODBC for "low level" development (outside of the COM environment) of SQL database applications. Use ADO for developing your business applications and use OLE DB for developing your data access infrastructure in the COM environment.

Client-Server Architecture

Client-server applications can cover a range of architectures and their components can be created using a wide variety of language-independent tools. This component-based strategy confers many benefits, such as:

Flexibility: A variety of performance and bandwidth requirements can be met since work can be distributed from the desktop to more powerful network servers.

Reusability: Component-based functionality can be shared and reused by many applications.

Ease of Maintenance: Complex projects can be compartmentalized into smaller component projects. Business logic is deployed on a centralized server, rather than scattered on desktops, simplifying change and reducing solution turnaround time.

Figure 11.1 shows the path taken in order for the user to access data in a database. The different application layers can be broken up in different ways, with some layers on the client machine and others on the server.

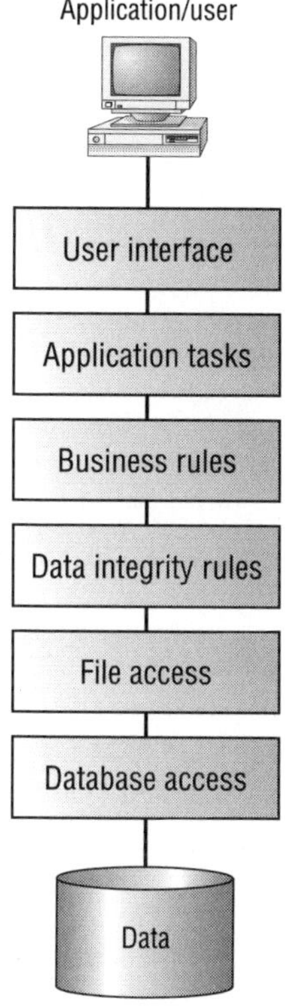

FIGURE 11.1: Computer application layers

The application tasks interact with and adhere to the business rules, which are further subject to compliance with the data integrity rules. The server retrieves data. When all of these layers reside on a single computer, you have a single-user application. Any client-server architecture separates the client side from the server side at any logical application layer boundary. For example, your user interface and application might reside on the client machine, while all of the business rules as well as the data integrity rules are handled and enforced by the server.

When to Use Client-Server Architecture

Generally speaking you want to consider using a client-server architecture in the following situations:

Data concurrency: Data needs to be "up-to-the-minute" accurate.

Concurrent users: Many people are using the same data at the same time and you need to avoid contention issues.

Volume: Tables are too large to manage on a smaller-scaled system.

Performance: Fetching and manipulating data needs to be handled quickly. Queries returning large result sets need optimum performance.

Security: You need to secure sensitive data adequately or to protect files from being inadvertently deleted.

Specialized features: You need to perform tasks above and beyond those offered by a desktop database.

Any of the above are valid reasons to consider using a client-server model. In general, you will deliver more secure and robust applications where the bulk of the data processing work is done on the server, rather than in the application.

Two-Tier Applications

A two-tier application consists solely of a client desktop and a back-end server. This is a common scenario where the data resides on a network server while the application, which might be built using Visual Basic, Access, or any other application, resides on the client machine and performs all of the business logic and presentation services. Another manifestation of the two-tier scenario is when both the data and the business services reside on the server. In this instance, the business logic is coded as Transact-SQL stored procedures on the server. Possible two-tier scenarios are shown in Figure 11.2.

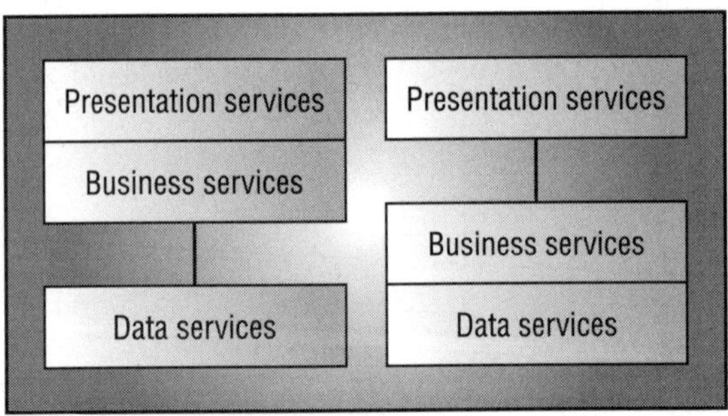

FIGURE 11.2: Two-tier applications

Three-Tier Applications

In a three-tier application, the processing is divided into three main components:

- Data services, which join tables and maintain database integrity
- Business services, which apply business rules
- Presentation services, which encompass the user interface and handle user input

Unlike in two-tier applications, business logic runs in a separate process that can be configured to run on the same server as the database or on a different server, as shown in Figure 11.3.

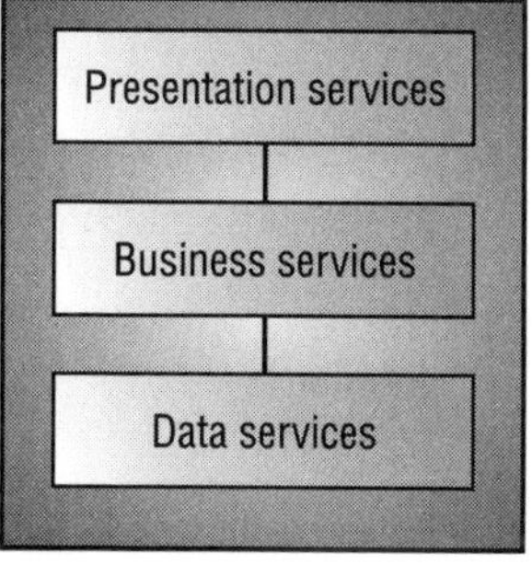

FIGURE 11.3: Three-tier application

One advantage of the three-tiered implementation is that it can span several databases, making limited use of database-specific features. You can use Microsoft Transaction Server (available as part of the Windows NT Option Pack) to host business services written in any language that can produce OLE objects.

The three-tiered application model requires you to partition your application into separate components by logically grouping the three different kinds of services. Services are networked together and can be shared among multiple applications. There may be some bleed between user services and business services and between business services and data services, where certain tasks overlap.

One big advantage to the three-tier implementation is that it is generally more scalable. You can alleviate contention for resources by locating business processes on one or more servers separate from the database. You can also partition databases on multiple computers. Of course, there's a price to pay—greater complexity and increased management.

A variation on the three-tier model is an Internet implementation, where the presentation services can be split onto a browser client and a Web server. Business services can run on the Web server as well, avoiding the overhead of crossing an additional process boundary. The main advantage to an Internet implementation is that anyone with a browser client can access the application, regardless of what platform they are on.

NOTE For more information on using SQL Server and the Internet, see Skills 9, 10, and 14.

The following are some of the things you need to consider when choosing how to implement your client-server application:

- Performance and scalability. If throughput requirements are high and optimum price/performance the goal, a two-tier implementation using business logic in stored procedures may work best. If your business services are resource-intensive and you need to use multiple servers with the application, then a three-tier implementation would be a better choice.
- If many different client platforms need to access your application, consider an Internet implementation.
- If you are skilled in a particular language or have existing code or applications, then choosing to implement in that language is going to cost less.
- Consider the administrative overhead required by each implementation as part of your plan.
- Some implementations require an application to be oriented to a specific database or language.

Understand all of the alternatives and the trade-offs for each before making a final decision and choosing an implementation. There is no single right answer that works for everyone in every situation.

Choosing an Interface

You may have already decided which interface to use as part of the process of deciding which client-server architecture to implement. There are three basic categories of interfaces.

Call-Level Interfaces A *call-level interface* is a set of function calls or APIs enabling client applications to interact with the server. This interface is usually implemented from C/C++ because of its reliance on pointers. It can then be called from languages such as Visual Basic that lack pointer support. SQL Server supports call-level interfaces through ODBC or through the older DB-Library APIs.

Object Interfaces With *object interfaces*, you use objects that can be created by your application to send and retrieve data from the database. Data is obtained through the manipulation of the object's methods and properties. There are several Microsoft object interfaces available, such as OLE DB, ADO, RDO, and DAO. ADO works with OLE DB as a higher-level object interface that avoids much of the programming work of writing directly to OLE DB, which also uses pointers extensively. Both RDO and DAO are older object interfaces whose destiny is to be eventually enfolded in ADO.

Embedded SQL *Embedded SQL* is an ANSI-standard programming interface allowing you to incorporate SQL statements into the source code of your application. Embedded SQL is somewhat slower than call-level interfaces for applications written in C. The advantage is that embedded SQL is portable and easy for Oracle, DB2, and Cobol programmers to understand.

What Is OLE DB?

OLE DB is the new COM interface data providers. It defines an object hierarchy and interfaces for manipulating data. Think of it as just an object version of the ODBC API. OLE DB abstracts the concept of tabular data so that all kinds of data sources can expose common OLE DB interfaces.

When you install SQL Server, the following three OLE DB providers are also installed:

- OLE DB provider for ODBC
- Microsoft SQL Server OLE DB provider
- Microsoft OLE DB provider for Jet

For a complete discussion of OLE DB, see Skill 12, *OLE DB Fundamentals*.

NOTE SQL Server distributed queries are a new feature in SQL Server that allows you to access data from multiple data sources that are stored in either the same or different computers. The data can be stored in multiple SQL Servers or be heterogeneous data stored in some other data source, such as a relational database. It can even be non-relational data stored in spreadsheets or text files. Distributed queries are designed to work with any OLE DB provider that implements the requisite OLE DB interfaces. See Skill 6, *Retrieving Data*, for more information on distributed queries.

Client-Side Design

Unfortunately there is no single design that is good for every application. Much depends on how complex your application is and how much data is being processed. You then need to weigh these factors against the capacity of your network and your server. Sometimes it's more efficient to split the workload between the client and the server by keeping local tables on the client. Good candidates for local tables might include:

- Tables with static data that rarely changes
- Data which fills list boxes and combo boxes that are frequently refreshed
- Data that does not need to be updated immediately on the server
- Data that needs several pieces in order to construct a complete transaction
- Complex reports that summarize and consolidate data

If you are using local lookup tables, you need to make sure that data is refreshed locally if and when it is ever changed.

Optimizing Data Access

There are two "golden rules" you need to follow when attempting to optimize your client-server application:

1. Execute queries entirely on the server—do not fetch data and process it locally.
2. Minimize the number of connections and the amount of data traveling across the network.

A server's strength is its ability to quickly and efficiently process data. This doesn't happen automatically—you need to construct your queries, forms, and reports accordingly.

For some operations, such as executing local functions on many rows, consider fetching the data into a temporary table and performing the necessary processing there. This will cut down on network traffic and speed up processing.

TIP

If you haven't already done so, add timestamps to your SQL Server tables. A timestamp field changes whenever data changes, so, when a timestamp exists, only one field has to be checked to determine whether there were changes to any of the other fields. This speeds up operations considerably, especially in tables with many fields.

Tips and Tricks

The following are some tips and tricks to optimize your client-server application:

- Fetch only needed data, not the entire table. Configure the SQL statements underlying your forms and reports with a `WHERE` clause to restrict the total number of rows returned. Stay away from filters—in effect, with a filter you're going to the well twice for the same data.
- Use unbound forms and fetch only the data needed to populate a single record. Users can only edit one record at a time, so it makes sense to fetch only one record. You can then create an Edit and a Save button, which will post any changes back to the server.
- Be aware of the difference between snapshots and dynasets. You may need to benchmark performance results in situations where you are fetching a lot of rows that don't need to be updated. Often dynasets will give better performance on large amounts of data since only the keys are fetched. Snapshots need to retrieve all of the data.
- Create your combo and list boxes on local tables wherever possible. Combo boxes and list boxes actually run separate queries to fetch data, so they will be faster and create less network traffic if they are based on local tables. You can always have a mechanism in place to refresh a user's copy of local tables if the data on the server changes.

- Don't use heterogeneous joins between local tables and server tables. If you have lookup tables that you use locally, don't join them to server tables to create reports. Instead have two copies of the lookup tables; one copy on the server for using in joins with other tables and the local copy for combo and list boxes where joins aren't needed.
- Stay away from built-in or user-defined functions in your queries. SQL Server does not support most of them, which means that data has to be fetched locally and processed line-by-line against the called function.
- Use transactions any time you need several operations to be processed as a single unit. Be aware that SQL Server does not support nested transactions, so these will be ignored.
- Use the `.FindFirst` method. This is slow in Jet but is processed efficiently with SQL Server.
- Be parsimonious when retrieving OLE and text (memo) fields since their large size increases network traffic. If you must include them on your forms, then make them "on demand only"—force the user to click a button to fetch and display them.
- Base reports on local tables except for reports that need to summarize large amounts of data or to use statistical functions not supported locally.
- Don't use sorting and grouping in queries fetching data for reports. The report engine needs to perform sorting and grouping locally, so there's no sense slowing things down by doing the same work twice.

TIP

Use the SQL Server Profiler utility in order to track your ODBC connections. You can configure the Profiler to monitor all server activity by creating traces used to analyze and resolve server resource issues. You can either view them on screen or save them to a file. This allows you to troubleshoot parts of your application that may be running too slowly. See Skill 8, *Using SQL Server Tools*, for more information on the Profiler.

Using the Older Query Libraries

When you work with SQL Server through the application side, you have a choice of data access techniques. A lot depends on the application and version you are using.

If you are using Microsoft Access, you can use DAO, ODBC, or ODBCDirect to query SQL Server data. If you are using Visual Basic Enterprise Edition, you can use all of the above plus ADO and RDO. No matter which application you use, you will be using Visual Basic for Applications (VBA), so the syntax used will be similar in many instances. Only the object models will vary.

ODBC

ODBC allows different types of application software to communicate with many types of database servers. It performs translation services between the application and the server so that the application does not need to be rewritten if you want to switch database servers. The ODBC components are the ODBC Driver Manager and the ODBC Driver, which sit between the application and the data source, as shown in Figure 11.4.

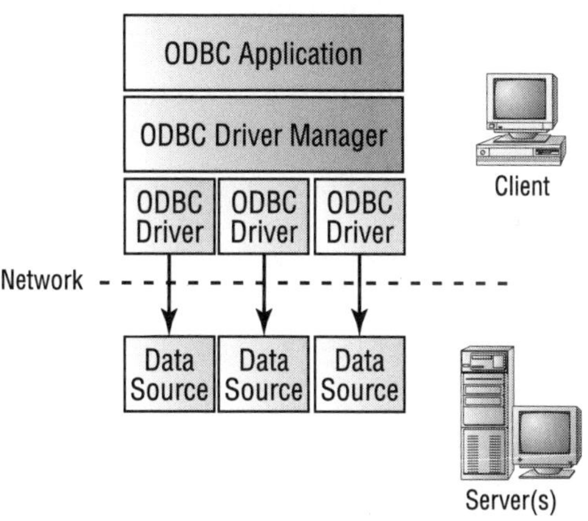

FIGURE 11.4: ODBC architecture

The way ODBC works is that the application calls the ODBC Driver Manager, which is then responsible for processing the application's request and figuring out which ODBC Driver to load to process the request. The ODBC Driver then translates the request into syntax that the database server understands. In order for the Driver Manager to do its work, you need to set up an ODBC data source using the ODBC Administrator (which is part of Windows and is accessible through the Control Panel).

WARNING ODBC drivers themselves are generally supplied by the database vendor, although some are supplied with various products, such as Microsoft Office. Make sure that you are using the most recent driver available and that all workstations are using the same version. Different versions of the same driver can cause erratic and unpredictable behavior.

When you set up a data source (or DSN), you need to choose between User DSNs and System DSNs. A User DSN will only be available to the user who is logged on to the network when it was created. A System DSN will be available to all users. Once you've configured your DSN, you're ready to go.

DAO

DAO (Data Access Objects) is a programmable hierarchy of objects with the DBEngine object as the parent object, as shown in Figure 11.5. DAO is used with the Jet database engine in order to work with Access tables. However, if you are using Access as a front-end for your application, you can also use DAO with linked SQL Server tables and views. If you are already familiar with programming DAO from using Access, you can continue to use it with SQL Server. However, of all the methods described in this skill, using DAO will be the slowest, since queries are processed by the Jet engine as well as by ODBC and SQL Server. You can avoid this in Access 97 by using ODBCDirect to bypass the Jet engine, which we will discuss later in this skill.

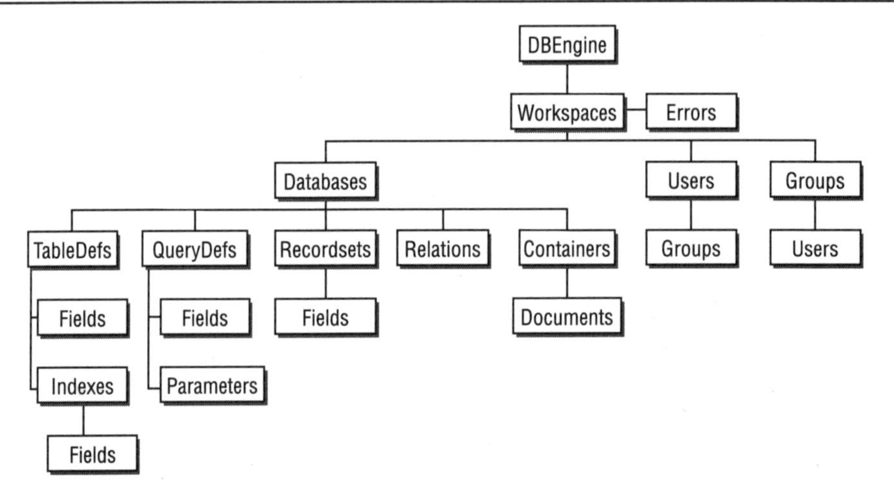

FIGURE 11.5: The DAO object hierarchy

Querying through DAO

In Figure 11.5, DBEngine represents a single instance of the Jet engine. The `Workspace` collection contains individual `Workspace` objects which define the security context of the session, while the `Databases` collection contains `Database` objects which also contain various collections of objects, all of which can be accessed programmatically through VBA.

When you link a SQL Server table or view, it shows up in the database container and can be manipulated in Access, appearing as though it were a native Access table, as shown in Figure 11.6. You can write queries, create forms and reports, and otherwise use the table the same way you would an Access table. This is good for prototyping and for some smaller applications but is not appropriate for more complex applications or larger tables, for performance reasons.

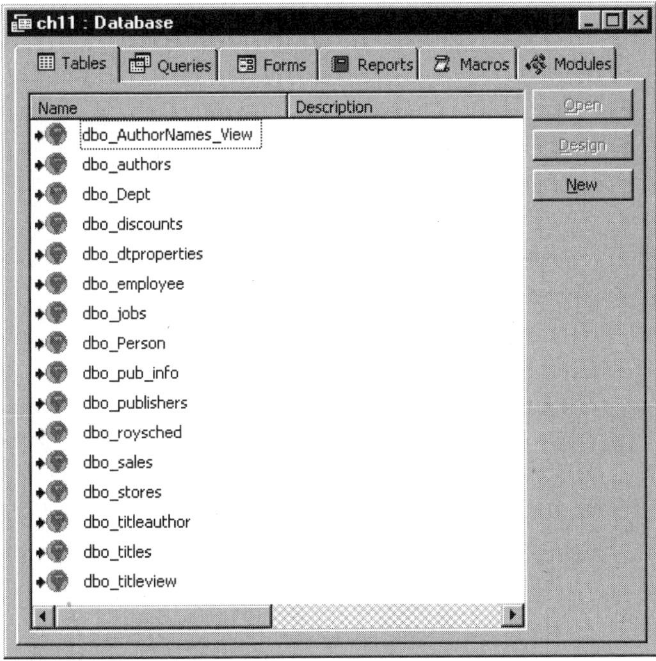

FIGURE 11.6: Linked SQL Server tables in Access

You can work with linked tables using the Access user interface. This makes it easy for an Access developer to create queries, forms, and reports based on your SQL Server data since no special knowledge is required. There is no apparent difference between Access and SQL Server tables since ODBC is providing all of the translation services. Although this may not be the most efficient way to work with data, it does have the advantage of being easy to use and can be a good way to rapidly build a prototype for a larger application.

The first step is getting connected to the server. You need to create a `Workspace` object and then a `Database` object first. Then after you connect, you can close the `Database` object and the connection will persist. The following code connects to SQL Server using integrated security (you don't have to pass a user ID and password). In this example we've set up a DSN named SQL-pubs that points to the pubs database on SQL Server as the default database.

```
Public Function CacheConnect() As Boolean
    Dim ws As Workspace
    Dim db As Database
    Dim strConnect As String

    On Error GoTo HandleErr
    strConnect = "ODBC;DATABASE=pubs;UID=;PWD=;DSN=SQL-pubs"
    Set ws = DBEngine.Workspaces(0)
    Set db = ws.OpenDatabase("", False, False, strConnect)
    db.Close
    CacheConnect = True

ExitHere:
    On Error Resume Next
    ws.Close
    Exit Function
HandleErr:
    CacheConnect = False
    Resume ExitHere
End Function
```

You can also link tables in code. The following procedure uses DAO to create a new `TableDef` object in Access and then connects to the server. The `.Connect` and the `.SourceTableName` properties then link to the authors table in the pubs database:

```
Public Sub ConnectAuthors()
    Dim db As Database
    Dim strConnect As String
    Dim tdf As TableDef

    strConnect = "ODBC;DATABASE=pubs;UID=;PWD=;DSN=SQL-pubs"
    Set db = CurrentDb
    Set tdf = db.CreateTableDef("Authors")
    tdf.Connect = strConnect
    tdf.SourceTableName = "authors"
    db.TableDefs.Append tdf
End Sub
```

If you use Access, you can design queries to run against SQL Server data. Any query you compose in Access SQL is translated by ODBC. One exception to this is the Access pass-through query, which bypasses the Jet engine entirely and is passed through to the server for processing. This allows you to run any type of query and to execute stored procedures.

To create a pass-through query in Access, create a new query and choose the Query ➢ SQL-Specific ➢ Pass-Through from the menu. Then you can either type the name of a stored procedure or type the appropriate Transact-SQL commands, as shown in Figure 11.7. You can set the ODBC connection string by selecting the `query` properties and clicking the builder button (the one with three dots) which will walk you through setting up the connection for your query.

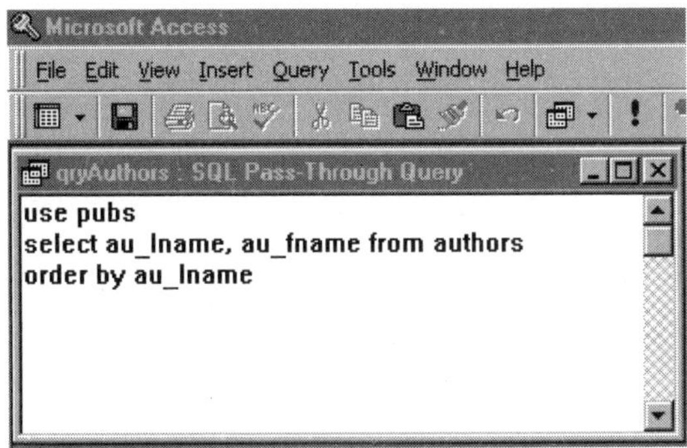

FIGURE 11.7: Creating a pass-through query in Access

You can also create a pass-through query in code. The following function inserts a record in the authors table by creating a non-persistent `QueryDef` object, which is then discarded after the code has run. You then set the `.ReturnsRecords` property to specify whether the query returns records or not. In this example, we are passing empty double quotation marks to the `CreateQueryDef` method, which causes the pass-through query not to be saved in the Access database container.

```
Public Function CreatePass-Through() As Boolean
    Dim db As Database
    Dim qdf As QueryDef
    Dim strConnect As String
    Dim strSQL As String
    Dim strErrors As String
    Dim errX As Error

    On Error GoTo HandleErr
```

```
    strSQL = "INSERT INTO authors (au_id, au_lname, " _
      & "au_fname, contract) VALUES ('111-22-3333', " _
      & "'Sherwood', 'Robert', 0)"
    strConnect = "ODBC;DATABASE=pubs;UID=;PWD=;DSN=SQL-pubs"
    Set db = CurrentDb
    Set qdf = db.CreateQueryDef("")
    With qdf
        .Connect = strConnect
        .ReturnsRecords = False
        .SQL = strSQL
        .Execute dbSQLPass-Through
    End With
    CreatePass-Through = True

ExitHere:
    Exit Function

HandleErr:
    CreatePass-Through = False
    For Each errX In Errors
        strErrors = strErrors & Err & ": " & _
          Err.Description & vbCrLf
    Next errX
    MsgBox strErrors, , "Errors in CreatePass-Through"
    Resume ExitHere
End Function
```

NOTE When you are writing pass-through queries in Access, you need to use SQL Server syntax, not Access SQL syntax. Although the two are similar, there are important differences. For example, the wildcard character in Access is the asterisk (*) whereas in SQL Server it's a percent sign (%). The syntax `Like 'A*'` in a `WHERE` clause will return all records starting with A in Access, and the syntax `Like 'A%'` will return the same records in SQL Server.

Using ODBCDirect

ODBCDirect is similar to DAO but allows you to connect to SQL Server data without actually loading the Jet database engine. This consumes fewer resources on the client side and can speed data retrieval by providing direct access to ODBC data sources. In addition, ODBCDirect provides access to certain server-specific features that Jet doesn't, such as specifying cursor location, specifying input, and checking return values when using stored procedures.

> **NOTE** ODBCDirect supports asynchronous queries, so you don't have to wait for the query to finish before performing other operations.

ODBCDirect supports batch updating, enabling you to cache Recordset object changes locally and then to submit these changes to the server in a single batch. You can also create simple cursorless result sets, or more complex cursors, depending on your needs. You can also run queries that return any number of result sets as well as limit the number of rows returned. ODBCDirect allows you to monitor all the messages and errors generated by the remote data source without affecting the performance of the executing query.

The ODBCDirect object model looks a lot like the DAO object model, as shown in Figure 11.8.

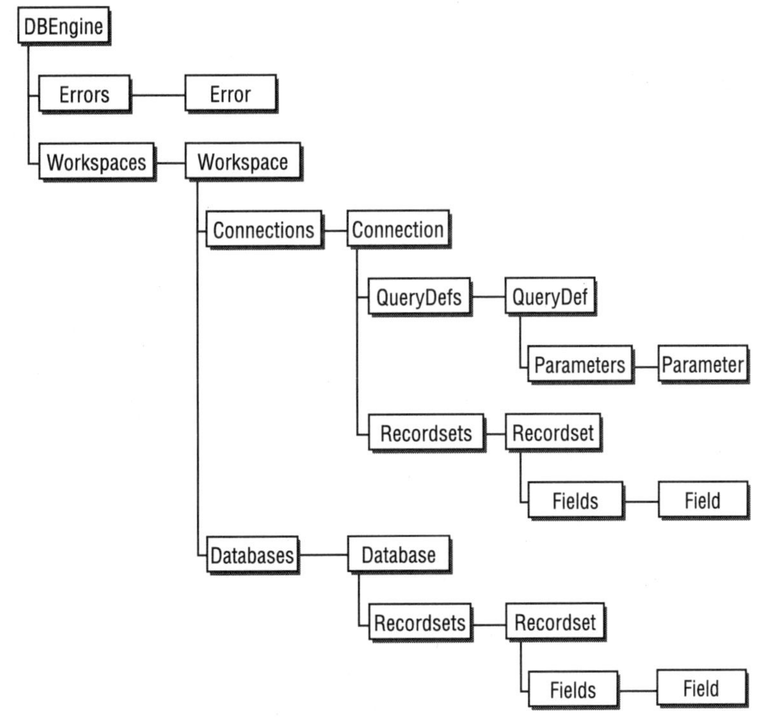

FIGURE 11.8: ODBCDirect objects

To create an ODBCDirect workspace, use the `CreateWorkspace` method and specify the constant `dbUseODBC` for the `type` argument. If you don't specify `dbUseODBC`, then a Jet workspace will open, since that is the default. If you want to change the default, set the `DefaultType` of the `DBEngine` object to `dbUseODBC`:

```
DBEngine.DefaultType = dbUseODBC
```

If you don't want to change the default type, you can open a single workspace using ODBCDirect:

```
Set ws = CreateWorkspace("ODBCws", CurrentUser(), "", dbUseODBC)
```

NOTE You can use both ODBCDirect workspaces and Jet workspaces in the same application.

An ODBC query is very similar to DAO, except that the SQL syntax used is not parsed by Jet, making it very like a pass-through query. Once you've set the workspace, use the `OpenConnection` method of the `Workspace` object to connect to the server. The following example opens an ODBCDirect workspace, connects to the server, and then creates a recordset to fetch data from the authors table.

```
Public Function ConnectODBCDirect() As Boolean
    Dim ws As Workspace
    Dim con As Connection
    Dim rs As Recordset
    Dim errX As Error
    Dim strConnect As String
    Dim strSQL As String
    Dim strErrors As String

    On Error GoTo HandleErr
    strConnect = "ODBC;DATABASE=pubs;UID=;PWD=;DSN=SQL-pubs"
    strSQL = "select au_lname, au_fname from authors"
    Set ws = CreateWorkspace("ODBCws", "Admin", "", dbUseODBC)
    Set con = ws.OpenConnection("ODBCconnection", _
      dbDriverNoPrompt, True, strConnect)
    Set rs = con.OpenRecordset(strSQL, dbOpenSnapshot)
    With rs
        If .RecordCount > 0 Then
            Do Until .EOF
                Debug.Print rs!au_lname, rs!au_fname
                .MoveNext
            Loop
        End If
    End With
    ConnectODBCDirect = True
```

```
ExitHere:
    On Error Resume Next
    con.Close
    ws.Close
    Exit Function

HandleErr:
    ConnectODBCDirect = False
    For Each errX In Errors
        strErrors = strErrors & Err & ": " & _
          Err.Description & vbCrLf
    Next errX
    MsgBox strErrors, , "Errors in ConnectODBCDirect"
    Resume ExitHere
End Function
```

ODBC errors are handled by Jet with the Errors collection, which can contain more than one error at a time. You can iterate through the collection to find out all the errors that may be returned by the server.

RDO

RDO (Remote Data Objects) provides a wrapper around ODBC and is only available with the Enterprise Edition of Visual Basic. It allows you to access SQL Server data more efficiently than DAO. RDO employs a hierarchical structure of programmable objects that looks a lot like DAO, as shown in Figure 11.9. The major difference between the two is that RDO objects are not persistent since there is no native file format it can save them to. The `rdoQuery` object provides a way to make queries persistent for the life of an application but no longer. RDO has more functionality than ODBCDirect and is much faster at retrieving and manipulating data than Jet is, so it's a clear front-runner if you are programming using the Enterprise Edition of Visual Basic 5. If you are using Visual Basic 6, use ADO.

RDO supports a wider variety of cursors and options for returning data to the application. Cursors supported by RDO include the following:

- Keyset cursors, which are similar to dynasets
- Dynamic cursors, which show deletions and additions to data as well as updates to data
- Static cursors, which are similar to snapshots
- Forward-only cursors, which allow you to move through in a forward direction only

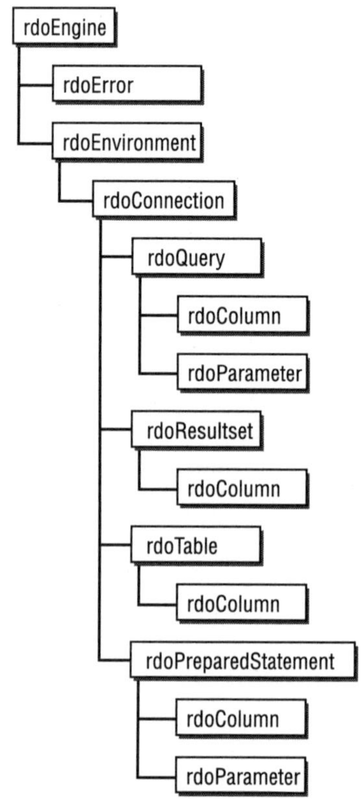

FIGURE 11.9: The RDO object model

- Cursorless result sets, which allow you to retrieve non-updatable records with little overhead
- Server-side cursors, where the set of keys is created on the server and downloaded across the network to the client only as the keys (and their associated records) are needed

NOTE Make sure your tempdb is big enough to handle the result sets that might be opened by simultaneous users if you are using server-side cursors since they are implemented in the server's tempdb database.

Options supported by RDO include the following:

- RDO supports multiple result sets for stored procedures that return more than one result set.

NOTE Multiple result sets are not supported for server-side cursors.

- You can set query limits by imposing a maximum size for the data returned by any single query.
- ODBC handles are exposed as the properties of objects, so that you can program some operations using RDO and speed-critical operations by working directly with the ODBC API.
- RDO can trigger events in your program, which allows you to write event-driven code.
- An RDO `ResultSets` object has the `GetClipString` method, which transforms a set of rows into a delimited string.
- An `RDO Column` object's `KeyColumn` property is True if the column is part of the primary key for the `ResultSet` object.

Querying through RDO

RDO's hierarchical structure provides an object-oriented view of SQL Server data and stored procedures as shown in Figure 11.9.

NOTE If you are writing new RDO code, use `rdoQuery` instead of `rdoPrepared-Statement`. Note that `RdoPreparedStatement` has been replaced by `rdoQuery` in RDO 2 and it is possible that it will be removed from the RDO object model in a future version.

The `rdoEngine` object is the parent object in the collection, much like the `DBEngine` object in DAO. The `rdoEngine` object contains collections of objects, which you need to reference starting with the topmost object, `rdoEngine`. The first thing you need to do in order to use RDO is to set a reference to it by opening a module window in Visual Basic and selecting the Tools ➢ References option from the Reference menu and checking the RDO 2 option, as shown in Figure 11.10.

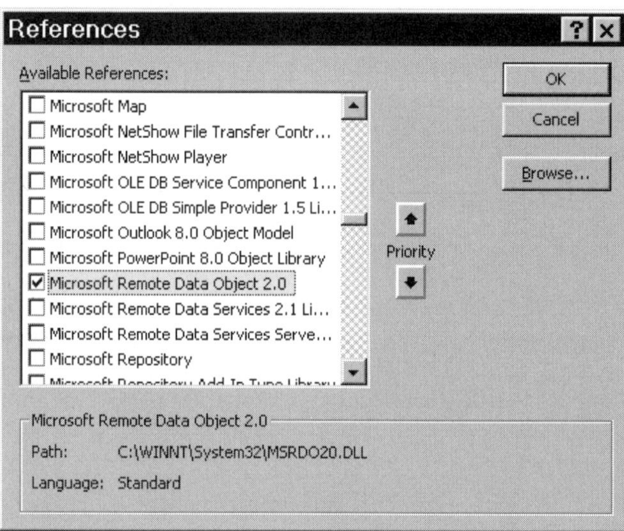

FIGURE 11.10: Setting a reference to RDO

Once you've set the reference, then RDO objects will show up in the Object Browser. You can then initialize the `rdoEngine` object, which allows you to set the default user name and password to use with the server. By setting the `rdoDefaultCursorDriver` property of the `rdoEngine`, you can specify which cursor library your application will use. Valid cursor library options are shown in Table 11.1.

TABLE 11.1: Cursor Library Options

Option	Description
`rdUseIfNeeded`	Default. RDO chooses which library to use. ODBC client-side cursors will be used if server-side cursors are not available.
`rdUseODBC`	Specifies the ODBC cursor library. Good for small result sets.
`rdUseServer`	Specifies the server-side cursor library. Good for large result sets but can cause extra network traffic.
`rdUseClientBatch`	Specifies the optimistic batch cursor library. Performs all operations in batch mode.
`rdUseNone`	No cursors. All result sets will be forward-only and read-only.

The default environment object, rdoEnvironments, is created the first time you use an RDO object. However, if your code is implementing multiple transactions or requires multiple users, then you need to create additional rdoEnvironment objects. Use the OpenConnection method of the rdoEnvironment object to initialize an rdoConnection object and connect to a database. This might prove to be slightly faster than using a previously created DSN. Figure 11.11 shows viewing rdoEnvironment events, methods, and properties.

NOTE You can use the rdoEngine.rdoRegisterDataSource method to create new DSNs in code.

You can use the WithEvents keyword to take advantage of RDO's events in your code. The following code illustrates declaring WithEvents in the declaration of the rdoConnection object:

```
Dim WithEvents mobjConnection as rdoConnection
Set mobjConnection = rdoEnvironments(0). _
     OpenConnection("pubs", Options:=rdAsyncEnable)
```

NOTE When it's time to close the connection, use the rdoConnection.Close method. This frees up resources on the server, so it's a good idea to close any connections you aren't using.

Once you're connected, there are two different ways to work with data. You can use the rdoConnection.OpenResultSet method to return a result set, or an rdoQuery object to access stored procedures or to run the same query multiple times with different parameters. The following will return an rdoResultSet object and create a cursor for the records:

```
Set mResultset = mConnection.OpenResultset( _
             txtSQL)
```

You can then use the WillExecute method of the rdoConnection to decide whether or not to let an RDO operation continue:

```
Private Sub mConnection_WillExecute( _
 ByVal Query As RDO.rdoQuery, Cancel As Boolean)
   Dim intRet As Integer

   If mfScreen Then
       intRet = MsgBox("Continue with execution of " & _
        Query.SQL & "?", vbYesNo + vbQuestion, _
        "RDOTest")
```

```
            If intRet = vbNo Then
                Cancel = True
            End If
        End If
    End Sub
```

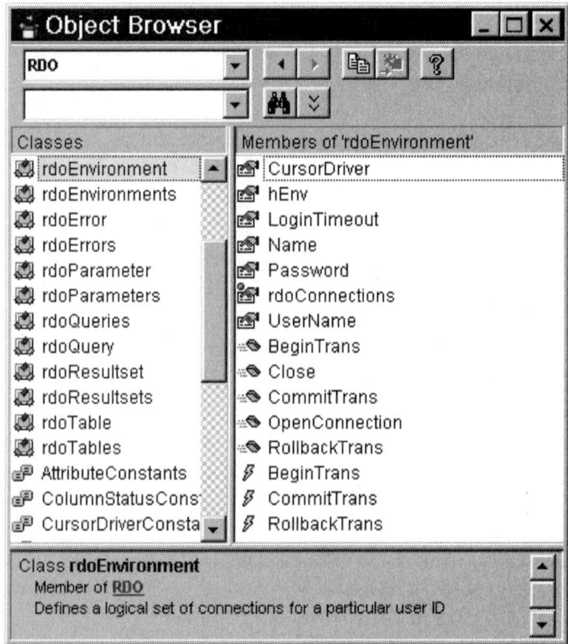

FIGURE 11.11: Using the Object Browser to view rdoEnvironment events, methods, and properties

If you are working with result sets, then the `QueryComplete` event of the `rdoConnection` object will fire. This allows you to process any results and determine which `rdoResultSet` objects have been returned. The `rdoColumn` objects of the `rdoResultSet` can be retrieved either by index or by name, as shown here:

```
Private Sub mConnection_QueryComplete( _
 ByVal Query As RDO.rdoQuery, _
 ByVal ErrorOccurred As Boolean)
    ' Process a resultset
    If ErrorOccurred Then
        DumpErrors
    Else
        lstResults.Clear
```

```
            With mResultset
                If Not .EOF Then
                    Do Until .EOF
                        lstResults.AddItem ( _
                         .rdoColumns(0).Value)
                        .MoveNext
                    Loop
                End If
            End With
        End If
    End Sub
```

If you are not using a forward-only cursor, the `rdoResultSet.MoveLast` method will force population of the result set:

```
mResultSet.MoveLast (rdAsyncEnable)
```

NOTE `MoveLast` can be executed asynchronously, immediately returning control to your application. The `rdoConnection.QueryComplete` event fires when the operation is complete on the server.

When you need to reuse the same query multiple times, use an `rdoQuery` object instead. Table 11.2 describes the options available that affect the behavior of the `rdoQuery` object.

TABLE 11.2: Options for rdoQuery

Property	Comments
`BindThreshold`	Specifies the maximum size of the largest column that can be retrieved. Larger data can still be read by using the `GetChunk` method.
`CursorType`	Specifies the cursor type. Can be `rdOpenForwardOnly`, `rdOpenKeyset`, `rdOpenDynamic`, or `rdOpenStatic`.
`HStmt`	The ODBC statement handle used for calling ODBC API functions.
`LockType`	Controls locking behavior. Can be `rdConcurReadOnly`, `rdConcurLock`, `rdConcurRowVer`, `rdConcurValues`, or `rdConcurBatch`. RDO will substitute a different lock type from the one requested if the server is unable to supply the requested lock type.
`MaxRows`	Maximum number of rows.
`QueryTimeout`	Number of seconds before the `QueryTimeout` event should be fired.
`RowsetSize`	Number of rows to be automatically retrieved when the result set is opened.
`SQL`	SQL statement or stored procedure to be executed.

When you need to execute a query more than once with different criteria, use the following syntax, which creates an `rdoQuery` object with a single parameter:

```
SELECT * FROM CUSTOMERS WHERE City = ?
```

You can then assign this SQL statement to an `rdoQuery`'s `.SQL` property, causing the `rdoParameters` collection to have one member. You need to set the value of the parameter before attempting to retrieve a result set:

```
qrySample.rdoParameters(0).Value = "Burbank"
```

RDO creates a temporary stored procedure on the server to execute `rdoQuery` objects. You can also use an `rdoQuery` object to directly execute stored procedures by setting the `.Execute` property plus the name of the stored procedure, where a question mark indicates the supplied parameter:

```
qrySample.SQL = "Execute mystoredproc ? "
```

Stored procedures with return values need a placeholder for the output parameter, as shown in the following example which executes the system stored procedure `sp_password`. Set the values of `rdoParameters(1)` and `rdoParameters(2)` before executing the query and read the result from `rdoParameters(0)` afterwards.

```
qrySample.SQL = "{ ? = call sp_password (?, ?) }"
```

To update data using the `rdoResultset` object, you use the `.Addnew`, `.Edit`, `.Update`, and `.Delete` methods, which work like their DAO analogs.

NOTE None of the Find family methods work with RDO. You can't use `FindFirst`, `FindNext`, or `FindLast`.

You can use the `.Updatable` property of the `rdoResultset` object to determine whether the user has permission to change data.

NOTE Check the `Updatable` property of the `rdoResultsets` object to see whether or not you have permission to change data in any given result set.

Here are some pointers when implementing RDO in your application:

- Use the smallest cursor feature set that makes sense for your application.
- Consider whether you can use a forward-only cursor, a read-only cursor, or both.

- Using stored procedures minimizes client-side load and network traffic.
- Use static batch cursors to group updates and send them to the server as a batch.
- Use the `.QueryTimeout` property to cancel long-running queries.

The ODBC API

Open Database Connectivity (ODBC) is a common language definition and a set of protocols that allow a client, such as Access, to interactively determine a server's capabilities and to adapt the processing to work within the functions supported by the server. ODBC sits between the application and the data and handles the communications between the two. If you are using Access as a frontend for your client-server application by linking directly to SQL Server tables or views, the ODBC layer is transparent—the linked tables look just like Access tables with a different icon. However, behind the scenes, the Jet Engine transparently converts your queries to the ODBC format and uses this standard for communicating with SQL Server.

SQL Server supports ODBC as one of the native APIs for writing C, C++, and Visual Basic applications that communicate with SQL Server, with the ODBC API communicating with SQL Server through C function calls. The SQL Server setup installs an ODBC driver for use with Microsoft SQL Server any time it installs the SQL Server client utilities. The SQL Server 7 ODBC driver is a Win32 ODBC 3.5 driver.

ODBC defines a core standard SQL grammar and set of function calls, with two levels of optional extensions. ODBC also includes mechanisms for calling server-specific features that are not included in the ODBC standard, which allows you to decide on the level of functionality you want to use when accessing a database server. You have the choice of using the least common denominator of functionality provided by ODBC or of exploiting the full capabilities of the server.

One of the design goals of ODBC is to hide the complexity of the underlying communications necessary for an application to retrieve data from a data source such as SQL Server. ODBC uses an abstraction that maps the data source name to a specific server so that the mechanics of drivers, server addresses, networks, and gateways are hidden from the user.

The SQL Server engine uses OLE DB for communication between internal components, such as the storage engine and relational engine, and for communication between SQL Servers when using remote stored procedures.

SQL Server includes an updated ODBC SQL Server 3.*x* driver that is compliant with the ODBC 3 standard and a beta release of the ODBC 3.5 Driver Manager.

The ODBC SQL Server driver fully supports Sphinx and SQL Server 6.*x* servers. Use ADO for developing business applications and OLE DB if you are developing a middle-tier data provider that needs to expose a private interface other than ADO or if you need to share rowsets with other OLE DB consumers. Use ODBC only for "low level" development (outside of the COM environment) of SQL database applications.

When writing ODBC API code, you'll be communicating directly with either the Driver Manager or the driver. In general, the Driver Manager handles connecting and disconnecting chores while the driver is concerned with the actual data retrieved from the server. You don't need to be concerned with directing your commands to the correct component. The ODBC libraries will automatically choose the driver or the Driver Manager as necessary.

The ODBC SQL Server driver includes a new set of SQL Server bulk copy functions that are identical to the DB-Library bulk copy functions. Some of the new features include:

- Descriptors allowing you to execute procedures using named parameters
- Diagnostic arrays to provide more detailed SQL Server error information
- Performance improvements by using quick rebinding by offset, allowing you to use an existing set of bindings with a new memory location
- Connection pooling to increase performance for applications that make and break the same connection to SQL Server

The ODBC SQL Server 3.5 driver fully supports programs using Active Data Objects (ADO), OLE DB ODBC provider, DAO, RDO, Active Server Pages (ASP), and Internet Database Connector (IDC).

Querying through the ODBC API

OLE DB providers that support command objects, such as the OLE DB ODBC provider, also define the command dialect to use in the text of commands. The OLE DB ODBC driver uses the DBGUID_DBSQL syntax, which is ANSI SQL with the ODBC escape sequences.

When using the OLE DB ODBC provider with the SQL Server ODBC driver, you can use any SQL syntax supported by the SQL Server ODBC driver and SQL Server (ANSI SQL supported by SQL Server, ODBC SQL syntax supported by the ODBC driver, and Transact-SQL syntax).

When targeting portability across different SQL-based OLE DB providers, use primarily ANSI and ODBC SQL syntax. To take advantage of the extensions to ANSI SQL offered by SQL Server, you can always use Transact-SQL syntax for OLE DB applications running against Microsoft SQL Server.

Writing directly to the ODBC API bypasses all but the essential connectivity and translation layers contained in the driver and Driver Manager. This requires the most extensive programming effort on your part. You need to write your code in C, C++, or through API calls in VBA. This means more complex code and more difficult code maintenance. The trade-off here is between the speed of your application and the time that it takes to complete it. Also bear in mind that, as the operating system changes, you're more likely to have to change ODBC API calls than code written using some of the other data access methods such as DAO and RDO.

In general, programming to the ODBC API involves a fixed series of actions:

1. Initialize the necessary data structures.
2. Send SQL statements to the server for execution.
3. Retrieve results from the server.
4. Destroy the data structures.

ODBC uses three main data structures: an environment, a connection, and a statement. The environment contains high-level information of interest to ODBC itself and you'll seldom, if ever, need to manipulate it after creating it. The connection contains information on the particular server—you need to somehow associate this to a Data Source Name (DSN). The statement relates to a particular SQL statement sent to the connection.

We'll see below how to create and use each of these data structures. Each data structure can be passed back and forth by means of a *handle*—a 32-bit address that can be stored in a VBA long integer. Use module-level variables for all handles so that they remain in scope between calls to the various functions that you declare.

Creating the Environment

To create an ODBC environment, your code needs to call `SQLAllocEnv`. If you have an application that frequently connects to and disconnects from various servers, you'll want to create the environment once in a function of its own, and have it available for multiple connections, one after the other.

NOTE

Aliasing is the process of assigning a new name to an API call in your Access code. It's generally a good idea to use an aliased name. VBA lets you have the same public procedure name in multiple modules. However, if you do this you will have to use the full `modulename.procedurename` syntax every time you wish to call the function.

`SQLAllocEnv` takes only a single argument, `hEnv`. The function uses this to return the environment handle, which is used in subsequent calls within that environment.

Making the Connection

The `ODBCConnect` function is an Access function that connects your application to a specific SQL Server via the ODBC API. It takes three arguments, as shown in Table 11.3.

TABLE 11.3: Arguments to ODBCConnect()

Argument	Meaning
`strServer`	Data Source Name to connect to. This must be set up with ODBC Administrator before running the function.
`strUID`	User ID to use when logging on to the server. Leave empty to use integrated security.
`strPassword`	Password to log on with. Leave empty to use integrated security.

```
Option Compare Database
Option Explicit

Declare Function oSQLAllocEnv Lib "odbc32.dll" Alias _
 "SQLAllocEnv" (phenv As Long) As Integer
Declare Function oSQLAllocConnect Lib "odbc32.dll" Alias _
 "SQLAllocConnect" (ByVal henv As Long, phdbc As Long) As Integer
Declare Function oSQLConnect Lib "odbc32.dll" Alias "SQLConnect" _
 (ByVal hdbc As Long, ByVal szDSN As String, ByVal cbDSN _
 As Integer, ByVal szUID As String, ByVal cbUID As _
 Integer, ByVal szAuthStr As String, ByVal cbAuthStr _
 As Integer) As Integer
Declare Function oSQLAllocStmt Lib "odbc32.dll" Alias _
 "SQLAllocStmt" (ByVal hdbc As Long, pHstmt As Long) _
 As Integer

' Possible ODBC return codes
Public Const SQL_INVALID_HANDLE = -2
Public Const SQL_ERROR = -1
```

```
Public Const SQL_SUCCESS = 0
Public Const SQL_SUCCESS_WITH_INFO = 1
Public Const SQL_STILL_EXECUTING = 2
Public Const SQL_NEED_DATA = 99
Public Const SQL_NO_DATA_FOUND = 100

' Null handles used by SQLError
Public Const SQL_NULL_HENV = 0
Public Const SQL_NULL_HDBC = 0
Public Const SQL_NULL_HSTMT = 0

' Miscellaneous constants
Public Const SQL_MAX_MESSAGE_LENGTH = 512
Public Const SQL_NULL_DATA = -1

Function ODBCConnect(strServer As String, _
    strUID As String, strPassword As String) _
    As Boolean
' Take a hard-coded ODBC data source, connect
' to it, and open a statement. Returns True on
' success, false on any error
    Dim intRet As Integer
    Dim strConnIn As String
    Dim strConnOut As String * 256
    Dim intConnOut As Integer

    On Error GoTo ODBCConnectErr
    ODBCConnect = True
    ' Allocate the environment
    intRet = oSQLAllocEnv(mlngHenv)
    If intRet <> SQL_SUCCESS Then
        ' ODBCErrorInfo processes any errors
        ' returned by the server
        Call ODBCErrorInfo(mlngHenv, _
            SQL_NULL_HDBC, SQL_NULL_HSTMT)
    End If
    ' Allocate the connection
    intRet = oSQLAllocConnect(ByVal _
        mlngHenv, mlngHdbc)
    If intRet <> SQL_SUCCESS Then
        Call ODBCErrorInfo(mlngHenv, _
            mlngHdbc, SQL_NULL_HSTMT)
    End If
    ' Connect to the server
    intRet = oSQLConnect(ByVal mlngHdbc, _
        strServer, Len(strServer), strUID, _
        Len(strUID), strPassword, Len(strPassword))
    strConnIn = ""
    If intRet <> SQL_SUCCESS Then
        Call ODBCErrorInfo(mlngHenv, _
            mlngHdbc, SQL_NULL_HSTMT)
```

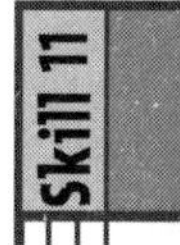

```
        End If
        ' Allocate the statement
        intRet = oSQLAllocStmt(ByVal mlngHdbc, _
            mlngHstmt)
        If intRet <> SQL_SUCCESS Then
            Call ODBCErrorInfo(mlngHenv, _
                mlngHdbc, mlngHstmt)
        End If
    ODBCConnectExit:
        Exit Function

    ODBCConnectErr:
        MsgBox Err.Number & ": " & Err.Description, _
            vbCritical, "ODBCConnect()"
        ODBCConnect = False
        Resume ODBCConnectExit
    End Function
```

The `ODBCConnect` function first uses `SQLAllocEnv` to set aside storage for an environment, and then `SQLAllocConnect` to set aside storage for a connection. `SQLAllocConnect` requires two arguments. The first is the environment handle from the call to `SQLAllocEnv`. The second is the connection handle, which the function will return after successfully setting aside storage space for the connection.

The call to `SQLConnect` does the actual work of connecting from our program to an individual SQL Server (or other ODBC data source). This function takes a number of arguments. Finally, we call `SQLAllocStmt` to set aside storage for a statement. This initializes the statement handle `mlngHstmt`, which can then be used to send SQL straight to the server. `SQLAllocStmt` takes two arguments: the connection handle to contain the statement, and the statement handle to be returned.

TABLE 11.4: Arguments to SQLConnect

Argument	Meaning
`hdbc`	Connection handle to use in making this connection
`szDSN`	Data Source Name (DSN) to connect to
`cbDSN`	Length of `szDSN`
`szUID`	User ID to log on to the server
`cbUID`	Length of `szUID`
`szAuthStr`	Password to log on to the server
`cbAuthStr`	Length of `szAuthStr`

As an alternative to using SQLConnect with the DSN of a server, you can use SQLConnectWithPrompt. This allows you to supply incomplete DSN information as part of the connect call. If the information is incomplete, the user is prompted via standard ODBC dialog boxes to supply the missing information. You can use the SQLDriverConnect API call to allow the user to select a data source at runtime.

```
Declare Function oSQLDriverConnect Lib "odbc32.dll" Alias
➥"SQLDriverConnect" (ByVal hdbc As Long, ByVal Hwnd As Long, ByVal
➥szConnStrIn As String, ByVal cbConnStrIn As Integer, ByVal
➥szConnStrOut As String, ByVal cbConnStrOutMax As Integer,
➥pcbConnStrOut As Integer, ByVal fDriverCompletion As Integer) As
➥Integer
```

The following code snippet will perform the connection:

```
strConnIn = ""
intRet = oSQLDriverConnect(ByVal mlngHdbc, _
    hWndAccessApp, strConnIn, 0, strConnOut, _
    255, intConnOut, SQL_DRIVER_PROMPT)
```

Table 11.5 shows the arguments to SQLDriverConnect.

TABLE 11.5: Arguments to SQLDriverConnect

Argument	Meaning
hdbc	Connection handle to use in making this connection.
hwnd	Window handle to anchor any required dialog box.
szConnStrIn	A (possibly incomplete) ODBC connect string.
cbConnStrIn	Length of szConnStrIn.
szConnStrOut	Storage for the actual connect string. If the function is successful, this will be filled in by the driver.
cbConnStrOutMax	Available length of szConnStrOut.
pcbConnStrOut	Actual length used in szConnStrOut.
fDriverCompletion	Flag that controls how the user will be prompted for more information if necessary. Use SQL_DRIVER_PROMPT to prompt the user for all necessary information.

Handling Errors

Every ODBC call returns an integer indicating the success or failure of the call. Possible values for this return value are shown in Table 11.6.

TABLE 11.6: ODBC API Return Values

Constant	Meaning
SQL_INVALID_HANDLE	One or more of the handles (environment, connection, or statement) supplied to the call was invalid.
SQL_ERROR	An error occurred within the ODBC layer.
SQL_SUCCESS	The call succeeded.
SQL_SUCCESS_WITH_INFO	The call succeeded, but further information is available via SQLError.
SQL_STILL_EXECUTING	An asynchronous call is still processing on the server.
SQL_NEED_DATA	The server is waiting for further information.
SQL_NO_DATA_FOUND	A call to SQLError found no further data.

Any ODBC call can post an error or multiple errors. One technique you can use is to check the return value after each call. If it's not SQL_SUCCESS, call the ODBCErrorInfo function, which will tell you about all of the errors and warnings that occurred during the call.

```
Sub ODBCErrorInfo(lngHenv As Long, _
    lngHdbc As Long, _
    lngHstmt As Long)

    Dim strSQLState As String * 5
    Dim strErrorMessage _
        As String * SQL_MAX_MESSAGE_LENGTH
    Dim lngNativeError As Long
    Dim intRet As Integer
    Dim intErrorLength As Integer
    intRet = SQL_SUCCESS
    Do Until intRet = SQL_NO_DATA_FOUND
    Debug.Print intRet
        intRet = oSQLError(lngHenv, _
            lngHdbc, lngHstmt, strSQLState, _
            lngNativeError, strErrorMessage, _
            SQL_MAX_MESSAGE_LENGTH - 1, _
            intErrorLength)
        #If FDEBUG Then
            If intErrorLength <= 255 Then
                MsgBox Left$(strErrorMessage, _
                    intErrorLength)
            Else
                MsgBox strErrorMessage
```

```
                End If
            #Else
                If intErrorLength <= 255 Then
                    Debug.Print Left$(strErrorMessage, _
                        intErrorLength)
                Else
                    Debug.Print strErrorMessage, _
                        intErrorLength
                End If
            #End If
        Loop
    End Sub
```

The `ODBCErrorInfo` function is able to report on errors generated on any of the ODBC handles, so it takes all of the current handles as arguments. In turn, it calls the `SQLError` API function to return information from the ODBC layer. Table 11.7 shows the arguments to this call. This procedure also uses the `FDEBUG` conditional compilation constant to decide whether to post the messages to the user interface or just to the Debug window.

TABLE 11.7: Arguments to SQLError

Argument	Meaning
`henv`	Current environment handle. Use the constant `SQL_NULL_HENV` if there is no environment handle.
`hdbc`	Current connection handle. Use the constant `SQL_NULL_HDBC` if there is no connection handle.
`hstmt`	Current statement handle. Use the constant `SQL_NULL_HSTMT` if there is no statement handle.
`szSQLState`	Current state of the SQL connection. String value supplied by the server.
`pfNativeError`	Native error code supplied by the server.
`szErrorMsg`	Native error message supplied by the server.
`cbErrorMsgMax`	Length of the `szErrorMsg` buffer.
`pcbErrorMsg`	Actual length used in the `szErrorMsg` buffer.

The SQL Server ODBC driver returns `SQL_ERROR` any time it encounters a severity 11 or higher error on the server. Errors of severity 10 or less return `SQL_SUCCESS_WITH_INFO` instead. During the process of connecting to a server, for example, several low-severity messages are returned. If you connect to the pubs database with FDEBUG set to a non-zero value, you'll get a message box for each of these messages:

- Changed database context to master
- Changed language setting to us_english
- Changed database context to pubs

Sending a Query

The end result of calling either ODBCConnect or ODBCConnectWithPrompt (assuming that there are no errors in connecting to the server) is to allocate a *statement handle* at the module level, mlngHstmt. This serves as a pipeline you can use to execute queries on the server. The simplest way to do this is to use the SQLExecDirect call, followed by the SQLFetch call. SQLExecDirect sends a query to the server and returns the results to a statement handle. SQLFetch fetches the next row of results queued up to a statement handle. Table 11.8 shows the arguments to SQLExecDirect.

TABLE 11.8: Arguments to SQLExecDirect

Argument	Meaning
hstmt	Statement handle to use for this query. This determines which server will handle the query. You must already have used SQLConnect or SQLDriverConnect to provide a valid connection to the server.
szSQLStr	SQL string to execute on the server. You must supply this in standard ODBC SQL.
cbSQLStr	Length of szSQLStr.

The SQLFetch function only has one argument—hstmt. This gives the statement handle to fetch data from. You must already have used SQLExecDirect to make results available on this handle.

In the following function, we've wrapped an example of doing this in the ODBCDebugFetch function, which prints the results of a SQL statement out to the Debug window.

```
Function ODBCDebugFetch(strSQL As String) _
    As Boolean
' Execute a SQL statement over an existing
' statement handle and print the results '
' to the Debug window. Returns true on
' success and false on any error
```

```
    Dim intRet As Integer
    Dim intCols As Integer
    Dim i As Integer
    Dim strRet As String * 1024
    Dim lngLength As Long

    ODBCDebugFetch = True

    intRet = oSQLExecDirect(ByVal mlngHstmt, _
        strSQL, Len(strSQL))
    If intRet <> SQL_SUCCESS Then
        Call ODBCErrorInfo(mlngHenv, _
            mlngHdbc, mlngHstmt)
    End If
    If intRet <> SQL_SUCCESS And _
        intRet <> SQL_SUCCESS_WITH_INFO Then
        ODBCDebugFetch = False
        GoTo ODBCDebugFetchExit
    End If
    ' Find the number of columns in the result
    intRet = oSQLNumResultCols(ByVal mlngHstmt, _
        intCols)
    If intRet <> SQL_SUCCESS Then
        Call ODBCErrorInfo(mlngHenv, mlngHdbc, _
            mlngHstmt)
    End If

    intRet = oSQLFetch(ByVal mlngHstmt)
    Do While intRet <> SQL_NO_DATA_FOUND
        For i = 1 To intCols
            intRet = oSQLGetData(ByVal mlngHstmt, _
                i, SQL_C_CHAR, ByVal strRet, _
                1024, lngLength)
            If intRet <> SQL_SUCCESS Then
                Call ODBCErrorInfo(mlngHenv, _
                    mlngHdbc, mlngHstmt)
            End If
            If lngLength = -1 Then
                Debug.Print Space(i) & "#NULL#"
            Else
              Debug.Print Space(i) & Left$(strRet, _
                lngLength)
            End If
        Next i
        intRet = oSQLFetch(ByVal mlngHstmt)
    Loop
ODBCDebugFetchExit:
    Exit Function
```

```
ODBCDebugFetchErr:
    MsgBox Err.Number & ": " & Err.Description, _
        vbCritical, "ODBCDebugFetch()"
    ODBCDebugFetch = False
    Resume ODBCDebugFetchExit
End Function
```

The `SQLExecDirect` function sends the SQL statement directly to the server for execution. Assuming it succeeds, the statement handle `mlngHstmt` now points to a data structure that can be used to retrieve results. We next use the API call `SQLNumResultsCols` to determine how many columns are in the result.

Looping through the entire set of results is done by calling `SQLFetch` repeatedly. Each call to `SQLFetch` loads another record into the statement handle, until finally `SQL_NO_DATA_FOUND` is returned. The inner loop uses the `SQLGetData` call to get the data out of each column of the result set in turn and then to dump it to the Debug window. `SQLGetData` provides a general purpose way to retrieve a column from the most recently fetched row of data. It takes the arguments shown in Table 11.9.

TABLE 11.9: Arguments to SQLGetData

Argument	Meaning
`hstmt`	Statement handle to get data from. You should already have used `SQLFetch` to make data ready on this statement handle.
`icol`	Column number of the data to retrieve. Columns are numbered starting at one.
`fcType`	C data type to use when fetching the data. The easiest thing to do from Access is to always use `SQL_C_CHAR` and depend on Access to convert from the returned string to the data type you want to use.
`rgbValue`	Storage for the data. If you're using `SQL_C_CHAR` for the type, this should be a string variable passed by value.
`cbValueMax`	Length of the storage buffer.
`pcbValue`	Length of the data actually returned.

After you've called `SQLGetData`, the first `pcbValue` bytes of the `rgbValue` buffer will contain the data returned by ODBC.

Binding Columns

As an alternative to using `SQLGetData`, you can bind columns to an ODBC statement. Just as binding a control on an Access form connects that control to a field in the underlying data source, binding in ODBC connects a variable in your code to a field in the ODBC statement. To simplify data management, you can define a user-defined type on the module's Declarations page, as shown in the following example:

```
' Type used to hold information from the Dieter table
Private Type Dieter
    intDieterID As Integer
    lngDieterIDLen As Long
    chrDieterName(50) As Byte
    lngDieterNameLen As Long
End Type
```

This type matches a single row in `tblDieters` in the database. For each field, we've provided storage for the returned data and storage for the length of the returned data.

`BindDemo` declares a particular variable of this type:

```
Dim typDieter As Dieter
```

After making a connection to the database and setting some options for the statement, here's the code that `BindDemo` uses to retrieve records from the table:

```
Declare Function oSQLSetStmtOption Lib "odbc32.dll" Alias _
 "SQLSetStmtOption" (ByVal hstmt As Long, ByVal fOption As _
 Integer, ByVal bparam As Long) As Integer
Declare Function oSQLExecDirect Lib "odbc32.dll" Alias _
 "SQLExecDirect" (ByVal hstmt As Long, ByVal szSqlStr As _
 String, ByVal cbSqlStr As Integer) As Integer
Declare Function oSQLBindCol Lib "odbc32.dll" Alias "SQLBindCol" _
 (ByVal hstmt As Long, ByVal icol As Integer, ByVal fCType As _
 Integer, rgbValue As Any, ByVal cbValueMax As Long, pcbValue _
 As Long) As Integer
Declare Function oSQLFetch Lib "odbc32.dll" Alias "SQLFetch" _
 (ByVal hstmt As Long) As Integer

' Constants used with SQLSetStmtOption
' and SQLGetStmtOption
Public Const SQL_QUERY_TIMEOUT = 0
Public Const SQL_MAX_ROWS = 1
Public Const SQL_NOSCAN = 2
Public Const SQL_MAX_LENGTH = 3
Public Const SQL_ASYNC_ENABLE = 4
Public Const SQL_BIND_TYPE = 5
Public Const SQL_CURSOR_TYPE = 6
Public Const SQL_CONCURRENCY = 7
Public Const SQL_KEYSET_SIZE = 8
```

```
Public Const SQL_ROWSET_SIZE = 9
Public Const SQL_SIMULATE_CURSOR = 10
Public Const SQL_RETRIEVE_DATA = 11
Public Const SQL_USE_BOOKMARKS = 12
Public Const SQL_GET_BOOKMARK = 13
Public Const SQL_ROW_NUMBER = 14

' Possible ODBC return codes
Public Const SQL_INVALID_HANDLE = -2
Public Const SQL_ERROR = -1
Public Const SQL_SUCCESS = 0
Public Const SQL_SUCCESS_WITH_INFO = 1
Public Const SQL_STILL_EXECUTING = 2
Public Const SQL_NEED_DATA = 99
Public Const SQL_NO_DATA_FOUND = 100

' Cursor types
Public Const SQL_CURSOR_FORWARD_ONLY = 0
Public Const SQL_CURSOR_KEYSET_DRIVEN = 1
Public Const SQL_CURSOR_DYNAMIC = 2
Public Const SQL_CURSOR_STATIC = 3

' Concurrency types
Public Const SQL_CONCUR_READ_ONLY = 1
Public Const SQL_CONCUR_LOCK = 2
Public Const SQL_CONCUR_ROWVER = 3
Public Const SQL_CONCUR_VALUES = 4

Function BindDemo()
' Demonstrates connecting to a server, binding columns,
' fetching results, and then disconnecting
    Dim booRet As Boolean
    Dim intRet As Integer
    Dim typDieter As Dieter
    Dim strSQL As String
    Dim strDieter As String
    Dim varDieter As Variant

    booRet = ODBCConnect("Food", "sa", "")
    strSQL = "SELECT * FROM tblDieters"

        ' Set the RowSet size on the statement
    intRet = oSQLSetStmtOption(mlngHstmt, _
        SQL_ROWSET_SIZE, 1)
    If intRet <> SQL_SUCCESS Then
        ' Not a disaster; it'll just use the default
        Debug.Print "Warning: Couldn't set Rowset Size"
        Call ODBCErrorInfo(mlngHenv, mlngHdbc, mlngHstmt)
    End If
```

```
' Set the cursor type for the statement
intRet = oSQLSetStmtOption(ByVal mlngHstmt, _
    SQL_CURSOR_TYPE, SQL_CURSOR_KEYSET_DRIVEN)
If intRet <> SQL_SUCCESS Then
    ' Not a disaster; it'll just use the default
    Debug.Print "Warning: Couldn't set Cursor type"
    Call ODBCErrorInfo(mlngHenv, mlngHdbc, mlngHstmt)
End If

' Set the concurrency type for the statement
intRet = oSQLSetStmtOption(ByVal mlngHstmt, _
    SQL_CONCURRENCY, SQL_CONCUR_ROWVER)
If intRet <> SQL_SUCCESS Then
    ' Not a disaster; it'll just use the default
    Debug.Print "Warning: Couldn't set Concurrency type"
    Call ODBCErrorInfo(mlngHenv, mlngHdbc, mlngHstmt)
End If

intRet = oSQLExecDirect(ByVal mlngHstmt, strSQL, _
    Len(strSQL))
If intRet <> SQL_SUCCESS Then
    Call ODBCErrorInfo(mlngHenv, mlngHdbc, _
        mlngHstmt)
End If
intRet = oSQLBindCol(mlngHstmt, 1, SQL_C_USHORT, _
    typDieter.intDieterID, _
    Len(typDieter.intDieterID), _
    typDieter.lngDieterIDLen)
If intRet <> SQL_SUCCESS Then
    Call ODBCErrorInfo(mlngHenv, mlngHdbc, _
        mlngHstmt)
End If
intRet = oSQLBindCol(mlngHstmt, 2, SQL_C_CHAR, _
    typDieter.chrDieterName(0), 50, _
    typDieter.lngDieterNameLen)
If intRet <> SQL_SUCCESS Then
    Call ODBCErrorInfo(mlngHenv, mlngHdbc, _
        mlngHstmt)
End If
intRet = oSQLFetch(ByVal mlngHstmt)
Do While intRet <> SQL_NO_DATA_FOUND
    strDieter = StrConv(LeftB(typDieter.chrDieterName, _
        typDieter.lngDieterNameLen), vbUnicode)
    Debug.Print typDieter.intDieterID, _
        typDieter.lngDieterNameLen, strDieter
    intRet = oSQLFetch(ByVal mlngHstmt)
Loop
```

```
    booRet = ODBCDisconnect()

End Function
```

As before, the SQLExecDirect call actually executes the query and sets up the result set. But now, before moving through the rows with SQLFetch, we call the SQLBindCol function. This function takes the arguments shown in Table 11.10.

TABLE 11.10: Arguments to SQLBindCol

Argument	Meaning
hstmt	Statement handle to use
icol	Column number to bind, starting at one
fcType	C data type of the column
rgbValue	Storage for the data returned from the column
cbValueMax	Length of the rgbValue buffer
pcbValue	Number of bytes actually returned by the most recent SQLFetch call

Once the column has been bound to a particular variable, each call to SQLFetch sets the variable to hold the data from the current row of the query results. You can read this value freely without needing to make a call to SQLGetData.

One additional thing you need to watch out for in this case, though, is Unicode. Strings are returned as arrays of bytes rather than as Access strings. You'll need to use LeftB and StrConv, as shown in the sample, to actually convert these strings to something that your Access code can use.

Dropping the Connection

When you are done with an ODBC connection, you should drop it. This will preserve resources on your local machine and keep your server from being bogged down by excess connections. There are calls to deallocate each of the data structures in turn, which you can wrap up in a single function:

```
Declare Function oSQLFreeStmt Lib "odbc32.dll" Alias "SQLFreeStmt" _
 (ByVal hstmt As Long, ByVal fOption As Integer) As Integer
Declare Function oSQLDisconnect Lib "odbc32.dll" Alias _
 "SQLDisconnect" (ByVal hdbc As Long) As Integer
Declare Function oSQLFreeConnect Lib "odbc32.dll" Alias _
 "SQLFreeConnect" (ByVal hdbc As Long) As Integer
Declare Function oSQLFreeEnv Lib "odbc32.dll" Alias "SQLFreeEnv" _
```

```
 (ByVal henv As Long) As Integer

' Possible ODBC return codes
Public Const SQL_INVALID_HANDLE = -2
Public Const SQL_ERROR = -1
Public Const SQL_SUCCESS = 0
Public Const SQL_SUCCESS_WITH_INFO = 1
Public Const SQL_STILL_EXECUTING = 2
Public Const SQL_NEED_DATA = 99
Public Const SQL_NO_DATA_FOUND = 100

' Null handles used by SQLError
Public Const SQL_NULL_HENV = 0
Public Const SQL_NULL_HDBC = 0
Public Const SQL_NULL_HSTMT = 0

Function ODBCDisconnect() As Boolean
' Disconnect from the module-level data source
    Dim intRet As Integer
    On Error GoTo ODBCDisconnectErr
    ODBCDisconnect = True
    ' Close the query and drop the statement
    intRet = oSQLFreeStmt(ByVal mlngHstmt, _
        SQL_DROP)
    If intRet <> SQL_SUCCESS Then
        Call ODBCErrorInfo(mlngHenv, _
            mlngHdbc, mlngHstmt)
    End If
    ' Close the connection
    intRet = oSQLDisconnect(ByVal mlngHdbc)
    If intRet <> SQL_SUCCESS Then
        Call ODBCErrorInfo(mlngHenv, mlngHdbc, _
            SQL_NULL_HSTMT)
    End If
    ' Free the connection memory
    intRet = oSQLFreeConnect(ByVal mlngHdbc)
    If intRet <> SQL_SUCCESS Then
        Call ODBCErrorInfo(mlngHenv, mlngHdbc, _
            SQL_NULL_HSTMT)
    End If
    ' Close the environment and free its memory
    intRet = oSQLFreeEnv(ByVal mlngHenv)
     If intRet <> SQL_SUCCESS Then
        Call ODBCErrorInfo(mlngHenv, _
            SQL_NULL_HDBC, SQL_NULL_HSTMT)
    End If
ODBCDisconnectExit:
    Exit Function
```

```
ODBCDisconnectErr:
    MsgBox Err.Number & ": " & Err.Description, vbCritical,
"ODBCDisconnect()"
    ODBCDisconnect = False
    Resume ODBCDisconnectExit
End Function
```

There are four steps to shutting down the ODBC connection entirely:

1. Use `SQLFreeStmt` to stop any query processing and discard the statement handle.
2. Use `SQLDisconnect` to break the connection with the server.
3. Use `SQLFreeConnect` to free the memory used by the connection handle.
4. Use `SQLFreeEnv` to free the memory used by the environment handle.

Three Ways to Update Data

Positioned updates and deletes provide a general purpose way to modify data via ODBC. They do require that you use `SQLExtendedFetch` to retrieve your data, however. If you're using `SQLFetch`, you'll need to find another alternative.

There are two other ways to update data via ODBC. One is to issue a single-row `UPDATE` statement, either by opening a second statement handle or closing the first one and reusing it. In the general case, you must know the value of a unique index to write this update. If you like, you can call the `SQLPrimaryKeys` function to determine the primary key of a table, and use this information in constructing the SQL statement to send to `SQLExecDirect`.

The other way to perform an update via ODBC is through the `SQLSetPos` function. If you issue this call with a parameter of `SQL_UPDATE`, it will take the values you have stored locally and send them back to the server via an ODBC-constructed stored procedure. Unfortunately, there's no way to do this in the general case in Visual Basic for Applications. To do an update this way, you must make use of ODBC Binding, the process of assigning retrieved data to local variables. This requires a foreknowledge of your recordset's structure to create an appropriate user-defined `Type` structure within Access.

In general, if you want to do updates, we recommend not trying to write direct ODBC API calls yourself. You should either use regular recordsets within Access, use the ODBC recordset wrappers with positioned updates and deletes, or use the Visual Basic Remote Data Objects discussed earlier in this skill. Any of these alternatives will allow you to update your data without needing to write large amounts of code.

Using SQL-DMO and SQL-NS

SQL-DMO and SQL-NS give you, the application developer, a way to get into SQL Server and manipulate server objects without having to physically open the Enterprise Manager on the server. Using these interfaces makes it possible to perform administrative actions programatically.

SQL-DMO

SQL Distributed Management Objects (SQL-DMO) allows you to automate the administrative functions of SQL Server from your application by allowing you to manipulate the properties and methods of an object instance. SQL-DMO is implemented as a dual-interface in-process server, which can be used from any OLE automation controller. SQL-DMO allows you to automate the following tasks:

- Any commonly performed administrative tasks
- SQL Server Agent jobs, alerts, and operators
- Installation and configuration of SQL Server replication

SQL-DMO is an object model that encapsulates a collection of SQL Server components. Thus, you can alter the properties of an instance of a SQL-DMO object to administer a server. SQL-DMO has three object types:

- An *object*, which references a single component
- A *collection*, which contains objects as members
- A *list*, which is a container object with a fixed membership

All SQL-DMO objects have properties, such as `Name` or `Count` (for collections). Most objects also expose methods, which perform actions on an instance, and a few have events, which can provide information to the client application. In order to use a SQL-DMO object in your application, you need to do the following:

1. Set a reference to the Microsoft SQL-DMO Object Library in your application.
2. Instantiate a new instance of the SQL-DMO object.
3. Configure the object to reflect the attributes of the desired SQL Server component.
4. Add the configured object to its collection.

The SQL-DMO object model is quite extensive; you can find it in Books Online. An abbreviated version is shown in Figure 11.12. There are three main branches for logically grouping database, agent, and replication tasks.

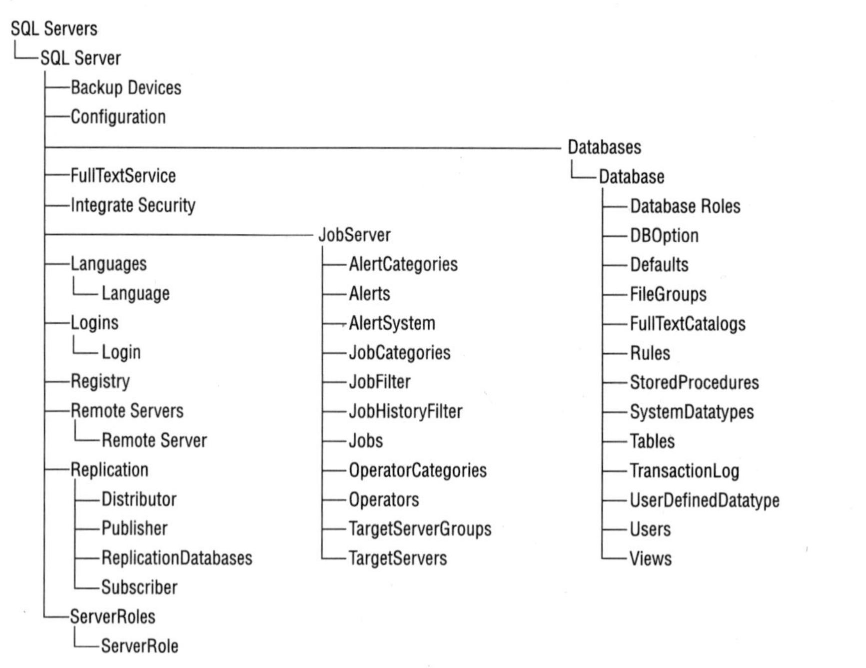

FIGURE 11.12: The SQL-DMO Database object model

The easiest way to work with SQL-DMO from your VBA application is to use the Object Browser to familiarize yourself with the objects you need to use to manipulate your server. Press F2 to load the Object Browser, then select the SQL-DMO object library. You can also search for specific objects, properties, or methods you are interested in, as shown in Figure 11.13. Clicking the question mark (?) icon will bring up online help for the selected item, which will give you further information, as shown in Figure 11.14.

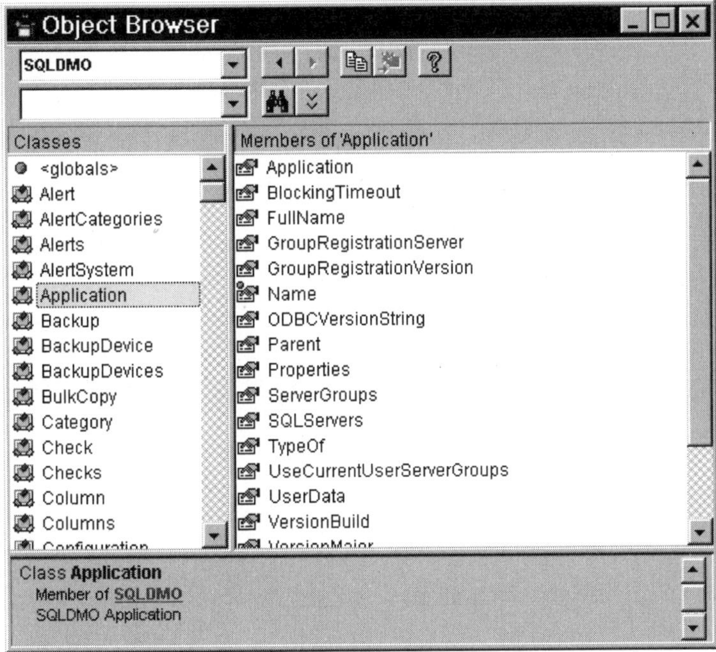

FIGURE 11.13: Using the Object Browser to obtain information about SQL-DMO

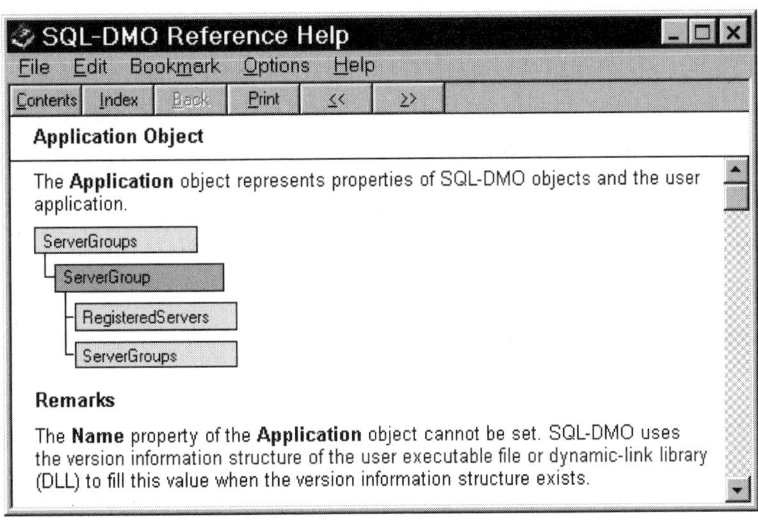

FIGURE 11.14: Obtaining online help for SQL-DMO

When declaring a SQL-DMO object in your VBA application, use the following syntax:

```
Dim objectname As SQLDMO.objecttype
Set objectname = SQLDMO.objecttype
```

or

```
Dim objectname As New SQLDMO.objecttype
```

This instantiates it on the same line. The first version gives you more control since you might not necessarily want to instantiate the object at the same time as you declare it. Once you've instantiated your object, you can then refer to its properties or run its methods using the following syntax:

```
objectname.objectproperty
```

or

```
objectname.objectmethod
```

To add a configured object to its collection, use the following syntax:

```
Parentobjectname.ParentCollection("ItemName").ChildCollection.Add
objectname
```

The following simple example illustrates this by adding a subtotal column to the Order Details table in the Northwind database that computes the unit price times the quantity:

```
Public Sub AddTotalsColumn()
    ' Declare and instantiate new
    ' SQL-DMO objects
    Dim oSQLServer As New SQLDMO.SQLServer
    Dim oColumn As New SQLDMO.Column

    ' Connect to the server
    oSQLServer.Connect

    ' Define the new column attributes
    oColumn.Name = "SubTotalNoDiscount"
    oColumn.DataType = "money"
    oColumn.ComputedText = _
     "CONVERT(money,  Quantity * UnitPrice)"
    oColumn.IsComputed = True

    ' Add the column to the Order Details Columns collection
    oSQLServer.Databases("Northwind").Tables _
     ("[Order Details]").Columns.Add oColumn
End Sub
```

NOTE

There are many other uses for SQL-DMO besides adding columns to tables. You can also create and run stored procedures, manage replication, and back up and restore databases, to name but a few. Unfortunately we don't have space to discuss SQL-DMO fully here—see Books Online for more information.

SQL-NS

Unlike SQL-DMO, which has been around for a while, the SQL-NS (`SQLNamespace`) object is completely new in SQL Server 7. Its purpose is to invoke the SQL Server Enterprise Manager user interface components from your client application. For example, you can run one of the Enterprise Manager wizards to administer your server.

The SQL-NS object model exposes four objects:

- `SQLNamespace`, which sets the local ID for the ISQLNamespace interface
- `SQLNamespaceObject`, which is the interface for each object in the `SQLNamespace`
- `SQLNamespaceCommand`, which is the command interface for a `SQLNamespace` object
- `SQLNamespaceCommands`, which is the collection of commands supported by an object

SQL-NS exposes the following properties:

- `CommandGroup`
- `CommandID`
- `Commands`
- `Count`
- `Handle`
- `HelpString`
- `Name`
- `Type`

SQL-NS exposes the following methods:

- `Execute`

- `ExecuteCommandByID`
- `ExecuteCommandByName`
- `GetChildrenCount`
- `GetFirstChildItem`
- `GetName`
- `GetNextSiblingItem`
- `GetParentItem`
- `GetPreviousSiblingItem`
- `GetRootItem`
- `GetSQLDMOObject`
- `GetSQLNamespaceObject`
- `GetType`
- `Initialize`
- `Item`
- `Refresh`
- `SetLCID`

In addition to its methods and properties, SQL-NS makes use of a great many constants as return values and parameters for its methods and properties. The following lists the main groups of SQL-NS constants. The complete list can be found in Books Online.

- `SQLNSCommandID`
- `SQLNSErrors`
- `SQLNSModality`
- `SQLNSObjectType`
- `SQLNSRootType`

Like SQL-DMO, the first step in using SQL-NS is to set a reference to the Microsoft `SQLNamespace` Object Library in your application. You can then use the Object Browser to investigate further, as shown in Figure 11.15.

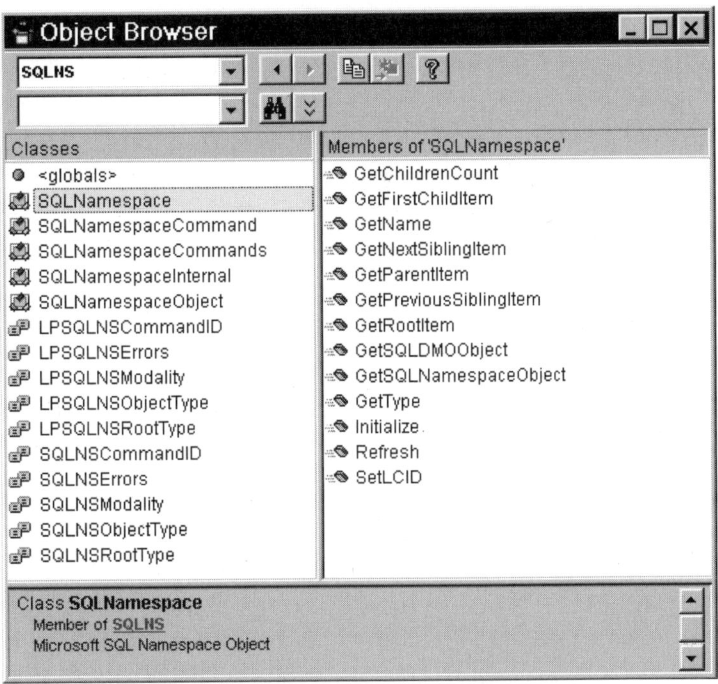

FIGURE 11.15: SQL-NS objects in the Object Browser

You then need to negotiate the hierarchy of objects to get to the one you want, as shown in the following example, which runs from the `Click` event of a Command button on a form to display the properties of the Northwind database. You need to initialize the `SQLNamespace` object, then get the root object, and keep going until you get to the object that you want to run a command on, in this case the Northwind database. The following procedure initializes the `SQLNamespace` object, which starts you off at the root (or the server). You get the root item and any children until you get to the level in the hierarchy where the command exists that you want to execute. The path to the command we want to execute is Server ➢ Databases ➢ Northwind. Once there, you invoke the `.Commands("Properties").Execute` method of the `SQLNamespaceObject` object, which displays the Properties dialog box in the Enterprise Manager.

```
Private Sub cmdNwindProps_Click()
    Dim lngRoot As Long
    Dim lngDatabase As Long
    Dim lngNwind As Long
    Dim oSQLNSObj As SQLNamespaceObject
```

```
        Dim oSQLNS As New SQLNamespace

        On Error GoTo HandleErr
        ' Initialize the SQLNamespace object
        oSQLNS.Initialize "Test", SQLNSRootType_Server, _
         "Server=KARIS;Trusted_Connection=Yes;", Me.Hwnd

        ' Get the root (Server) object
        lngRoot = oSQLNS.GetRootItem

        ' Get the databases
        lngDatabase = oSQLNS.GetFirstChildItem(lngRoot, _
         SQLNSOBJECTTYPE_DATABASES)

        ' Get the Northwind database
        lngNwind = oSQLNS.GetFirstChildItem(lngDatabase, _
         SQLNSOBJECTTYPE_DATABASE, "Northwind")

        ' Set a SQLNamespaceObject to execute the command
        Set oSQLNSObj = oSQLNS.GetSQLNamespaceObject(lngNwind)
        oSQLNSObj.Commands("Properties").Execute

    ExitHere:
        On Error Resume Next
        Set oSQLNSObj = Nothing
        Set oSQLNS = Nothing
        Exit Sub

    HandleErr:
        MsgBox Err & ": " & Err.Description, , _
         "Error in cmdNwindProps_Click"
        Resume ExitHere
    End Sub
```

Note that, when working with the `SQLNamespace` object, it expects you to send it the `.Hwnd` property (or window handle) of a form when you initialize it. This argument is listed as optional, and it's possible that some commands will execute OK without it, but others will not. The example code shown here is being called from a form, so we can pass it the form's window handle (`Me.Hwnd`).

The next function shows how to run the Maintenance Plan Wizard from your application. You need to initialize the `SQLNamespace` root object, then execute the command on the `SQLNamespaceObject` object, which in this case happens to be the Northwind database. In this case we're executing by using the `ExecuteCommandByID` method, which takes the intrinsic constant SQLNS_CmdID_TOOLS_MAINT_PLAN for the Maintenance Plan Wizard.

```
Public Function RunSQLDBMaintWiz() As Boolean
' Run the Database Maintenance Plan Wizard
    Dim oSQLNS As New SQLNS.SQLNamespace
    Dim oSQLNSObj As SQLNS.SQLNamespaceObject
    Dim lngRoot As Long
    Dim lngDatabases As Long
    Dim lngPubs As Long

    On Error GoTo HandleErr
    ' Initialize root object
    oSQLNS.Initialize "Test", SQLNSRootType_Server, _
     "Server=KARIS;Trusted_Connection=Yes;", Me.Hwnd

    If oSQLNS Is Nothing Then
        MsgBox "SQLNamespace could not be initiated.", , _
         "Can't Connect to Server"
        GoTo ExitHere
    End If

    ' Get Databases, then the Northwind database
    lngRoot = oSQLNS.GetRootItem
    lngDatabases = oSQLNS.GetFirstChildItem(lngRoot, _
     SQLNSOBJECTTYPE_DATABASES, "Databases")
    lngPubs = oSQLNS.GetFirstChildItem(lngDatabases, _
     SQLNSOBJECTTYPE_DATABASE, "Northwind")

    ' Execute Tools Maintenance Plan command of SQLNamespaceObject
    Set oSQLNSObj = oSQLNS.GetSQLNamespaceObject(lngPubs)
    oSQLNSObj.ExecuteCommandByID SQLNS_CmdID_TOOLS_MAINT_PLAN, _
     Me.Hwnd, SQLNamespace_PreferModal
    RunSQLDBMaintWiz = True

ExitHere:
    On Error Resume Next
    Set oSQLNSObj = Nothing
    Set oSQLNS = Nothing
    Exit Function

HandleErr:
    MsgBox Err & ": " & Err.Description, , _
     "Error in RunSQLDBMaintWiz"
    RunSQLDBMaintWiz = False
    Resume ExitHere
End Function
```

TIP

The constants needed for the `ExecuteCommandByID` method can be found in the Object Browser.

As you can see from these two samples, programming SQL-NS can give your applications enormous power and flexibility since you can run commands directly upon the Enterprise Manager itself. We've only scratched the surface here, but you should by now have a good idea of how to start building robust applications to manage your SQL Server by using SQL-NS and SQL-DMO.

Declaring local `SQLNamespace` and `SQLNamespaceObject` variables caused problems in the beta version of SQL Server 7. The workaround is to declare them as module-level variables instead.

Are You up to Speed?

Now you can...

- ☑ configure a multiple-tier client-server application
- ☑ use DAO, ODBCDirect, and RDO to manipulate data
- ☑ use SQL-DMO and SQL-NS from your application

SKILL 12

Fundamentals of OLE DB

- OLE DB
- ActiveX Data Objects

In this skill, we'll investigate OLE DB, which provides the glue between SQL Server data and the applications that use it. OLE DB is central to the SQL Server 7 implementation, since it's even used for communication between the core database engine and the rest of the product. In this skill, we'll learn a bit about OLE DB in general and look at the ActiveX Data Objects (ADO) model that is implemented on top of OLE DB.

OLE DB

OLE DB is the centerpiece of the strategy known as Microsoft Universal Data Access. For SQL Server purposes, you can think of OLE DB as the low-level plumbing between SQL Server components. It also provides a way for other programs to retrieve data from SQL Server. In this section, we'll take a brief look at the concepts behind OLE DB, and then at the interfaces that it makes available.

SQL Server 7 ships with OLE DB version 2 and a fully OLE DB 2-compliant data provider for SQL Server data.

What Is OLE DB?

OLE DB is a set of COM interfaces used to make data available to clients that are interested in it. COM, the Component Object Model, is an overall standard for interconnections between different programs and services that forms the basis of Microsoft's ActiveX technologies.

OLE DB partitions the world into data providers and data consumers. Anything that can store data can, at least theoretically, be an OLE DB data provider. Data consumers are programs that use data from OLE DB data providers. In the SQL Server box you'll find both data consumers and data providers. SQL Server ships with a native OLE DB data provider to make SQL Server data available to any OLE DB data consumer and most of the SQL Server utilities—for example, osql—are data consumers.

You may recognize the similarities between OLE DB and the earlier ODBC standard. Both are intended to make it possible to retrieve data from multiple data sources in a vendor-neutral fashion. You might think of OLE DB as ODBC Mark II—it was created based on the experience that Microsoft gained working with ODBC and then extended to support a wider variety of both consumers and providers. On the consumer side, OLE DB is supplied as a set of COM interfaces, making it easy to use from a variety of clients (as well as making it easy for Microsoft to support within the operating system). On the provider side, OLE DB is designed to be more flexible than ODBC, so that even such diverse data stores as Exchange mailboxes and text files could have OLE DB providers written for them.

NOTE OLE DB is built to allow easy integration with ODBC data sources. The OLE DB Software Developers Kit (SDK) ships with an OLE DB data provider that can retrieve data from any ODBC data source.

Connecting to SQL Server with OLE DB

Before you can connect an application to SQL Server via OLE DB, you must configure the driver properly on the client computer. Fortunately, for many developers this will be just an extension of their experience with ODBC. That's because the SQL Server OLE DB driver is designed to retrieve all of the information that it needs from an ODBC DSN. So creating an OLE DB connection is as simple as creating an ODBC connection. Let's walk through the steps you'll need to take to do this.

The process starts with running the ODBC Data Sources applet from the Windows Control Panel.

Choose System DSN or File DSN and click the Add button. (You'll usually want a system DSN. File DSNs are generally required only for internet access or user-level security.)

Choose the SQL Server driver and click the Finish button.

After you choose a driver, the control panel applet hands control over to that driver. The SQL Server driver asks for some configuration information, starting with the dialog box shown in Figure 12.1. We'll walk through the configuration dialog boxes with some typical information filled in. In this case, we're creating a new data source to refer to the pubs database on a computer named Moocow. The description is optional; the name and server are required.

The next dialog box, shown in Figure 12.2, lets you set the security options for the new connection. For a discussion of SQL Server security, see Skill 16, *Managing SQL Server Security*. You need not fill in a username and password here; in fact, you probably shouldn't if you're concerned about security since whatever you fill in will be saved with the connection. Check the Connect To SQL Server checkbox and SQL Server will attempt to connect when you click Next. Fill in as many options as possible in the remaining dialog boxes based on information in the server.

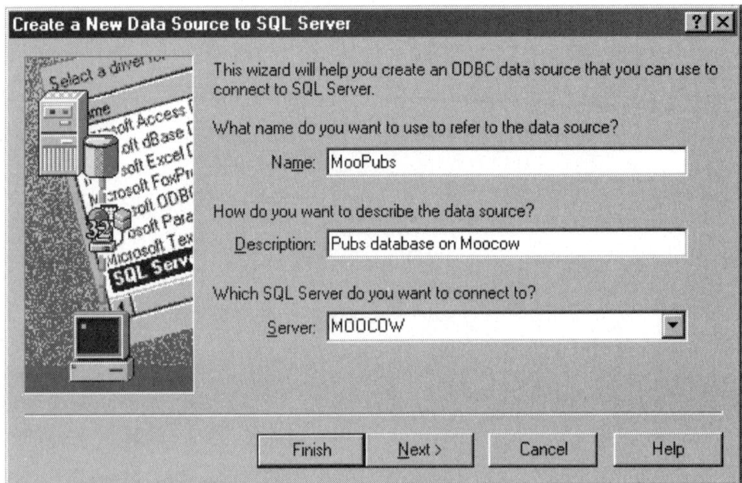

FIGURE 12.1: Naming a new connection

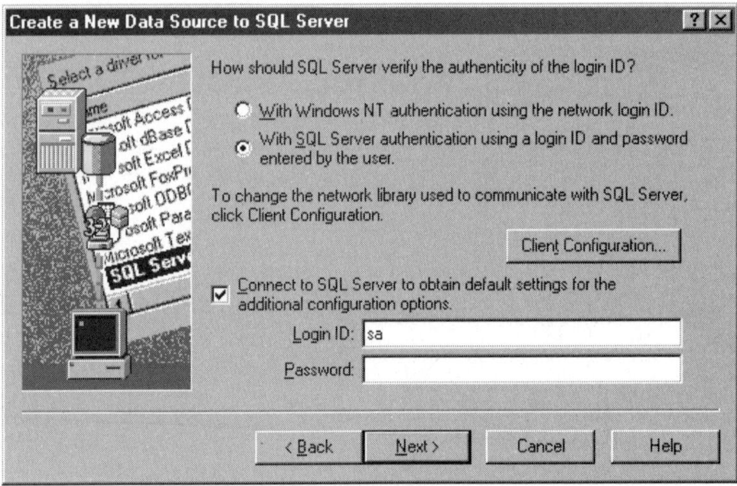

FIGURE 12.2: Setting security options

The next dialog box, shown in Figure 12.3, lets you set the default database to be used by this connection (if you don't set one, it will default to the master database), and it lets you choose a level of ANSI compatibility. If your server is configured for automatic failover, you can also choose to use a backup server if the primary server isn't available.

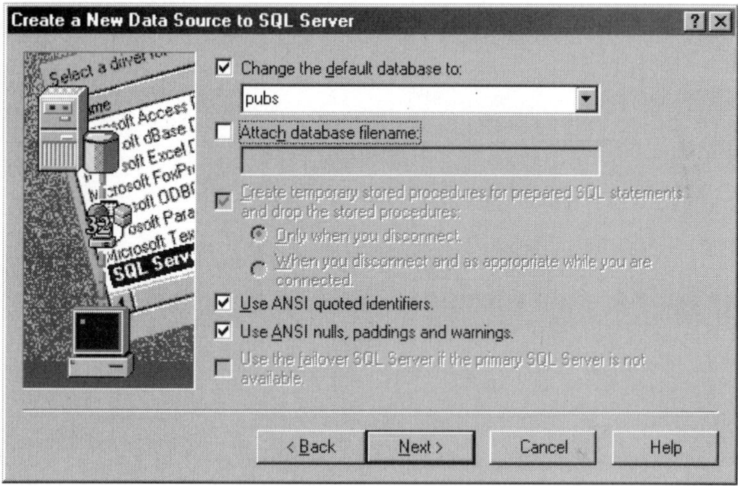

FIGURE 12.3: Setting the default database

The final dialog box, shown in Figure 12.4, lets you set some miscellaneous options:

- The language to use for system messages returned by SQL Server
- Whether to use a translation driver on data stored on the server
- Whether to format dates and currency using local settings
- Whether to log long-running queries and driver statistics

When you click Finish, you'll be presented with a summary dialog box listing the options that you chose when setting up this connection. This summary dialog box also has a button that allows you to test the new connection before saving it, letting you backtrack to make changes if necessary. It's a good idea to test new connections before saving them.

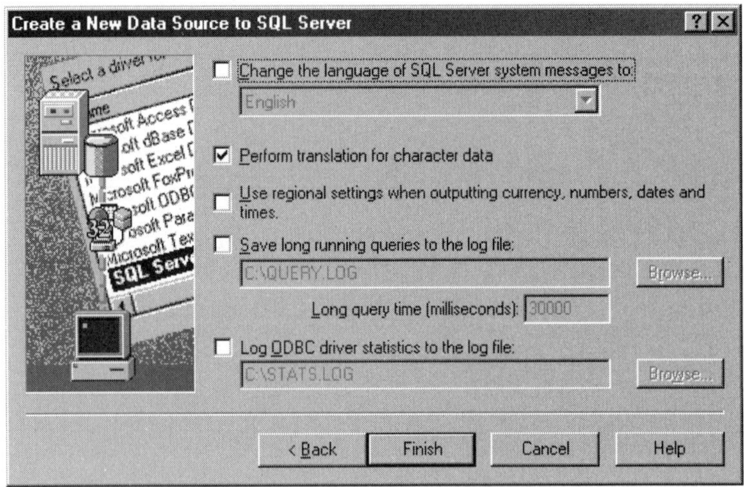

FIGURE 12.4: Setting miscellaneous options

OLE DB Interfaces

OLE DB is not a monolithic standard that must be entirely implemented by every OLE DB data provider or consumer. Rather, it is a set of component object model (COM) interfaces. Each interface defines a related set of actions with some relation to data. OLE DB providers need not supply an implementation for every interface, nor must OLE DB consumers work with every interface. Providers and consumers are free to pick and choose the interfaces that make sense for their particular needs.

NOTE Interfaces are basically indivisible. That is, if a particular OLE DB data provider provides an implementation for one method in an interface, you can safely assume that it implements all of the methods in that interface.

Table 12.1 lists some of the OLE DB interfaces defined by version 2 of the OLE DB standard.

TABLE 12.1: Selected OLE DB Interfaces

Interface	Explanation
`IColumnsInfo`	Provides a simple interface for the most commonly used column metadata
`IColumnsRowset`	Returns complete metadata about the columns in a rowset
`ICommand`	Provides methods to implement commands (queries)
`ICommandPrepare`	Provides methods for command optimization and compilation
`IDBCreateSession`	Creates a new session with a particular data provider
`IDBInfo`	Provides information about the keywords and literals that a data provider supports
`IErrorInfo`	Returns information about data access errors
`IRowset`	Provides methods for fetching and navigating through data represented as rows and columns
`IRowsetChange`	Provides methods for adding, updating, and deleting rows
`IRowsetIndex`	Exposes index functionality for a rowset
`IRowsetInfo`	Provides information on the capabilities of a particular rowset
`ISQLErrorInfo`	Returns native error information from SQL databases
`ITableDefinition`	Exposes DDL (Data Definition Language) capabilities
`ITransaction`	Implements transactional capabilities for a data provider

The OLE DB specification is still evolving, and we expect it to continue to define new capabilities after SQL Server is released. Although documentation for OLE DB is included in the SQL Server Books Online, you should refer to the Microsoft Universal Data Access Web site (`http://www.microsoft.com/data`) for the latest OLE DB information.

TIP

If you're doing low-level OLE DB programming, you should know that the SQL Server driver defines several custom interfaces. These include `ISQLServerErrorInfo` for returning specific information on system errors and `IRowsetFastLoad`, which is an interface to `.bcp`.

ActiveX Data Objects (ADO)

Unless you're doing direct COM programming in C++ to create an OLE DB data provider or consumer (a subject for an entire book in itself), you're unlikely to use OLE DB directly. Instead, you'll probably call ActiveX Data Objects (ADO), a set of objects implemented using the OLE DB interfaces. You can use ADO from Visual C++, Visual Basic, or any other development environment capable of setting a reference to a type library and using the objects contained in that library. ADO supplies dual interfaces so that ADO objects can be used with either early binding or late binding. This makes ADO objects available to development environments that do not support early binding, such as VBScript.

SQL Server 7 ships with ADO version 2.

ADO Overview

ADO can handle most of your data access tasks. Depending on the underlying OLE DB provider, you will have some or all of these features available in an ADO application:

- Batch updating
- Parameters and return values for stored procedures
- Multiple cursor types, including client- and server-side and even backend-specific cursors
- Recordset caching on client or server
- Limits on the number of rows returned from a query
- Support for multiple recordsets from a single command

ADO Objects

If you've worked with older Microsoft data access libraries such as Data Access Objects (DAO) or Remote Data Objects (RDO), ADO's object model will seem somewhat familiar. However, as Figure 12.5 shows, the object hierarchy is not nearly as complex in ADO as it was in previous libraries. ADO has been designed so that most objects can be created directly without navigating through the object hierarchy. This simplifies your code and results in a smaller memory footprint for most ADO applications.

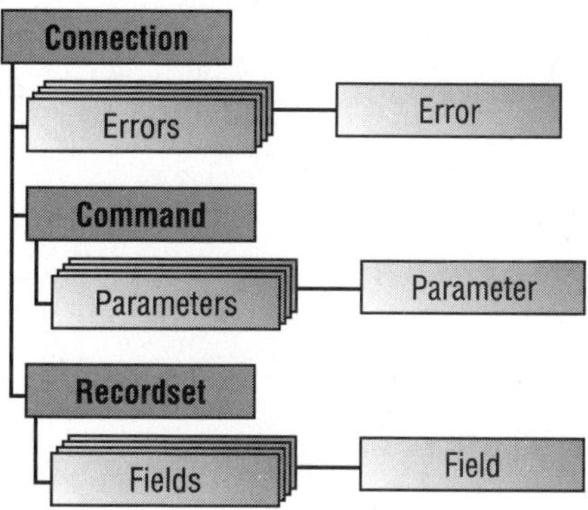

FIGURE 12.5: ADO object hierarchy

In addition to the objects shown in Figure 12.5, the Connection, Command, Recordset, and Field objects each have a Properties collection of Property objects. This enables your code to easily scan through the properties of these objects.

Connection Object

The Connection object represents an open connection to an OLE DB data source. You can create a Connection object and use it to create other objects further down the ADO object hierarchy. However, if you only need a single recordset from a particular connection, it's probably more efficient to just create the recordset directly.

You choose which data source a particular connection will point to by using its `ConnectionString` property. This can either be a Data Source Name (DSN) that you've previously defined or a string of arguments and values using this syntax:

```
Provider=providervalue;Data Source=datasourcevalue;User=uservalue;
Password=passwordvalue;File Name=filenamevalue
```

The `providervalue` argument specifies the name of the OLE DB provider to use. The `datasourcevalue` argument specifies a data source; for example, the name of an ODBC data source when you're using the ODBC provider for OLE DB. The `uservalue` and `passwordvalue` arguments specify a user identity to use for this session. The `filenamevalue` specifies a file containing connection information; for example, an ODBC file data source.

All of these arguments are optional. You can include additional arguments in the `ConnectionString` property, in which case they are passed to the OLE DB provider without any alteration by ADO.

Table 12.2 details the methods and properties of the Connection object.

NOTE In Table 12.2 and following tables, the Type column indicates whether a particular listing is a property (P), method (M), or collection (C) of the parent object.

TABLE 12.2: Connection Object Details

Name	Type	Explanation
`Attributes`	P	Bitmapped property that indicates whether the data source supports retaining commits and retaining aborts
`BeginTrans`	M	Begins a transaction
`Cancel`	M	Cancels a pending asynchronous `Open` or `Execute` method
`Close`	M	Terminates the connection with the data source
`CommandTimeout`	P	Number of seconds to wait for a response from the data provider when using the `Execute` method
`CommitTrans`	M	Commits a transaction
`ConnectionString`	P	Data source name or arguments to use for this connection
`CursorLocation`	P	Controls whether cursors are created on the client or the server
`ConnectionTimeout`	P	Number of seconds to wait for a connection after executing the `Open` method
`DefaultDatabase`	P	Database that other objects for this connection should use
`Errors`	C	Collection of Error objects
`Execute`	M	Executes a command on the connection without creating a Command object
`IsolationLevel`	P	Constant indicating the isolation level of transactions in this connection from those in other connections
`Mode`	P	Sets to one of `adModeUnknown`, `adModeRead`, `adModeWrite`, `adModeReadWrite`, `adModeShareDenyRead`, `adModeShareDenyWrite`, `adModeShareExclusive`, or `adModeShareDenyNone` to indicate the permissions for this connection
`Open`	M	Initializes the connection with the data source
`OpenSchema`	M	Obtains schema information from the provider

TABLE 12.2 CONTINUED: Connection Object Details

Name	Type	Explanation
`Provider`	P	OLE DB provider used for this connection
`RollbackTrans`	M	Rolls back a transaction
`State`	P	Constant indicating whether the connection is open or closed
`Version`	P	Version of ADO

Recordset Object

A Recordset object represents a set of records retrieved from a data provider (similar to the DAO RecordSet and RDO ResultSet objects). Because this is the object that allows you to retrieve data directly, it's indispensable to ADO processing. ADO allows you to open a Recordset object directly or to create one from a Connection or Command object.

ADO Recordsets support four types of cursor (although, of course, not all cursor types will be available from all data providers):

- A dynamic cursor lets you see changes to the data made by other users and supports all types of movement that don't rely on bookmarks. It may allow bookmarks if the data provider supports them.
- A keyset cursor is dynamic but does not let you see records added or deleted by other users (it does allow you to see changes to the data made by other users). Keyset cursors support bookmarks and all other kinds of movement through the recordset.
- A static cursor provides a frozen copy of the data at the time the recordset was opened. Additions, changes, and deletions by other users have no impact on the recordset since it is never refreshed after it is created. Static cursors support bookmarks and all other kinds of movement through the recordset.
- A forward-only cursor is a static cursor that only allows you to move forward through the recordset. This is ADO's default cursor.

ADO recordsets support both immediate and batch updating. However, in the current implementation they do not support the optimistic batch-updating methods supplied by RDO.

Table 12.3 lists the methods and properties supplied by the ADO Recordset object. Remember, not all of these will apply to every recordset. The methods and properties that are relevant depend on both the recordset type and the underlying data provider.

TABLE 12.3: Recordset Object Details

Name	Type	Explanation
AbsolutePage	P	Number of data pages into the recordset of the current record
AbsolutePosition	P	Ordinal position of the current record in the recordset
ActiveConnection	P	Connection this recordset was created from
AddNew	M	Prepares a new record to be added to the recordset
BOF	P	True if you have moved before the beginning of the recordset
Bookmark	P	Unique identifier for the current row of the recordset
CacheSize	P	Number of records that are cached in local memory
CancelBatch	M	Cancels all pending changes in the recordset
CancelUpdate	M	Throws away an AddNew or Edit without saving changes
Clone	M	Produces a second recordset identical to the current recordset
Close	M	Closes the recordset
CursorLocation	P	Constant indicating the location of the cursor used for this recordset
CursorType	P	Constant indicating the type of cursor used for this recordset
Delete	M	Deletes the current record
EditMode	P	Enumerated value indicating whether the current record is being edited
EOF	P	True if you have moved past the end of the recordset
Fields	C	Fields collection of the recordset
Filter	P	Allows you to select a subset of the recordset to work with
GetRows	M	Fills the local record cache
LockType	P	Controls the type of locks placed during editing
MarshalOptions	P	Controls the marshalling of records to the server for a client-side recordset
MaxRecords	P	Maximum number of records to be returned in the recordset
Move	M	Moves to an offset from the current record

TABLE 12.3 CONTINUED: Recordset Object Details

Name	Type	Explanation
MoveFirst	M	Moves to the first record
MoveLast	M	Moves to the last record
MoveNext	M	Moves to the next record
MovePrevious	M	Moves to the previous record
NextRecordset	M	Returns the next recordset from the current Command object
Open	M	Opens a recordset
PageCount	P	Number of data pages in the recordset
PageSize	P	Size of a single data page
RecordCount	P	Number of records in the recordset. May return adUnknown (-1) if ADO cannot determine how many records are in the recordset
Requery	M	Reruns the original query that created the recordset
Resync	M	Synchronizes the recordset with the underlying data
Save	M	Persists the recordset to a file
Sort	P	Specifies the field to sort the recordset on
Source	P	Source of the recordset
Status	P	Array of values containing the results of batch update operations
Supports	M	Operator to determine which operations a recordset supports
Update	M	Commits the work since an Edit or AddNew method
UpdateBatch	M	Commits all pending changes on a batch cursor

Field Object

A Field object represents a single column of data in a recordset. Once you've retrieved a recordset, you'll usually work with fields to read the data in the recordset. However, since the Fields collection is the default property of the recordset, you won't often see its name in your code. The following two lines of code produce an identical result:

```
Recordset.Fields(0).Value
Recordset(0)
```

Table 12.4 shows the methods and properties available from the Field object.

TABLE 12.4: Field Object Details

Name	Type	Explanation
`ActualSize`	P	Size of the data actually stored in the field
`AppendChunk`	P	Stores a chunk of data in a long binary field
`Attributes`	P	Bitmapped value indicating some of the characteristics of the field, including whether it may be updated and whether it is valid for long binary operations
`DefinedSize`	P	Maximum data the field can store
`GetChunk`	P	Retrieves a chunk of data from a long binary field
`Name`	P	Name of the field
`NumericScale`	P	Scale (number of digits to the right of the decimal point) for a numeric field
`OriginalValue`	P	Value in the field before another user changed it
`Precision`	P	Precision (total number of digits) for a numeric field
`Type`	P	Constant indicating the data type of the field
`UnderlyingValue`	P	Value currently stored in the database for this field (might have changed since the field's `Value` property was set)
`Value`	P	Data stored in the field

Command Object

Think of a Command object as a single instruction to your data source to produce data. Depending on the backend, this might be a SQL query, a stored procedure, or something else entirely.

The easiest way to use a Command object is to create an independent Command object, set its other properties, and then set its `ActiveConnection` property to a valid connection string. This will cause ADO to create an implicit Connection object for use by this command only. You can also set the `ActiveConnection` property to an existing Connection object.

TIP Depending on whether you're using a connection string or a Connection object, the `ActiveConnection` property might be a string or an object. Be sure to use the `Set` keyword in the latter case.

Table 12.5 shows the methods and properties of the Command object.

TABLE 12.5: Command Object Details

Name	Type	Explanation
`ActiveConnection`	P	Connection to execute this command on
`Cancel`	M	Cancels a pending asynchronous command
`CommandText`	P	Text (SQL statement) of the command
`CommandTimeout`	P	Number of seconds to wait for a response from the data source
`CommandType`	P	One of `adCmdText`, `adCmdTable`, `adCmdStoredProc`, or `adCmdUnknown`
`CreateParameter`	M	Creates a new Parameter object
`Execute`	M	Executes the command and returns any recordset(s) it generates
`Prepared`	P	If set to True, causes the data provider to save a compiled version of the command on the first execution
`Parameters`	C	Collection of Parameter objects
`State`	P	Constant indicating whether the object is open

Parameter Object

A Parameter object represents a single parameter for a Command object. This might be a run-time parameter in a SQL query or an input or output parameter in a stored procedure. If you know the properties of a particular parameter, you can use the `CreateParameter` method to make appropriate Parameter objects for a Command object, which allows you to initialize parameters without any server-side processing. Otherwise, you must call the `Refresh` method on the Command object's Parameters collection to retrieve parameter information from the server.

Table 12.6 lists the methods and properties for Parameter objects.

TABLE 12.6: Parameter Object Details

Name	Type	Explanation
`AppendChunk`	M	Stores data in a long binary parameter
`Attributes`	P	Bitmapped set of attributes for the parameter
`Direction`	P	Indicates whether a parameter is input, output, both, or a return value from a stored procedure
`Name`	P	Name of the parameter
`NumericScale`	P	Scale (number of digits to the right of the decimal point) for a numeric parameter
`Precision`	P	Precision (total number of digits) for a numeric parameter
`Size`	P	Maximum data a parameter can hold
`Type`	P	Constant indicating the data type of the parameter
`Value`	P	Current value of the parameter

Error Object

An Error object represents a single error. Since one data access operation can generate multiple errors, Error objects are contained in an Errors collection. If the last operation succeeded, this collection will be empty. Otherwise, you can use the `For Each` operator to examine each Error in turn.

Note that if there is no valid Connection object, you will have to use the Visual Basic Err object instead. This is the case if you've directly opened a recordset using a connection string, for example.

Table 12.7 lists the properties of the Error object.

TABLE 12.7: Error Object Details

Name	Type	Explanation
`Description`	P	Text of the error
`HelpContext`	P	Help topic for the error
`HelpFile`	P	Help file for the error
`NativeError`	P	Original ODBC error number
`Number`	P	Error number
`Source`	P	Object that raised the error
`SQLState`	P	Original ODBC `SQLState` constant

Using ADO

One typical use for ADO is to allow clients to retrieve data over an Internet connection. There are, of course, many ways to accomplish this, but one possible Microsoft-only solution uses ADO in conjunction with Active Server Pages (ASP). Active Server Pages are an example of *server-side scripting*: They contain commands that are processed at the server before the results are sent to the client. When a client browses to an ASP page on an Internet server running Microsoft Internet Information Server (IIS), the server sends the page to local libraries for processing. These libraries produce static HTML, which is then returned to the client. If there are ADO objects on the ASP page, these objects are instantiated and destroyed entirely on the server; they are never returned to the client.

To show the data from a table using ADO, we could save the following ASP file on a server running IIS:

```
<HTML>
<HEAD>
<TITLE>SQL Server In Record Time</TITLE>
</HEAD>
<BODY BGCOLOR=#FFFFFF>
<%
Dim Con
Dim Rst
Dim i
Set Con= Server.CreateObject("ADODB.Connection")
Con.Open "pubs"
Set Rst = Con.Execute("SELECT * FROM authors")
%>
<P>
<TABLE BORDER=1>
<TR>
<%For i = 0 to Rst.Fields.Count - 1 %>
      <TD><B><%= Rst(i).Name %></B></TD>
<%Next %>
</TR>
<%Do While Not Rst.EOF %>
      <TR>
      <%For i = 0 to Rst.Fields.Count - 1 %>
           <TD VALIGN=TOP><%= Rst(i) %></TD>
      <%Next%>
      </TR>
      <%
    Rst.MoveNext
Loop
Rst.Close
```

```
Con.Close
%>
</TABLE>
<BR>
<BR>
</BODY>
</HTML>
```

NOTE For this script to work, it must be in a directory managed by IIS and named with an .asp extension. An ODBC DSN named "pubs" must also exist and be pointed at the pubs sample database.

The above sample uses a persistent connection to the database to retrieve the recordset. Alternatively, if we were only interested in this single response from the server, it would be faster to create the recordset directly, using this equivalent ASP file:

```
<HTML>
<HEAD>
<TITLE>SQL Server In Record Time</TITLE>
</HEAD>
<BODY BGCOLOR=#FFFFFF>
<%
Dim Rst
Dim i
Set Rst= Server.CreateObject("ADODB.Recordset")
Rst.ActiveConnection="pubs"
Rst.Open "SELECT * FROM authors"
%>
<P>
<TABLE BORDER=1>
<TR>
<%For i = 0 to Rst.Fields.Count - 1 %>
      <TD><B><%= Rst(i).Name %></B></TD>
<%Next %>
</TR>
<%Do While Not Rst.EOF %>
      <TR>
      <%For i = 0 to Rst.Fields.Count - 1 %>
           <TD VALIGN=TOP><%= Rst(i) %></TD>
      <%Next%>
      </TR>
      <%
    Rst.MoveNext
Loop
```

```
Rst.Close
Con.Close
%>
</TABLE>
<BR>
<BR>
</BODY>
</HTML>
```

TIP In addition to the help in the SQL Server Books Online, you'll find ADO samples in the Active Server Pages component of Internet Information Server.

Are You up to Speed?

Now you can...

- ☑ **identify the benefits of OLE DB**
- ☑ **use ActiveX Data Objects (ADO) to retrieve data from SQL Server**

SKILL 13

Programming SQL Server

- DB-Library
- Open Data Services
- Embedded SQL for C
- ActiveX automation

We've seen how to develop client applications that make use of SQL Server data and how to use Transact-SQL to place pieces of applications directly on the server. Now we'll look at the various ways in which programs running on the server computer can interact directly with SQL Server. This can be done by using DB-Library, Embedded SQL for C (ESQL), or Open Data Services. We'll also look at the syntax used to create ActiveX objects from within Transact SQL scripts.

You can also program SQL Server using SQL Distributed Management Objects (SQL-DMO) or SQL NameSpace (SQL-NS). These technologies are covered in Skill 11, *Creating Client-Server Applications*.

DB-Library

DB-Library (often referred to as *dblib*) provides dedicated interfaces for communication with SQL Server from either the C language or Visual Basic. Historically, DB-Library has been very important as a data access tool for SQL Server, but with version 7 it is being de-emphasized. The version of DB-Library that ships with SQL Server 7 is practically unchanged from the version that shipped with SQL Server 6.5. This may be because it is a very server-specific tool. You can only use DB-Library to retrieve data from Microsoft SQL Server, and you can only use it within C or Visual Basic. The emphasis now is on more universal solutions, and for new applications you should consider alternatives such as OLE DB and ADO (discussed in Skill 12, *OLE DB Fundamentals*).

However, there is a wide legacy base of applications using DB-Library, and you may some day be called on to maintain one of these applications. Also, DB-Library can provide a quick way to get something up and running if you don't need client or server interoperability. To gain some familiarity with the way these applications work, we'll examine both the C and Visual Basic versions of DB-Library.

DB-Library for C

DB-Library for C is a set of functions, contained in either a DLL or a static-linked library, for performing some specific actions from a C program to a Microsoft SQL Server. These include:

- Opening and closing connections
- Sending a query to the server

- Retrieving data generated by a query
- Using scrollable cursors on the server
- Bulk-copying data to and from the server
- Managing two-phase commit on the server
- Executing stored procedures on the server

This may appear to be a small subset of SQL Server operations. However, since you can do almost anything on the server with a Transact-SQL query or a stored procedure, including launching jobs, you can indirectly do almost anything from DB-Library that you could through any other means of talking to the server.

To use DB-Library for C, you need Microsoft Visual C++ version 4 or later, or a 100 percent compatible compiler. Given the difficulties of managing compiler compatibility, we recommend that you use the latest version of Microsoft Visual C++ (version 6 as of this writing).

There are also versions of DB-Library available for 16-bit C for Windows 3.1 and DOS. Because we view those operating systems as obsolete, we won't explicitly discuss those versions here. A full installation of SQL Server 7 includes 16-bit sample applications.

TIP The SQL Server CD includes Visual C++ make files for each of the samples, so you can build them for Windows 95 or Windows NT on either Alpha or Intel platforms.

Using DB-Library for C

Using DB-Library for C requires writing code for five separate steps:

1. Connecting to the SQL Server
2. Submitting Transact-SQL statements to the server
3. Processing results from the server
4. Handling server messages and errors
5. Disconnecting from the server

Each of these tasks is covered in more detail below.

Connecting to SQL Server

Connecting to a SQL Server using DB-Library for C requires three steps:

1. Allocating a login record using the `dblogin()` function
2. Filling in fields in the login record
3. Connecting to the server with the `dbopen()` function

These steps are shown in the following code fragment:

```
CString strServer,          // SQL Server
        strLogin,           // login
        strPassword;        // password

// Prompt the user for connection options
cout << "Type the SQL Server to connect to: ";
cinstr (strServer);
cout << "Type your login: ";
cinstr (strLogin);
cout << "Type your password: ";
cinstr (strPassword);

// get a login record
PLOGINREC pLoginRec;
pLoginRec = dblogin();
if (pLoginRec == NULL)
{
    cout << err << "Could not allocate a login record" << endl;
    return (1);
}

// fill the login record
DBSETLUSER (pLoginRec, strLogin);       // set the login
DBSETLPWD (pLoginRec, strPassword);     // set the password
DBSETLAPP (pLoginRec, "Sample App");    // set the app name
DBSETLHOST (pLoginRec, "Sample App");   // set the host name

// attempt to connect to SQL Server
PDBPROCESS pDbproc;
pDbproc = dbopen (pLoginRec, strServer);
dbfreelogin (pLoginRec);
if (pDbproc == NULL)
{
    cout << err << "Could not connect to SQL Server '" <<
     strServer << "'" << endl;
    return (1);
}
```

The `dblogin()` function is designed solely to allocate an empty `PLOGINREC` structure. This structure contains all of the required and optional fields that can be used in connecting to a SQL Server. For each of these fields, DB-Library provides a function to set the member to a particular value. Table 13.1 shows these functions. All of the fields are initialized to `NULL`.

TABLE 13.1: Functions for Setting PLOGINREC Members

Function	Data set by this function
DBSETLUSER	Username.
DBSETLPWD	Password.
DBSETLHOST	Workstation name.
DBSETLAPP	Application name.
DBSETLNATLANG	National Language option.
DBSETLPACKET	Packet size for the SQL Server Tabular Data Stream protocol (TDS). The server may modify this if it is unable to allocate a large enough buffer.
DBSETLSECURE	Call to set secure connection mode.
DBSETLTIME	Timeout value.
DBSETLVERSION	Used to choose between SQL Server 4.2 and SQL Server 6 compatibility.
BCP_SETL	Call to enable bulk copy operations.
DBSETLFALLBACK	Call to indicate that a failover server can be used.

Once you've allocated a `PLOGINREC` structure and filled in the fields you want to initialize (at least the username and password), you can call the `dbopen()` function to actually connect to the server. The `dbopen()` function allocates a `PDBPROCESS` structure, which is used by the rest of the program to communicate with the server. If you've called the `DBSETLFALLBACK` macro and the requested server isn't available, `dbopen()` will attempt to connect to a failover server.

TIP You can supply `NULL` instead of the server name in the call to `dbopen()` to connect to a local SQL Server.

Once you've connected to the server, the information in the `PLOGINREC` structure is no longer needed. At this point, you can call the `dbfreelogin()` function to release the memory used by this structure. Alternatively, you can reuse a single

PLOGINREC structure throughout a program, to connect to one or more servers and free it when you exit the program.

Sending SQL to the Server

When you have created a valid PDBPROCESS structure, you can use it to communicate with the server. To send a SQL statement to be executed, you must do the following:

1. Call the dbuse() function to specify the database to use.
2. Call the dbcmd() function to build your SQL statement.
3. Call the dbsqlexec() function to execute the SQL statement.

The next code fragment shows these three steps:

```
// use the "pubs" database
dbuse (pDbproc, "pubs");

// construct command buffer to be sent to the SQL server
dbcmd (pDbproc, (char *)"select au_id, au_lname, au_fname, phone,");
dbcmd (pDbproc, (char *)" address, city, state, zip");
dbcmd (pDbproc, (char *)" from authors");

dbsqlexec (pDbproc); // send command buffer to SQL server
```

The dbuse() function is equivalent to the Transact-SQL USE statement. It specifies the database to be used for subsequent SQL statements. Each time you call dbuse, the command and result buffers in the PDBPROCESS structure are reinitialized.

Each time you call dbcmd(), the string supplied is concatenated into the PDBPROCESS command buffer. If you make a mistake and need to clear this command buffer, you can call dbfreebuf(). After a call to dbsqlexec(), the next call to dbcmd() automatically clears the command buffer and starts over.

The dbsqlexec() function sends the entire contents of the command buffer to the server to be executed. After calling dbsqlexec(), you can proceed to retrieve the result set from the server.

TIP

The dbsqlexec() function is synchronous—that is, your program will wait for it to succeed or fail. For asynchronous queries with DB-Library for C, you can use the dbsqlsend(), dbdataready(), and dbsqlok() functions.

Processing Results from the Server

Processing results retrieved using DB-Library for C is also a three-step job:

1. Call `dbresults()` to determine when results are available.
2. Call `dbbind()` to bind SQL result columns to local program variables.
3. Call `dbnextrow()` to actually retrieve the results.

These steps are shown in this code fragment:

```
// Variables used to store the returning data
char       au_lname[41];
char       au_fname[20];
char       id[12];
char       phone[13];
char       address[41];
char       city[21];
char       state[3];
char       zip[6];
RETCODE    result_code;

// check the results from the SQL server
while ((result_code = dbresults(dbproc)) != NO_MORE_RESULTS)
{
     if (result_code == SUCCEED)
     {
            // when we have results, bind the columns to variables
            dbbind (dbproc,       1, NTBSTRINGBIND, (DBINT) 0,
            (char *)id);
            dbbind (dbproc,       2, NTBSTRINGBIND, (DBINT) 0,
            (char *)au_lname);
            dbbind (dbproc,       3, NTBSTRINGBIND, (DBINT) 0,
            (char *)au_fname);
            dbbind (dbproc,       4, NTBSTRINGBIND, (DBINT) 0,
            (char *)phone);
            dbbind (dbproc,       5, NTBSTRINGBIND, (DBINT) 0,
            (char *)address);
            dbbind (dbproc,       6, NTBSTRINGBIND, (DBINT) 0,
            (char *)city);
            dbbind (dbproc,       7, NTBSTRINGBIND, (DBINT) 0,
            (char *)state);
            dbbind (dbproc,       8, NTBSTRINGBIND, (DBINT) 0,
            (char *)zip);

            // now process the rows
            while (dbnextrow(dbproc) != NO_MORE_ROWS)
```

```
                {
                        printf ("Author ID:  %s\n",   id);
                        printf ("Last Name:  %s\n",   au_lname);
                        printf ("First Name: %s\n",   au_fname);
                        printf ("Address:    %s\n",   address);
                        printf ("City:       %s\n",   city);
                        printf ("State:      %s\n",   state);
                        printf ("Zip Code:   %s\n",   zip);
                        printf ("Telephone:  %s\n",   phone);
                        printf ("\n");
                }
        }
        else
        {
                printf ("Results Failed\n");
                break;
        }
}
```

The `dbresults()` function tells you whether results are ready to return from the server. Typically the return will be either `SUCCEED` or `NO_MORE_RESULTS`. The latter indicates that all the SQL statements in the batch have finished executing. It can also return `FAIL` if there's a network or server error.

WARNING Always call `dbresults()` until it returns `NO_MORE_RESULTS`. Otherwise, subsequent functions that use the same `DBPROCESS` structure will only return an error that tells you that results are pending.

The `dbbind()` function provides a mapping between the columns in the SQL Server result set and local variables in your C program. Each call to this function identifies for DB-Library a particular variable that you want to have results copied to. Finally, the `dbnextrow()` function actually transfers data from the result set to the bound variables. When all the rows have been transferred, `dbnextrow()` returns `NO_MORE_ROWS` and you're done processing that query.

Handling Messages and Errors

DB-Library for C manages errors and informational messages by way of a pair of callback functions. You call the `dberrhandle()` and `dbmsghandle()` functions to install your own callbacks, as shown in the following code fragment.

TIP If you forget to call these functions, errors and messages will not be reported to your application.

```
main ()
{
// Install error and message handlers
dberrhandle((DBERRHANDLE_PROC)err_handler);
dbmsghandle((DBMSGHANDLE_PROC)msg_handler);

// Main logic goes here
}

// Error and message handlers
int err_handler(PDBPROCESS dbproc, int severity, int dberr,
 int oserr, char * dberrstr, char * oserrstr)
{
     if (dberrstr != NULL)
            printf("DB-LIBRARY error:\n\t%s\n", dberrstr);

     if (oserr != DBNOERR)
            printf("Operating-system error:\n\t%s\n", oserrstr);

     if ((dbproc == NULL) ||       (DBDEAD(dbproc)))
            return(INT_EXIT);
     else
            return(INT_CANCEL);
}

int msg_handler(PDBPROCESS dbproc, DBINT msgno, int msgstate,
 int severity, char * msgtext)
{
     printf("SQL Server message %ld, state %d, severity %d:\n\t%s\n",
                   msgno, msgstate, severity, msgtext);
     return(0);
}
```

Your error handling function will be called for both DB-Library and operating system errors. DB-Library will pass in the six arguments shown in Table 13.2.

TABLE 13.2: DB-Library for C Error Handler Arguments

Argument	Contains
dbproc	The DBPROCESS structure affected by the error
severity	Severity of the error
dberr	Error number
oserr	Operating system error number (if any) or DBNOERR
dberrstr	Printable description of the DB-Library error
oserrstr	Printable description of the operating system error

You must return one of three values when you're done dealing with the error:

- `INT_CANCEL` returns `FAIL` from the function that originally caused the error.
- `INT_EXIT` returns `FAIL` from the function that originally caused the error if the program is running under Windows. If the program is running under DOS, it causes the application to terminate.
- `INT_CONTINUE` causes the program to wait for one full timeout period and then retry the failing operation. If the error was not the result of a timeout, this is treated as `INT_CANCEL`.

WARNING Don't call DB-Library functions from within an active error handler. If any errors occur within these functions, your code may get stuck in an infinite loop.

The message handling function in your application receives messages and errors from SQL Server itself. This function receives the eight arguments shown in Table 13.3. When you are done with the message, your function must return a value of zero.

TABLE 13.3: DB-Library for C Message Handling Arguments

Argument	Contains
`dbproc`	The `DBPROCESS` structure affected by the error
`msgno`	Message number from the SQL Server sysmessages table
`msgstate`	Message error state number
`severity`	Severity of the error
`msgtext`	Text of the message
`srvname`	Server name
`procname`	Name of the stored procedure that generated the error or a zero-length string if the error did not come from a stored procedure
`line`	Line number in the batch or stored procedure that generated the error or zero if a line number cannot be determined

Disconnecting from the Server

When you are done using the DB-Library for C functions, you should call the `dbexit()` function. This function closes all of the open `DBPROCESS` structures and returns their memory to the operating system. Alternatively, to close a single `DBPROCESS` you can call the `dbclose()` function.

DB-Library for Visual Basic

DB-Library for Visual Basic provides Visual Basic wrapper functions for a large number of the DB-Library for C functions. It does this through two objects:

- The `vbsql.bas` module contains global constants, type declarations, and API declarations that a Visual Basic program can use to call DB-Library functions.
- Because previous versions of Visual Basic did not support callbacks and, even in Visual Basic 5, callbacks are difficult to program, the `vbsql.ocx` custom control provides events that will fire for DB-Library errors and messages.

NOTE Since it relies on an ActiveX control, DB-Library for Visual Basic requires the 32-bit version of Visual Basic 4 or Visual Basic 5.

WARNING DB-Library for Visual Basic **should not** be used for new applications. RDO 2 and ADO both supply a superset of DB-Library for Visual Basic functionality. For more information on RDO, see Skill 11, *Creating Client-Server Applications*. And for more information on ADO, see Skill 12, *OLE DB Fundamentals*.

Using DB-Library for Visual Basic

Using DB-Library for Visual Basic requires writing code for the same five processes as DB-Library for C:

1. Connecting to the SQL Server
2. Submitting Transact-SQL statements to the server
3. Processing results from the server

4. Handling server messages and errors
5. Disconnecting from the server

Each of these tasks is covered in more detail below.

Connecting to SQL Server

Connecting to a SQL Server using DB-Library for Visual Basic requires three steps:

1. Add the global module and custom control to your Visual Basic project.
2. Call `SqlInit` to initialize the library.
3. Call `SqlOpenConnection` to connect to a server.

To add the module and custom control to the project, you must use Visual Basic's Project ➢ Components menu to browse to the `VBSQL.OCX` control. Then create a Visual Basic form and place an instance of this control on the form. Last, import the `VBSQL.BAS` module to your Visual Basic module.

TIP `VBSQL.OCX` is not installed by default. You'll need to copy it from the `x86\BINN` folder on the SQL Server CD to your hard drive, and then use `regsvr32.exe` to register it before you can use it.

The form with the `VBSQL.OCX` control must remain loaded during the entire time that you are communicating with the server. However, the form need not be visible.

The code fragment shows the code needed to connect to a server:

```
Dim glngSqlConn As Long
Dim glngRc As Long
Dim gstrVersion As String
Private Sub Form_Load ()
    gstrVersion = SqlInit()
    If gstrVersion = "" Then
        Stop
    End If
    glngSqlConn = SqlOpenConnection("MyServer", "sa", "password", _
     "WSName", "AppName")
    If glngSqlConn = 0 Then
        Stop
    End If
End Sub
```

The SqlInit() function initializes the DB-Library data structures and sets up your error and message handlers. It returns the DB-Library version number. The SqlOpenConnection() function accepts the standard connect parameters (server name, username, password, workstation name, and application name) and returns a unique identifier for the connection.

If SqlInit() returns an empty string or SqlOpenConnection() returns zero, then initialization failed and your application should not proceed. In the example above, we simply stop executing code if this happens.

Sending SQL to the Server

Once SqlInit() and SqlOpenConnection succeed, you can send statements to the Server. Using DB-Library for Visual Basic, this is a two-step process.

1. Call the SqlUse() function to specify the database to use.
2. Call the SqlSendCmd() function to execute the SQL Statement.

The next code fragment shows these two steps:

```
Dim strSql As String

' use the "pubs" database
glngRc = SqlUse(glngSqlConn, "pubs")

' Send a command to the SQL server
strSql = "select au_id, au_lname, au_fname, phone," & _
  " address, city, state, zip") & _
  " from authors"

glngRc = SqlSendCmd (glngSqlConn, strSql)
```

The SqlUse() function is equivalent to the Transact-SQL USE statement. It specifies the database to be used for subsequent SQL statements.

Unlike DB-Library for C, DB-Library for Visual Basic does not contain an internal command buffer. You simply create a Visual Basic string containing the SQL to be executed and call the SqlSendCmd() to send this string to the server to be executed. After calling SqlSendCmd(), you can proceed to retrieve the result set from the server.

Processing Results from the Server

Retrieving results from the server is also simpler with DB-Library for Visual Basic. You simply call the SqlNextRow() and SqlData() functions to retrieve the data:

```
Dim intCol As Integer
Do Until SqlNextRow(glngSqlConn) = NOMOREROWS
    For intCols = 1 To SqlNumCols(glngSqlConn)
        Debug.Print SqlData(glngSqlConn, intCol)
    Next intCol
Loop
```

The SqlNextRow() function returns the next row of results from the server or the special NOMOREROWS value when there are no further rows to retrieve. The SqlData() function simply retrieves the value from the specified column of the current row. The data is always returned as a string, and null values are returned as zero-length strings.

Note that both of these functions take as an argument the return value from the SqlOpenConnection() function. This is generally true of DB-Library for Visual Basic functions.

Handling Messages and Errors

DB-Library for Visual Basic manages errors and informational messages by posting events to the VBSQL.OCX ActiveX control. You are responsible, of course, for writing your own code in these events. The sample code shown here can get you started.

```
Private Sub Vbsql1_Error(ByVal SqlConn As Long, _
 ByVal Severity As Long, _
 ByVal ErrorNum As Long, _
 ByVal ErrorStr As String, _
 ByVal OSErrorNum As Long, _
 ByVal OSErrorStr As String, _
 RetCode As Long)
    MsgBox ("VBSQL Error: Sev:"  _
     & Severity & "Error:" & _
     & ErrorNum & " - " & ErrorStr)
End Sub

Private Sub Vbsql1_Message(ByVal SqlConn As Long, _
 ByVal Message As Long, ByVal State As Long, _
 ByVal Severity As Long, ByVal MsgStr As String, _
 ByVal ServerNameStr As String,  _
 ByVal ProcNameStr As String, ByVal Line As Long)
    MsgBox ("Msg:" & MsgStr & " - State:"  _
     & State & " - Severity:" & Severity  _
```

```
    & " : " & Message)
End Sub
```

The arguments to these functions are shown in Tables 13.4 and 13.5.

TABLE 13.4: DB-Library for Visual Basic Error Handler Arguments

Argument	Contains
SqlConn	Connection affected by the error.
Severity	Severity of the error.
ErrorNum	Error number.
ErrorStr	Printable description of the DB-Library error.
OSErrorNum	Operating system error number (if any) or DBNOERR.
OSErrorStr	Printable description of the operating system error.
RetCode	Set to 0 to return FAIL from the original function or 1 to try the function again if it was a timeout problem.

TABLE 13.5: DB-Library for Visual Basic Message Handling Arguments

Argument	Contains
SqlConn	Connection affected by the error.
Message	Message number from the SQL Server sysmessages table.
State	Message error state number.
Severity	Severity of the error.
MsgStr	Text of the message.
ServerNameStr	Server name.
ProcNameStr	Name of the stored procedure that generated the error or a zero-length string if the error did not come from a stored procedure.
Line	Line number in the batch or stored procedure that generated the error or zero if a line number cannot be determined.

Disconnecting from the Server

When you're done using DB-Library for Visual Basic functions, you need to call both the SqlExit and SqlWinExit functions:

```
SqlExit
SqlWinExit
```

Open Data Services

While DB-Library and SQL Distributed Management Objects (SQL-DMO, covered in Skill 11, *Creating Client-Server Applications*) can both be used on client machines as well as on the server, Open Data Services (ODS) is a server-side-only programming library. With this C-based API, you can create servers that users can connect to directly, as well as new extended stored procedures that can be called from within SQL Server.

ODS-based servers allow you to leverage the SQL Server client-handling code. They share with SQL Server itself the net libraries and client-side connectivity that allows clients to log in to a server. The ODS library passes requests from clients to event handlers in your ODS server. ODS servers can manage and respond to many simultaneous clients.

ODS Server Applications

An ODS server application can often be thought of as a gateway: a server that passes on requests to another server, possibly with some intermediate processing. For example, you could write an ODS application that runs on the same computer with a SQL Server, accepts SQL statements from clients, uses the DB-Library `dbsqlexec()` function to execute these functions on the server, and returns the results back to the client. Your gateway could then perform additional tasks, such as logging statistical information about the peak hours for client requests.

TIP SQL Server installs several sample ODS applications that you can use as the basis for your own development. They're particularly useful as examples of creating and installing extended stored procedures.

ODS Server applications respond to various events that are generated by clients. These include:

- Connect events, which occur whenever a new client logs on to the server
- Language events, which occur when a string to be processed arrives from a client
- Remote stored procedure events, which occur when a remote stored procedure is invoked by either a client or another server application
- Status events, including client attention requests and client disconnects
- ODS events, including start, stop, sleep, restart, and exit of ODS servers

Building ODS server applications is beyond the scope of this book. If you'd like to learn more about the tasks involved in building ODS server applications, refer to Books Online and the sample code supplied with SQL Server.

Extended Stored Procedures

ODS applications can also supply extended stored procedures to SQL Server. An extended stored procedure appears to client applications just like any other stored procedure: It can be called from Transact-SQL batches just by entering its name or from ODBC or DB-Library clients. The code for an extended stored procedure, though, does not reside in SQL Server. Rather, it's implemented as an external dynamic-link library (DLL). Each function in the DLL becomes an extended stored procedure. The ODS library is used to communicate between the DLL and SQL Server.

Returning Data

Extended stored procedures will often have to send data back to the client that invoked them. This requires both telling SQL Server about the structure of the data set and actually sending the data. Four ODS functions are used to accomplish this:

- `srv_describe()` defines a column's name, number, and size.
- `srv_coldata()` specifies the storage location for a column's data.
- `srv_setcollen()` is used to set the current size for a column's data.
- `srv_sendrow()` sends a row of data to the client.

The following code fragment shows the use of these functions:

```
typedef struct xp_info {
    DBCHAR name[MAXNAME];
    DBCHAR usage[MAXLEN];
} XP_INFO;

XP_INFO Xps[] =
{
    "xp_one",
    "usage: xp_one",
    "xp_two",
    "usage: xp_two",
};
...
sprintf(colname1, "spname");
```

```
srv_describe(srvproc, 1, colname1, SRV_NULLTERM, SRVCHAR, MAXNAME,
 SRVCHAR, 0, NULL);

sprintf(colname2, "spusage");
srv_describe(srvproc, 2, colname2, SRV_NULLTERM, SRVCHAR, MAXLEN,
 SRVCHAR, 0, NULL);

for (i = 0; i < 2; i++) {
        srv_setcoldata(srvproc, 1, Xps[i].name);
        srv_setcollen(srvproc, 1, strlen(Xps[i].name));

        srv_setcoldata(srvproc, 2, Xps[i].usage);
        srv_setcollen(srvproc, 2, strlen(Xps[i].usage));

        srv_sendrow(srvproc);
    }
```

The arguments to `srv_describe()` are shown in Table 13.6.

TABLE 13.6: Arguments to srv_describe()

Argument	Meaning
`*srvproc`	Pointer to the `srvproc` structure for the current client. SQL Server will supply this when it calls the extended stored procedure.
`colnumber`	Column being described. This numbering is one-based. Columns should be described in order.
`columnname`	Name of the column. This can be null, since columns are allowed to be unnamed.
`namelen`	Length of the column name. You can also use the constant `SRV_NULLTERM` to indicate that the name is null-terminated.
`desttype`	A constant specifying the type of data. ODS supplies constants for all the common types.
`destlen`	Maximum length of the data.
`srctype`	Type of the variable holding the source data.
`srclen`	Maximum length of the source data.
`*srcdata`	Pointer to the variable holding the source data.

Building Extended Stored Procedures

To build an extended stored procedure, you must follow a particular template. SQL Server will call the stored procedure only if it has a proper declaration and it expects a particular set of return values. Here's a template you can use to build an extended stored procedure:

```
SRVRETCODE xp_template(srvproc)
SRV_PROC *srvproc;
{
    int paramnum;
    paramnum = srv_rpcparams(srvproc);

    // Process parameters
    // Do other work

    srv_senddone(srvproc, SRV_DONE_MORE, 0, 0);

    return(XP_NOERROR);
}
```

All extended stored procedures should be defined to return a SRVRETCODE. This can be either XP_NOERROR, if all is well, or XP_ERROR, if any error occurs during the extended stored procedure.

SQL Server will pass your extended stored procedure a srvproc structure containing information about the client that invoked the procedure. The stored procedure in turn passes this back as an argument to other ODS functions to identify the connection that is being serviced at any given time. This allows extended stored procedures to be safely invoked simultaneously by other clients.

If your extended stored procedure expects to be passed parameters, you can call the srv_rpcparams() function to get a count of the parameters. You call srv_paramdata() to retrieve a particular argument and srv_paramlen() to retrieve the length of the argument.

When your extended stored procedure is done with its work, it needs to call srv_senddone() to notify the client that processing is finished. The value you pass as the second argument should be SRV_DONE_MORE, if the extended stored procedure succeeded, or SRV_DONE_MORE | SRV_DONE_ERROR, if an error occurred.

Registering Extended Stored Procedures

Before users can run an extended stored procedure, the system administrator must use the addextendedproc stored procedure to register it. The system administrator should also grant permissions to run the stored procedure. If you ship a DLL containing extended stored procedures to other servers, you'll probably want to include a registration script with it, similar to the one shown here:

```
sp_addextendedproc 'xp_template', 'template.dll'
go
grant exec on xp_template to public
go
```

Embedded SQL for C

Embedded SQL for C (ESQL) provides another way to execute Transact-SQL statements from the C programming language. Unlike DB-Library or ODS, though, ESQL requires a precompilation step. That is, you embed the SQL statements directly within your code and then call a special program that transforms those statements into a syntax that your C compiler can understand, before you can compile the program

ESQL is mainly of historic interest at this point. It was the original standard method of using SQL from C programs, but if you're starting from scratch, DB-Library probably makes more sense. However, because you may have legacy code to maintain, or applications from other database servers that you need to port to Microsoft SQL Server, it's worth a quick look at how ESQL works.

Embedded SQL for C was not upgraded for SQL Server 7. You should not rely on it for new applications.

ESQL programs actually look fairly simple when you first write them. By default, the source code has an extension of `.sqc`. Here's a simple bit of ESQL that retrieves and prints a single field from a database:

```
#include <stddef.h>
#include <stdio.h>
#include "gcutil.h"
int main (
    int argc,
    char** argv,
    char** envp)
{
```

```
    EXEC SQL BEGIN DECLARE SECTION;
    char first_name[50];
    char last_name[] = "White";
    EXEC SQL END DECLARE SECTION;

    EXEC SQL SET OPTION LOGINTIME 10;
    EXEC SQL SET OPTION QUERYTIME 100;

    EXEC SQL CONNECT TO MOOCOW.pubs
     USER sa.;

    EXEC SQL SELECT au_fname INTO :first_name
    from authors where au_lname = :last_name;

    printf("%s\n", first_name);

    EXEC SQL DISCONNECT ALL;
}
```

All of the statements in capitals are instructions to the ESQL precompiler. You can see, for example, that you can type in a SQL statement to be executed as a part of the source code. (The `:first_name` syntax specifies a variable to be used at that point in the statement.)

Once you've written your ESQL program, you have to run it through the precompiler. This is a program that converts the nice simple ESQL code into horrid low-level C code. The precompiler is named `nsqlprep`, and the syntax for calling it is simple:

```
nsqlprep <source file>
```

If your source file is named something like `sample.sqc` then the precompiler will create `sample.c` from it. Here's a bit of the C file created from our simple example:

```
#line 24
/*
EXEC SQL SELECT au_fname INTO :first_name
    from authors where au_lname = :last_name;
*/
#line 25

#line 24
{
```

```
#line 24
     sqlastrt((void far *)pid, (void far *)0, (struct tag_sqlca far
*)sqlca);
#line 24
     sqlaaloc(1, 1, 4, (void far *)0);
#line 24
     sqlasetv(1, 0, 462,(short) SQLLENMAX(sizeof(first_name)),(void far
*)&first_name, (void far *)0,0L);
#line 24
     sqlaaloc(2, 1, 4, (void far *)0);
#line 24
     sqlasetv(2, 0, 462, (short) SQLLENMAX(sizeof(last_name)), (void
far *)last_name, (void far *)0, (void far *)0L);
#line 24
     sqlxcall(24, 4, 2, 1, 60, (char far *)"  SELECT au_fname from
authors where au_lname = @p1          ");
#line 24
     SQLCODE = sqlca->sqlcode;
#line 24
     sqlastop((void far *)0L);
#line 24
}
#line 26
```

Fortunately, if you're working with ESQL, you never really need to look at this form of your code. Just write the simple stuff, precompile it, and use your C compiler to finish the job.

NOTE At runtime, ESQL uses a runtime library to issue DB-Library statements. That's another reason that you should write directly to DB-Library if you have the choice.

Using Automation Objects from Transact-SQL

As you saw in Skill 11, *Creating Client-Server Applications*, SQL-DMO allows ActiveX clients to use objects created and maintained by SQL Server. But SQL Server can also play the other role in an automation scenario. There is a set of extended stored procedures (contained in `Odsole70.dll`) that allows SQL Server to function as an automation client from within a Transact-SQL batch. In this section, we'll learn how to use the SQL Server automation stored procedures to create, to manipulate, and to destroy objects from an ActiveX server.

SQL Server as an ActiveX Client

There are six stored procedures that are used to manipulate ActiveX objects from other servers:

- `sp_OACreate` is used to create new Automation objects.
- `sp_OAGetProperty` returns the current value of a property from an object.
- `sp_OASetProperty` sets a new value for a property of an object.
- `sp_OAMethod` executes a method of an object.
- `sp_OAGetErrorInfo` returns extended information on any error.
- `sp_OADestroy` destroys an Automation object and frees its memory.

A seventh stored procedure, `sp_OAStop`, stops the automation execution environment. It's not necessary to call this procedure. If you stop SQL Server, it automatically stops any automation.

Automation objects are automatically destroyed at the completion of a Transact-SQL batch, so all operations on a single object must be contained within a single batch.

WARNING If you're using these stored procedures to call an object from an automation server created with Visual Basic, you should ensure that all procedures within the Visual Basic project contain appropriate error trapping. Untrapped errors can cause unpredictable and potentially severe SQL Server problems.

Creating Automation Objects

To create a new Automation object, you call the `sp_OACreate` stored procedure. For example, if you have a custom server that exposes an object with the class name `Business.Invoice`, you can create an instance of that object by using the following Transact-SQL batch:

```
DECLARE @obj int
DECLARE @hret int

EXEC @hret = sp_OACreate 'Business.Invoice', @obj OUTPUT
```

If the object creation succeeds, then `@hret` will be non-zero. If creation fails, you can call `sp_OAGetErrorInfo` to retrieve more detailed error information.

Using Automation Objects

Once you have created an Automation object, you can manipulate its methods and properties. Supposing that the Business.Invoice object has a Customer property and a Post method, our example could proceed with this code:

```
DECLARE @property varchar(255)

- Set the customer name
EXEC @hret = sp_OASetProperty @obj, 'Customer', 'PQR Inc.'

- Display the customer name
EXEC @hret = sp_OAGetProperty @obj, 'Customer', @property OUTPUT

- Post the invoice
EXEC @hret = sp_OAMethod @obj, 'Post'
```

Destroying Automation Objects

When you've finished using an Automation object, you should destroy it. In our example, we could destroy the Business.Invoice object with this line of Transact-SQL:

```
EXEC @hret = sp_OADestroy @object
```

Are You up to Speed?

Now you can...

- ☑ **create DB-Library applications using C++ or Visual Basic**
- ☑ **create an extended stored procedure using Open Data Services**
- ☑ **use Embedded SQL to execute SQL statements from a C program**
- ☑ **create and manipulate Automation objects using Transact-SQL**

SKILL 14

Using Replication

- Plan replication strategy
- Configure a server for replication
- Publish data
- Subscribe to data
- Monitor replication
- Implement heterogeneous replication
- Replicate over the Internet

Replication is one part of SQL Server that has seen tremendous enhancements from previous versions. *Replication* can be most simply defined as making copies of your data to different locations and then automatically synchronizing the data so that all copies end up with the same data values. You have a wide variety of options to choose from depending on the needs of your application. You can implement replication between a source database and a destination database, when those databases are located on the same server, or when they are located on different servers connected by LANs, WANs, or the Internet. Databases need not be directly connected; changes can be stored and forwarded as needed. You can schedule replication or carry out synchronization on demand.

NOTE In addition to SQL Server, you can also replicate to heterogeneous databases, such as Microsoft Access and Oracle. We will cover heterogeneous replication with Microsoft Access later in this skill.

Replication is an efficient way to distribute data to multiple sites. Even with all its new features, SQL Server replication is still based on its traditional publishing and subscribing metaphor, in which a server makes data available by publishing it. The server is the *publisher* of the data, making published data available for replication. The publisher sends copies of all changes to the published data to the *distributor*. The distribution server contains the distribution database, which receives all changes to the data, stores them, and transmits them to the *subscribers*. The subscription server maintains destination databases, which receive the published data and maintain their own replicas. A subscriber can subscribe to some or all of the publication server's publications.

NOTE The distribution server can be the same computer as the publication server or a different computer.

SQL Server offers several replication technologies:

Snapshot replication Data stored at the publisher replaces data at a subscriber on a periodic basis. The initial synchronization involves copying all of the data at the source to the destination, and then snapshots of changed data, known as a *scheduled table refresh*, are sent after that. This is a good solution if you do not need your data to be constantly up-to-date or if you are infrequently connected to the publisher. It also requires much less overhead than transactional replication.

Transactional replication The source database log file is used to distribute committed transactions within seconds of their occurrence. `INSERT`, `UPDATE`, and `DELETE` statements are distributed to the destination servers; the actual data is not. Changes are sent in the order in which they were committed, ensuring that they are received by the subscriber in the same order in which they were applied at the publisher. Transactional replication is a good solution where transactional consistency is important.

Merge replication Multiple sites make changes to data independently of the publisher and then synchronize with the publisher, which distributes the changed data to the other sites. Merge replication is useful for mobile applications, such as the traveling salesman scenario, where users are not continuously connected to the server yet need to insert data to the server. Merge replication does not guarantee transactional consistency, so it's best suited for partitioned or disconnected applications.

The Microsoft Distributed Transaction Coordinator (MS DTC) provides a graphical management interface for replication that provides the ability to manage transactions, recording important operational events in the system log.

Planning Replication

Planning replication often requires juggling the conflicting needs of different applications and environments. There is no single solution that will meet the needs of every application, and often you will find that you have conflicting needs in the same application. If your application requires transactional consistency, then this conflicts with the need for site autonomy. Another important issue you face in planning replication is the need to partition data to avoid data conflicts, which occur when the same record is updated in different locations. Data conflicts generate extra administrative work since they must somehow be resolved for the data to be consistent across multiple sites.

Choosing the Right Replication Strategy

SQL Server offers a wide variety of solutions to choose from when selecting the right replication strategy. If you need up-to-the-minute, guaranteed-accurate data, then transactional replication is what you should consider first. If site autonomy is important, then merge replication would be the right answer. The other factors you need to weigh would be the avoidance of conflicts—do you need to partition your data? In other instances, data may need to be kept current even though the users are disconnected, making it impossible to guarantee transactional consistency at all times.

Understanding Transactions

There are three levels of transactional consistency that you need to consider when working with replication:

Guaranteed tight consistency All sites are guaranteed to have the exact same data at the same time, as though the data had been changed at only one site.

Guaranteed loose consistency All sites are guaranteed to have the same data, but not necessarily all at the same time. In other words, all the sites eventually get the same data but, at any single point in time while data is being modified, they do not have the same data.

No guaranteed consistency Data is changed in ways that would not have happened had the data been changed at only one site.

The main difference between tight and loose consistency is whether the data values are consistent at the same instant in time or not. With no guaranteed consistency, data is never expected to be consistent. If you employ a tight consistency model and have multiple remote sites participating in replication, using a two-phase commit makes any change to the data dependent on the other sites being able to commit the transaction. If one server goes down, then none of the sites will be able to get any work done. On the other hand, having no guaranteed consistency between sites means that the data at any given site could be wildly out of sync with data at the other sites, causing work to stop for other reasons.

Partitioning Data to Avoid Conflicts

Conflicts are to be avoided whenever possible since they always result in some site's data being overwritten or rolled back or in the loss of guaranteed transactional integrity. Partitioning is a useful strategy for avoiding conflicts. This solution works well with multiple disconnected sites. Each site receives data that is partitioned from other sites and is a subset of the entire database. For example, a salesperson on the road has a segregated set of records that reflects her territory and customers and omits the data relevant to other territories. In this case you have both transactional consistency and site autonomy since the other sites have entirely different subsets of the data.

There are two types of partitions:

- Horizontal partitions, in which certain rows are selected from the total
- Vertical partitions, in which certain columns are selected from the total

You can also combine the two. If you choose a distributed, loosely consistent replication model, then you should design your application so that conflicts are the exception, rather than the rule.

Using the NOT FOR REPLICATION Option and Uniqueidentifier

When you have set the `NOT FOR REPLICATION` option on identity values in your table columns, then SQL Server will maintain the original identity values on rows added during replication. If a row is added by another user, then the identity value will increment in the normal way. When that row is replicated to a subscriber, the identity value stays the same when the row is inserted into the subscriber's table and does not affect the next value at the subscriber; it does not cause the value at the subscriber to be reseeded. This is useful when you partition your data.

When defining your tables for later replication, use the `uniqueidentifier` data type with the `NEWID()` function when you need to generate a unique ID for a row. The `uniqueidentifier` is guaranteed to be globally unique and you cannot exhaust the list of values. `NEWID()` will generate a new value automatically for each row added to the table. The downside is that GUIDs are cumbersome, difficult to use in queries, and aren't useful for tables built around incremental ID values. A GUID's format looks like this:

```
2338F4BB-4B08-11D1-853F-00Q04FBFE9BX
```

If you need incrementing values, then combine the `uniqueidentifier` column with a normally incrementing column.

Replication Components

Replication consists of the following parts:

- A *publisher* is the server that makes data available to other servers. It maintains information about all publications in a database. Each publication has a single publisher, although multiple subscribers can update it.
- A *subscriber* is a server that stores replicas and sends or receives changes from the publisher. Subscribers can also become publishers to other subscribers.
- The *distributor* is the server on which the distribution database is located. Its role varies depending on which type of replication you use. The distributor does not necessarily have to be the same server as the publisher.
- An *article* consists of the data to be replicated and can contain data from a stored procedure or table that has been marked for replication.
- A *publication* is a collection of one or more articles. Articles can consist of entire tables or filtered (partitioned) tables. Subscribers subscribe to publications, not to individual articles.
- A *subscription* is created on a subscription server to obtain the publications marked for replication.

TIP

Subscribing to articles is allowed in SQL Server 7 for backwards compatibility only. However, you should consider migrating any old subscriptions to the publication level since the user interface no longer supports it.

NOTE

Any SQL Server can be configured to perform the roles of publisher or subscriber of replicated data. You can install the replication components on separate computers to balance workloads and improve performance.

NOTE

There is no peer-to-peer (or multimaster) topology in SQL Server replication. This is quite different from the replication model used in Microsoft Access where all members of a replica set are more or less equal and any member of the replica set can be designated as the Design Master if the need arises. In SQL Server, there is only one publisher and one master database for any number of subscribers. The ability of subscribers to make updates to data is not the same thing as being a publisher.

There are two basic types of subscriptions:

- *Push subscriptions*, where the publisher propagates (or pushes) the changes to a subscriber. Push subscriptions are good for applications where you need to send changes to subscribers as soon as they occur, for publications needing higher security, and for publications that need to be scheduled. There is higher processor overhead at the publisher with a push subscription.
- *Pull subscriptions*, where the subscriber requests changes from the publisher. Pull subscriptions are good for mobile users dialing in for changes, for publications needing less security, and where there are a great many subscribers, such as Internet/intranet applications.

TIP A single publication can support both push and pull subscriptions simultaneously.

Types of Replication

There are three basic types of replication to choose from:

- Snapshot replication
- Transactional replication
- Merge replication

Each type has different capabilities and attributes for transactional consistency and site autonomy. You can configure your application by partitioning your data then choosing which of the different types of replication are suitable—you are not restricted to a single type since an application can support a mixture of replication types. In the same application, you can configure some of your data to use transactional replication, some snapshot replication, and some merge replication, depending on whether your data needs tight consistency or not. Figure 14.1 shows the spectrum of choices available on a scale ranging from loose consistency to tight consistency.

You may also have two or more of the following Replication Agents depending on which type of replication you use:

- Each publication has its own *Snapshot Agent*, which prepares snapshot files of published tables and stored procedures and records synchronization status information.

- Each transactional publication has its own *Log Reader Agent*, which moves marked transactions from the transaction log on the publisher to the distribution database.

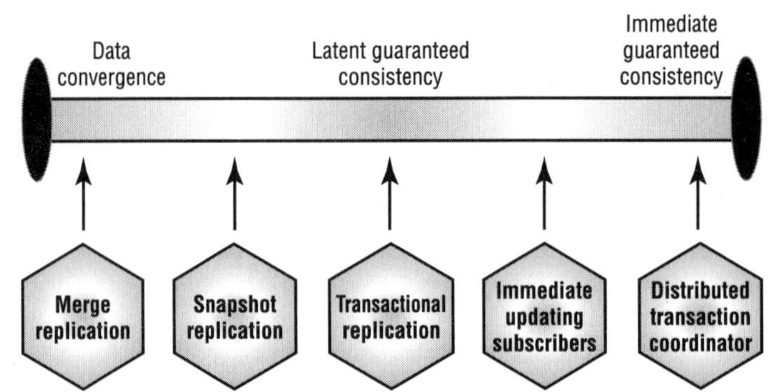

FIGURE 14.1: Replication options based on data consistency

- Both transactional and snapshot subscriptions have a *Distribution Agent*, which moves the transactions and snapshot jobs from the distribution database to subscribers.
- Each merge subscription has its own *Merge Agent* to apply initial snapshot jobs held in publication database tables to subscribers and to merge incremental data changes occurring after the creation of the initial snapshot.

Snapshot Replication

Snapshot replication copies a snapshot of the publication data to the destination server, overwriting any data that may have previously existed. When you initially configure replication, SQL Server can automatically synchronize all the data at all destination servers by copying snapshots to them. Since snapshot replication does not involve continuous monitoring of the transaction log on source servers, it requires less overhead to implement. You can set up scheduled table refreshes at specified intervals to update the data at the subscribing servers. This bulk transfer of data will replace any existing data on the subscriber. This works well in situations where you might have subscribers who are not well connected to the server and who do not need up-to-date data at all times.

NOTE

Unlike replicated tables in a transactional system, replicated tables in a snapshot replication system do not require primary keys.

You need to schedule snapshot replication carefully to minimize user impact. The Snapshot Agent locks the entire table while it uses the bcp utility to export the table. No other users will be able to edit the data in the table while the Snapshot Agent is working, so you need to schedule snapshots accordingly.

TIP

Allocate sufficient disk space in the replication working directory. The default working directory uses the C$ share with a complete path of \\<computer>C$\Mssql7\Repldata. Any snapshots created will be the same size as the published table, so you need at least as much disk space in the replication working directory as you have allocated for the tables at the publisher. There must be enough space to store all snapshots from all publications simultaneously.

You can set up snapshot replication using the Enterprise Manager, system stored procedures, or SQL-DMO. Before you start, you need to take the following steps:

1. On the publisher, you need to set the server's publication options and install a distributor.
2. On the distributor, you need to install a distribution database.
3. For each subscriber, you need to install a subscriber database and to set the server's subscription options.

We'll cover setting up these options later in this skill.

Transactional Replication

When you need tight consistency between sites, you need to consider transactional replication, which is based on monitored changes in the transaction log of the source server. Any modifications, such as `INSERT`, `UPDATE`, and `DELETE` statements, are then distributed to destination servers.

The way transactional replication works is that a Log Reader Agent monitors the transaction log of each database participating in replication. When the Log Reader Agent finds replicable transactions, it hands them off to the distribution database, which holds them until they can be distributed to the subscribing databases in the other participating servers. Any changes made to tables are sent to the destination server in the order in which they are committed, so that the subscribers will receive them in the same order that they were applied at the publisher. Only committed transactions are sent to destination servers and users are not excluded from accessing the destination tables while they are being updated.

The publication database's transaction log holds the transactions marked for replication until the log reader moves them into the distribution database. Then the log reader truncates the transaction log of the distribution database. Once this occurs, the transaction log of the publication database can also be safely truncated, which purges only transactions not marked for replication.

There are three things you need to do before setting up transactional replication:

1. Make sure all the tables involved in transactional replication have primary keys.
2. Make sure that the transaction log has enough space allocated since a published database transaction log generally requires more space. The log can't be truncated past the oldest published transaction that has not been passed into a distribution database. This is not a major problem on SQL Server 7, since you can set the log database to grow as necessary.
3. Make sure the distribution database has enough space to store all of the transactions posted since the last snapshot. For example, if you schedule the Snapshot Agent to run once a week, you need to have enough disk space to store the snapshot plus all of the transactions that occur during the week.

TIP You can replicate text and image data types in transactional replication using the `INSERT`, `UPDATE`, and `DELETE` statements. Logged text operations using `WRITETEXT` and `UPDATETEXT` with the `WITH LOG` option can also be replicated. For more technical details on replicating text and image data, see Books Online.

You can implement transactional replication using the Enterprise Manager, system stored procedures or SQL-DMO. Before you start, you need to take the following steps:

1. On the publisher, you need to set the server's publication options and install a distributor.
2. On the distributor, you need to install a distribution database.
3. For each subscriber, you need to install a subscriber database and to set the server's subscription options.

Immediate Updating Subscribers The Immediate Updating Subscribers option allows subscribers to update data as long as the update can be immediately applied at the publisher using the two-phase commit protocol. This means that there is no loss of transactional integrity. If the update is successful, then the publisher propagates those changes to any other subscribers when the next snapshot refresh occurs. This gives you more site autonomy than would be possible if all the subscribers needed to immediately accept the change, as they would with a full two-phase commit. This is a good choice for applications that tend not to have high update rates and in which changes do not need to be immediately applied at all the subscribers.

The benefits of Immediate Updating Subscribers are:

- There are never any conflicts since the subscriber can update, insert, or delete data only if it can perform a two-phase commit with the publisher.
- Updates are replicated to other subscribers through snapshots or transactional replication.
- The updating subscriber can continue to work without having to wait for the successful update to trickle down via the next snapshot.
- The updating subscriber does not need a distribution database or log reader or to otherwise get involved in administering replication.
- There are fewer failure points with every site than with full two-phase commit.
- Transactional consistency is guaranteed.

The Microsoft Distributed Transaction Coordinator (MS DTC) manages the two-phase commit using the Transact-SQL `BEGIN DISTRIBUTED TRAN[SACTION]` statement. Triggers at the subscriber capture transactions and submit them to the publisher using a remote stored procedure call within the two-phase commit. These triggers are created by using the `NOT FOR REPLICATION` parameter of the `CREATE TRIGGER` statement so that changes applied by the Distribution Agent do not themselves cause the trigger to fire. The triggers take care of calling the `BEGIN DISTRIBUTED TRAN` statement and handle executing remote procedure calls to the publisher. Other stored procedures at the publisher apply changes if there are no conflicts with changes made at the publisher. If there are conflicts, then the transaction is rolled back at both the publisher and the subscriber. Conflicts are detected by detecting differences in the timestamp column. If a timestamp column does not already exist, then one will be added when the publications and subscriptions are enabled for replication.

TIP The Immediate Updating Subscribers option is only supported for SQL Server 7 databases residing on different servers. Updates to multiple databases on the same server do not use MS DTC. In addition, each table must have a primary key.

Replicating Stored Procedures There are two different ways you can replicate stored procedures in SQL Server 7:

Procedure execution The procedure execution is replicated to all subscribers, regardless of whether or not individual statements in the stored procedure were successful. Data at the subscribers cannot be guaranteed to be consistent with data at the publisher since changes made to data by the stored procedure may occur within multiple transactions.

Serializable procedure execution The procedure execution is replicated only if it is executed within the context of a serializable transaction. Data at the subscriber is guaranteed to be consistent with data at the publisher.

When a stored procedure is replicated, no new data changes or procedure executions are replicated until the stored procedure finishes execution. The stored procedure definition at the publisher is propagated to each subscriber by default, but you can modify it at the subscriber if you want different logic to be executed at the publisher and subscriber.

Synchronous Transactions

Synchronous transactions are new in SQL Server 7 and can be used with either transactional replication or snapshot replication. With synchronous transactions, a subscriber can modify replicated data if the transaction can be performed using a two-phase commit with the publisher. This allows you to bend the old rules where data could only be updated at the publisher and not the subscriber. Unlike in merge replication, where each site must communicate with all of the other sites, the subscriber need only communicate the changed data to the publisher. The changed data will eventually get replicated to the other subscribers, sooner if you are using transactional replication and possibly later if you are using snapshot replication.

continued

The two-phase commit is automatic and, if it is successful, the subscriber can work with the changed values right away. However, if the publisher is not available, then data cannot be updated on the subscriber. The subscriber also does not need a distribution database since the publisher will handle the task of propagating the changed data to the other subscribers. This also has the advantage of preserving transactional consistency since the two-phase commit ensures that the data is updated as though it were on the publisher.

Distributed transactions are implemented by the Microsoft Distributed Transaction Coordinator (MS DTC). Triggers created at the subscriber submit them to the publisher via a remote stored procedure call within a two-phase commit. You can enable synchronous transactions using the Enterprise Manager or by using the stored procedures in both transactional and snapshot replication.

Merge Replication

Merge replication, or bidirectional replication, is a new capability in SQL Server 7. It allows data to be updated independently at multiple sites where the sites then synchronize with each other later. It does not guarantee transactional consistency and is not a good choice for applications with a high volume of updates with a strong likelihood of conflicting with each other. Merge replication works well with applications that do not need transactional consistency, that are loosely connected, or where multiple inserts are performed that do not conflict with each other.

The most common topology is the hub-to-spoke topology in which a central distributor controls synchronization. You can also configure multihub topologies and mix hub-spoke and multihub configurations. Merge replication scales well for large topologies by supporting various subscribers. A site can be a republisher, local subscriber, global subscriber, or anonymous subscriber.

In merge replication, the publisher creates the publication, but all subscribers may update data. You can configure your own conflict resolution criteria so that the publisher doesn't automatically win in any conflicts with a subscriber (the default). Merge replication utilizes the Snapshot Agent to prepare snapshot files containing schema and data, to store it in the distributor, and to record synchronization jobs in the publication database. The Merge Agent applies the initial snapshot, merges incremental data changes, and handles any conflicts by applying rules that you create.

SQL Server makes several important changes to tables and database schema when a table is published using merge replication:

- A unique column (`rowguid`) is added for each row in the table, which allows the row to be uniquely identified across multiple copies of the table. If a `uniqueidentifier` column already exists, then SQL Server will use it for the unique identifier.
- Triggers are installed to track data changes and record them in merge system tables.
- System tables are added to the database to support data tracking, synchronization, and conflict resolution.

The initial snapshot copies the current publication to new subscribers since they must contain tables with the same schema and data as the tables at the publisher. Snapshots are only applied to new subscribers; other subscribers already participating in merge replication will not be affected.

TIP If you have a very large publication, you can load a snapshot manually from a tape or other storage device instead of sending it over the network.

The following are some design issues that need to be considered before you implement merge replication:

- Use the `uniqueidentifier` data type and avoid using identity columns since multiple sites will insert records that have the same sequential values. These rows will conflict when merged, because duplicate values are not allowed in an identity column.
- Remove all timestamp columns from any table to be published via merge replication. Since timestamp values are automatically generated by the local server, changes to timestamp columns at the subscriber could never be applied at the publisher (or vice versa).
- Design for merge replication to ensure that application integrity is preserved at the publisher, despite the changes being made at subscribers. No change should be allowed to violate integrity constraints when applied at the publisher.

- Maintain primary key references when specifying tables by including tables that contain the primary key references. Inserts to tables with foreign keys referencing primary keys in missing tables will fail, although updates to the existing rows will succeed since updates don't need to add a new key value.
- Provide support for text and image data types by using the `UPDATE` statement to explicitly update them. The `WRITETEXT` and `UPDATETEXT` statements alone will not propagate changes to other sites.

You can use the Enterprise Manager, system stored procedures, or SQL-DMO to configure merge replication, which we will cover later in this skill.

Conflict Resolution and the Conflict Wizard

With merge replication, there will sometimes be collisions with conflicting data written to the same record at different sites. Conflict information is stored at the publisher site by copying the losing record into a *conflict table* that has the same structure as the original table. Information about which tables have related conflict tables is stored in the system table called sysmergearticles. The name of the conflict table is Conflict_UserTable. If there are delete conflicts, these are stored in a table called MSmerge_delete_conflicts.

The following lists some possible conflicts that may occur with merge replication:

- Two sites attempt to insert a row that has the same key value. If each succeeds, then a conflict occurs at synchronization.
- One site inserts a row with a foreign key value while another site deletes the corresponding primary key row.
- Locking problems

Merge replication uses site priority in order to determine which are the winning and losing records. Each subscription is assigned a priority number between zero (the lowest priority) and 100 (the highest priority). Basically the subscription with the highest priority change wins and the subscription with the lowest priority loses. No changes made at the highest priority replica ever get undone by the conflict resolution mechanism. Of course, this does not prevent lower priority replicas from making subsequent changes to the winning row on the next pass, which will then propagate back without a conflict.

In case of a tie where replicas are assigned equal priority, then the first one in is determined to be the winner. The lineage shows which replica created each version of a row. The publisher can then determine the priority of the changes based on which replica made a particular version, based on the lineage. For example, you have two subscriber replicas, Rep-1 and Rep-2, each with a priority of 50. They have both merged with the publisher at the hub (which has a priority of 100) and all have the same data. The following sequence of events illustrates the first-in tiebreaker:

1. Rep-1 makes a change to row 10.
2. Rep-1 merges with the publisher and uploads the new row 10. The lineage at row 10 in MSmerge_contents shows that Rep-1 made the current version of the row.
3. Rep-2 makes a change to row 10—it's the old row 10 since it hasn't yet merged with the publisher.
4. Rep-2 merges with the publisher and tries to upload its version of row 10.
5. Rep-2 loses and its changes are not uploaded to the publisher because Rep-1 got its changes in first. The conflict is logged at the publisher and Rep-2 gets the new version of row 10 from the publisher.

The "first in to the publisher" rule only applies to replicas of equal priority. If Rep-2 had a higher priority than Rep-1, then its changes would have been merged to the publisher and Rep-1's changes would have been overwritten. Rep-1 would have been updated on a subsequent merge with the publisher.

Anonymous subscriptions are always treated as having a priority of zero, so they automatically lose in any conflict. If an anonymous subscription propagates a non-conflicting change, then the hub assumes authorship of the change. If you set up a single hub with only anonymous subscriptions, then all changes done at the hub can be thought of as being permanent since they will never be undone. Changes at a non-hub are tentative until synchronized with the hub, at which time they either become permanent or are rejected.

NOTE

If you like you can override the default priority-based conflict resolution scheme by providing your own custom resolver. Use Transact-SQL to create stored procedures to execute at each publisher. For details on how to create a custom-resolver stored procedure, see Books Online.

Implementing Replication

Once you've designed your application and figured out which types of replication are necessary in your application, your first step towards implementation is to configure the server.

Configuring the Server

You can configure the server using the Configure Publishing and Distribution Wizard. To load the wizard from the Enterprise Manager, expand the Server folder so that a server is active and choose Tools ➢ Replication ➢ Configure Publishing and Subscribers. The opening dialog box informs you that you can specify your server as a distributor, configure it as a distributor, or configure it as a publisher. You then need to specify your server as a distributor or else designate another server as the distributor. We'll take the current server, as shown in Figure 14.2.

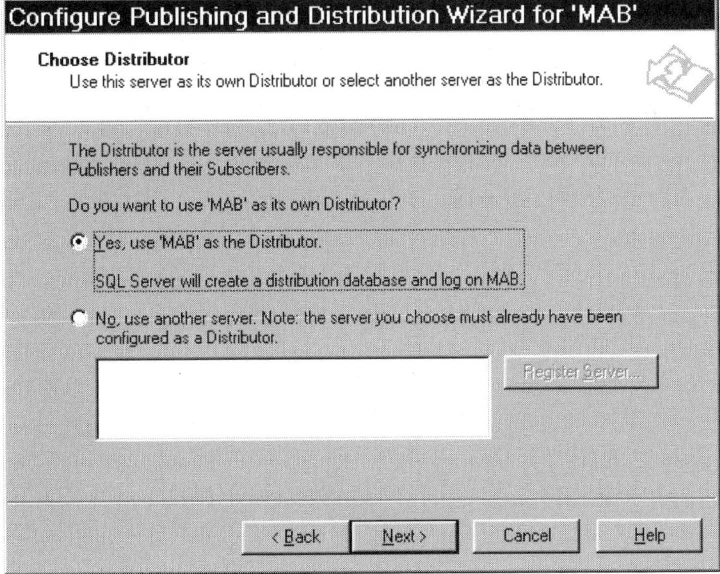

FIGURE 14.2: Configuring the server as a distributor

After you've designated your server as the distributor, you need either to accept the default settings, which are listed in the box on the next wizard page, or to customize your settings. We've chosen the default settings, as shown in Figure 14.3.

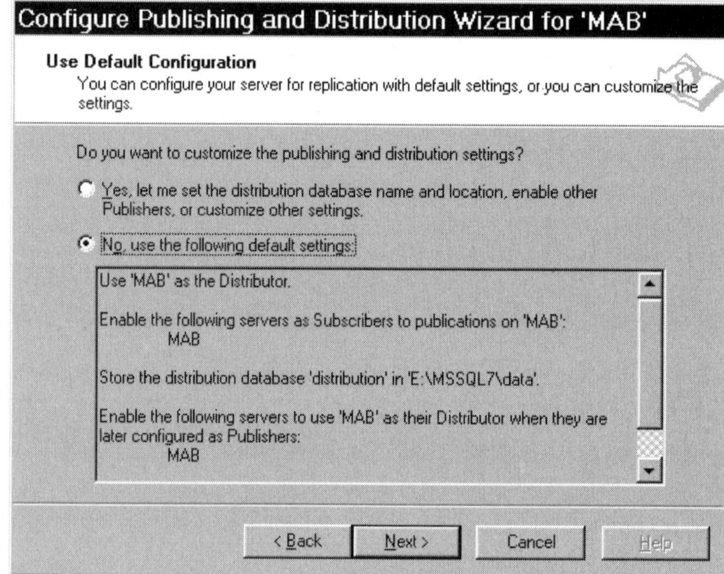

FIGURE 14.3: Setting default configuration options for the distributor

Once you click the Finish button, the wizard will create the distribution list and log and set other configuration options. You may also receive a dialog box asking you if you want to configure the SQL Server Agent service to start automatically when the computer is started. Click Yes; if the Agent isn't running, you won't be able to synchronize.

Once you've finished configuring the distributor, SQL Server will add the Replication Monitor to the console tree, as shown in Figure 14.4. The Replication Monitor allows you to view publishers, publications, subscriptions, schedules, events, and history for each Replication Agent as well as to set up and monitor alerts for replication events.

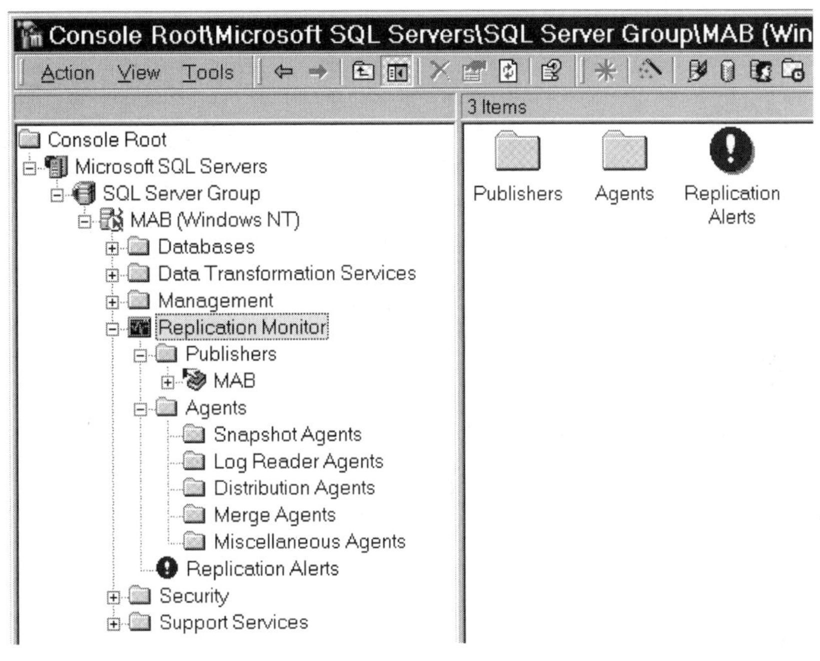

FIGURE 14.4: Replication Monitor is added to the console

You can later change any of the options you've chosen by expanding the folder until the Replication Monitor folder is visible, then right-click it and choose Distributor Properties from the shortcut menu. This will bring up the dialog box shown in Figure 14.5. Note that there are five separate tabs and many more options than shown in the wizard. The wizard is good for getting you started, but you'll want to investigate these properties further. You can use this dialog box not only to set the properties of the distributor but also to enable databases for publication, to set up subscribers and publishers, and to configure security through the publication access list. Security is discussed later in this skill.

You can also use the replication system stored procedures to work with replication. To configure a server to be a distributor, execute the `sp_adddistributor` stored procedure using the master database:

```
sp_adddistributor  @distributor = 'KARIS'
```

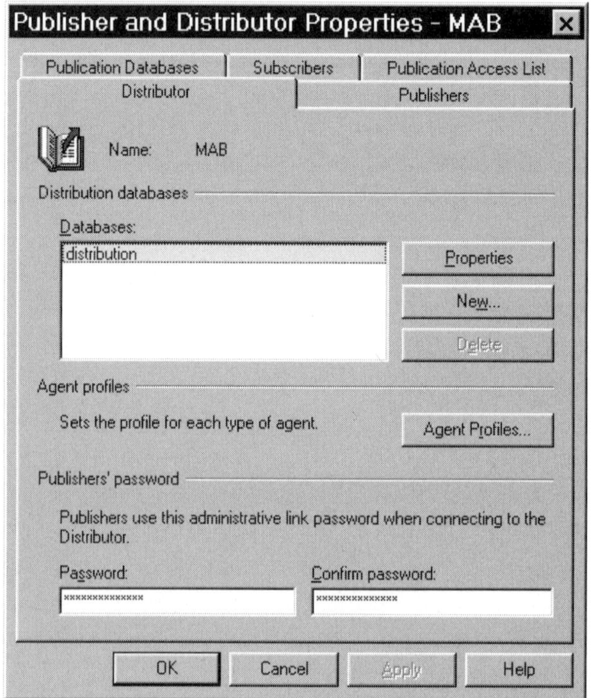

FIGURE 14.5: Publisher and Distributor Properties dialog box

Once you've specified that the server is to be a distributor, use the stored procedure sp_adddistributiondb to create a new distribution database.

```
sp_adddistributiondb @database = N'distribution',
    @data_folder = N'C:\MSSQL7\DATA',
    @data_file = N'distribution.mdf',
    @data_file_size = 3,
    @log_folder = N'C:\MSSQL7\DATA',
    @log_file = N'distribution.ldf',
    @log_file_size = 1,
    @min_distretention = 0,
    @max_distretention = 24,
    @history_retention = 24,
    @security_mode = 1
```

You then need to execute sp_adddistpublisher at each server using the distributor that you want to be a publisher:

```
sp_adddistpublisher  @publisher = N'KARIS',
```

```
@distribution_db = N'distribution',
@working_directory = '\\KARIS\C$\MSSQL7\ReplData',
```

There are other arguments for these stored procedures but, since we're working with Windows NT in these examples, the defaults are sufficient and don't need to be spelled out. For more information, see Books Online.

Enabling a Database for Replication

Let's use the Northwind database as an example of enabling replication. To enable the Northwind database for replication, choose Tools ➢ Replication ➢ Configure Publishing, Subscribers, and Distribution. Then click the Publication Databases tab on the Publisher and Distributor Properties dialog box, as shown in Figure 14.6. In the figure, the Northwind database is now enabled for merge replication.

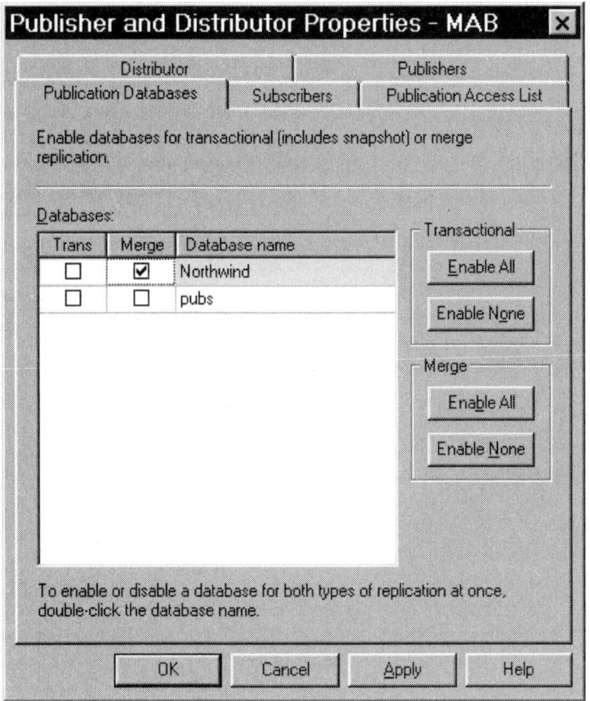

FIGURE 14.6: Enabling a database for replication

You can also run the stored procedure `sp_replicationdboption` to enable a database for replication:

```
sp_replicationdboption @dbname = Northwind,
    @optname = 'publish',
    @value = true
```

Publications and Subscriptions

Any SQL Server can participate in any of the three roles of replication as a publisher, a distributor, or a subscriber, or in any combination of the three. You also need to determine what sets of replicated data your subscribers will receive. You can subscribe to some or all of the publications offered as well as partition tables (vertically, horizontally, or both) so that subscription servers only see a subset of the publisher's data. In this section we'll discuss working with publishers, distributors, and subscribers.

Publishing Data

In order to publish data, you need to select the tables and stored procedures to be included and to make the publication available to subscription servers. You can create one or more publications from each database on a publication server. You can't span databases—each publication must contain articles from a single database. SQL Server ships with several wizards to help you with the process (to view these, choose Tools ➢ Wizards ➢ Replication) as well as replication menu options (choose Tools ➢ Replication). In addition, there are right-click, context-sensitive options available when replication components are selected in the main console.

You can use the SQL Server Enterprise Manager to create a publication by selecting a server to be the publisher (as shown in the previous example) and then running the Create Publication Wizard to create the actual publication.

The Create Publication Wizard

The Create Publication Wizard walks you through the steps of enabling and configuring a database for replication. You select tables or stored procedures to be the articles published and specify what kinds of subscriptions are allowed, the initial synchronization strategy, and formats. Additional specifications you perform with the wizard include the following:

- Whether to use snapshot or transactional replication

- Whether to allow synchronous update subscriptions
- Whether to allow publications to pull subscriptions and, if so, whether to allow anonymous subscriptions
- Whether to filter the data in the article
- Whether to always maintain a snapshot of the publication at the server
- Whether the data will be published in native SQL Server format or in text format for non-SQL Server subscribers

In addition, you can use the wizard to carry out the following:

- Enable Internet subscriptions.
- Set up various publication options, such as name and description.
- Set up scheduling for the Snapshot Agent.

To use the Create Publication Wizard, choose Tools ➢ Wizards ➢ Replication ➢ Create Publication Wizard. Figure 14.7 shows the opening dialog box of the Create Publication Wizard. We'll create a publication from the Northwind database.

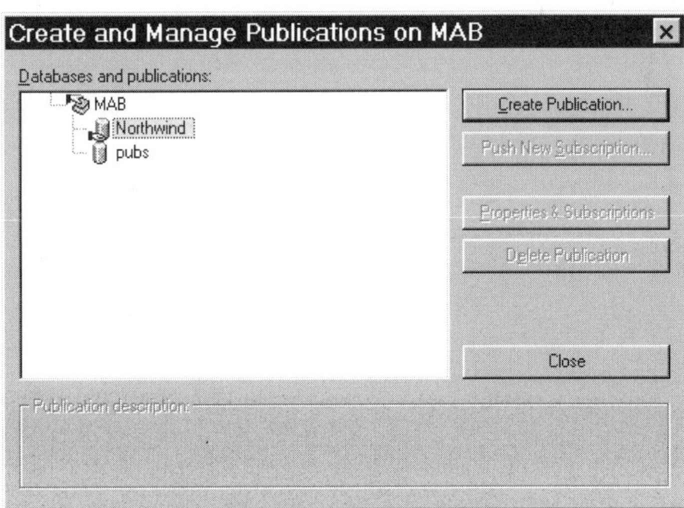

FIGURE 14.7: The Create Publication Wizard

The introductory dialog box to the wizard states that you can use the wizard to create the publication from the data in Northwind and set its filters and properties. The first option you need to choose is whether the publication type is going to be snapshot, transactional, or merge. We'll create a snapshot publication, as shown in Figure 14.8.

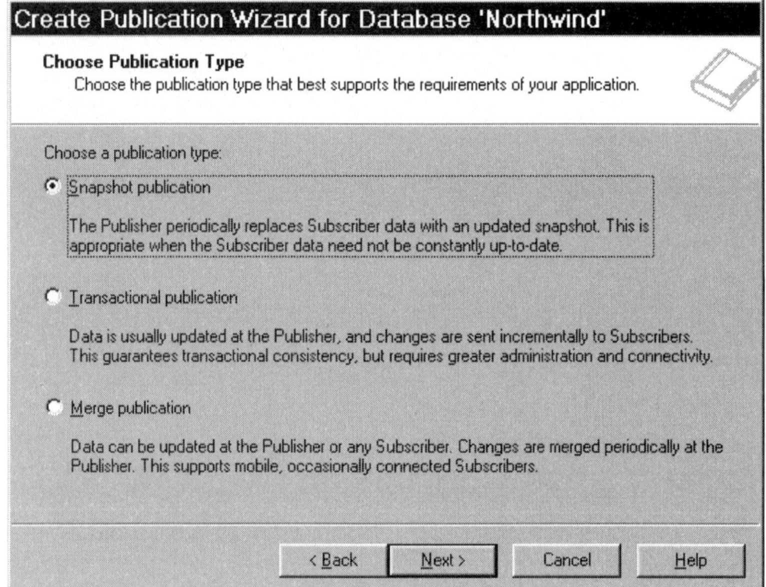

FIGURE 14.8: Specifying a snapshot publication

The next option asks whether you want immediate updating subscribers or not. This would involve using the Microsoft Distributed Transaction Coordinator to implement a two-phase commit between the publisher and subscribers, which you wouldn't want unless your servers were very tightly connected. We'll choose No for this option.

You then need to specify whether or not all subscribers will be SQL Servers. If other databases will be subscribing, the files will be larger. We'll be covering Access subscribers later in this skill, so we'll choose to have all subscribers be SQL Server subscribers.

Next you need to specify the articles to include in your publication, as shown in Figure 14.9. We'll choose to publish the Customers table.

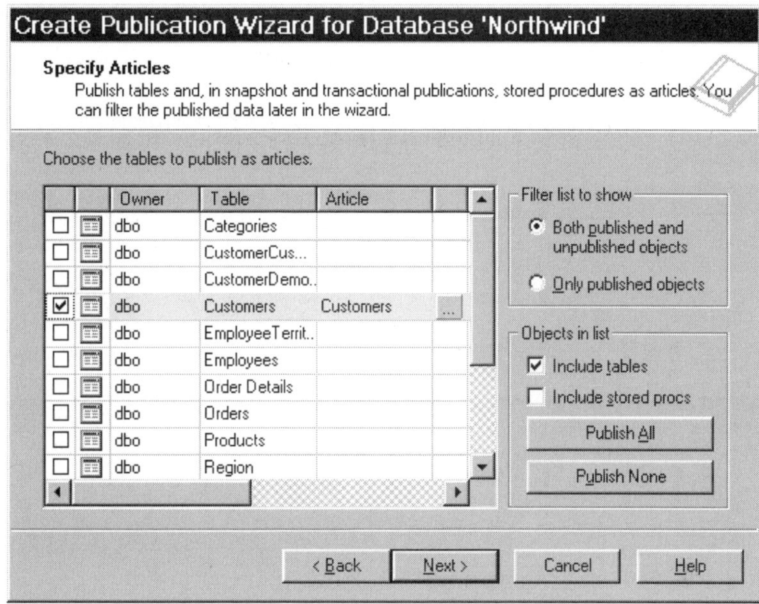

FIGURE 14.9: Selecting the articles to include

You can set additional options for this article by clicking the builder button to the right of the Customers article. You can rename the article on the General tab—we've renamed this article SnapParisCustomers. Clicking the Snapshot tab lets you fine-tune other options for this article, as shown in Figure 14.10.

The next wizard dialog box lets you set the name for the entire publication, as shown in Figure 14.11.

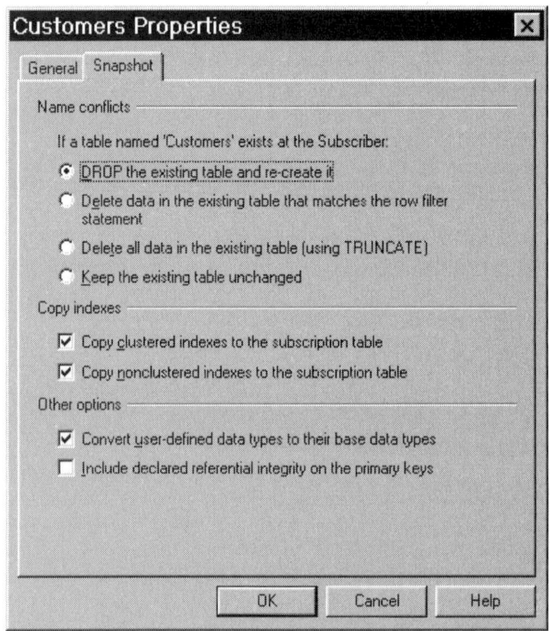

FIGURE 14.10: Setting snapshot options for the replication article

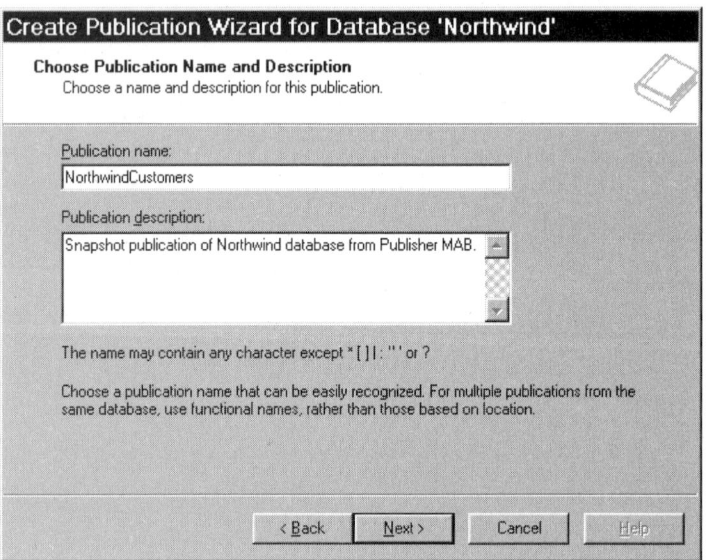

FIGURE 14.11: Naming the publication

You will next be asked if you want to use the default properties of the publication or if you want to define custom properties or data filters. If you elect to filter the data, you can select which articles you want to filter. Figure 14.12 shows filtering the columns. Only the checked columns will be included in the publication.

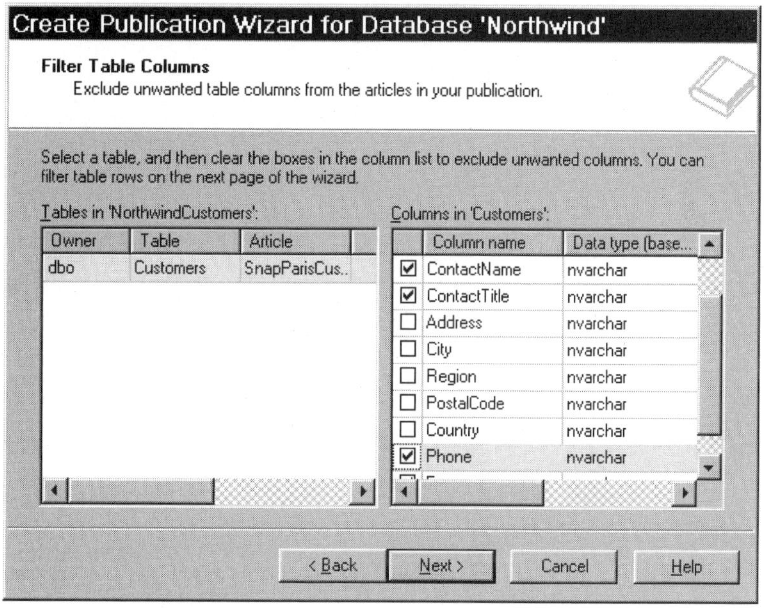

FIGURE 14.12: Selecting the columns on which to filter the article

To filter rows, click the builder button on the Filter Table Rows dialog box. This will bring up the Specify Filter dialog box, where you can type in a `WHERE` clause, as shown in Figure 14.13.

Then you can elect whether or not to allow anonymous subscriptions. The next dialog box allows you to set the Snapshot Agent schedule by clicking the Change button, as shown in Figure 14.14. The Snapshot Agent creates the files necessary to initialize new subscriptions.

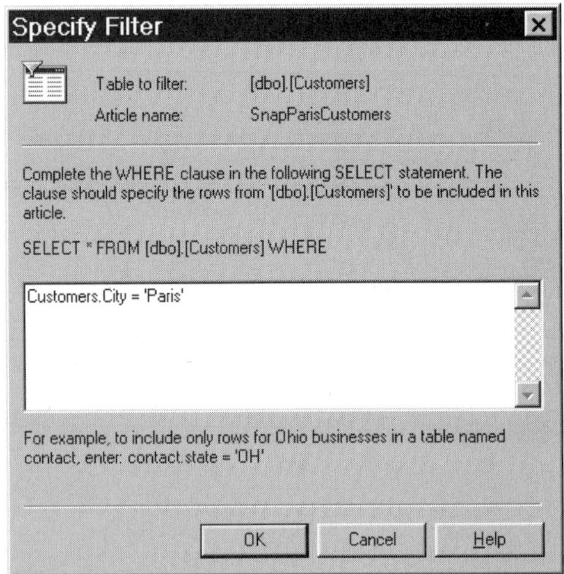

FIGURE 14.13: Filtering by row

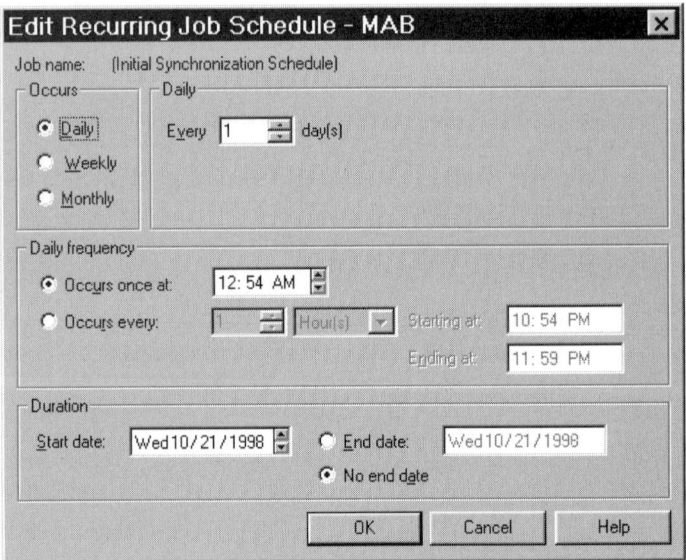

FIGURE 14.14: Scheduling the Snapshot Agent

The Distribution Agent can run at the same time as the Snapshot Agent. If the Distribution Agent runs and there is not a snapshot available it will wait (if it is running continuously) or shutdown with a message stating a snapshot is not yet available.

You then can choose the publication access list that you want to use for the publication. This sets the security context. You can use either the default (the publisher's list) or customize your own. We'll select the publisher's list, as shown in Figure 14.15.

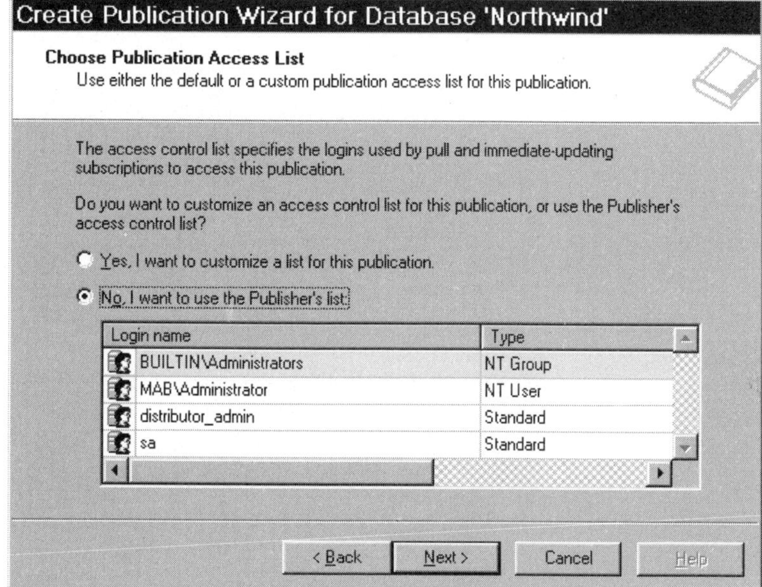

FIGURE 14.15: Choosing the publication access list

The final wizard dialog box summarizes all the options you've chosen along the way. You can always click the Back button and change any options you're not happy with before you click the Finish button.

The Create Publication Wizard will then set the publication properties, create the publication, add the articles, exclude marked columns, set filters, and start the Snapshot Agent. When it is done, you will then be returned to the Create and Manage Publications dialog box, where you can elect further options, as shown in

Figure 14.16. You can always get back to this dialog box by selecting Tools ➢ Replication ➢ Create and Manage Publications from the main console menu.

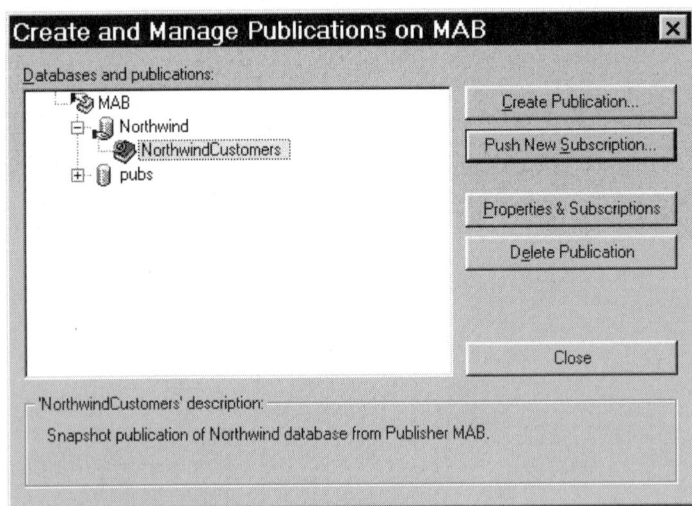

FIGURE 14.16: The Create and Manage Publications dialog box

If you want to push the subscription to another server, you need to link to that server, which we will discuss in the next section in this skill.

If you prefer, you can also use stored procedures to perform the same tasks. To create a snapshot publication, use the `sp_addpublication` stored procedure against the Northwind database:

```
sp_addpublication @publication = 'SnapCustomers',
    @sync_method = 'native',
    @repl_freq = 'snapshot',
    @description = 'Snapshot of Northwind Customers',
    @status = 'active',
    @allow_push = 'true',
    @allow_pull = 'true',
    @allow_anonymous = 'false',
    @enabled_for_internet = 'false',
    @independent_agent = 'false',
    @immediate_sync = 'false',
    @allow_sync_tran = 'false',
    @autogen_sync_procs = 'false',
    @retention = 60,
    @default_access = 'true'
```

Once you've created the SnapCustomers snapshot, then you need to run the `sp_addpublication_snapshot` stored procedure to make it a snapshot and set other properties:

```
sp_addpublication_snapshot
    @publication = 'SnapCustomers',
    @frequency_type = 4,
    @frequency_interval = 1,
    @frequency_relative_interval = 1,
    @frequency_recurrence_factor = 0,
    @frequency_subday = 4,
    @frequency_subday_interval = 5,
    @active_start_date = 0,
    @active_end_date = 99991231,
    @active_start_time_of_day = 0,
    @active_end_time_of_day = 235959
```

These two stored procedures create the shell of the publication but don't add any articles to it. In order to add an article, you need to run the `sp_addarticle` stored procedure. The following will create an article out of the Customers table with no partitioning or filters:

```
sp_addarticle @publication = 'SnapCustomers',
    @article = 'Customers',
    @source_table = 'Customers',
    @destination_table = 'Customers',
    @type = 'logbased',
    @creation_script = null,
    @description = null,
    @pre_creation_cmd = 'drop',
    @schema_option = 0x0000000000000031,
    @vertical_partition = 'false',
    @ins_cmd = null,
    @del_cmd = null,
    @upd_cmd = null,
    @filter = null,
    @sync_object = null
```

If you want to create a merge publication, use the stored procedure `sp_addmergepublication` as follows:

```
sp_addmergepublication @publication = 'MergeCustomers',
    @description = 'Merge publication of Northwind Customers',
    @retention = 60,
    @sync_mode = 'native',
    @allow_push = 'true',
```

```
    @allow_pull = 'true',
    @allow_anonymous = 'false',
    @centralized_conflicts = 'true'
```

Once you add the merge publication shell, you then need to create a snapshot and articles, as we did in the previous example.

To create a transactional publication, execute the sp_addpublication stored procedure with repl_freq set to continuous:

```
sp_addpublication @publication = 'TransNorthwindCustomers',
    @restricted = 'false',
    @sync_method = 'native',
    @repl_freq = 'continuous',
    @description = 'Transactional publication of Customers',
    @status = 'active',
    @allow_push = 'true',
    @allow_pull = 'false'
```

Then execute sp_addpublication_snapshot to create the Snapshot Agent and then add the articles you want to publish.

Subscribing to Publications

Subscribing to a publication means a subscription server agrees to receive a replica of the publication or articles from the publication server. There are two types of subscriptions:

- Push subscriptions, which are performed from the publication server where replicas are pushed out to subscription servers
- Pull subscriptions, where the subscription server pulls a replica from the publication server. There are several kinds of pull subscriptions, such as anonymous subscriptions and Internet-enabled subscriptions. These are created at the subscriber but must be enabled at the publisher.

The type of subscription you choose is determined by whether you are administering the publication server or the subscription server. If you are administering the subscription server, you won't be able to create a pull subscription unless they have been allowed at the publication server.

When you set up your subscription options, an initial automatic synchronization creates an identical copy of the publication database in the subscriber database. After that, you can schedule additional synchronizations.

Linking a Server

In order to push a subscription to a subscriber, you first have to configure that subscriber as a linked server. Expand the Security pane until you see the Linked Servers icon, right-click it, and select New Linked Server from the menu. The linked server does not have to be a SQL Server—you can choose from the drop-down list of provider names, as shown in Figure 14.17. We'll create a link to an unsecured Access database. The Access database is not secured, so we don't need to worry about security settings.

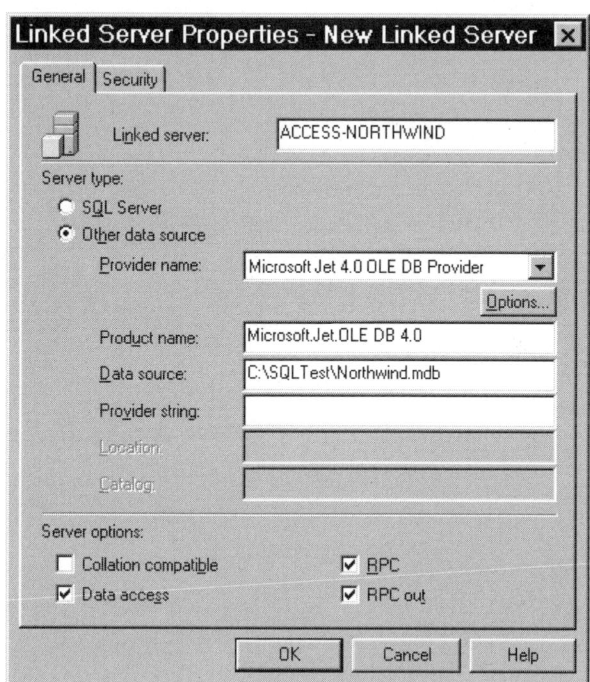

FIGURE 14.17: Setting up a new linked server

Configuring the Subscriber

Once you've set up your new linked server, choose Tools ➢ Replication ➢ Configure Publishing, Subscribers, and Distribution from the menu and click the Subscribers tab. Click the New Subscriber button and select OLE DB Data

Source. This will bring up the Enable Non-SQL Server Subscriber dialog box, as shown in Figure 14.18. This step is required to enable the linked server for replication. The database is not secured, so the default login is Admin (with no password).

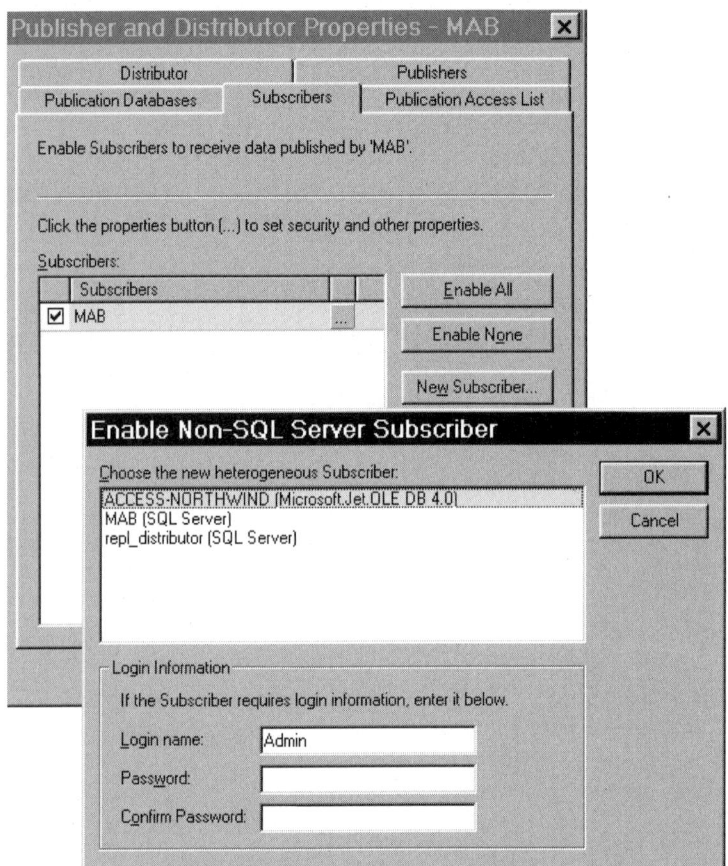

FIGURE 14.18: Enabling the linked server as a subscriber

Once you've configured a server, you can then push the subscription to a subscriber. When changes to the data are made at the publisher, a Distribution Agent will attempt to connect to the subscriber to propagate the changes. If the subscriber is not available, the agent will retry 10 times before posting an error to the Replication Monitor. If you have scheduled the Distribution Agent, it will retry again on the next round. Changes to the data will be persisted in the distribution database until either they have been propagated to all subscribers or the retention period has been exceeded (the default is 60 days).

Adding a Pull Subscription

A pull subscription is created from the subscriber, not the publisher, by pulling in a replica of a publication from the publisher. Only other SQL Server subscribers can pull subscriptions using the Enterprise Manager. The Distribution Agent and the Merge Agent run at the subscriber, not the publisher, which can result in a reduction in the amount of processing overhead at the distributor. The subscriber decides which publications are received and configures all the scheduling.

Before you pull a subscription, you need to first create a destination database at the subscriber. Then right-click the database and select Tools ➢ Replication ➢ Pull Subscription on *ServerName*. Click Pull New Subscription to bring up the Pull Subscription Wizard. The Pull Subscription Wizard will then present you with a list of servers and publications, as shown in Figure 14.19.

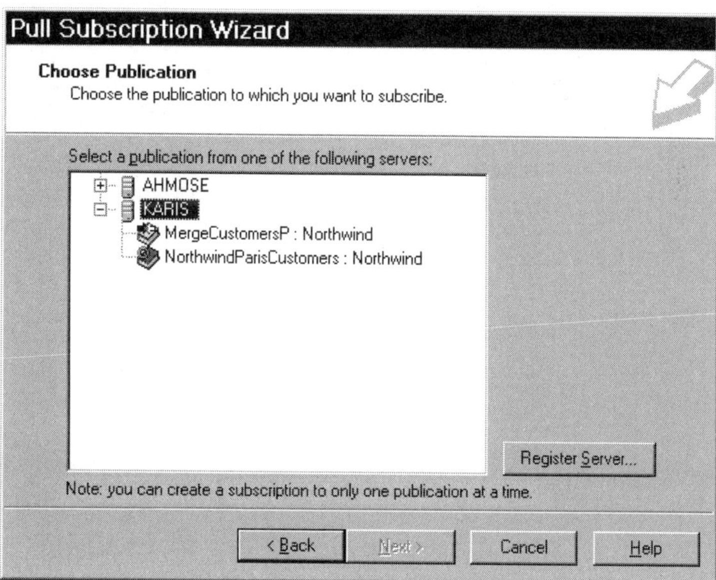

FIGURE 14.19: The Pull Subscription Wizard

Select the server and then select the database in which you want the subscription to appear. Specify the Synchronization Agent Login and then the database in which the subscription will be created. You can elect to create a new database, as shown in Figure 14.20.

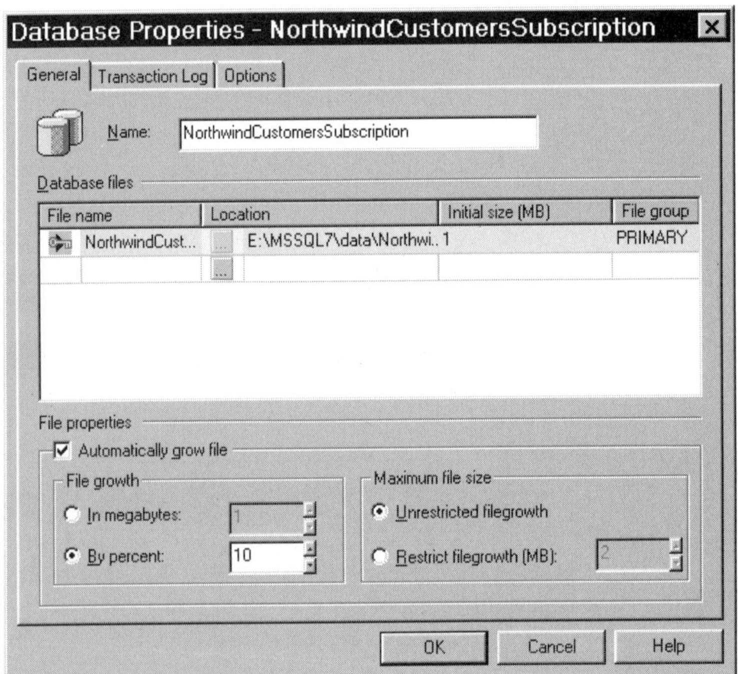

FIGURE 14.20: Creating a new database for the subscription

You can then start the subscription immediately or when scheduled. You can change the schedule by clicking the Change button on the Set Distribution Agent Schedule dialog box, as shown in Figure 14.21.

You will then be asked whether the subscription should be anonymous or not. For this example we can choose No, since we already have a linked server set up. You will then see the Start Required Services Status dialog box, which indicates that the Agent is running. On the last wizard dialog box is the summary screen. When you click the Finish button, the pull subscription is created, along with the database specified to contain it.

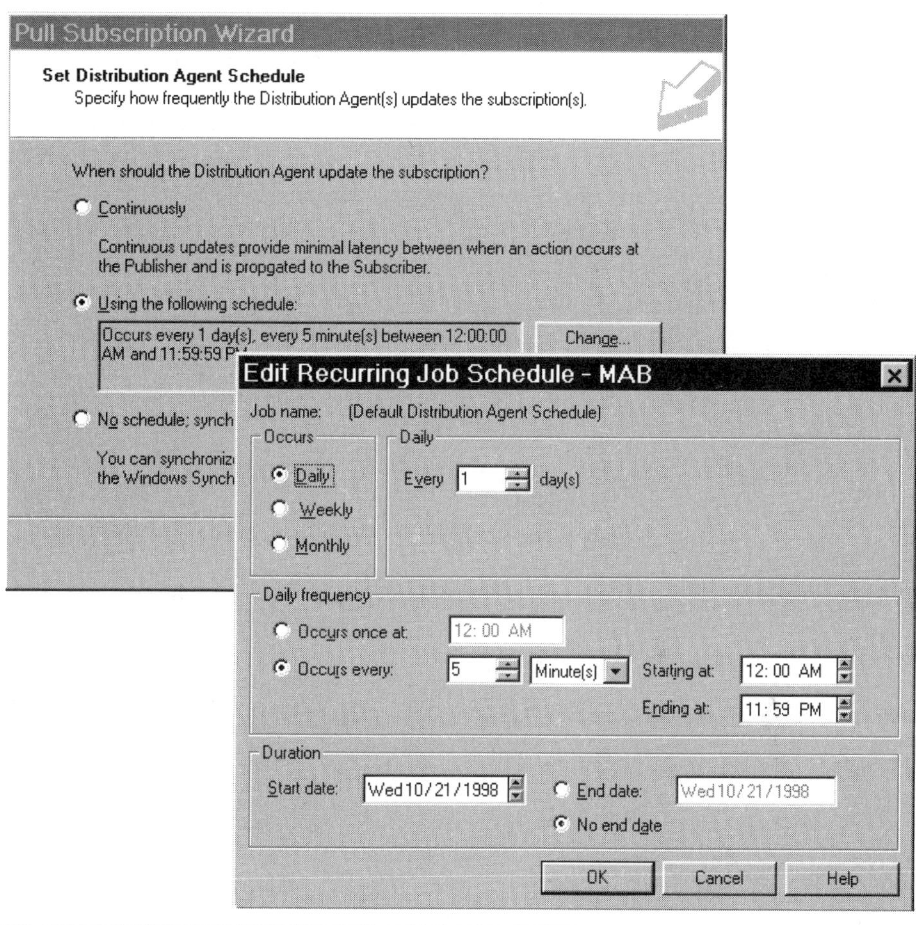

FIGURE 14.21: Setting the Distribution Agent Schedule

Adding an Anonymous Subscription

In a normal subscription, information about each subscriber is stored at the publisher. With an anonymous subscription, detailed information is not stored at the publisher. Anonymous subscriptions allow you to have a large number of subscribers without the overhead of maintaining the extra information, and such subscriptions are also necessary if you want to allow Internet subscribers.

Anonymous subscriptions are always initiated by the subscriber, which is responsible for synchronization chores. However, the publisher needs to be enabled for anonymous subscriptions and the server can't be previously registered as a subscriber at the publisher. To create an anonymous subscription, follow the steps to create a pull subscription as described earlier in this skill. After specifying the articles to publish, click the Let Subscribers Pull Subscriptions checkbox and then click the checkbox labeled Yes, Allow Anonymous Subscriptions to this Publication. The Pull Subscription Wizard will create an anonymous subscription automatically if the subscriber is not already registered at the server.

Modifying Pull and Anonymous Subscriptions

You can modify pull and anonymous subscription properties from the subscribing server by selecting Tools ➢ Replication ➢ Pull Subscription To, from the menu. Then select the subscription from the database folder and click the Properties button. Click the Distribution Agent Properties button. This brings up the dialog box shown in Figure 14.22, which shows the General tab. You can then change the schedule by selecting the Schedule tab, set notifications on the Notifications tab, and manage the steps (such as running the various agents) by selecting the Steps tab.

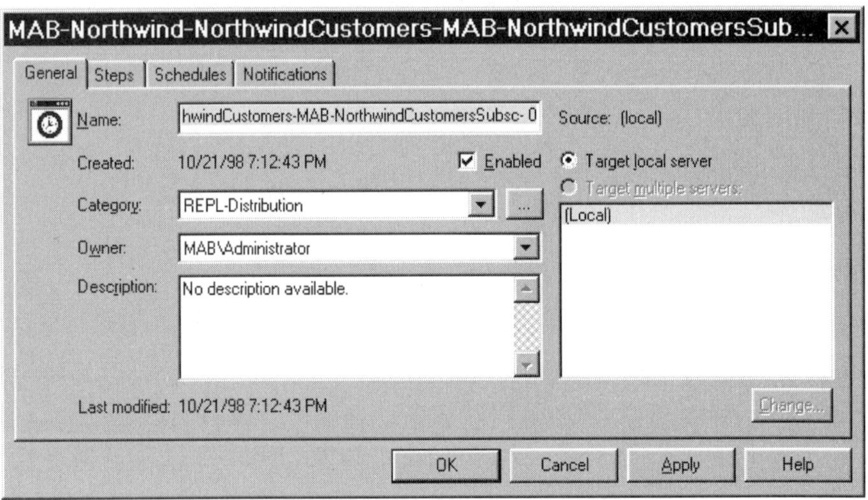

FIGURE 14.22: Modifying subscription properties

Deleting Pull and Anonymous Subscriptions

If you want to delete a pull or anonymous subscription, you must do so from the subscriber. After you have deleted the subscription, you need to drop the database manually in a separate step. Select Tools ➢ Replication ➢ Pull Subscription and expand the database containing the subscription you want to delete. Click the publication and the subscription and then click Delete Subscription.

You can delete a snapshot pull or anonymous subscription using Transact-SQL by executing the `sp_dropsubscription` stored procedure to delete the subscription and then the `sp_dropsubscriber` to remove the subscriber's registration entry, as shown here:

```
sp_dropsubscription @publication = 'NorthwindParisCustomers',
    @article = 'all',
    @subscriber = 'AHMOSE',
    @destination_db = 'Northwind'
sp_dropsubscriber @subscriber = 'AHMOSE'
```

If you want to disable publications that allow anonymous snapshot subscriptions, execute the `sp_droparticle` stored procedure for each article in the publication, `sp_droppublication` to delete the publication, and `sp_replicationdboption` to disable replication of the current database.

Managing Replication Security

Replication security has improved dramatically from earlier versions of SQL Server, with much easier-to-use built-in features, such as required roles for replication actions, restricted logins to a publication, password protection for the distributor, and security for immediate updating subscribers. You no longer need to know NT security, to know in advance the server names of approved subscribers, or even to configure replication at the subscribers. We won't discuss security in detail. For a complete discussion of SQL Server Security, see Skill 16, *Managing SQL Server Security*.

There are several built-in roles for administering security. Table 14.1 lists the roles and the replication tasks associated with those roles.

TABLE 14.1: Replication Security Roles

Role	Replication Action
sysadmin	Configure distribution, enable databases for replication, configure publishing, create publications, create push subscriptions, monitor replication, update default or custom publication access list, drop subscriptions
db_owner	Create publications, create push subscriptions, update custom publication access list, drop subscriptions, Log Reader Agent logging into publisher, Log Agents logging into subscriber

In addition to the specified roles, logins in a publication's access list can create pull subscriptions, log in to the publisher, or log in to the distributor publication.

Publication access lists allow you to specify NT groups or standard logins that can subscribe to a specific publication. The publication access list is created automatically when you configure a server for publishing and distribution. The default logins in the publication access list are distributor_admin, sysadmin, and db_owner, as shown in Figure 14.15.

You can modify this list from the dialog box shown or by using either of the two system stored procedures `sp_grant_publication_access` and `sp_revoke_publication_access`.

```
sp_grantpublication @publication = 'pubs',
    @login = 'public'

sp_revoke_publication_access @publication = 'publication',
    @login = 'login'
```

If you want to further restrict a publication, you can create your own publication access list to control just that one publication. If a Replication Agent's login does not exist in either the default or a custom publication access list, it won't be able to get in. If you have configured the publisher and distributor on separate servers, logins must exist on both the publisher and distributor publication access list.

You can also restrict access to a distributor by applying a password to the login distributor_admin. Use either the Enterprise Manager or the `sp_changedistributor_password` system stored procedure to do this—manually changing the password can cause publications using a local distributor to fail. You can change the password in the Enterprise Manager by selecting Tools ➢ Replication ➢ Configure Publishing, Subscribers, and Distribution and clicking the Distributor tab. Fill in the password, enter the confirmation string at the bottom of the dialog box, and click the Apply button, as shown in Figure 14.23.

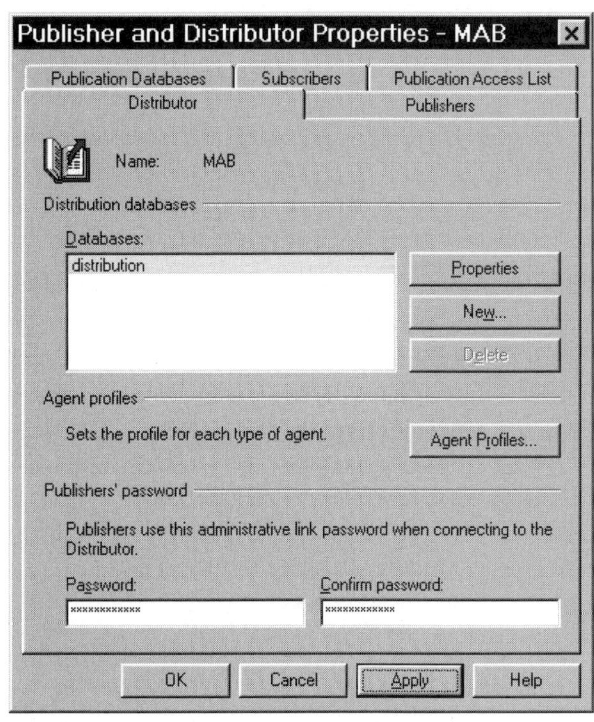

FIGURE 14.23: Set a distributor password

Monitoring Replication

The Replication Monitor lets you view the status of Replication Agents and helps troubleshoot problems with a distribution server. The Replication Monitor is activated when you configure a server as a distributor and will allow you to set up and monitor replication alerts, monitor Replication Agents, and view that distributor's list of publishers, publications, and subscriptions. There are also command-prompt utilities available for monitoring replication.

You can also use the Microsoft Windows NT Event Viewer to view SQL Server messages.

The Replication Monitor

The Replication Monitor is only activated when your server is enabled as a distributor. You can use the Replication Monitor to do the following:

- View lists of publishers, publications, and subscribers.
- View scheduled Replication Agents and monitor their status and history.
- Configure and monitor replication alerts. You can define tasks or send e-mail to respond to specific alerts.

If you are monitoring publishers and subscribers, you can use the Replication Monitor to display a list of all the publishers that use the server as a distributor. You can also display lists of publications for individual publishers. If you select a single publication, you can monitor registered subscriptions and the various agents involved (the agents will vary depending on the type of publication).

To monitor a publisher, expand the Replication Monitor and the Publishers folder. Click a publication. A list of objects will appear in the right-hand Results pane. You can double-click any object to get more details, as shown in Figure 14.24, which shows the Snapshot Agent history for the NorthwindCustomers publication.

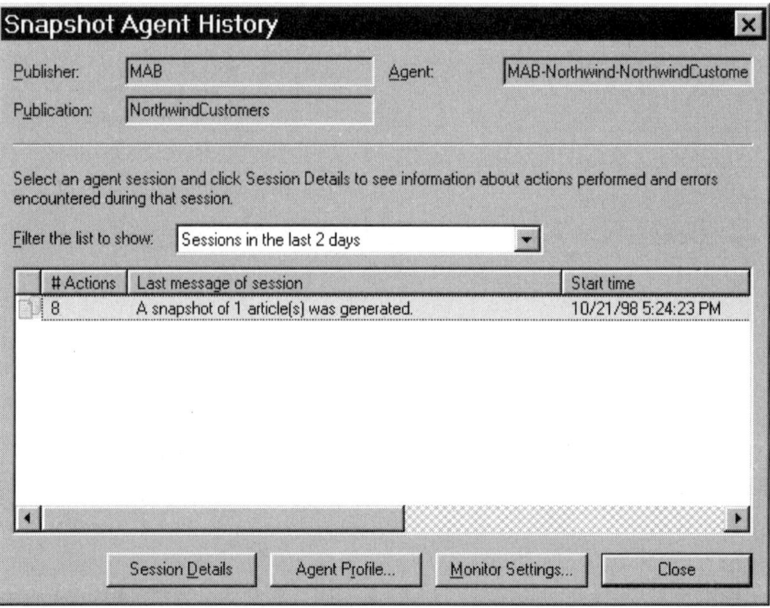

FIGURE 14.24: Snapshot Agent history

The Agents

The Replication Monitor allows you to graphically administer agent activity. You can view a list of all the Snapshot, Log Reader, and Distribution Agents supported by a distributor and monitor details about the current activity and the task history of each agent. When you expand the node for a particular agent, all agents of that type are displayed and you can then drill down to more detailed activity of a specific agent. Replication in SQL Server is handled by the following agents:

- Snapshot Agent
- Log Reader Agent
- Distribution Agent
- Merge Agent

The *Snapshot Agent* performs the initial snapshot of data upon the initial synchronization. If you are using snapshot replication, then the Snapshot Agent also moves replication data from the publisher to the distributor. You can use the Replication Monitor to display a detailed list of all the Snapshot Agents on the server by drilling down to it using the Enterprise Manager.

The Snapshot Agent can also run as a command-prompt utility whose executable file can be found in the `\Mssql7\Binn` directory. The syntax is:

```
snapshot [-?]
-Publisher publisher
-PublisherDB publisher_database
-Publication publication_name
[-BcpBatchSize bcp_batch_size]
[-Continuous]
[-DefinitionFile def_path_and_file_name]
[-Distributor distributor]
[-DistributorLogin distributor_login]
[-DistributorPassword distributor_password]
[-DistributorSecurityMode [0|1]]
[-LoginTimeOut [login_time_out_seconds]]
[-MaxBcpThreads]
[-Output [output_path_and_file_name]]
[-OutputVerboseLevel [0|1|2]]
[-PublisherLogin publisher_login]
[-PublisherPassword publisher_password]
[-PublisherSecurityMode [0|1]]
[-QueryTimeOut [query_time_out_seconds]]
[-ReplicationType [1|2]]
```

The *Log Reader Agent* is responsible for moving replicated transactions or data from the publisher to the distributor. You can use the Enterprise Manager or the command-prompt utility (also found in the `\Mssql7\Binn` directory). The syntax is:

```
logread [-?]
-Publisher publisher
-PublisherDB publisher_database
[-AsynchLogging]
[-Buffers number_of_buffers]
[-Continuous]
[-DefinitionFile def_path_and_file_name]
[-Distributor distributor]
[-DistributorLogin distributor_login]
[-DistributorPassword distributor_password]
[-DistributorSecurityMode [0|1]]
[-HistoryVerboseLevel [0|1|2]]
[-LoginTimeOut [login_time_out_seconds]]
[-MessageInterval message_interval]
[-Output [output_path_and_file_name]]
[-OutputVerboseLevel [0|1|2]]
[-PacketSize packet_size]
[-PollingInterval polling_interval]
[-PublisherSecurityMode [0|1]]
[-PublisherLogin publisher_login]
[-PublisherPassword publisher_password]
[-QueryTimeOut [query_time_out_seconds]]
[-ReadBatchSize number_of_transactions]
[-ReadBatchThreshold read_batch_threshold]
```

The *Distribution Agent* moves replicated transactions or data from the distribution database to the subscription database for both transactional and snapshot replication. You can use the Replication Monitor to display a list of all the Distribution Agents on the server in the Result pane. The Distribution Agent command-prompt utility will configure and begin a replication Distribution Agent. The syntax is:

```
distrib [-?]
-Publisher publisher
-PublisherDB publisher_database
-Subscriber subscriber
[-BcpBatchSize bcp_batch_size]
[-Buffers number_of_buffers]
[-CommitBatchSize commit_batch_size]
[-CommitBatchThreshold commit_batch_threshold]
[-Continuous]
[-DefinitionFile def_path_and_file_name]
[-Distributor distributor]
[-DistributorAddress distributor_address]
```

```
[-DistributorLogin distributor_login]
[-DistributorNetwork distributor_network]
[-DistributorPassword distributor_password]
[-DistributorSecurityMode [0|1]]
[-ErrorFile error_path_and_file_name]
[-FileTransferType [0|1]]
[-FtpAddress ftp_address]
[-FtpPassword ftp_password]
[-FtpPort ftp_port]
[-FtpUserName ftp_user_name]
[-LoginTimeOut [login_time_out_seconds]]
[-MaxDeliveredTransactions number_of_transactions]
[-MessageInterval message_interval]
[-NoTextInitOnSync]
[-Output [output_path_and_file_name]]
[-OutputVerboseLevel [0|1|2]]
[-PacketSize packet_size]
[-PollingInterval polling_interval]
[-Publication publication]
[-QueryTimeOut [query_time_out_seconds]]
[-QuotedIdentifier quoted_identifier]
[-SubscriberCatalog subscriber_catalog]
[-SubscriberDatabasePath subscriber_path]
[-SubscriberDataSource subscriber_data_source]
[-SubscriberDB subscriber_database]
[-SubscriberLocation subscriber_location]
[-SubscriberLogin subscriber_login]
[-SubscriberPassword subscriber_password]
[-SubscriberProviderName subscriber_provider_name]
[-SubscriberProviderString subscriber_provider_string]
[-SubscriberSecurityMode [0|1]]
[-SubscriberType [0|1|2]]
[-SubscriptionTableName subscription_table]
[-SubscriptionType [0|1|2]]
[-TransactionsPerHistory [0|1|...10000]]
```

The *Merge Agent* reconciles differences when changes are made in multiple replicas when posting them back to the publisher. You can select a distribution server and use the Replication Monitor to display a list of all the Merge Agents installed on the server. The Merge Agent command-prompt utility will configure and begin a replication Merge Agent, which applies initial snapshots and merges data changes.

```
replmerg [-?]
-Publisher publisher
-Publication publication
-Subscriber subscriber
```

```
-SubscriberDB subscriber_database
[-Continuous]
[-DefinitionFile def_path_and_file_name]
[-Distributor distributor]
[-DistributorAddress distributor_address]
[-DistributorLogin distributor_login]
[-DistributorNetwork distributor_network]
[-DistributorPassword distributor_password]
[-DistributorSecurityMode [0|1]]
[-ExchangeType [1|2|3]]
[-FastRowCount [0|1]]
[-FileTransferType [0|1]]
[-FtpAddress ftp_address]
[-FtpPassword ftp_password]
[-FtpPort ftp_port]
[-FtpUserName ftp_user_name]
[-HistoryVerboseLevel [0|1|2]]
[-LoginTimeOut [login_time_out_seconds]]
[-OutputVerboseLevel [0|1|2]]
[-PublisherAddress publisher_address]
[-PublisherDB publisher_database]
[-PublisherLogin subscriber_login]
[-PublisherNetwork publisher_network]
[-PublisherPassword publisher_password]
[-PublisherSecurityMode [0|1]]
[-QueryTimeOut [query_time_out_seconds]]
[-SubscriptionType [0|1|2]]
[-SubscriberLogin subscriber_login]
[-SubscriberPassword subscriber_password
[-SubscriberSecurityMode [0|1]]
[-Validate [0|1|2]]
```

You can change the monitoring properties of these agents by right-clicking the Replication Monitor. You can then choose the Refresh Rate and Settings option or the Select Columns option.

The executables for the agents are:

- Log Reader Agent: `logread.exe`
- Snapshot Agent: `snapshot.exe`
- Distribution Agent: `distrib.exe`
- Merge Agent: `replmerg.exe`

You can invoke the Distribution Agent through the ActiveX interface `sqldistx.dll` and the Merge Agent through `sqlmergx.dll`.

Monitoring Alerts

SQL Server Agent works hand-in-hand with the Windows NT Application Event Log, watching for an event that matches a defined alert. Once an alert is detected, SQL Server Agent will respond by executing a task that you have previously defined for that alert. SQL Server provides predefined alerts, which correspond to common error conditions, when a server is configured as a distributor. Table 14.2 lists the errors and alerts, most of which enter additional information in the sysreplicationalerts system table.

TABLE 14.2: Alerts

Message ID	Predefined alert	Causes alert to fire:
14150	Replication: Agent success	An agent shuts down successfully.
14151	Replication: Agent failure	An agent shuts down with an error.
14152	Replication: Agent retry	An agent shuts down after unsuccessfully retrying an operation: agent encounters an error such as server not available, deadlock, connection failure, or time-out failure.
20574	Replication: Subscriber has failed data validation	A Distribution or Merge Agent fails data validation.
20575	Replication: Subscriber has passed data validation	A Distribution or Merge Agent passes data validation.
20572	Replication: Subscription reinitialized after validation failure	The response job 'Reinitialize subscriptions on data validation failure' successfully reinitializes a subscription.
14157	Replication: Subscription cleaned up.	An inactive subscription was deleted.

You can use these alerts to do more than just put up a message box; you can create jobs to respond to the alert. Additional information about the alert is stored in sysreplicationalerts, so it's easy to use. There are also predefined jobs for common alerts; you just need to configure the alert to use the job.

To view existing alerts, expand the Replication Monitor and click Replication Alerts. You will see a list of alerts in the right-hand pane. Double-click the Replication: Agent Failure alert. This will bring up the dialog box shown in Figure 14.25. You can either fill in the options to enable the alert, create a custom message, or click the Response tab to generate a response, as shown in Figure 14.26. The response can include notifying an operator by e-mail, pager, or NET SEND.

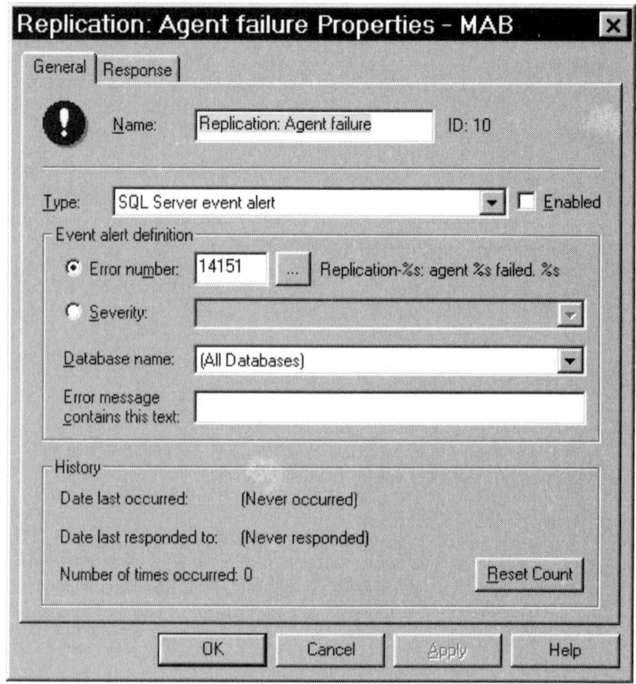

FIGURE 14.25: The Replication: Agent Failure alert

To define a new alert, expand the Replication Monitor and right-click Replication Alerts. Select New Alert and fill in the options.

If you need to view the Windows NT Application Event Log to see the alerts posted, choose Programs ➢ Administrative Tools (Common) ➢ Event Viewer from the Start menu on your computer. From the Event Viewer menu, choose Log ➢ Application. You will then see a list of events, as shown in Figure 14.27. If there is an error (indicated by the red stop icon), you can double-click the error to see more details, as shown in Figure 14.28.

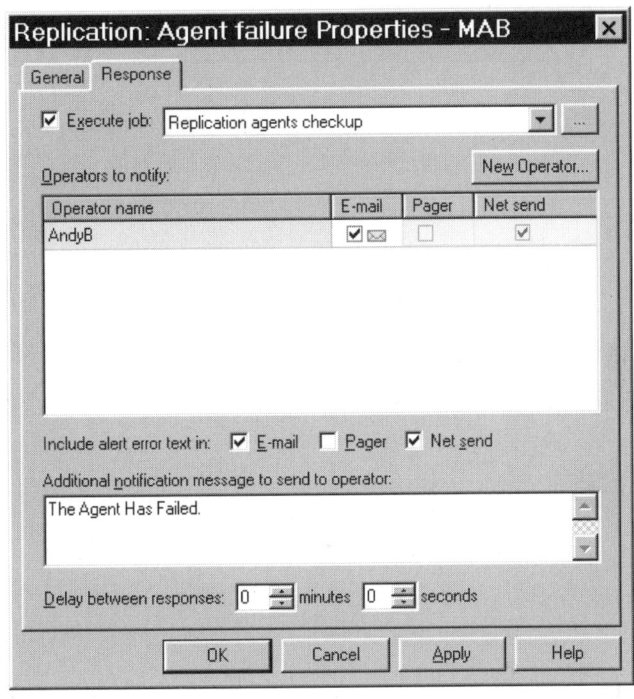

FIGURE 14.26: Generating a response to an alert

Event Viewer - Application Log on \\KARIS

Log View Options Help

Date	Time	Source	Category	Event	User	Computer
9/7/98	1:12:51 PM	MSSQLServer	Server	17055	Administrator	KARIS
9/7/98	1:09:58 PM	Perflib	None	1000	N/A	KARIS
9/7/98	1:06:32 PM	SQLServerAgent	Service Control	101	N/A	KARIS
9/7/98	1:05:57 PM	MSSQLServer	Server	17055	N/A	KARIS
9/7/98	1:05:51 PM	MSSQLServer	NETLIB	19020	N/A	KARIS
9/7/98	1:05:51 PM	MSSQLServer	NETLIB	19020	N/A	KARIS
9/7/98	1:05:51 PM	MSSQLServer	NETLIB	19020	N/A	KARIS
9/7/98	1:05:51 PM	MSSQLServer	NETLIB	19020	N/A	KARIS

FIGURE 14.27: The Windows NT Application Event Log

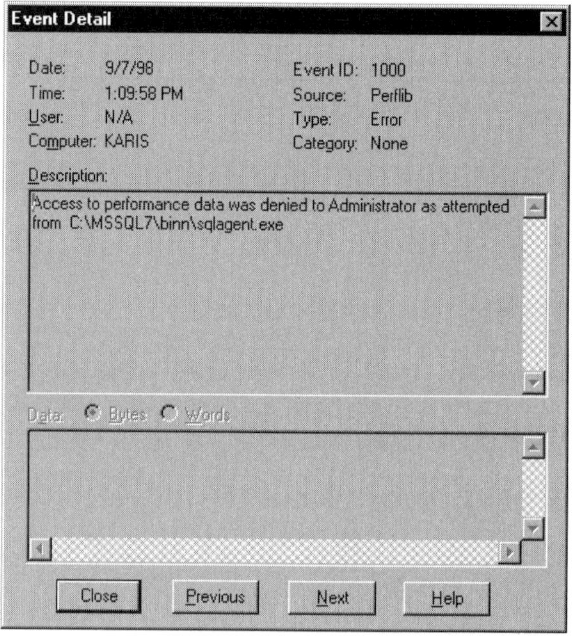

FIGURE 14.28: Event Detail from the Windows NT application event log

Performance Tips

There are many things you can do to increase replication performance. The following are some tips:

- Publish only the amount of data required. Publishing more data than is required consumes additional resources within the distribution databases and lowers the throughput for the required data.
- Configure the distributor on a dedicated machine. This reduces processing overhead on the publication server, resulting in performance gains for both the publisher and the distributor.
- Increase memory on the distribution server: 64MB or more can greatly improve performance.

- If you have numerous subscribers, reduce their distribution frequency. Stagger the initial times of Distribution Agents so that they don't all attempt to start at once. If the distributor has multiple processor capability, run a separate Distribution Agent for every publication/subscription pair.
- Minimize the log history and retention period. This reduces overhead on the distribution server.
- Enable pull subscriptions when practical. This increases distributor performance by moving distribution processing to subscription servers.
- Enable anonymous subscriptions when practical. Anonymous subscriptions (a variety of pull subscriptions) are run at the subscription server, freeing up resources on the distribution server. This also reduces overhead on the publishing server, which does not have to maintain information about anonymous subscribers.
- Use multiprocessor computers to take advantage of the multithreaded architecture of SQL Server Replication Agents.
- Optimize your database design to include replication considerations. Reduce filter rows when defining articles and minimize the use of horizontal partitions, which can be a minor detriment to performance.

Heterogeneous Replication

Heterogeneous replication is the ability to replicate between different databases. This capability is new with SQL Server 7. This topic merits a book by itself, so in this part of the skill we're going to focus mainly on replication between Microsoft Access databases and SQL Server.

Replication with Microsoft Access

You can now replicate directly to Microsoft Access 2000 (Jet 4) subscribers from SQL Server. Jet supports merge replication, which means you can update data from Access or from SQL Server and merge the changes. There are several steps you need to take, which are summarized as follows:

1. Create a linked server to point to the path and filename of an Access database by right-clicking the Linked Servers icon in the Enterprise Manager and selecting New Linked Server, as shown earlier in this skill. Select

Microsoft Jet 4 OLE DB Provider in the drop-down list box for Provider Name. This and the data source are the only required arguments. The data source can be either a normal Access database (one that is not enabled for replication by Jet) or one that is not created yet—you just supply a path and filename. SQL Server will create the `.mdb` for you when it initializes the subscription.

NOTE You can't use a previously existing Jet replica for a SQL Server subscription because SQL Server needs to install its own reconciler, which is different from the one Jet uses.

2. Next click the Security tab. If your Access environment is unsecured, map the remote user ID to Admin, with no password. If it is secured, type in the user ID and password of a user who has permission to administer the database. When you're through, click OK and the linked server will be created.

TIP If you are working with a secured Access database, you need to configure the Registry to use the correct workgroup information file (or system database) for the Access application. The full pathname for the Registry entry is: `HKEY_LOCAL_MACHINE\SOFTWARE\Microsoft\Jet\4.0\Engines\SystemDB`

3. Next you need to enable the new linked server for replication. Choose Tools ➢ Replication ➢ Configure Publishing, Subscribers, and Distribution from the main console menu. Click the Subscribers tab and the New Subscriber button. This will bring up the Enable New Subscriber dialog box. Select OLE DB Data Source and click OK. This will then bring up the Enable Non-SQL Subscriber dialog box, as shown earlier in this skill. Select your new linked server and click OK twice.
4. You are now ready to push the subscription to Access. Choose Tools ➢ Replication ➢ Push Subscription To Others, from the main console. Expand the Database folder that holds the publication and select it from the available list. Click the Push New Subscription button, which will load the Push Subscription Wizard.
5. Click Push New Subscription. After the first introductory screen, select your linked server from the list of available servers, as shown in Figure 14.29, and click the Next button.

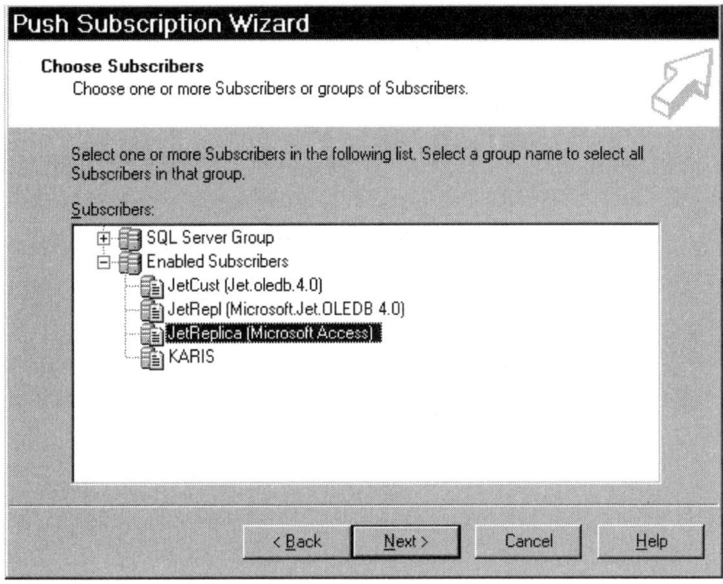

FIGURE 14.29: Choosing the subscriber

6. The next dialog box asks you to schedule the updates between the two replicas. It defaults to updating every hour, which you can change if you want. You can then initialize the subscription immediately or start it as scheduled. A third option lets you skip the initial snapshot if the Access `.mdb` already has the schema and data. You then need to set the priority of the two replicas, as shown in Figure 14.30. The default is to have the SQL Server database retain the highest priority.

The next dialog box allows you to start the SQL Server Agent if it is not already running. The final screen summarizes the options you have set. Click Finish to create the subscription.

NOTE

There are bound to be some incompatibilities between SQL Server and Jet, although both the Jet development team and the SQL Server team have tried hard to minimize the conflicts. Certain constraints and referential integrity rules won't be applied, such as cascading updates and deletes. Access 2000 was still in beta while this book was being written, so as of this writing the complete list has not been finalized.

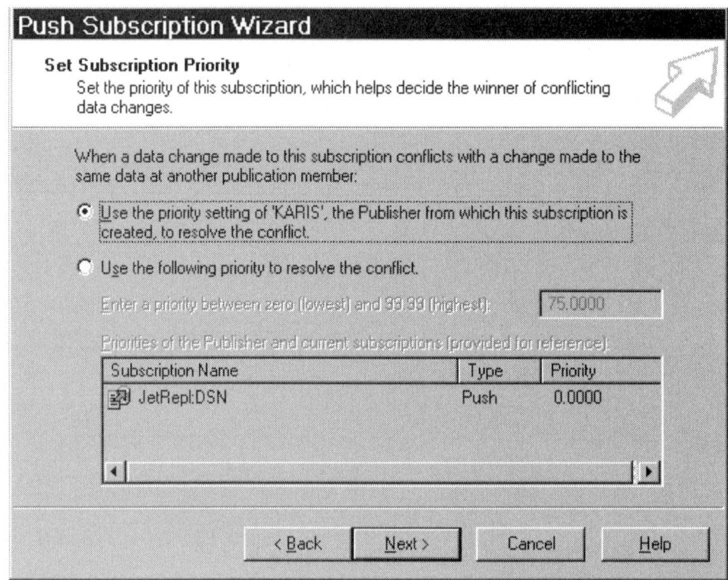

FIGURE 14.30: Setting the conflict resolution priority

Replicating between Different Versions of SQL Server

You can replicate with SQL Server 6.*x* servers with the following limitations:

- A SQL Server 6.5 publisher can use a Sphinx distributor. When upgrading from SQL Server 6.5 to Sphinx, you must upgrade the distribution server before you upgrade the publishing server.
- Sphinx replication supports only push subscriptions to SQL Server 6.*x* servers, not pull subscriptions.

ANSI to OEM Replication

You can replicate between two SQL Servers with different code pages unless you are using SQL Server 6, in which replication can only occur between servers that have the same code page.

All data that is sent to ODBC subscribers from SQL Server is in the ANSI code page (ISO 8859-1). An ODBC subscriber must translate the data to its native code page. Follow these steps to define an ANSI-to-OEM translation:

1. In Control Panel, click the 32-bit ODBC icon.
2. Select the data source.
3. Click Configure.
4. Click the Translation tab and then clear the Configure Translations To Connection checkbox.
5. Click Convert ANSI to OEM Characters and click OK.

Replicating Data to the Internet

Once you've configured SQL Server for Internet replication, you can publish articles according to the type of subscription you have chosen (push, pull, or anonymous). If your network has a firewall, both the publisher and distributor need to be on the same side of the firewall. You also need to enable the TCP/IP protocol on each server where the Distribution and Merge Agents execute. The Distribution and Merge Agents execute at the distributor for push subscriptions and at the subscriber for anonymous and pull subscriptions.

Setting Up Pull and Anonymous Subscriptions

Make sure that the distributor and the Internet Information Server (IIS) are installed on the same server and that the FTP home directory on IIS is the working folder. Configure the Distribution and Merge Agents at the subscriber with the correct file transfer information. The FTP addressing includes the FileTransferType, FtpAddress, FtpPassword, FtpPort, and FtpUserName. Set the address using the Distribution Agent utility from the command prompt at the distributor.

Once you've set up and configured your server, you can publish on the Internet using the Enterprise Manager. Create a publication in the normal way. Make sure to select Yes on the Allow Anonymous Subscribers dialog box and the Anonymous Subscribers Can Create Subscriptions dialog box. Select the Allow Snapshots To Be Downloaded Using FTP option.

To set further subscription options, choose Tools ➢ Replication ➢ Create and Manage Publications. Expand the folders until the subscription you have just created is showing. From the Create and Manage Publications main dialog box, click the Properties and Subscriptions button. Select the Subscription Options tab and fill in the options as shown in Figure 14.31.

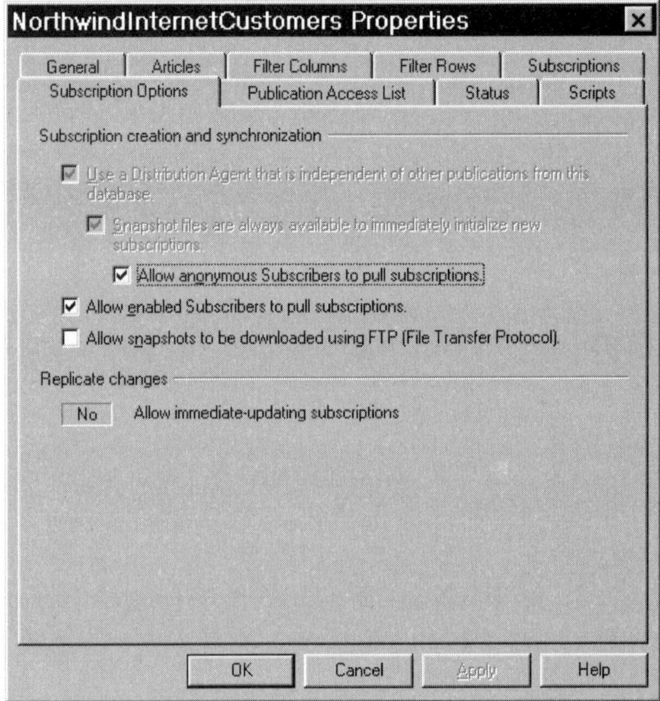

FIGURE 14.31: Setting subscription options for Internet subscribers

You can also use stored procedures to publish on the Internet. To publish a snapshot, execute the `sp_addpublication` stored procedure with the `enabled_for_internet` option set to True to enable Internet subscriptions. The following will add a publication called SnapCustomers and enable it for Internet publishing.

```
sp_addpublication @publication = 'SnapCustomers',
    @restricted = 'false',
    @sync_method = 'native',
    @repl_freq = 'snapshot',
    @description = 'Snapshot of Customers.',
```

```
        @status = 'active',
        @allow_push = 'true',
        @allow_pull = 'true',
        @allow_anonymous = 'true',
        @enabled_for_internet = 'true',
        @independent_agent = 'false',
        @immediate_sync = 'true',
        @allow_sync_tran = 'false',
        @autogen_sync_procs = 'false'
```

If you wanted to publish to the Internet using transactional replication, change the repl_freq argument to @repl_freq = 'continuous'.

The following would create a merge publication:

```
sp_addmergepublication @publication = 'MergeCustomers',
    @description = 'Merge publication of Customers',
    @retention = 60,
    @sync_mode = 'native',
    @allow_push = 'true',
    @allow_pull = 'false',
    @allow_anonymous = 'false',
    @enabled_for_internet = 'true',
    @centralized_conflicts = 'true'
```

Are You up to Speed?

Now you can...

- ☑ **plan replication strategy**
- ☑ **configure a server for replication**
- ☑ **publish data**
- ☑ **subscribe to data**
- ☑ **monitor performance**
- ☑ **implement heterogeneous replication**
- ☑ **replicate over the Internet**

SKILL 15

Administering a Server

- Operators and alerts
- SQL Mail
- Jobs
- Using the logs
- DBCC

It would be nice if you could just set up a database server and forget about it. Unfortunately, although SQL Server 7 requires less administration than any previous version, it still requires some. In this skill we'll look at the various tasks a SQL Server administrator should be expected to perform: setting alerts to watch for problems on the server, configuring the integration of SQL Server with electronic mail, and managing SQL Server jobs. We'll also see how to extract useful information from the logs that SQL Server maintains and investigate the proper usage of the DBCC utility that's designed to help you recover from server and database problems.

Automating Administration

Let's face it, the easiest way to keep a complex product such as SQL Server running is to have it run itself. With SQL Server 7, Microsoft has gone to great lengths to automate administration. For example, SQL Server 7 will request more memory from the operating system when it's needed and give it back to the operating system when it's not. It will also make extra locks available to databases on a similar dynamic basis. Previous versions of SQL Server required the server administrator to manually adjust these and many other parameters to keep the server running smoothly.

However, there are some things that the server administrator still has to do on their own. For example, there's no way SQL Server can know what you consider an adequate amount of free space on your server. This number depends on many factors, including how many users you have on the server, what other software it's running, and how large the hard drives on the server are.

Given that it's not feasible to automate server administration 100 percent, the next best thing is to automate as much of the administration as possible. SQL Server includes several features that are designed to allow you to automate server administration:

- Alerts can be sent to designated operators depending on server performance.
- SQL Server can interface directly to your electronic mail system.
- Jobs can be used to schedule the performance of repetitive sequences of commands.

We'll look at each of these features in the following sections.

Alerts

SQL Server alerts provide a means for the server to notify administrators when some particular situation occurs. Alerts are handled by the SQL Server Agent, an independent Windows NT service (the SQLServerAgent service) whose job it is to monitor the Windows NT application log (of course, on Windows 95, SQL Server Agent runs as a program rather than a service). The agent constantly scans the log for events posted by SQL Server, comparing them with a list of criteria that you program by defining alerts. When the agent finds a matching event, it can:

- Send electronic mail to one or more operators.
- Send messages to one or more operators' pagers (the pagers must be set up with an electronic mail gateway).
- Use `NET SEND` to notify one or more operators directly over the network.
- Run a SQL Server job.

Since the agent uses the application log, rather than interfacing directly with SQL Server, it's not limited to responding to events raised by the SQL Server software itself. You can use the agent, for example, to respond to events from the Windows NT Performance Monitor.

Operators

Alerts are only sent to SQL Server operators. An operator is a particular user, designated by using the Operators node in SQL Enterprise Manager (this node is located under Management, SQL Server Agent). To create a new operator using SQL Enterprise Manager, right-click Operators and choose New Operator. Figure 15.1 shows the dialog box used to define a new operator.

The minimum you must do to define a new operator is to assign it a name. However, to have any notifications sent to this operator, you must tell SQL Server how to get messages to the operator:

- For e-mail notification, specify an electronic mail address that the SQL Mail account can reach.
- For pager notification, specify an electronic mail address that the SQL Mail account can reach.
- For direct Net popup notification via `NET SEND`, specify an account name on your network.

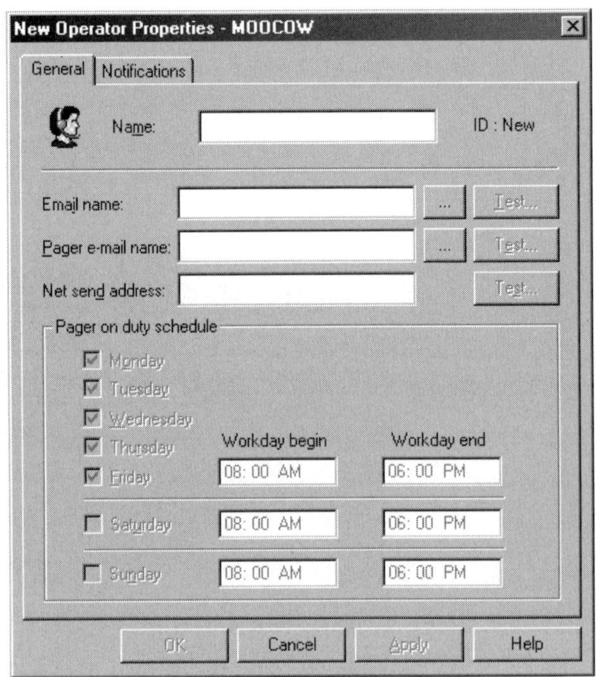

FIGURE 15.1: Defining a new operator

You can test each of these options by clicking the associated Test button. You don't have to save the operator before testing.

Despite what the user interface may lead you to believe, SQL Server has no direct knowledge of pagers built in. Pager notifications are sent just as any other electronic mail. It's up to you to install a gateway service on your mail server that can reach your paging company. All of the major paging vendors offer such gateways.

You can also use the New Operator dialog box to indicate which alerts should trigger notification to this operator and which methods of notification should be used for each alert. Figure 15.2 shows our new operator enabled to receive notifications of three alerts by electronic mail, two by pager, and one by a direct `NET SEND` command.

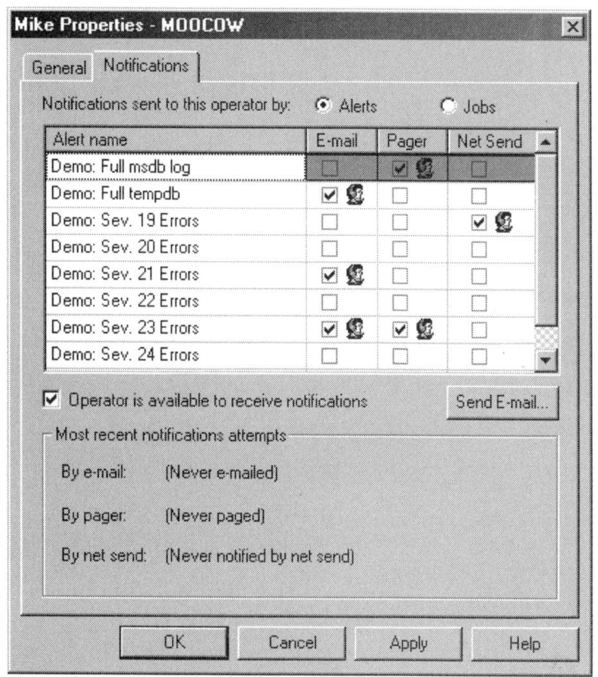

FIGURE 15.2: Choosing alerts for an operator

TIP Before you can use e-mail or pager notification, you must configure the account used by SQL Mail, which we'll discuss later in this skill.

To create an operator using Transact-SQL, you invoke the `sp_add_operator` stored procedure:

```
sp_add_operator 'name' [,enabled] [,'email_address'] [,'pager_address']
[,weekday_pager_start_time] [,weekday_pager_end_time]
[,saturday_pager_start_time] [,saturday_pager_end_time]
[,sunday_pager_start_time] [,sunday_pager_end_time] [,pager_days]
[,netsend_address] [,category]
```

For the most part, these options simply echo those shown on the dialog box in Figure 15.1. The `enabled` argument, like other SQL Server Boolean arguments, can take the value of 0 for False or 1 for True. The time arguments are defined using a

24-hour clock and the format *HHMMSS*. The `pager_days` argument is a bit flag defined by summing constants from this list:

- 1 Sunday
- 2 Monday
- 4 Tuesday
- 8 Wednesday
- 16 Thursday
- 32 Friday
- 64 Saturday

To create the same operator we created in the previous example, we could use this Transact-SQL statement:

```
sp_add_operator 'Mike Gunderloy2', @enabled=1, @email_address='MikeG1',
➥@pager_address='MikePage', @weekday_pager_start_time=060000,
➥@weekday_pager_end_time=150000, @sunday_pager_start_time=070000,
➥@sunday_pager_end_time=180000, @pager_days=43, @netsend_address='Mike'
```

NOTE The `sp_add_operator` stored procedure and the other stored procedures dealing with alerts and operators can only be run in the msdb database.

You can designate one operator as a Fail-Safe Operator. This is the operator who will be paged for any alert if no other operator can be paged, either because sending pages to those operators fails or because there is no operator designated to page at the particular time that the alert occurs. You can only designate a Fail-Safe Operator by using SQL Enterprise Manager. To do so, follow these steps:

1. Right-click SQL Server Agent and select Properties.
2. Select the Alert System tab.
3. Choose the operator who will be your Fail-Safe Operator from the combo box.
4. Choose the methods of notification to be used for fail-safe notifications.

Figure 15.3 shows this dialog box.

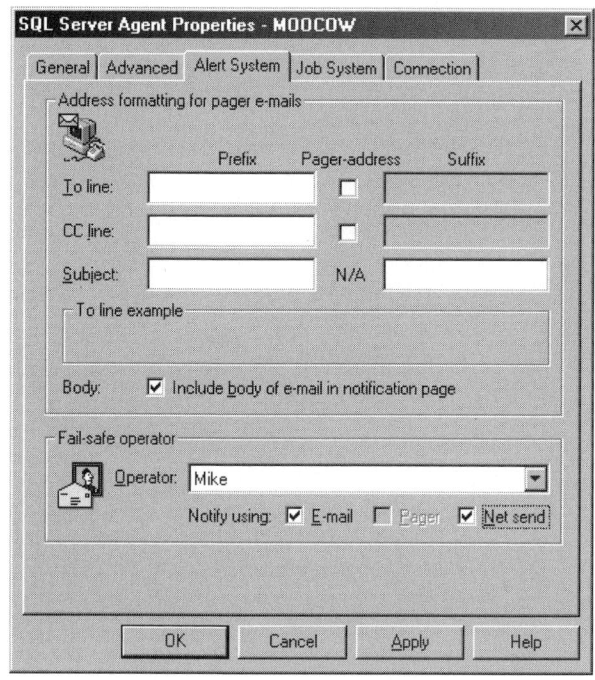

FIGURE 15.3: Selecting a Fail-Safe Operator

TIP If you need to change the properties of an operator after creating the operator, you can right-click the operator in SQL Enterprise Manager and choose Properties, or you can run the `sp_update_operator` stored procedure.

Setting Alerts

Operators would not do much good without alerts to trigger notifications. To create an alert with SQL Enterprise Manager, expand the SQL Server Agent node, right-click Alerts, and choose New Alert. This will open the dialog box shown in Figure 15.4.

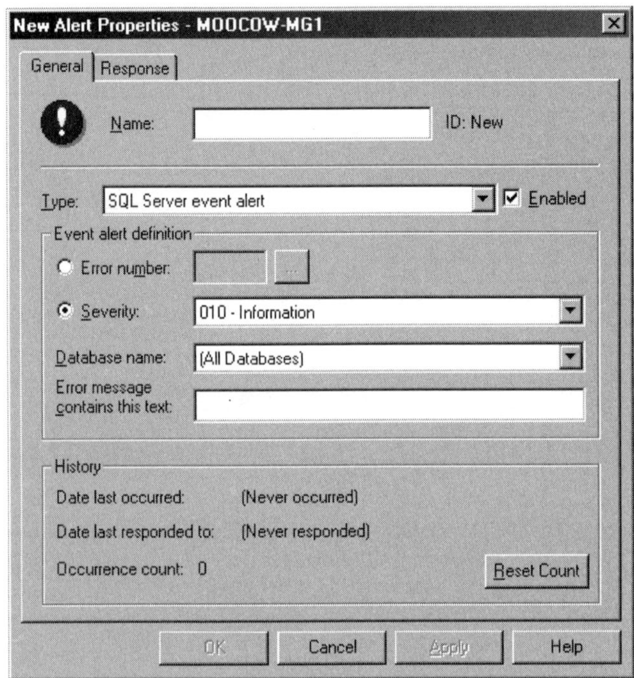

FIGURE 15.4: Defining an alert with SQL Enterprise Manager

You can define alerts based on either the particular error or an entire group of errors. To select a group of errors based on severity, choose the appropriate severity from the combo box. Table 15.1 shows the possible error severity values for SQL Server 7.

TABLE 15.1: Error Severity Classes

Severity	Explanation
1	Miscellaneous system information
7	Notification: Status information
8	Notification: User intervention required
9	User-defined errors
10	Information
11	Specified database object not found

TABLE 15.1 CONTINUED: Error Severity Classes

Severity	Explanation
13	User transaction syntax error
14	Insufficient permission
15	Syntax error in SQL statement
16	Miscellaneous user error
17	Insufficient resources
18	Non-fatal internal error
19	Fatal error in resource
20	Fatal error in current process
21	Fatal error in database processes
22	Fatal error: table integrity suspect
23	Fatal error: database integrity suspect
24	Fatal error: hardware error
25	Fatal error
110	Non-sysmessages server information
120	Non-sysmessages server warning
130	Non-sysmessages server error
140	Abnormal server termination

TIP SQL Server ships with alerts preconfigured on severities 19 through 25. To use these alerts, just assign them to operators.

If you choose to set an alert on a particular error, clicking the button next to the error number box opens another dialog box that lets you search for errors by number, name, or severity. You can fine-tune alerting by specifying an individual database to watch for the error or by specifying particular text that must appear in the body of the alert.

Once you've decided what to watch for in order to generate an alert, you can use the Response tab of the same dialog box, shown in Figure 15.5, to specify the actions that SQL Server Agent should take when the alert occurs.

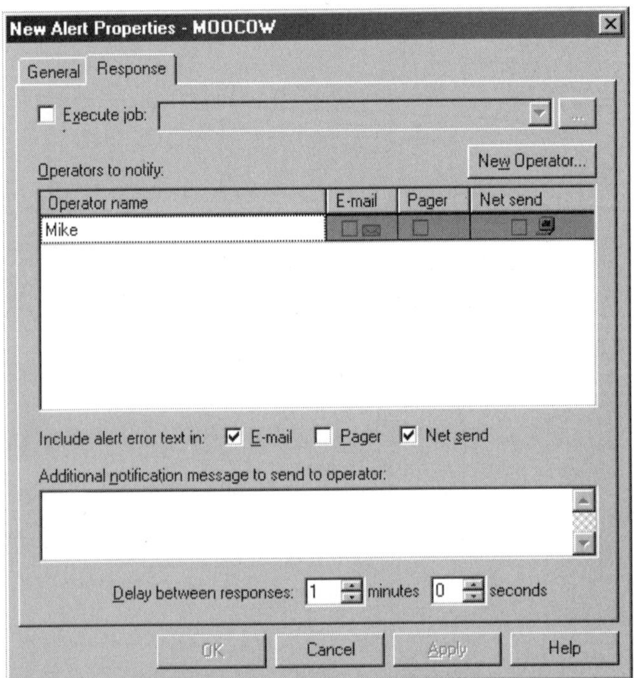

FIGURE 15.5: Selecting operators for an alert

Note that you can specify a minimum cycle time for the alert. This helps prevent users' electronic mailboxes from filling up if something happens that causes SQL Server to generate the same error over and over again in a loop. If you prefer, you can execute a job in response to an alert, instead of or in addition to notifying operators. We'll cover jobs later in this skill.

Of course, you can also create an alert using Transact-SQL. The general syntax for the `sp_add_alert` stored procedure is

```
sp_add_alert 'name', message_id, severity [, enabled]
➥[,delay_between_responses] [,'notification_message']
➥[,include_event_description_in] [,database] [,event_description_
➥keyword] [,job_id] [,'job_name'] [,raise_snmp_trap] [,performance_
➥condition] [,category]
```

These options exactly parallel those in the dialog box from SQL Enterprise Manager. The `include_event_description_in` argument specifies which types of notification will be sent with the full event description and must be set to `NONE`, `EMAIL`, `PAGER`, or `BOTH`.

SQL Server also includes a wizard for creating new alerts. Just like all the other wizards, you can run this wizard from the Tools ➢ Wizards ➢ Select Wizard dialog box. Choosing the Create Alert Wizard (under Management) walks you through a series of dialog boxes that prompt you for the same information as the New Alert dialog box or the `sp_add_alert` stored procedure. Figure 15.6 shows the closing screen for this wizard.

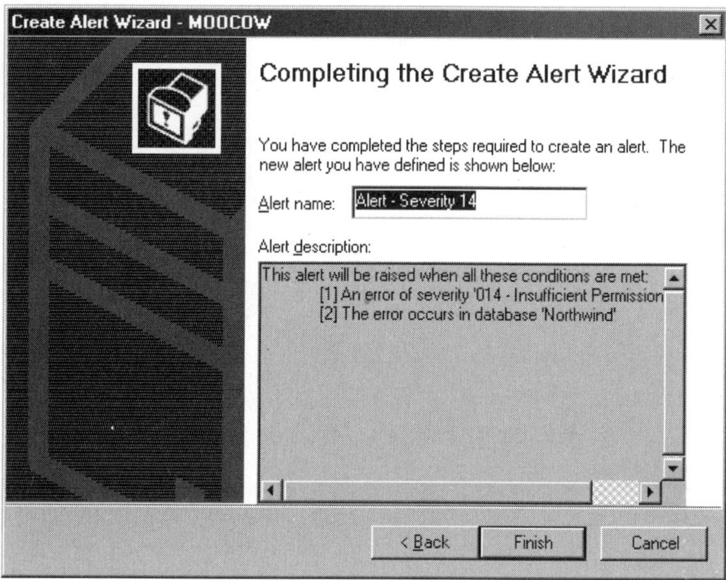

FIGURE 15.6: Creating a new alert with the wizard

Integrating Alerts with Windows NT

SQL Server includes a command-line utility, `sqlalrtr70.exe`, that can raise error conditions on the local SQL Server. You can use this utility in conjunction with alerts to create notifications for a wide variety of conditions from any program that can shell out to a command-line utility. For example, you might want to send an alert whenever the free space on your server's C: drive drops below 100MB.

To start the process, run the Windows NT Performance Monitor utility, and select View ➢ Alert to see the current list of Performance Monitor alerts. Select Edit ➢ Add to Alert. This will open the dialog box shown in Figure 15.7.

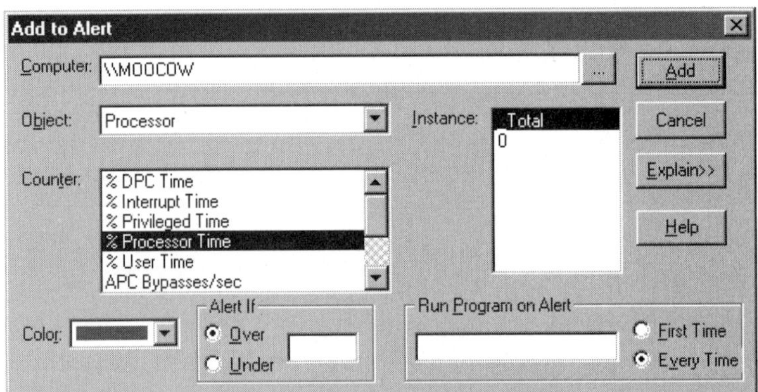

FIGURE 15.7: Adding a Performance Monitor alert

Once you've selected the appropriate Performance Monitor counter and threshold, you need to enter a command line to run the `sqlalrtr70` program. This command line takes the following form:

```
sqlalrtr70.exe /Eerror_number [/Sserver_name] [/Ppassword]
[/Ddatabase_name] [/Vseverity]
```

WARNING The arguments (`/E`, `/S`, `/P`, `/D`, and `/V`) are case-sensitive.

Once you've added the Performance Monitor alert, you should use SQL Enterprise Manager to add an alert on the error number that you specified in the command line for `sqlalrtr70.exe`. When the Performance Monitor alert is triggered, it will run `sqlalrtr70.exe`. This program will log on to your server and use the `RAISERROR WITH LOG` command to place an event message in the application log. In turn, SQL Server Agent will read this message, execute the alert, and send the appropriate notifications.

Event Forwarding

With all the processes involved in dealing with alerts, you might worry about the load on the server to handle this processing. Fortunately, SQL Server provides an easy way to remove this load from your main database server through *event forwarding*. With event forwarding, you specify an *alerts server* to handle alerts from other SQL Servers. All unhandled events are forwarded to this server for processing. This has several benefits. First, the processing load for events can be largely removed from the computers that are responsible for retrieving data. Second, in a large organization, you can use a single alerts server to centralize alerts handling from a wide variety of databases.

Forwarding alerts from your whole enterprise to a single server creates a potential single point of failure. You may want to investigate hardware or software redundancy options for this server.

To specify an alerts server, you can use the Advanced tab of the SQL Server Agent Properties dialog box in SQL Enterprise Manager. This dialog box, shown in Figure 15.8, lets you choose a server to handle events that are not handled locally. You can choose a server that you've already registered with SQL Enterprise Manager or choose New Forwarding Server from the combo box to register a forwarding server from here. You should also choose a minimum severity level for events to be forwarded. We suggest using a fairly high severity level here, to avoid generating excessive network and server traffic.

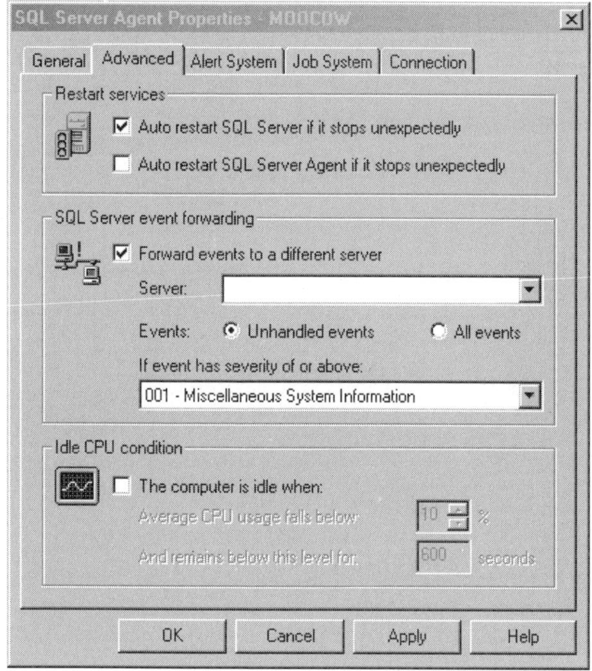

FIGURE 15.8: Designating an alerts server

SQL Mail

One of the most powerful administrative tools for SQL Server is the ability to integrate the server with your mail system. SQL Mail is a component of SQL Server that is designed to communicate with any MAPI-compliant mail server. This might include a workgroup post office created with Windows NT, a Netware mail server accessed via Windows NT Gateway Services for Netware (GSNW), or a Microsoft Exchange Server. Once you've set up SQL Mail, you can use it to handle alerts notifications, as discussed in the previous section of this skill. There are also several extended stored procedures that let you use SQL Mail directly from Transact-SQL scripts.

NOTE For our examples, we've used a Microsoft Exchange Server. For information on setting up SQL Mail with other servers, see the *Administering SQL Server* manual in your SQL Server documentation.

Setting Up SQL Mail

The key to setting up SQL Mail properly with Exchange is to make sure you have a valid Exchange mailbox for the SQL Server to use. This mailbox must be available to the default SQL Server account. To set up SQL Mail, follow these steps:

1. In SQL Enterprise Manager, right-click SQL Server Agent and choose Properties. On the General tab, you'll find the user account that the service uses to log on to Windows NT. In our example, this is the user called Administrator, as shown in Figure 15.9. If your SQL Server is set to use the system account, you may encounter problems with SQL Mail. In that case, we suggest that you specify a user account here.
2. Have your Microsoft Exchange administrator create a recipient for SQL Mail to use. On our test machine, this is the SQL Mail recipient, shown in Figure 15.10. Assign permissions for this recipient to the Windows NT account you determined in step 1.

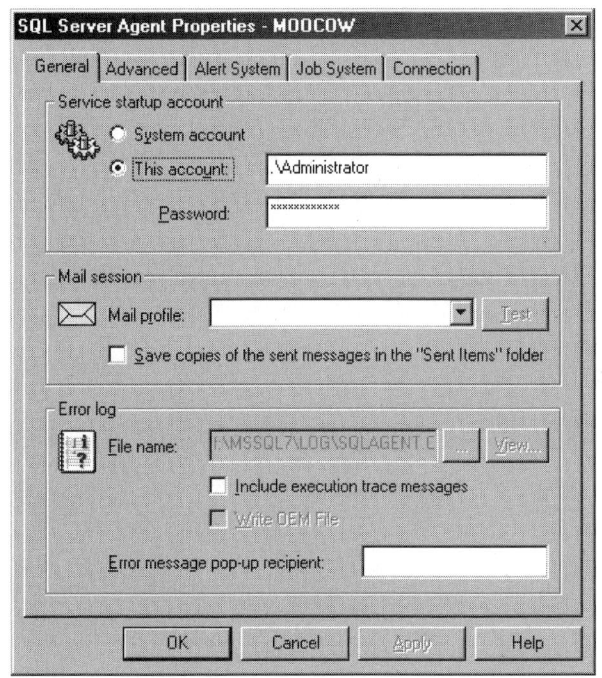

FIGURE 15.9: Determining the logon user

3. Log on to the SQL Server computer using the Windows NT account that SQL Server is configured to use. Create an Exchange profile to log on to the Exchange account created in step 2 (the steps for creating this profile will vary depending on which version of the Exchange client you're using, but you can always do this by right-clicking your Inbox). We named this profile SQLMail.

4. In SQL Enterprise Manager, right-click SQL Mail and choose Properties. This will display the dialog box shown in Figure 15.11. Specify the name of the profile you created in step 3.

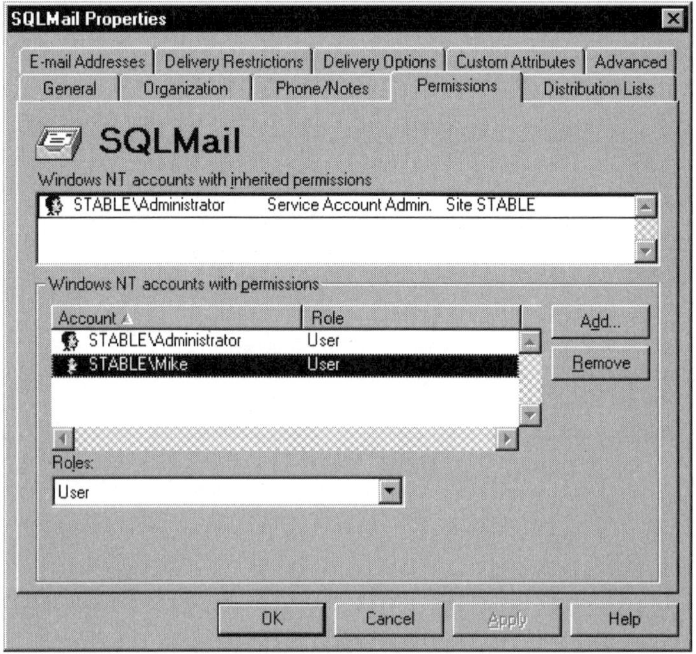

FIGURE 15.10: Configuring the Exchange account

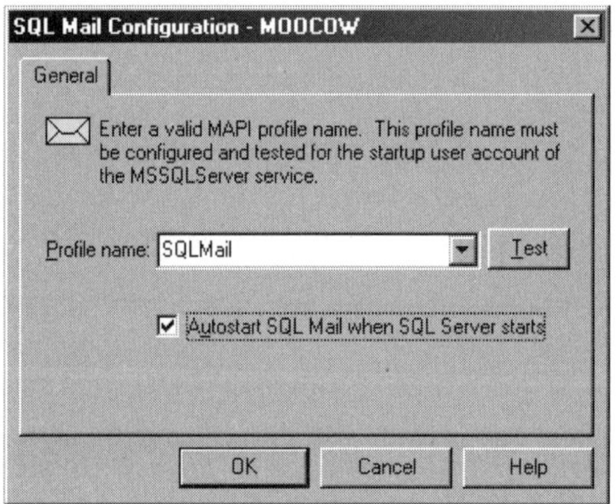

FIGURE 15.11: Selecting the Exchange profile to use

5. In SQL Enterprise Manager, right-click SQL Server Agent, choose the Advanced tab, and check the box for "Autostart SQL Mail when SQL Server starts."

At this point, the SQL Mail icon in SQL Enterprise Manager should be green, indicating that the mail service successfully started.

Sending Mail from SQL Server

SQL Server provides an extended stored procedure, `xp_sendmail`, which can be used to send nearly anything from SQL Server to a mail recipient. As shown here, `xp_sendmail` takes a lot of arguments:

```
xp_sendmail 'recipient' [;…n] [,'message'] [,'query'] [,attachments]
➥[,'copy_recipient' [;…n]] [,'blind_copy_recipient' [;…n]] [,'subject']
➥[,type] [,<attach_results>::= {'TRUE' | 'FALSE'}] [,<no_output>::=
➥{'TRUE' | 'FALSE'}] [,<no_header>::= {'TRUE' | 'FALSE'}] [,width]
➥[,separator] [,<echo_error>::= {'TRUE' | 'FALSE'}] [,set_user]
➥[,dbuse]
```

You probably recognize most of these arguments as being the standard mail message properties you'd set when sending a message from a mail client program. Table 15.2 lists these arguments and their use.

TABLE 15.2: Arguments to xp-sendmail

Argument	Explanation
`recipient`	Recipient of the mail. You may specify multiple recipients separated by semicolons.
`message`	Text of the message to send.
`query`	A SQL Server query used to generate a result set to be sent as an attachment to the mail.
`attachments`	Filename of a file to be attached to the mail message.
`copy_recipient`	Recipient of a cc: copy of the mail. You may specify multiple copy recipients separated by semicolons.
`blind_copy_recipient`	Recipient of a bcc: copy of the mail. You may specify multiple blind copy recipients separated by semicolons.
`subject`	Subject of the mail message.
`type`	MAPI message type. If you're not using custom message types on your system, you should leave this set to the default of `NULL`.
`attach_results`	Set to True to return the results of a query as an attachment to the message. If you specify a list of attachment filenames, the first name on the list is used for the attachment. Otherwise, SQL Server will generate a name for the attachment.

TABLE 15.2 CONTINUED: Arguments to xp-sendmail

Argument	Explanation
no_output	Set to True to suppress a confirmation message to the session that called xp_sendmail.
no_header	Set to True to leave off the header row from any query results.
width	Line width to use for any query results. Defaults to 80 characters.
separator	Character to use between columns in the result set.
echo_error	Set to True to append any errors to the query instead of sending them to the server error log.
set_user	User whose security context should be used to run a query.
dbuse	Database to run the query in.

As an example, the following Transact-SQL statement could be used to send a simple message to a mail recipient:

```
xp_sendmail @recipients='MikeG1', @subject='SQL Server Warning',
➥@message='The server will shut down at midnight for maintenance'
```

The results of this statement are shown in Figure 15.12.

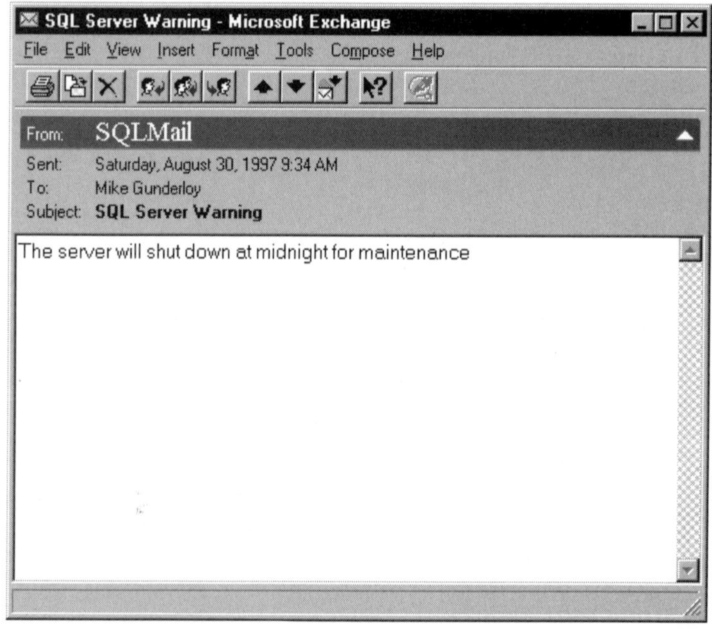

FIGURE 15.12: Simple message from SQL Server

To send the results of a query to a user, you'll need to specify the `@query` and `@dbuser` arguments. For example, you can send the contents of the authors table from the pubs database with a statement such as this:

```
xp_sendmail @recipients='MikeG1', @subject='Current authors',
➥@message='Here is the current author list', @query='SELECT * FROM
➥authors', @dbuse='pubs', @width=250
```

Figure 15.13 shows the results of executing this statement.

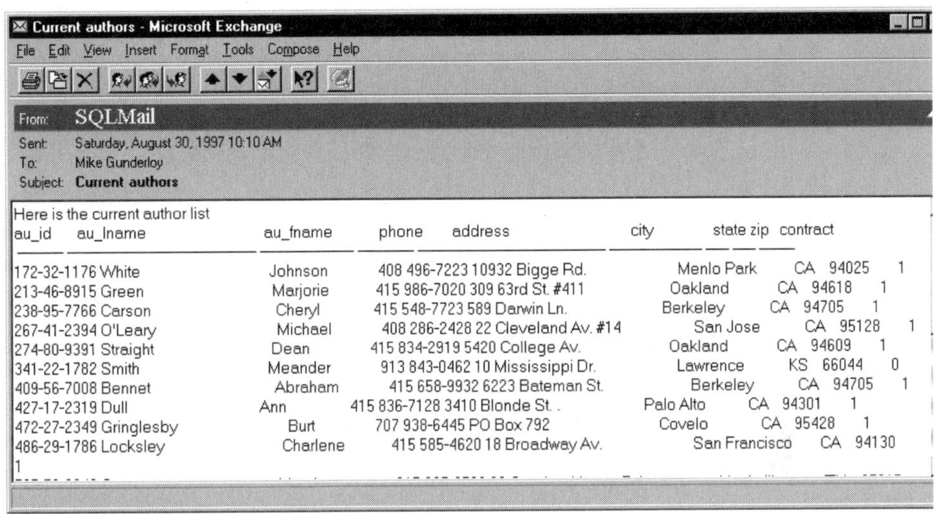

FIGURE 15.13: Simple result set from SQL Server

You can also send the results as an attached file, by specifying `@attach_results=TRUE`. Figure 15.14 shows the results of the previous statement after adding this argument.

Execute permission on `xp_sendmail` defaults to the sa user only. You should be extremely cautious about granting permission to any other user, since the `attachments` argument can be used to send any disk file from the server as an attached file. The potential security ramifications are quite severe. If you wish to allow non-sa users to use `xp_sendmail`, consider creating a stored procedure that calls `xp_sendmail` without exposing the `attachments` argument and grant permission on that stored procedure instead.

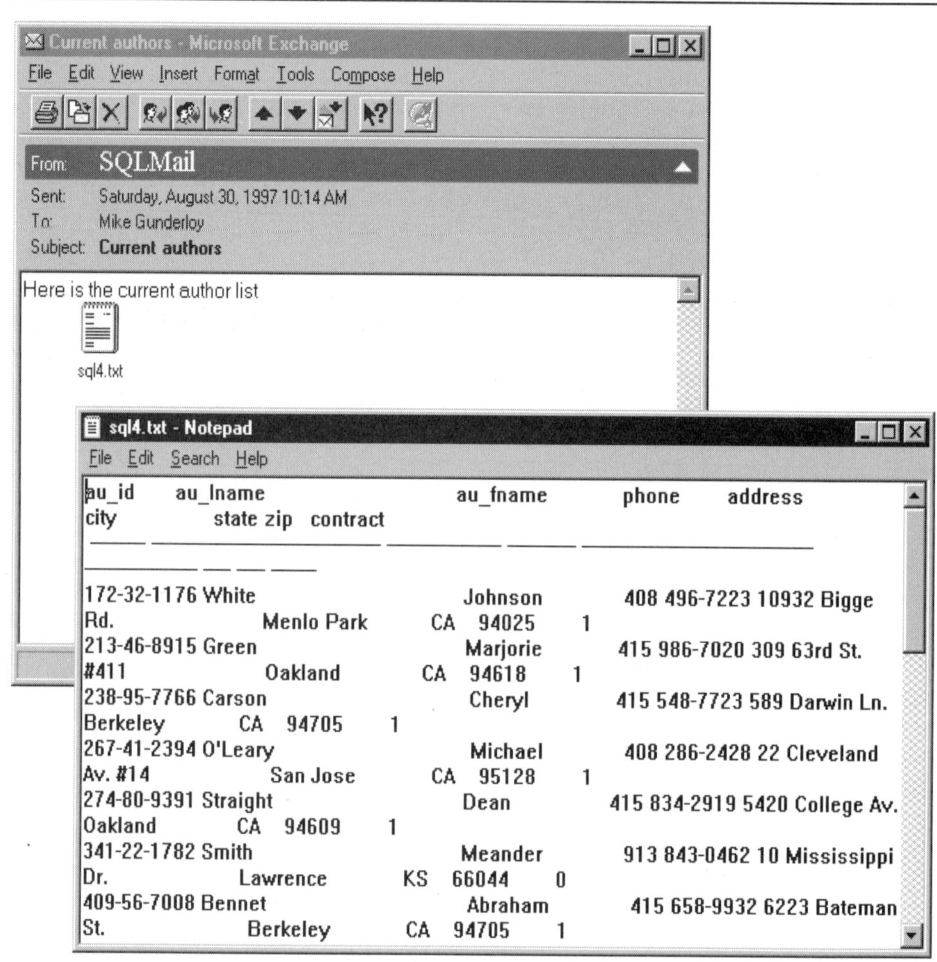

FIGURE 15.14: Attached result set from SQL Server

Processing Queries via SQL Mail

You can also set up SQL Server to automatically process queries that are sent to the server by electronic mail and to return the results by electronic mail. The stored procedure `sp_processmail` is used to read waiting messages and create their result sets (this stored procedure calls lower-level extended stored procedures to interface with the mail system). The sp_processmail stored procedure takes five arguments:

```
sp_processmail [subject] [,filetype] [,separator] [,set_user] [,dbuse]
```

The subject argument specifies the subject line that SQL Server should look for in incoming messages. The default is to process all messages. The filetype argument specifies an extension to be used when sending results back and separator specifies the separator to use between columns in the result. These default to .txt and the Tab character respectively. The set_user and dbuse arguments allow you to specify a user context and database to process the queries with. By combining the subject and dbuse arguments, you can direct different groups of user queries to different databases.

For example, you might set as a convention that all queries with the subject line of QueryPubs represent queries to be run against the pubs database. A user who knows the mail account that is assigned to your SQL Mail utility could then send a mail message to the server with that subject and the following text:

```
SELECT au_fname, au_lname FROM authors
```

On the server, you would then run this stored procedure:

```
sp_processmail @subject='QueryPubs', @dbuse='pubs'
```

The incoming message (and any others with the same subject line) would be executed against the pubs database. The result is that a mail message containing the results of the query will show up in the user's Inbox. To automate the process, you could create a job to run the stored procedure on a regular basis (see the next section in this skill). This can provide a powerful mechanism for ad hoc querying available to users connected via slow links or the Internet.

Jobs

Jobs are an enhanced version of tasks from previous versions of SQL Server. A job is a series of steps that will be carried out by the SQL Server Agent, either on demand from the SQL Enterprise Manager interface or at a scheduled time. There are five types of steps that you may use in a job:

- Transact-SQL steps
- CmdExec steps (shelled programs)
- VBScript steps

- JavaScript steps
- Replication steps (Distribution, Log Reader, Merge, and Snapshot)

TIP You can mix different types of steps in a single job.

In this section, you'll learn how to create jobs, to set their properties, and to use the various types of job steps.

Creating a Job

In most cases you'll want to use SQL Enterprise Manager to create jobs. There are stored procedures, `sp_add_job`, `sp_add_jobstep` and `sp_add_jobschedule`, that can create a job, but the visual programming interface in SQL Enterprise Manager is much easier to use. To create a job, expand the SQL Server Agent node, right-click Jobs, and select New Job. To define the job and its schedule, you'll need to fill in all four tabs.

The General tab, shown in Figure 15.15, defines the job itself. Here you can name the job, specify which servers it should run on, and provide a job description. Job categories are a concept for organizing groups of jobs to make it easier to find the one you want to work with at any given time. By default, only [Uncategorized (Local)] is available here. You can create your own job categories by right-clicking Jobs and selecting Job Categories when you're in SQL Enterprise Manager.

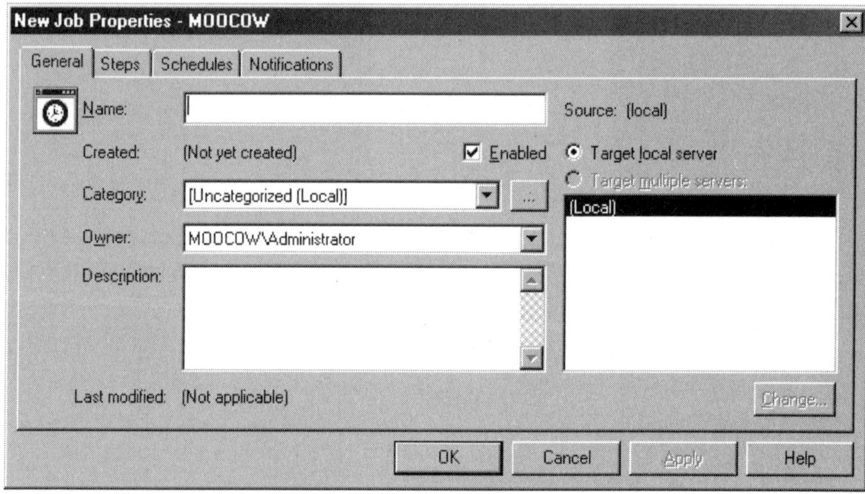

FIGURE 15.15: General options for a new job

The Schedules tab, shown in Figure 15.16, allows you to define when your job will be run.

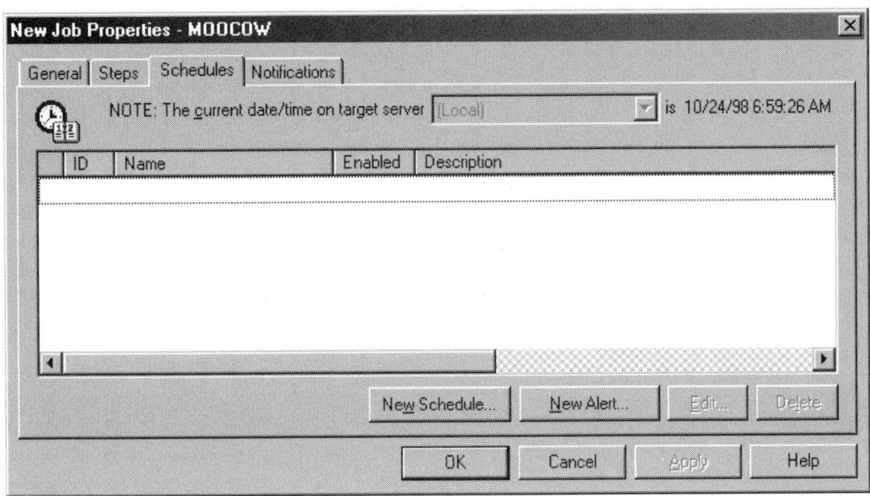

FIGURE 15.16: Scheduling options for a new job

Clicking the New button gives you a rich set of options for creating job schedules. You can run jobs with these scheduling options:

- Automatically, whenever SQL Server Agent is started (Autostart jobs)
- Once, at a particular time and date
- Daily, weekly, monthly, or even hourly
- Indefinitely or until a specified ending date

Although you can define multiple schedules for a job, be sure that they don't overlap. SQL Server Agent can only run one instance of a particular job at any given time. If you attempt to start a second instance while the first instance is still running, this attempt will fail.

The Notification tab controls what will happen after SQL Server Agent finishes running the job. This tab is shown in Figure 15.17. You can choose notification via electronic mail, pager, or direct `NET SEND`, as well as by recording information in the Windows NT application log. Each of these notifications can be sent if the job is successful, if it fails, or on completion of the job. You can also choose to automatically delete the job when it's completed.

Skill 15

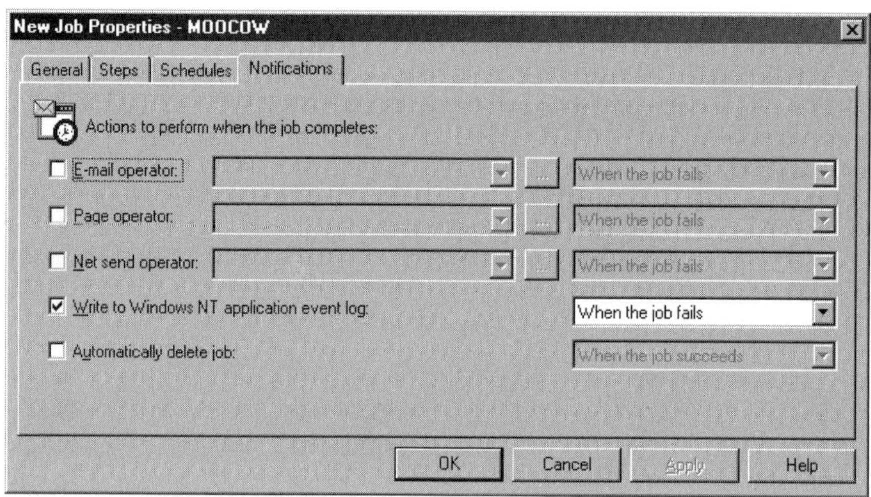

FIGURE 15.17: Notification options for a new job

You use the Steps tab, shown in Figure 15.18, to define the steps that will be processed as a part of this job. In our example, we've defined a job consisting of two steps. First, it runs a batch file on the server. Then, it sends a file by invoking the `xp_sendmail` extended stored procedure. Each type of step has its own editing dialog box, which we'll discuss in the following sections.

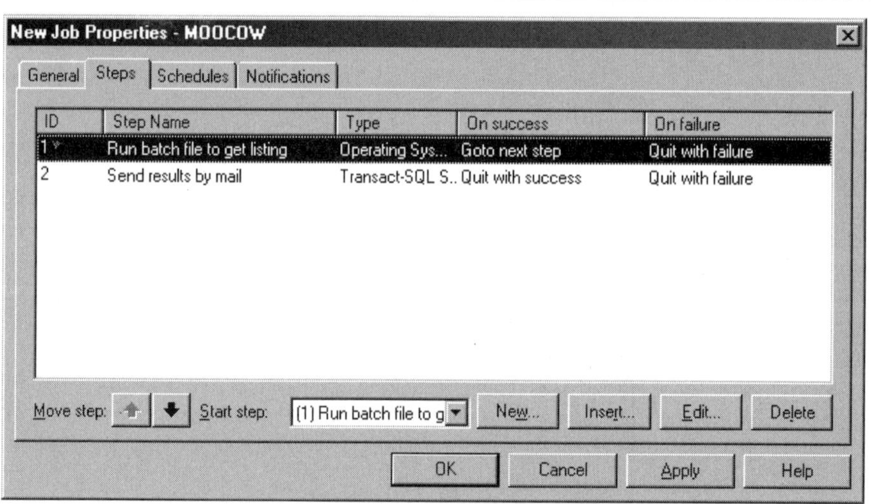

FIGURE 15.18: Defining steps for a new job

Transact-SQL Steps

A Transact-SQL step can execute any SQL statement against any database on the server. This makes the entire Transact-SQL language, including batches, stored procedures, and extended stored procedures, available for use in jobs. In our sample job, we use a Transact-SQL step to call the `xp_sendmail` extended stored procedure, as shown in Figure 15.19. When you're entering new text, the Parse button is available to check the syntax of your Transact-SQL statement.

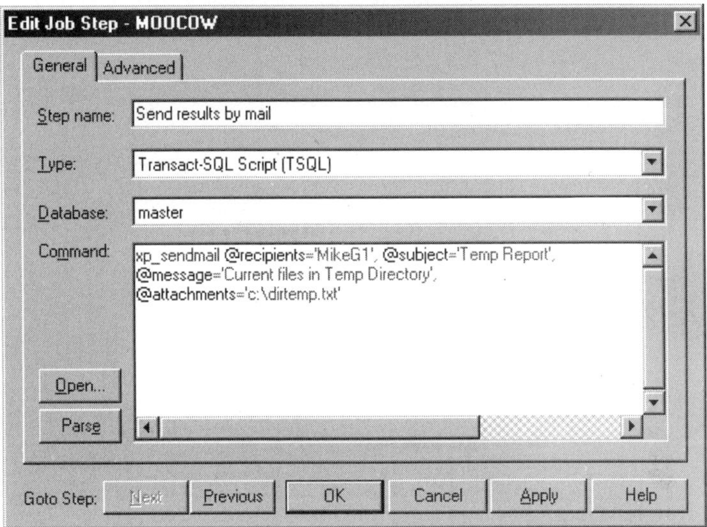

FIGURE 15.19: Defining a Transact-SQL step

You can use the Advanced tab of this dialog box to specify an output file for the results of the statement or to specify a user whose security context should be used when executing the statement. By default, Transact-SQL steps are executed by the sa user in the master database.

Whenever you define a step, you can also use the Advanced tab to define the branching possibilities for the step. Whether a step succeeds or fails, you can choose one of these actions:

- Go to the next step.
- Go to a particular step.
- Quit the job, reporting either success or failure.
- Retry the step.

CmdExec Steps

CmdExec steps represent operating system commands to be carried out in a Windows command window. These can be commands or the names of batch files—anything that would be valid if typed at the command line. Figure 15.20 shows a CmdExec step from our sample job, which runs a batch file and sends its output to a specified file.

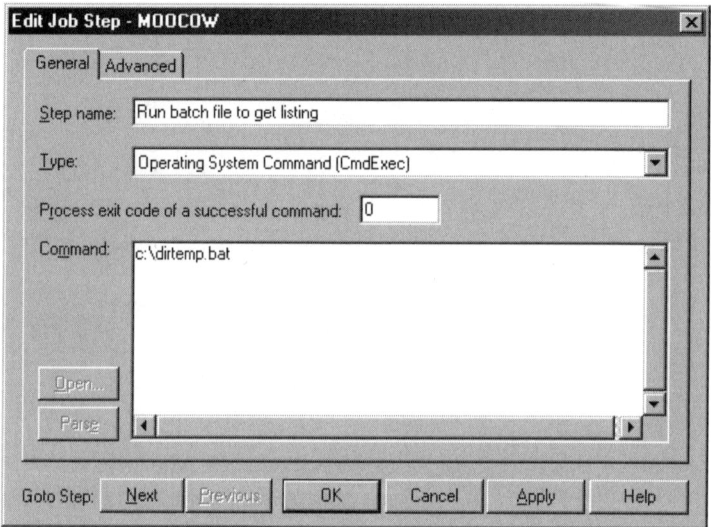

FIGURE 15.20: Defining a CmdExec step

CmdExec steps in jobs that are owned by users other than sa are run on Windows by the SQLServerAgentCmdExec account, which is created when you install SQL Server. By default this account is a member of the Users Local group. You can control the operating system access for jobs created by non-sa users by manipulating the security of this account.

CmdExec steps in jobs that are owned by sa are run on Windows with the same user account that SQL Server Agent itself uses. This account normally belongs to the System Administrators group on the server.

WARNING You should be extremely cautious about allowing non-sa users any access to jobs owned by sa, since they might edit the job and execute unintended commands as an administrator.

Script Steps

SQL Server can also run active scripting languages such as VBScript or JavaScript as part of a job. Since these languages are general purpose, this opens up many possibilities. For example, you can use SQL-DMO objects within VBScript to perform server management operations, either on the local server or on a remote server.

Defining a script step requires selecting the scripting language and typing in the script. Figure 15.21 shows an example of a VBScript step within a job.

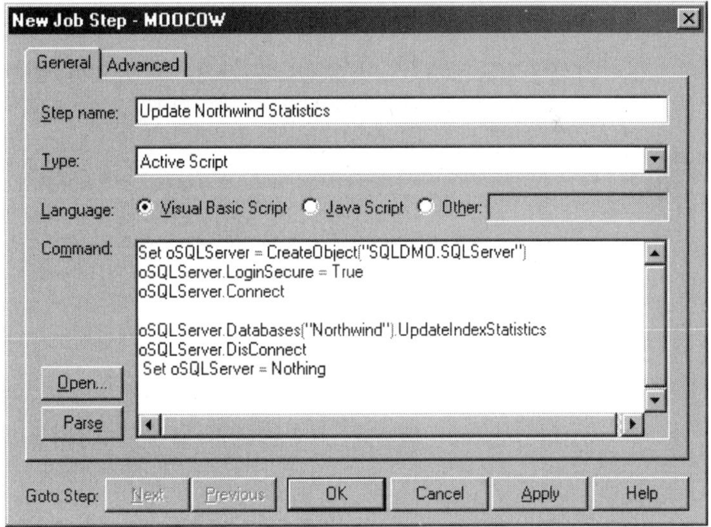

FIGURE 15.21: Defining a script step

Uses for Jobs

Because jobs have the entire Transact-SQL language available to them, as well as the entire command language and any ActiveX Automation server (through scripting commands), they are practically unlimited in flexibility. As you work with your server, you'll find many uses for jobs in automating repetitive actions. Here are a few suggestions to get you started:

- Configuring automated nightly backups
- Shelling to an external disk defragmentation utility
- Sending administrators updated lists of objects owned by users
- Creating disk-space reports showing the growth of databases
- Network testing by using the `ping` command to check other hosts

Analyzing Operations

As an administrator, you'll set up as much automated support as possible. But there are times when you have no choice but to analyze events to determine what went wrong. SQL Server provides several tools for analyzing the operation of your server. There are several different logs maintained by the server. In addition, the DBCC utility commands can help you check individual databases or objects for possible inconsistencies.

Logs

During the normal course of operations, SQL Server writes to three logs: the SQL Server error log, the Windows NT application log, and the database's own transaction log. Each of these logs is useful for particular tasks.

The Error Log

The error log is a text file maintained by SQL Server. By default, this file is `C:\MSSQL7\LOG\ERRORLOG`. SQL Server keeps the previous six error logs with extensions of `.1`, `.2`, and so on. If you want to save more history than this, you'll have to arrange to copy out old logs before SQL Server can overwrite them, perhaps by running a nightly or autostart job.

TIP

You can view the error logs directly in SQL Enterprise Manager by expanding the SQL Server Logs node under the Management node.

Figure 15.22 shows a portion of a SQL Server error log. As you can see, SQL Server records informational messages in this log, as well as errors. Any errors are identified with their severity as well as their text.

Date	Source	Message
1998-10-24 06:03:33.88	kernel	Microsoft SQL Server 7.00 - 7.00.593 (Intel X86) ...
1998-10-24 06:03:33.91	kernel	Logging SQL Server messages in file 'f:\MSSQL7\log\ERRORLOG'.
1998-10-24 06:03:33.91	kernel	All rights reserved.
1998-10-24 06:03:33.91	kernel	Copyright (C) 1988-1997 Microsoft Corporation.
1998-10-24 06:03:34.19	kernel	SQL Server is starting at priority class 'normal'(1 CPU detected).
1998-10-24 06:03:34.19	kernel	initconfig: Number of user connections limited to 32767.
1998-10-24 06:03:34.38	kernel	User Mode Scheduler configured for thread processing
1998-10-24 06:03:35.64	server	Directory Size: 8099
1998-10-24 06:03:35.65	spid1	Using dynamic lock allocation. [500] Lock Blocks, [1000] Lock Owner
1998-10-24 06:03:35.68	spid1	Opening file f:\MSSQL7\data\master.mdf.
1998-10-24 06:03:35.68	spid1	Starting up database 'master'.
1998-10-24 06:03:35.74	spid1	Opening file f:\MSSQL7\data\mastlog.ldf.
1998-10-24 06:03:35.87	spid1	Loading SQL Server's Unicode collation.
1998-10-24 06:03:35.92	spid1	Loading SQL Server's non-Unicode sort order and character set.
1998-10-24 06:03:36.12	spid1	4 transactions rolled forward in database 'master' (1).
1998-10-24 06:03:36.14	spid1	0 transactions rolled back in database 'master' (1).
1998-10-24 06:03:36.29	spid1	Opening file f:\MSSQL7\DATA\model.mdf.
1998-10-24 06:03:36.29	spid1	Starting up database 'model'.
1998-10-24 06:03:36.41	spid1	Opening file f:\MSSQL7\DATA\modellog.ldf.
1998-10-24 06:03:36.57	spid1	Clearing tempdb database.
1998-10-24 06:03:36.66	spid1	Creating file f:\MSSQL7\DATA\TEMPDB.MDF.
1998-10-24 06:03:36.96	spid1	Closing file f:\MSSQL7\DATA\TEMPDB.MDF.
1998-10-24 06:03:37.10	spid1	Creating file f:\MSSQL7\DATA\TEMPLOG.LDF.

FIGURE 15.22: The SQL Server error log

TIP

SQL Server Agent maintains its own log of information. You can view this log from SQL Enterprise Manager by right-clicking SQL Server Agent and choosing Display Error Log.

The main use of the SQL Server error log is to give you a picture of what else might have been happening when a particular error occurred (perhaps one that triggered an alert). It provides you an overall view of the server's activity.

The Application Log

SQL Server also writes error information to the Windows NT application log. This is the information that is processed by SQL Server Agent when you set an alert. It also provides a good way to look for interactions between SQL Server and other processes. For example, if you're having errors using `xp_sendmail` and you can't find anything wrong with the calls to the extended stored procedure, you should check the application log. You might find that Exchange itself has placed additional useful diagnostic information in this log. Figure 15.23 shows a portion of a Windows NT application log.

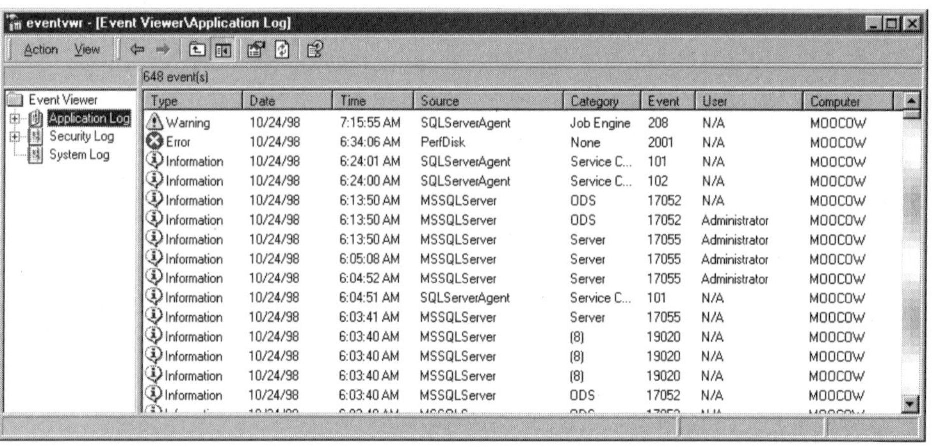

Type	Date	Time	Source	Category	Event	User	Computer
Warning	10/24/98	7:15:55 AM	SQLServerAgent	Job Engine	208	N/A	MOOCOW
Error	10/24/98	6:34:06 AM	PerfDisk	None	2001	N/A	MOOCOW
Information	10/24/98	6:24:01 AM	SQLServerAgent	Service C...	101	N/A	MOOCOW
Information	10/24/98	6:24:00 AM	SQLServerAgent	Service C...	102	N/A	MOOCOW
Information	10/24/98	6:13:50 AM	MSSQLServer	ODS	17052	N/A	MOOCOW
Information	10/24/98	6:13:50 AM	MSSQLServer	ODS	17052	Administrator	MOOCOW
Information	10/24/98	6:13:50 AM	MSSQLServer	Server	17055	Administrator	MOOCOW
Information	10/24/98	6:05:08 AM	MSSQLServer	Server	17055	Administrator	MOOCOW
Information	10/24/98	6:04:52 AM	MSSQLServer	Server	17055	Administrator	MOOCOW
Information	10/24/98	6:04:51 AM	SQLServerAgent	Service C...	101	N/A	MOOCOW
Information	10/24/98	6:03:41 AM	MSSQLServer	Server	17055	N/A	MOOCOW
Information	10/24/98	6:03:40 AM	MSSQLServer	(8)	19020	N/A	MOOCOW
Information	10/24/98	6:03:40 AM	MSSQLServer	(8)	19020	N/A	MOOCOW
Information	10/24/98	6:03:40 AM	MSSQLServer	(8)	19020	N/A	MOOCOW
Information	10/24/98	6:03:40 AM	MSSQLServer	ODS	17052	N/A	MOOCOW

FIGURE 15.23: The application log

Writing to the Logs

Ordinarily, SQL Server takes care of writing information to the error log when an error occurs. But there are times when you might want to write your own information to these logs. Transact-SQL provides the `RAISERROR WITH LOG` statement for these occasions:

```
RAISERROR msg_str, severity, state WITH LOG
```

Here msg_str is a message string explaining the error in human-readable form, severity is an error severity level (which must be from 19 to 25 for logged messages), and state is an arbitrary number from 1 to 127 which you can use to represent the state of the system when the error occurred. The error will be written to both the error log and the application log.

TIP You can also add your own custom error messages to the sysmessages table, using the sp_addmessage stored procedure, and raise them by number.

The Transaction Log

In addition to the error and application logs, SQL Server maintains a transaction log with a complete log of activity for each database on the server. The information in this log is not, however, stored in a form that's useful to administrators. The main use of the transaction log is to support rollback and rollforward operations, as discussed in Skill 5.

DBCC

DBCC is the Microsoft Database Consistency Checker. DBCC provides a whole raft of statements that you can execute in Transact SQL. These statements can carry out the following:

- Perform maintenance tasks.
- Check the status of the server.
- Validate the data stored by the server.

We'll look at a few of the uses of DBCC in this section. For a complete listing of all the DBCC statements, see the SQL Server Books Online.

Checking Databases

The DBCC CHECKDB statement is the easiest way for a server administrator to investigate the status of a particular database. Hardware or software failures could damage the files that a database is stored in, for example, and it's useful to be able to check for such damage. When you run DBCC CHECKDB, it checks the following:

- Index and data pages are correctly linked.
- Indexes are properly sorted.

- Pointers are consistent.
- Page offsets are reasonable.

It performs these checks for every table and index in the database. It will also attempt to repair any errors found. The basic syntax to use is as follows:

```
DBCC CHECKDB ('database_name')
```

Figure 15.24 shows part of the results for running DBCC CHECKDB on the sample Northwind database.

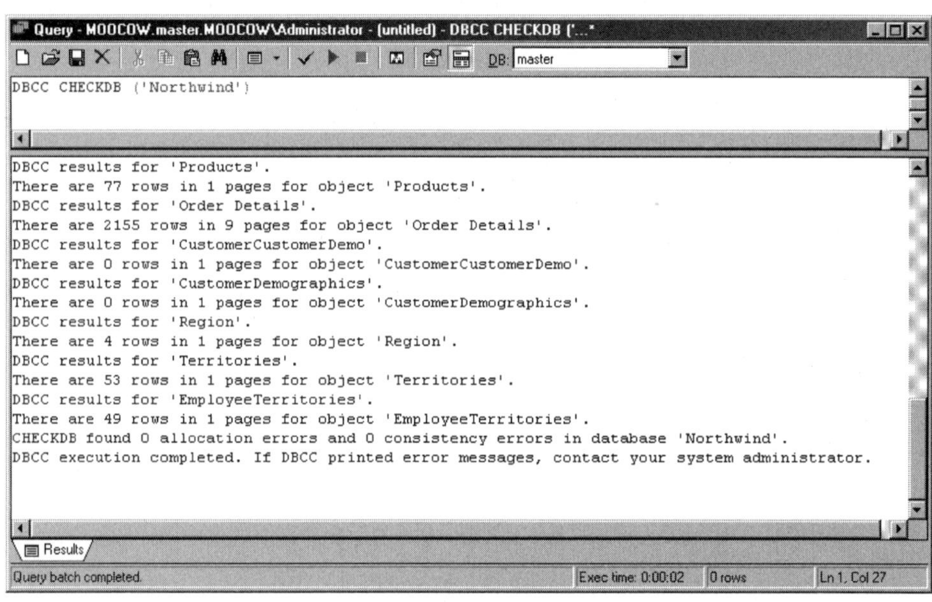

FIGURE 15.24: DBCC CHECKDB output

Checking Tables

You can also use DBCC to check an individual table by using the DBCC CHECKTABLE statement. This statement performs the same checks as DBCC CHECKDB but only on a specified table. You must execute it within the context of the database containing that table. For example, if you switch to the pubs database and execute DBCC CHECKTABLE ('authors'), you'll see output similar to this:

```
DBCC results for 'authors'.
```

```
There are 23 rows in 1 pages for object 'authors'.
DBCC execution completed. If DBCC printed error messages, contact your
system administrator.
```

Miscellaneous DBCC Uses

Some of the other available DBCC statements include the following:

- `DBCC DBREINDEX` rebuilds indexes for tables in a database.
- `DBCC PINTABLE` can load a table permanently into memory so that it can always be accessed quickly. This command is best saved for small lookup tables, since pinning a large table can prevent other queries from getting enough buffer space to run efficiently.
- `DBCC SHOWSTATISTICS` will show index distribution statistics for a particular table.
- `DBCC SHRINKFILE` can recover empty space if you've deleted a lot of data from a particular database.
- `DBCC TRACEON` can be used to set debugging flags. Typically you would only execute this statement if Microsoft Technical Support suggests it.

Are You up to Speed?

Now you can...

- ☑ **create operators and alerts**
- ☑ **send notifications to operators using e-mail or pager**
- ☑ **call alerts from Windows NT Performance Monitor**
- ☑ **configure SQL Mail**
- ☑ **use SQL Mail to send messages and result sets**
- ☑ **create and manipulate jobs**
- ☑ **view the error and application logs**
- ☑ **use DBCC to check object consistency**

SKILL 16

Managing SQL Server Security

- How SQL Server security works
- Users, groups, and roles
- Permissions
- Implementing security

You will need to implement some kind of security on your SQL Server database, whether you are concerned with outright theft or merely want to keep users from inadvertently destroying sensitive data. There are several options to choose from, depending on your environment and needs. In this skill you will learn how to:

- Design and implement security for your application
- Work with NT users and groups
- Create roles to fine-tune security
- Apply the appropriate permissions on database objects

How SQL Server Security Works

SQL Server uses a new, highly flexible security model that is tightly integrated with Windows NT security. There are two basic stages a user passes through when working with SQL Server:

- The *authentication* stage, when a user logs on and is validated by the system
- The *permissions validation* stage, which controls the activities that the user is allowed to perform once they've been authenticated

There are two ways to authenticate users:

- *Windows NT Authentication mode.* Users don't have to log on twice. They are authenticated only once, when logging on to NT. SQL Server also supports assigning permissions to NT users and groups.
- *SQL Server Authentication mode.* User logins are defined in SQL Server and users are required to log on using a SQL Server username and password.

NOTE If you are using SQL Server for Windows 95/98, you must use SQL Server Authentication mode. Windows NT Authentication mode is not supported for any other operating system than Windows NT.

Once users can access SQL Server, they need to have permissions assigned to them so that they can perform tasks in SQL Server. You can assign permissions directly to users or you can assign them to NT groups if you are using NT

Authentication. In addition, you can create SQL Server *roles* which can contain any number of groups, users, or even other roles to more narrowly define your security needs. SQL Server also ships with predefined server and database roles, which simplify the task of assigning permissions. We'll cover roles and permissions later in this skill.

NOTE The two authentication modes replace the Standard, Integrated, and Mixed security of earlier versions. Use Windows NT Authentication mode when you want Integrated security and SQL Server Authentication mode when you want Standard or Mixed, which have been combined in this version.

Security Architecture

If you use Integrated security with Windows NT, you can map permissions directly to users or assign them to NT groups where the users inherit the permissions of the group. Likewise, you can assign permissions to SQL Server roles, to NT groups, or to users. The structure of the users, groups, and roles is hierarchical—SQL Server roles can contain other groups and roles as well as users. It is often possible to map this structure fairly closely to the organizational chart of the corporation you are implementing security for. Figure 16.1 shows how you can map NT users and groups to SQL Server users and roles and still map SQL Server users and roles independently of NT users and groups.

The hierarchical model simplifies managing security since you only need to apply settings once to the group or role, instead of redundantly for each user. Users inherit permissions assigned to the group or role.

TIP Even if a group or role only has one member, it's better to create a group or role for that user rather than assign permissions to the user directly. If you have assigned permissions to a user and that user leaves the company, then you would need to reconstruct that user's entire set of permissions for a new user. If you assign permissions to roles, you only need to delete the old user and create a new user account, adding it to the role. The new user will be able to take over where the old user left off.

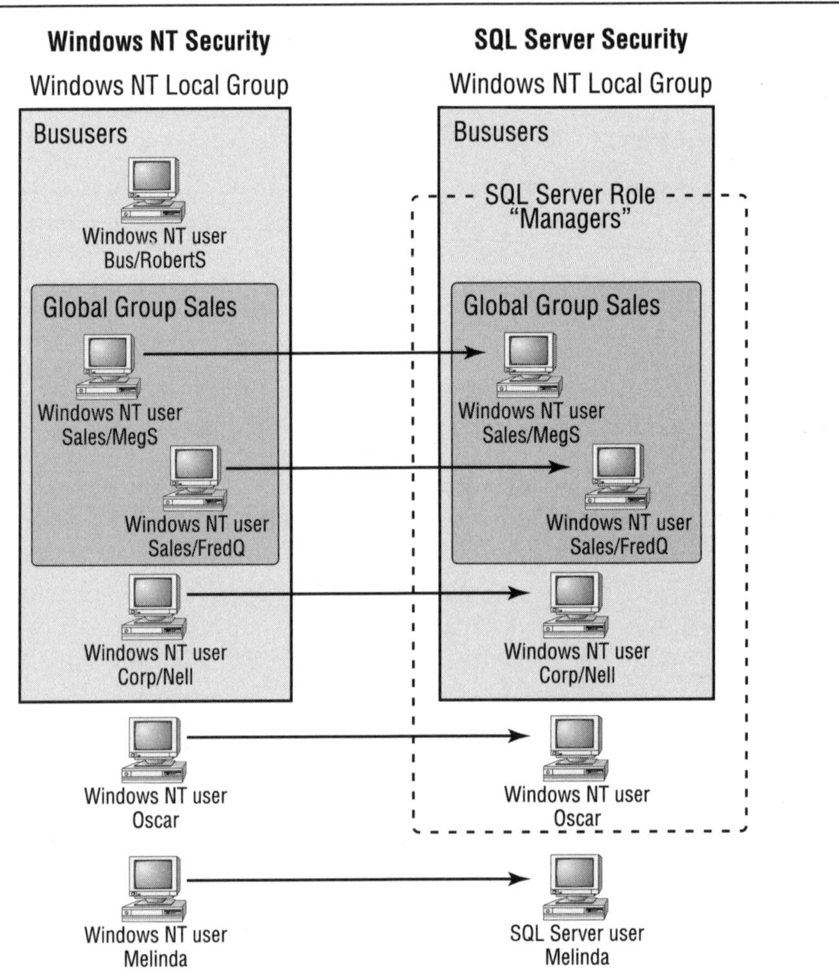

FIGURE 16.1: Windows NT security groups

Windows NT Authentication Mode

When you configure your SQL Server to operate in Windows NT Authentication mode, SQL Server assumes a trust relationship with NT Server in which the assumption is made that NT has authenticated the user's account name and password when they logged on to NT. SQL Server then checks the user account and any NT group accounts the user may be a member of to see if that user is allowed to work in the database.

Windows NT Authentication is preferable to SQL Server Authentication mainly due to its tight integration with the NT security mechanism. Windows NT also provides more secure validation and encryption of passwords, auditing, password expiration, minimum password length, and account lockout after an invalid password.

NOTE Changes to NT users and groups are automatically reflected in SQL Server, so they don't have to be administered separately. If changes are made to the permissions of a connected user, those changes will only become effective the next time the user connects to SQL Server.

SQL Server Authentication Mode

If you configure SQL Server Authentication mode, then SQL Server will require an additional login to verify whether that person has a valid account and password previously defined in SQL Server. If there is no account set up for that user, then an error will occur and the user will not be logged on.

Use SQL Server Authentication mode for mixed security (where you want to use both NT accounts and SQL Server accounts), for backwards compatibility, or with older applications. You also need to use SQL Server Authentication mode for connections from non–Windows NT clients and Internet clients.

In general, SQL Server Authentication can be easier to administer for simple applications that do not have extensive security needs and where you don't need to control the activities of individual groups or users.

Permission Validation

Once the user is authenticated, there must be a SQL Server account in each database that is used to apply SQL Server permissions for that user. If no account exists, then the user will default to the permissions mapped to the guest account (if one has been defined). The SQL Server account can be mapped to either the person's NT user account, a group, or a SQL Server user account mapped to their SQL Server login account. All activities the user is allowed to perform are governed by the permissions assigned to that security account, whether they are entering ad-hoc queries, working through a front-end application, or choosing menu options in SQL Server.

NOTE Requiring a user account in each database prevents a user from logging on to SQL Server and then using any database they please!

Whether you use Windows NT or SQL Server Authentication, you need to create SQL Server user accounts in all databases that map to logins.

Behind the scenes, all of the activities a user performs (or attempts to perform) are communicated to the server through Transact-SQL statements. Each time the server receives a Transact-SQL statement, it checks to make sure the user has permissions to execute that particular statement. If they don't, then an error is returned.

Users, Groups, and Roles

When you set up security in your SQL Server application, you need to either add NT accounts for logins, users, and groups, if you are using Windows NT Authentication, or to create SQL Server logins, users, and groups, if you are using SQL Server Authentication. You then need to use predefined SQL Server roles and also possibly custom SQL Server roles to further fine-tune security.

Working with NT Users and Groups

No matter which form of authentication you use, users will need a valid NT login account before they will be able to access SQL Server, if your server is running under Windows NT. You have the option of granting permissions to a Windows NT group to connect to SQL Server, or you can grant permissions to individual users, if an NT group should not be granted collective permissions.

About Windows NT Groups

Windows NT has both global and local groups. An NT local group can contain global groups but not vice versa. Global groups are created on NT Server only and contain user accounts from that domain—they can't contain users from other domains. Local groups contain user accounts from their own domain as well as usernames from other trusted domains.

Windows NT has predefined local groups—Administrators, Users, and Guests—which are always available (unless you remove them). These groups function much the same way that SQL Server roles do: you can assign users to them to reduce the administrative overhead of having to assign permissions to individual users.

Add a Windows NT Login to SQL Server

You need to specify the Windows NT domain or computer name when you grant access to a Windows NT user, as in the following example using the `sp_grantlogin` stored procedure. In this example, the NT domain is AHMOSE and the username is Charmian.

```
sp_grantlogin 'AHMOSE\Charmian'
```

When you grant an NT group access to connect to SQL Server, you need to specify the domain or computer name, followed by a backslash, and then the group name, the same way you did for an NT user above. However, if you are granting access to one of the built-in Windows NT groups, you need to specify it using BUILTIN, as in the following example, which uses `sp_grantlogin` to add the NT Administrators group:

```
sp_grantlogin 'BUILTIN\Administrators'
```

To add an NT login from the Enterprise Manager, expand the Security folder, right-click Logins, then select New Login. Fill in the options, as shown in Figure 16.2.

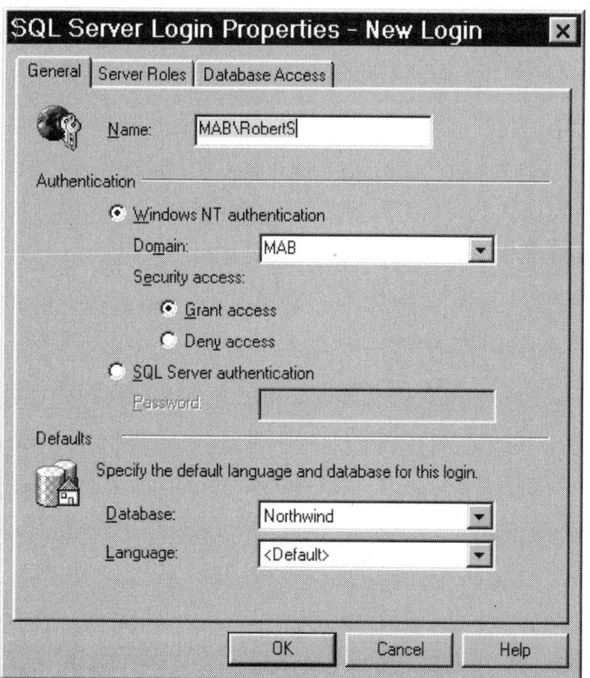

FIGURE 16.2: Adding an NT login to SQL Server

If you want the new user to be able to perform server administrative tasks, click the Server Roles tab and select the roles you want the new user to be a member of, as shown in Figure 16.3.

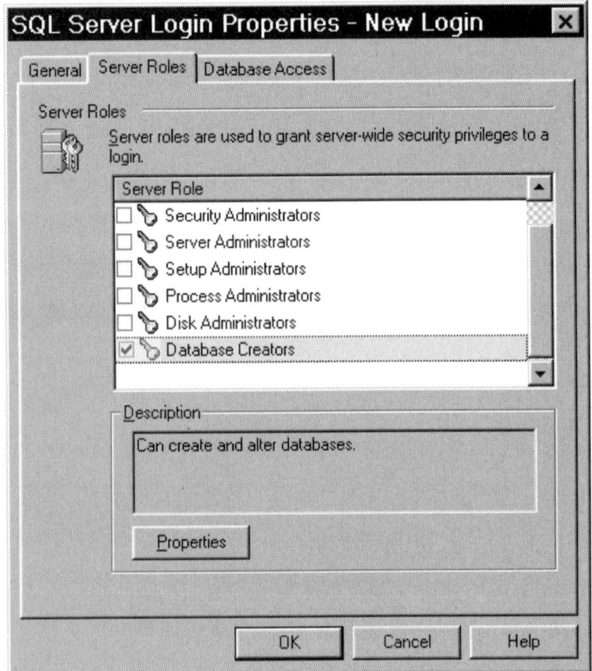

FIGURE 16.3: Adding the login to a server role

To grant the new user access to databases, click the Database Access tab and select the databases you want the new user to be able to have access to, as shown in Figure 16.4. You can also set permissions in each of these databases by assigning the user to one or more database roles.

TIP If you want to add an NT group, just type the group name instead of a username. You can add NT groups to server roles and grant them access to databases in the same way you do users.

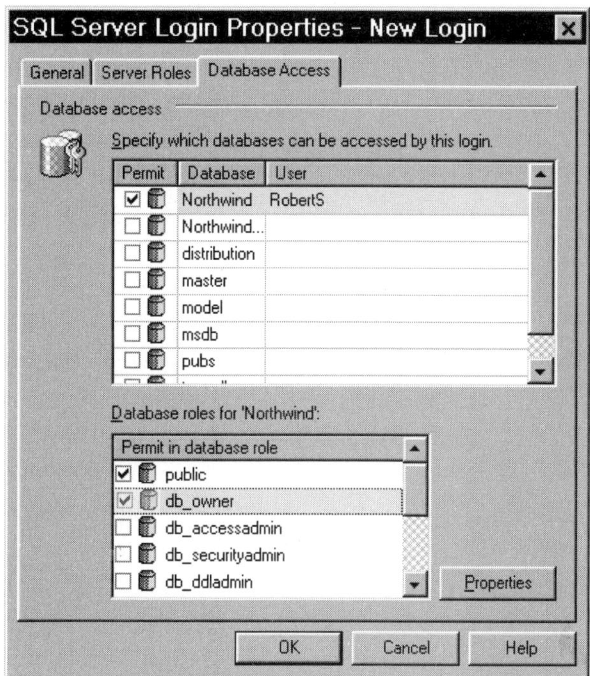

FIGURE 16.4: Granting access to databases

Use the `sp_grantdbaccess` stored procedure to add the new user (the `sp_adduser` stored procedure exists only for compatibility with older versions of SQL Server). The syntax is:

```
sp_grantdbaccess login, name_in_db
```

The *`login`* argument is the name of the login for the new account in the database and the *`name_in_db`* argument is the optional name for the account in the database. If you don't specify the *`name_in_db`* argument, then the NT login name will be used. If later on you want to remove an account, use the `sp_revokedbaccess` stored procedure.

```
sp_grantdbaccess 'AHMOSE\RobertS'
```

Working with SQL Server Users and Logins

If you aren't planning to use NT Authentication, you need to create your own SQL Server logins.

Naming Rules for SQL Server Logins, Users, Roles, and Passwords

Logins, users, roles, and passwords can contain from 1 to 128 characters. You can use letters, symbols, and numbers as long as the name does not contain a backslash and is not an empty string or `NULL`. However, it's best to stay away from symbols, which might cause you to have to use delimiters when writing Transact-SQL statements. Delimiters are double quotation marks or square brackets. You'll have to use delimiters if the login, user, role, or password contains or begins with a space, begins with a dollar sign ($), or begins with the "at" (@) character.

Adding a SQL Server Login

If your system is configured to run in SQL Server Authentication mode, then you need to add logins, which are separate from your users' NT logins. To add a login using the Enterprise Manager, follow the same steps you took above in adding an NT login. Select SQL Server Authentication and fill in the username and password, as shown in Figure 16.5. Set the other options by clicking the Server Roles and Database Access tabs.

In Transact-SQL, you can add a login by using the `sp_addlogin` stored procedure. The syntax is:

```
sp_addlogin login, password, database, language, login_pid
```

If you don't specify any of the arguments other than the login argument, then the password will default to `NULL` and the default database for that user will be the master database. If you want your user to have an initial password of "cobra" and to default to the Northwind database, use the following syntax:

```
sp_addlogin 'Iras', 'cobra', 'Northwind'
```

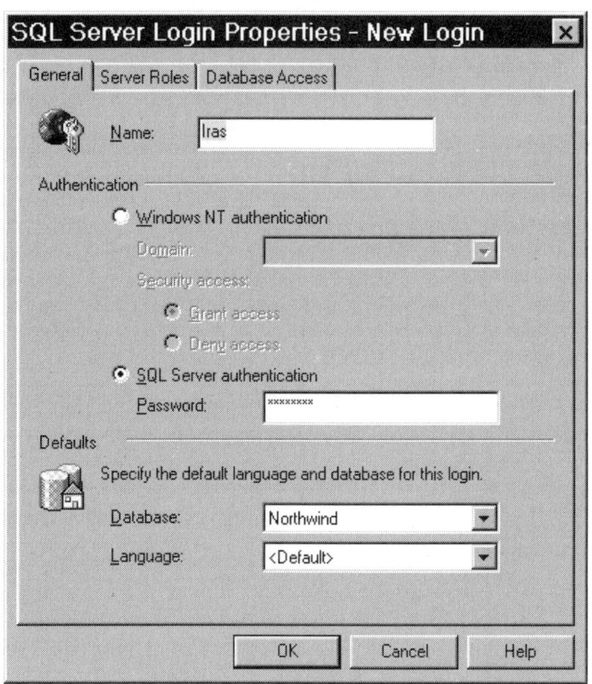

FIGURE 16.5: Creating a SQL Server login

Adding a Linked Server Login

If you are using distributed queries or remote procedure calls where SQL Server connects through an OLE DB provider, SQL Server may need to provide a valid login name and password for use on the remote server. SQL Server maps the current SQL Server login at the linked server level to a remote login and password on the remote provider. If the other server is a SQL Server using NT Authentication mode, then it can use the NT security credentials and does not need to use a predetermined login mapping. However, SQL Server running on Windows 95/98 and other providers (such as Jet) cannot use NT Authentication when used as linked servers. You can use the `sp_addlinkedsrvlogin` stored procedure to set up the mapping, as shown in the following example, which maps the NT/SQL Server user Charmian to the Jet login, Admin (which has no password).

```
sp_addlinkedsrvlogin 'JetCustomers', false, 'Charmian', 'Admin', NULL
```

You can also use the Enterprise Manager to perform the mapping, as shown in the section on linked servers in Skill 14, *Using Replication*.

About the sa Login

The sa (or system administrator) login is mainly provided for backwards compatibility with earlier versions of SQL Server. In SQL Server 7, it is mapped to the sysadmin fixed server role and cannot be changed or deleted. By default, it is installed with no password, so you should take care to set one. Create your own logins and add them to the sysadmin role instead of relying on sa when you need system administrators. Use sa only as a backdoor if other system administrators are unavailable or have forgotten their passwords.

WARNING If you rely on sa and you forget the password, you will have to reinstall SQL Server.

Using the Guest User Account

The guest account is for users who do not have their own account in a database. However, you have to create and enable the guest account in each database where you want it to be used. You can add permissions and roles to the guest user as if it were any other user account.

Using Roles

You can create roles in SQL Server, assign users to the roles, and have them inherit the permissions of the role. There is no restriction to the number of roles a user can belong to, unlike earlier versions of SQL Server, which restricted users to being a member of only one group and forced you to use aliases to work around this restriction. There are also fixed roles, which are built into SQL Server. You can nest roles, but don't get carried away: there's a performance penalty if your nesting scheme gets too complex.

Creating a SQL Server Role

If you use NT Authentication, you may have security needs which are not met by the existing NT groups. Alternatively, if you use SQL Server Authentication, you may need to create the equivalent of groups to simplify security administrative tasks. Roles fill these needs admirably—you can create a role in SQL Server, assign permissions to the role, and add users to the role so that they can perform the actions assigned to that role. A couple of possible scenarios where you would find roles useful are:

- Your company hires outside consultants to work on various projects side-by-side with in-house developers. They are members of a Consultants group in NT. Some, but not all, of these consultants need to work with your SQL Server application, but you do not want them to have access to sensitive data. You can create a role that precisely defines the activities of these developers in your application and add only those developers to the role who are involved in the project.
- A group of employees who are members of diverse NT groups are involved in a common project which has tables and views created just for that one project. You can create a role that has the necessary permissions to work with the tables and views involved and then add the users to the role.
- You are working in a mixed environment where your application needs to run on Windows 95/98.

To create a new role using the Enterprise Manager, expand the database so that the Roles folder is showing. Then right-click Roles and select New Database Role. Fill in the options, as shown in Figure 16.6. Name the role and add the users you want to be able to use the role.

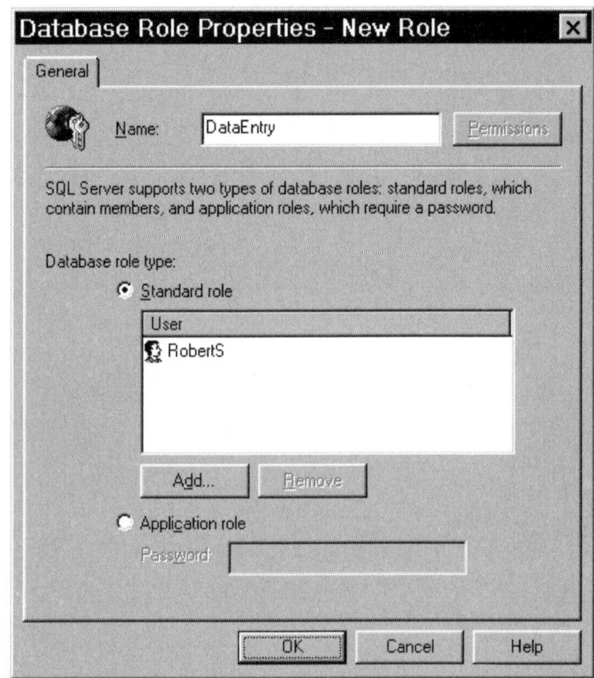

FIGURE 16.6: Creating a database role

You can also set permissions for the role after you have created it. Right-click the role and click the Permissions button. This will bring up the Permissions tab, where you can set permissions on all the database objects, as shown in Figure 16.7.

The syntax in Transact-SQL for adding a new role is:

```
sp_addrole role, owner
```

The following example will create the SpecialProjects role and make Charmian the owner:

```
sp_addrole 'SpecialProjects', 'Charmian'
```

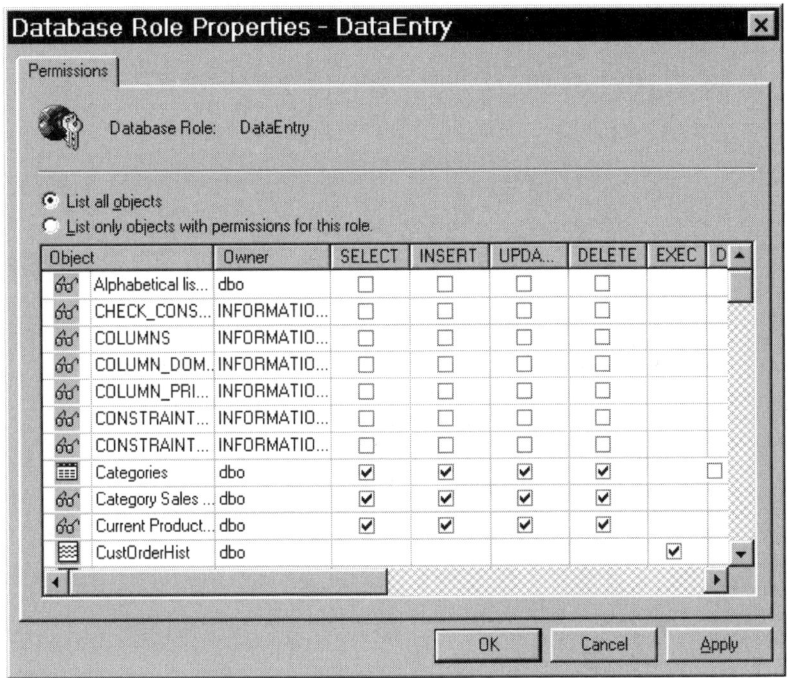

FIGURE 16.7: Setting permissions for the new role

Fixed Server and Database Roles

Fixed server and database roles are built-in roles in SQL Server and you cannot alter them in any way—you can only add users, groups, or other roles to them. Fixed server and database roles provide for more flexibility and improved security compared to using the old system administrator (sa) login. The fixed server roles are listed in Table 16.1.

TABLE 16.1: Fixed Server Roles in SQL Server

Role	Description
dbcreator	Can create and alter databases.
diskadmin	Can manage the disk files.
processadmin	Can manage the processes running in SQL Server.

TABLE 16.1 CONTINUED: Fixed Server Roles in SQL Server

Role	Description
serveradmin	Can configure the server-wide settings.
setupadmin	Can install replication and manage extended procedures.
securityadmin	Can manage the logins for the server.
sysadmin	Can perform any activity in the SQL Server installation. This role spans all the other roles.

Server roles exist outside of individual databases. In order to add a user, the user must already have a login account that you can add to the role. To add a user to a fixed server role using the Enterprise Manager, expand the server and click Server Roles. Select the role you want to add a user to and right-click it, selecting the Properties option. Fill in the blanks, as shown in Figure 16.8.

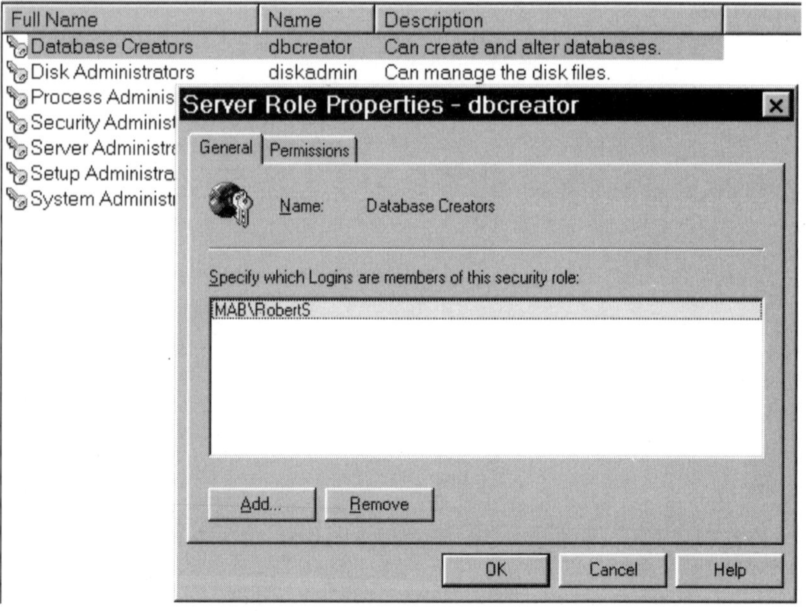

FIGURE 16.8: Adding a user to a fixed server role

You can also use the `sp_addsrvrolemember` stored procedure to add a user to a fixed server role, as shown in the following example where the NT user Charmian is added to the sysadmin role:

```
sp_addsrvrolemember 'KARIS\Charmian', 'sysadmin'
```

NOTE Windows NT users who are members of the NT Administrators group at the time that you install SQL Server are automatically members of the sysadmin role and don't need to be manually added to it.

In addition to the server roles, there are also database fixed roles, which exist in individual databases instead of across the whole server. Like server roles, database roles cannot be altered. Table 16.2 lists the fixed database roles in SQL Server.

TABLE 16.2: Fixed Database Roles in SQL Server

Role	Description
db_accessadmin	Can add or remove NT users and groups and SQL Server users in the database
db_backupoperator	Can back up the database
db_datareader	Can see any data from all user tables in the database
db_datawriter	Can add, change, or delete data in all user tables in the database
db_ddladmin	Can add, modify, or drop objects in the database
db_securityadmin	Can manage role membership and can manage statement and object permissions in the database
db_denydatareader	Cannot see any data in the database
db_denydatawriter	Cannot change any data in the database
db_owner	Can perform the activities of all the database roles as well as maintenance and configuration activities

To add a user to a fixed database role using the Enterprise Manager, expand the database and click the Roles folder. Select the role you want to add a user to and right-click it, selecting the Properties option. Click the Add button to add a new user, as shown in Figure 16.9.

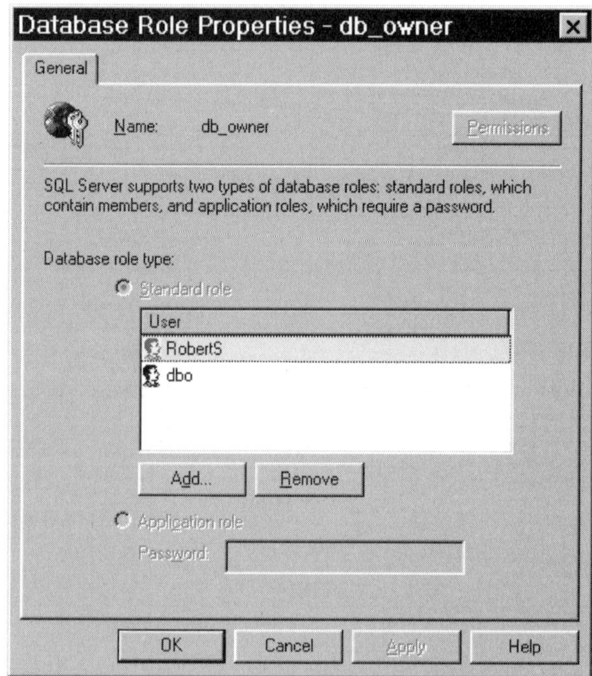

FIGURE 16.9: Adding a user to a fixed database role

TIP You can also add a user to a role by selecting the user in the Users folder and editing its properties.

You can use the `sp_addrolemember` stored procedure to add a user to a role, as in the following example where the user KARIS\Charmian is added to the `db_accessadmin` role:

```
sp_addrolemember 'db_accessadmin', 'KARIS\Charmian'
```

The Implicit Owner Role

There are roles in SQL Server that are implied but not named. For example, the owner of an object, such as a table, view, or procedure, has full permissions on that object and can also manage permissions on that object for other security accounts.

Therefore it is a good idea to make sure that nobody owns an object for which you don't want them to have those permissions. You can use the `sp_changeobjectowner` stored procedure in Transact-SQL to change ownership of any object in the database:

```
sp_changeobjectowner object, owner
```

If you want to change ownership of the database itself, use the `sp_changedbowner` stored procedure:

```
sp_changedbowner login, drop_alias_flag
```


The Public Role

The public role is a special role that cannot be dropped. Every database user belongs to public, so you don't need to assign users, groups, or roles to it. Every SQL Server database contains the public role, including master, msdb, tempdb, and model.

The dbo (Database Owner)

The dbo is a special user account inside each database, which is mapped to the sysadmin fixed server role. What this means is that if you are logged on as user Bob, you are a member of the sysadmin role, and you create an object, that object's owner will be dbo; not Bob. You can't delete the dbo account and it's only mapped to sysadmin, not to the database owner (`db_owner`).

Database Object Owners

If you create an object in a database and you are not a member of the sysadmin role, then you own that object. What this means is that you can administer security on that object, granting others permission to use it. In fact, if you want others to use objects you create, you have to grant them permissions or they will be unable to access the object.

The Create SQL Server Login Wizard

So far we've gone through all the steps to grant logins a piece at a time, but the SQL Server Login Wizard, shown in Figure 16.10, can wrap the whole process up for you all at once. It allows you to carry out the following:

- Choose the authentication mode used to connect to SQL Server

- Add either an NT or SQL Server login
- Add the login to a fixed server role
- Add the user to one or more databases

FIGURE 16.10: The SQL Server Login Wizard

To run the wizard, choose Tools ➢ Wizards ➢ Database ➢ Create Login Wizard and follow the steps to completion.

The Application Role

The application role is a special role that can be created to support the security needs of a front-end application. SQL security is implemented at the database level, which is the best way to control user activities inside the database. However, you may have situations where you want to customize security, based on the requirements of your application rather than the individuals who use it. The way it works is that the application itself activates the application role, and any person using the application will gain any permissions granted to the application role.

The application role exists only for a particular application—you can't add users to an application role. Since application roles do not have users the way regular roles do, they require a password in order to be authenticated. The application itself provides the password to activate the role and thus gain access to the database objects. The user will have only those permissions granted to the application role—any permissions they may have individually under NT or SQL Server, which are distinct from the application role, will be ignored.

An application role is a good way to keep users from working directly with the data in SQL Server. For example, you have an application that uses Excel to query data in your SQL Server. You do not want the users of your Excel application to be able to query data directly by using the SQL Server Query Analyzer or any other tools they may have. There is a high likelihood that if they were allowed to do so, they could negatively impact performance by writing a query that returned too much data or, in a worst case scenario, inadvertently deleting data. These are the types of scenarios that the application role is designed to prevent.

The users are associated with the application role when they use the application. Application roles override a user's default permissions as long as the user is connected to the database through the application. For example, user Bob normally has permission to edit data in the Customers table. Bob connects to the database using an application role which has read-only permissions on the Customers table. Bob now has read-only permissions on the Customers table for the duration of that session while he is connected via the application role—his edit data permissions have been suspended.

TIP

If you are using Windows NT Authentication mode and a user logs on with an application role, Windows NT auditing of the user account will still take place. If you are using SQL Server Authentication, use an application role only for applications that don't require auditing.

To create an application role using the Enterprise Manager, expand the Database folder and then right-click the database in which to create the application role. Select New ➢ Database Role and enter the name of the new role. Select the Application Role option, and enter the password, as shown in Figure 16.11. This creates an application role. You can then set the permissions for the role the same way you would for a regular database role.

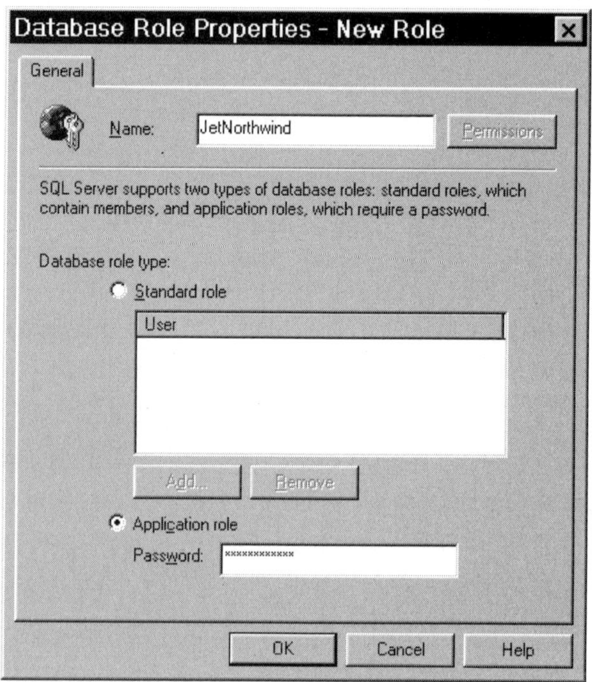

FIGURE 16.11: Creating an application role

To create an application role using Transact-SQL, use the `sp_addapprole` stored procedure:

```
sp_addapprole [@rolename =] 'role', [@password =] 'password'
```

For example, the following would add an application role for an Access application with a password of MongooseAhoy:

```
sp_addapprole 'NewJetRole', 'MongooseAhoy'
```

Managing Users, Groups, and Roles

Once you've set up security, you need to be able to view it and modify it if need be. SQL Server 7 makes this very easy to do through the Enterprise Manager and through the system stored procedures.

Managing Logins and Users

You can view information for each login, including the name of the user associated with that login, the default database, the user's SID (if an NT user), and the language associated with the database. However, you can't view the password—it's encrypted and stored internally. If you ever need to delete a login, you need to delete the user first.

To view information about logins, expand the server group down to the Security folder and click Logins. Right-click the login you are interested in and select Properties. You can also change the information on the General tab. For example, if you have a SQL Server login and a user has forgotten their password, you can set a new password, as shown in Figure 16.12.

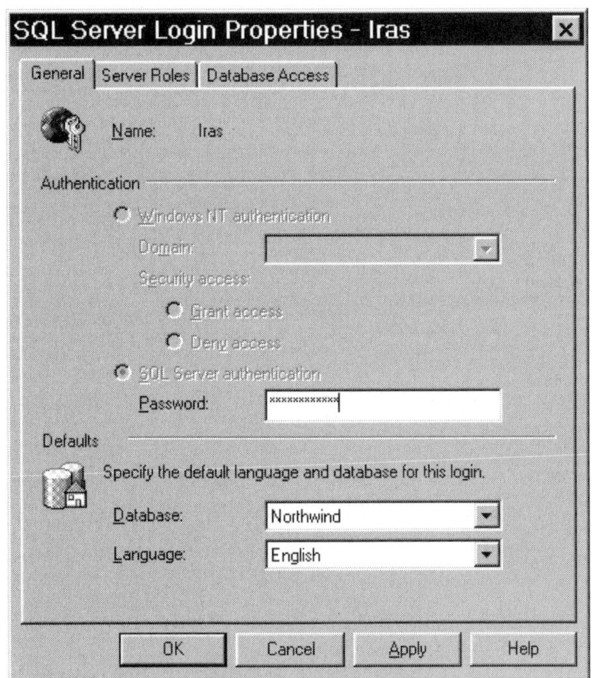

FIGURE 16.12: Modifying login information

You can also use the `sp_helplogins` stored procedure to return information about a login.

```
sp_helplogins @LoginNamePattern = 'KARIS\Charmian'
```

The output looks like this (the SID has been elided):

```
LoginName              SID            DefDBName  DefLangName   AUser Remote
---------------------- -------------- ---------- ------------- ----- ------
KARIS\Charmian 0x01050 … 7EE030000 Northwind  us_english    yes   no

LoginName              DBName         UserName            UserOrAlias
---------------------- -------------- ------------------- ------------
KARIS\Charmian         Northwind      db_accessadmin      MemberOf
KARIS\Charmian         Northwind      db_owner            MemberOf
KARIS\Charmian         Northwind      KARIS\Charmian      User
```

If you have a SQL Server login, you can use the `sp_password` stored procedure to change it. Members of the sysadmin role can change the password of other users without having to know the old one, as in the following example, which uses `NULL` for the `old_password` argument and sets the new password to Sneferu.

```
sp_password [[@old =] 'old_password',] {[@new =] 'new_password'}
[,[@loginame =] 'login']

sp_password NULL, 'Sneferu', 'Iras'
```

NOTE You can change passwords only for SQL Server logins but not for NT logins.

To view information about database users, expand the database and click Users. Right-click the user you are interested in and select Properties, as shown in Figure 16.13.

You can use the `sp_helpuser` stored procedure.

```
sp_helpuser @name_in_db = 'Iras'
```

The output looks like this:

```
UserName GroupName    LoginName DefDBName          UserID SUserID
-------- ------------ --------- ------------------ ------ --------
Iras     public       Iras      Northwind          10     7
```

If you need to view the current NT accounts in the database, use the `sp_helpntgroup` stored procedure:

```
sp_helpntgroup
```

The output looks like this (the SID has been elided):

```
NTGroupName  NtGroupId SID                 HasDbAccess
------------ --------- ------------------- ------------
Developers   11        0x0105 … C030000   1
```

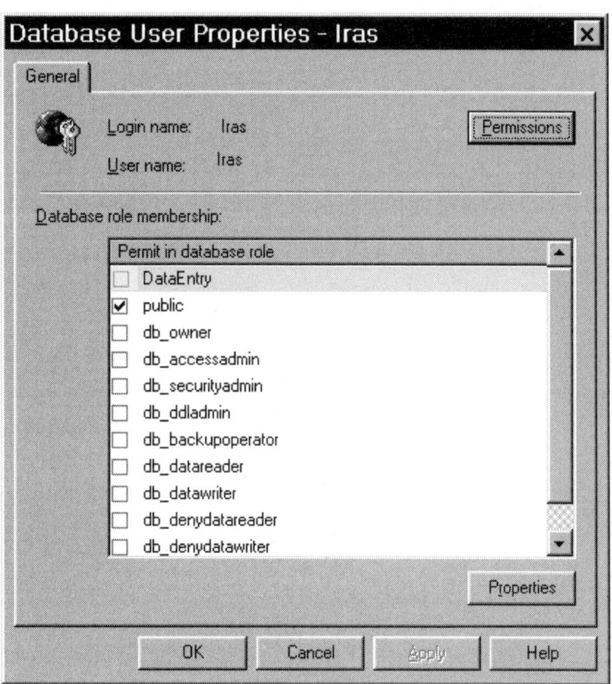

FIGURE 16.13: Information about database users

Removing Logins and Users

If your company is anything like most companies, users will come and go and you will eventually need to remove logins and users from SQL Server. If you are using NT Authentication, you should remove the user's NT account first. Then remove any user accounts in SQL Server databases and, finally, remove the SQL Server login.

Removing a user account from a database automatically removes the permissions that were defined for them—you don't need to do this in a separate step. However, you won't be able to do this if the user owns any objects. You can transfer objects to another user by running the `sp_changeobjectowner` system stored procedure or drop them entirely.

If you remove the user account and do not remove the login, the user can still log on to the database through the guest account, if one exists.

To remove a user using the Enterprise Manager, expand the database and click Users. Right-click the user you want to remove and click Delete. Click Yes to confirm.

To remove a user using Transact-SQL, use the sp_dropuser stored procedure, as in the following example, which removes the user Iras:

```
sp_dropuser @name_in_db = 'Iras'
```

To remove a login using the Enterprise Manager, expand the server down to the Security folder and click Logins. Right-click the login you want to remove and click Delete. Click Yes to confirm.

You can deny access to an NT user and group by clicking on the Deny Access option under Authentication or by running the sp_denylogin stored procedure.

To remove a SQL Server login using Transact-SQL, use the sp_droplogin stored procedure, as in the following example, which removes the login Iras:

```
sp_droplogin @loginame = 'Iras'
```

To remove a Windows NT login using Transact-SQL, use the sp_revokelogin stored procedure, as in the following example, which removes the login KARIS\Charmian:

```
sp_revokelogin @loginame = 'KARIS\Charmian'
```

Managing Roles

Another part of managing security is adding and removing users within roles. To view or modify the members of a database role using the Enterprise Manager, expand the database folder and select Roles. Right-click the role you are interested in and select Properties. You can now add users or remove users from the role, as shown in Figure 16.14.

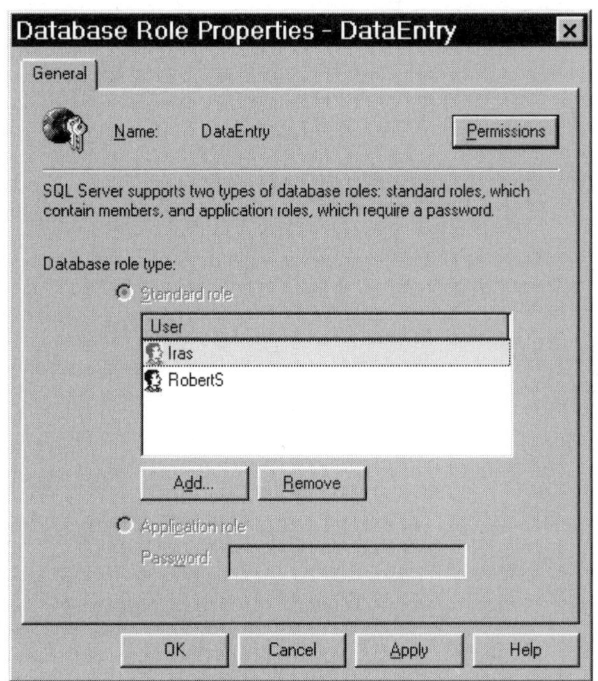

FIGURE 16.14: Modifying database roles

You can also use the sp_helpuser stored procedure to view information about a database role, as in the following example, which returns information about the DataEntry role.

```
sp_helpuser 'DataEntry'
```

The results look like this:

```
Group_name                 Group_id Users_in_group            Userid
-------------------------- -------- ------------------------- -------
DataEntry                  16400    JetNorthwind              8
DataEntry                  16400    RobertS                   5
DataEntry                  16400    KARIS\Charmian            6
```

To remove a user from a role, use the sp_droprolemember stored procedure, which will remove the user RobertS from the DataEntry role:

```
sp_droprolemember 'DataEntry', 'RobertS'
```

To delete a role entirely using the Enterprise Manager, select it from the list of Roles and right-click it. Select Delete and click Yes to confirm.

To delete a role using Transact SQL, use the sp_droprole stored procedure, as shown in the following example, which deletes the DataEntry role:

```
sp_droprole 'DataEntry'
```

TIP You won't be able to delete a role if it has members. Delete all the members first and then you will be able to delete the role.

To view or modify the members of a fixed server role using the Enterprise Manager, expand the server down to the Security folder and select Roles. Right-click the role you are interested in and select Properties. You can now add users or remove users from the role, as shown in Figure 16.15.

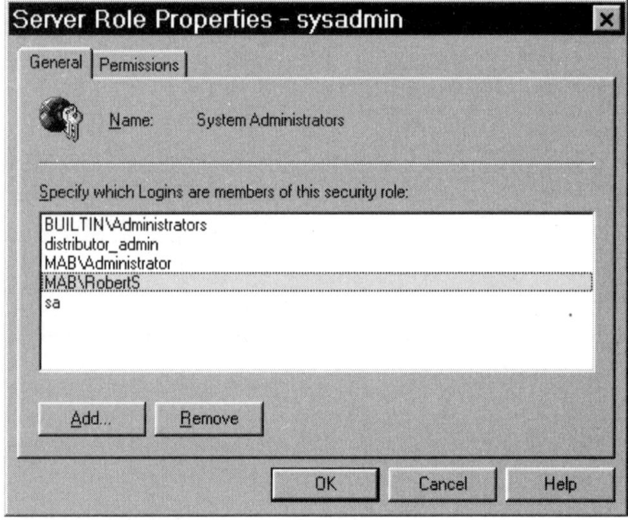

FIGURE 16.15: Modifying fixed server roles

You can also use the sp_helpsrvrolemember stored procedure to view information about a fixed server role, as in the following example, which returns information about the sysadmin role.

```
sp_helpsrvrolemember 'sysadmin'
```

The results look like this (the SIDs have been elided):

```
ServerRole      MemberName                  MemberSID
--------------- --------------------------- ----------------------
sysadmin        BUILTIN\Administrators      0x01020 … 0020000
sysadmin        distributor_admin           0x5221E … 7853907
sysadmin        KARIS\AndyB                 0x01050 … B030000
sysadmin        KARIS\Charmian              0x01050 … E030000
sysadmin        sa                          0x01
```

To remove a user from a fixed server role, use the stored procedure, as shown in the following example, which removes user Charmian from the sysadmin role:

```
sp_dropsrvrolemember 'KARIS\Charmian', 'sysadmin'
```


Permissions

What a user can do after connecting with SQL Server is determined by permissions granted to the user directly or inherited by the user through membership in groups or roles.

You need to set appropriate permissions for the users in your database in order for them to perform actions that view or modify data, change the database definition, or perform system maintenance tasks. They must have the appropriate permissions to perform any activity, regardless of whether the activity is communicated with SQL Server through typing in Transact-SQL commands directly or through an application.

Since you may have many users in your database, it simplifies administrative tasks to assign permissions to groups or roles rather than individual security accounts.

There are three kinds of permissions in SQL Server:

- Object permissions
- Statement permissions
- Inherited or implied permissions

Object permissions are permissions set on objects, such as tables or views, that would allow users to interact with the object. Statement permissions are applied to the statement itself, such as the `CREATE VIEW` statement, which would allow a user to create a view. Inherited or implied permissions are those permissions which are inherited by a user as a result of being added to a role or group or by virtue of the fact that they are the owner of an object. For example, any member of the sysadmin role inherits full permissions to do anything in a SQL Server installation. Similarly, the owner of a table can perform any action on the table, such as altering its definition, modifying its data, or controlling the way other users work with the table. Implied permissions can't be modified or applied to other accounts or roles.

Grant Permissions

There are two types of permissions in SQL Server: object permissions and statement permissions. You grant permissions on database objects in order to allow users to interact with those objects. You also grant permissions on statements to allow users to interact with data. Examples of statements of this sort for which you can grant permissions are:

- `SELECT`
- `INSERT`
- `UPDATE`
- `DELETE`
- `EXECUTE`

Other types of statements allow users to manipulate database objects. For example, you can grant permissions on these statements:

- `CREATE DATABASE`
- `CREATE DEFAULT`
- `CREATE INDEX`
- `CREATE PROCEDURE`
- `CREATE RULE`
- `CREATE TABLE`
- `CREATE VIEW`

There are also statements that don't require any permissions, such as `PRINT`, while yet others cannot be assigned permissions at all. For example, the `SHUTDOWN` statement is part of the sysadmin role and cannot be independently assigned to another user, group, or role. Fixed and implicit role permissions cannot be added to or revoked and you never interact with them directly.

To grant permissions using the Enterprise Manager, select the object in the Details pane, right-click, and select All Tasks ➢ Manage Permissions. Click List All Users/DB Roles and select the permission to grant each user. A check indicates a granted permission, as shown in Figure 16.16.

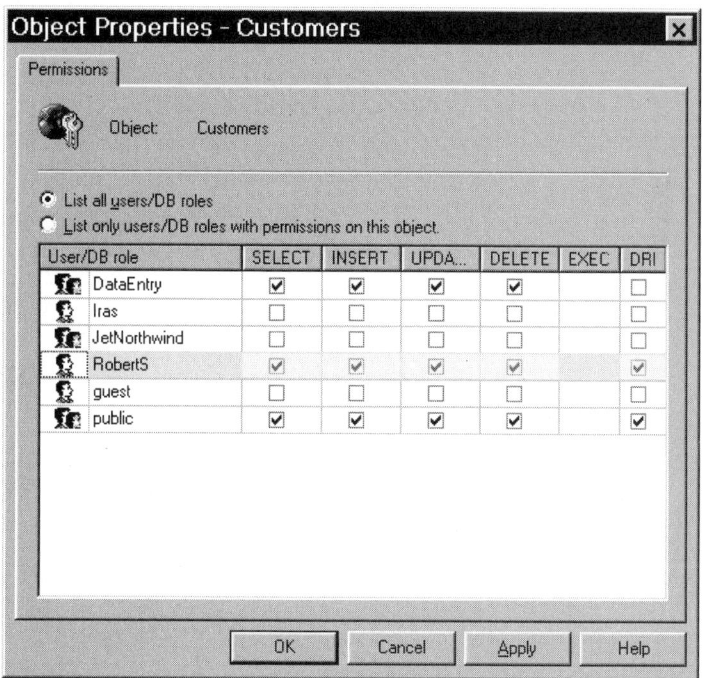

FIGURE 16.16: Granting object permissions

To grant permissions using Transact-SQL, use the GRANT statement. For permissions on statements, use the following syntax:

```
GRANT {ALL | statement[,...n]}
TO security_account[,...n]
```

For permissions on objects, use the following syntax:

```
GRANT
     {ALL [PRIVILEGES] | permission[,...n]}
     {
            [(column[,...n])] ON {table | view}
            | ON {table | view}[(column[,...n])]
```

```
            | ON {stored_procedure | extended_procedure}
    }
TO security_account[,…n]
[WITH GRANT OPTION]
[AS {group | role}]
```

Members of the sysadmin and db_securityadmin roles can grant any permission in the database. Otherwise, permission to use GRANT depends on the object and the permissions being granted. The owner of an object can grant permissions on that object. You can grant permissions to multiple users, roles, or groups at the same time for both objects and statements. The following shows granting permissions on multiple statements to Iras, AndyB, and Charmian:

```
GRANT CREATE DATABASE, CREATE TABLE
    TO Iras, AndyB, [KARIS\Charmian]
```

The following shows granting INSERT, UPDATE, and DELETE permissions on the authors table:

```
GRANT SELECT
    ON authors
    TO public
GO
GRANT INSERT, UPDATE, DELETE
    ON authors
    TO Iras, AndyB, [KARIS\Charmian]
GO
```

TIP

When granting multiple permissions, start at the bottom of the permission hierarchy. Grant basic permissions to groups that everyone belongs to, such as the public group, then fine-tune by granting broader permissions to specific users or roles. For example, grant SELECT to the public group first, then grant INSERT, UPDATE, and DELETE to more exclusive groups or roles.

Deny Permissions

There are times when you need to deny permissions to certain users, groups, or roles. Denying a permission removes a permission that has been previously granted and deactivates that permission if it has been inherited from another role. Additionally, it ensures that the user, group, or role will not inherit that permission in the future, even if they are added to a role that has that permission assigned to it. For example, user Bob has been granted DELETE permissions on the authors table. Bob is also a member of the Developers role, which has full permissions on the authors table. If you deny the DELETE permission to Bob, then Bob will not be able to delete a row in the authors table even though he is still a member of the Developers role. If Bob is later added to the Administrators role, which also has full permissions on the authors table, he will be unable to inherit the DELETE permission from the Administrators group. Once you deny Bob the DELETE permission, he will be unable to delete a row from the authors table from that point on, either directly or through inheriting the permission from any present or future group or role Bob may be added to.

TIP You can extend denying permissions to roles as well. For example, you might have subgroups of users, such as summer employees, interns, or temps, who you do not want to see certain tables or views but who need to be members of more general groups or roles in order to do their jobs. To meet this need, you can create a special role called RestrictedData. Deny permissions to key objects to the RestrictedData role and add these employees to it. This technique enables you to restrict their permissions without having to explicitly and redundantly deny them for each individual employee or worry that they will inherit permissions to sensitive data that you do not want them to have from other roles.

To deny permissions using the Enterprise Manager, right-click the object in the Details pane, click All Tasks ➢ Manage Permissions, and select the List All Users/DB Roles option. Select the permission to deny each user. An "X" indicates a denied permission, as shown in Figure 16.17.

To deny permissions using Transact-SQL, use the DENY statement. To deny permissions on statements, use the following syntax:

```
DENY{ALL | statement[,...n]}
TO security_account[,...n]
```

For example, if you don't want your temporary employees creating new tables, you can deny that permission from the SpecialProjects role:

```
DENY CREATE TABLE
TO SpecialProjects
```

To deny permissions on objects, use this syntax:

```
DENY
     {ALL [PRIVILEGES] | permission[,...n]}
     {
             [(column[,...n])] ON {table | view}
             | ON {table | view}[(column[,...n])]
             | ON {stored_procedure | extended_procedure}
     }
TO security_account[,...n]
[CASCADE]
```

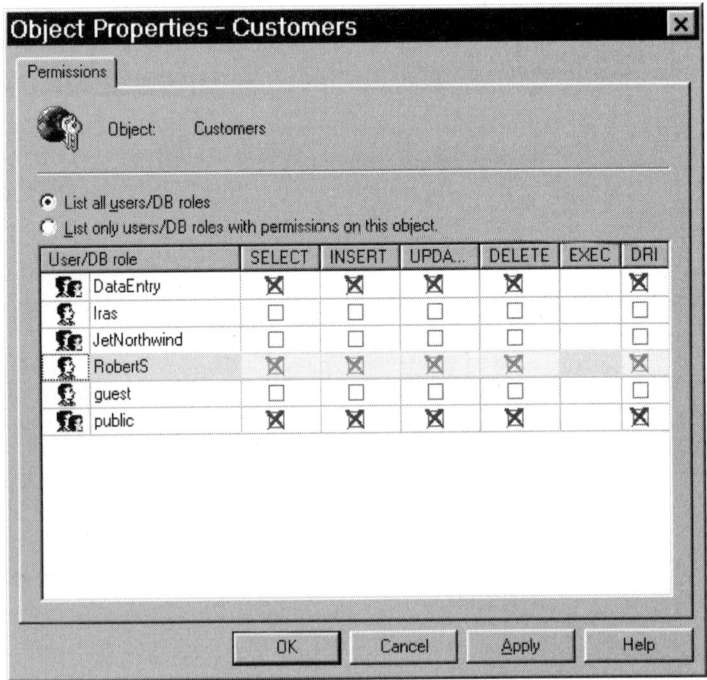

FIGURE 16.17: Denying object permissions

To deny permissions for the RestrictedData group to modify the data in the authors table, use the following syntax:

```
DENY INSERT, UPDATE, DELETE
     ON authors
TO RestrictedData
```

Revoke Permissions

Revoking a permission is similar to denying a permission since both will remove a granted permission, but there is a key difference. Revoking a permission will not prevent the permission from being inherited from another group or role. For example, if you revoke `DELETE` permissions on the authors table from user Bob and later add Bob to the Administrators role, which has full permissions on the authors table, then Bob will be able to inherit the `DELETE` permission from the Administrators group. You can revoke permissions from NT and SQL Server users, groups, and roles.

To revoke permissions using the Enterprise Manager, right-click the object in the Details pane, select All Tasks ➢ Manage Permissions, and select the permission to revoke for each user. An empty box indicates a revoked permission, as shown in Figure 16.18, where everyone has revoked permissions.

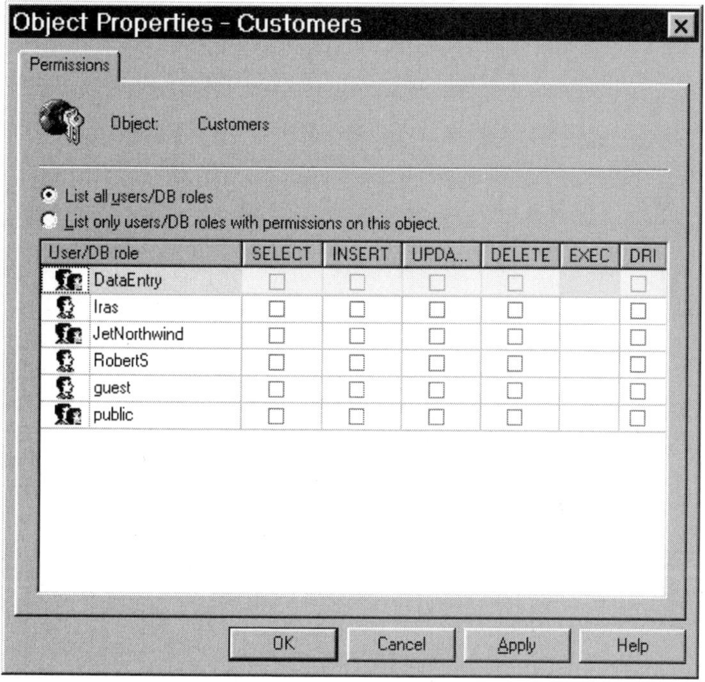

FIGURE 16.18: Revoking object permissions

NOTE The Permissions checkboxes are three-way toggles: empty means revoked, a check means granted, and an X means denied.

To revoke permissions using Transact-SQL, use the `REVOKE` statement. To revoke permissions on statements, use the following syntax:

```
REVOKE {ALL | statement[,...n]}
FROM security_account[,...n]
[AS {group | role}]
```

For example, right now you don't want your trainee Iras to be able to create tables. Later on, when she has proved her competency, you intend adding her to the Developers role. Revoking the CREATE TABLE permission now will enable Iras to inherit it later on:

```
REVOKE CREATE TABLE, CREATE DEFAULT
     FROM Iras
```

To revoke permissions on objects, use this syntax:

```
REVOKE [GRANT OPTION FOR]
{ALL [PRIVILEGES] | permission[,...n]}
     {
              {[(column[,...n])] ON {table | view}
              | ON {table | view}[(column[,...n])]
              | {stored_procedure | extended_procedure}
     }
{TO | FROM}
     security_account[,...n]
[CASCADE]
[AS {group | role}]
```

Again, you don't want trainee Iras to be able to modify data in the Customers table until later on:

```
REVOKE INSERT, UPDATE, DELETE
     ON Customers
     FROM Iras
```

Using WITH GRANT OPTION

WITH GRANT OPTION allows you to give the grantee the ability to grant an assigned object permission to other users. For example, if you want members of the Developers role to be able to grant permissions to other users or roles to update data in the Products table, use the following syntax:

```
GRANT UPDATE
     ON Products
TO Developers
WITH GRANT OPTION
```

When Charmian wants to take advantage of her membership in the Developers role to grant UPDATE permissions to Iras, Charmian must use the AS option:

```
GRANT UPDATE
     ON Products
TO Iras
AS Developers
```

Charmian can't grant INSERT or DELETE permissions to Iras since they weren't included in the original WITH GRANT OPTION statement to the Developers role.

If at some point you want to revoke or deny UPDATE permissions for the Developers role on the authors table, use the CASCADE syntax to remove the permission from all of the grantees:

```
REVOKE UPDATE
     ON Products
FROM Developers
CASCADE
```

WARNING Use WITH GRANT OPTION with caution: once you have granted permissions using WITH GRANT OPTION, you have no control over which security accounts will receive that permission in the future.

Encrypting Views and Stored Procedures

You can use the WITH ENCRYPTION option in Transact-SQL to encrypt a view or a stored procedure. This secures the view or stored procedure by scrambling the definition so it can't be read. The following will create an encrypted stored procedure:

```
CREATE PROCEDURE author_encrypted
WITH ENCRYPTION
AS
SELECT * FROM authors
```

If you execute the stored procedure, it will return all of the rows from the authors table. However, if you attempt to use the stored procedure sp_helptext to read the definition:

```
sp_helptext author_encrypted
```

the result set will be:

```
The object's comments have been encrypted.
```

continued

If you try to get around it by querying the syscomments and sysobjects tables:

```
SELECT comment.id, comment.text
FROM syscomments comment, sysobjects obj
WHERE comment.id = obj.id
    AND obj.name = 'author_encrypted'
```

the result set will be

```
id          text
----------- ----------------------
949578421   LysåvùO_Oéf:3j"ØË&V÷KÔÑmî êù™[+GãRÁ_çpóÔôq…ø
2Ä_ÈgyÅ¯†:ò_Œk 1Ì‘ãAh_«/É¤_Ù5LÄ÷'ë

(1 row(s) affected)
```

Implementing Security

Implementing security in your SQL-Server database requires careful planning. You need to evaluate the needs of your users and what kind of security would be appropriate for the kind of application you are building. This is best done at the outset of a project during the design phase, so it can be tested and verified during development, and not as a last-minute rush job where holes and omissions might jeopardize your data or cause it to fall into the wrong hands.

Design Considerations

You need to evaluate each object or statement in relation to the roles or users who will be granted permissions on it. For example, granting all permissions on a payroll table to the Accounting role could be a really bad idea if you don't want all members of Accounting to see confidential salary information. In this situation, there are several ways you can protect the confidential salary data, depending on whether or not you want to restrict some or all members of Accounting from seeing the salary column:

- Grant permissions to the Payroll table to the Accounting role and exclude the salary column. This would not allow any members of Accounting to read salary data.

- Create two views: one that excludes the salary column and one that includes it. Grant permissions to individual users for the appropriate view. This will protect the salary information from users you don't want to see it, but it could be time-consuming to administer.
- Create a separate role, AccountingRestricted, deny permissions to the salary column for the role, and add those members of the Accounting group who you don't want to have access to the salary to the AccountingRestricted role. This gives you both security and flexibility since it is easy to administer. It will also protect the salary column from being read by those users in the future, no matter which roles they may be subsequently added to.

You also need to consider statement permissions when evaluating your security needs. Granting liberal statement permissions can potentially cause server-wide problems later. For example, you have granted CREATE DATABASE permissions to your Developers group under the assumption that they know what they are doing. Down the road a new developer is hired and experiments with various server options, including creating databases, using up all the hard-disk space on the server. There are several options you could consider for curbing this problem:

- Deny CREATE DATABASE permissions to the Developers role. This would have the effect that any member of Developers would be forever unable to create a new database, which could be too drastic. If you deny the permission to the new developer directly, you then have to remember to revoke the deny later when they know what they're doing. This could get tedious to administer if you do it more than once or if there are other statement permissions you want to deny trainees.
- Revoke CREATE DATABASE permissions to the Developers group. If certain members of Developers needed to create databases, you could create a new role and grant CREATE DATABASE permissions to it. The disadvantage of this technique would be that you would have two nearly redundant groups with many users in both to administer. Revoking the permission to the new developer directly wouldn't be a good idea in case they might inherit it from membership in another role.
- Create a new role, RestrictedDevelopers, and deny CREATE DATABASE permissions to the role. Add any members of the Developers group you don't want creating new databases to it. This has the advantage of flexibility since you can also restrict other permissions to the role and the new developer can be removed from the group at any time. You also avoid having two nearly redundant groups, since the trainees would likely be fewer in number than

the number of seasoned developers who could be trusted to create databases.

Examples and Scenarios

When planning security, you need to list all the items and activities that need to be restricted. Next, list all the groups and users who will need to access the database. Then you cross-reference the two lists to determine the appropriate levels of permissions for the various groups and users on the database objects and statements. If you are using NT Authentication, there may not be an exact match between the NT groups and the groups necessary to restrict data in your application, so you will need to create roles to assign users or groups to. The following examples will discuss some of the issues you need to consider when designing security.

NOTE There is no single, right way to implement security in a database. Each database application will be unique based on the sensitivity of the data, the needs of the users, and countless other factors. Don't expect to get it right the first time around. Implementing security on a complex database application will take time and adequate testing to ensure that a robust application is delivered. Test your security by giving it to others to break—don't trust yourself to test, since you may not be aware of all of the potential security holes your users will undoubtedly find.

Single-User Database

A single-user database is the easiest to implement. The assumption here is that one person will do everything: create objects and databases, work with data, and perform administrative chores on the server.

The first thing is to choose whether or not to use NT Authentication or SQL Server Authentication. If you choose NT Authentication, then the user will not have to log separately to SQL Server. Regardless of whether you use NT or SQL Server Authentication, once you add an account for this user, grant them membership in the sysadmin role and your job is done. Members of sysadmin have full permissions on the server and on any databases, objects, or statements.

Single-Location Company Database

An orders database for a small company in a single location is going to have more complex security needs than a single-user database. Your first consideration will be whether or not to use NT or SQL Server Authentication. NT Authentication will probably be best if there are already groups and users established that you can use. This will give you the most robust security, providing NT security has been set up correctly.

You then need to evaluate the groups and users relative to the tasks they need to perform. Then consider creating roles for the tasks and mapping the users and groups to the roles. Likely roles would include those listed in Table 16.3.

TABLE 16.3: Possible Roles for an Orders Database

Role	Tasks
Administrator	Perform backups, restores, archiving, and server maintenance.
Developer	Create new tables, views, stored procedures. Needs access to all objects.
Sales	Create new orders and view sales history.
Personnel	Work with employee data only.
Management	Read all data only.
Accounting	Work will all data, including payroll and accounting.

In addition to these roles, there might also be other roles, such as clerical workers in Accounting, who might have access to only a subset of the data. List out all the possible roles and then match them up with the actual tables, views, and procedures they need to have permissions for. If you design this process on paper first and verify it, it will save time later by acting as a blueprint when you go to implement security on your database.

TIP

Always design security around roles and never around individual users. This will save an enormous amount of time administering security since you won't have to worry about individual permissions. This holds true even if you only have one user assigned to a role. When that user leaves the company and a new user replaces them, all you need to do is remove the old user's account and add the new user to the role.

Distributed Corporate Database

If your database is going to be shared across multiple NT domains or across a WAN, then NT Authentication makes the most sense. In this case, you let NT handle the basic security chores of domain and user validation. You will then need to map your roles to users and groups the same way you would for the orders database listed above.

If you are using replication to share data, then you also need to take into consideration which users can set up and administer replication as well as which servers can participate in synchronization.

Securing a Database for the Internet

If you want to use a SQL Server database over the Internet, then you must use SQL Server Authentication. Users connecting to your SQL Server database will need to type in an ID and password and cannot be authenticated by their home server. As far as security goes, the Windows Sockets Net-Library has been enhanced to work with Microsoft Proxy Server and provide secure communication across the Internet. Proxy Server is tightly integrated with NT Authentication, so you can block access to restricted sites by ranges of IP addresses, domains, or individual users. You can use Proxy Server to prevent unauthorized users from connecting to your private network by controlling all the permissions and accesses to the listening port. This will protect any sensitive data you might have.

NOTE

See Skill 9, *Publishing SQL Server Data to the Web*, for more information on using SQL Server databases over the Internet.

Are You up to Speed?

Now you can...

- ☑ select the appropriate authentication mode for your security needs
- ☑ add login and user accounts to SQL Server
- ☑ create users, groups, and roles
- ☑ grant, deny, and revoke permissions to database objects and statements
- ☑ plan and implement security for a wide range of databases

SKILL 17

SQL Server Optimization and Configuration

- Optimize databases, tables, and queries
- Tune memory and manage stored procedures
- Retrieve and set configuration options
- Optimize data operations

As an application designer, your work doesn't stop with having a way to input and retrieve data that your users want to work with. You also need to make sure that the application runs quickly enough to be useful. In this skill, we'll look into some common ways that you can optimize your SQL Server applications.

Optimizing Your SQL Server Application

You need to think about optimizing your SQL Server application at the design stage, when you're first starting out. As you progress and build more objects, then you can think about optimizing individual parts of it, such as a query that doesn't perform well.

Designing an Optimized SQL Server Application

The first thing you need to consider when designing a SQL Server application is where you are going to locate the running code. Is most of the work going to be done by the application or the server? In most cases, the logical three-tier application development model is the one that makes the most sense for a SQL Server application, where the bulk of the code involving data services and business services resides on the server.

NOTE See Skill 12 for a complete discussion of three-tier application development.

No matter which object interface your application uses (OLE DB, ADO, RDO, or DAO) make sure you are using it effectively without creating unnecessary overhead and degrading performance. Use the SQL Server Profiler (which has replaced SQL Server 6.5's SQL Trace utility) to examine the traffic generated by your application. Sometimes merely tweaking an option or property in the object interface is all you need to optimize the number of extra commands that the interface is generating.

When designing your application, you want to take full advantage of the relational database model, which means starting off with a normalized database design. You may decide to denormalize later for a specific reason (such as your database is used primarily for decision support and reporting), but you should always selectively denormalize specific tables for a good reason rather than just starting out with unnormalized data. In general, normalization avoids the need to update the same data in multiple places and avoids introducing errors due to inconsistent data.

When you've designed and normalized your table structure, implement the data rules on the server to make them visible to all users of the database, rather than hiding them in application logic. This will guarantee that data integrity is enforced and that errors due to faulty application enforcement do not arise. Implement the following built-in features of SQL Server to automatically maintain data integrity:

- Utilize `CHECK` constraints to ensure valid column values.
- Implement `PRIMARY KEY` and `UNIQUE` constraints to guarantee uniqueness of rows.
- Use `IDENTITY` columns when you need to generate a unique row identifier.
- Use `DEFAULT` and `NOT NULL` constraints to make sure that necessary column values are entered.
- Implement `FOREIGN KEY` constraints to ensure that rows in dependent tables are not orphaned and always have a matching value in the master table.
- Use user-defined data types for consistent column definitions.
- Implement `TIMESTAMP` columns for concurrency checking between multiple user updates.

TIP

If you use `char` data types in columns where there will be null values, you should consider changing it to a variable-length `varchar` data type. Unlike previous versions, SQL Server 7 will use all of the space to store the value, even if it is null. Of course, if there are no nulls and if all the column values are the same length or the lengths don't vary by much, then fixed-length `char` columns will be more efficient.

TIP

Remember that you can now store character strings up to 8KB in length in `char` and `varchar` data types whereas you used to need to use the `image` data type. The `char` and `varchar` types are more efficient and give you more flexibility.

Retrieving Data

The first rule for efficient database performance is "Fetch only the data you need." Create `WHERE` clauses to restrict the number of rows returned and don't issue a `SELECT * FROM` statement—select only the columns you are going to use. You can avoid unnecessary network traffic by filtering data at the server rather than sending it to the client to be filtered. Data that is fetched needs to be buffered by the application, which may not be able to handle an unrestricted load. In addition, buffering large amounts of data that the user isn't going to use is a waste of time and resources.

Make sure that you utilize the right kind of cursor for the work that you are doing. Use a server cursor when you need to fetch a small subset or block of rows from a large result set. SQL Server fulfills each block request as needed and does not hold locks between block fetches on server cursors. You can also use server cursors for positioned updates.

If you are going to use all the results from a `SELECT` statement, then use a default result set instead of a server cursor. A default result set requires a single round trip between the server and the client, whereas multiple calls to fetch individual blocks of rows from a server cursor will result in multiple round trips.

You can also take advantage of the advanced features of the SQL language itself to manipulate data efficiently. A single advanced SQL statement is going to perform certain tasks more efficiently than multiple simple SQL statements combined with application logic. Some of the advanced features of SQL you can use include these:

- Create an `UPDATE` statement to modify rows in one table based on related values in other tables.
- Utilize `JOIN` capabilities, such as `INNER`, `CROSS`, `LEFT OUTER`, `RIGHT OUTER`, and `FULL OUTER`.
- Create subqueries to be used in expressions.
- Utilize the `CASE` syntax for conditional logic.
- Use the `CUBE` and `ROLLUP` functions to produce multidimensional aggregates.

Some other tips for optimizing data include these:

- Make sure that you commit transactions as soon as possible. Since SQL Server uses page locks for most operations, you want to make sure to release those locks as quickly as possible to minimize impact on other users.

- You can also use statement batches to send multiple SQL statements to the server at one time, minimizing the number of round trips to the server.
- Use parameter arrays for repeated operations by calling `SQLBindParameter` and `SQLSetStmtAttr`.
- Use stored procedures, which are compiled into an optimized execution plan. This can save a significant amount of time when executing.
- Create indexes appropriately.

Optimizing Databases

SQL Server 7 boasts a more direct relationship between the server and the Windows file system, which results in greater scalability and robustness. Earlier versions of SQL Server used the concept of a device and a segment on top of the operating system files, whereas SQL Server 7 consists of two or more files, each file being used by only one database. Files cannot be shared by multiple databases.

A SQL Server database will have at least two files: a data file and a log file. The transaction log is very different from earlier versions in that it consists of one or more log files, each containing a contiguous set of log records. Unlike earlier versions, the log file isn't represented as a system table and its data pages don't compete for space in the memory cache with the pages of other tables. The new design is more robust and enables more data to be logged without degrading performance.

Databases can now automatically grow in size. When you create a database, you can specify a growth increment and maximum size. Or you can have the database autogrow as needed by not specifying a maximum size. In this case the database can grow until it has filled all available space on the disk. This cuts down on the need for a system administrator to manage the database size. See Skill 2, *Managing Databases*, for more information on initializing your databases.

You can also distribute your data over multiple physical disk drives to improve performance, which is called striping. The data is striped across multiple physical devices using NT's disk management facilities to achieve maximum throughput. NT also offers RAID (redundant array of independent disks) levels to protect against the failure of a hard disk.

RAID

RAID, which is available only on Windows NT, is a disk system that comprises an array of multiple disk drives to improve performance, reliability, and storage capacity. There are six RAID levels, each of which uses a different algorithm to implement fault tolerance.

You can use the following to protect against data loss and improve performance:

- Hardware-based RAID above level 0
- Windows NT–based disk striping and striping with parity
- Windows NT–based disk mirroring and duplexing

For more information on RAID, striping, and mirroring, see Books Online and your Windows NT documentation.

If your database spans multiple servers, you might want to consider replication to move data between servers. See Skill 14, *Using Replication*, for more information on replication.

Partitioning Data

Partitioning data consists of splitting a large table into smaller tables, thus improving performance for data retrieval, backup, and rebuilding indexes. You don't necessarily have to physically place each table on its own individual disk drive. You can improve query performance by placing one table on one drive and its related tables on a separate drive. Queries involving joins between the two tables utilize multiple disk heads to read the data at the same time. You can use filegroups (discussed next) to specify disk placement.

Hardware Partitioning

Hardware partitioning lets you optimize your database based on the available hardware. For example, multiprocessors allow many queries to execute at the same time through multiple threads of execution. Or parallel multiple processors can run a single query faster by scanning separate tables by different threads.

You can also get faster data access with a RAID device, which allows data to be striped across multiple disk drives with more read/write heads accessing the data at the same time.

Horizontal Partitioning

Horizontal table partitions break a table into multiple tables with identical columns but fewer rows. For example, a large table of sales data could be broken out by region, date, or other criteria, depending on how the data is analyzed. If you do this, you'll have less flexibility later on if you want to summarize sales data by some other criteria. You'd want to avoid later having to create a bunch of Union queries to join tables so that you can summarize data by some criteria other than the ones you initially split them up on.

Vertical Partitioning

Vertical table partitions break a table into multiple tables with fewer columns in each table. Normalizing your data naturally gives you a certain level of vertical partitioning when you break out redundant data into lookup tables joined by primary and foreign key relationships. You can also split rows arbitrarily so that, instead of one table with many columns, you end up with two tables with fewer columns related one-to-one with each other. This can speed up query performance in some situations but not always if the partitions are very large, since analyzing data from multiple partitions requires additional queries to join them back together again.

Using Filegroups

You can create filegroups to group database files together to improve query performance and to support parallel queries by placing data and indexes on filegroups located on specific disk drives. Filegroups placed on separate disks can each have their own disk controller. This speeds things up considerably, especially if the computer has multiple processors and can perform parallel data scans. You can create a table on a specific filegroup rather than the default filegroup. You can also create `text`, `ntext`, and `image` columns on a filegroup other than the one that contains the base table. All of these strategies allow you to increase the parallelism of retrieving stored data.

You can also back up and restore individual files or groups rather than backing up and restoring an entire database. No database file can be a member of more than one filegroup. All pages in tables, indexes, `text`, `ntext`, and `image` data are allocated to the filegroup that you specify.

You can't specify log files as part of a filegroup—log space is managed separately. The two types of filegroups are:

- The default filegroup contains the primary data file and any other files not put into other specified filegroups. The system tables are part of the default filegroup, as are pages for tables and indexes that are not part of user-defined filegroups.
- User-defined filegroups, which you can specify by using the FILEGROUP CREATE DATABASE or ALTER DATABASE statements.

You can create an additional filegroup using the Enterprise Manager when you create a database by entering a second filename under the default filename, as shown in Figure 17.1, and filling in a new name under the File Group option. Click the builder button next to the filename to locate the file in a specific directory, as shown in Figure 17.2. Note that you can also specify a different file for the transaction log by clicking on the Transaction Log tab.

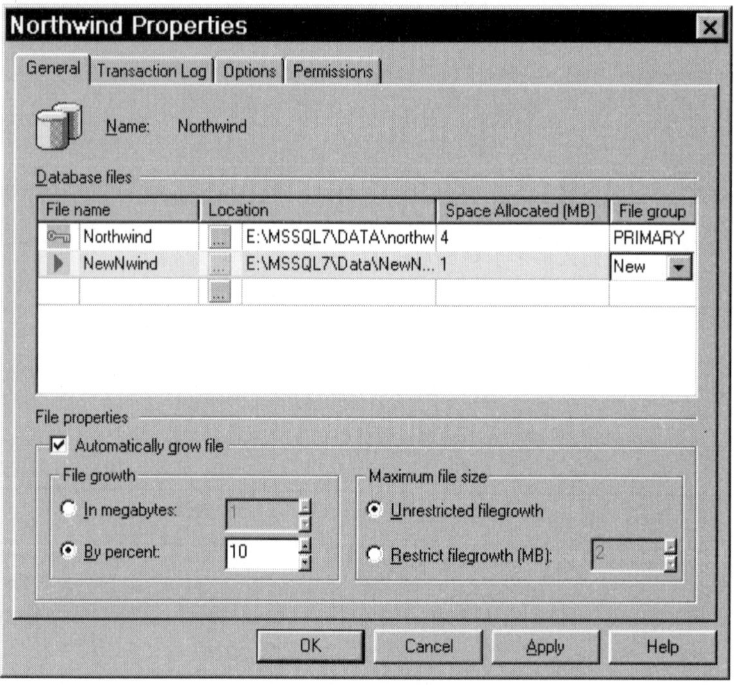

FIGURE 17.1: Creating a new filegroup

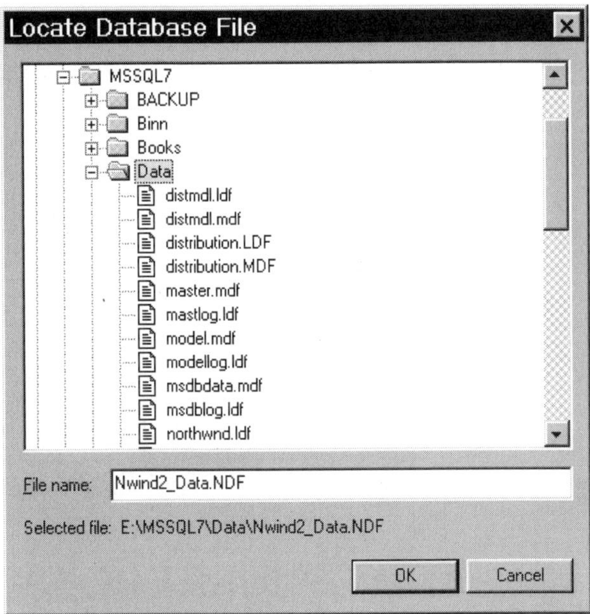

FIGURE 17.2: Locating the filegroup

To create a new table on a filegroup using the Enterprise Manager, create the table normally and optionally specify the filegroup by selecting it in the Properties dialog box. You can bring up the Properties dialog box by right-clicking or choosing the toolbar button, as shown in Figure 17.3.

To place an existing table in a different filegroup, right-click the table and select Design Table. From here on you will use the same steps as placing a new table on a filegroup—bring up the Properties dialog box and fill in the filegroup name.

You may find that you don't need to create filegroups; performance is adequate as it is. If so, then all files are included in the default filegroup, with SQL Server allocating data within the database.

The default filegroup needs to be large enough to hold all of the system tables as well as any other tables not contained in user-defined filegroups. If you turn off autogrow or the disk runs out of space, the default filegroup won't be able to add new catalog information to the system tables. User-defined filegroups can also run out of space. If this occurs, turn autogrow back on or delete other files on the disk to free up enough space.

Skill 17

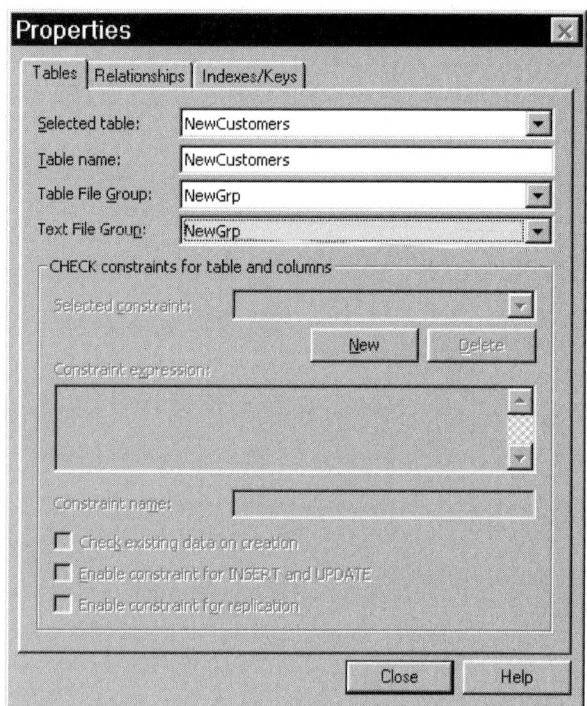

FIGURE 17.3: Placing a table on a filegroup

You can use Transact-SQL to create a table on a filegroup by using a `CREATE TABLE` statement with an `ON` clause, as shown here. This creates a LocalCustomers table on the NewGrp filegroup:

```
CREATE TABLE NewCust
(
    CustID int, CustName varchar(20)
)
ON NewGrp
```

You can also create a non-clustered index on a different filegroup from the one the table resides on. This can give you performance benefits since data and index information can be read in parallel by multiple disk heads, providing of course that the filegroups can make use of different physical drives with their own controllers. Your safest bet is to spread tables and indexes across all available filegroups since you can't predict the timing or type of data access that will take place. This guarantees that all disks are being accessed and simplifies administration.

You can move a table from one filegroup to another by creating a clustered index for that table on a different filegroup. You can then drop the old table, leaving the table in its new filegroup.

WARNING If you use multiple filegroups to split tables and indexes, they must all be backed up together and then you must create a transaction log backup. Otherwise you may never be able to restore from the backup since not all of the indexes would be backed up.

Verifying Database Integrity with DBCC

The DBCC (database consistency checker) utility allows you to verify that your database is consistent. You should use the `DBCC CHECKCATALOG` statement as part of your regular maintenance routine to check the logical and physical consistency of your database. `DBCC` checks for consistency in and between system tables. The syntax is:

```
DBCC CHECKCATALOG [('database_name')]
[WITH NO_INFOMSGS]
```

The `CHECKCATALOG` statement makes sure that every data type in syscolumns has a matching entry in systypes and that every table and view in sysobjects has at least one column in syscolumns. The `database_name` argument is the database being checked, and the `WITH NO_INFOMSGS` argument suppresses the display of informational messages (error messages will still be displayed).

You would use the following syntax to run DBCC on the pubs database:

```
DBCC CHECKCATALOG pubs
```

The following is the output from the `DBCC` statement where there are no errors:

```
DBCC results for 'pubs'
DBCC execution completed. If DBCC printed error messages, contact your
system administrator.
```

For more information on DBCC, see Skill 15, *Administering a Server*.

Optimizing Tables

The best course of action to optimize tables is a good, normalized database design. As noted above:

- Utilize CHECK constraints to ensure valid column values.
- Implement PRIMARY KEY and UNIQUE constraints to guarantee uniqueness of rows.
- Use identity columns when you need to generate a unique row identifier.
- Use DEFAULT and NOT NULL constraints to make sure that necessary column values are entered.
- Implement FOREIGN KEY constraints to ensure that rows in dependent tables are not orphaned and always have a matching value in the master table.
- Use user-defined data types for consistent column definitions.
- Implement timestamp columns for concurrency checking between multiple user updates.

Optimizing Queries

The query processor in SQL Server 7 supports new execution strategies and parallel query execution, using an improved costing model and new plan selection techniques, which allow it to choose from a larger set of execution plans. The net result for the developer is an increase in speed for the processing of complex queries and support for very large databases.

Another new feature in SQL Server 7 is that the system database tempdb expands automatically as needed by any query that requires a large amount of temporary space. However, that doesn't always guarantee optimal performance. It's often not enough to add memory or processors or to tune the server to cure performance problems. You need to analyze the queries and application as well as analyzing updates the application is submitting to the database and how they interact with the database schema. Slow query performance can be caused by the following:

- Slow network communications
- Insufficient memory at the server
- Not enough available memory overall

- Lack of or outdated statistics
- Lack of useful indexes
- Lack of useful data striping

When troubleshooting query performance problems, you also need to make sure that the problem isn't due to other components such as a slow network, which can be detected by using the Performance Monitor.

There are several tools that will help you gather information to allow you to determine how a query is being executed and which indexes are being utilized. Use the SQL Server Profiler to help nail down your slow queries. You can also use the `SET` statement to enable the `SHOWPLAN`, `STATISTICS IO`, and `STATISTICS TIME` options. The `SHOWPLAN` option describes the method chosen by SQL Server when the query optimizer retrieves data. The `STATISTICS IO` option reports information on number of scans and logical and physical reads for each referenced table. The `STATISTICS TIME` option displays the milliseconds required to parse, compile, and execute the query. You can also turn on the Graphical Execution Plan option in the SQL Server Query Analyzer. All this information will help you determine if you can improve performance by rewriting the query, changing the indexes, or modifying the database design.

Query Statistics

Monitor your queries using the SQL Server Profiler or the Graphical Execution Plan in the Query Analyzer and make sure that your queries have enough statistics and are up to date. Queries are up to date if no `UPDATE` operations have taken place. Statistics regarding the distribution of values in a column are created automatically on indexed columns, but you can also create them manually on unindexed columns. Statistics are used by the query processor in determining the optimal strategy for executing a query, and the additional statistics on non-indexed columns involved in join operations can improve performance.

Analyzing Queries

The SQL Server Query Analyzer allows you to query SQL Server databases. In addition, you can view a graphical representation of the query's execution plan, view the results in a table-like grid, view statistics about an executed query, or execute multiple Transact-SQL scripts and stored procedures. In addition, you can obtain online help both for the Query Analyzer and for Transact-SQL. Many previous limitations have been removed, such as table limitations—a query can now reference up to 32 tables and an unlimited number of internal work tables.

To analyze a query and see a graphical representation of its execution plan, click Query and select Display Execution Plan, as shown in Figure 17.4. Note that you can select different query elements by clicking to see additional statistics.

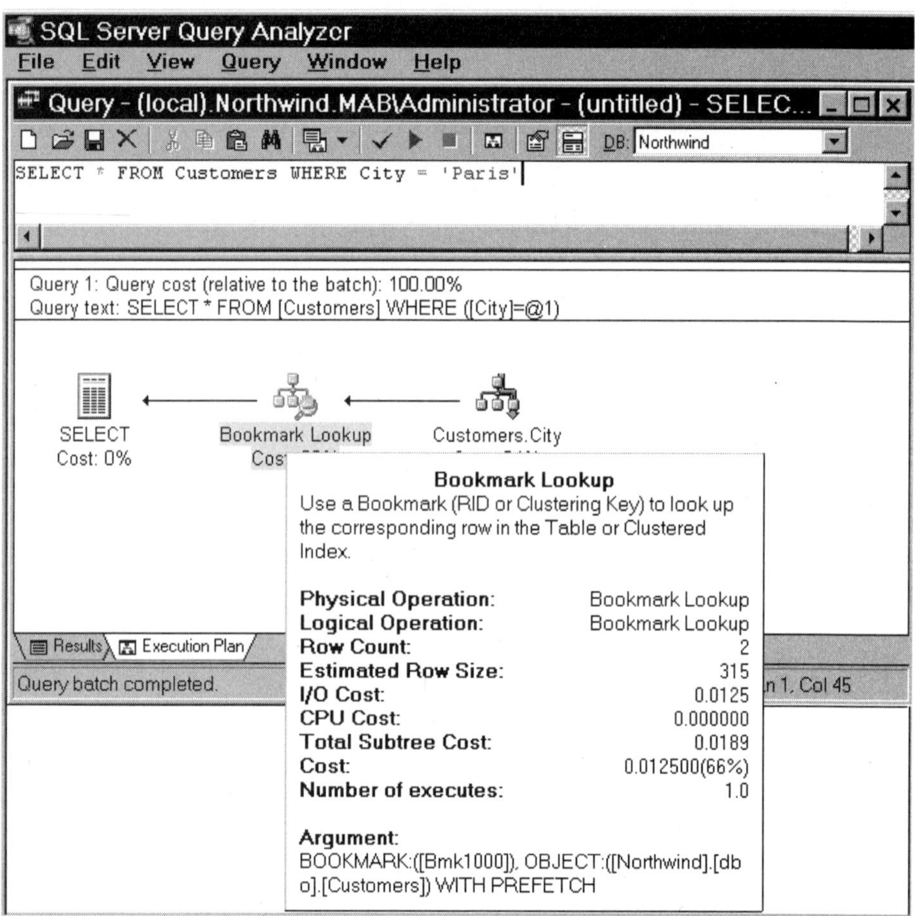

FIGURE 17.4: The SQL Server Query Analyzer execution plan

The Transact-SQL statements `SHOWPLAN_TEXT` and `SHOWPLAN_ALL` are used to produce statement and query execution plans. When `SHOWPLAN_TEXT` or `SHOWPLAN_ALL` is set, queries and statements are not executed. Instead, the server returns a result set that is the detailed query execution plan as a set of rows. These rows are a tabular representation of a tree structure. The Showplan tree structure uses one row for each node in the tree. Either option pauses query execution and shows information about the query instead. Use the information returned in the results to rewrite your queries to optimize SQL Server performance. When you're done, setting SHOWPLAN_ALL OFF will resume normal query execution.

```
SET SHOWPLAN_ALL ON
GO
SELECT * FROM Customers
GO
```

The output looks like this:

```
StmtText
-----------------------
SET QUOTED_IDENTIFIER OFF
SET ANSI_NULLS ON
 SET ANSI_PADDING ON
 SET ANSI_WARNINGS ON
 SET STATISTICS PROFILE ON

(4 row(s) affected)

StmtText
-----------
SET SHOWPLAN_ALL ON

(1 row(s) affected)

StmtText
--------------
SELECT *
FROM Customers

(1 row(s) affected)

StmtText
------------------------------
  |-Clustered Index
Scan(OBJECT:([Northwind].[dbo].[Customers].[PK_Customers]))

(1 row(s) affected)

StmtText
---------------
SET STATISTICS PROFILE OFF

(1 row(s) affected)
```

Displaying the Query Execution Plan

When you display the execution plan, the query is not actually executed, just analyzed, and the results display how the statements would have been executed as a series of operators. The icons are shown in Tables 17.1 and 17.2. This works for individual DML and Transact-SQL statements as well as compile-time information about stored procedures, triggers invoked by a batch, and the called stored procedures and triggers invoked to an arbitrary number of calling levels. The query execution plan uses icons to represent SQL Server's execution of specific statements and queries.

If you analyze a series of statements that create objects, such as tables, subsequent statements involving those objects will return errors because the objects don't actually exist yet.

TABLE 17.1: Graphical Showplan Icons for Physical Operators

Icon	Physical operator
	Assert
	Bookmark Lookup
	Clustered Index Delete
	Clustered Index Insert
	Clustered Index Scan
	Clustered Index Seek
	Clustered Index Update
	Collapse

TABLE 17.1 CONTINUED: Graphical Showplan Icons for Physical Operators

Icon	Physical operator
	Compute Scalar
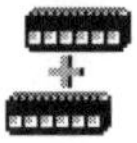	Concatenation
	Constant Scan
 T-SQL	Deleted Scan
	Filter
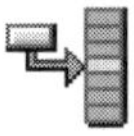	Hash Match
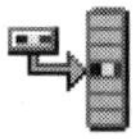	Hash Match Root
	Hash Match Team
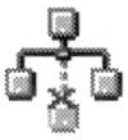	Index Delete
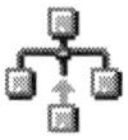	Index Insert
	Index Scan
	Index Seek
	Index Spool
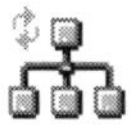	Index Update
 T-SQL	Inserted Scan

TABLE 17.1 CONTINUED: Graphical Showplan Icons for Physical Operators

Icon	Physical operator
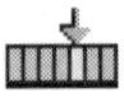	Log Row Scan
*	Merge Interval
	Merge Join
	Nested Loops
	Parallelism
	Parameter Table Scan
	Remote Delete
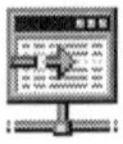	Remote Insert
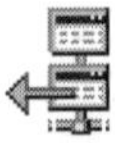	Remote Query
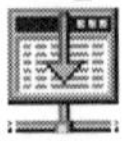	Remote Scan
	Remote Update
	Row Count Spool
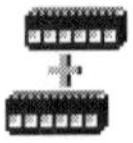	Sequence
	Sort
*	Split

TABLE 17.1 CONTINUED: Graphical Showplan Icons for Physical Operators

Icon	Physical operator
	Stream Aggregate
	Table Delete
	Table Insert
	Table Scan
	Table Spool
	Table Update
	Top

*Not all icons were available at this writing.

TABLE 17.2: Graphical Showplan Icons for Cursors

Icon	Cursor physical operator
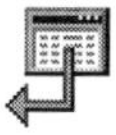	Dynamic
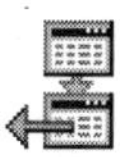	Fetch Query
	Keyset
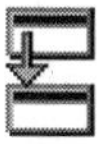	Population Query
	Refresh Query
	Snapshot

The graphical execution plan output is read from left to right and from top to bottom, showing the query or statement order of execution in a tree structure. The icons represent logical and physical operators used in each part of the query as different nodes in the tree structure. Rules with arrowheads connect each node to its parent node in the tree. The tree structure is determined by the type of statement being executed. Figure 17.5 shows the graphical execution plan output for a more complicated query against the pubs database.

NOTE If a query contains multiple statements, then an execution plan for each statement is drawn.

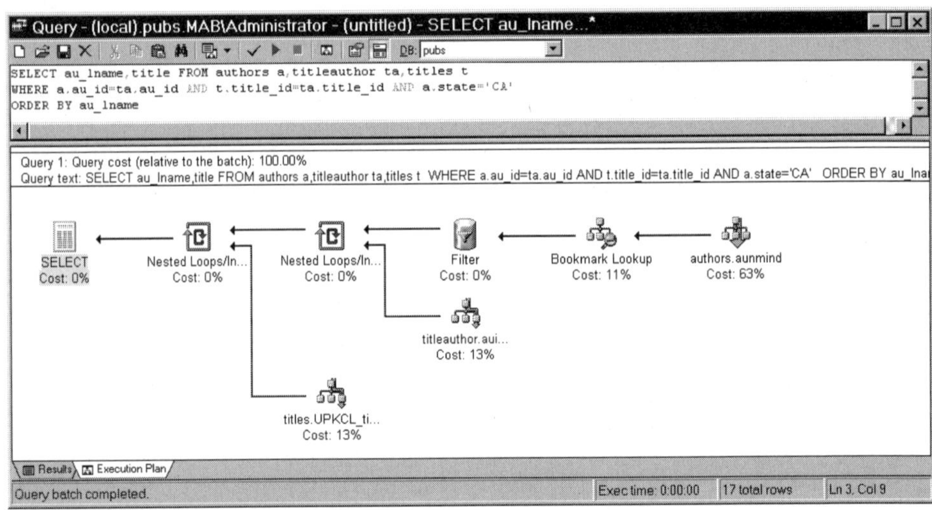

FIGURE 17.5: The graphical execution plan of a complex query

Tuning Queries

No matter what you do, there will always be those queries that are resource-intensive and take a long time to execute. For example, queries with highly non-unique `WHERE` clauses and those returning large result sets are intrinsically costly. Here are a few suggestions for tuning:

- Add more memory.
- Add more processors. Multiple processors can make use of parallel queries.
- Rewrite the query so that it's not so complex or doesn't return so many rows.
- If you are using cursors, see if you could use a more efficient cursor type or do away with cursors altogether. Some cursors can be replaced by `GROUP BY` or `CASE` statements or by using a subquery.
- Place any loops inside the query, not the application. This will cut down on round trips between the application and the server. Make use of temp tables to replace loops where the body of the loop contains a parameterized query.
- Don't use multiple aliases for a single table to simulate index intersection. SQL Server automatically considers index intersection and can make use of multiple indexes on the same table in the same query.
- Don't use query hints unless you've tested them first. The query optimizer will likely come up with a better execution plan.
- Set query options with the query governor to prevent long-running queries from executing. You can set the maximum number of seconds that a query is allowed to execute. The default value of zero means that all queries are allowed to take as long as they need to run. You can change the value using the `sp_configure` stored procedure or the Enterprise Manager. The setting change takes place immediately. To change the query governor cost limit option using the Enterprise Manager, right-click the server and click Properties. Click the Server Settings tab. Under Server Behavior, select or clear Use Query Governor To Prevent Queries Exceeding Specified Cost. In the box (shown in Figure 17.6), specify a non-zero, non-negative value, which the query governor will use to disallow execution of any query that has a running length exceeding that value.

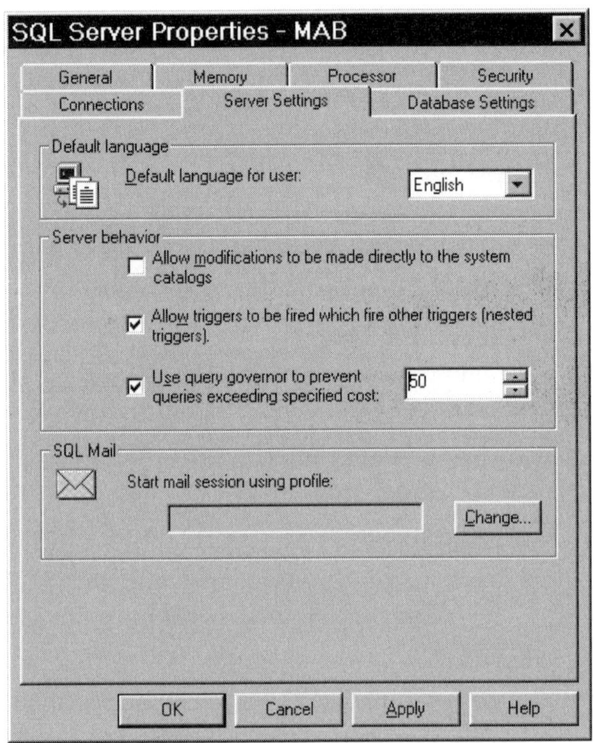

FIGURE 17.6: Changing the query governor cost limit option

Index Tuning

One of the things you can do to improve the performance of your database is to utilize efficient index design. The SQL Server Query Optimizer's job is to select the most efficient index for any given query. So your design strategy should be to provide a good selection of indexes for it to use, when doing so will result in optimal performance. However, using indexes incorrectly can result in worse performance, not better, so the Query Optimizer may not use an index if it will negatively affect performance.

When you create indexes, you should observe some of the following guidelines:

- Use one statement when writing a query to update rows, rather than multiple queries updating the same rows.
- Once you've written your queries, analyze them with the Index Tuning Wizard, discussed below.
- When you create a clustered index, use an integer key column and set it to be a unique, non-null, or identity column.
- Create indexes on all columns used in queries.
- Don't create indexes on columns with few unique values.

The Index Tuning Wizard is available to help you analyze your queries and suggest efficient indexes. SQL Server ships with the Index Tuning Wizard, which allows you to create indexes without having to know a whole lot about the structure of the database, the hardware components, and how applications interact with it.

The Index Tuning Wizard has the following capabilities:

- Allows you to use the Showplan cost formula to compare, contrast, and select indexes
- Uses a trace file or SQL Script to recommend a set of indexes
- Analyzes index use and cost
- Graphically displays the effect of a recommended index configuration
- Allows you to implement the recommended configuration
- Provides scheduling capabilities to implement indexes either immediately or as a batch

To use the Index Tuning Wizard, select Tools ➢ Wizards ➢ Management ➢ Index Tuning Wizard. The introductory screen tells you that the wizard will assist you in identifying the server, database, and workload to analyze, to select the tables to tune, to analyze the data, to make recommendations, and to implement them. The second wizard dialog box asks you to select the server and database it's going to use, as shown in Figure 17.7. Note that you can also elect to keep all existing indexes and to perform an exhaustive analysis of the workload.

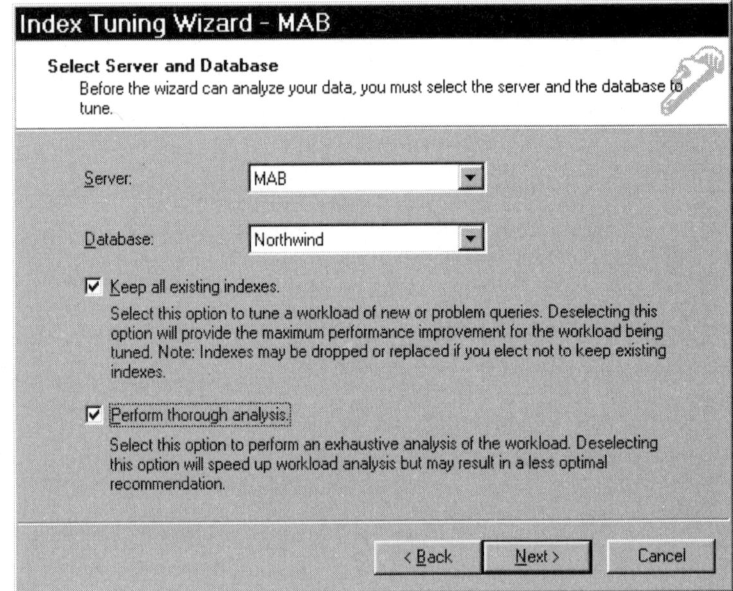

FIGURE 17.7: Selecting the server and database using the Index Tuning Wizard

The next wizard screen prompts you for a trace file. If you don't already have one, select the option to create one on your own. This will open the SQL Server Profiler. You'll have to start the wizard again after you create the trace. Choose File ➢ New Trace from the menu. You can then fill in the trace properties, as shown in Figure 17.8.

Figure 17.9 shows the dialog box for selecting events that you want to trace. There are also additional tabs for selecting Data Columns and Filters.

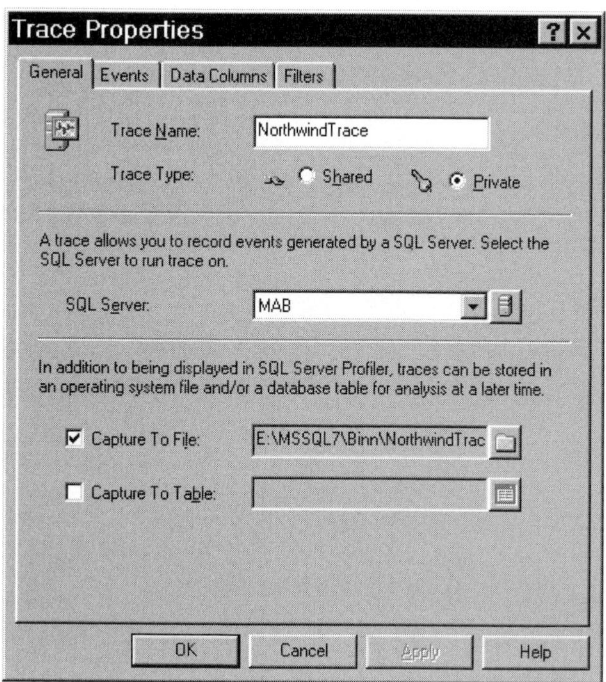

FIGURE 17.8: Filling in trace properties

Once you've created the trace, it will start running. You can close down the profiler and start the Index Tuning Wizard over again. Once you get past the introductory screens, designate the workload file you just created, as shown in Figure 17.10. The Advanced button allows you to set a maximum number of queries to tune (the default is 32,767) and to specify the maximum amount of space for the recommended indexes and the maximum columns per index.

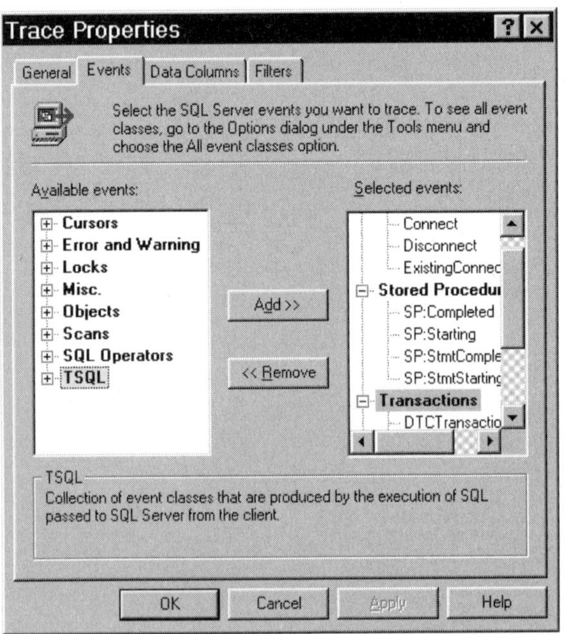

FIGURE 17.9: Choosing events for the trace

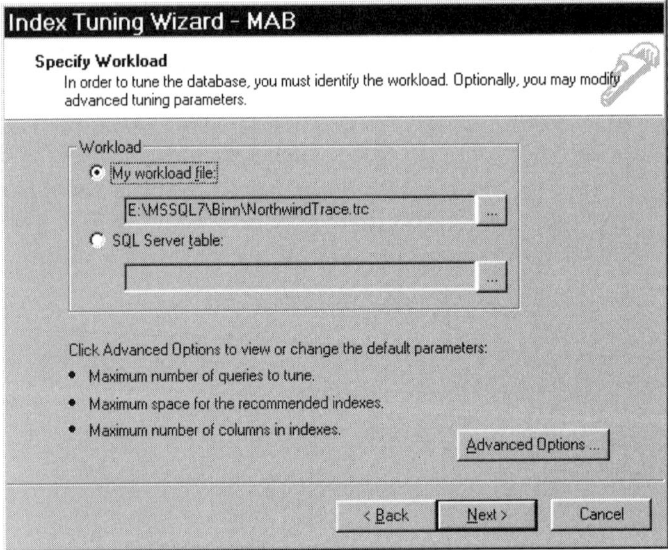

FIGURE 17.10: Specify the trace file in the Index Tuning Wizard

The next dialog box allows you to select the tables to analyze. All of the tables are selected by default, as shown in Figure 17.11.

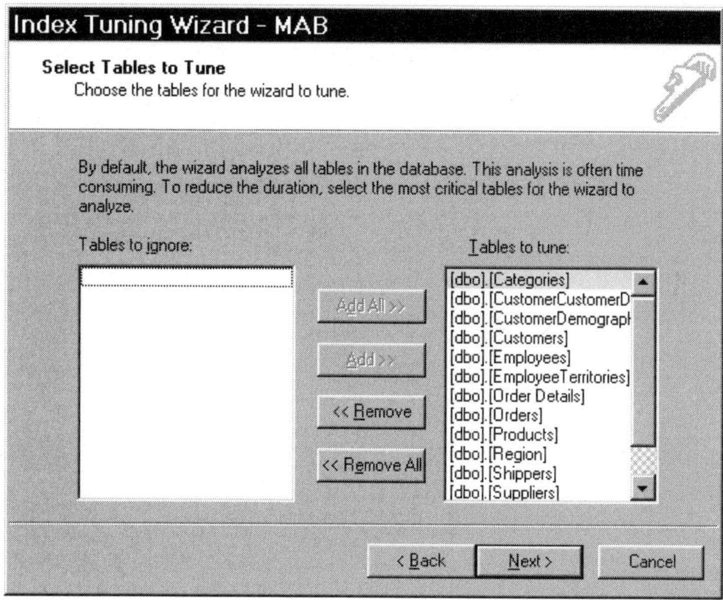

FIGURE 17.11: Selecting the tables to tune in the Index Tuning Wizard

The index tuning wizard will then present its index recommendations, which are shown in Figure 17.12. Clicking on the Analysis button will show the reports that the Index Tuning Wizard creates, as shown in Figure 17.13. You can save them to a tab-delimited text file for later use.

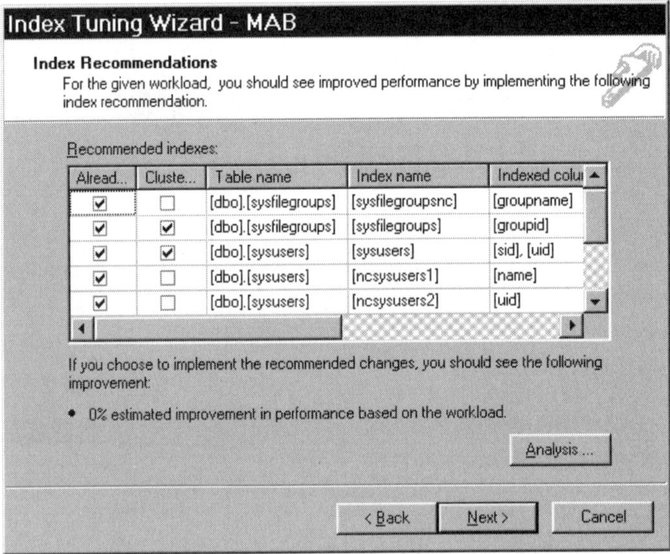

FIGURE 17.12: The Index Tuning Wizard's recommendations

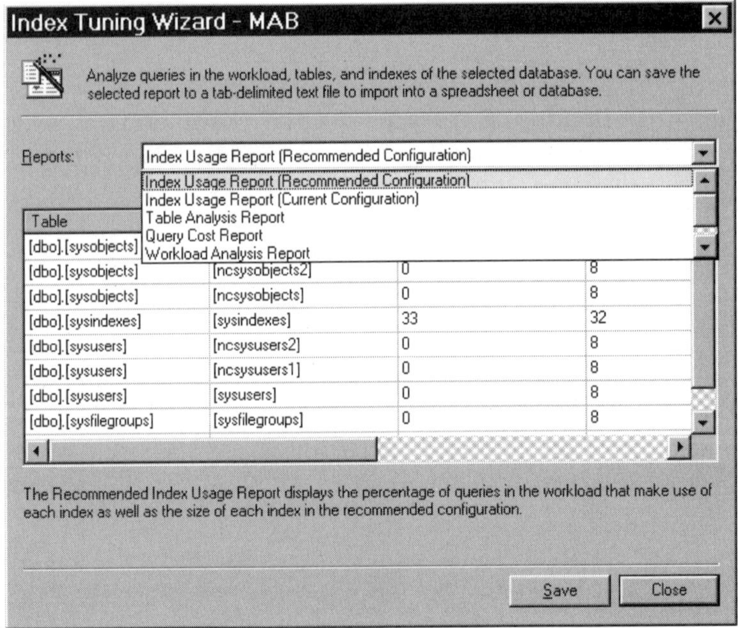

FIGURE 17.13: Reports created by the Index Tuning Wizard

The next wizard dialog box then prompts you to apply the changes (which you can schedule for a later time) or to save a script file, as shown in Figure 17.14. Clicking on the Finish button on the final Index Tuning Wizard dialog box will complete the process and implement the changes.

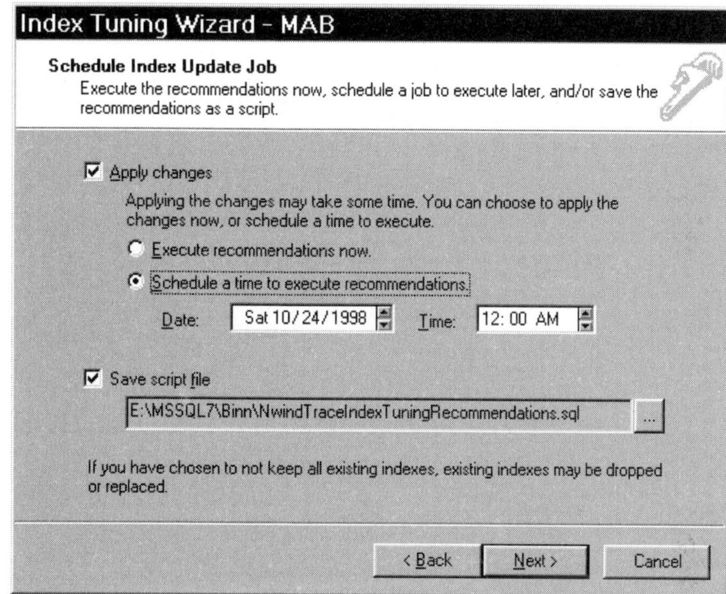

FIGURE 17.14: Scheduling the Index Tuning Wizard's recommended changes

Optimizing Application Performance

One thing you can do right off the bat to improve application performance with SQL Server is to ask for less data with a restrictive `WHERE` clause that limits the amount of data returned to the application. This will filter the data at the server, while reducing network traffic. Also, avoid selecting unnecessary columns (`SELECT * FROM...`), which requires the server to return all column data whether or not your application actually requires it.

Use stored procedures in place of queries stored in your application to save processing time while executing. A client execution request to a stored procedure is more efficient than a Transact-SQL statement sent directly to the server.

Processing data on the server is almost always faster than moving data to the client to perform the processing.

If you are using ODBC, make sure that you set query options correctly prior to executing the query. If you leave statement options set to their defaults, SQL Server will calculate the most efficient way to send the data.

Make sure that your application buffers any rows from a default result set that are not used immediately but may be needed later. Don't be tempted to request a default result set and to fetch rows from the server only as needed—this can tie up the connection to the server and block other work in the same transaction. The server will hold locks on the unfetched rows, preventing other users from updating the data.

Take time to user-proof your application as follows:

- Create forms that do not allow users to fill in options to generate long-running queries and do not allow user input within a transaction.
- Allow for query cancellation by the user. Make sure to issue the required number of `ROLLBACK` and `COMMIT` statements, since merely canceling a query does not automatically roll back or commit a transaction or free up locks.
- Set query and lock timeouts in the application to prevent long-running queries and avoid distributed deadlocks. Once the client application requests locks, the SQL Server lock manager will hold them until they are released by the application, blocking other transactions.
- Keep transactions as short as possible.
- Manage connections efficiently.
- Test the application with the full projected concurrent user load—problems that won't show up during preliminary test may emerge once you've loaded all the data and start banging on it with the full contingent of users.
- Use server-side block cursors for situations where the user wants to select specific rows from a large result set. This allows SQL Server to fulfill each block request as needed without holding locks between fetches.
- Use server cursors for positioned updates or to delete a fetched row.

TIP

Server cursors are generally more expensive than a default result set since a default result set requires only one round trip to the server—each block fetch requires a separate round trip. Dynamic cursors require a primary key or unique index while keyset and static cursors use up temporary storage at the server. Use a default result set when you need to fetch a single row by primary key and a server cursor when you need to fetch rows in reasonably sized blocks.

Transactions

Keep your transactions as short as possible since long-running transactions do not scale well when there are many users. Running a transaction causes the database to hold locks on shared resources until it commits, locking out other users and increasing the chances of a deadlock.

NOTE

Deadlocks occur when two or more users have locks on separate objects and each wants a lock on the other's object. Each waits (in vain) for the other to release their lock. When this happens, neither transaction can release the locks they hold until they commit or roll back, but they can't do either because they require a lock held by the other transaction in order to continue.

The following are some hints to speed up transactions:

- Commit changes as soon as possible. Break up large transactions into smaller ones so that changes are committed as quickly as possible and locks are released.
- Use statement batches to send multiple Transact-SQL statements to the server, reducing the number of network round trips to the server.
- Use the ODBC `SQLParamOptions` function to allow parameter arrays for repeated operations. This lets you have multiple parameter sets for a single Transact-SQL statement sent to the server as a batch, reducing the number of network round trips to the server.
- Use the SQL Server Profiler to capture calls sent from client applications to SQL Server. You may find some unexpected application overhead due to unnecessary calls to the server, as well as opportunities for placing statements being sent separately in batches.

Configuring and Tuning the Server

SQL Server boasts configuration options that have been considerably streamlined and simplified. The server automatically and dynamically adjusts its memory and lock resource usage by default, increasing allocated resources when necessary, without over-committing, and decreasing resource usage when no longer needed. You can usually run SQL Server out of the box without changing the default settings for server components unless you have a special situation, such as adding a new server or changing network connections. We'll discuss manually setting server options in this section.

Setting Configuration Options

SQL Server also lets you manually adjust configuration options using the Enterprise Manager. However, you should modify only one option at a time and test the results by restarting the server so that you can easily reverse the change if there's a problem or if it doesn't perform as anticipated.

To display and manage configuration options using the Enterprise Manager, follow these steps:

1. Right-click the server you want to configure and click Properties. This will bring up the dialog box shown in Figure 17.15.
2. Click the tab of the option you want to set. The following are the available option tabs:
    - General—Sets autostart properties and specifies any startup parameters
    - Connections—Sets maximum concurrent users, default connection options, and remote server connections
    - Memory—Configures the amount of memory used by SQL Server
    - Server Settings—Sets the default language, server behavior, and SQL Mail session profile
    - Processor—Specifies which processors will be used, maximum worker threads, and the number of processors to use for parallel execution of queries
    - Database Settings—Sets default index fill factors, backup and restore options, and recovery interval
    - Security—Sets the authentication mode and startup service account

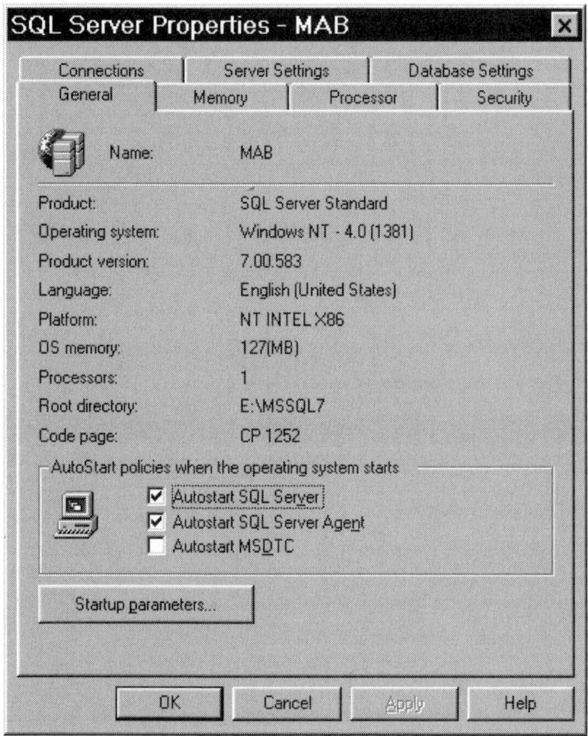

FIGURE 17.15: Setting configuration options

3. Select and change the appropriate configuration option and then click OK.
4. Restart SQL Server if necessary.

You can also use `sp_configure` system stored procedure to configure advanced systems options. The syntax is:

```
sp_configure [[@configname=]'name'] [,[@configvalue=] 'value']
```

TIP Use the `RECONFIGURE WITH OVERRIDE` statement with `sp_configure` for the change to take place immediately. Otherwise, the change won't take effect until after you restart the server.

The available configuration options are listed in Table 17.3. Advanced options are marked with an *A*, self-configuring options are marked with *SC*, and options requiring a server restart are marked with *RR*.

TABLE 17.3: Configuration Options

Configuration option	Minimum	Maximum	Default
affinity mask (A, RR)	0	2147483647	0
allow updates	0	1	0
cost threshold for parallelism (A)	0	32767	5
cursor threshold (A)	–1	2147483647	-1
default language	0	9999	0
default sortorder id (A, RR)	0	255	52
extended memory size (A, RR)	0	2147483647	0
fill factor (A, RR)	0	100	0
index create memory (A)	704	1600000	1216
language in cache (RR)	3	100	3
lightweight pooling (A, RR)	0	1	0
locks (A, RR, SC)	5000	2147483647	0
max async IO (A, RR)	1	255	32
max degree of parallelism (A)	0	32	0
max server memory (A, SC)	0	2147483647	2147483647
max text repl size	0	2147483647	65536
max worker threads (A)	10	1024	255
media retention (A, RR)	0	365	0
min memory per query (A)	0	2147483647	1024
min server memory (A, SC)	0	2147483647	0
nested triggers	0	1	1
network packet size (A)	512	32767	4096
open objects (A, RR, SC)	0	2147483647	500
priority boost (A, RR)	0	1	0
query governor cost limit (A)	0	2147483647	0
query wait (A)	0	2147483647	600

TABLE 17.3 CONTINUED: Configuration Options

Configuration option	Minimum	Maximum	Default
recovery interval (A, SC)	0	32767	0
remote access (RR)	0	1	1
remote login timeout	0	2147483647	5
remote proc trans	0	1	0
remote query timeout	0	2147483647	0
resource timeout (A)	5	2147483647	10
scan for startup procs (A, RR)	0	1	0
set working set size (A, RR)	0	1	0
show advanced options	0	1	1
spin counter (A)	0	2147483647	0, 10000
time slice (A, RR)	50	1000	100
Unicode comparison style (A, RR)	0	2147483647	196609
Unicode locale id (A, RR)	0	2147483647	1033
user connections (A, RR, SC)	0	32767	0
user options	0	4095	0

To use `sp_configure` to change options, use the following syntax:

```
USE master
EXEC sp_configure 'recovery interval', '3'
RECONFIGURE WITH OVERRIDE
```

Optimizing Server Performance

For the most part, you can let SQL Server automatically tune most of the server configuration options by leaving them set to their default values. If you feel it's necessary, you can configure the following components:

SQL Server memory: Set the minimum server memory, maximum server memory, maximum worker threads, and index create memory configuration options.

I/O subsystem: Set the maximum asynchronous IO and recovery interval configuration options.

NT options: Set NT options to maximize throughput, configure server tasking, and configure virtual memory.

You can use the SQL Server Performance Monitor counters to determine if an adequate amount of memory is allocated. If an inadequate amount of memory is allocated to the data cache, then the server will read data from disk, which is much slower.

NOTE Use Windows NT Performance Monitor to track SQL Server page faults. Click Add Data and update the following: in the Object box, select Process; in the Counter box, select Page Faults/sec; and in the Instance box, select SQLSERVER.

To load the Performance monitor, choose Programs ➢ Microsoft SQL Server 7 ➢ Performance Monitor, from the Windows Start menu. This loads the Performance Monitor, as shown in Figure 17.16.

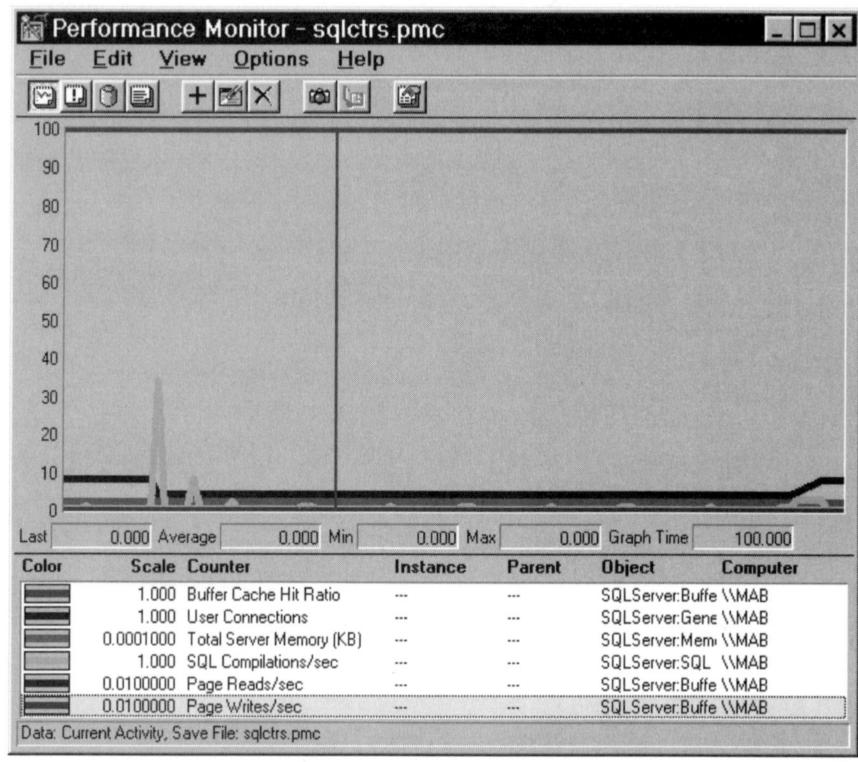

FIGURE 17.16: The SQL Server Performance Monitor

You can use the Performance Monitor to view the performance of various objects and to do the following:

- View and dynamically change charts reflecting current activity. Display counter values that are updated at a frequency you define.
- Simultaneously view data from any number of computers and create log files containing data about objects on different computers.
- Export data from charts, logs, alert logs, and reports.
- Add system alerts that list events in the alert log and notify you either by reverting to Alert view, logging the event in Event Viewer's application Log, or issuing a network alert.
- Run a predefined program in response to counter values going over or under a value you define.
- Form archive logs by appending selected sections of existing log files to a single file.
- View current-activity reports or create reports from existing log files.
- Save individual chart, alert, log, and report settings, or save the entire workspace setup.

You can add objects and counters to the chart by choosing Edit Add To Chart from the Performance Monitor menu. This will bring up the dialog box shown in Figure 17.17. Expand the Object drop-down list for a list of objects to add, and expand the Counter list to add new counters.

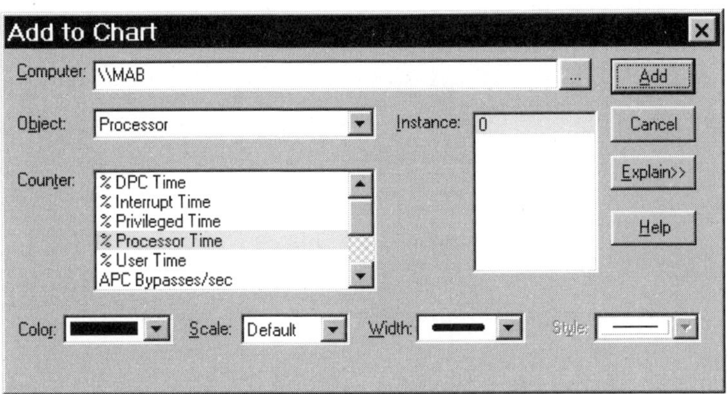

FIGURE 17.17: Adding objects and counters to the SQL Server Performance Monitor

Are You up to Speed?

Now you can...

- ☑ design an optimized application
- ☑ use Showplan to optimize queries
- ☑ use filegroups
- ☑ use DBCC
- ☑ set configuration options and tune memory
- ☑ use the SQL Server Performance Monitor

APPENDIX A

Installing SQL Server

This appendix will walk you through installing and, if necessary, uninstalling SQL Server 7.

Prerequisites

In order to install SQL Server, your computer must meet certain hardware and software requirements, as shown in Table A.1. The disk space requirements are the maximum required—your computer may already share components with other programs.

TABLE A.1: Hardware and Software Requirements for Installing SQL Server 7

Item	Requirement
Computer	DEC Alpha and compatible systems.
	Intel or compatible (Pentium 166MHz or higher, Pentium PRO, or Pentium II).
Memory (RAM)	Enterprise Edition: 64MB minimum.
	Other Editions: 32MB minimum.
Disk drive	CD-ROM drive.
Hard disk space	SQL Server 180MB (full).
	SQL Server 170MB (typical).
	SQL Server 65MB (minimum).
	SQL Server 90MB (management tools only).
	OLAP Services 50MB.
	Microsoft English Query 12MB.
Operating system	Enterprise: Microsoft Windows NT Server Enterprise Edition version 4 or later with SP4 or later.
	Standard/Small Business: Windows NT Server 4 or later with SP4 or later, Microsoft BackOffice Small Business Server, or an operating system listed above.
	Desktop/Management Tools only: Windows NT Workstation 4.0 or later with SP4 or later, Microsoft Windows 95/98 (or an operating system listed above).

TABLE A.1 CONTINUED: Hardware and Software Requirements for Installing SQL Server 7

Item	Requirement
Internet software	Microsoft Internet Explorer version 4.01 with SP1 or later.
Network software	Windows NT or Windows 95/98 built-in network software. Additional network software is not required unless you are using Banyan VINES or AppleTalk ADSP. Novell NetWare client support is provided by NWLink.

NOTE The installation instructions in this appendix were correct at the time of writing. Changes may have been made, however, with the final release of the product.

Services User Accounts

SQL Server, SQL Server Agent, and the Distributed Transaction Coordinator need to be assigned to a Windows NT user account in order to run. You can assign a single local system account or a domain account to all three services. If you assign a local system account, which has no network access rights, SQL Server will be restricted from interacting with other servers. Interactions include remote procedure calls, replication, backing up to network drives, joins involving remote data sources, and SQL Mail. If you assign a domain account, it must:

- Be a member of the Administrators local group
- Have a password that does not expire
- Log on as a service
- Have service rights set on the SQL Server computer with all logon hours allowed

Network Protocols

SQL Server Setup installs all of the Net-Libraries onto the computer and allows you to configure the ones you need. The network libraries are DLLs that perform network operations required by specific IPC mechanisms. You can change these configurations at any time by running the SQL Server Network Utility. By default, SQL Server listens on the standard pipe, \\.\pipe\sql\query, for Named Pipe

Net-Library connections. You can change this or drop it later to listen only on other Net-Libraries.

The TCP/IP Sockets Net-Library allows SQL Server to communicate by using standard Windows Sockets as the IPC method across the TCP/IP protocol. Windows 95/98 uses this method, so if you are installing on Windows and set SQL Server to listen on TCP/IP, type the TCP/IP port number in the Port number box. The default is 1433, which is the socket number assigned to SQL Server by the Internet Assigned Number Authority (IANA). If you set SQL Server to listen on a proxy server using Microsoft Proxy Server over TCP/IP Sockets, type the proxy server address in the Remote WinSock proxy address box when you set up the TCP/IP Sockets Net-Library.

Before You Install...

If you're upgrading, it is a good idea to back up an existing SQL Server 6.*x* before you start. In addition, you should shut down all services, including those dependent on SQL Server, the NT Event Viewer, and Regedt32.exe. You should already have created a domain user account and be logged on to the system under a user account with administrative privileges.

TIP

Before installing, perform a dry run, going through the setup program without finishing. This will give you an idea of the questions you will be asked so that you can make the appropriate selections when you run the setup program for real. Make sure to press the Cancel button and not the Finish button when you've reached the last screen!

You need to decide on a character set, sort order, and Unicode collation options before you start. Changing it later is a big hassle since you will need to rebuild any databases and reload the data. Your character set, sort order and Unicode collation options should be consistent across all of your servers in order to ensure that server-to-server activities complete successfully.

TIP

For detailed information on selecting the character set, Unicode collation, and sort order that is appropriate for your installation, see Books Online. You can read it from the installation CD before installing SQL Server.

Installation Options

There are many options open to you when installing SQL Server. Some of them determine which other options are available later on.

- Name, Company, and Serial Number. Use the name of the person who will be administering the server as well as the product ID.
- Convert Existing Data. If you have existing SQL Server 6.*x* data, you can automatically run the Upgrade Wizard when the install completes. If you say no, you can always run the wizard later.

There are three types of installations you can choose from:

- Typical
- Compact
- Custom

Typical is recommended for most users. It installs all of the SQL Server management tools and documentation. It does not include full-text search, development tools, or samples.

Compact is recommended for computers with only the minimum available disk space. It installs the bare minimum configuration necessary to run SQL Server, with none of the SQL Server management tools or documentation.

Custom is recommended for expert users and allows you to change any or all of the default options, such as:

- Install upgrade tools
- Install replication support
- Install full-text search support
- Install client management tools
- Install online documentation
- Install development tools
- Install samples
- Set character set
- Set sort order
- Set Unicode collation
- Install network protocols

Components

The following SQL Server program files can be installed:

- The SQL Server relational engine, core tools, bcp, isql, osql, ODBC, and DB-Library (required)
- The SQL Server Upgrade Wizard
- Support for replication
- Full-text search

The following management tools can be installed:

- The Enterprise Manager, used to administer the server
- The Profiler, used to monitor database activity
- The Query Analyzer, which allows you to enter Transact-SQL
- MS DTC (Microsoft Distributed Transaction Coordinator), used to extend database transactions across multiple servers
- The Replication Conflict Resolver
- The Client Connectivity component, which is used to communicate between clients and servers and includes the network libraries for ODBC, OLE DB, and SQL-DMO
- Online Documentation, including Books Online, Quick Tour and What's New

The following development tools can be installed:

- Header files and libraries (`*h` and `*.lib`) needed for developers creating programs using ODBC, DB-Library, Open Data services, SQL-DMO, Embedded SQL for C, and MS DTC
- The Virtual Device Interface DLLs required to back up and restore from a virtual device

You can choose to install any or all of the following:

- DBLIB (DB-Library)
- DTS (Data Transformation Services)
- ESQLC (Embedded SQL for C)

- MS DTC (Microsoft Distributed Transaction Coordinator)
- ODBC (Open Database Connectivity)
- ODS (Open Data Services)
- OLEAut (OLE Automation)
- Repl (Replication)
- SQL-DMO (SQL Distributed Management Objects)

Unattended Installation

You can create a setup initialization file to run the SQL Server Setup program without being prompted. This is useful if you need to do multiple installations with the same options. You can also use Microsoft Systems Management Server 1.2 to perform unattended installations if you are running Windows NT.

The files you need are located on the SQL Server to both install and uninstall SQL Server, as shown in Table A.2. You can also create custom setup initialization (`.iss`) files to automate any set of installation options.

TABLE A.2: Files Needed for Unattended Installation

Command file	Initialization file	Action
`sql70ins.cmd`	`sql70ins.iss`	Installs a typical installation of SQL Server.
`sql70cli.cmd`	`sql70cli.iss`	Installs the SQL Server management tools
`sql70rem.exe`		Removes SQL Server

To run an unattended installation, use the following syntax from the command prompt:

```
start /wait D:\x86\setup\setupsql.exe -f1C:\InstallScripts\
➥SQL7.iss -SMS -s
```

The `-f1`*`<initialization file path>`* argument selects an unattended setup initialization file. Do not use a space before the file path.

The `start /wait` command, together with the `-SMS` option, return control to the command prompt only after SQL Server Setup finishes.

The `-s` flag causes the Setup program to run in silent mode with no user interface.

The setup initialization file specifies all the options you might choose when installing SQL Server. There are three of them included on the installation CD, which you can edit. You can also create a new setup initialization file if you need other initialization options. You can also create a custom command file to point to your initialization file.

Take the following steps to create a custom command file:

1. Open `SQL70ins.cmd` in Notepad.
2. Change the current `.iss` file path after each instance of the `setupsql` command to point to a custom setup initialization file.
3. Save the file with the `.cmd` file extension.

If you use SMS 1.2 to automatically install SQL Server on multiple servers, you can use the `Smssql70.pdf` file included on the CD. This will automate creating a SQL Server package in SMS. `Smssql70.pdf` includes instructions for running the three setup command files included on the SQL Server compact disc. To run a custom command file that you have created, make a copy of `Smssql70.pdf` and edit it to run your command file.

Run SQL Server Setup

Installing SQL Server is very easy if you've done your homework and figured out which options you need. Place the CD in the drive and select whether you are installing the Database Server – Full Product, the Desktop Edition, SQL Server 7 OLAP Services, or English Query, as shown in Figure A.1.

The next dialog box asks whether you will be installing to a local machine or to a remote machine. Select the appropriate option for your install.

After the usual license agreements and filling in your name, company name, and serial number, select whether you wish a Typical, Minimum, or Custom installation, as shown in Figure A.2. Selecting Custom will let you choose which components you want to install. For example, Full-Text Search is not a default for a typical install. You can also choose a different destination folder for the program and data files than the ones suggested by clicking the Browse button.

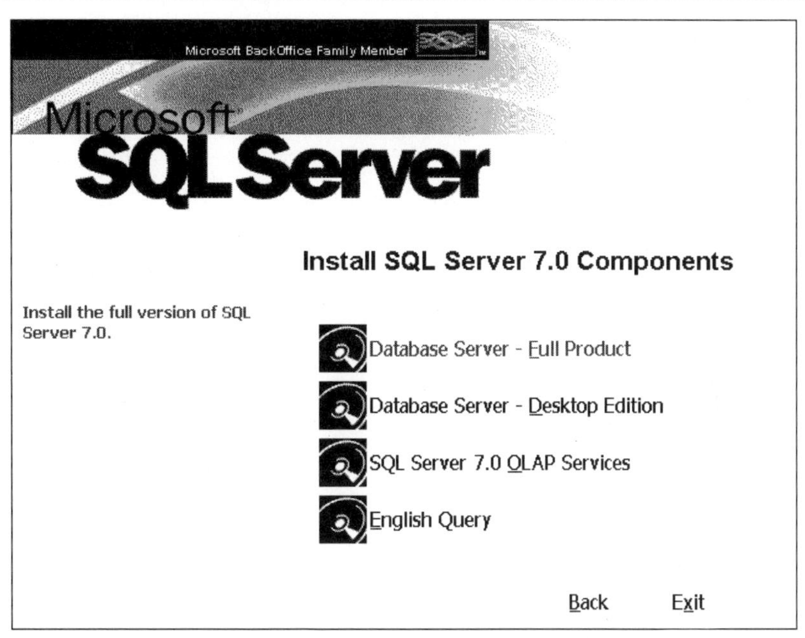

FIGURE A.1: Select which SQL Server components to install.

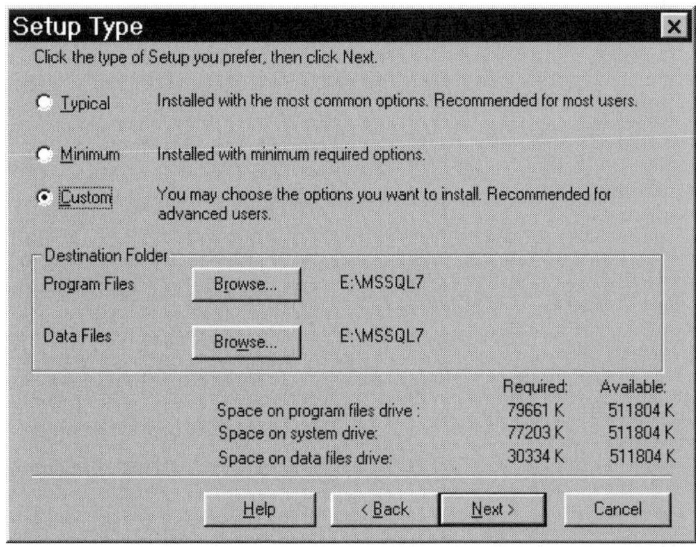

FIGURE A.2: Selecting a Typical, Minimum, or Custom installation

You can now select the components you wish to install, as shown in Figure A.3. We've selected all available components here.

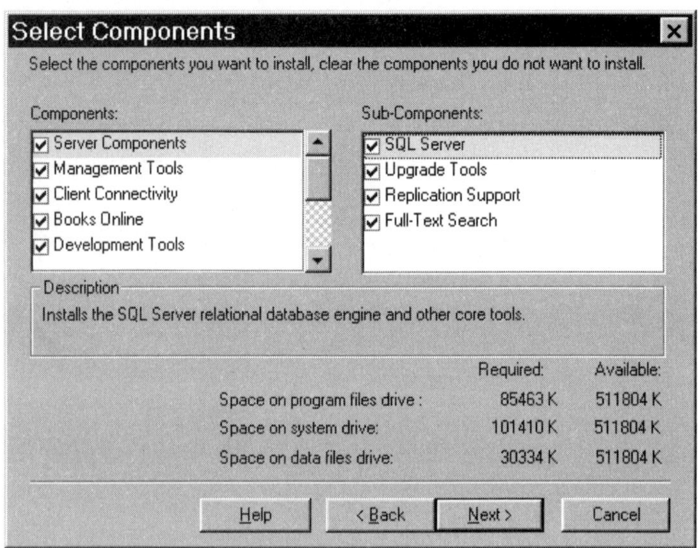

FIGURE A.3: Selecting components

The next dialog box allows you to set the options for the character set, sort order, and Unicode collation, as shown in Figure A.4.

The next dialog box allows you to set the network libraries you will be using, as shown in Figure A.5.

Figure A.6 shows setting up the SQL Server Services Accounts for all services or separate accounts for SQL Server and SQL Agent. You can choose either an NT domain user account or a local system account. SQL Server will then map the accounts you have specified.

After you set the services accounts, there will be an additional dialog box to allow you to backtrack and confirm your settings before continuing on with the install. Once all the files have been copied, you will be prompted to restart your computer.

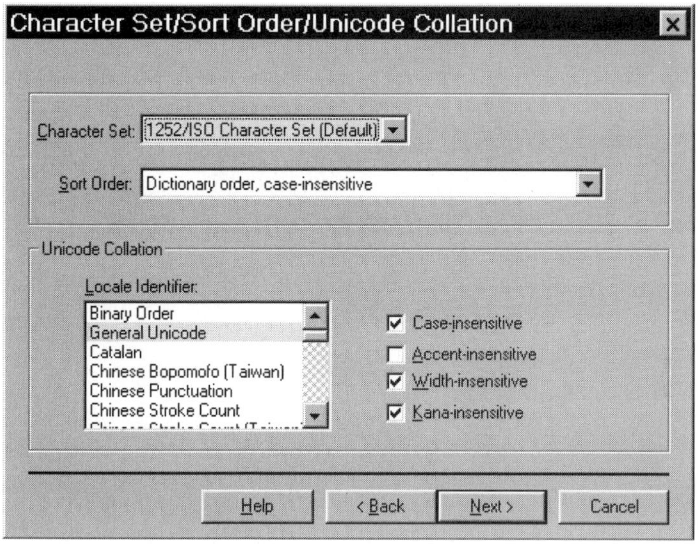

FIGURE A.4: Character set, sort order, and Unicode collation options

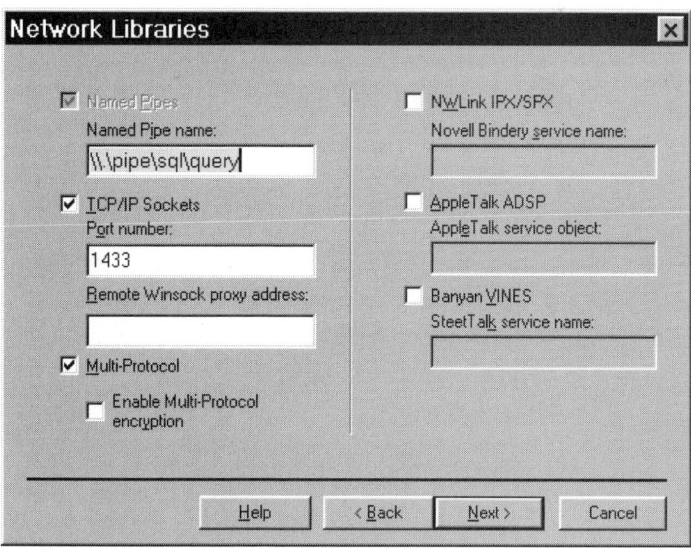

FIGURE A.5: Network library options

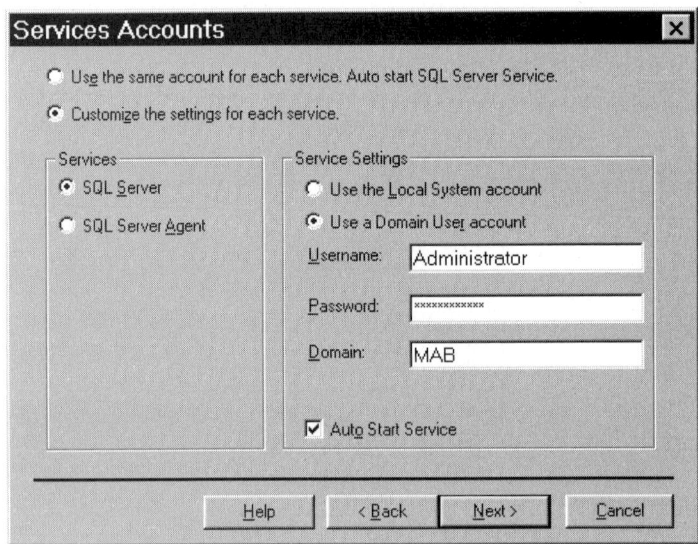

FIGURE A.6: Setting SQL Server Services Accounts

Upgrading from Previous Versions of SQL Server

Upgrading from SQL Server 6.*x* is a breeze with the SQL Server Upgrade Wizard. However, you have to know what the prerequisites are for upgrading and be familiar with the available upgrade options and their possible consequences for your SQL Server 6.*x* databases before you proceed.

Prerequisites

The only versions of SQL Server that you can upgrade are 6.0 and 6.5. If you have an earlier version, you must upgrade it to either 6.0 or 6.5 before you start. You also must have Windows NT version 4 with Service Pack 4 already installed or later in order to upgrade.

SQL Server requires about 148MB of disk space. However, if you plan on upgrading, you will need at least 200MB of free disk space available on the computer where the server is located. You should also review the other hardware and software requirements listed for installing SQL Server.

See the sidebar "Calculating Disk Space Needed for Upgrading" for more information on space requirements.

Shut down SQL Server and make sure that replication is stopped and that the log is empty. Set the system administrator's default database to master. It's also a good idea to back up the database in case something goes wrong and you need to revert to the old version.

If you are running Windows NT Server, then you can install the full product. If you are running Windows NT Workstation, Windows 95, or Windows 98, you must install the Desktop Edition.

Set `tempdb` to at least 10MB on the SQL Server 6.*x* you are upgrading to prevent the upgrade objects scripts from causing the upgrade process to fail.

TIP

If you are upgrading a replicated database, make sure to upgrade the Distributor before upgrading the other servers. Sphinx replication is designed to support existing SQL Server 6.5 publishers and subscribers in addition to Sphinx replication servers, although you won't be able to take advantage of many of the new features until you have upgraded all of the servers in your replication topology.

Calculating Disk Space Needed for Upgrading

The SQL Server Upgrade Wizard will examine the current SQL Server 6.*x* installation and estimate how much disk space is necessary to upgrade to SQL Server 7. This is only an estimate, not an exact requirement. The Database Information Utility will estimate the size of the SQL Server 7 databases and logs and the amount of disk space required for `tempdb`. To run the Database Information Utility, follow these steps:

1. On the Start menu in SQL Server 7, click SQL Server Upgrade Wizard.

continued

2. Click Next.
3. Click Named Pipe, then click Next.
4. In Export server (6.*x*), in the Server Name box, enter the name of the local or remote computer on which SQL Server 6.*x* resides.
5. In the Administrator Password ('sa') box, enter the sa password for SQL Server 6.*x*, then click Next.
6. Unless you have changed it, the system administrator password for SQL Server 7 is blank.
7. Include the databases to upgrade. Move any database not to be included in the disk space estimation to the Exclude list, and then click Next.
8. Click Use the Default Configuration or Edit the Default, then click Edit.
9. The SQL Server Upgrade Wizard layout utility appears, showing the proposed layout of the SQL Server 7 data files.
10. Click Advanced.
11. Click an object in Proposed 7.0 database layout to view details in Object details.
12. The Drive summary field shows the estimated size of all of the SQL Server 7 data files and the free disk space left on all of the local fixed disks. On the Options menu, select "Freespace includes 6.*x* files" to view the free space that would exist if the SQL Server 6.*x* data files were deleted.
13. Click Accept to return to the Database Creation dialog box and Cancel to exit.

Upgrade Checklist

Make sure you have completed the following tasks before upgrading your existing SQL Server 6.*x* application:

- Back up your existing databases so that you can restore them if necessary.

- Install the latest SQL Server Service pack if you use replication.
- Set `tempdb` to at least 25MB in your SQL Server 6.*x* installation.
- Set the memory option to an appropriate amount in your SQL Server 6.*x* installation. Do not set the memory option to use much more than half the available memory.
- Ensure that all database users have logins in the master database, which holds system logins.
- Stop replication and make sure that the log is empty.
- Shut down all applications, including all services dependent on SQL Server.
- If you copied your SQL Server 6.*x* databases to a new computer to perform the upgrade, you may need to update the new 6.*x* master database.
- Change references from the earlier server name to the current server name in the 6.*x* master database.
- Update the device file locations in the SQL Server 6.*x* master database.
- Install SQL Server 7.
- Make sure that you upgrade all databases with cross-database dependencies.
- Assign a username and password to the MSSQLServer service in your SQL Server 6.*x* and SQL Server 7 installations, instead of using the local system account.

You can install SQL Server 7 on the same machine with SQL Server 6.*x*, but don't install it in the same directory.

The SQL Server Upgrade Wizard Upgrade Options

The SQL Server Upgrade Wizard will take care of most of the drudgery of upgrading for you. But before you upgrade, familiarize yourself with the available options. Some options depend on how you install SQL Server 7 and thus determine other options. There are two ways the upgrade can take place:

- Side-by-side on a single computer. The upgrade takes place on a single computer using a disk-to-disk named pipe connection, tape drive, or network share to transfer data. If you have enough disk space you can use a direct pipeline. If not, the Version Upgrade Wizard can export the old catalog data, objects, and databases to a tape backup or network share while you reclaim the disk space occupied by SQL Server 6.*x*. The Version Upgrade Wizard can then import and upgrade the catalog data, objects, and databases into SQL Server 7.

- From one computer to another. Install SQL Server 7 on one computer and connect to the computer with the existing SQL Server 6.*x* installation. The upgrade uses a named pipe connection, tape drive, or network share to transfer the data.

TIP

If you are upgrading from one computer to another, both computers must be in the same network domain.

Whether you are on one computer or two, you will need to identify both the import server and the export server. The import server will always be the name of the computer on which you are running the Upgrade Wizard. The export server will be the name of the SQL Server 6.*x* server. It defaults to the computer you're running the wizard on, but you can change it if necessary.

TIP

If you are upgrading a replication server, you must use the side-by-side single computer method.

There are two data transfer methods that SQL Server can use:

Named pipe This gives the best performance and is the most reliable. However, it takes more disk space.

Tape backup Use this when you're low on disk space. The Upgrade Wizard will back up the SQL Server 6.*x* databases, then delete all of the 6.*x* devices before creating the SQL Server 7 data files.

WARNING

The Upgrade Wizard will delete all of the SQL Server 6.*x* devices, not just the ones being upgraded.

NOTE Both the tape backup option and the named pipe option use the default named pipe, //./pipe/sql/query.

VERIFICATION

The Upgrade Wizard creates output logs in case any of the objects could not be imported due to errors or compatibility problems. In addition, the wizard will validate successful object data transfer in 6.*x* before the upgrade and in the SQL Server 7 database after the upgrade by creating and comparing lists of all objects, including the number of rows in each table, security, schema, and stored procedures. It will also perform a checksum for each column in every table both before and after the upgrade to verify that data values have not changed.

The Upgrade Wizard does not report any differences in objects that are there by design. For example, certain stored procedures might not import due to errors in the objects or compatibility problems. These errors are reported in the SQL scripts that show the source code of the objects, the error messages received from SQL Server 7 when it tries to create them, and also in the output of the verification process.

Databases and Log Files

You don't need to upgrade all of your databases at once; you'll be presented with a list and you can choose to upgrade some databases at a later time. The master and msdb databases are not explicitly selected for upgrading. If you run the Upgrade Wizard again after some of your databases have been upgraded, the previously upgraded ones will default to the excluded list. You can move it back to be included if you want to upgrade it a second time.

There are three options for creating the SQL Server 7 database and log files:

1. Use the default database configuration where the Upgrade Wizard estimates how much space is necessary to hold the objects and data and

creates database files of the estimated sizes. The wizard also creates a log file for each database twice the size of the total of all log segments allocated to the database in SQL Server 6.*x*.

2. Use the databases and logs that you have already created in SQL Server 7. The Upgrade Wizard will not create any user databases—you must create the necessary databases and logs before you start.

3. Provide a SQL script file that the wizard can use to create the necessary user databases and logs.

Database Options

Remember that data may take up more disk space in SQL Server 7 than it did in SQL Server 6.*x*. The wizard estimates this growth. You can edit the default configuration of the SQL Server 7 database in the wizard. You can change:

- The name and path
- The initial size of the file
- Whether the file can autogrow or remain a fixed size, as well as the autogrow increment
- The maximum size

Configuration Options

There are several configuration options in the master database that you can upgrade as well:

- SQL Server 7 server configuration for login and remote login registrations and server configuration options. SQL Server 6.*x* configurations that are not used in SQL Server 7, or are not recommended to be set to non-default values, are not transferred.
- All replication settings, such as articles, subscriptions, and publications of each selected database, plus the distribution database, are transferred and upgraded.
- All scheduled SQL Executive tasks are transferred and upgraded so that SQL Server 7 can run them in SQL Server Agent.

ANSI Nulls

There is a difference in the way SQL Server 6.*x* and SQL Server 7 handle the `ANSI_NULLS` option, which controls both database default nullability and comparisons against null values. In 6.*x*, the `ANSI_NULLS` option in objects is resolved during query execution; in SQL Server 7, it is resolved when the object is created. You must explicitly choose the setting you want for all objects in the databases you are upgrading so that the Upgrade Wizard can create them using the setting you have chosen. If you enable `ANSI_NULLS` in SQL Server 7, the comparison operators `EQUAL` (=) and `NOT EQUAL` (<>) always return `False` when one of its arguments is null. If you disable `ANSI_NULLS`, then these operators return `True` or `False` depending on whether both arguments are null.

Quoted Identifiers

SQL Server uses the `QUOTED_IDENTIFIER` setting to determine whether double quotation marks (") delimit a character string (the `OFF` setting), or an identifier (the `ON` setting). You might need quotes delimiting an identifier such as a column name with spaces or punctuation in it. An example would be the following statement:

```
SELECT "x" from T
```

If `QUOTED_IDENTIFIER` is on, then x is a column; if it's off, x is the constant string x and equal to the letter x. `QUOTED_IDENTIFIER` takes its behavior according to how the option was set when the object was created—changing `QUOTED_IDENTIFIER` later does not change the behavior of a previously created stored procedure. When the Upgrade Wizard re-creates database objects in SQL Server 7, it creates them with the `QUOTED_IDENTIFIER` setting you specify, either On or Off. If you're not sure and think you may have a mixture, then click Mixed. With this setting, the Wizard will first convert all objects with double quotes with the On setting and then go back and convert any objects that failed to be created on the first pass with the `QUOTED_IDENTIFIER` in the Off setting.

Tape Backup Options

If you perform a tape backup, you must select the tape drive and choose how the Upgrade Wizard will handle backing up and deleting 6.*x* objects. You need to specify the device for the data transfer so that the Upgrade Wizard will transfer all the data you are upgrading to that drive before the SQL Server 7 databases are created. You can also elect to back up the 6.*x* devices, which is separate from the transfer to tape that the Upgrade Wizard uses to complete the upgrade. The wizard will prompt you to back up the devices manually, through NT Backup, or by copying them to a shared network directory.

If you elect to back up SQL Server 6.*x* devices to tape, make sure to remove the tape backup and insert a blank tape before continuing. The Upgrade Wizard will format the tape before it begins the data transfer part of the upgrade—any data on that tape will be overwritten.

You can also elect to be prompted before deleting the 6.*x* devices if you do not wish to back them up.

Switching between SQL Server 6.*x* and SQL Server 7

Although you can have both SQL Server 6.*x* and SQL Server 7 installed on the same computer, only one of them can run at a time. Once you finish running the Upgrade Wizard, SQL Server 7 will be the active version, even if you have not upgraded all of your databases. If you have enough disk space, you can leave 6.*x* on your computer until you're sure all of your databases upgraded successfully.

If you want to switch from one version to the other, use the Microsoft SQL Server-Switch application on the start menu or run `vswitch.exe`, which is located in the \Mssql7\Binn folder.

Don't try to switch between versions while the Upgrade Wizard is still running. This is in the category of warnings like "don't run with scissors," but it's probably worth repeating anyway.

Removing SQL Server 6.*x*

At some point you're going to want to remove SQL Server 6.*x* from your computer. You can remove it by running the SQL Server Setup locally, from the CD, or from a shared network drive.

Make sure to switch to SQL Server 6.*x* so that it is the active server when you remove it. If SQL Server 7 is the active server, and you try to remove SQL Server 6.*x*, then part of each will be removed and your registry will be corrupted.

Once you remove SQL Server 6.*x*, you will not be able to reinstall it on the same computer with an existing SQL Server 7 installation.

Configuring SQL Server after Upgrading

The Version Upgrade Wizard won't do everything for you—there are a few configuration tasks that you need to take care of when the wizard is done. You can use the Enterprise Manager to:

- Register the server and add it to a server group
- Set security options
- Set configuration options

If you need to change network support, add a language, rebuild the master database, or change the character set and sort order, you need to use the Setup program. This will update the Registry in a safe manner.

Don't use the NT Registry editor to reconfigure SQL Server installations: Use either the Enterprise Manager or the SQL Server Setup program. This will protect the integrity of the Registry from inadvertent changes.

Uninstalling SQL Server

There may come a time when you will want to uninstall SQL Server. Fortunately, this is very easy to do.

To uninstall SQL Server, stop all services by double-clicking the Service Manager in the Windows Taskbar, as shown in Figure A.7. Once you have done that, you will need to close the Service Manager itself.

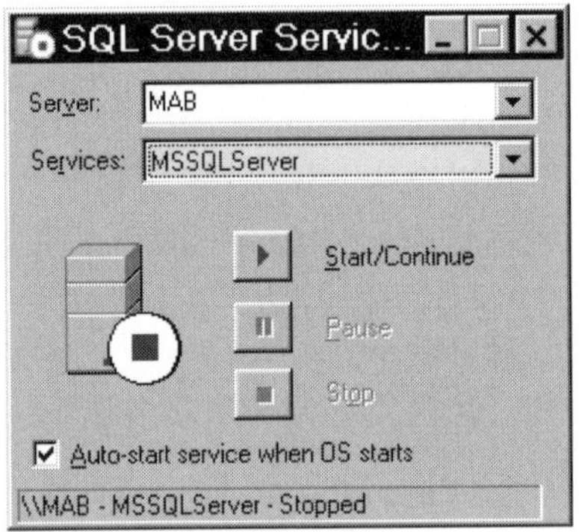

FIGURE A.7: Stop all services using the Service Manager

Choose Programs ➢ Microsoft SQL Server 7 from the Windows Start menu, and select the option Uninstall SQL Server 7. You will be asked to confirm that you want to completely remove SQL Server 7 and all of its components. Click Yes.

You may be prompted that certain DLLs which are no longer being used will also be removed, as shown in Figure A.8. You may safely remove those DLLs.

Figure A.9 shows the final uninstall dialog box after all of the files have been removed. However, you can delete \MSSQL7 folder to get rid of the rest of them. The Uninstall Wizard will not delete your \Backup, \Binn, \Data, and \Repldata folders.

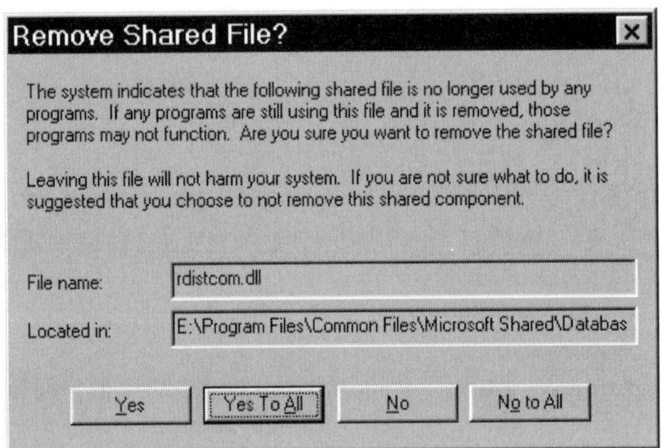

FIGURE A.8: Removing shared components

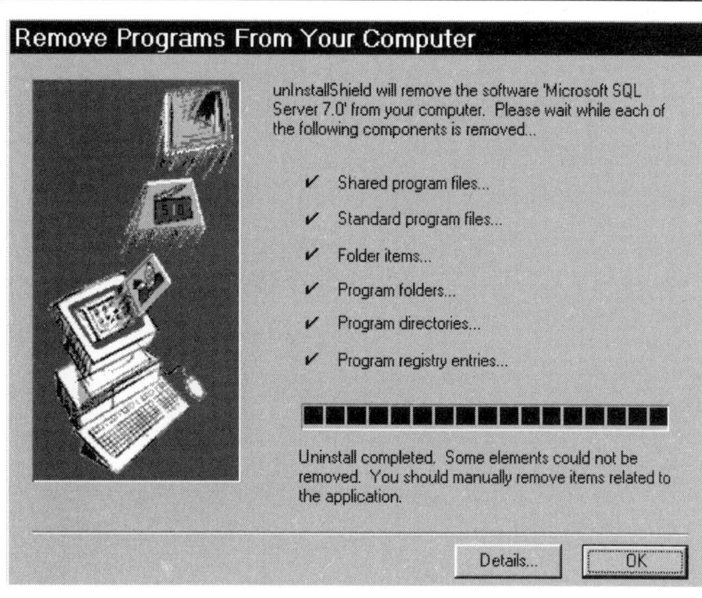

FIGURE A.9: SQL Server is uninstalled.

APPENDIX B

SQL Server Samples

SQL Server 7 includes many samples designed to help you understand how the product works. In this appendix, we'll take a look at those samples and sort out which ones are most useful. The samples are divided into two classes. First, there are sample databases that get installed into the server itself. Second, there are developer samples that show you how to program applications using SQL Server.

TIP In addition to the samples shipped with the product, there are also other sample files and white papers available on the SQL Server Web site (`http://www.microsoft.com/sql/default.asp`). We won't cover those here, but it's worth checking out. You'll find samples for the OLAP server, among other interesting offerings.

Sample Databases

SQL Server ships with two full-blown sample databases: pubs and Northwind. Northwind is a new addition to SQL Server, based on the sample that has shipped with Microsoft Access for years. The other sample, pubs, has been around SQL Server for several versions now. Both databases include fully developed schemas, sample data, and other objects.

pubs

Figure B.1 shows the schema of the pubs database. This database contains information related to a fictional publishing company and its book projects.

In addition to the tables shown in the schema, pubs also contains some useful views, stored procedures, and user-defined datatypes.

You'll also find pubs useful simply because it's been in SQL Server, essentially unchanged, for many versions. There are many books and articles that use pubs for their examples, since it's the one database that everyone can be expected to have. In fact, most of the examples in Books Online draw on this sample database.

The pubs data set is fairly small, since it's used mainly to demonstrate syntax issues. The largest tables in this database have only about 25 rows.

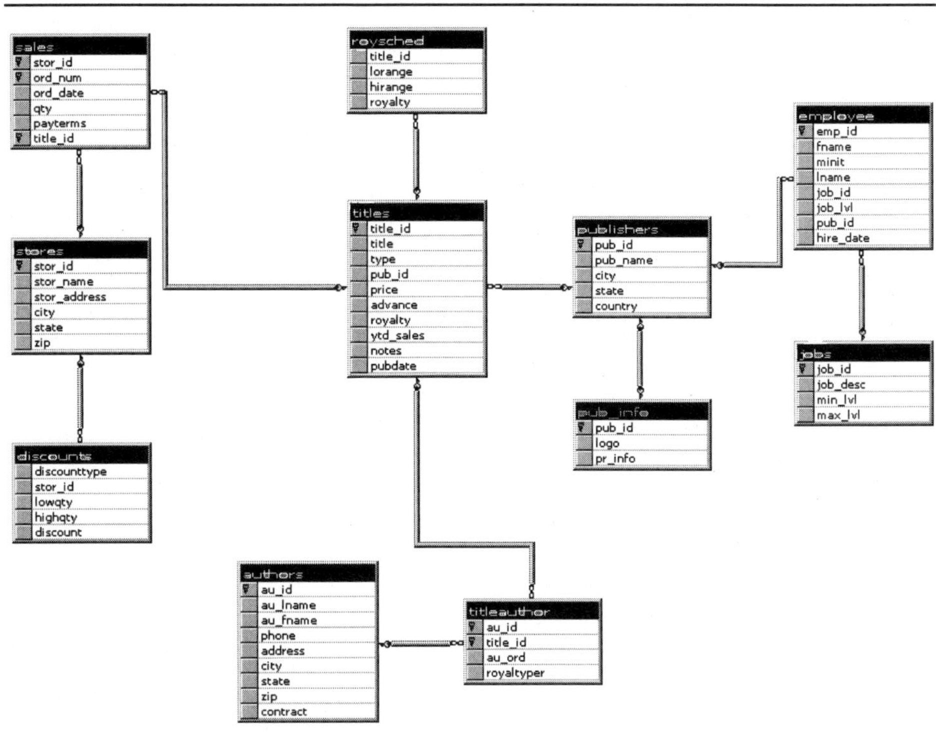

FIGURE B.1: pubs schema

Northwind

The Northwind sample database makes its first appearance in SQL Server 7, though it's based on the sample of the same name that's shipped in all versions of Microsoft Access. This is a typical customers and orders database. Figure B.2 shows the schema of the Northwind sample database.

The Northwind sample contains more data than the pubs sample—over 2000 rows of order detail information. While this is not a staggering amount, it is enough to allow you to construct queries complex enough to analyze with the graphical Showplan, among other things.

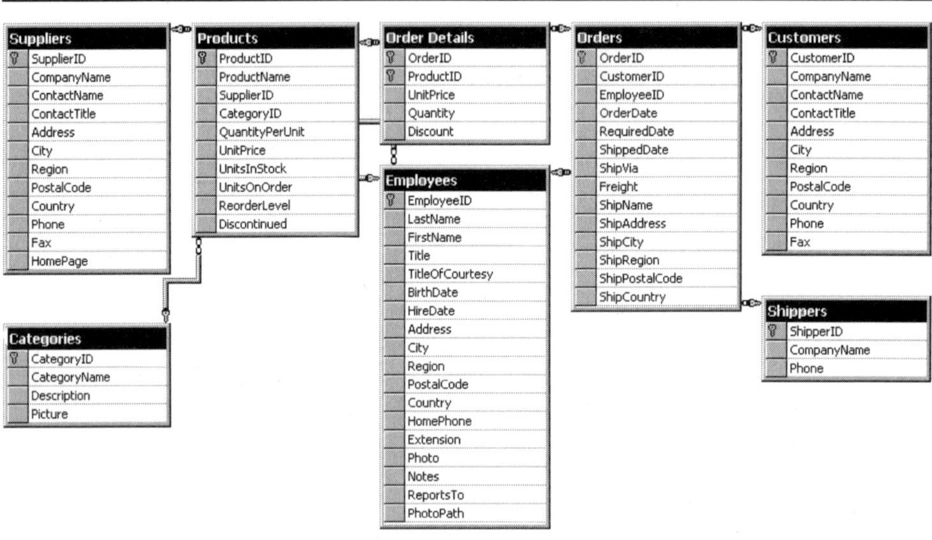

FIGURE B.2: Northwind schema

If you're looking for examples of queries using Northwind, one good place is the Microsoft Access online help. The version of Northwind that ships with SQL Server is practically identical to the Access version, so you should be able to try many of the same queries.

If you install Microsoft Access or Microsoft Visual Basic, you'll get the Access version of Northwind. With this and the SQL Server version you'll find it's easy to test heterogeneous replication with Jet and Data Transformation Services.

Developer Samples

SQL Server also includes many sample projects aimed at developers of applications that include SQL Server as one of their components. Some of these, like the ESQL samples, have not been revised for this version of SQL Server. Others, like the OLE DB samples, are brand new. In this section, we'll review the available samples. You shouldn't hesitate to borrow code from the samples: That's what they're there for.

You'll find all of the samples mentioned here in the Mssql7\DevTools\Samples folder on the SQL Server CD. By default, they won't be installed to your hard drive, but you can just copy them over with Windows Explorer. Each technology has its own subfolder under that root, as listed in Table B.1.

TABLE B.1: Available Samples

Folder	Technology
Ado	Active Data Objects
Dblib	DB-Library for C
Dts	Data Transformation Services
Esqlc	Embedded SQL for C
Dtc	Distributed Transaction Coordinator
Odbc	Open Database Connectivity
Ods	Open Data Services
Oleauto	OLE Automation (COM)
Sqldmo	SQL Distributed Management Objects
Sqlns	SQL Namespace
Sqlrepl	Replication

Generally, the samples shipped with SQL Server require either Visual Basic 4.0 or later, or Visual C++ 5.0 or later.

ADO Samples

SQL Server ships with two samples designed to introduce ADO. The first of these is an introductory sample constructed as a Microsoft Visual Basic project. This sample lets you submit queries to an arbitrary SQL Server, and see the result set. It's built using ADO to submit the queries via the OLE DB driver.

The other ADO sample demonstrates basic ADO operation in Active Server Pages. It lets you work with the data in the Northwind sample database over the Internet. In order to use this sample, you'll need to install Internet Information Server on your network.

DB-Library Samples

For DB-Library, SQL Server provides samples that will work in 32-bit Windows, plus some for 16-bit Windows and MS-DOS. You can investigate the latter on your own if you need the compatibility for old client machines. We recommend upgrading everything to 32-bit Windows, though.

SQL Server includes these 32-bit samples for DB-Library for C:

- `SQLTESTC` provides a simple console application that demonstrates retrieving data.
- `SQLTESTN` provides a GUI-based sample with the same functionality.
- `TEXTCOPY` shows how you can deal with text and image data.
- `SQLCURS` demonstrates using cursors from DB-Library.
- `SQLEXAMP` is a more full-featured command-line processor.
- `EXAMPLE8` shows how to work with stored procedures and parameters.

These samples will compile on either Intel or Alpha processors.

DTS Samples

SQL Server ships with five samples that demonstrate how you can use Data Transformation Services from within your own code, rather than from the SQL Enterprise Manager user interface.

- `DTSEXMP1` is a simple Visual Basic project that uses DTS to fill a table based on the results of a query in the pubs database.
- `DTSEXMP2` is another Visual Basic project. This one uses DTS to retrieve information and create an Excel pivot table.
- `DTSEXMP3` is a more complex Visual Basic project that demonstrates ad-hoc construction of DTS objects. The user can choose an ODBC database and use DTS to execute arbitrary SQL Statements or transformation scripts against it.
- `DTSTASK` is a Visual C++ program that implements a custom DTS task in a DLL. It's not a complete sample, but there are comments to show you which parts should be extended if you base production work on it.
- `DTSXFORM` is also a Visual C++ sample. This one implements a custom DTS Transform in a DLL.

Embedded SQL for C Samples

SQL Server ships with eight Embedded SQL for C samples. These are provided in the form of `.sqc` files, which are the files that need to be precompiled if you're using this technology. They demonstrate techniques ranging from simple selects to executing stored procedures. Our recommendation is that you stay away from Embedded SQL for C, since it's now obsolete. You should be looking at DB-Library or OLE DB instead.

MS DTC Samples

There are three samples included to show you what you can do with the Microsoft Distributed Transaction Coordinator. Each of these samples demonstrates using MS DTC from a different technology:

- DB-Library
- ODBC
- Transact SQL

In each case, you'll see how to set up and then commit distributed transactions.

ODBC Samples

The ODBC samples are largely unrevised for this release, since this technology is now on the verge of becoming obsolete. You should probably be using OLE DB instead of ODBC for most applications. However, if you do need to get into the low-level business of ODBC, these samples are available:

- The `bcp` sample indicates using the `bcp` API.
- The `compute` sample demonstrates using a Transact SQL `COMPUTE` clause from ODBC.
- The `loaddata` sample demonstrates a technique for quickly and efficiently inserting new data into a set of tables.
- The `mfcperf` sample integrates ODBC with a C++ MFC application.
- The `tran` sample indicates the use of cursors from ODBC.

Open Data Services Samples

SQL Server provides four C++ samples that show you how to call Open Data Services. These are most useful if you're planning to develop extended stored procedures.

- `xp_hello` constructs an extremely simple extended stored procedure.
- `xp_param` constructs a stored procedure that interacts with parameters.
- `xp_dblib` shows how you can make a new connection to the server that calls an extended stored procedure by using DB-Library.
- `xp_odbc` is similar to `xp_dblib`, but uses ODBC for the new connection to the server.

OLE Automation Samples

The OLE Automation samples weren't revised for SQL Server 7, and the techniques they demonstrate are largely obsolete. Now that you can write VBScript directly in SQL Server jobs, you're unlikely to need the techniques demonstrated in these samples.

SQL-DMO Samples

SQL Server includes samples demonstrating the use of SQL Distributed Management Objects from Visual Basic, C++ and straight C. Of these, you'll likely find two of the samples most useful.

- The Visual Basic `explore` sample uses SQL-DMO to retrieve information about most of the objects in the SQL Server hierarchy. The interface allows you to "drill down" into objects and see the details of the objects that they contain.
- The C++ `dmoping` sample shows how you can use SQL-DMO within an environment that includes SQL Servers of various different versions.

SQL-NS Samples

SQL Server ships with four samples for SQL NameSpace, two each for Visual Basic and C++.

- The `dbprop` sample (available for both C++ and Visual Basic) demonstrates how you can retrieve the database properties for a specified database.

- The `dumptree` sample (for C++ only) iterates down the entire SQL Namespace, dumping each object it comes to.
- The `browse` sample (for Visual Basic only) also lets you drill down into the entire Namespace, but it does it interactively via an Explorer-like interface. This is the most developed of the samples.

Unlike the other Visual Basic samples on the SQL Server CD, the `browse` sample requires Visual Basic 6.

Replication Samples

SQL Server ships with three different sets of replication samples. These are all designed to show you how you can extend replication beyond what's built into the product.

- The `replctrl` samples show how you can use the SQL Merge and SQL Distribution controls in either Visual Basic or C++ applications.
- The `resolver` samples show you how to write custom conflict resolvers for a variety of situations.
- The `samppub` samples demonstrate how to tie a third-party data provider into SQL Server replication.

Index

Note to the Reader: First level entries are in **bold**. Page numbers in **bold** indicate the principal discussion of a topic or the definition of a term. Page numbers in *italic* indicate illustrations.

A

D

N

Q

R

T

U

W